HUNGER

MARTÍN CAPARRÓS

HUNGER

THE OLDEST PROBLEM

TRANSLATED FROM THE SPANISH BY
KATHERINE SILVER

MELVILLE HOUSE
BROOKLYN • LONDON

HUNGER

First published in 2015 by Editorial Anagrama
Copyright © Martín Caparrós, 2014
Translation © Katherine Silver, 2019
All rights reserved.

This new and revised edition has been prepared especially
for English language publication.

First Melville House Printing: January 2020

Melville House Publishing
46 John Street
Brooklyn, NY 11201

and

Melville House UK
Suite 2000
16/18 Woodford Road
London E7 0HA

mhpbooks.com
@melvillehouse

ISBN: 978-1-61219-804-0
ISBN: 978-1-61219-805-7 (eBook)

Library of Congress Control Number: 9781612198040

Designed by Euan Monaghan
Printed in the United States of America

1 3 5 7 9 10 8 6 4 2

A catalog record for this book is
available from the Library of Congress

"Try again. Fail again. Fail better."

SAMUEL BECKETT, *Worstward Ho*

CONTENTS

A NOTE ON THE 2020 ENGLISH EDITION

Hunger was first published in Spanish in 2014 and has since been translated into many languages. For this first English edition, some figures, some insights have had to be updated.

In the years following this book's original publication, the situation for millions of the world's hungry appeared to be slightly improving, their number diminishing gradually but continuously. But recent statistics have shown that the number of hungry people in the world has begun to increase again. The explanations are many and debatable, but the main questions remains the same: how can we live in a world that, despite its capacity to feed all of its inhabitants, cannot provide millions of people with enough food to live and live healthfully? Why does hunger, humankind's oldest problem, remain its biggest problem? Why have we not solved an epidemic that kills more people than malaria, tuberculosis, and AIDS combined? If we have made advances toward containing and eradicating those afflictions, why do we struggle to do so for world hunger?

We've tried, we continue to try, but we've failed, and we continue to fail. In June 2019, in a lecture given before the Food and Agricultural Organization, Graca Machel, the widow of Nelson Mandela, stated the world was nowhere near achieving a global goal to end hunger and malnutrition by 2030 because decision-makers are not held to account. "We are not doing enough on the pace and level of investment," she told the Thomson Reuters Foundation after her lecture, "and we're not going to get there."

This is why I still believe that hunger should be our main concern, that a world without hunger, the most joyful goal I can imagine, is one we have to keep investing in making happen. And I still think that, in order to achieve it, the first step is to know hunger, the second to understand what has kept us from solving it—those are the purposes of this book, along with another: to galvanize. But writing itself cannot act; the choice to do so is, perhaps, yours alone to make after reading.

Martín Caparrós
Madrid, June 2019

INTRODUCTION

1

There were three women: a grandmother, a mother, an aunt. I'd been watching them for a while as they milled around the hospital cot; as they slowly collected their two plastic plates, their three spoons, their small, sooty pot, their green bucket, and handed them to the grandmother. And I kept watching while the mother and the aunt tied up their blanket, their two or three little T-shirts, and their rags into a cloth so the aunt could place it on her head. But I shook when I saw the aunt lean over the cot, lift up the baby boy, and hold him in the air, then look at him with a strange expression on her face, as if puzzled, as if incredulous, then place him on his mother's back the way children in Africa are carried, on their mothers' backs—their legs and arms spread, chest pressed against the mother's back, head turned to one side—and the mother tied him on with another cloth, the way small children are tied to their mothers in Africa. The child stayed in its usual place, ready to return home. Dead.

It wasn't any hotter than usual.

I think this is when this book originated, a few years ago when I was in a town deep in Niger, sitting with Aisha on a straw mat in front of the door to her hut—with midday sweat, on dry earth, under the shadow of a spindly tree, within earshot of children scattering about—as she told me about the single ball of millet she ate daily, and I asked her if that was true, that she only ate one ball of millet a day, and that's how we had our first cultural misunderstanding:

"Well, every day I can."

She spoke while lowering her eyes in shame, and I felt like such an ass. Aisha was thirty or thirty-five years old; she had a concave nose, sad eyes, and a lilac fabric covering the rest of her face. We kept talking about food and her lack thereof, foolishly unable to see that I was face-to-face with the most extreme form of hunger. After a few hours full of surprises, I asked her—for the first time, a question I would subsequently ask so often—what she would ask for if she could ask for anything, if a wizard told her he would grant her any wish. It took Aisha a while to respond to a question she'd never even dreamed of.

"I would ask for a cow that would give lots of milk, so I could sell a little of the milk and buy what I need to make *puff-puffs* [fritters] to sell in the market, and then I'd be able to get by, more or less."

"But let's say this wizard could give you anything, anything you want."

"Really, anything?"

"Yes, whatever you want."

"Two cows?"

She said this in a whisper, then explained, "With two, then I'd really never be hungry."

It was so little, I thought at first.

Only later did I realize that it was so much.

2

There's nothing more frequent, more constant, more present in our lives than hunger—and yet, for most of us, there's nothing further removed from us than real hunger. We know hunger, we're used to hunger: we feel hungry multiple times a day. But the distance between that repetitious, daily hunger we feel—one that we can repeatedly satisfy—and the desperate hunger that is never satisfied, is an entire world. Hunger has always been the force behind social change, technical progress, revolutions, counterrevolutions. Nothing has had a greater influence on human history. No illness, no war has killed so many people. There is no plague as lethal, and at the same time as avoidable, as hunger.

For so long, I had no idea.

My vision of true hunger, in my earliest imaginings, was a little boy with a swollen belly and stick-thin legs in an unknown region once called Biafra, an ephemeral place that declared its independence from Nigeria on May 30, 1967—the day I turned ten. During the war that ensued, nearly two million people died from starvation. It was then that I first heard an even more brutal word for hunger: famine. By the time I'd turned thirteen, Biafra no longer existed. What it left behind could be seen on the screens of those black-and-white television sets: children surrounded by flies, their faces shadowed by death.

Throughout the following decades, I would become more and more accustomed to this repeated, insistent. This is one reason I always imagined writing a book that would give a harsh, horrifying portrait of famine. I would accompany an emergency relief team to some wretched African locale, where thousands of people were dying of starvation. I would describe it in brutal detail, the worst of all horrors, then say that we mustn't lie to ourselves—or allow ourselves to be lied to—that situations like this one are only the very, *very* tip of the iceberg and that reality is quite different.

I had it planned and perfectly thought out, but during the years I spent working on this book there were no random outbreaks of famines; rather, I discovered that famine, as a temporary and cruel catastrophe, appears only when there's a war or a natural disaster. More often, hunger is a fact of life: endless scarcity in the Sahel, limited nourishment for Somali and Sudanese refugees, seasonal floods in Bangladesh. While it is good that widespread famine no longer suddenly erupts, these calamities have often been the only opportunity to see starvation—as broadcasted images—by those who didn't suffer it. Commonplace hunger, that is so much more difficult to show: the millions and millions of people who go hungry every day, and suffer and slowly perish because of it. It's not the tip of the iceberg, but the iceberg itself that this book attempts to consider.

We all know there is hunger in the world. We all know there are approximately 800 million people—the estimates vary—who experience hunger every day. We have all read or listened to these estimates, and we either don't know what to do or don't want to do anything with them. If eyewitness accounts—the story in the raw—ever made a difference, they don't anymore.

So what's left? Silence?

Aisha told me that with two cows her life would be different. How can I explain that? Must I explain that? Nothing made a stronger impression on me than the realization that the cruelest poverty, the most extreme poverty, is the one that robs you of the possibility of thinking differently: thoughts without horizons, thoughts without desires, thoughts that condemn you to inevitable sameness.

I ask, I want to ask, but I don't know how to ask, if you can imagine what it is like not knowing if you will be able to eat tomorrow? And this if you can imagine a life made up of one day after another of not knowing if you will be able to eat tomorrow? A life that consists, above all, of this uncertainty, the anxiety of this uncertainty, and the effort of figuring out how to alleviate it, not being able to think about anything else because every thought is tinged with the thought of hunger? A life that is so constricted, so short, so painful, and so frequently a struggle?

So many forms of silence.

This book has many problems. How to tell about this "otherness," about what is so far away? It is probable that you know someone who has died of cancer, someone who has been the victim of violence, someone who has lost a love, a job, a point of pride; it is improbable that you know someone who lives with hunger, who lives with the threat of dying of hunger. That is the fate of so many millions of people so far away: people we don't know how—or wish—to imagine.

How to tell about so much misery without falling into the miserabilism of other people's suffering? Why even highlight such misery in the first place? To tell about misery is often a way to make use of it. Certain types of shameless people use the misfortune of others to convince themselves that they aren't so bad off after all. The misfortune of others—their misery—is used to sell, to hide, to create confusion, to assume that individual destiny is an individual problem.

And, above all, how to struggle against the degradation of words such as "millions go hungry," which *should* mean something, provoke something, produce certain reactions. For the most part, however, words no longer galvanize. If we could give words back their meaning, maybe things could actually change.

This book is a failure, because every book is a failure. But above all, because an exploration of the greatest failure of the human species can do nothing but fail itself. Contributing to this, of course, are my own limitations, doubts, inabilities. Be that as it may, it is a failure I am not ashamed to own. True, I should have listened to more stories, thought up more questions, understood much more. But sometimes failing is worth the effort.

Fail again, and fail better.

Jean Ziegler, the former special rapporteur for the United Nations' Right to Food mandate, once wrote:

> The destruction, every year, of dozens of millions of men, women, and children through hunger constitutes the scandal of our century. Every five seconds a child under ten years old dies of hunger on a planet that is overflowing with riches. In

its present state, world agriculture could feed twelve billion human beings, almost twice the current population. Therefore, it is not inevitable. A child who dies of hunger is a murdered child.[1]

Thousands and thousands of failures. Every day, twenty-five thousand people in the world—in this world—die of hunger-related causes. If you, dear reader, take the trouble to read this book, if you are swept up and it takes you, let's say, eight hours to read from beginning to end, around eight thousand people will have died. Eight thousand people dead in eight hours. If you don't take the trouble, those people will still die, but you will have the good fortune of not knowing about it. Maybe knowing this fact will make you not want to read this book. Perhaps I would feel the same way if I hadn't started writing it. Maybe you think that, in general, not to know who these people are, not to know how nor why they have died, would be best.

(Just so you know, in the thirty seconds it took you to read that paragraph, eight or ten people died of hunger—*only* eight or ten, that's not so bad, is it?)

But before you decide to look away, allow me a question that I have asked myself and will pose again and again in this book, the one question that stands out, the one question that rings most loudly, the one question that never ceases to urge me forward:

How the hell do we manage to live with ourselves knowing that these things are happening to others?

NIGER: FORMS OF HUNGER

1

I had spoken to her earlier: five or six hours earlier, when her very skinny little boy was still alive, asleep but moaning.

"A doctor told me I need to be patient, he might get better."

"And he might not?"

"I don't know, I don't know."

Kadi is twenty years old—"maybe around twenty," she said—and Seydou was her only son. She told me she'd gotten married late, around sixteen.

"That's late?"

"Well, the rest of the girls in the village got married at thirteen, twelve, ten."

Kadi told me that they married her to a neighbor who didn't have much of anything. Apparently, nobody else wanted her.

"I don't know why. Maybe because I'm so skinny, maybe they thought I wouldn't be any good at having children."

She told me that Yussef is a good husband but it's very hard for them to find food because they have no land, so he has to find work wherever he can; and it was hard for her to get pregnant but at last she did and you can't imagine how happy we were, she told me, and how scared because how were they going to raise him; but if everyone else does it, they could, too, and how happy they were that it was a boy, and they named him Seydou, and he grew so well, Kadi told me, that when he was really little he grew a lot and they were so happy.

"But then, a few days ago, he got this diarrhea, you can't imagine how horrible it was, it didn't stop. So I took him to see the marabout."

Like many countries, Niger was founded on the kinds of political circumstances that have carved the world. Plans to take over what was then part of the kingdom of Bornu and turn it into French Niger were first formed in 1885, at the infamous Berlin Conference where European leaders met to partition Africa into colonial states. And like the creation of modern Niger, the French exploited what they believed was the ignorance of the population to remain in charge, completely unaware of their own ignorance in the process.

In any case, the creation of Niger was the result of unfortunate circumstance, which gave way to a nation of infertile, almost subsoiled land. A few miles beyond its southern border, in Nigeria, oil gushes out of the ground, which serves no benefit to the people of Niger, who have no right or access to it. Without resources, its citizens go hungry. There's usually something cruel about these countries, which are—or so they tell us—so deeply ours that we should love them with our souls and protect them with our lives.

Niger is possibly the most representative country of the Sahel, a swath of land more than three thousand miles long and about six hundred miles wide that traverses Africa from the Atlantic Ocean to the Red Sea, just below the Sahara. In fact, Sahel means "coast" or "shore"—in this case, of the desert. This flat semiarid region witnessed the flourishing of some of the most powerful kingdoms of Africa, such as the Mandinka or Mali Empire in the fourteenth century, when the masters of Timbuktu built one of the most important cities of the time, trading salt from the desert to the north for slaves from the jungles to the south. This region now includes parts of Senegal, Mauritania, Algeria, Burkina Faso, Mali, Chad, Sudan, Ethiopia, Somalia, and Eritrea. It covers almost two million square miles, and is home to nearly a hundred million people, a lot of scrawny livestock, poor crops, a minimum amount of industry, very little infrastructure, and more and more exploitable minerals.

The Sahel is also the region that gave a different meaning to the word *emergency*, used for extraordinary, unexpected events. In the Sahel, every June, millions of people face an emergency: they are left with no food; starvation looms.

The next year, the same thing happens. And the next, and the next, but each time, it's different.

The Sahel is, among other things, the victim of a cliché, the cliché that asserts that its inhabitants don't eat because there's no possible way for them *to* eat; that assumes hunger to be a structural problem, irredeemable, almost ontological; that they are hungry because there's no way they couldn't be poor, godforsaken souls.

Hunger in the Sahel is omnipresent, but it turns brutal during the time of year called the *soudure* in French and the *hunger gap* in English. This lasts several months when the grain from the previous year's harvest has run out and the following year's crop is just coming out of the ground. Then governments either ask for help or don't, international agencies warn of the danger and mobilize their resources or don't, and millions eat or don't, and here, in the district hospital of Madaoua, three hundred miles from Niamey, Médecins Sans Frontières (MSF) is erecting a new tent every two or three days because more and more malnourished children keep arriving. The Intensive Care Malnutrition Center (CRENI, *Centre de Récupération et d'Éducation Nutritionnelle Intensif*) planned for the treatment of approximately one hundred children; however, there are already more than three hundred, and they keep coming. Nothing out of the ordinary: same as every year. Last year, out of approximately ninety thousand children under five living in the Madaoua district, twenty-one thousand were treated for malnutrition at this center and its satellites; that's almost a quarter of the children in the region. A week before I had arrived in Madaoua, fifty-nine children died of hunger and hunger-related illnesses.

Kadi was the mother with the dead baby on her back. So, when the child became ill, Kadi explained, the marabout gave them some ointments to rub on his back and some leaves to make him tea. The marabout is not only the village's Muslim holy man, he is also someone who plays a decisive role in what was once called a *witch doctor*, a term now politically corrected to *traditional doctor*. Kadi did what he told her to do; the diarrhea didn't stop. A neighbor told her about the hospital and said she should bring him there. Kadi came more than six days ago, and they took care of her and her baby, but what she doesn't understand is why they told her that he got sick because he didn't eat enough.

"I always fed him. First, I nursed him, then I started giving him food. We always gave him his food. Sometimes my husband and I didn't eat, we ate very little, but we always gave him his food: he never cried, he always had his food."

Wary, suffering, is what Kadi told me.

Kadi pointed the blame outward. "My son eats. If he got sick, it's because of something else. Maybe a magician or a witch did it. Maybe he swallowed too much dust the other day when that large herd passed through the village. Or it's Kadi's envy, because her little boy died, and they were born at the same time. I don't know what it is, but it can't be because of food, because he eats."

"What do you give him to eat?"

"What do you mean, what? Fura."

She said this as if it were obvious. I didn't tell her that *fura*, a ball of fermented millet flour and water that is the daily meal for most peasants in Niger, isn't enough to nourish a one-and-a-half-year-old child, for it lacks nearly everything the child needs. Kadi was upset, offended.

"Here they tell me he's like this because I didn't feed him. They obviously don't understand. When I hear that, it scares me, and I feel like running away."

To put it more clearly: to eat a ball of millet every day is to live on bread and water.

To go hungry.

Hunger is an uncanny word. It has been used so many times in so many different ways, and it means so many different things. We know hunger and yet we have no idea what hunger is. We say hunger and hear hunger so much that it has been worn out, turned into a cliché.

Hunger is a multifarious word. In Spanish, it's *hambre* (which also gets stirred up with *hombre* [man], *hembra* [woman], and *nombre* [name]: weighty words), the equivalent to hambre in English is of course *hunger*. Yet English accommodates the Latin word for hunger, *famen*, with words like *famished*, which means an extreme hunger, and *famine*, which is extreme widespread hunger. The Spanish word for famine, however, is *hambruna*: hunger happening together, in the same place, simultaneously. No words are heavier, yet it is so easy to remove the burden of their weight.

Hunger is a deplorable word. Third-rate poets, sixth-rate politicians, and hacks of all sorts have used it so often and so casually, it should be forbidden. Instead of forbidden, it's been gutted. "World hunger"—as in, "So what do you want to do, end world hunger?"—is a sarcastic expression used to sum up how laughable certain intentions are. The problem with those worn-out concepts, polished to a sheen for facile use, is that if you were to one day suddenly back up and examine them more deeply, the whole meaning of the word would blow up in your face.

Hambre in Spanish is a feminine noun that means—according to those who say that words have meaning—three things: "Desire or necessity to eat; scarcity of basic foods, causing shortage and general misery; appetite or burning desire for something." An individual physical state, a reality shared by many, a personal sensation: it would be difficult to think of three more distinct definitions.

But *hunger* is a word that the relevant technocrats and bureaucrats usually avoid. They probably consider it too brutal, too rustic, too graphic. Or, to be generous, they don't consider it sufficiently precise. Technical terminology usually has one clear advantage: it doesn't provoke feelings. They, and the organizations they work for, tend to prefer this. So they talk about *nutrition deficiency, undernourishment, malnutrition, food insecurity*—and the terms end up getting confused or confusing those who read them.

First of all, I would like to explain what I mean when I use the word *hunger*. Or, at least, what I'm trying to say, which is this: we eat sun. Some eat so much more sun than others. To eat is to be "solarized." To eat—to take in nutrition—is to absorb solar energy. Charged photons are constantly falling on the surface of the planet, and through that mystifying process of photosynthesis, plants trap them and transform them into digestible material. Ten percent of the land surface of the earth, about six million square miles—one half acre for each human being—is being used to do just this: grow plants that produce chlorophyll, which transforms the electromagnetic energy of the sun into chemical energy, a reaction turns the carbon dioxide in the atmosphere and the H_2O stored in plants into breathable oxygen and edible carbohydrates. In the final analysis, everything we eat, directly and indirectly—through the meat of animals that eat them—are vegetable fibers charged by the sun. This is the energy we need to replenish and reconstitute our own strength. It enters the body in various forms: fats, proteins, and carbohydrates; liquids and solids. The amount of energy each body consumes is measured in calories, what physics defines as the amount of energy needed to increase the temperature of one gram of water by one degree centigrade. In order to function, a body needs a large quantity of energy, so to measure consumption, we use a thousand calorie unit: kcal. An individual's caloric need varies based on age and situation. But, roughly speaking, a baby in his or her first year needs to eat approximately 700 kcals a day, 1,000 a day from one to two years old, and 1,600 from ages two to five. An adult needs between 2,000 and 2,700 kcals, depending on their body, the climate they live in, and the work they do. The World Health Organization (WHO) says that an adult who does not eat a minimum of 2,200 kcals a day does not replenish the energy he/she expends: that is, he/she does not feed him/herself. This is an average, a convention, one that helps us grasp the bigger picture.

An adult who doesn't manage to consume 2,200 kcals of food a day goes hungry. A child who doesn't consume 700 or 1,000 kcals a day, according to their age, goes hungry. Hunger is a process, a battle the body wages against the body. When a person does not consume those 2,200 kcals a day, they feed on themselves. A hungry body is a body that is eating itself—that's the long and the short of it.

When a body consumes less than it needs, it first taps its sugar reserves, then moves on to its fat reserves. The body begins to move more slowly, then becomes lethargic. It loses weight and its immune system grows weaker. It becomes susceptible to viruses that cause diarrhea. Parasites the body is no longer capable of expelling settle in the mouth and cause pain; bronchial infections make breathing difficult and cause pain. Finally, the body begins to lose scarce muscle mass; it can no longer stand up and soon will no longer be able to move: pain. It curls up; it shrivels; the skin folds and cracks: pain. The body cries quietly; not moving, it waits for the end.

Few people—too many people—die directly of hunger; many more die of illnesses or infections that are fatal because their bodies have been weakened by lack of food and are unable to fight them effectively; these are illnesses or infections that a person who eats normally would never even notice. Few people—too many people—die directly of hunger. Half the children who die before their fifth birthday in a country like Niger die of hunger-related causes.

Including Kadi's baby.

2

These are deaths that never appeared in the newspaper. They can't: newspapers would collapse under their weight. Newspapers can only report the unusual, the extraordinary.

I was speaking with a woman named Aï who was telling me that she used to wonder what fathers were for, what it was like to have one, what life was like for children with fathers. Aï didn't see that much difference: she and her cousins lived together in the yard of her grandparents' house, and their lives were the same even though they had a father. Later, much later, they told her that if her father, who had died two or three days after she was born, was still alive, maybe she would have gone to school. She was glad she didn't have a father.

"I didn't want to go to school."

Her cousins who had a father didn't go either. Just maybe, she thinks now, if she'd had a father they wouldn't have married her off so young. Or maybe they would have.

When they told her she was going to get married, Aï was still a little girl running around and playing with her girlfriends; on full-moon nights they'd sing and dance with a drum or just clapping their hands. Other days she'd fashion dolls and pots and plates and a cow and some camels and houses from clay, and they'd play house: practicing what they would become. The rest of the time, played house without playing: she cleaned, fetched water, looked after her brothers and sisters, and cooked.

"What did you imagine your life would be like when you grew up?"

"Nothing. I didn't imagine anything. I wanted to get married. The only thing I imagined was getting married, what else could a girl do . . . But not so soon . . ."

When she turned ten, her family married her to her first cousin; her uncle paid fifty thousand francs—an amount worth a hundred dollars—for the bride price, ten thousand francs for the clothes and the trousseau, and all of them organized the party. Aï had a good time, but when the moment came to go to the house of her husband/cousin, she was terrified.

"He was a man, a grown-up."

Niger has one of the highest rates of child marriage in the world: although it is illegal, a quarter of all girls get married before they are fifteen. The marriage of a daughter is, among other things, a source of income for the family: the greater the need (the greater the hunger), the greater the temptation to marry the girl for the bride price, to eat for a few more days and have one less mouth to feed.

"I looked at him and was scared. And he did more than just look at me."

Aï tried to escape many times. At first she'd go to the home of her mother and grandmother, but they always sent her back, and each time her uncle/father-in-law and her husband/cousin beat her to teach her a lesson. Aï started escaping into the countryside, hiding in some out-of-the-way spot, but they always found her. The last time, her father-in-law told her very calmly that if she ran off again, he would personally slit her throat, and Aï believed him. Sometimes, when her uncle was sleeping, Aï would run her finger along the blade of the mango-wood machete; two years later she had her first daughter. Three boys would follow.

"Do you still live with your husband?"

"Yes, of course I live with him."

"Do you get along?"

"Without problems."

Aï thought that she might've been twenty-five, but she looked younger. Her face was a complicated structure, full of subtleties and nuance: she had a blue and green scarf with white flecks wrapped around her head, large eyes, thick lips, a tribal scar in the shape of a flower on her left cheek, earrings in her ears and nose, and a necklace of colored beads around her neck.

"He works hard, and often. And he's changed. He doesn't hit me anymore."

Her life, on the other hand, was still the same. Every morning, Aï got up around six, washed, prayed, before setting to grind the millet into edible balls. It took an hour and a half to pound the grain with a wooden mortar and pestle to separate out the edible portion, then two hours to grind it into flour. Then, with a three-gallon bucket on her head, she would fetch water from the well about three hundred yards from her house, hoping it would be enough and she wouldn't have to make a second trip. Though lately her daughter had been able to do that.

"Doesn't she go to school?"

"No, we can't afford it. And she has a father."

I wasn't sure if she was being ironic.

Fire is another problem: she or one of her sons had to gather enough branches to boil the water she'd use to mix the millet flour, adding a splash of milk, if there were any. Around noon, when the heat was unbearable, Aï would bring water in a clay jar to her husband, Mahmouda, in the field where he worked. They had three plots that Mahmouda worked because their oldest boy at the time was still too young. But that year, Aï said, two older boys were able to assist with the planting. But only with the planting.

"They're still too little to do anything else, poor things."

By the time they are five, more than half the children in Niger suffer from stunted growth as a result of malnutrition. If they survive their childhood, they will have more illnesses, fewer possibilities to work or enjoy life, and a shorter and poorer life than if they had eaten well those first few years. It's that simple.

Aï's house was 150 square feet of dirt surrounded by a crude and irregular adobe wall about six feet high. Inside, there were two three-by-three rooms; the granary was conical structure, also of adobe, with a pointed thatch roof. But when I visited, life was lived outdoors: Aï's daughter ground grain in a mortar that was as tall as she was, Aï's boys were running around, and she and I were sitting on the ground on a straw mat, talking, while a goat nursed her kid in the yard.

To thresh and winnow the grain, separate out the seed and grind it. The inhabitants of rich countries—The rich inhabitants of other countries—buy it already done.

We were in Kumassa, one of many villages near the regional capital, Madaoua. The village consisted of twenty or thirty huts like this one, with dirt streets and empty lots in between. There is a village like this every mile or so surrounded by the plots of land the inhabitants cultivate; then, every dozen miles, there's a larger town with a market and a few government offices. This is the classic structure, the fabric of the agrarian world where walking is the only way to get from one place to another.

When I observed these villages, I had a hard time imagining them being any different a thousand years ago: their streets were the spaces left over between houses where the children, goats, chickens played and bones and feathers and dust swirled; a little boy walked by, rolling an old tire, two others brandished sticks, still others ran around with no apparent direction. Someday, in some town somewhere, someone is going to decipher the meaning of the directions children take when they're running around, and that person is going to understand the world.

The mosque in the middle of the village was a nine-by-nine-foot room with a little tower that had been painted, a long time ago, green or blue. Women ground grain in their wooden mortars, others walked by with babies tied to their backs, including a twelve-year-old girl. Others gathered around the well with large, brightly colored jerry cans, to wash or chat or to just fetch water. Others sat talking next to the road on a tree trunk—worn down, polished by their buttocks and the buttocks' of their elders, centuries of buttocks; next to them was a store, another adobe hut, with three walls instead of four. Its owner sold eggs, tea, used jerry cans, and cigarettes. A young man walked by leading a cart pulled by a donkey loaded with firewood, his wife on top of the pile; an ethnic Fula shepherd wearing a *tengaade*, a round straw hat with a pointed top, carried a very long walking stick to herd along some emaciated goats and long-horned cows; a pickup truck drove slowly by a dozen or so people piled in the back, their legs hanging out, bodies pressed together, some sitting on boards hanging over the edges so more people could fit.

When Aï's husband Mahmouda finished eating under the shade of a tree in the field, she returned home, cleaned up, and looked after the children. She liked to nap during the early afternoon; the heat made it impossible to do much else. Until the evening, when she started cooking the millet paste—something like polenta—which on good days she could mix with sautéed onions, maybe a few tomatoes, even one or two gumbo or baobab leaves.

"We sit down to eat before the sun goes down, here in the yard. I don't particularly care, but my husband doesn't like to eat when it's dark; he likes to be able to see. But many days this year, we had nothing to eat for our evening meal."

It all happened, Aï told me, because Mahmouda wanted to improve their situation: he sold part of the millet he had harvested in October so that he could plant onions in December; the fertilizer and seeds were expensive, but then the harvest was good and they were hopeful.

"But when we went to sell the onions, they paid us very little. They said there were too many, who would want them, and said we had to agree to sell for the price they offered or eat them all ourselves, and we ended up with almost nothing. And then when we had to buy millet, the prices kept rising."

"So what happened?"

"We're in debt."

"In debt?"

"My husband asked to borrow money from a friend of his."

A loan of fifty thousand West African francs, roughly fifty dollars. And as they didn't make back even half of that, Aï didn't know how they were going to repay it.

"What are you going to do?"

"I don't know. Let's hope next year's harvest is better."

Though she told me her husband's friend was a good man, Aï worried that if they couldn't repay him, he would take their land, or at least a parcel of it. And then they would have no way to grow enough food.

"But the worst part is, this year my husband couldn't even plant. When it was time, we'd already eaten all the grain, we didn't have any left for seed. Or to eat. So now he's working a rich person's land so we'll have something to eat."

"How are you going to eat next year?"

"Ah, that's a long way away."

In 2012, nongovernmental organizations (NGOs) and other agencies that work in Niger helped feed about 400,000 children, though it is estimated that more than one million needed their services. In 2017, according to the World Food Programme, who have operations in Niger, the number of children fed has risen, but so has the number of children that have died from starvation. The trouble is that these agencies and NGOs can only cover so much territory. In a country with no health care system, not even birth records, children die and are buried as though they never existed.

Aï's youngest son, Ismael, was fourteen months old and spent fifteen days at the clinic in Madaoua; when he got there, he weighed less than nine pounds, severely malnourished. He recovered, but Aï was anxious that it would happen again.

"Now every week I have to take him for his checkup and to get my bag of food. I do it, but I can't keep doing it forever. I don't want to always get my little bag of food. If my son has to eat, I want him to eat well at home."

Ismael was wearing a blue-and-white wool cap and happily sucking on a melting bar of Plumpy'Nut, a food supplement. It was just under a hundred degrees.

I had gone to Niger to write a piece on the cereal banks that were prolif-erating throughout the region. They seemed like a good idea. NGOs were encouraging women in villages—in hundreds of villages—to organize community granaries; if they did that, they would be given several tons of millet as startup capital. During the *soudure*, members could take a loan out of the millet that they needed to survive. When their husbands finished the harvest, the members were supposed to return the loaned millet, adding an additional small amount as interest.

This initiative had two apparent benefits, the most obvious was that it gave women power in their communities they had never had before. But Aï told me that in her village and in other villages the banks ran into problems because too many women didn't pay back the loans—they didn't want to or couldn't pay them back—and the banks were left without any grain capital. Most of them stopped lending and began to sell. Even so, the banks did some good: they kept the price at 30 to 40 percent below the market and, by doing so, forced the merchants to keep their prices down as well. But in many cases, this eventually backfired: the merchants, through local front men and small-time corruption, bought the grain so they could resell it at whatever price they wanted, which led them to control market prices.

This had been just before the economic crises that engulfed so many of the donor countries, and the number of grain suppliers dwindled. If the banks ran out, there would be no rescue efforts. Many banks had to close—including the one in Aï's village.

"Are you afraid you won't have enough food, or don't you think about that?"

"Of course I think about it. Nights when I have nothing to give my children, it's all I think about."

"Do you think about how you could get more food?"

"I don't know. I just think."

What can one think about when one doesn't have enough to eat? Aï never had enough food, she'd never been in a city, she never had electricity or running water or a gas stove or a toilet; she never gave birth in a hospital, never watched television, never wore pants, never had a watch or a bed, never read a book, never read a newspaper, never paid a bill, never drank a Coke, never ate a pizza, never chose her future, never thought her life could be any different than it is.

There is no room for these thoughts when all you can think about is whether you will eat the next day.

3

One of the oldest tricks in the book is to talk—when that's all there is to do—in terms of an impersonal, almost abstract hunger, hunger as a noun, a subject in its own right. The struggle against hunger. The reduction of hunger. The scourge of hunger. But hunger doesn't exist apart from the people who suffer it. Yet people who suffer hunger are never the subject.

Perhaps if one person—one single person, with a name, a personal history, a face—died of hunger, it would be a scandal. It would be reported in all the newspapers, on cable news, and discussed avidly on social media. The world would talk about that person, mourn them with genuine sadness. Government officials would say that this is intolerable, should never happen again, and they would promise to take urgent measures. The pope would appear on his balcony and make the sign of the cross—maybe even draw a line, a thunder bolt on a summer afternoon, though not from a storm.

Technical terminology eschews emotions. In general, bureaucrats prefer not to say, or write, the word *hunger*. In fact, they prefer not to talk at all about malnutrition, undernutrition, things like that, and in order to pretend they are speaking when they'd rather keep quiet, they invented the term *food insecurity*.

In truth, what they invented was the opposite concept: *food security*. The 1996 World Food Summit in Rome, organized by the Food and Agriculture Organization of the United Nations (FAO), stated that "Food security exists when all people, at all times, have physical and economic access to sufficient safe and nutritious food that meets their dietary needs and food preferences for an active and healthy life."[1]

Let's suppose that those terms are used out of professional conscientiousness, in order to define the object of study more precisely. Or out of political correctness, to avoid offending. Let's suppose they're used with a view to the greater good, to be able to better carry out the tasks at hand. Whatever the intention, the result is that the problems of billions of people turn into a text that only a few understand, while the majority remain ignorant. In short: bureaucratese becomes an obstacle to general knowledge, which is the most fertile kind of knowledge.

Herein another of those prodigies of bureaucratic language: a concept that only has meaning because of what it negates. Nobody who regularly has such access ever thinks about food security; only those who don't, ever do, and even then, only when they can. Hence the operative idea is not "food security" but rather its opposite. Food insecurity is one of the saddest euphemisms in an era of sad euphemisms.

In a world where security is held up as *the* supreme value, one that justifies so much horror and cuts short so much debate, including food as a form of security is a commendable effort. We can assume that we are all threatened by insecurity. Security is the "human rights"—the hegemonic discourse—of our times. If it was appropriate in 1948 to say that food was a human right—and even more so in the seventies and eighties—now it has become a condition of security. Then we'd have to talk about a world that has traded human rights for security; well employed, and applied in proper doses, terrorism perpetrated by the bad guys has served this purpose and many more.

The result of the most extreme form of food insecurity is "severe acute malnutrition," which we could call, in order to understand each other, famine. Famines are what we think about when—if ever—we think about hunger. We think about them because they show up in the newspaper or on television when something happens or rather, several days later—something like an earthquake, a flood, a drought, a plague of locusts, an armed conflict; when millions of people cannot eat because food disappears or the population flees or because the supply chain has been interrupted.

These are circumstances that make it impossible to plant or harvest, the roads become impassable or occupied, and the state becomes fully dysfunctional. The hungry become refugees, clients, beggars of international assistance. They huddle in fields and around food distribution centers waiting for handouts. They have no resources of their own, zero autonomy, they wholly depend on others' actions. If those others stop acting, they die within a few days.

Every year, in different ways, famines affect some fifty million people. This seems like a lot, it is a lot; but it's nothing compared to those who suffer from "structural malnutrition."

"Structural malnutrition" is a cold, fittingly contemporary concept that describes a rather unimpressive situation. It contains no drama, no catastrophe, no spectacular disaster that erupts into view, but rather the insidious normality of lives in which not getting enough to eat is business as usual.

In what Guy Debord referred to as "the society of the spectacle" there is no way to make a spectacle out of malnutrition. They're only numbers. But numbers aren't as sexy as the photograph of an emaciated child. Famines are easier to explain: the fury of nature, the cruelty of a tyrant, the devastation of war. Malnutrition, on the other hand, is pure bureaucracy, the banality of evil. And it's most of the story.

"Structural malnutrition" is chronic: it stretches across time. Rather than being a single event, it is many people's norm. It can't be seen but is always there, passed on from mother to child, sustained across decades in the poorest of countries. In one way or another, it affects approximately two billion people: almost a third of the men and women on the planet.

Those—let's just say—two billion people suffer from what bureaucrats call *food insecurity* sensu stricto: sometimes they eat enough, though they are never certain that they will, and sometimes they don't. By definition, eating comes and goes; the slightest change in their circumstances—the loss of a job, the outbreak of a conflict, a weather event—is all it takes for one person—for millions—not to know if they are going to eat the following day.

Those—let's just say—two billion men and woman suffer from malnutrition. In general, the poorest don't eat enough nutrient-rich food— meat, eggs, fish, milk, vegetables, fruits, and vegetables—and they suffer the consequences. The technicians define malnutrition sensu stricto as inadequate nutrition essential for healthy growth, even if there are enough calories. The result is what Jean Ziegler calls "invisible hunger."[2]

One of the most common consequences of malnutrition is iron-deficiency anemia, where red blood cells, lacking iron, cannot produce enough hemoglobin, which allows them to carry oxygen through the blood. According to the WHO, there are about 1.6 billion people who suffer from various forms of anemia. Mostly mothers: one out of every five maternal deaths is due to iron-deficiency anemia.

Then there is vitamin A deficiency, which, according to the WHO, leaves up to half a million children blind every year (half of them dying within twelve months of losing their sight), and provides an easy breeding ground for malaria or rubella.

Every year, maternal iodine deficiency causes twenty million poor children to be born with brains that were not able to develop fully, resulting in low IQs. Zinc deficiency results in the impairment of motor function and a predisposition to infections: diarrheal disease, so often lethal, affects zinc-deficient bodies with much greater violence. *The Journal of Health, Population, and Nutrition* blames these maladies for the deaths of eight hundred thousand children every year.

And so on and so forth.

Then there are the most wretched of the earth, the epitome of the malnourished, those who do not consume the requisite amount of protein and calories to reproduce the energy spent: the malnourished who are chronically undernourished.

Here's hunger in all its splendor: more than 821 million starving people, neatly packaged as statistics.

But even here, there is a hierarchy of starvation. While an undernourished adult can recover without suffering serious consequences, it's the youth that hunger affects most brutally. One out of every five children under five will die of malnutrition, and those who are malnourished but survive will suffer physical and mental growth stunting. A child under five who doesn't eat enough will have forever lost the opportunity to be healthy.

Hunger in the youngest is often a result of hunger in the mother. Women constitute half the world's population and 60 percent of the hungry: there are many cultures in which more of the little food there is goes to the men: gendered hunger. Each and every day, three hundred women die in childbirth due to anemia. A thousand more die each day due to nutritional deficiencies.

That is why, every year, 20 million children are born underdeveloped and begin their lives underweight, and they carry on like that because the poorly nourished bodies of their mothers are unable to produce enough milk. This is the most vicious of all circles: malnourished mothers raising underdeveloped children. Hunger during the first thousand days of life never ends.

Or it does end, brutally, before its time. Each year, more than three million children die from hunger and diseases—diarrhea, rubella, malaria—that would be mere anecdotes in the life of a well-nourished child.

Three million children are more than eight thousand dead children every day, more than three hundred every hour, more than five in one minute.

4

Madaoua was, until a few years ago, tedious in its tranquility. When I was there in 2011, the town then consisted of five dirt streets that flooded every time it rained, as well as goats and children and that guileless energy so typical of a market town. That was before the war in Mali had spilled over the border, and the town became overrun with jihadists from the north or from Nigeria, nobody really knows. In the few months before I arrived, there had been bombings, kidnappings, armed confrontations. White people like myself couldn't go out unaccompanied. The surprising thing is that this didn't happen before, where poverty has existed in a state of perfect resignation.

"What if one day a wizard came and said you could have anything you want, what would you ask for?"

"I don't believe in wizards, sir. I only believe in God, the one God, and his prophet, Mohammed."

The clinic in Madaoua consisted of several rooms painted blue, ochre, and green in a large empty lot on the outskirts of town; tents had been set up around these rooms to care for more patients because the place had surpassed capacity. When I paid a visit, there were signs of an impending sandstorm; the birds shrieked as they circled around the baobab tree, and Mariama, sitting under the tree, waited for something to happen. Better put: for something to stop happening. Her grandson Abdelaziz had died an hour before, and she had no way to tell his parents. The boy was underweight, ate very little, and had had a fever for two weeks. The mother stayed in the village. She wanted to come but she had other children to look after. His father—her son—had come yesterday with her and the child only to turn right around and leave. He had to return to the village, Mariama told me, so that the next day he could sell his only goat at the market. His plan had been to return with a bit of money to purchase food while the boy was still in the hospital. Still alive. The grandmother, Mariama, had nothing more to do, no money for food, and no way to inform his son or the boy's mother that Abdelaziz had died, that his little body was lying in the cot, covered with a yellow cloth, waiting for somebody to do something.

"God sent me this fate, so I must deserve it. Some have to be unhappy so others can be happy. That's life, you know."

They know. Niger spends $5 per inhabitant per year on health care, as opposed to the $8,600 the US spends. The migration of those who know or can and want to escape misery and disease produces more disease, more misery. Wealthy countries that place obstacles, walls, machine guns, boats to stop desperate migrants, happily welcome the few professionals who manage to get some training in those wastelands.

In the Madaoua clinic there were eight doctors—a luxury because they are paid by Doctors Without Borders—who covered three shifts and took care of four hundred hospitalized children. Two doctors per eight-hour shift, about seventeen children to see per hour.

Abdelaziz slept with his grandmother, Mariama. He liked to play with other children, she said, but he tired quickly. And he ate very little; even when there was food, he didn't eat enough. He was her daughter's second; the first, born underweight, died after a few days. It was a difficult year, not much to eat, Mariama said. Then Abdelaziz was born, about four years earlier, then a girl two years later, and now, a few months ago, another girl, who's also sick.

"That's why my daughter stayed, to take care of her."

She, on the other hand, Grandma Mariama, had eleven children, she explained. She counted on her fingers and knuckles, repeated names, frowned.

"Now I have four left: two men and two women."

The rest, three girls and four boys, died when they were little: three when they were between a year and a year and a half, just after they were weaned; another, when he was older, during a rubella epidemic. There was one, she said, who died when she was older, already married.

"I was sad, but it's God's will, what can we do," she told me with nervous laughter.

I was disturbed by an inconvenient idea: that in Madaoua, every adult—every one of those men and women waiting with their children for them to be cured of hunger, everyone walking along the dirt road next to the hospital, selling SIM cards or *puff-puffs*, every nurse, every patient—was a survivor, someone living on borrowed time. It took some sort of good fortune, providence, for a child to survive and grow to adulthood—an idea that effectively negated any concept of acquired right, the idea that those still alive were the ones who'd escaped death: delinquent debtors, squatters in their own lives.

This is why white people like myself sometimes want to believe that things aren't as bad as they seem to us: we're used to it; their dead didn't remain with them the same way ours remained with us. It must be a way of alleviating our guilt, lightening the load. That morning, watching that silent, dignified procession—mother, aunt, and grandmother with their baby who'd just died—I fell into that trap for the umpteenth time, the trap of thinking that within this cultural framework (which must have existed in Europe until a century ago) a couple knew that in order to guarantee themselves the requisite number of offspring, they needed to produce a few extra, and they accepted this with a certain degree of ease.

And now, talking to Mariama, I churned it over and didn't know how to ask. Finally, I found a way that seemed tolerable.

"When you started having children, did you know that some would die, did you expect it?"

"No, I didn't think about it," she said and gave me a strange, suspicious look. "Nobody has children so that they'll die. That would be an insult to God."

In Niger every woman gives birth to an average of seven children—the highest fertility rate in the world; and for every thousand children born in Niger, eighty five of them will die before the age of five. If statistics were an exact science, each Nigerien woman would lose one child. But it doesn't work like that: fewer die in the cities, more in the countryside.

Nine out of every hundred Nigerien children dies before the age of five; in wealthy countries, it's one out of every one hundred and fifty.

Another woman I met in the clinic, Hussena, told me she thought she ought to stop having children.

"I've already had a lot. It gets harder and harder the older I get . . ."

Hussena was in the clinic because her twin girls got sick: fever, vomiting, not even really crying anymore. Her local marabout gave them some herbs, but they didn't help; by the time they got to the hospital, their breathing was laborious and they were severely underweight. One of them died the previous morning and Hussena had been praying for the other to survive. She was holding her, the remaining twin, in her arms. The child wasn't crying; she blinked and pressed her lips together, her features barely moving. The faces of undernourished children resemble those of sad old men: as if death were staking its claim by marking them with time that never passed.

Sadness, apathy, full-body resignation.

The twins were born ten months earlier; they were Hussena's twelfth and thirteenth children. Hussena was already forty-five years old and told me she never thought her life would be like this.

"When I was little I played with mud dolls and fed them, I always fed them. I thought life would be like that, that things would be good, but this is what's happened and I have to accept it."

"What would make things good?"

"To have food, a few clothes, a little money for expenses."

"Why is it like this?"

"I don't know. My husband works and works, but we never get there. . ."

"Why?"

"I don't know. I've asked myself many times, but I never know."

They talk about the drought. Whenever they talk about hunger in Niger, in the Sahel in general, they always talk about the drought. It's true, weather is a factor: for example, the drought last year, notorious climate change, things like that.

For millennia, ever since the invention of agriculture, humans have depended on the weather, feared the weather. In order to believe they could control it—or at least, attenuate its effects—they invented gods and offered them their goods, their lives, their destinies. A little more than a century ago, they learned how to predict, sometimes even with a bit of accuracy. But there were still events that defied their predictions: hurricanes, droughts, and other freak phenomena whose causes they couldn't understand.

With the advent of the Scientific Revolution in the fifteenth century,

and later the Age of Reason in the eighteenth century, it became difficult
to invent more gods to explain how things worked. Climate change has
brought gods back into the picture as prime movers of these shifts in
weather patterns—rises in temperatures, drops in temperatures, reduction of the Arctic ice cap, increase in the Antarctic ice cap, heat waves,
cold spells, cyclones, tsunamis—but now we are the gods, as pitiful as
that is.

Consider how, without irrigation, a drought would make farming
impossible. Of course, where there is need, there is money to be made, and
as long as farmers depend on irrigation, executives for irrigation companies will turn a profit. At least in Western countries, many farmers will
receive subsidies to have at least some income during periods of drought.
In Madaoua, during a recent period of draught, there were neither irrigation systems in place nor subsidies to pay out. Seydou, Abdelaziz, Has-
sana, and several others all starved to death.

"Whose fault is it?"

"Me and my husband's. We should have gotten food."

"Why? Is there something you should have done that you didn't?"

"We'd have more money if we had something to sell."

"Why don't you?"

"Because we don't have any money to start with."

"Why?"

Hussena looked at me in silence and with so much sorrow. I shut up.

People often think that Africa is ridden with fatal diseases. The fact
is, there are just as many here as anywhere else, but here they're fatal
and elsewhere they're not. A few years ago, I had malaria; I spent a few
days in a modern Western hospital, was given the best treatment, and
that was the end of it. A person in North America with AIDS knows can
take retroviral medications for preventing that condition from becoming
terminal. An African with AIDS knows that most likely he or she won't
be able to pay for the medications and will die within a few years. The
same goes for typhoid, diarrhea, tuberculosis, and many other diseases,
diseases that kill millions of Africans a year; in order to be deadly, it
must attack a body that is not only malnourished but has no chance to
receive treatment.

The degree of danger posed by disease has always been, to a certain
degree, but never so much as now, a question of class. With the development of modern medicine and the growth of the pharmaceutical
industry, having money is the most important variable that determines
whether you will be treated and cured.

Hussena also had a twin sister; when they were six or seven they started going to the madrassa, the Qur'anic school where the marabout taught them to recite *Surahs* by heart. When the marabout said the twins were good students, their father decided to send one to the public school, and asked him to choose which one. The marabout said he couldn't, that it had to be the father's choice. The father also couldn't and tried to send both. Hussena finished elementary school; when she wanted to continue, her father said he couldn't manage.

"He told me he couldn't and he asked me to forgive him. It was the only time I saw him do anything like that. He was sad."

Hussena was old—seventeen—when she got married to a boy she met at a cousin's wedding: he watched her all afternoon, then finally went up to her and told her that he wanted to marry her. She told him to talk to her father, which he did. Hussena said it was better to get married that way, by choice and not so young. And she's happy she married that man, in spite of everything.

Hussena's first three were boys, who grew well; the five following ones died. They were born weak, she explained, and small: they didn't have the strength to live. When the third one died, the old woman in the village told her that she was having babies too frequently because she got pregnant two or three months after giving birth and then stopped nursing, and her baby had to eat something else and then got sick and died; moreover, Hussena was so weak and skinny from so many births that the babies came out smaller and smaller, more and more fragile. Hussena understood, but she kept getting pregnant.

"What did you think when your babies kept dying, one after the other?"

"I don't know, I wondered why God didn't want my children to live, I tried not to get pregnant. I went to the marabout and to help prevent me from getting pregnant, he gave me a *gris-gris*, a cord of animal skin you tie around your waist to cure illnesses or ward off other evils.

"That stopped you from getting pregnant?"

"Yes, it did."

"How?"

"That's just how it is. It's our tradition."

Every so often, Hussena gave me a sweet, gentle smile full of the compassion one feels toward someone who doesn't really understand even the simplest things.

Over the next twelve years, Hussena had six more children, two of them twins, and they were all born healthy, but then one of the twins died.

"And to think how difficult that birth was."

I asked her if they were easier now or at the beginning.

"At the beginning, I was stronger. Everything becomes more difficult with age . . . Now when I'm pregnant, all my work is much harder."

The earlier births were at home and more peaceful, she said, but when she was pregnant with the twins, two years ago, she had very little food and was very weak, and when she went into labor she fainted, and they brought her unconscious to the hospital in Madaoua on a motorbike, "And that's how I got this," she told me, pointing to a horrible burn scar on her ankle. "The muffler, that's what did it. That's what I get for riding on those things."

The doctors told her that the problem was that she'd eaten too little— she explained, they didn't say little; they said *too* little—and that's why the twins were born so weak, and that now she had to feed them well. She said, yes, of course, yes. The day she was leaving she summoned up the courage to ask them how she was going to feed them well, and they told her she had to nurse them, but to do that, she'd have to eat well so she'd have a lot of milk.

"Imagine that."

To imagine her fear, her doubts, how she'd often eat less so her children wouldn't go without, but the doctors warned that if she ate any less the twins would get sick and now what was she supposed to do.

"If I don't eat, my milk won't be any good. But if I eat, my children won't eat. So if I eat to have good milk, I'm saving the youngest ones and forsaking the others. What for? So that when the little ones grow up the same thing will happen to them?"

"What did you do?"

"I don't know, I didn't know what to do. Sometimes I ate, sometimes I didn't. For all the good it did . . ."

She looked at the ground. Her daughter Hussina in her arms, whimpers.

"Sometimes I hate having children."

I wondered if I should ask any more questions. I felt embarrassed, ashamed. But she had one more thing to say.

"I hate it because I'm afraid they'll hate me for making them live like this."

It was here, on arid plains like these, that mankind was born. It's easy here to reflect upon the advantages of leaving one's place of origin: of emigrating, changing, flying away. It's easy; they say we were born here and they say—now they say—we were born from a drought; that several million years ago—the number is discussed and revised, nothing is more changeable than the past—some monkeys who lived in the trees had to come out of the trees because drought made their habitual food scarce.

They had to stand up on two legs, walk, run, go make their livelihood on that arid plain. Those who knew how, survived; after millions of years, their ability to remain upright allowed them to carry a heavier head and, with time, even to use it. Then came those stone axes, those six million gods, veal cutlets and mashed potatoes, the scribbles we call letters. We come from that drought; but none of this tells us where we're going.

"Are you religious?"

"I'm Muslim."

"Why do you think God made a world where so many people don't have enough to eat?"

"I don't know, I have no way to know. But every chance I get, I ask God to give me food."

"Does God listen to you?"

"Yes, he listens. And sometimes he gives and sometimes he doesn't."

"Couldn't God have just as easily created a world where everybody had enough to eat?"

"God created it this way, where some are rich and others poor, and the poor have to pray to him to have something to eat."

"You mean, if there weren't so many poor people, fewer would pray to God . . ."

"I don't know, I don't understand these things."

"Maybe God created the poor so there'd be people who needed him."

"Maybe." She laughed.

I had a feeling she'd never thought of it, but the idea seemed interesting. My mistake was to continue.

"Isn't that kind of selfish of him?"

"God isn't selfish," she said, once again entrenched in her certainties. "Sometimes when I ask, he gives. And when he doesn't, I'm sure he has a good reason."

Nigerien peasant families are precision mechanisms of units of production: the husband works the land, laboriously cultivates a plot, and provides the family with grain; the woman procreates, doesn't work in the field, takes care of the house and the children, prepares the food; very rarely she tends to a few yards of land, almost sand, where she grows accessory edible plants, like okra. Sometimes there are complementary activities: the man can work in someone else's field when his doesn't provide enough, or he can even emigrate for a limited amount of time; the woman can try some kind of *petit commerce*, which, if she can acquire the initial capital, would probably consist of mixing and frying and selling *puff-puffs*.

The family has to produce enough children to guarantee continuity: the daughters are given to other families in exchange for a payment of money—the bride price—and they leave; the sons guarantee the survival of the parents when these can no longer work. In exchange, the mother, now grandmother, takes care of the children and the house, and the father, now an old man, is in possession of some supposed wisdom that gives him symbolic power that keeps him alive.

Here's another one of those difficult choices: in a country where the rate of infant mortality is among the three highest in the world, a family that doesn't have lots of children runs the risk of not having enough sons to work when the father no longer can. If they have more, however, more might survive than they are able to feed. It's a difficult balance: have fewer children in order to be able to feed them; have enough so that they can support you in your old age.

In the wealthy world, where it is assumed that the state and other sources of funding are there to take care of us in our decadence, having children has turned into a search for personal or emotional realization, a form of symbolic continuity; in the poor world, it is—also, still—the primary strategy for survival.

All of this, obviously, is a blueprint, but one followed by almost every family in places where the complications and confusions of roles in contemporary Western families is utterly foreign.

Compared to our innovations, which imply new roles and relationships, the structures of these families seem simple and immutable.

The temptation: to consider it logical that they are grounded in a society with the same modes of production, rhythms, and problems as their great-grandparents.

Agrarian life: bound to what never changes.

The first goal of any human, of any group of humans, is to eat. Ten thousand years ago, everybody used most of their energy to do just that. Then societies began to specialize. Now, in the richest ones, only 2 or 3 percent of the population works the land to produce food. In many African countries, peasants continue to make up between two-thirds and three-quarters of the population. The proportion of farmers in a society is a cruel measure of wealth—or "development."

Eight out of every ten Nigeriens live in the countryside. It is difficult for us to imagine a society based on subsistence agriculture. This is not a society in which people who own land and machinery grow a lot of plants to sell to others, but one in which people who possess almost nothing grow plants, then see how much they get to eat.

"If a wizard came and said you could ask for anything you want, what would you ask for?"

"Food. Food every day. That's what I'd ask for."

Hussena had a black scarf tied around her head, a gold ring in her right ear, attentive intelligent eyes; on her checks, she had the parallel scars of her tribe, a seed necklace around her neck; her body was severely underweight, her hands rough; there was one prominent, almost white, callous at the base of both her thumbs where she held the pestle every day, two hours a day, for forty years. Thirty thousand hours of crushing millet seed, grinding millet seed, then converting millet seed into their only food.

"When you were a child, was there more or less food than there is now?"

I meant it as a general question, if things were better or worse than before; her answer took a different tack.

"No, there was more because we didn't have so many children. Then we had many children, but some died. Now, with the rest of our living children, there's much less."

We think of agriculture as an ancient activity. In the richest countries of Europe, agriculture is a craft, an anachronism, which the state makes an effort to maintain and subsidize so as not to lose traditions, that is, culture. In the granaries of Balkans, and the more or less rich countries of the New World—Canada, Australia, Brazil, Argentina—it has become the business of a very few. In the United States, where the farm lobby wields a certain amount of power, that sector accounts for only a single percent of the gross national product.

In general, and just before we really give it any thought, agriculture seems like something faintly contemptible, the most outdated, least dynamic human activity. We forget one small detail: we still haven't discovered a way to produce food other than transforming solar energy into food for plants and, in turn, fuel for animals.

Decades of efforts in sophisticated laboratories, thousands of ideas and patents, vast quantities of colorings, flavorings, scents, sweeteners, without changing the fact that everything we eat is still the fruits of the earth or what other animals have done with the fruits of the earth.

Moreover, agriculture still consists of five basic processes: selecting usable plants, managing water, renewing and enriching the soil, protecting the crops from pests, and using labor to harvest. Nor is the quantity of plants that large. There are around 400,000 plant species, of which 200,000 are edible, and we regularly eat about 200: grains, roots, tubers, fruits, vegetables, herbs, nuts, spices. Today—and on average, because the proportions vary greatly by location—the meat and milk of animals fed

on these agricultural products, along with fish, only provides a third of
provide of all protein consumed by humans. Plants make up the rest. In
fact, 90 percent of our calories comes from fifteen vegetable species; 60
percent being derived from three plants: rice, corn, and wheat.

The food and agriculture industry accounts for only 6 percent of the
world economy; a mere trifle, ten times less than the service sector. The
interesting part is that this trifle determines everything else. Of the
approximately 7.5 billion people on the planet, about 2.5 billion are farmers. Demographics, economic weight, and real need stand strangely far
away from each other.

Agriculture in poor countries, the shovel and hoe variety, is very
physically demanding work—work in which men can claim the advantage: women can make an effort, do a bit here and there, but men are the
ones who have to feed their families. This, in turn, creates a certain idea
about life. The subjugation of women had a very specific counterpart: in
exchange—in the dialect of master and slave—the man gave her food. In
more progressive societies it is simpler and more feasible to break from
this idea; here, it's more complicated. But it must not be easy to be a man
here either: to have to provide and not be able to, to be constantly failing.

Salou, Hussena's husband, was not among the poorest of the poor: he had
two small plots of land, half a hectare each, where he grew millet. If the
drought wasn't extreme, if the locusts didn't ravage, each plot could yield
about sixty bundles of millet. In the best years, one bundle could contain
thirty-three pounds of grain; in a bad year, only one or two.

"It varies that much?"

"Yes, you never know. Never."

Hussena and I did the math. In a very, very good year, each plot could
yield five hundred pounds of millet. A large family like his needed at
least two *tias* (around three pounds) of millet per day. Three times 365 is
1,095. So even in an exceptionally good year, it's still short by a month or
so, which means they'd have to buy more. And that isn't even counting
all the other expenses: salt, sugar, tea, a tomato or two, clothes, shoes,
transportation, kerosene for the lamp, tools, medicine.

Hussena explained, "My job is to make the millet last. Salou plants it,
tends to it, harvests it, gives it to me. Then I have to take care of it. Sometimes we fight, and he tells me to give him more food. But he never hits
me, almost never. I tell him: Do you want to keep eating during planting time? We have to eat a little less now so it will last till then. Finally,
he understands. But I'm also afraid of making a mistake. I'm afraid I'll

count wrong and it won't last as long as it has to; it'll run out sooner: that's happened a few times."

"Have you ever made a mistake in the opposite direction and had extra?"

Hussena laughed and looked at me with that combination of surprise and compassion. "Any year that isn't perfect, the food would run out after six or seven months. Not to even mention years like last year, when a bundle didn't contain even a pound of grain. To supplement, many farmers tried to plant onions, but that required money for seed, and fertilizer, not to mention the shortage of water. The rest of the time, Salou looked for odd jobs, but employment, even temporary, was never guaranteed. So, sometimes we eat and sometimes we don't. Sometimes a neighbor gives me husks and I make a soup for my children. Sometimes we find leaves on trees. Sometimes, not even that . . ." Again she laughs at my surprise. This man, she must think, he doesn't understand anything about life.

"Do you ever eat anything other than millet?"

"Sometimes on Saturdays, market day, we can buy something else."

"What?"

"Some potatoes, cassava."

"What's your favorite food?"

"I prefer rice. But I can almost never buy it. When there's some in the market, a *tia* costs fifteen hundred francs. Millet costs eight hundred francs. That's too much."

Eight hundred francs per *tia*. A few months ago, at harvest time, two pounds of millet was selling for seventy. That was the moment the merchants were waiting for: they bought it from peasants in debt, held onto it, speculated, and waited, because they knew that every other year, hunger arrived.

"But this year I ate some beef."

There was a wedding, she told me, a rich relative, and she ate a piece of meat: beef, she told me, beef.

In all my drafts of this chapter on Niger, the title was always "Structural Hunger": hunger rooted in profound conditions, almost an ontology. This was a country where hunger would be, in a certain way, a geographic, climatic destiny: an arid region with limited productivity that doesn't manage to feed its inhabitants. That is the image one has of the Sahel in general, of Niger in particular, and it took me a long time to realize that I was abdicating to a particular ideology. There's no such thing as structural, inevitable hunger. There are always causes, reasons, decisions.

When they say "structural," they mean predestined, immutable.
More tricks of bureaucratese.

"What makes you feel good, when are you happy?"

"When I have enough to eat and enough to give my children, then I'm happy. Those are my best moments."

VOICES OF THE TRIBE

How?

It all depends on your point of view. Orson Welles is the Third Man, a dealer in diluted antibiotics in post-war Vienna, and Joseph Cotton, his old friend, reproaches him for what he does. They are at the very top of the Ferris wheel at the Prater Amusement Park; Welles answers him, suggesting he stop being so melodramatic.

"Look down there. Would you feel any pity if one of those dots stopped moving forever?"

Seems like an excess of cynicism, though cynicism always seems excessive. What's excessive, above all, is the fact that as he says it, he is looking at them from afar: they are dots. To avoid cynicism, we don't look.

How the hell?

No, I'm not talking about those sons of bitches who don't give a damn. Sometimes I feel like killing them, I think, *How the hell can they lie like that,* I don't understand them. How can they be so uncaring, to look at a famished child with those big eyes and that sad face and not care? No, they should lock up those sons of bitches for being such sons of bitches. I couldn't do that, not give a fuck about anybody; that's right, I give, our company has a policy that at the end of every fiscal year we give a certain amount, not always the same amount, it depends on how business has been, because really you can't be such an asshole that you know these things are going on and you don't do anything, right? Especially if you've been lucky and are doing well, you have a little money, a family. That's why we have to give, we all have to give, everybody as much as they can, just to know that.

How the hell do we manage?

To wonder where I'm going to eat tonight. To wonder what I'm going to eat tonight. To wonder who I'm going to eat with tonight. To wonder the same thing, the things I'm used to wondering.

To wonder if I'm going to eat tonight.

How the hell do we manage to live?

No, but really: with all these disasters right here, around the corner, you're giving me a hard time about children in Africa? Could it be that you don't want to deal with what's right in front of you? Maybe that's your escape?

How the hell do we manage to live knowing?

They don't say: hunger is the mise-en-scène of the fact that we don't care that there are other people suffering in the world. They don't say: of the fact that we don't care that there *are* others.

I'm not making a judgment, I'm just stating one. Maybe it's better not to care. Maybe it's sheer foolishness to waste time or play God and think about others. We must consider this possibility, discuss its pros and cons.

How the hell do we manage to live knowing these things?

Sometimes I swear I get the urge to go out with a bazooka and kill everybody. Everybody, you hear me, not leave a single person standing; it infuriates me to see those guys filling their pockets with the rewards of other people's sweat, with other people's suffering; man, those guys who starve millions, standing there like kings on top of a pile of corpses, I swear I'd kill them all if it would help anything. But what would I gain? Seriously, what can you do? Really, what can you do to change this shitty system? Even if you had absolute power, total control, there's still no way to drag them out of their bunkers and their banks and their airplanes and their—

How the hell do we manage to live knowing these things are happening?

5

First it was hunting slaves, then trading them: starting in the fifteenth century certain Arabs and certain Europeans finished off a large portion of the population of Black Africa, as much as half according to some estimates. The European invasion at the end of the nineteenth century

destroyed what was left of African economies, leaving their local industries demolished, their trade in shambles, their lands occupied, their
food crops replaced by crops needed in the metropolis.

When independence came, the Europeans took everything they could
away with them. In most countries, the situation was difficult: weak
infrastructure, few people with any training, lack of capital to invest in
any of that—and, of course, political and social conflicts. But everything
got worse in 1989 when the Washington Consensus and the World Bank
and the International Monetary Fund (IMF) "convinced"—with threats
regarding their foreign debt—most African governments to reduce the
state's involvement in certain sectors.[3] One of these was agriculture,
which continued to be the principal economic activity of a large part of
the continent, and the one that fed most of its inhabitants.

The market will oversee an improvement of conditions, repeated
the leaders of the World Bank and the IMF. In the meantime, the state
should stop subsidizing farmers or guaranteeing a minimum offtake of
their products and price regulations—all this on the pretext of helping
them integrate into the "global free trade system."

In many countries, leaders accepted this policy without much resistance:
farmers didn't have enough power to exert any influence. And anyway, agriculture was an archaic activity that wasn't worth promoting; it was, according to Western experts, the reason so many Africans lived in poverty.

Later, the World Bank itself would claim that agricultural subsidies
are four times more effective in reducing hunger than any other kind.
But between 1980 and 2010, the proportion of international aid to Africa
designated for agriculture dropped from 17 to about 5 percent. The
United States and Europe, in the meantime and without aid, subsidize
their farmers to the tune of $300 billion annually.

The IMF also applied pressure on Africans to abandon family farms
that grew products for local consumption and turn those lands over to
the cultivation of products for the world market: coffee, tea, cotton, soy,
and peanuts. The foreign currency obtained from these exports would
help these countries pay their foreign debt—or the interest on their foreign debt—and, by the way, render them captive to international markets
manipulated by the most powerful countries and companies.

During that thirty-year period, the opening of markets in many
countries allowed for the import of cheaper food—subsidized by the
governments where they were grown—to replace locally grown food.
This was one of the global markets' greatest acts of violence: without
any buyers for their products, millions of peasants in the world's poorest countries lost the shirts they never had off their backs. In addition,

their countries lost all hope of producing their own food and, as corollary, of not depending on the prices, whims, and impositions of the "market."

The importation of food also deepens regional differences within countries: most of it remains in the big cities, especially the coastal cities, where national wealth is concentrated. Of the fifty poorest countries in the world, forty-six import—from wealthy countries—more food than they export. For more than a century Africa had exported food; after 1990, it started to import more than it exported.

In 1986, at the start of the Uruguay Round of trade negotiations, John R. Block, former Secretary of Agriculture for the Reagan administration, said, "The idea that developing countries should feed themselves is an anachronism from a bygone era. They could better ensure their food security by relying on US agricultural products which are available, in most cases, at lower costs."[*]

It seemed obvious: the United States and Europe could grow food better and more cheaply, so Africans—and other poor people—should stop doing it and get other jobs so they can spend their incomes on imported food. Though it was never clear what jobs they would get. In some cases, rudimentary factories were built to take advantage of cheap labor, but mostly, there was nothing. As a result, the big cities were swamped with the unemployed, and the countryside with peasants who had neither land nor the means to grow anything.

Two out of every three Africans are still peasants. Those who live in a subsistence economy eat what they grow, though this is never enough because their land and their tools and their input produce little. As a result, they never have any surplus to invest in increasing their output.

In 1970 it was estimated that ninety million people in all of Africa were undernourished. In 2010: more than four hundred million.

At the clinic, I saw only one father among the dozens of mothers. He was an older man, around fifty—the national life expectancy age. Several of his children had already passed on. He was at the clinic that day because his three-year-old son had been hospitalized for malnutrition. The boy's three older brothers had died more or less at the same age.

The father was weeping. His name was Yusuf and he tried tenaciously to maintain his dignity. He did not bend over to cry, he did not hide his face in his hands, he did not wring his eyes with his fingers; he wept with his face lifted, the tears falling down his deeply lined cheeks. Yusuf told me that his first wife couldn't get pregnant; his second one could, but she had children who couldn't survive. He didn't say so, but I suspected he blamed himself—but I didn't have the heart to ask him.

"I thought I'd send him to school so he'd study, find a good job, carry out the dream I once had. I can't be anything, but maybe he would be able to."

Yusuf was wearing a white shirt, dirty and stained from the days he'd spent at the clinic; his feet were cracked with age, and the tears kept falling slowly, silently.

"He can't, he won't be able to."

Yusuf cried for his son but he also cried for himself. "What am I going to do?" he asked, "What am I going to do when I'm old, what am I going to do all alone?"

The future, for the most part, a threat.

Little black plastic bags blew across the field. Little black plastic bags from the market that fly in and out of every nook and cranny of Niger, escapees from modernity that arrive here only as residues.

The future, for the most part.

Niger is just under 400,000 square miles, yet less than a quarter of it is arable land. Pastoral nomads live in the rest, raising about twenty million heads of goats, sheep, donkeys, camels, zebus. The price of medicine for these animals—antiparasitics, vaccines, vitamins—multiplied when the IMF forced the government to close its National Veterinary Office and open the market to multinational corporations. Since then, more and more nomads have lost their herds and been forced to flee to the outskirts of Niamey, or to the capital cities in surrounding countries, such as Abidjan and Cotonou. It was also the IMF that forced the Nigerien government to shut down its grain warehouses—containing about forty thousand tons of grain, mostly millet—that had been tapped when frequent droughts or plagues of locusts or the annual *soudure* brought hunger to the population. The IMF thought such government intervention distorted the market; the government, strangled by its foreign debt, had to agree.

Niger is among the world's largest producers of uranium; its reserves in Arlit, in the middle of the desert, are the fourth largest in the world, But for many years, a French state company, Areva, had the monopoly on mining it, and little tax was paid back to the Nigerien state. But this changed in 2007 when new deposits were found near the town of Azelik and then President Mamadou Tandja decided not to award Areva with a presumed contract, but instead declared that the Nigerien government would form a mining partnership with a Chinese mining company. Areva's inevitable protests were ignored, as they were again when two years later yet another uranium deposit was discovered in Imouraren. Areva's ire at not being awarded any further contracts had plenty to do with France being the most "nuclear" country in the world: almost half of the uranium required to power the atomic power plants that supply three-quarters of France's electricity comes from Niger.

In February 2010, President Tandja began negotiations with the Chinese to exploit the new site. A few days later, however, Nigerien army Lieutenant General Salou Djibo led a military coup that unseated Tandja, who had been in power for ten years, claiming it for himself. As soon as he took power, the lieutenant general broke off negotiations with China, reaffirmed his country's "gratitude and loyalty" to France, and awarded Areva the disputed contracts.[5] The following year, elections brought Mahamadou Issoufou, a mining engineer who worked for Areva, to power.

At the beginning of this century, the World Bank prepared a plan to build an irrigation system that would make an additional four hundred thousand hectares arable, a tenfold increase of arable land, and a guarantee that all of the country's inhabitants would eat. With uranium money, such a project could have been paid for, but in awarding the contracts to Areva, not a single penny came their way.

The land is dry: only 4 percent of the arable land in Africa has some kind of irrigation, this compared to almost all the comparable land in Europe and North America, and half in Asia. In the north of Brazil, the World Meteorological Organization compared the yields of five contiguous acres planted with beans, one with irrigation and the other with rainwater; the one that depended on rainwater produced 110 pounds, the other that used irrigation produced thirty-three hundred. A little engineering goes a long way.

The land is impoverished. The vast majority of peasants still work with no tools other than their hands, their legs, and a hoe. Experts claim that when traction doubles, so does the amount of land that can be cultivated.

Among the peasants, most of them cannot afford fertilizer or are not able to sell their products elsewhere because there are not enough trucks or roads, which is why when they are lucky and have extra grain, it often rots in poorly ventilated warehouses. According to the FAO, 25 percent of the world's harvests are destroyed by rodents or poor storage—most, of course, in those countries, where the silos are either poorly built or nonexistent.

In few arenas is the inequality so glaring, so grotesque, as in agriculture: the basic industry that supplies us with food.

The director of an NGO based in Niamey, who asked me not to use his name, said, "I feel outraged when they say that the Sahel can't feed itself. Of course it can; you just need policies and politicians for whom that is a priority. Large international donors talk a lot about corruption, and they are right. But it's also their fault. If I give you ten francs to buy a pencil and then I never make you show me that pencil, I'm not going to keep giving you the same ten francs every year so you can buy the same pencil. That's what they do: they give and give and give, knowing that their money is ending up in the worst pockets, because it's convenient for them in order to maintain their policies and their business in the region. It's a mutually beneficial relationship, and not only economic. A corrupt government that is going to give in easily when an American or European company arrives to do business is not only convenient for them, there's also something more structural. It's in their interest to keep local governments dependent on their 'humanitarian' aid. And it's the same with the governments: it's in their interest to keep the population dependent on that aid, and at the same time distracted. It's difficult for people who are always threatened by hunger to look carefully at what their leaders are doing. The more difficult a population's circumstances, the less they dig. In addition, those people learn to live on handouts; instead of thinking about how to produce their own food, they wait for some official or some bank to bring it to them. I'm not saying it's always like that, but . . ."

A nurse at the hospital in Madaoua told me about a mother—one among many, she said—who for months had been keeping her son a little below minimum weight so they would keep giving him nutrition supplements and a little food—a bag of millet, a few liters of oil—for her and the rest of the family. The following day the nurse introduced me to her and we had a brief conversation.

"They tell me your son isn't getting better, that he's still underweight."

"That's right, he's not getting better, poor thing."

"Could it be that's because he doesn't eat all his food?"

"No, I give him everything, doctor, everything. I think he must be under a curse. It must be a curse, doctor."

There were also women who found out where and when different NGOs were distributing food and would walk for hours to obtain it. Some need it for their children—one packet of Plumpy'Nut costs 150 francs (a quarter of a dollar) in the market in Madaoua—others need it to sell so they can buy other things to eat.

Hunger in Niger—and in many other countries in Africa, Asia, and the Americas—is not "structural." Though maybe it is, because nobody built structures that would make sure there wasn't hunger. Here, without going any farther, the soil isn't very good, but with fertilizers, herbicides, tractors, and irrigation, everything would be different.

Hunger in Niger—as in so many other countries—is a consequence of plunder. If, during the one hundred years before independence, something of what had been produced had been accumulated; if, afterward, some of Areva's uranium had been used to increase agricultural yield, then there would be tractors, some irrigation, a few roads, perhaps even light industry. Ways to improve lives—even slightly; ways to eat a little more often.

In their book, *Enough: Why the World's Poorest Starve in an Age of Plenty*, former *Wall Street Journal* journalists Roger Thurow and Scott Kilman recount the unbelievable tragedy of a great success. In 2002 Ethiopia had already seen several years of increasing agricultural yields, this due to seed improvements, the use of some fertilizers, tractors, and a minimum amount of irrigation. That year Ethiopia had become the second largest producer of grain on the continent, after South Africa. But nobody had ever thought about what to do with so much grain. The quantity surpassed local demand; the roads to the ports were destroyed or cut off by the war in Eritrea; nobody—either in the government or the private sector—had money to buy and store the grain; there weren't even any silos to store it in. There were millions of hungry people in certain areas of the country, but the roads to them were impassable, and only airplanes of international aid agencies were able to reach them—mostly from the United States, carrying grain from the United States, in accordance with their laws. The country was full of grain that nobody could use, and the United States arrived with its own grain: tons and tons of grain bought at very high prices from US farmers.

In some regions, there was simply too much grain; the markets were flooded with cheap wheat, and in a few days, the price dropped to two dollars per two hundred pounds. Most farmers lost so much that the following year they didn't have any money to buy seeds, fertilizer, or—the privileged fuel for their water pumps: the majority of the land was left fallow. The harvest of 2003 was one of the smallest in the last several decades, and hunger spread throughout the country. "'I knew that when I cut the size of my farm, I was contributing to the food shortage,'" a farmer named Bulbula Tulle told Thurow. "'It's horrible. But at least I'm not losing money.'"[6]

Romeo Momo, the director of MSF in Niger, had been working in the region for two years. He was born and grew up in Mali, trained in a number of organizations, and is an expert on the Sahel. Momo spoke calmly but firmly, with conviction.

"It's true, there are more or less natural and demographic components that make life more difficult. There's always the threat of plagues, such as locusts and sparrows, who can arrive one night, one morning very early when the field is just about ready, and take everything. And then there are issues related to the last few decades of history. Some of the nomads who roamed the area with their flocks became sedentary and added to the demographic pressure, reducing the space for the remaining nomads to settle, and so forth. Since there are fewer animals, there's less fertilizer, and the chemical fertilizer replacements are expensive, so yield decreases. The soil has been degraded, there's less rain, the population has increased. So the land that used to produce enough food to eat, no longer does . . ."

In the last twenty years, the population of Niger has grown by four percent, yet agricultural production can only accommodate two percent of that growth. With more people, the land gets divided up into smaller and small plots. Before, the system worked because the peasants would keep adding terrains that were a little farther away from their villages, with land that was a little drier, a little less fertile. But now they no longer can: everything is occupied. This also prevents them from letting their land remain fallow. Each plot yields less, so each plot can rest less often, so each plot yields less, and so forth, until the yields decrease so much that the peasant can no longer live from his or her labor. For centuries, land could only be sold to relatives or, in the worst case, to neighbors. Forty years ago this regulatory mechanism broke down, and land began to be sold on the famous market: rich people in the cities—government officials, businessmen—started buying it, and many peasants found themselves with an asset that didn't yield enough to meet their needs but was worth some money; in their desperation, the chance to sell was tempting—first one acre, then another, then the last one. And they were left with nothing, but still had to live, now as pariahs, with a relative or, finally, as immigrants to the slums of Niamey or Abidjan.

"So it is," said Momo as we spoke about this problem. "But this has been going on for forty years. A solution should have been found."

Hussena and Salou had two grown sons over twenty-five who were still living with them. Getting married was expensive and they hadn't been able to raise the money for the bride price, the party, and the gifts. Hussena told me that she was thinking of asking a relative for a loan to cover a wedding for her eldest, who had grown more and more impatient; if the harvest this year isn't bad, said Hussena, she was going to try. If not, she worried that he would leave and never return.

"Where will he go?"

"He says he wants to go to Niamey, but he doesn't know how to get there, he doesn't know anybody . . ."

"Have you been to Niamey?"

"No, and I don't know anybody there. Where would I go?"

"How do you imagine it?"

"I don't know, a very big place."

"Where people are better or worse off?"

"There it's very different. They're much better off. They have electricity, water, food. In the city, there's always food; their lives are much better. In the city, everybody's lives are much better."

This is how she imagines a city that is crammed full of shanties, garbage dumps, beggars, cripples, outcasts.

"You wouldn't want to go live there?"

"I'd go, but to live in Niamey, you have to start with something."

She explained it to me patiently: imagine that she and her husband and their sons—or even without their sons, for theoretically they could leave them in the village—go to Niamey to live. They would need money to get there, and then, when they arrived, they would have to have something to eat the first few days before they found work, if they found work, and anyway, where would they sleep? She'd heard that in the city you can't just go and bed down anywhere, you need to rent a room. And because they don't have that kind of money, they can't go. Going to the city to make a new life for yourself is for people who already have something. That's why she thinks her son should stay with them. And anyway, she says, lowering her voice, as if she weren't really going to say it, there's another thing: "Children who leave forget their parents."

6

When it did rain the fields would be full of men and women, hoeing the ground to plant the seeds. The soil would still put up a fight, though it would be softened by the wetness. I was there in Madaoua the day after a rainfall.

"You can't believe how happy we were when we saw the first drops," a man named Ahmad tells me with a triumphant smile, "and we saw that they were good."

"It seemed like it was never going to come. Each year it seems like it is never going to come, and it finally does, and then the next year it seems like it's never going to come."

"And it always does?"

"No. Sometimes it doesn't."

Or, to put it another way: the rain came when it came, regardless of how bad it was desperately needed. Rain that falls or doesn't, a swarm of locusts that sweep through, a merchant who hoards and raises prices: these make the difference between life and death for dozens, thousands. Being rich means you have options, a certain amount of backup, not to live always on the verge of disaster. It means you have a wider arena to move in, where there's room even to fall, where even if you've fallen, you're somewhere. Poverty is living on a knife's edge—the slightest stumble, and you fall off.

Wristwatches weren't common apparel, but Ahmad had a big one on his right wrist—digital, square, heavy, metal, flashy; he glanced down at it every once in a while, as if to make sure it was still there, as if to see that I saw that he was looking at it, looking at him, a man with a wrist-watch. The fact that the time of day matters—not abiding by hours so much as marking them—is an important change in a culture; peasants who have spent centuries measuring time without clocks suddenly have to confront new situations, where the time of day is a piece of information. And, of course, they like to show that off.

Ahmad was twenty-eight years old and had a basic primary school education: he could read, write, do arithmetic. He also had a wife, three children, a father, a mother, three brothers, four sisters, and a multitude of nieces and nephews; among all of them, they owned three half-acre plots, two of full acre plots, and one quarter of an acre plot shared among four men. This makes him wealthier than almost all of his neighbors.

"Don't go getting any wrong ideas, my man. Nobody gives me anything. I break my back."

Ahmad worked the land with his father and two of his brothers. Farming the arid soil to produce food was a long process. In April, before planting, they would burn the field to remove the weeds and prepare the soil, which was already depleted from long years of overuse. Then came the most labor-intensive part: making rows with hand plows, in this case, long sticks with small knives on the end. That was a common sight here: a stick and a man breaking through the earth's crust. In May, before the first rains, they would sow the seeds, planting dry, and wait to spread the fertilizer until they knew if it was going to rain, allowing for the seeds to sprout. They were wealthy, but not wealthy enough to waste fertilizer on hope. Two or three weeks later, if it did rain, the first sprouts would begin to appear. Fertilizer was very expensive; even if it was just cow manure, there were fewer cows because there was less unoccupied land for the nomads to graze their animals. So now it had to be purchased, and great care had to be taken how it got spread around. After a month, they would weed and apply more fertilizer, if there was any left, and then wait yet another month and a half or even two, praying for rain, and praying as well that when it should rain, that the sparrows or locusts wouldn't come and devour everything. If it all worked out, they could harvest and make up the bundles. But even then, in every field, no matter the distances, there are struggles: what isn't eaten by the grazing goats of shepherds dries up from drought. Even if the crops manage to survive, the land must be worked eight to ten hours under a brutal sun, with only a break at noon to pray and a single ball of millet for lunch.

"Is it very tiring?"

"Very."

"Does it leave you much time to think?"

"Yeah, a lot. I can think things over many times."

"What do you think about?"

"What I think about most, what I think about all the time, is when I am going to finish, how much is left to do. And often I think that one day I have to get the money to buy myself a plow and a couple of cows or a camel to pull the plow. Then my work will be so much easier . . ."

A wheel plow made by the village blacksmith cost about 35,000 francs, almost seventy dollars. And it wasn't very sturdy, Ahmad told me, but if you took care of it, it could last, though, he admitted, they almost always broke. A good could cost 60,000 or 80,000 francs, and you needed a pair of cows to pull it, which costs no less than 150,000. Maybe 200,000 or 250,000 would be enough. That is: $400 or $500.

"That's a lot," he said, and sighed.

Small-scale farming is hereditary; it's very unlikely, unless things go very badly, that the son of a farmer would give up his father's land. He would take it over and live the same life as his father, repeating, conserving.

It is a destiny, I thought: a destiny.

And then I understood that destiny is an idea that comes from other times, an idea that comes from farming.

If he had a plow, Ahmad told me, he could grow a little more and work more quickly, and with his free time he could work planting other fields, or buy another small plot—because he would be able to do everything faster and better—and that would give him the energy to take his trips or, as they called it here, his "exoduses." Every year, once or twice a year, Ahmad would go to Nigeria for a few months to make money for his family. Nigeria was very close, less than ten miles away, and the borders were porous: he told me that the Boko Haram groups in the Sahel use them a lot.

For many years Niger remained outside of regional conflicts, but not anymore. Acts of terrorism have placed it on the military map of the world. In February 2013 it was reported that the United States had set up a drone base on the outskirts of Niamey, a base for the weapon that is changing the way wars are fought, and that is the clearest expression of the extreme military differences between the rich and the poor: the poor fight with their bodies and the rich with machines they control from far away.

A US official refused to say how many Predator drones were there, but did insist that their deployment was temporary and "for now they are only being used for surveillance." But the move involved Niger in the war and placed its government in an uncomfortable position. "We welcome the drones," President Mahamadou Issoufou said at the time. "Our countries are like the blind leading the blind. We rely on countries like France and the United States. We need cooperation to ensure our security."[7]

That's not the only reason: aid and cooperation with the West comprises 40 percent of the Niger state budget and this, like everything, comes with a price.

Ahmad and other young men from the village would cross the border, during the harvest season of rice and corn in Nigeria. As in many other poor countries, the old mechanism whereby men leave, move around, travel, while the women remain bound to the land, had remained intact. Actually, the women would take one long trip: when they got married, they left their homes to live in their husband's villages. And then, short of a catastrophe, that was it.

In Niger, a peasant's labor was worth 2,000 francs a day—four dollars; in Nigeria, this rate could be as high as 4,500 francs—almost ten dollars. With some of what he earned, Ahmad would buy socks or flashlights from a Chinese wholesaler in Kano and try to sell them in the villages. And every ten or fifteen days he would send a little money—sometimes through a friend who was returning, sometimes through a bank, which takes more than 10 percent—to his wife so the family could eat.

"And if I didn't love my land, I would stay in Nigeria to work. But I can't, I can't just abandon it; it's my father's land, my grandfather's . . ."

It wasn't just that Ahmad didn't want to, it's that his family wouldn't let him. Last year, the owner of a Nigerien farm offered him permanent work. And it wasn't to sweat with hoe in hand but rather to do the accounting. Ahmad was excited, but of course, the first thing he did was ask for his father's permission. His father reminded him of his uncle, who had gone to work in Nigeria years before and never come back, never even sent anything. His father told him he didn't want him to disappear from their lives.

Remittances from migrants are a savage way to redistribute wealth, mixed in with even slightly more savage exploitation. Poor people go to wealthy countries to do the jobs locals don't want to do, and in exchange they send that money to their own countries. Hundreds of millions of migrants in the world send hundreds of billions of dollars back to their countries of origin. In Niger, one out of every thirty men works in Nigeria, Ghana, Benin, or the Ivory Coast, sending home about $100 million a year. Many remain; others leave and come back.

They are, also, a poor form of globalization. The implosion in Libya, for example, after the fall of Gaddafi, not only spread jihadists throughout the region, it also prevented a quarter of a million Nigeriens who had gone there to work from sending money home: more misery through very remote causes.

Ahmad wasn't going to give up; he affirmed that he would get ahead. He knew that with effort, with many sacrifices, he could make farming this land work. He wasn't afraid of the effort or the sacrifices. His body was already showing signs of wear, his daily uniform, a white and yellow shirt with big hippie flowers and a pair of pants, were stained and full of holes. He did have his wristwatch.

Ahmad managed. But even if he could cultivate all of his land, and sometimes supplement that with a crop of onions in December or the okra the women occasionally tried to grow, or even his temp jobs in Nigeria, it would never be enough.

"We almost always eat now. But not always. The children always eat. Almost always."

Ossame, his two-year-old son, was just released from the hospital in Madaoua where he had been treated for acute malnutrition. Ahmad didn't believe it, that it couldn't have been that, that the doctor must have made a mistake.

"Who do they think they are?" he asked me rhetorically. "When Ossama got there, he weighed fifteen pounds. We give them their piece of ball every day. It's just that here everything depends on so many things. Sometimes I think I can't think about so many things. About whether it'll rain, about seed, fertilizer, Nigeria, my brothers, if this and that and the other. A man can't think about so many things."

"What's your favorite dish, the food you like to eat most?"

"Balls of millet."

"Really? Is it better than chicken?"

"Chicken? I could never eat chicken. Is that strange to you?"

It was springtime. The old tree trunks were alive with new leaves, the shrubs were green, the millet was sprouting in the fields; I had gone to Niger during the rainy season, and the unrelentingly dry landscape was softening, becoming more livable. But it is, also, the *soudure*; it is cruel that just when nature experiences a modicum of abundance, humans suffer the most extreme scarcity.

A friend of Ahmad's walked by, and they started chatting. This friend told Ahmad that he heard that in the villages on the other side of Madaoua, the millet was growing tall and strong. Everything is green, said his friend, and Ahmad nodded. I had just been through those villages: newly planted fields, very few shoots; I told him so.

"No, sir, you must be wrong. We know that they're going to have a good harvest there."

You can't argue with somebody who knows. But you can think, perhaps, of the need for mythology: a bit farther away, always farther away, there's something (better), something one deserves but doesn't have. This is what makes, among other things, modernity, as well as religion. This is what makes history.

When he wanted to pamper himself—when he could pamper himself—Ahmad went to the home of some relatives in Madaoua for a day or two to rest and watch television.

"I watch the news and soccer. I'm a fan of Real Madrid. Do you know that team? Real Madrid?"

He repeated himself, slowly, as if to explain. He went on to tell me that one day he would be independent, have his own land, a television set, his two oxen to plow his land. And that recently he almost managed it—the oxen, he said, he almost got them—because he'd worked a lot and sold many flashlights in Nigeria and he had a little money and he could think about buying them, but then he got tempted.

"What do you mean you got tempted?" I asked, playing along, and he smiled with his jumbled teeth and held onto the mystery.

"I got tempted. You know what I did?"

I wonder when that very contemporary definition of "doing something" with one's life started making the rounds: to "give meaning," to use it for something. Something other than eating, working, procreating, believing, forgetting, dying. For millennia, few ever thought about that; for the vast majority, living was more than enough. But now it doesn't seem to be—one has to do something else.

It seems like an urban idea. My prejudice: for a peasant bound to his land it is easier to imagine continuity, more difficult to imagine radical change. Or more difficult to desire it, because there were always wars, migrations, cataclysms: change as threat.

"You don't know. How could you know," Ahmad said, before reverting to his mysterious silence for another minute. Then, like someone throwing a bomb, he spoke again. "I got married. Now I have a second wife."

Ahmad was so proud—his smile spread across his face. He told me that he got married seven months ago with his first cousin, a seventeen-year-old, and that the wedding was beautiful, there was a lamb and singing and dancing and now he had to work much more because it would not be easy to support two women, but he would manage it, he told me.

"Why did you get married again?"

"Because I felt like it."

"You don't like your wife anymore?"

He explained it to me: his group of friends were nine boys from the village who did everything together, who knew each other forever, played together, studied together, worked together, and many of them went to Nigeria together, and they were real and true friends. And out of the nine, six already had a second wife, and he didn't want to be left behind.

"They teased me, laughed at me. They acted as if they were better than me."

It would be easier, simpler, to be able to write that Ahmad didn't manage to buy his long-desired plow because of the socioeconomic situation and the global inequalities and the gross injustices—and that's true, but it's also true that he had his opportunity and he chose not to take advantage of it. Or, in fact, he chose to take advantage of it in another way.

"We had such a good time at the wedding. Almost two days of partying, everybody was there—friends, family."

What with the bride price and the gifts, the wedding cost almost 200,000 francs: exactly what he would have spent on the plow.

"But now they get along well, the two of them, there's no problem. And my friends know they have to take me seriously."

"It's not too much work, having two wives?" I asked just what he was expecting and so giving him the chance to shine.

"For as long as God grants me health, there won't be any problem."

He looked at his wristwatch and got up to leave. Busy man.

7

That time, once again, there were problems with the harvest. In 2004 drought and a plague of locusts had reduced the yield of millet, but what really made thousands and thousands of Nigeriens go hungry was a twofold increase in the price. The price on international markets rose due to speculation on the Chicago Mercantile Exchange (CME), and a lot of grain went to Nigeria, where the demand was constantly growing. But local prices increased above all because of the maneuvers of twenty or thirty large-scale merchants who control trade in Niger. They were the ones who took advantage of the government's withdrawal from the market to manipulate it: they raised the price of millet, hoarded tons for when it rose again, then raised it again. They had no reason to concern themselves with the well-being of the population; all they cared about, with the full force of the logic of their logic, was to make more money.

At the end of 2004 ever-increasing numbers of people were left without any food or money to buy it. Cows and goats died by the thousands: for many Nigeriens, the beginning of the final disaster is the death of their animals. But President Mamadou Tandja was campaigning for reelection, which he won at the end of that year; the crisis was happening, but the government was careful not to mention it for fear of losing votes, for the same reasons malnutrition and infant mortality were not a central theme of the national political agenda. The Department of Nutrition of the Ministry of Health had spent a year without a leader.

"The famine label is not neutral. How a 'crisis' is interpreted determines how it should be acted upon. Whether a situation is or is not characterized as 'famine' influences how much money can be spent, where and how it should be spent, and who should administer relief funds and operations," wrote Benedetta Rossi in "The Paradox of Chronic Aid."[8]

Tandja's government decided to play dumb so he wouldn't be taken for daft or useless. That's why they denied the obvious; that's why they didn't ask for the aid they needed. A classic scenario that repeats itself every certain amount of time. Ethiopia, 1984–85, for example: half a million dead.

Just like the famines in North Korea should be cautionary tales about what a dictatorial state does when its sole concern is to remain in power, the Nigerien famine of 2005 should serve to illustrate what the market does when it operates as it wishes. But the famine served other purposes as well.

At that time, Niger had some fourteen million inhabitants, of which almost three million were children under five years old. Every year two hundred thousand of those children died, and half of those deaths were associated with undernourishment. But in 2005, children under five were dying at a higher rate than in any war: five out of every ten thousand every day.

MSF was there, almost by accident. They had arrived three years earlier to carry out a vaccination campaign against rubella in the district of Maradi, one of the most fertile and productive regions in the country, and they had discovered that the number of malnourished children surpassed any previous estimate. So they decided to intervene.

"We didn't carry out any study," Stéphane Doyon, an officer in the MSF's Sahara base told me, "we were working in the region and we saw the number of malnourished children. It was an illness nobody was paying any attention to. They paid attention if there was a catastrophe with the weather or war; if not, nothing."

The situation only got worse. In April 2005 they already knew that 20 percent of the children under five in Maradi were suffering from severe acute malnutrition. (In general, not much is known about hunger in adults: why they don't die right away, why they last for several years, continue to deteriorate, die of other causes. But that year, another organization calculated that the mothers of these children had a proportionately high level of malnutrition.)

However, the government refused to intervene, or pressure the grain wholesalers, or ask for help. When asked about the famine, Niger's president, Mamdou Tandja, outright denied that it was happening, telling reporters: "The people of Niger look well-fed, as you can see."

In his essay, "Building the Case for Emergency," Xavier Crombé, a French expert with MSF, explained that the first thing they had to do to support an efficient intervention in that famine was "to construct an object of public health concern: infant-child malnutrition in Niger" and turn it into a main subject. And he recounts the steps they took to do so: collect data, sift through them, understand them, disseminate them, and propose possible solutions. This is how things work in the world: there are subjects that are accepted as priorities, and others that aren't. "Constructing concern" is only the first step, but it is a fundamental one: "to bring the disease into social existence," say those who do it. Turn it into an unavoidable emergency.[9]

It took some time, but they managed. It was already August and the children were dying by the thousands when President Tandja finally asked for help—and distributed a little of the millet he was hoarding. Then began the dance of the donors: I need so much; okay, I'll give you half; no, please, the situation is very difficult; but it's already the middle of the year and I've already allocated the entire budget; don't you see the children are dying; but if I give you more it will line people's pockets; you can't say no now, you should have thought of it sooner; okay, so what do you want in return; we'll send a project your way; okay, whatever you want, but make it fast.

It's charity—from those who are making off with the beggar's possessions. Uranium, let's say. And a situation that never ceases to remind the victims who has the power. An African government asks "the world" for help during an emergency. So "the world" sets its mechanisms in motion, leading to discussions, tugs-of-war, haggling, and finally ends with the sending of food and medicine and maybe a clinic: the world is going to "save lives," which, it's understood, the country itself cannot save. But that country should, after all, thank the kind gentlemen who agreed to save it once they'd made off with everything they wanted.

That year, 2005, in the Department of Maradi, MSF treated sixty thousand severely malnourished children.

A body that feeds on itself. A body that consumes itself, which is why the most visible sign of malnutrition is called "wasting." The more advanced the process, the more mass a person loses and the less chance there is for survival. The body weakens, intestinal absorption decreases, kidneys shut down, the immune system weakens. At this critical moment of the disease—disease?—kwashiorkor usually appears as edema on the legs, arms, and face, as does marasmus, which causes severe emaciation.

Most people treated for severe malnutrition are children under the age of five—the most critical, most vulnerable stage of life. When malnutrition has still not reached the state of marasmus or kwashiorkor, it can be recognized through other symptoms. The most classic is the reduction of weight in proportion to height: the child's weight is compared to the average weight of children of the same height who are well fed.

But what has come to be used most commonly, because it is easy and precise, is the measure of the mid-upper arm circumference (MUAC): if the perimeter of the arm of a child measures less than 125 centimeters, the child is said to suffer from severe acute malnutrition (SAM); if it measures less than 115, the malnutrition is only severe, according to one commonly used set of definitions.

For decades the treatment for children with severe acute malnutrition—those who were literally dying of hunger—consisted of hospitalizing them and trying to feed them by mouth or intravenously. It was a costly solution—in resources, infrastructure, and personnel—as well as fairly ineffective: depending on the place and circumstances, between one-third and one-half of these children died. About twenty-five years ago, scientists reviewed the process and finally understood that the kind of food they were giving not only didn't cure them but sometimes, because of the demands it made on the weakened bodies, actually killed them.

In 1986, a French student named Michel Lescanne completed his training as a food-processing engineer with a study on "the feasibility of a cracker functioning as a nutritional supplement for the populations in poor countries." The son of a dairy engineer in Normandy, after his studies, Lescanne began to work in the family business where, convinced he had a mission, he helped develop protein tablets called Novofood, which were used in several African emergencies.

Lescanne then founded his own business, Nutriset, which would "dedicate itself to research on humanitarian nutrition, developing innovative solutions for the treatment and prevention of malnutrition." In 1993 he began the industrial production of enriched powdered milk, F-100 therapeutic milk, specifically designed to feed hungry children. It contained one hundred calories in each one hundred centiliters, and was quickly and abundantly put into use in food emergencies. But it had several problems.

For starters, the children, who had to follow a strict regime of F-100 every four hours in doses determined by their condition, required hospitalization. Because the milk spoiled quickly, it had to be prepared up to eight times a day. Many children fell victim to hospital-acquired diseases, infections, exposed as they were to the filth of hundreds of mothers camping out among babies with diarrhea. The hospitals weren't equipped to keep the hungry children there for three or four weeks, and the mothers couldn't spend a month away from their homes, where they had other children, a husband, and work to do. Many of them spent a few days, then left once their children seemed better. Some even took a supply of F-100 with them, and when they prepared it with dirty water and left it out in the African heat, it made them even sicker. Many children were back a few days later, worse than before—or they died at home.

In 1994 Lescanne proposed to André Briend, a physician specializing in nutrition at the Research Institute for Development (IRD) in Paris, that they work together to develop a better product. For more than two years they experimented with all kinds of ingredients, but none had the necessary longevity, flavor, and ease of handling. Until, the legend says, one morning while eating breakfast, Briend went into ecstasy over a jar of Nutella, which had the consistency he was looking for. The legend doesn't go so far as to claim that he shouted "Eureka!" but this is said to be the genesis of a paste made of peanuts, which, when enriched with milk, sugar, fat, vitamins, and minerals, could be eaten without preparation, tolerated high temperatures, and could last for two years in an aluminum packet. Plus, it tasted good. They called it Plumpy'Nut, the first in a line of Plumpy products, and a food that would have an everlasting impact on the treatment of child malnutrition.

Dr. Steve Collins, an Irish nutritionist, carried out the first experiments in Malawi and Ethiopia in 2002 and 2003. But the campaign carried out by MSF in Niger in 2005 was Plumpy'Nut's great launching pad, turning it into the most well-known ready-to-use therapeutic food (RUTF).

At first MSF workers had their doubts. Some doctors felt uncomfortable with the new protocol: to hospitalize the children for a few days until they recovered to a certain degree, then send them home with their dose of Plumpy; they did not like releasing a patient in that state; they complained that they were offering incomplete treatment.

But the outcomes, let it be said, were extraordinary: not only were they able to treat ever-increasing numbers of cases of malnutrition, they also achieved a nine-out-of-ten recovery rate from famished to healthy in children, which before then had been unheard of.

And they could treat a previously untreatable population: those with moderate acute malnutrition. The moderately malnourished are never hospitalized; their situation does not require constant medical attention. But, since these cases were more numerous, more children with that condition died.

The MSF campaign that year was only the beginning; thousands of centers now treat children with moderate acute malnutrition on an out-patient basis with the famous Plumpy.

Two years later, in 2007, the WHO, UNICEF, and the World Food Programme (WFP) issued a joint statement declaring it the best treatment for child malnutrition.

Success always produces unexpected consequences. The MSF experts, having taken on their role as researchers of new methods, began to think that it wasn't enough to supply Plumpy'Nut to the acutely malnourished, both severe and moderate. Faced with an entire population always on the verge of malnutrition, to look for and find a food supplement that would prevent their condition from worsening would not only save a lot of lives but also a lot of money in doctors, hospital infrastructure, and hospitalizations, money that could be used to distribute more supplements.

As Doyon explained, "Giving it to everybody, in a way, is cheaper than picking and choosing whom to give it to. Personnel expenses are reduced because there is no need for complicated decision-making, and many fewer children arrive at the hospitals with more complications that are more serious and more expensive to treat. So, the mortality rate is sharply reduced because they were treated before their organisms became severely compromised."

Doyon would go on to say that that the greatest risk to children was right after they weaned, when they stopped receiving the nutrition they needed to develop and, instead, filled their bellies with water and flour. At that point, they needed, above all, animal proteins, fruits, and vegetables, which is precisely what they didn't receive.

MSF contacted Lescanne and asked him to develop a version of Plumpy for this purpose. In 2007, Plumpy'Doz, a more diluted supplement, which comes in weekly packets and is taken three times a day, was ready for testing. They started in several villages in the Maradi region; a few months later they saw that those who had not taken it had gotten sick, and died, at double the rate of those who had.

"In addition," Doyon told me, "this allows us to improve other aspects of medical care for these children. For example: it's not easy to get a mother to walk six miles to have her baby immunized, but if she has to get her food supplement, she will go, and once there, vaccinations seem like a good idea. As well as other preventative treatments."

Prepared food supplements were not only an important advancement in the struggle against malnutrition; they were also turning into a gigantic business.

At the end of the nineties, an economist who was born in India and worked in the United States, C. K Prahalad, defined a new business opportunity: large companies should address the needs of an enormous mass of consumers whom nobody pays any attention to. He called them "BoP," or "bottom of the pyramid": the four billion people who live on less than two dollars and fifty cents a day.[10]

Prahalad, who studied at Harvard and taught at the University of Michigan, insisted that this could be good business, and that business, government, and international organizations should stop seeing these people as victims and start seeing them as demanding consumers; such a strategy, he said, would bring more than copious returns on their investments.

It's what many multinational companies, such as Ericsson or Sony, already do, designing mobile phones with graphic commands for illiterate Africans; or Unilever, which sells a shampoo in India that lathers better in cold water, for those who don't have hot water.

The industry of food supplements could be placed in this category, though at first most of the customers would not be the end consumers but rather the governments and organizations that help them. The industry could, however, apply pressure on them to buy and distribute their products.

In 2012 Nutriset produced almost fifteen thousand tons of Plumpy'Nut, ten times more than the previous decade. Lescanne made millions which, they claimed, were reinvested in research and development. In 2008, faced with criticism for these profits as well as the tight control they wielded over the patents for their products, Nutriset rolled out a franchise system: local producers—only ever in poor countries—could use the brand name, the know-how, and the technical support in exchange for a commitment to buy machinery, packaging, and certain ingredients —vitamins and minerals—from the home company. In this way, small Plumpy factories sprung up in a dozen African countries. The equation, however, didn't work that well. Here, in the Sociéte de Transformation Alimentaire of Niger (without going too far), they produce the paste with local peanuts, but bring palm oil from Malaysia, sugar from Argentina, cacao from the Ivory Coast purchased in Europe—and because of the scale of production, the local paste ends up costing more than the French one. In any case, the treatment is still expensive: a six months' supply of Plumpy'Doz costs about fifty dollars per child, this in a country where the people who need it live on less than a dollar a day.

Embarrassed, and a bit on the sly, I tasted it one afternoon at the hospital in Madaoua. Plumpy is gooey, greasy, very edible, a bit like peanut nougat; quite salty for a sweet.

And Abdoul, a two-year-old with a wide face and an underweight body, ran to ask me for it. I gave it to him, and he laughed so much as he smeared his face with that brown paste and licked himself clean.

Some said that Plumpy was a brand typical of an era of substitutes: sweetness without sugar, coffee without caffeine, butter without cholesterol, bicycles that don't go anywhere, cigarettes without smoke, sex without physical contact, nourishment without food: a way of pretending that these children who don't eat, eat, that those millions of impoverished people are going to stay alive.

Its success provoked debate. There was, above all, those who questioned the use of a palliative cure for a structural problem, in other words, "a medical response to a social problem," the famous Band-Aid for a hemorrhage.

MSF claimed they know, but that they also knew that their task—their opportunity—was not to reduce malnutrition but rather to avoid associating it with as many deaths as possible; that's difficult but it's all they could do. To be doctors was to accept that limitation.

The children—and their parents—still don't have food. Hunger continues unabated, but it kills less often.

Dr. Steve Collins, the pioneer, was also concerned, "I didn't want to usher in a new world order where the poor depend on food supplements from Europe or the United States."[11]

Plumpy is, when all is said and done, only a partial remedy for a disease that has no reason to exist: it is the most avoidable, the most curable of all known diseases.

Hunger kills more people every year—every day—than AIDS, tuberculosis, and malaria combined, and it doesn't exist. Hunger has none of the mystery, the inscrutable shadow realm, the unmanageable aspects of disease: impotence in the face of the incomprehensible. Hunger is too well understood, even though it doesn't exist: it's a human invention, our invention.

And it could so easily be our unbelievable past.

8

That's when I got sick: a week in the shadows. Even with a bed, electricity, running water, a toilet, a fan, a mosquito net, medicines, a doctor from Andalucía, some faith in medicines and science, those days of vomiting and diarrhea and fever and nightmares were punishing. I tried—and I failed—to imagine how it was for any of those men and women and boys and girls in those Nigerien villages, without electricity or running water or a toilet or a fan or a mosquito net or medicines or doctors, without the slightest certainty: there, often, people died from this.

I believed—I assumed at least—that I wouldn't get better. I spent days horizontal, aching so much it felt like I'd been beaten with baseball bats, getting up only to expel the contents of my guts. I expelled and expelled, drinking sips of water and having nightmares in which I would be wandering around a city that was too symmetrical and never ended, then I would expel more: I sweated, shat, vomited. I sweated more, I tossed and turned on the wet mattress; and I felt so hungry, an insistent demand from the mouth of the stomach, a constant insistence from a void that, after insisting so long, turned into pain. I did not eat for six days because I was nauseous and I shat and vomited everything I ingested; my body wouldn't absorb anything. Outside, life went on, and I paid less and less attention to it. Again and again I imagined, eagerly, the possibility of taking a long drink of cold water: one endless chug—which I couldn't actually do, because I'd expel that too. But I kept imagining it—at least I still had the desire. My hunger: the writing of this book was taking its revenge on me, I was embodying it, and I thought, in my confusion, that I wanted to understand, record what was happening to me, that I should take advantage of being sick to observe my hunger, but I just couldn't. My body had turned into my enemy: I was its hostage.

A note from that time: The sensation that something isn't right. That I should be better able to record what I'm feeling, that this would help me better understand the situation of hunger, help me describe it. The sensation that I cannot. Illness: The sensation that I am losing myself. But to what?

Advanced societies exchanged the venture of the social body for the venture of the individual body. Now, for men and women in prosperous countries, the limit, the unexplored territory, is no longer the *terra incognita* yet to be discovered or the adventurous tomorrows yet to be built, but rather the body: the body—one's own body—is the unknown, which, in all its mystery, can give us everything or take it all away. My hunger, during that time, was the hunger that belonged to a wealthy person from a Western society: it's not that society prevented me from obtaining food, rather that my body prevented me from dealing with it.

From time to time, I thought about the irony; from time to time, I thought again that I should concentrate and try to record what was happening to me: how my body coped with hunger. Hunger is, more than anything, an extreme consciousness of the body, and a fog in the mind. But at the time I didn't understand that much: I was so weak, incapable of thinking much about anything, lethargic, cross, in pain. I could feel every small movement, every threat from my stomach, my intestines, the various buzzings in my head, the groggy cries of my body. I had moments of rage and tantrums, others of desperation. I had many moments when I cared about nothing

"I've lost almost fifteen pounds," I told a nurse.

"Your wife is going to cry."

She told me this as though she were informing me of an oncoming storm.

I was sick in Madaoua during Ramadan: for an entire lunar month, it was ordained that everyone would go twelve hours a day without eating, days with temperatures reaching over one hundred degrees in the shade without a drop of water. To fast is to give something precious to a god—to deny oneself something one wants—and thereby obtain from him something in exchange. It is repaid with pleasure or satisfaction, something we care about deeply: the well-being of a relative, the success of a harvest or a battle, the guarantee that we will eat, the salvation of the soul we believe we have. Yet to me, to commit such an unnatural act is nothing more than a brutal expression of influence from the powerful to the meek.

God plays with his own—and with others. I was still sick and yet I carried on, separate from the sounds of the parties every night that entered through my window. In the meantime, every day, the hospital received sixty to seventy children with malaria, acute anemia, convulsions, pneumonia, severe diarrhea—all consequences of hunger. Pascual, a Spanish doctor, told me that that week, they'd again had fifty-odd deaths, and he was exhausted.

A different afternoon, Manuela, a nurse, also Spanish, told me that they were filled to overflowing, and they couldn't treat everybody and they had to choose; that it's monstrous but that there were children with little chance of recovery and so they would focus on those whose chances were better.

Manuela explained, "In order to stand it, you have to think about those you save. If you think all the time about those who die, you can't go on. But if you don't think about them, you would be strange, a machine. When you get home, often, that's when everything hits you, you realize how powerful it's all been. Here there's no time for that, no space, you live as if what you're living here were normal. Then one day you go home."

I started to recover. I went outside where I had—almost without realizing it—the strange sensation that I had learned something that I should know: the sensation that I had touched true misery. Not the misery of those who lived on the fringes of the wealthy, but that of those who lived where there is nothing, who had spent centuries eating what they could—that ball of millet, who pray each night that tomorrow they could eat—*inshallah*—that ball of millet.

A constant struggle for the most basic, if two cows was the thing you wanted most in the world. That misery that also consisted of not believing or having learned or even suspected that other lives were possible. It was not only a shrinking of material boundaries but also mental ones; a shrinking of the field of the imaginable.

And then, the most stringent meaning of the word *survival*: thousands and thousands of people wake up every day to see if they can find something to eat. The most concise meaning of the word *survival*: it's not easy, with that idea of the word, under those conditions, to think of anything long term—one month, three months, a year and a half, a century. In the future, being able to feed yourself will have become a luxury.

ON HUNGER: ORIGINS

1

According to legend, Diogenes the Cynic was caught one day masturbating in public. He was scolded loudly but refused to apologize.

"Oh, so you think it isn't right to banish sexual desire like this? What would you say if I could banish hunger by rubbing my belly?"

They understood him but they had no answer. Because he couldn't; to banish hunger you need food, and to have food, you need land to grow it and people to harvest it, and who owned the land, who grew the food, who got to eat it was the cause of so many wars, so much change: one of the prime movers of history.

We'll never really know how we began, but there are hypotheses. In his book *Cocinar hizo al hombre* [Cooking Made Us Human], Faustino Cordón Bonet claims it was because we didn't know how to do what others did; when our ancestors were primates hopping around in the trees looking for shoots and an unfortunate insect or two, there were a few who were better at hanging from the branches. Therein the origins of the larger apes: animals that developed powerful arms and torsos to travel from branch to branch, took over that desirable territory, and threw out the others; our ancestors, meek and meager, had to make a living on the ground.[1]

With that defeat, it is said, man began.

Others say that now—with overpopulation, climate change, the depletion of soil and water—"the food wars" will come. Food wars have always existed, and always will. There are only moments of relative calm between battles, during which the winners have so resolutely won that they don't have to fight in order to continue enjoying their triumph.

Humanoids, now on the ground, had to make a virtue out of necessity: they learned to walk better, developed more powerful feet, and made some refinements in those arms and hands they no longer needed for hanging: they could start to handle a primitive tool, a rock, a bone, a stick. This phase—this process—would last for millions of years and produce a couple of decisive results: erect posture, in consequence of the new habitat, which allowed them to carry tools they no longer had to discard in order to climb trees; and a larger degree of community because, fearful and facing new dangers in their new habitat, those primates had to take care of and support each other. Hence, also, evolution in their forms of communication: the first attempts at language.

With this equipment, which would supplement the obvious limitations of the human body—we are not especially strong, we can't jump or run like others, we don't have particularly good vision or senses of smell or hearing, we don't have powerful claws or teeth—those ancestors began to expand their sources of food. With certain sticks they could kill certain animals, with others they could dig up roots and tubers, with stones they could break the bones they found to eat the marrow; their bodies became accustomed to other foods, which in turn transformed them.

A mob: animals grunting and jumping around a smaller or weaker or deader animal, fighting over it, tearing it apart, eating it in chunks: the first images of hunger.

Sociability increased when it occurred to those inept hunters that they should do the same thing any trader on the stock exchange does today: diversify their risks. Those ape-men couldn't purchase a range of stocks but they could form alliances with other ape-men, their cousins and neighbors, and share whatever they all got every day. When someone didn't get enough on a particular day, they still ate because the others had. Out of this fear of not being able to eat, societies were formed, bonds strengthened. The principle of reciprocity was a form of equality: I give to you, you give to me, but what I give you I expect to be given back something of equal value. Trust and mistrust.

According to Bonet, hunger was their daily condition. Three or four million years ago, hominoids lived by the skin of their teeth, suffered privations and dangers, spent their lives looking for food. Mostly, they ate a variety of plants and the flesh of dead animals: they were, more than anything, carrions. The more animal fats and proteins they ate, the more the size of their heads and brains increased, and their better developed brains allowed them to obtain better food, which increased their brain capacity, and so forth. The brain-to-body ratio most common in animals, expanded exponentially in humanoids, and those bodies needed ever increasing amounts of food for their disproportionate brains.

But the human body is an archaism; it is designed for very different times and lives, when there might or might not be food; the leaves or animals that were supposed to feed our ancestors were difficult to find, a question of chance: sometimes yes, sometimes no.

Our metabolism and physiology were also established at that time. That's why satiety doesn't last long, why we have certain hormones that constantly need to be fed; this everlasting anxiety, this permanent fear of the consequence of having no food was the way to prepare for the moments when no food was to be had. It is what we usually call hunger: the combination of physical signals that demands food.

(However, in order to withstand periods of forced fasting, a system of reserves was also established: humans, like most animals, can store energy in the form of fat.)

And then, less than a million years ago, and who knows how—there are abundant hypotheses—those animals discovered the power of fire.

(Many millennia later, when those animals began to think they were so smart, they would celebrate this discovery as the beginning of their existence. Fire—according to their myths, including Prometheus—made them human, distinguished them from beasts.)

It's probable that fire was not, at first, used for cooking, that those ape-men first used it to protect themselves from the cold and other animals, and that it was only by chance that they discovered that some food tasted much better after it had fallen into the flames. By cooking their food, however, they established a fundamental difference: they were the first animals not to eat what they obtained but rather what they transformed and improved. Therein culture—one of the first forms of culture—was interposed between the meat of that creature and their stomachs: cooking made us human.

Those males and females learned to hunt and cook together, to have more time to think about something other than hunting and food, to help one another, to take care of their offspring—who, with such big heads, were born prematurely in order to be able to pass through their mothers' pelvises—to develop those languages that finally turned them into men and women.

Hunger, for some of them, began to be something that didn't happen all the time.

To think about that time can make you dizzy: to make the effort to imagine those half-clad ladies and gentlemen, wandering through the forests and across the plains, eating a few mouthfuls here a few there, without the least idea of past or future, is to remember, in contrast, everything we have invented.

Cooking, among other things, greatly expanded the boundaries of what was edible: large numbers of plants and animals, which humans couldn't digest raw, became edible when cooked. That's when our ancestors became truly omnivorous.

This process took thousands of years. To acquire new foods was to take over the world: the more I eat it, the more I make it mine. That's when we began to become machines that eat everything, as we do today. We eat animals, plants, and minerals: roots, rinds, stems, leaves, fruits, flowers, grains, mushrooms, algae, mollusks, fish, birds, bird embryos, reptiles, insects, and, from our fellow mammalians, their meat, blood, and skin, the marrow and even the glandular secretions that we call milk or cheese—and enormous quantities of a ground-up rock we call salt.

That capacity—that ability to fight hunger—is one of the main reasons that within a span of a hundred thousand years, the number of humans has gone from around one hundred thousand to the 7.7 billion we are today: an explosion that is the best test that the species—as a species—has functioned.

There's nothing more dishonest than being—than thinking as—a species.

This increase was a long and sinuous process. We suppose that temperatures rose, ecosystems changed, animals became scarce, and those hunters became gatherers. The hunter-gatherers had strict systems of birth control—which included, of course, infanticide—to maintain the delicate balance between persons and food. It is still unclear if they somehow lost control and thus were forced to think up new ways to feed themselves, or if new ways they discovered allowed them to let go of control: another case of the chicken or the egg.

In any case, the increase became an explosion when agriculture began. This was one of the great moments—and the great mysteries—of human history, though there are historians who say it was, above all, one of the great moments of women's history. About ten or twelve million years ago, different people in different places—the Middle East, Central America, China, New Guinea, tropical Africa—discovered more or less simultaneously what they could do to make those plants they searched for grow where they decided they should grow. They could remove their seeds, bury them, and wait—and, while they were at it, invent gods to ask for rain. The bit about the gods, of course, didn't come on its own; some gentlemen appeared who claimed they knew how they could talk to them and explain their babblings and contradictions. Priests and religions were, in a way, the parasites of those primitive grains.

At the same time, those humans discovered that they could do the same thing with animals: domesticate and raise them in order to make use of their meat and their milk and their eggs—as well as their labor power, which served to make more food.

It is difficult, now, when there is nothing more traditional that to cultivate the land, to think about a time when agriculture was the peak of modernity, the recent invention that was changing so many lives. They were, of course, afraid: the new is always scary to the majority. Many believed that plowing Mother Earth was an act of brutal violence: dug up, wounded, conquered by her children, she would one day take her revenge. Many mythological stories lament this intolerable violence: this the most primitive form of militant environmentalism.

It was a radical change: nobody had ever before been assured of having food a few months into the future. Along with that certainty came the necessity to remain in a particular place until those seeds bore their fruit. Thus appeared the first villages, where they could settle and wait. Thus appeared the idea of the future as a time when things one could predict would come to pass. Thus appeared the possibility to think about those things and make plans.

And thus appeared the necessity to find ways of preserve that grain. One of the great and often forgotten changes in history arrived when humans learned how to store food. Again, chicken and egg: perhaps they began to find ways to produce more and then confronted the problem of storing it, or more probably they began to find ways to store it and so looked for ways to obtain more than they needed for today and tomorrow. So they produced more and expanded their storage capacity and discovered new ways to produce more and so forth: our societies.

We began to be—for better or worse, or for nothing at all—what we are.

Those humans started to eat at certain predictable times of day. This was an extraordinary step, one that could be taken only because they believed their access to enough food meant they didn't have to eat whenever they could—as they'd always done, as all other animals still do.

Constant hunger is the original condition of humans. And the relief of knowing that for a few hours it will not be necessary to look for more food is a decisive cultural conquest. We are more *human* when our bellies are fuller. And we are more *human* the less time we have to spend filling them. The process of civilization is a path that leads from spending all our time getting food to spending the least amount of time possible.

This story is still relevant today.

2

Out of laziness, ignorance, or who knows what other great virtue, we are inclined to think that history could only ever have been as it has been. It's the oldest trick in the book played by those who would rather we accept the world as it is: whatever was, is what it had to be—and what is, is also what has to be or, moreover, it is the only option. What would the world be like if, say, it hadn't occurred to a gang of early hominids that what they used and consumed was theirs, their possession, their property, but rather belonged to everybody because everybody wanted it and needed it? What if they had preferred not to make the effort to work and had continued to be nomadic slackers? What if nobody had had enough fear or imagination or ambition or intelligence to tell their companions—convince their companions—that that huge ancient tree was a superior being, a "god" they could ask things of?

In the first villages—the first cities—the ability to store food produced another extraordinary innovation: free time, idleness as a demonstrable idea. Humans no longer had to spend all their time obtaining food because they knew that their food was there, growing in the fields, fattening up in the farmyard. Those men and women could devote time to other things: sewing, tanning hides, making pottery, traveling, fighting, conversing, taking naps, conspiring, loving, betraying each other. Special skills—trades—developed, as well as differences.

The existence of food reserves also made others want them, and since they had to be protected, individuals appeared—the strongest, the most ambitious—who specialized in doing just that. The community agreed to give them what they needed in exchange for defending them, and hence they acquired power.

It was a long process: due to food surpluses, some people no longer had any part in producing it, and they settled down into bigger houses—that we would one day call palaces—and those in towns became different from those in the countryside, and the rich became different from the poor. Wealth accumulated in those new places, those first cities. Whoever controls the granary, controls those who want to eat that grain. Whoever has some control, wants to control more, by inventing structures that guarantee that they can maintain control. That's when, here and there, the first states began to appear.

The new Mesopotamian states already had enough power to construct canals and dikes on a scale never seen before, which in turn allowed them to plant and harvest on such a grand scale: obtain more food, hence more power.

And classes formed, differences, inequalities. The most important innovation was that some ate and others didn't. Until then, human tradition had been the more or less equal sharing of scarcity and abundance among the whole tribe. No longer. And those who produced the food—whose hands got dirty, whose backs broke plowing the land—tended to be those who had less to eat.

The innovation: that some ate and others didn't.

Societies organized around agriculture reduced the rich and complex diet of early humans to a diet of "staple foods," such as what predominates today in many poor societies. A particular grain or tuber became the habitual, repeated daily food of a large portion of the population—complemented by a sauce made of whatever vegetables are available, maybe a piece of meat, hunted or raised, every once in a great while.

It's true, many more ate, but they ate poorly. Curiously, the great Neolithic revolution, the great technical leap forward that would usher in change like no other in human history, made those humans smaller and more fragile as it made them more civilized. Moreover, it put them to work from sunup to sundown, for a boss.

The diet of their hunter and gatherer ancestors was rich in vegetables and a bit of lean meat; the first farmers moved on to eat more carbohydrates and sugars. Their bodies felt it: within a few centuries, those peasants lost about eight inches of height and five years of life. And, due to the sweetening of their diet, they came to know cavities, another invention of our culture, and arthritis, due to their work on the farm, not to mention other diseases. The first epidemics took place.

These men and women were much more intelligent, and they lived in infinitely more complex societies; they had kings and gods and prostitutes and soldiers, they had ideas about the world, and they reproduced boldly; but they were shorter and lived a shorter amount of time. These are the strange paradoxes of "progress." They weren't hungry anymore—they weren't always hungry anymore—but they began to be poorly nourished.

This could be a version of a contemporary discussion: the progress of the Neolithic—the discovery of agriculture—worsened the quality of food for some people. But forty centuries later, it has made it possible for there to be forty times more of us. What of that?

Does the species improve if the lives of individuals worsen?

Simultaneously, this harvested food, which was eaten by the chiefs and generals and priests and emperor king gods who ruled over those people, became more and more specialized. Those were the years—about ten thousand of them ago—when the difference between high food and low food appeared: between the table set with various products in complex preparations—already sometimes produced by the first specialists—and the peasants' or craftspersons' or soldiers' bowl, which contained one food, the same food every day, prepared by the women of the house. Thanks to those other foods, the powerful became fat—and fat became a sign of power. The poor were thin—a sign of powerlessness.

And, of course, hunger survived, in so many places.

A single-food diet not only worsened their nutrition, it also brought serious dangers. On almost every occasion this food source failed—due to drought, war, flooding, freezing—hunger became unstoppable. The first known record of famine is an inscription on the tomb of the monarch, Ankhtifi, of Upper Egypt, from four thousand years ago, which reads: "The whole of Upper Egypt died of hunger and each individual had reached such a state of hunger that he ate his own children."

They invented bread. Making bread is an achievement that implies thousands of years of research—an extraordinary adventure. To plant seeds, harvest the plants, grind the grain, turn it into dough, shape it, bake it; four or five extremely complex technologies—four or five stunning discoveries—put into play so that Mediterranean humans would produce their emblematic food. So much so that in the *Iliad* and the *Odyssey*, Homer often refers to humans as "eaters of bread."

There were gods. Humans—afraid, needy—had created gods. One of the functions of these gods—one of their most important functions—was to guarantee the harvest. And if not, in the worst-case scenario, when there was no other solution, to give them something to eat:

> And the children of Israel said unto them, Would to God we had died by the hand of the LORD in the land of Egypt, when we sat by the flesh pots, *and* when we did eat bread to the full; for ye have brought us forth into this wilderness, to kill this whole assembly with hunger.
> "Then said the LORD unto Moses, Behold, I will rain bread from heaven for you; and the people shall go out and gather a certain rate every day, that I may prove them, whether they will walk in my law, or not.[2]

Improvements in farming techniques increased the population, forcing more and more people to go in search of new lands to feed themselves. Some lands were not as fertile as the first, and they had to struggle to invent new methods. For instance, a peasant would clear a plot of land, then burn it, and those ashes were the fertilizer that allowed them to grow food for one or two years; when the land was depleted, the peasant did the same to a neighboring plot, and so forth. A few years later, they could return to the first plot and begin the cycle again. Even so, the mechanism worked only if there was a lot of land available, that is, if there weren't many people. But numbers kept increasing, and this was the beginning of the great migrations, and the occupation of more and more territory.

In the Mediterranean world of the Roman Empire, where there was no longer any spare land, peasants discovered that things worked better when they integrated animal husbandry and agriculture: the animals complemented their diet, fertilized the land with their manure, and helped them cultivate it. The animals, however, had stiffer and stiffer competition: slaves tended to be cheaper and sometimes more efficient.

In Asia, in the meantime, rice cultivation expanded. In certain regions—in the southeast, southern China, parts of India, Korea, Japan—two or three harvests a year were possible. The system needed many people to work the land, but it produced a lot of food and could feed them. The Far East became the most populated region on the planet.

The idea of high food and low food reached its peak in Rome. Certain imperial banquets in Rome symbolized—and still do today, two thousand years later—the quintessence of the gastronomic extravagance of the wealthy: Trimalchio's banquet in *The Satyricon*, with its sows' udders, oyster-stuffed goose, flamenco tongues, and pork carved into the shape of birds, is still one of the most colorful examples of that difference. If the value of cooking consists of transforming food into iconography, then a false creature is created for the sake of culture. Nature is cooked, processed.

But Rome also established a model for food distribution that still functions in our societies: *assistentialism*, otherwise known as welfare, dependency, or clientelism. First all citizens, and finally all inhabitants, had the right to free or highly subsidized—according to the moment— staples: grain, bread, and oil. The state protected against hunger, a system that sometimes didn't work, but often did.

"Only in Rome does the State feed the poor. In the East, the poor are considered a bother, and if they cannot buy their own bread, they are left to die of hunger," wrote Mark Anthony in a letter thirty years before the birth of Christ. To do so they organized, for the first time, a global, integrated food system: the grain the leaders in Rome distributed to the poor was brought from Sicily or Egypt, the oil from Hispania or Syria. And they were well aware—and said so—that they did so to buy peace: that food was like a war tribute paid to a beaten enemy, quiet but never asleep, the people of the city of Rome.

That's also where there appeared the word that still now refers to the practice of modest distribution: each Roman with power had hundreds or thousands of people less wealthy than he, who followed him and obeyed him and received, in return, favors: his clients.

The system would outlast them.

3

Since the beginning of civilization, hunger has been one of the most powerful weapons—an extreme way of wielding power. To conquer a city by cutting off its food supply until hunger defeated it; to win the appreciation or tolerance of a population by doling out food to prevent hunger—and so many others.

Hunger was a threat because it never ceased to be a presence. Hunger—the possibility of hunger—was, for millennia, the norm of all cultures.

In her excellent book, *Hunger: An Unnatural History*, Sharman Apt Russell summarizes the three stages originally set out by anthropologist Robert Dirk, that occur when the threat of famine appears. Russell, paraphrasing Dirk, writes,

> People are excited and may become more gregarious. They may share more, setting up such things as communal kitchens. They may migrate. Emotions increase. There is irritability and anger, political unrest, possible rioting, and looting. There may be more religious ritual, increased devotion, and mystical acts. In the second stage, resistance is directed against the hunger itself, as opposed to its cause. People conserve energy rather than expend it. They are less social, their actions focused on obtaining food. Small, closed groups, such as the family unit, become the most effective way to survive. Friends and extended family may need to be excluded. Stealing is common. Organized political work diminishes, although there may be random acts of aggression and violence. In this social disorder, people turn more trustingly to authority. [...] The last phase is marked by a collapse of all cooperative efforts, even within the family. This can happen gradually. The elderly are the first to be sacrificed and then young children. People become physically as well as emotionally exhausted, sitting for long hours, staring at nothing, saying nothing. Disaster brings out the very best and the very worst in people; it exaggerates what is already there.[3]

Hunger was what was already there.

"In this year a severe famine oppressed almost all of the Gauls. Many dried and ground into powder grape seeds and oat chaff and fern roots and mixed a little flour with it and made bread; many cut straw and did the same. Many who had no flour ate different herbs, which they gathered, and in consequence swelled up and died." Gregory of Tours—who later was sainted—wrote this in his *History of the Franks*, a sixth-century work.[4]

Hunger was then just another part of life—just like sleep, fornication, death, family—as persistent as nature, as powerful as anything that exists without a shadow of a doubt. The Middle Ages in the West was a world trapped by hunger. The collapse of the Roman administrative and commercial structures, the decrease in population, the loss of agrarian technology all conspired to reduce the production and circulation of food to the lowest possible levels.

In a world where each region had to support itself, where communication and transportation were an infrequent luxury, it was enough for the harvest in one region to fail—due to plagues, droughts, wars, the pillage of an unscrupulous lord—leaving its hundreds, thousands, tens of thousands of inhabitants to die of hunger.

There were no states to distribute anything. Every once in a while, the Catholic Church stepped in, but it was much more effective in establishing the rationale, the justification for hunger. In a world ruled by an all powerful god, anybody could have asked themselves why there was not enough food, why that god did not provide. The Catholic response was that hunger was the just punishment for those who had in some way offended God.

Sometimes, that god was so generous that his priests took care of the lost, needy, underfed flocks. But in Medieval iconography, the hungry were depicted as a warning to the believers: this is what awaits you if you do not accept His reign, His rules, His power, if you do not follow His orders. Hence, they were not objects of pity or sympathy but rather contempt and horror, examples of the wages of amorality, sloth, and the weakness of sinners. Warnings, cautions from gods but delivered by men.

Some machines work better than others; no ideology has ever worked that didn't convince the hungry that they were to blame for their hunger: *mea culpa, mea maxima culpa.*

During those same years in more prosperous regions, the Islamic kingdoms spread, occupying most of the north of Africa, the south of Europe, the Middle East, and Central Asia. They improved agricultural production with new techniques of crop rotation, large irrigation projects, mills, and the incorporation of cultivars they brought from all over the world. Sugar cane, rice, bananas, citrus fruits, eggplants, coconut palms, and melons fed the largest cities of the time, such as Baghdad and Córdoba, with their million inhabitants, this at a time when London had only ten thousand, and most of them ate poorly. According to Rodulfus Glaber, the French monk, in his famous account of the ninth-century famines in Western Europe,

> Rain fell so continuously everywhere that for three years fur-
> rows for seed could not be properly driven. [...] This aveng-
> ing famine began in the Orient, and after devastating Greece
> passed to Italy and thence to Gaul and the whole English
> people. [...] After men had eaten beasts and birds, under the
> pressure of rampant famine, they began to eat carrion and
> things too horrible to mention. Some tried to escape death by
> eating the roots of the forest and the herbs of the stream, but in
> vain, for there is no escape from the wrath of the vengeance of
> God except to God himself. It is terrible to relate the evils which
> then befell mankind. [...] Alas, a thing formerly little heard of
> happened: ravening hunger drove men to devour human flesh!
> Travelers were set upon by men stronger than themselves,
> and their dismembered flesh was cooked over fires and eaten.
> Many who had fled from place to place from the famine, when
> they found shelter at last, were slaughtered in the night as food
> for those who had welcomed them. Many showed an apple
> or an egg to children, then dragged them to out-of-the-way
> places and killed and ate them. In many places the bodies of
> the dead were dragged from the earth, also to appease hunger.
> This raging madness rose to such proportions that solitary
> beasts were less likely to be attacked by brigands than men.
> The custom of eating human flesh had grown so common that
> one fellow sold it ready cooked in the market-place of Tourmis
> like that of some beast. When he was arrested he did not deny
> the shameful charge. He was bound and burned to death. The
> meat was buried in the ground; but another fellow dug it up
> and ate it, and he too was put to death by fire.

Cannibalism was somewhat extraordinary, but not hunger. In the thou-sand years after the fall of the Roman Empire, ten years rarely passed without some region of Europe—or many—suffering from terrible famine. But widespread famine was still sporadic: the norm continued to be hunger as a constant and permanent threat, the horizon of daily life.

This was not linear, of course, not always the same; it was, instead, a mad dash among variables: the tools and techniques of working the land improved, new lands were farmed, more food was produced, and then the population grew, until that very growth made the food scarce—or a war or a plague would break the very precarious equilibrium.

(One of those cycles of impoverishment and famine began at the beginning of the fourteenth century and ended in 1348 with the appearance of a disease that found a weakened population—the Black Plague killed a quarter of the population in Europe.)

In these societies, where so many went hungry, some of those who didn't would sometimes impose hunger on themselves: hunger as a means of purification. The monotheistic religions maintain intense relationships with hunger: all try to enforce certain fasts, controlled forms of experiencing hunger, in order to demonstrate that a god—and his lackeys—can force us to do whatever they want. Ways of abusing ourselves to pay homage to an absolute power.

Religion imposes itself by standing in opposition to nature. It is "culture" in its most extreme sense: a culture that doesn't translate this world but rather creates others. Fasting is a triumph of culture, a monument to the hubris of culture. According to religious thinking—thinking that imagines the existence of something better than humans, or rather, that we humans are an inferior species—eating is a debility. We would be better if we didn't have to eat. The need to eat was always thought of as a low and heavy burden; superior beings were free of it. In the Christian tradition, it is never stated that God ate anything, as opposed to the Greco-Roman gods, who were so anthropomorphic, they ate nectar and ambrosia. Fasting is for angels—the Christians said—who are beyond nature.

To fast is to accept an interruption in the natural order, to allow a cultural order to be imposed; but that cultural, religious order is presented as supernatural or, even better, preternatural: prior to all nature, the genesis of all nature. Nature is decadence—the flesh is decadent, feeding it is decadent—and the supernatural improves and corrects it.

There's nothing more vulgar than eating to appease hunger.

But for most of the population, gluttony was not a sin; it was a miracle. A few ate a lot; the many continued to eat poorly and little. Meat was almost exclusively a privilege of the nobles, who kept hunting rights for themselves; for more than two thousand years, food for the majority of Europeans was so cursory, so monotonous, that they were left at the mercy of any and all misfortune.

For centuries, hunger was due to a lack of food: primitive farming techniques, harvests lost to weather or wars. But it was also, to a large extent, due to food without sufficient nutrition: chronic, constant undernourishment. At the Hôtel-Dieu, the great hospital in medieval Paris, many of the sick were cured with no medicine besides a short stay: some called it a miracle. Many years later it was discovered that their health improved because at the hospital they ate bread made with a more nutritious wheat than the black bread—made of barley and rye hulls—that they could afford at home.

The food of the rich, the food of the poor: for most of the Middle Ages, high-class food overflowed with spices: peppers, cloves, cinnamon, ginger, saffron—because almost nobody could afford them. After the sixteenth century, when world markets made spices cheaper, a new and delicious cuisine based on butter, fresh vegetables, and other products arose and was available—in the cities, to a chosen few. These were scaled reproductions of the basic differences: to have or not to have, to eat or not.

In addition, the doctors of the day supported this setup. Many erudite treatises, such as *Régime de santé pour les pauvres facile à tenir*, by Jacques Dubois, explained that the poor should restrict themselves to the food that corresponded to them—above all the black bread, onions, garlic, leeks, garbanzos, grits, a bit of bacon, soups—and leave the delicacies to the lords who knew how to eat them. It was, they said, for their own good: their stomachs were not accustomed to those birds, those fish, those sweets, that fresh fruit, those refined flavors, and they would not know how to digest them and would fall ill, die because they wanted to eat them. The Spanish writer Francisco de Quevedo would later mock this assessment in *La vida del Buscón* [The Life of a Swindler]: "Master Cabra sat down and said grace. They ate a meal that lasted forever, without beginning or end. From wooden bowls they drank broth that was so clear, Narcissus would have been in greater danger than at the well."

To deal with hunger, those who suffered it invented imaginary places, lands of happiness where the houses were made of ham, their roofs of salmon and bass, and, as Quevedo noted, "in the streets huge geese are roasted on spits and they turn themselves and are followed closely by a white garlic sauce and they settle themselves down on those tables covered with white tablecloths, next to the jugs overflowing with wine."[5] It was alternately called Cocagne, Cuccagna, Jauja, a Cornucopia, and it was always far away, beyond the sea. The curious thing is that one day some more or less Spanish sailors believed they had found it. America wasn't such a big deal, but the products that came from there changed the food of the world forever. Potatoes, tomatoes, corn, pepper, and so many others gave the poor some comfort, but there was no cornucopia: hunger continued and their diets again deteriorated.

More or less the same thing happened again: improvements in agriculture and a demographic explosion made more people eat less variety of foods and nourish themselves less.

That was when Jonathan Swift wrote his *A Modest Proposal*, one of the great satires of history, as a suggestion for decreasing hunger in Ireland—by eating the hungry:

> The number of souls in this kingdom being usually reckoned one million and a half, of these I calculate there may be about two hundred thousand couple whose wives are breeders; from which number I subtract thirty thousand couple, who are able to maintain their own children, (although I apprehend there cannot be so many, under the present distresses of the kingdom) but this being granted, there will remain an hundred and seventy thousand breeders. I again subtract fifty thousand, for those women who miscarry, or whose children die by accident or disease within the year. There only remain an hundred and twenty thousand children of poor parents annually born. The question therefore is, How this number shall be reared, and provided for? which, as I have already said, under the present situation of affairs, is utterly impossible by all the methods hitherto proposed. For we can neither employ them in handicraft or agriculture; they neither build houses (I mean in the country) nor cultivate land: they can very seldom pick up a livelihood by stealing till they arrive at six years old; except where they are of towardly parts, although I confess they learn the rudiments much earlier; during which time they can however be properly looked upon only as probationers: As I have been informed by a principal gentleman in the county of Cavan, who protested to me, that he never knew above one or two instances under the age of six, even in a part of the kingdom so renowned for the quickest proficiency in that art.
>
> I am assured by our merchants, that a boy or a girl before twelve years old, is no saleable commodity, and even when they come to this age, they will not yield above three pounds, or three pounds and half a crown at most, on the exchange; which cannot turn to account either to the parents or kingdom, the charge of nutriments and rags having been at least four times that value.
>
> I shall now therefore humbly propose my own thoughts, which I hope will not be liable to the least objection.
>
> I have been assured by a very knowing American of my acquaintance in London, that a young healthy child well nursed, is, at a year old, a most delicious nourishing and

wholesome food, whether stewed, roasted, baked, or boiled; and I make no doubt that it will equally serve in a fricasie, or a ragoust.

I do therefore humbly offer it to public consideration, that of the hundred and twenty thousand children, already computed, twenty thousand may be reserved for breed, whereof only one fourth part to be males; which is more than we allow to sheep, black cattle, or swine, and my reason is, that these children are seldom the fruits of marriage, a circumstance not much regarded by our savages, therefore, one male will be sufficient to serve four females. That the remaining hundred thousand may, at a year old, be offered in sale to the persons of quality and fortune, through the kingdom, always advising the mother to let them suck plentifully in the last month, so as to render them plump, and fat for a good table. A child will make two dishes at an entertainment for friends, and when the family dines alone, the fore or hind quarter will make a reasonable dish, and seasoned with a little pepper or salt, will be very good boiled on the fourth day, especially in winter.[6]

Hunger was also present at the beginning of the French Revolution. A day laborer in Paris earned less than twenty *sous* a day; a four-pound loaf of bread, which was almost his entire food for the day, cost more than fifteen. More than a hundred years later, the French social reformist and historian Louis Blanc wrote of this plight in his *Histoire de la Révolution Française*: "In the meantime, the people of Paris were literally dying of hunger. Every day, deep in those dark neighborhoods where unrest threatens and pallor lingers, at four in the morning there emerged groups of women, children, and old people clamoring loudly that they wanted to live. A loaf of bread was a victory. And what bread it was! A mass whose black color, filthy taste, and fetid scent spoke loudly of flour poisoned with murderous mixtures. Who will tell of the desperation of a mother when the head of her child, dead from starvation, falls on her lap."[7] Hence, those revolts began when thousands of Parisians were begging for bread, and they received one of the least appreciated *boutades* of history in response: "Let them eat cake."

Thus began a revolution that, in some ways, continues to this day.

INDIA: TRADITIONS OF HUNGER

KOLKATA

1

It was the wineskin that caught my eye. An ancient looking wineskin that was being filled with water by an Indian man on a Kolkata street, and I tried to remember how long it had been since I'd seen an actual wineskin, how long since I'd recalled that ancient word to designate a present object rather than as part of the parable from the Bible about new wine in old wineskins. But I saw the wineskin and spent a while with its Spanish word, *odre*, rolling around my tongue, tasting it, savoring it, mourning all those words left orphaned of what they once meant and without the weight of an object to balance them, words that have slowly descended into gibberish. (Will someone, one day, pick up those sounds, recover the way the tongue presses up against the teeth between the *d* and the *r*, and make it mean something else?)

Sometimes I am baffled by the fact that I often find the disappearance of a monument, a landscape, an artifact, a word, more difficult than that of a person. The sensation—subjectively real—that the monument or landscape or word is unique, irreplaceable, and that a person is just a person, one among so many. At the corner, a very old man is squatting as they do in the East—his feet firmly planted on the ground, his rear low, his knees a little higher—surrounded by hundreds of potatoes and more potatoes overflowing a wicker basket full of potatoes. Potatoes, of course, roll, returning to the ground from whence they came.

Kolkata is like a European city from the first half of the twentieth century: a maze of right angles formed from small sidewalks and wide streets, four- and five-story buildings like the kind you find on the coast of the Mediterranean. But Kolkata is no different than any other city in that it exists in a state of constant re-creation, layer upon layer of reformation. It has commercial modernity—cars, lights, street signs—in addition to the disaster of thousands upon thousands of the most wretched of the earth—walking, crawling, the animals, the smells. Our cities eliminated the smells they must have had for centuries, but on that Kolkata street, where I watched the man fill the wineskin, the smell of manure mixed with the smell of a body and the smell of piss and the smell of putrefaction and the smell of coconut soap and the smell of burning firewood and oil and garbage and the smell of incense and the smell of spices and the smell of shit, all seemingly out of place and oversaturated with meaning.

Then there were a couple of streets lined with small shops full of recycled computers parts, televisions, CDs, radios, car radios, DVDs, cell phones. Objects of the last twenty years made to last four or five, rescued by demographic pressure: just because I can't buy tomorrow's computer doesn't mean that I can't use one that worked the day before yesterday. Going against one of the most indispensable requirements of consumerist modernity, dozens of men sat on benches along the sidewalk screwing, soldering, taking apart, and putting back together what was meant to be used and thrown away. Among twenty or thirty computer carcasses in different stages of dismemberment, two sticks of incense fragranced the air. Computers are objects that only emit an odor when they are new. The scent of incense went unchallenged.

For centuries, millennia, merchandise was divided into perishables and nonperishables; food and drink ran out, a shirt would finally wear out, but nobody bought a bed or a cart or a pot thinking that they would soon have to buy a new one. Duration was consubstantial with those objects. More recent capitalism has managed to give everything the same value as food or drink: they are to be consumed, they are consumable. *Consume* is a very rugged word.

That's why now, I suppose, the world is so much more of merchants: because nothing is bought once and for all, because everything has to be bought and sold indefinitely.

Sometimes, when I walk down these streets that in so many countries have become marketplaces, I freak out. Thousands and thousands of—let's just assume—similar T-shirts, similar flip-flops, thousands and thousands of purses, sports shoes, brushes, balls, pots, screwdrivers, all purchased by thousands and thousands of people, all just as similar, all earning the same daily dollar to be spent at this or another market, to purchase T-shirts, flip-flops, brushes, pots, rice, to come back another day to sell or purchase from those remaining thousands and thousands of—let's just assume—similar T-shirts, flip-flops, thousands and thousands . . .

They don't do anything; they wait, chat, earn their tiny profit margin. They are only slightly less useless than the rest. They add nothing to those T-shirts or cables or bananas or sports shoes or candies; those things would be the same without them. What would happen if this so notoriously unnecessary activity—commerce—disappeared?

What good are merchants if all they do is obtain things at wholesale, jack up the cost, and sell their wares to people who otherwise do not have a choice but to pay the higher rate? Like pundits, who are nearly as useless, merchants are efficient intermediaries at best. But merchants exist, survive, and are growing in ever increasing numbers. In rich countries this kind of commerce is more or less camouflaged throughout the landscape: in stores, shopping malls, the Internet. In any other country, it is clearly the first and often only recourse: when a child doesn't know what to do, he or she sells mangos or pencils or bags on the street, degree zero of urban economic activity. The streets exist as a space where thousands of people can earn their living by buying and selling.

Doing away with mercantilism however, is not so easy. Sovietism tried by turning private vendors into a horde of civil servants—lifeless, bored, even less productive—and they could never really solve the problem of the distribution of goods. But even if a good solution were discovered, what would those millions of people do who now make a living off it? Would they find some useful, productive employment? Would a labor force and a social force be liberated that would change everything? Or, rather, would the streets be filled with more beggars and scavengers?

Beggars and scavengers.

Streets full of beggars and scavengers.

Twenty years have passed since I was last in Kolkata; at that time, I wrote a book about India, *Dios mío* [My God]; already then, this city of horrors perplexed me. Twenty years later I am still surprised by the ease with which Indians coexist with the misery of others.

Streets full: of scavengers, of beggars.

And the way they sit in the dust of the streets: curled up, shrunken, defensive, their arms wrapped around their knees, their head sunk between their knees, one foot on top of the other, as if taking care of each other. A rickshaw driver at rest: it's two in the afternoon, the heat is stupefying. A rickshaw driver in Kolkata runs shoeless, his bare feet on the asphalt, or whatever's there. Throughout the years his feet may have stepped on everything one can step on in this world.

In Kolkata there are indolent cows who stop traffic, pigs rolling around in the frequent piles of garbage, crows who steal food off tables—some windows have screens to prevent such thefts—even more thieving and rabid monkeys, chickens clucking in their death cages, docile dogs (strangely docile) and millions and millions of men and women: fourteen million men and women.

Some eat every day. Some even eat animals. At the central market in Kolkata the animals to be eaten are animals until they are eaten. Flayed, boned, cut up in pieces, vacuum-sealed, shrouded in some kind of cellophane: the meat we eat in our countries does everything it can to distance itself from the animal it once was. Lest anybody think about the cow's sad eyes when they eat a steak, the tender bleating of a lamb when digging into a gigot. In the poorest countries, animals are still animals until the very last moment; without refrigeration, without a cold chain, it is the only way to guarantee that they'll arrive fresh to the table. In the poorest countries, in any case, the poorest never eat animals.

In Niger, cow meat is a luxury food. In India, it is a forbidden food.

Soon after my arrival back in the city, I wandered to the cacophonous market. A sparrow swooped down, poked around the animal pieces, searched for scraps from one stall to the next; fifteen or twenty of us—suddenly paralyzed, silent, in suspense—watched it scavenge. The bird departed; the voices, the shouting returned, as did the movement, the smells, and we all smiled, confused, as if embarrassed. I considered saying something about the drudgery of routine and the pleasure of breaking it, but I kept quiet, not really knowing how I would have said such a thing, and instead asked a vendor for a small bag of strange-looking nuts.

My thoughts returned to the brief visit of the sparrow. And then I continued on.

A man at a stall tucked away, hidden from easy view, was selling little red fish from a tank decorated with plastic furnishings. The superfluous: a giant leap for culture. "The superfluous, a very necessary thing," wrote Voltaire, without needing to at all. The superfluous is the sign of a great change: to acquire something you didn't need, to pass from a state of pure urgency to that state of—even slight—privilege in which you can spend a few coins to own a little red fish, to keep it in an ornamented tank. A fish that one keeps as a pet rather than eats as food, this is the conquest of the right to the superfluous, the opposite of hunger. To be hungry is to live *with* the strictly necessary, to live *for* the strictly necessary, to live *in* the strictly necessary—to live without superfluity.

Hunger is when you need to eat the little red fish.

One of the great myths of India is that it is a *vegetarian* country. Swamis say that cows are sacred in the Hindu religion, yet some of the oldest and most sacred of Hindu texts, such as the Rig Veda or Brahmana, written more than three thousand years ago, include banquets where beef is served to guests. In one book of Brahmana, the "Shatapatha," a Hindu sage named Yajnavalkya advises against eating the cow or the ox, lest it lead to sin and destruction. Nonetheless, Yajnavalkya states in the same passage, "I, for one, eat [the flesh of cow and ox], provided that it is tender."[1]

In the Hindu religion, it is considered bad karma to subject other creatures to violence, and many follow the advice of another ancient text, the Tirukkural, which asks, "How can someone possess kindness if one eats meat from another body to grow one's own?"[2] Instead they suggest that vegetables are easier to digest and allow one to live lives that are "longer, healthier, more productive," that the Earth is suffering and that by not eating animals, one prevents some of that suffering.

While *vegetarian* connotes one who does not eat meat, the word itself was first published in 1850, in London. Most Indians are not vegetarian out of a lifestyle choice, but out of poverty—they don't have the means to buy meat such as chicken or beef. Or, if they have a cow or two, they don't have the luxury of killing it to eat it; they need to keep it to produce the milk they drink, the butter they use for cooking, the manure they burn, the power to farm. What a strange destiny these sacred, nutritious animals have, that they can be squeezed, depleted, overworked but not killed. Could it be a metaphor?

I'm impressed by the ease with which we swallow the most diverse products: the most complex processes. Such a large amount of history, of stories, are huddled in one bite of beef or one chicken wing or one shrimp. But, above all, the ease of thinking that this is simply life, without realizing that for thousands of years it wasn't like this, that for billions of people it is still not like this. Is it a waste to be so privileged that we can't even remember how privileged we are?

There are many ways to consider that question, but I think one decisive factor that ought not to be discounted is the triumph of mobility, which began in the early twentieth century, and created a world where the norm is that everything moves. Before 1900 paved roads were uncommon, and there weren't cars or trucks or highways to drive on them. And obviously there were no airplanes, or motorbikes, or submarines, or subways. Not only were there very few means of transportation; people didn't move much. Almost everybody lived in cities that were on a human scale, in small towns, or in the countryside, where one went everywhere on foot. Later we learned to consider it normal to be constantly moving: every morning I travel ten miles to get to work; every vacation four hundred or four thousand go to get broiled at some picture-postcard beach. It's odd how humans, who were a fairly sedentary animal, became big movers. And the same thing happened with food. There was always trade, but until a century ago, only the very necessary or very valuable got transported. Now everything circulates: Italian grapes are sold in Russian groceries, Camembert is imported from France to India, and Chinese pigs are fattened up on Argentine soy—and billions still don't eat meat.

Eating animals is almost always a luxury. "Except for rare exceptions," writes the French anthropologist Bruno Parmentier,

> basic human food consists of grains, all over the world, in every country and culture. But grain doesn't have enough protein to satisfy all our needs. The first thing that is added, everywhere, are legumes [...]. Then come the starches and beans. When the standard of life rises, fats are added [...]. And finally, only when the standard of life really takes off, in come meat and other animal products, such as eggs and milk products. [...] To eat a steak then is outright planetary madness.[3]

The inhabitants of more or less wealthy countries eat the opposite of this diet, what the vast majority of humanity has eaten since the beginning of time. It is a radical cultural shift, and it doesn't seem like we pay much attention to it. Every time we have a salad with our steak, or French fries with our hamburgers, or corn chips with our beef burritos, we are turning millenarian habits on their heads by putting a piece of animal as the centerpiece, accompanied by those carbohydrates and plant fibers.

I think we don't realize how ostentatious this is. I think any Indian, any African, and many South Americans would notice it immediately. Because, for the majority of the inhabitants of the Other World, the system remains the same: the global consumption of food seems quite varied, but three-quarters of the food consumed on the planet is rice, wheat, and corn; rice alone makes up half the world's food.

That means: half of all the food humans eat is rice.

Rice. Something not even the Nigerien woman Hussena could afford to eat.

Outside of the West, eating animals is shifting from a luxury to a standard right. In 1980 the Chinese, for instance, ate on average thirty pounds of meat per person per year; now it's one hundred and twenty. And they enjoy it tremendously. Eating meat is an aspiration for those having recently achieved a modicum of prosperity: they eat it to show that they are prosperous, that they can do the same as the rich people, that all things carnivorous are theirs too. With it, they acquire the diseases they hadn't suffered till now: cardiovascular disease, cancer of the digestive system, high cholesterol. They also add to the climate disaster: cows' farts, filled with methane, are an environmental nightmare, making up almost one-fifth of greenhouse gas emissions.

We are in competition with meat. Animals didn't used to eat the same food as humans. In his book *Cannibals and Kings*, the American anthropologist Marvin Harris suggested that the taboo against eating pigs in two of the three great monotheistic religions was due to them competing with humans for the same food. Or, rather: eating pigs was considered wasteful, as opposed to eating cows, sheep, goats, who ate plants humans couldn't eat and, therefore, transformed those inaccessible calories into something we could swallow.[4]

Not any longer. Now 75 percent of animal feed could be consumed by humans: soy, corn, and other grains.

This is a more or less recent innovation. Cows always ate grass. Around 1870, however, when there were boats with cold storage capacity, the British began to buy US beef, whose cows fed on corn and other grains. This resulted in, what was claimed at the time, a fattier and tastier meat. Until the Second World War, grain-fed meat was rare and made up only 5 percent of world beef production, a luxury reserved for the wealthiest people in Europe and the United States. But by the fifties, with its increase in agricultural production, the United States was looking for a way to get rid of its surplus. Multinational food corporations applied pressure to place this grain-fed beef on the world's tables; now, most beef produced in the world functions on that model. And the herds multiply. Half a century ago there were 700 million in the world; today there are 1.4 billion.

Then we have those huge chicken and pig factories. Brazil, the world's top chicken exporter, has to import grain to feed its infinite number of chickens. Every year seven billion chickens are born on their poultry farms; every year Brazilians kill as many chickens as the entire human population of Earth. The United States and China kill a few, as well, but they eat them all themselves.

The problem is that you need four vegetable calories to produce one calorie of chicken, six to produce one of pig, and ten vegetable calories to produce one calorie of beef or lamb. It's the same thing with the water: 1800 gallons of water are needed to produce one pound of beef. An acre of good land can produce about twenty pounds of beef. An acre of good land can also produce over three hundred and fifty pounds of soybeans. In other words, in order to produce beef for a few, resources that could feed many need to be used. In other words, meat establishes a brutal inequality. In other words, to eat meat is to not give a damn about other people.

During the last several decades, meat consumption has increased twice as much as the population; the consumption of eggs, thrice as much. Around 1950, fifty million tons of meat were eaten each year; now, almost six times more—and it's supposed to double again by 2030.

Livestock now use 80 percent of the agricultural land in the world, 40 percent of the world's grain production, and 10 percent of the water on the planet. Meat is powerful.

Meat is the perfect metaphor for inequality.

But meat's moment—this historical blink of an eye, this lapse—might be coming to an end.

Lester Brown, a pioneering environmental analyst, says that when they ask him how many people the Earth can support, he answers with another question, "'At what level of food consumption?' Using round numbers, at the US level of 800 kilograms of grain per person annually for food and feed, the 2-billion-ton annual world harvest of grain would support 2.5 billion people. At the Italian level of consumption of close to 400 kilograms, the current harvest would support 5 billion people. At the 200 kilograms of grain consumed by the average Indian, it would support 10 billion."[5]

Meat is a battle flag and a proclamation: the world can be used like this only if few of us use it. If everybody wants to use it like this, it just won't work.

Exclusion is a necessary, but never sufficient, condition.

(If it weren't that I can't, that I am a lost cause, because I've been stuffing myself for half a century with Argentine *asado*, because I can make believe that my gesture wouldn't do any good, the only possible conclusion here would be the announcement of my decision to never eat steak again. The opposite—what I'm doing—is to show my abject inconsistency. We Argentines, however, can claim to be a rather strange avant-garde of a trend that might not even exist. For more than a century, Argentina was synonymous with meat, the country par excellence of excellent meat, the largest consumer of beef in the world; not anymore. When I was born, an average Argentine chowed down over two hundred pounds of beef per year, more than a half a pound of beef day; now, the average has since slimmed to around a hundred pounds. The reasons also seem like precursors: the competitiveness of soy that made it more profitable to grow it than use the land for pasture; the resulting increase in price; the broadening of gastronomic horizons, which has offered a range of alternatives; and health concerns. But here, in India, many of its inhabitants think they are choosing vegetarianism freely. Indians consume eleven pounds of meat—any meat—per year per person: ten times less than the Chinese. And they think they are choosing it: the miracle of ideology.)

2

Twenty years ago, one person's ideological commitments made a lasting impression on me. Mother Teresa's hospice stood next to a temple to Kali and it was there for people to die—a little more peacefully. Mother Teresa founded it in 1951 after a Muslim businessman sold her the mansion for a few rupees because he admired her and because, he said, he wanted to give back to God a little of what God had given to him—or something like that.

At that time, the walls were painted white and covered with prayer sheets, virgins in niches, crucifixes, and a photograph of Mother Teresa with Pope John Paul II. "Let us make the Church present in the world today," proclaimed a sign right underneath. The men's ward was sixteen yards long and eleven wide. There were two platforms made of cheap tiles along the two long sides; on each platform were fifteen cots, and on the floor between the two platforms, another twenty. The cots were sky blue, pillows covered in a darker hue. There were no sheets. On each cot lay a skinny body waiting for the moment of death.

In those days, volunteers at the hospice collected dying people in the streets and brought them to their blue cots, cleaned them up, and got them ready for a tidy death.

"Those on the platform are a little better, and some of them might even survive." That's what Mike told me, a thirty-year-old Englishman with a ponytail who insisted on speaking to me in choppy French. "Those down below are the ones who aren't going to last; the closer they are to the door, the worse they are."

In the hospice ward, moans could be heard, but not very many. A boy— maybe a boy, maybe he was thirteen or maybe he was thirty-five—with almost no flesh on his bones and a brutal wound on his head, shouted, "*Babu, Babu.*" Richard, a volunteer as big as two wardrobes, blond, from Milwaukee, with manners like a small-town American priest, understanding but strict, gave him little taps on the back. Then he brought a tin cup with water to an old man next to the door. The old man wasn't moving and his head was hanging off the cot. Richard moved it back, but the old man flung it off again.

"He's doing very poorly. He came yesterday and we took him to the hospital but they wouldn't admit him."

"Why?"

"Money."

"Aren't the hospitals public?"

"In the public hospitals, they don't give you a bed for four months.

They're useless. There's a private Christian hospital nearby with a quota for bed space they need to reach, but not surprisingly all full right now, so when we went there, they said no. We're not in the States here; here people die because there's no way for them to get treatment."

Richard told me about someone who had come with a broken leg; they couldn't take care of him, and he died of an infection. He wanted to tell me about other cases: it's nothing unusual, he explained, that somebody dies without putting up much of a struggle.

"We can't cure them. We aren't doctors. We have a doctor who comes in twice a week, but we don't have enough equipment or medicines. The only thing we do is comfort them, look after them, give them affection, offer them a dignified death."

At that time, Mother Teresa was already Mother Teresa, famous throughout the world, full of donations and resources, which she didn't use to pay for medical services at her headquarters.

That time, I ended my visit, and wrote,

> I would like to be able to describe Mother Teresa's hospice as the most noble and enlightened of places, but after a while the whole thing started to bother me, particularly that sanctimonious idea of collecting the dying from the streets to give them a clean death. If they want to do something for these people, I'd rather they helped them live better, not die better. It's true, on one hand, that dealing so much with death makes one see death as a road to someplace else and so, maybe, it matters how you get there, though I don't think one cot more or a few scabs less makes much of a difference. But still I can't help thinking that her hospice is an extreme example of Catholic charity: to alleviate the most visible symptoms of social blasphemies without touching on the causes of those blasphemies.

There were a lot of things I still didn't know. Afterward, I found out that Miss Agnes Gonxha Bojaxhiu, also known as Mother Teresa of Kolkata, was a bellicose version of her namesake saint, who held a couple of very strong opinions, among which was that the suffering of the poor is a blessing from God. "It is very beautiful for the poor to accept their lot, to share it with the passion of Christ," Christopher Hitchens quotes her as saying. "I think the world is being much helped by the suffering of the poor people."[6]

Perhaps that is why the nun asked those affected by the ecological disaster of the Union Carbide plant in Bhopal to "forget and forgive" instead of asking for reparations. Perhaps that is why she went to Haiti in 1981 to receive a Legion of Honor award from the dictator, Jean-Claude Duvalier—who had donated a lot of money to her—and explain that Baby Doc "loved the poor and was adored by them."[7] Perhaps that is why the nun went to Tirana to place a wreath of flowers on the monument to Enver Hoxha, the Stalinist leader of the poorest and most repressive country in Europe. Perhaps that is why she defended a United States banker who had given her a lot of money before he was imprisoned for defrauding hundreds of thousands of small investors. And so forth.

At that time in Kolkata, in 1994, I also didn't know how Miss Agnes had used that aura of sanctity she had known how to obtain: such saintly people can say whatever they want, whenever and wherever they want to. She used this halo to carry forward her largest campaign: the fight against abortion and contraception. She had already said as much in Stockholm in 1979 in her Nobel Peace Prize acceptance speech, "I feel the greatest destroyer of peace today is abortion." And later, speaking to the National Prayer Breakfast in Washington, DC, in February, 1994, she said, "These poor people maybe have nothing to eat, maybe they have not a home to live in, but they can still be great people when they are spiritually rich." And this, "And abortion, which often follows from contraception, brings a people to be spiritually poor, and that is the worst poverty and the most difficult to overcome."[8]

That afternoon, Cardinal James Hickey explained very clearly that her "cry to love and her defense of unborn life are not empty phrases, because she serves the suffering, the hungry, and the thirsty, and she welcomes the unwanted child with open arms."[9] The nun served this purpose, among others.

But she played another important role. Everybody—countries, groups of friends, volleyball teams, task forces—needs a pure being, someone who shows them that not everything is lost, the do-gooder. There are many different do-gooders, such as a compassionate public figure, a savior of the whales, an aging humanitarian, a self-sacrificing doctor: we have to believe in something. The Good is necessary, a condition of existence. And the world makes sure to find the Good Ones, exalt them, squeeze every last drop out of them. And that's why—but not only why— Miss Agnes occupied such an important place: the universal do-gooder.

And she still occupies it. Despite some of our attempts to tell a bit about her history of corruption and bribes, nobody listens: it's better and easier to keep thinking she was better even than Lassie. That works for a lot of people. Above all because it serves the purpose of reaffirming a couple of basic ideas. One: that this life is the path to another, better one, closer to the Lord. That's why what matters here is not what happens to us but how we prepare ourselves for the next one: by being meek, submissive, resigned. That's why the nun's first project was a hospice, a place to die clean. Miss Agnes was flooded with prizes, donations, and grants for her religious enterprises. And she never made the accounts of her enterprises public, though it's known, because she often said so, that she founded about five hundred convents in one hundred countries—but she never opened a clinic in Kolkata.

As we were saying: the nun's main idea, which she peddled around the world, was that the suffering of the poor was a gift from the All Powerful. Here it is again: "It is very beautiful for the poor to accept their lot, to share it with the passion of Christ. I think the world is being much helped by the suffering of the poor people." There is the core, the foundation. Two thousand years of theological lies summed up in two sentences. Not bad. "There is something beautiful in seeing the poor accept their lot . . ." And render to Caesar the things that are Caesar's, and hunger that gives dignity to the hungry. Or so the good nun said.

Now she has a replacement, Cardinal Bergoglio, as good as Lassie but more powerful, who managed to rescue an institution in free fall. Thanks to the Peronist pope, the Catholic Church has once again become a heavyweight in the battle for meaning.

Thanks also to him, a way of seeing the world that trains millions in obedience and acceptance of what they don't understand—what they are told by "those who know," those who have the power to know—has recovered its strength.

But the Christian religion, despite everything it has done, could never reach the heights of the Hindu religion in its ability to pacify the poor. That's the role of religion, more than anything: if you are living a shitty life, working your ass off, eating a little less than what's absolutely necessary, you need to follow a higher order, a belief that explains and justifies it all, a belief that explains the fact that there are a few people who have everything and run things and decide issues of life and death. But not only that. You also need a belief that explains the madness of death and convinces you that this isn't the end. But not only that. You also need a belief that explains the reason for or at least the origin of so much evil in the world. But not only that.

When the New Testament says that blessed are the poor for theirs is the kingdom of heaven, they are taking a big step. For the first time, a Western religion imagined that being poor had an added value of innocence, which would reward anyone boasting this condition with the Kingdom of Heaven, and this should comfort them and allow them to put up with the hellhole of their lives—merely an uncomfortable but necessary step toward another so much more attractive one. Hinduism, on the other hand, is more radical. It offers nothing, not even the glorification of poverty; its culture never thought to pretend that it held any value at all. Instead, it establishes once and for all that if you are poor, if you suffer, if you are hungry, it is because you are paying for—suffering the consequences of—crimes you committed in previous lives. Hence, it's your fault; hence: tough shit. What they call *karma* is the best invention of a theosophy that for centuries has allowed a small group of honchos to control so many millions of perennially destitute wretches.

This is India, and it is pure potential and they like to say they are the largest democracy in the world—and they are. They don't like to say that they are the country with the most undernourished people in the world—and they are. That the largest democracy has the largest mass of hungry people should be an awkward coincidence. But maybe it isn't.

3

Hunger is rather confusing. Numbers vary; it is extremely difficult to calculate with any precision how many men and women are hungry. Most live in countries with precarious governments that are incapable of keeping track of a good part of their citizenry, and organizations that try to count, use statistical calculations instead of detailed censuses.

The United Nations agency responsible for estimating "world hunger" is the Food and Agriculture Organization (FAO). They study agricultural inventories, importation and exportation of food, national consumption of food, economic difficulties, and social inequalities, and, from there, they determine the supposed availability of food for each individual: the difference between caloric necessity and caloric availability gives them the number of undernourished.

Over the course of the last few decades, the FAO has managed to significantly reduce the number of undernourished in the world by changing their method of calculation. They'd done the same thing previously. In 1974, according to the statistics they've published, their experts estimated that there were approximately 460 million hungry people in the world. This was more or less what other organizations were saying, such as the World Health Organization (WHO) and the United Nations International Children's Emergency Fund (UNICEF). They also warned that within ten years that number could reach as high as 800 million; in 1989 they confirmed just how close their predictions had come: there were, they said, 786 million hungry people.

This equation—subtracting caloric availability from caloric necessity—is workable, and there aren't others that work any better; it is so approximate that it becomes flexible: the results are so hypothetical that they can be corrected according to the needs of the moment. In 1990, for instance, the FAO revised their previous calculations, announcing that the statistical method they had been using was flawed and now they knew that in 1970 there hadn't been 460 million hungry people but rather double that amount: 941 million. This further allowed them to say that the 786 million at that moment in 1990 did not mean an increase in hunger but rather the opposite. There were, in fact, 155 million fewer hungry people: a great achievement.

Ten years later, in 1999, they said there were 799 million hungry people, hence hunger had continued to increase. Where, then, were the other million that make 800 million? Until they again revised their own numbers and said that in fact in 1990 there had been 818 million rather than 786 million, and therefore those 799 million meant a decrease. Again, we'd won.

But the best was yet to come. In 2011, there had still been 848 million hungry people in 1990; in 2012, that number reached 1 billion, and in 2013, 1.015 billion. If now there is a serious humanitarian crisis in the world, it is retrospective malnutrition in 1990.

One can assume that statistical methods have improved considerably over the last thirty years, but it is difficult to imagine that they have changed so much as to allow for a retrospective discovery of 160 million hungry people that nobody had previously counted. Or, if not, how can one take statistics seriously that allow for such a high margin of error?

We know there is nothing more variable than the past, but it is unusual to see it change so quickly, and so obviously. But we also know that all changes in the past are a response to the needs of the present. The 2014 numbers are particularly weighty: they were the last to be published before 2015, when the Millennium Development Goals (MDGs) of the United Nations should have been reached.

The goals were announced at the Millennium Summit in New York on September 8, 2000. The first and most pompous was: "To eradicate extreme poverty and hunger,"[10] though the specific target was to "halve, between 1990 and 2015, the proportion of people living on less than $1.25 a day."[11] This was the proportion of the total population, not the absolute number of persons, that should be halved, as compared to 1990. Hence, if the percentage of hungry people then calculated had not been halved, one possible solution was to increase the percentage of hunger by raising the proportion of the total population—at the time—and thereby improve the results—now. If the original calculation of hungry people on the planet was based on a global population of 5.5 billion people, let's say 20 percent of that, and you could determine that that number was actually 24 percent of 5.7 billion, then if the actual number of hungry people on the planet were calculated to be 1 billion people, you could write that off as having lowered the number from 1.36 billion rather than 1.1 billion, nearly 260 million more people saved from living on less than $1.25 a day. It seems like gobbledygook; it is gobbledygook.

The war against hunger consists of many nonsenses.

However, FAO's numbers are those that are respected, and used—also in this book—among other reasons because they are the only ones around. Changes to them not only function to reassure the world's great powers and convince their underlings how well their policies have been working, but they are also used to decide the fate of billions of dollars in aid and distributions. These numbers underpin what is known in good bureaucratese, as "policy continuity" and the "allocation of resources."

If we accept—provisionally—more recent revised FAO figures, then there are currently 795 million hungry people: more than 11 percent of the world's inhabitants, one out of every nine people in the world. If hunger were not so carefully distributed, one out of every nine people would necessarily include one of your uncles, several of the people you work with, a few childhood friends or classmates, some of your fellow commuters, maybe even you.

But it's not one man or woman out of every nine—or it is in one way and not in another. Hunger clearly is not distributed among one out of every nine inhabitants of the planet; it is perfectly concentrated in the poorest countries, which in bureaucratese is called the "developing countries," and here I call the Other World.

(Nobody says "underdeveloped" anymore. That word, so classic, is of recent coinage. It appeared in English around the end of the nineteenth century, but was used only to mean an underexposed photograph. Harry Truman was the first to use it in a sociological context, stating in his inaugural address, "We must embark on a bold new program for making the benefits of our scientific advances and industrial progress available for the improvement and growth of underdeveloped areas. More than half the people of the world are living in conditions approaching misery.

Their food is inadequate. They are victims of disease. Their economic life is primitive and stagnant. Their poverty is a handicap and a threat both to them and to more prosperous areas."[12])

The threat still exists, fortunately for some. And it is still referred to by some as "Third World," another obsolete concept. To say Third World only made sense when there were two others: the supposed First World—the capitalist bloc as it was constituted after the Second World War—and the Second World—the Soviet Bloc, which started to be assembled in the wake of that war, the Chinese Revolution, and the African and Asian independent movements. The Third World was, at that time, that dissimilar conglomeration of countries that were not in the First or Second Worlds, that were neither rich nor Soviet.

The Second World, as we know, no longer exists, so there can't be a third. But the planet is still clearly divided. There is a rich bloc, and it's northern—increasingly less so—and Western, where the quality of life is infinitely superior, and which still largely determines politics and economics.

Then there is the Other World: the poor, the poorest.

There are countries whose membership in the Other World is debatable. There are fifty, for starters, that can assert their undeniable right to belong: they are those on the list of "least developed countries," a category invented by the United Nations fifty years ago to define the poorest of the poor.

Out of the fifty-four African nations, thirty-four qualify as Other World. In addition to Niger are Angola, Benin, Burkina Faso, Burundi, Central African Republic, Chad, Comoros, Democratic Republic of Congo, Djibouti, Equatorial Guinea, Eritrea, Ethiopia, Gambia, Guinea, Guinea-Bissau, Lesotho, Liberia, Madagascar, Malawi, Mali, Mauritania, Mozambique, Rwanda, São Tomé and Príncipe, Senegal, Sierra Leone, Somalia, Sudan, South Sudan, Tanzania, Togo, Uganda, and Zambia.

There are also thirteen in the Asian-Pacific region—Afghanistan, Bangladesh, Bhutan, Cambodia, East Timor, Kiribati, Laos, Myanmar, Nepal, Salomon, Tuvalu, Vanuatu, Yemen—and one in the Americas: Haiti. Four more—Botswana, Cape Verde, Maldives, and Samoa,—were recently moved over to "developing countries."

Those countries—with their more than 750 million people, 11 percent of humanity—account for 0.5 percent of the world's riches.

They are the hard core, the indisputable. To them can be added other countries, according to the United National Development Program (UNDP), that score low on their Human Development Index (HDI): Bolivia, Burundi, Dominican Republic, Egypt, El Salvador, Fiji, Gabon, Guatemala, Guyana, Honduras, Indonesia, Kenya, Kirgizstan, Micronesia, Mongolia, Morocco, Namibia, Nicaragua, Nigeria, Pakistan, Papua New Guinea, Paraguay, Philippines, Sri Lanka, Surinam, Swaziland, Zimbabwe, Syria, Tajikistan, Thailand, Turkmenistan, Uzbekistan, Vietnam, and even one European country, the poorest of all: Moldavia.[13]

(Or, forget all those names and remember one frivolous criterion: the Other World consists of all those countries whose combined gross domestic product is less than the fortune of the richest person in the world: Jeff Bezos.)

Remaining are the large mixtures: five countries whose development is moving world markets—the BRICS: Brazil, Russian, India, China, South Africa—and have huge numbers of impoverished citizens. In fact, almost half the world's undernourished people live in China or India. Differences—and membership—don't always respect national boundaries. Between the Chinese coastal (and wealthy) city of Shanghai, and its most interior (and impoverished) city of Kashgar, there is more distance than between France and Turkey; Iraq to Russia; further apart still than Nigeria to Spain.

And the same thing happens, in a way, in the supposedly middle-class countries like Argentina or Mexico, or even, among the new poor in the wealthiest countries.

They all live in different ways in the Other World.

In the Other World, there are no solid houses, no sewers, no hospitals or schools that cure or teach, no dignified work, no protective state, no guarantees, no future.

In the Other World there is not enough food for everybody. This, above all.

Of the 795 million and counting hungry people on the planet, 780 million of them reside in the Other World. They have no money, no property, carry no weight; they usually have no way to influence the decisions of those who make the decisions. There was a time when hunger was a shout, but contemporary hunger is, above all, silence: a condition of those who have no possibility of speaking. Those of us who eat, speak—with our mouths full. Those who don't eat, usually remain silent. Or they speak where nobody listens.

Of those 780 million undernourished people in the Other World, about 50 million are victims of an unusual situation: an armed conflict, a merciless dictatorship, a natural or weather disaster—droughts, floods, earthquakes. That leaves 730 million who go hungry for no particularly extraordinary circumstance other than that they happen to be part of a social and economic order that denies them the possibility of feeding themselves.

According to FAO, 50 percent of the world's hungry are small farmers with a small plot of land, 20 percent are landless peasants, 20 percent are urban dwellers, and 10 percent are shepherds, fishermen, and foragers.

Since 2007—it is assumed, calculated—something changed radically in the world's population: for the first time in history, more people live in cities than in the countryside. The most obvious explanation is that millions of people flee the countryside each year because, overall, peasants are still the poorest. Of the 1.2 billion people who live in "extreme poverty"— according to the World Bank, on less than $1.25 a day—three-quarters live in the countryside: 900 million extremely poor peasants.

Landless peasants and those with only a small plot of land are hunger's favorite prey; three out of every four don't have enough to eat. The rest are residents of those new sites of poverty in the peripheries of large cities—the slums, *favelas*, *bidonvilles*, shantytowns, *villa miserias*.

Hunger is one of the main reasons that life expectancy in Spain is eighty-two years and in Mozambique, fifty; eighty-three in Japan and fifty-seven in Zambia; and that there are people born with every chance to live twice as long as others who are born somewhere else, in another society. I can't think of any more brutal form of injustice.

(It's about defining what is fatal, what is "legitimate" to die from and what not. In reality, the biggest scandal is the fact that every year, every month, every day, thousands and millions of people die who shouldn't die or, better said, who wouldn't die from what kills them if they didn't live in poor countries, if they weren't so poor. It's about thinking about the greatest possible privilege: to live where others die. And then we have to think about all the rest of it: about those difficult lives, that anguish, that enormous waste.)

The numbers are brutal—and they could fill pages and pages. But numbers are often, also, the refuge of certain scoundrels. What if there were 100 million rather than 842 million hungry people? What if there were 24 million? And what if there were 24? Would we then say, okay, it's not so bad? When does it start to get bad? Numbers are the alibi for pathetic relativism. If it is happening to very many, it's bad; if to many, it's kind of bad; if to fewer, it's not so bad. If this book were brave—and if I were brave—we wouldn't include a single number.

But we're not: I take refuge, scoundrel that I am, in the shelter of numbers.

BIRAUL

1

There were three doctors standing around the toddler: the Greek doctor, Maria, and two Indians. There were also two nurses and in back of us, sitting on a small red bench, crying like one sings a sad song, the mother of the toddler—barefoot, wearing a red sari. The toddler was emaciated, not moving, her eyes wide open, an oxygen mask on her face.

The toddler arrived yesterday with severe diarrhea, vomiting, extreme weakness, and did not show signs of improvement the following day. The mother in back, sings her sad song.

"Forget everything you've seen on television," a veteran from Médecins Sans Frontières told me right after I arrived.

"This is something else. Here you almost never see those horrible scenes of swollen bellies and legs as thin as bones. Here you won't see children like skeletons surrounded by flies. Here's it's different."

Here is, generally speaking, India. But in particular, it's Biraul, in the state of Bihar, one of the poorest. Bihar could be the tenth most populated country in the world, but it is not a country; it's a state. There are a hundred million inhabitants, almost one-third of the entire population of the entire United States, crowded into 62,000 square miles of land—a little smaller than the state of Wisconsin. The plains here are actually fertile: if nature cooperates, a rice crop and a wheat crop can grow in one year. The greatest Indian empire rose here three thousand years ago; Buddhism, twenty-five hundred years ago; fifteen hundred years ago: the most prestigious universities of the day.

"Really, forget all of it. Here, hunger is very different."

The toddler's name was Gurya, the fifteen-month-old daughter of a nineteen-year-old woman named Rahmati who told me that she didn't understand what was happening to her daughter. Rahmati had another daughter, four years old, and this older girl was supposedly fine and healthy. Rahmati is Muslim and talks a lot about God and why He allows such maladies and sufferings. Why God is always close at hand in such places allowing this to happen.

"Do you think God is angry at you?"

"Yes, He's angry."

"Why?"

"I don't know, how can I know?"

"What do you think?"

"I'd prefer not to think about it. Now, all I want is for my daughter to get better. That's why I'm here in this hospital. Then we'll see."

Gurya had the flaky rash and protruding belly caused by the nutritional disorder kwashiorkor: a condition most children under five don't survive.

Rahmati was thin, brittle, with a ring in her left nostril that meant she was married. She wore copper bracelets, a threadbare red sari, thick black eyebrows, and eyes that continuously darted around. Rahmati lived nearby, she told me, in a village three hours away by foot.

Rahmati was never educated. When she was a child she assisted her mother in the house and sometimes she helped her father retrieve algae from a local pond. The algae he sold at market. They didn't have any land or other way of earning a living, Rahmati told me. They almost always ate; sometimes a day or two would go by without a meal, but eventually something edible would find its way to their stomachs.

When she turned thirteen, Rahmati began to get impatient; one after the other, her friends in the village were getting married, and she wasn't. Finally, her parents arranged a marriage with the son of her mother's cousin; the man was about ten years older, and when the moment arrived, Rahmati was terrified. To save money, they had to share the wedding with her sister: not even the most important day of her life would be wholly hers. In addition to a wife, each groom received a cow; to buy them, her father had to ask for a loan he finished paying off only many years and a lot of privations later.

After the wedding, Rahmati's husband left; there was no work in the village and he'd heard that in Delhi he could find something; there he painted houses so he could save a few rupees to begin his married life. Rahmati stayed at home; for her, everything had remained the same, though it hadn't. She could no longer play like a child, wander around, have fun, because she was no longer a child but a married woman. Her first year of marriage was very boring. Then her husband returned and took her to his parents' home, where things got much worse. Her mother-in-law bossed her around, forced her to do all the work and take care of her sisters-in-law. When the first baby was born, the family welcomed her happily; but they were very disappointed when a second girl was born; her mother-in-law insulted her. An Indian couple needs to have sons who will support them in their old age; daughters leave and on top of that, they have to pay a dowry.

Rahmati's days were all the same. The family rose at dawn when she would begin to prepare the rice for the day. The rice, full of bugs, had to be cleaned. Days with only rice were woeful; a scoop of lentils or slices of a tomato could lift the spirits, but those things weren't easy to come by. Sometimes, she added some wild leaves for flavor. In order to cook, she had to make a fire. Sometimes they could afford prechopped wood at the market; other days, she had to borrow from a neighbor or collect her own—but forest wood was getting harder and harder to find. If Rahmati had a cow, she could have used its manure for fuel; a neighbor who owned a calf sometimes gave her a little. Rahmati told me that if she had all the money in the world, she'd buy a cow.

"Oh, yes, I'd buy a cow, I'd have milk," she said, her face shining.

"How much does a cow cost?"

"About twenty-five thousand rupees."

Which is about $500, an impossible amount. And she says her life would be so different.

"Imagine, a cow! Everything would change if I had a cow. It would give me milk, which costs about twenty-five rupees per liter, and I'd have manure and I could have a calf and I could sell a little milk and buy rice and vegetables and who knows what else. Yes, everything would be very different if I had a cow."

For the first time her voiced rose, emitting a little enthusiasm. Then she remembered the state of her daughter, and went in to check on her; a while later, when she returned to the yard where we had sat talking on a small straw mat, suffocating in the heat, beset by flies, her sadness had returned.

Rahmati lived with her husband and her mother-in-law and a brother-in-law and her two daughters in a hut made of logs and reeds. It used to have a sheet metal roof, but that broke and they couldn't afford to replace it. Out in front of the hut, they ate breakfast every day at 8:00 a.m., then her husband would leave to try and find work: a field to plow, a wall to paint, something so he could earn the hundred rupees—less than two dollars—that it cost for them to eat the following day. Rahmati would stay with their two girls, clean them, wash their clothes: she always has some clothes to wash. The less clothes you have the more clothes you have to wash, Rahmati told me. When she finished, she could go play for a while with the girls and did not have to think about anything else. Afterward, sometimes, all three would take a nap. At noon they would eat what was left over from the morning, then she would either carry on with her chores or visit a neighbor; later, when her husband returned, she served him a little more rice for dinner, maybe even a piece of *roti* flatbread.

"Do you ever do anything different?"

"Well, no. Every day is the same, except when there's a wedding or a religious celebration. On Fridays my husband goes to the mosque, but I can't."

"Why not?"

"Because that's what our religion says, that women don't go."

"Do you ever feel like going?"

"No, because I don't want to disobey my religion."

So I asked her what her favorite moment of the day was, and she didn't understand the question. I repeated it—I asked the interpreter to repeat it—and Rahmati responded, again, that she doesn't understand; she didn't have a favorite moment, everything was more or less always the same.

This was a common sentiment that I heard while I was in Biraul, I asked about a dozen women what they do with their free time, but this idea of free time bewildered them, and so I would have to explain it in other terms. After I did, they would tell me that in the afternoon, when they finished everything they had to do in the house, they would go visit a neighbor, and that if there were anything recreational—a wedding, a funeral, a birth, a religious celebration—they were sporadic.

But on some days, if the husband was unable to find work, and thus get paid enough to purchase another day's meal, even the monotonous routine could be broken and the day would be filled with something else: anxiety. Without owning land, peasants don't have the option of growing something for their subsistence. While they lived very close to the earth—and here it was fertile—it was always other people's land that they would work, but to actually acquire the kind of food they were growing, they had to go through the market, suffer its fluctuations, pay the intermediaries.

"Sometimes my husband doesn't get work and there's no money, and the neighbors don't want to lend me any, or they don't have any, either, or they already lent me too much, so there's nothing."

(Rahmati's husband usually spent hours at a time standing in a kind of empty lot at the entrance to the village where the men would wait for somebody to hire them. Rahmati says that sometimes there were ten, twenty, thirty of them, and that sometimes they would get hired but often they didn't, and so her husband would spend the day under the tree in the vacant lot, thinking—I didn't know, but I imagined—what he would say to Rahmati when he returned without a rupee, without a pound of rice. Or thinking, perhaps—I didn't know, but I imagined this too—that if Rahmati said anything to him, he'd shut her up with a slap. Or maybe thinking—again, I couldn't be certain—how good it was to be married to a woman who knew to keep quiet when there was nothing to eat.)

Rahmati probably did keep quiet, but when she described how hard it was to fall asleep while hungry, I couldn't imagine that keeping quiet was easy.

Her daughter Gurya didn't cry; she remained still and quiet, her eyes wide open, an oxygen mask over her face. Here, now, was the MSF stabilization clinic in Biraul, a town consisting mostly of a couple of very long, winding streets full of shops and small stalls that lead to a Durga temple, a pond where the old folks and buffalos bathed, open fields where the children played cricket. Almost everything was sold on the main street: live chickens, light bulbs, motor bikes, modems, even farming tools forged by a local smithy. There was always a traffic jam: an ox-drawn cart, for example, blocked the street in front of the clinic, dozens of motorbikes and rickshaws were honking their horns, dozens of men and women were trying to get by, trying to find a crack they could slip through.

"Sometimes I think that if I didn't wake up, everything would be so much easier. But then I think of my daughters, about what would happen to them without me. Then I say, okay, I have to go on. But it's too difficult and there's no solution."

I always thought, without really thinking about it, that those faraway places—far away on the map, far away from known locations, far away from my history—were progressively emptier, more devoid of people. It was purely magical thinking: the middle of nowhere is packed, swarming with people. Thousands and thousands of people in this section of the ends of the earth, which is how the world will end: not with a bang but a honk. One day somebody is going to honk one horn too many and everything is going to explode. It will almost be peaceful: no fire storm, no horrific and deafening roar, no Earth splitting in two. Just one honk of a horn—probably in Biraul or maybe in Kolkata—and the world will cease to be.

The MSF clinic in Biraul was next to the town, along with the Primary Health distribution center, and the MSF food supplement warehouse.

These were located in a field that spread out around a massive tree; in Africa, in India, trees know how to find ideal locations where the world arranges around them. It was hot; the patients—the children and their mothers—waited under the tree for their turn to be seen.

Compared to normal medical facilities in an Indian village, this was a Disneyland: thirteen beds in two very clean rooms with white walls, windows, fans, mosquito nets, and an isolation ward with three more beds. There was a child in each bed with his or her mother; they usually stayed four or five days, until the child's health stabilized, and could begin outpatient care. Six doctors, ten nurses, space, medicine, furniture, instruments, cleanliness.

The stabilization clinic was packed. Every day one hundred, two hundred mothers arrived. They usually came because their children had a persistent cough or a fever that wouldn't go down, or just showed signs of general fatigue. Many would first go to the Indian run primary care ward; it was when the nurses there saw that the child might be malnourished, that the child and mother were sent to the folks at MSF. Others, having heard about the MSF clinic, went directly there, where they were received by three or four young Indian medical attendants and were subjected to a very strict protocol: each child was weighed in a hanging harness, then measured length- and widthwise on a table. After taking these measurements, the attendants wrapped the tape measure around their arm to determine if they were officially malnourished. That was the decisive moment; in just a few minutes, the little boy or girl either received MSF attention or not: a diagnosis that if inaccurate could continue a life or end it.

At the stabilization clinic, a mother saw me flip a light switch and asked my permission to do it as well. She had never before flipped a light switch. She flicked the plastic button fearfully, not knowing what occult forces she was about to unleash.

Less than fifty miles to the north of Biraul is Nepal, the Himalayas. But in Biraul, mountains were unimaginable: there everything was flat: wheat and rice, fertile lands waiting for rain. It was a surprise. I had imagined an arid plain and found lush fields. The problem was not that it wasn't productive; the problem, as it turned out, was for whom.

They say that before the English arrived, the inhabitants were poor but survived, and that it was the tax system of the crown that led to the concentration of land ownership, to the peasants being dispossessed. Tax collectors confiscated the land of millions of peasants in arrears, turning them into rural proletarians and themselves into large landowners. And although the owners' names may have changed over the past two centuries, the structure of ownership has remained. In the sixties and seventies there was a lot of social unrest, and the government approved agrarian reform laws that should have given land to those without. They were never carried out, however, because the bureaucrats who should have done it were the landowners themselves, and they found ways to keep their holdings. Poverty increased—as if more were needed—along with the increase in population; there are now one thousand people for every square mile. More than half are under twenty-five—a new record. And the consequences of men and women reproducing often because they know most will die.

The state of Bihar is like a concentrate, a bouillon of India—and India has more hunger than anywhere in the world. A quarter of the hungry people in the word live—if it can be called living—in India: about 195 million Indians don't manage to eat what they need, the 2,100 daily calories that all experts recommend as the minimum amount of energy the human body needs. Some get less; many, many millions get a lot less. I had been informed that in Biraul hunger was different—it didn't kill. Bihar is like a microcosm of India where hunger tends not to be acute: millions of people have spent many generations becoming accustomed to not eating enough. They have developed, throughout the generations, the ability to survive while eating almost nothing, thereby demonstrating the adaptive virtues of our species. Human beings survived, conquered territory, because they were able to adapt to so many things; here they adapted to almost not eating and, for this reason, millions are short and scrawny—bodies that have learned to subsist on little.

Small women who give birth to very small babies, children who reach a year old weighing nine pounds—who are too malnourished to even learn to walk. A resounding failure: Darwinian adaptation in all its sadness. The ability of humans to adjust to an undernourished life and thereby produce bodies—and brains—that require much less.

Chronic malnutrition—they explain—doesn't kill you in one fell swoop, but it also doesn't allow you to live as you should: reduced bodies, deficient minds. Millions waste their lives so they can continue to live.

2

I asked him what he liked to eat. That's all I asked, but when I did he looked at me with poorly concealed anger.

"I don't like to eat one thing or another; what I like is to eat. I'm poor,

I can't be thinking about eating something in particular. I eat whatever I can: roti, a plate of rice, whatever. What I like is being able *to* eat, is for my family to be able to eat."

He told me his name was Kamless, that he was twenty-six years old; he was also skinny, short, and strongly opinionated. Kamless and Renu, his wife, had just arrived at the MSF health clinic with their toddler son Manuhar in their arms.

Kamless said it took four or five hours to get there from his village by foot, though it was only a two-and-a-half hour journey if they were able to come via bicycle. Then, stupid me, I asked why they didn't always come on a bicycle. Kamless again glared at me with focused disdain— or perhaps desperation. "Because the bicycle isn't mine, it belongs to a neighbor, and sometimes he lends it to me and sometimes he doesn't. This morning, I begged him and he still said no."

Anyway, Kamless told me, it didn't matter; it was nothing for him to walk four or five hours, a couple of times a year he went to Punjab to work in the rice or beet harvest, and he had to travel overnight standing on a train as packed as a cattle car. Now *that,* he told me, was a journey.

In Punjab, he could get paid up to five thousand rupees a month. But in Biraul, where his family was, he could only expect to earn up to a hundred rupees for a day of bricklaying or farmwork, but that work was never guaranteed.

"Do you like to go to Punjab?"

"No, I like to be home, with my family."

"Would you like to move there with your family?"

"If I take them, it will be too expensive, I'd have to rent a room, and that alone would cost me a thousand rupees. I couldn't do it."

He told me that he was always having problems with his neighbor, the one with the bicycle, because his neighbor was rich, and there were always problems with the rich.

"Not with the poor?"

"With the poor, too, but it doesn't bother you as much."

"How rich is he?"

"He owns land, cows."

"How many cows?"

"Two, and a buffalo. He's rich. I used to have a cow too. When we got married, Renu brought a cow as a dowry. But I had to sell it. I had to sell everything to try to cure my son."

However, he still was never able to take him to see a good doctor. Manuhar was barely able to move: he was nothing but bones and couldn't even hold up his head.

"We didn't need more children, we already had two, we thought about going to family planning so that they'd tell us what to do. But we wanted to have a girl . . . and look at what happened to us."

All for wanting—contrary to common sense—a girl.

Kamless looked at me as if to say, *I told her I know I just wanted to make her happy.* He told me that the rich neighbor told them that Manu was ill because he hadn't eaten well, but Kamless didn't believe it because his other children ate the same, only drinking more milk. This time, Renu didn't have enough milk, that was the only difference.

"You didn't give him milk?"

"Yes, when we could. We asked our neighbor, from his cow. Sometimes he gave us and sometimes he didn't."

"What happened when he didn't?"

"We gave him our food."

Their food, he says, is rice. Almost always just rice.

"Would he eat it?"

"Yes, usually."

The doctors told them they could treat their son's malnutrition, and for two weeks they gave him Plumpy'Nut. But they also discovered a brain lesion they were not able to treat at the clinic, and were told they would take Manu to the hospital in Darbhanga.

"The problem is we don't have the money to take him there. People with a lot of money, like our neighbor, they can go to the doctor whenever they want. We almost never can. My poor son . . . when we want to go to a doctor, we first have to find the money for the bus, then for the doctor, then for the medicines the doctor gives us. We almost never can."

"What do you plan to do?"

"What do we plan to do? What do we *plan* to do?"

Kamless seemed like an intelligent man, capable of understanding that I was using words that didn't always correlate to his language.

"Yes. What are you going to do?"

Kamless shook his head. "What do you think I should do?"

India is a proud country, one of the oldest in the world, one of the biggest in the world, a great culture that has returned to center stage because it is going to be, or so they say, a great power. That's why, among other reasons, Indians don't like to accept the fact that half their children go hungry, and that this hunger and this poverty occurs in a whisper, as if it were something far away, almost conjectural—but something that can be seen all the time, in every village, on every street corner.

That's why, in 2008, when then prime minister Manmohan Singh said for the first time in his speeches that so many people suffering from malnutrition was a "national shame"[14] and a "curse that we must remove"[15] millions were shocked, as if it were the first they'd ever heard of a large birthmark on their left cheek.

Even so, India has for years had a series of mechanisms designed to improve the nutrition of children, and adults. The most well-known are the *anganwadis*.

An anganwadi, meaning "courtyard shelter," is a type of rural child-care center, paid for by a welfare system, which offers vaccinations and food to the poorest children. Almost all towns and neighborhoods in India have their own anganwadi. There are more than a million of these small centers managed by almost two million workers—mostly women. According to the government, they reach about sixty million children and ten million new mothers. It is obvious, however, that they do not function as they should. Many are closed; at others, beneficiaries complain that they do not give them the promised food, or that they give it out once a week instead of every day, or some other variation on the theme of neglect.

Besides the anganwadis, Below Poverty Line (BPL) cards constitute the largest Indian welfare system. They allow for the purchase of around eighty pounds of rice a month at two or four rupees a pound. Official studies say that half of those who should have the card, don't. Kamless does: when his father died he managed to convince an official to give him one. What makes up the poverty line is a subject of much discussion in India; some call it the "starvation line," because the government places it at fifty cents to the US dollar—thirty rupees—per person per day, less than half of what is usually used, equivalent to $1.25.

Ineptitude and corruption make it so that laws, no matter how lovely, don't do much good. Some studies indicate that two-thirds of the $12 billion spent annually in India to help the poorest of the poor remain "en route," in the pockets of civil servants, businessmen, intermediaries, and other wealthy people. Crime isn't the whole story; there's also a lot of inefficiency. But awareness of the weight of corruption on the system is so widespread that the most important citizen movement to have appeared in the country in the last few years is India Against Corruption, led by Indian social activist Anna Hazare, which uses, among other forms of pressure, the Gandhian hunger strike: hunger as a twisted weapon.

In the meantime, the system flourishes. Kamless told me about how each time he had to go to Punjab to work, he needed to borrow money for the trip and leave something for his family.

"I ask Salim, the owner of the store in my village. He lends me two thousand rupees, and I pay him back when I return. The problem is that I have to pay him double what he gives me and, in the meantime, I have to leave him my ID as collateral."

Salim—along with so many other merchants in so many other villages—used that ID as ration cards to purchase subsidized grain at wholesale, which he then turned around and sold at the market price. He did this with dozens of ID cards. In a money-makes-money trade, he could claim the rations because he bribed an employee of the state-run granary, who, in turn, also had enough money to bribe the person who hired him for the job. It is a classic racketeering job, but at least for Salim it is legal: he works with valid ration cards. Others don't even bother with legality; it is easy to buy IDs from corrupt officials. This is how things work in India, everything is possible because nothing seems totally impossible, rules are made to be bent out of shape in order to make things work. Whatever those things might be.

Manu was crying nonstop—tortured. He didn't want us to forget about him, Renu said, and she lifted up one of his limp hands. Kamless observed this then turned back to me.

"If I had all the money I wanted, what I'd do is open a shop, at the door to my house, to sell fruit. That way I could be home with the fruit, and I could save a little money for the future, and then my children could eat fruit once in a while."

"Do you think it's fair that some people have a lot of money and others so little?"

"It's not a question of fair or not. Those who have money, have money, so who cares if it's fair or not."

Kamless was worried, also, because his house was built on public land—the government's land, he told me—and he's afraid they'll throw him off one day.

"Governments always do what's good for them. If one day they want the land for one of their own, for a friend of theirs, they'll throw you off, and who are you going to complain to?"

The base of the pyramid—millions and millions at the base of the pyramid—are the landless peasants. Many never had land; many lost theirs during the Empire; many others have lost theirs more recently to debt. Many—who knows how many, such things are never recorded—have been expelled from the acre or half acre, which the government gave them in the sixties or seventies, by the henchmen of some rural landowner or political boss—or both. Peasants who seek redress have a good chance of ending up with a bullet in their head. Or, best-case scenario, standing in front of a local judge who is a friend of the plunderer or bought off by the plunderers—or, to wed the practical and the pleasant, a friend bought off by the plunderer—and they'll send him home but not before showing appropriate disdain at his poverty, at his inferiority.

"There are days I feel like going out and beating everybody up, hurting them, killing them, just so they know how it feels. But then I think, what will I gain, and I stay in my corner."

"What do you think, what would you gain?"

"Nothing. They'd lock me up and I'd have nothing. What could I possibly gain? But I still feel like doing it."

3

It was the dry season. The monsoon was due to arrive in two months and everything would then be inundated with water. Floods, impassable roads, apocalyptic rains, bugs, diseases—it would be even harder to get food. In India, life was ruled by the seasons, the natural cycles, broadsides of nature, hunger that came and went on a whim. Here, lives passed and so many seemed the same.

Anita was seventeen years old, scrawny, with crooked teeth, a pug nose with a gold ring in the left nostril, and a red dot in the middle of her forehead; she was wearing a saffron-colored sari lightly touched with green. Her daughter, Kajal, was nine-months old and had long, tangled hair; she was brought in weighing only six pounds, and couldn't hold up her head. Anita picked her up, caressed her—but she looked at her with strange irritability, just like her mother, at times resembling a caged animal, who also seemed to look at the world with a peculiar irritation.

I asked Anita if it had always been like this, if she had seen the same anxiety in her mother.

"I don't know, my mother died a long time ago."

"When?"

"Years, I don't know. A while before I got married, when I was still a child."

"What do you remember about her?"

"I don't know, watching her do things, work. I'd like to remember her at some moment when she wasn't working."

Anita told me about the first time she recalled being hungry and realized that she wasn't going to get anything to eat, and she shouted at her mother that she was bad and should give her food, and her mother slapped her. Then she watched her mother cry and she told her that it was the opposite, that the one who should have cried was her because her mother had slapped her, and then her mother laughed and cried, and then she didn't understand anything that was going on.

Anita was, according to her words, from the lower caste and didn't have much of a chance to remedy her and her family's problems.

"I never went to school. The lower castes, they don't go to school."

"What did you think when you saw that other children went to school?"

"Nothing. I played with the other children, or I went with my mother to the fields for the harvest, worked a little. I never thought anything about school."

"What does lower caste mean?"

"When you don't have land or money or a house or enough food, that's what lower caste means."

Anita didn't say that it also meant not being able to marry people in higher castes, not being able to live with people from higher castes, not being able to work in certain jobs or be accepted in different social settings just because of being from a lower caste. The Indian constitution prohibits this kind of discrimination; Indian life maintains it—strongly.

"Did you have enough to eat when you were little?"

"Sometimes I did, sometimes I didn't. Sometimes we ate twice instead of three times a day, sometimes only once. Sometimes not even once, and the children cried."

"You didn't cry?"

"No, I didn't. What for? What good would it do? I knew my father was doing everything he could to feed us."

"What did you want to be when you grew up?"

"Nothing, I didn't want anything."

"What did you imagine?"

"Nothing, I just let time pass."

"Did you think that when you grew up you'd have nice clothes, a big house?"

"No, I never thought about those things. Other castes think about those things."

Anita's father didn't have a steady job; he helped his neighbors farm their land and pasture the buffaloes, and so the neighbors gave him a little grain, milk, manure. Now her husband works, when he can, in a brick factory.

"Sometimes he works," Anita said, "sometimes he doesn't."

"Why does he sometimes not work?"

"I don't know, because he doesn't feel like it."

"Don't you tell him that you need him to work?"

"If I do, then we fight."

"How do you fight?"

Anita stopped talking, looked down, caressed her daughter's hair. Her irritability was turning into extreme discomfort. A gentleman didn't ask such questions, not even a journalist. I was about to tell her to drop it, that it didn't matter, when she said that he shouted at her and hit her. She said it very quietly.

"Have you told your brother that your husband hits you?"

"No."

"Why not?"

"Because he can hit me if he wants. That's why he's my husband and I'm his wife."

"What can you do to him?"

"Nothing."

"Would you rather be a man?"

"I don't know."

"Do you wish your daughter was a boy?"

"Yes."

"Why?"

Anita stood up, straightened out her sari, made to leave; she didn't want to talk to me anymore. I understood. I felt ashamed and apologized, leaving me in the patio of the stabilization clinic, where the flies were king.

The flies. Some bold and brooding wise man—let's say in Pergamum, 212 BCE; in Yucatan, eight hundred years later; in Bologna, 1286—must have posited that it was the flies that in some way, still unknown to mankind, brought hunger. Because the flies are there: whenever there's hunger, there are flies.

For decades, the Indian public health services have managed to create for themselves an accurate image of dysfunctionality. Potential patients know that health centers usually lack medicines or don't care or are closed or you have to give somebody money under the table—though there's usually not even a table. Sometimes, of course, they treat you well, but that is neither the norm nor the perception of the majority. None of this is happenstance. India spends one of the smallest percentages of gross national product on health care of any country: about 2 percent, as opposed to 10 percent in Argentina or Israel, and 14 percent in

Mexico. But, of this amount, only one-third is spent on public health—as opposed to 60 percent in Argentina, Mexico, and Israel. It's a real statement—of principles.

It is also a form of archaism. For millennia, there was no cure for many diseases. But in places like Biraul, there still isn't. The MSF can only do so much, it's a palliative response to an infrastructural problem. In Biraul, the MSF and Indian clinics are full of patients, if something other than an obvious emergency happens to someone, he or she wouldn't get seen. Even if that same person lived in a city, his or her chances of being examined would also be very low—the public hospitals were overflowing.

This was a place where it was possible to die from diseases that didn't kill other people in other places.

Anita returned shortly after and was willing to chat a bit further. She told me that she had come here in the first place because a neighbor in her village told her about this place, that they would see her daughter for free.

Anita explained, "I didn't believe her, but she insisted, so finally I came."

"And was it free?"

"Yes. I brought her, and they took good care of her. They told me that she was like that because she ate so little. She can barely swallow the milk I give her."

"Do you nurse her?"

"No, I can't. I couldn't even when she was a newborn because I didn't have any milk. I was dry."

Anita looked down at her chest: dry.

"So I give her formula. When I can get it."

"Did they tell you she was malnourished?"

"Yes, that's what they said: malnourished."

Until about twenty or thirty years ago, it was believed that one of the basic causes of malnutrition in so many children was that they didn't eat enough protein because their mothers didn't know how to feed them, and several international organizations ran huge campaigns to teach them how to properly feed their children—with food they didn't have. It sounds sinister, but at the time it was framed very scientifically.

Benedetta Rossi, an anthropologist specializing in Africa who teaches at the University of Birmingham, explained.

> The divide between humanitarian assistance and development actions has functioned as a *modus operandi* of the system, and debates have articulated around "the paradox of chronic

emergency" in policy documents and in the press releases of aid institutions. These debates have been well meaning. They constituted attempts to enroll supporters in the arguments and strategies perceived as most effective in the fight against hunger and poverty. Neither of these positions was inherently "wrong." Free food distributions, arranged and financed by donors and international organizations, do not address the structural causes of widespread malnutrition. But indeed, as the partisans of humanitarian assistance remind us, they save lives that would otherwise be lost while we wait for the results of development action, which have often proven misconceived, or even counterproductive.[16]

In 2009, the Indian government decided to cease the importation of Plumpy'Nut and instead administer locally prepared hot foods to its malnourished youth. In an act of what seemed like hunger nationalism, according to *India Today*, Pratibha Patil, then president of India, made a statement against the distribution of Plumpy'Nut to Indian Parliament on June 4, 2009, stating "Malnutrition has emerged as a major health challenge needing urgent response. Hence the nutrition delivery program will be comprehensively revamped to bring it under the watch of panchayat institutions and move to provision of hot cooked meals in anganwadis."[17]

Patil went on to state that India has its own malnutrition profile, and it doesn't make sense to use a product designed for different realities. The government says they don't want to "medicalize" the problem of malnutrition; the state shouldn't cure it but instead prevent it, stop it from happening—and that's what the subsidies are for, the meals in the schools, the network of anganwadis. But the truth is that with all that, there are more than eight million suffering from acute malnutrition in addition to the sixty million chronically undernourished children.

Patil also stated that because Plumpy'Nut was a foreign product, it could be the beachhead for an invasion of large multinational laboratories and that anyway they should manufacture the paste with local products from local businesses. But they didn't. MSF had been trying to prove the usefulness of this cure by using it: the center in Biraul would be, from this point of view, a pilot program attempting to show its healing virtues. The Indian government did not officially approve, though for the moment they tolerated it.

Their figures are conclusive: children treated with Plumpy'Nut, many of whom arrive in desperate conditions, have a much lower mortality rate, less than 3 percent.

The treatment works. Malnutrition, so lethal, is easy to treat if the necessary measures are taken. But they aren't. The state won't do it. Without intending to, the Plumpy'Nut imbroglio demonstrated the cruelty of inequality, the violence of a social model. Face-to-face with the few who have been treated and cured is their responsibility for the millions and million who have not—who don't even know that they should.

I wondered if Anita knew.

Anita had told me that she had been here for eleven days, but that the doctors wanted to keep her Kajal even longer. Anita said her daughter seemed better and that she needed to go home.

"My husband wants me back home. He came two days ago and told me I had to come home. But I told him I didn't have any money for the bus, and neither did he. He told me he was going to come back today so we could leave."

"Why does he want you to leave?"

"Because my sister-in-law is sick and has to go to the hospital, so I have to go back to take care of her children, the house, my husband, everything."

"Is all that more important than your daughter's recovery?"

"I think my daughter is fine now."

"But the doctor says she's not."

"I want to go. I don't like being here. And my husband wants me to."

"Don't you care if Kajal gets better?"

"Of course I do, but my husband told me Kajal would get better if we came home."

Anita, with her face like a caged animal, doesn't really understand but suspects that understanding wouldn't help much either.

"Do you think your husband knows more than the doctor?"

"I don't know. He's my husband."

She stood up again.

"Who do I have to talk to so I can go home?"

The biggest struggle for those working at MSF-Biraul was not against any disease: it was against the resistance their patients—the parents of their patients—have to believing in a disease that so closely resembled their normal state. This is the cruelest cruelty of malnutrition: frequently those who suffer it don't recognize it.

They don't know, they don't want to know, they can't know, they aren't able to fully grasp, that life could be any different.

Due to malnutrition, more than half of all children in this region do not develop fully, and many suffer from illnesses they either wouldn't have ever had or that wouldn't have affected them seriously if they had been well fed; some also die from complications from those diseases, but the MSF's most important work consists of convincing mothers that malnutrition can be alleviated.

So they devote a large part of their efforts to chasing after reluctant parents, convincing them that they must stick to the treatment; they call them, send transportation to bring them, seek them out incessantly— everything the state would never do. They also set up "mobile clinics" that carry personnel, equipment, and medicines to the farthest reaches of the district.

"I used to get so pissed off, sometimes I still do, but I've learned to empathize."

I was told this by Maria, the Greek doctor, after asking what it was like to deal with people like Anita who went against her advice.

"I've come to realize that it's much more difficult for them to realize what's happening to their children. For example, the indicator we always use for malnutrition is the MUAC, or mid-upper arm circumference. If it's 4.7 inches, the child is malnourished; if it's 4.9 inches, the child is not. But while we know this, the mother does not . . ."

"What do they tell you when you say they're malnourished, that they have a disease they didn't even know existed?"

"Usually they're full of doubt. They doubt the diagnosis, they doubt your expertise, they doubt a treatment that doesn't come in the form of pills or injections. They say, no, real doctors give you injections. And the mothers don't want to stay because they have so much to do at home that seems so important."

"Do you think they don't care about their children or that they don't think they're in danger?"

"They do, they care about their children. They walk for hours to get them treatment, they accept the treatment even if they don't understand and sometimes don't even believe the child's in danger, but they also have to take care for the rest of their family; they have other children at home, maybe a cow, and they know that if they stay much longer, one of those children will get sick and die, or the cow will, and then the family budget will tank . . . And sometimes they have to choose. I've seen them. It's horrible, but they end up choosing what they think will be best for everybody."

Which isn't the case if the doctor who is consulting them is a woman. Maria—thirty years old, energetic, olive-skinned, with spiky hair—told me that she would often see somebody, ask questions, examine them. At some point a male nurse entered the office and the parent of a patient would exclaim, "You're finally here, doctor, I've been waiting for you."

Maria told me she sometimes wished she didn't have to see their faces.

"What do you mean?"

"I mean when I go to bed, when I am eating, whenever I lower my guard, I can see the face of a sick infant, a malnourished little girl, a dying boy."

She told me about a recent infant who had died, a little girl severely malnourished, eighteen months old, with such an acute respiratory infection, she could barely breath. "It was a Friday; we spent all day Saturday working on her, we stabilized her, we were saving her, but on Sunday morning her father came and said they had to leave. I insisted they stay, I fought, I told him that if they took her away, she would die, but her father told me that he was her father and that he knew what to do. I was sad, depressed, but what else could I do? On Monday morning we sent someone to go check on the girl, which was about two hours by car from here, and they told us she had died the night before. I still see her, the face of the little girl we could have saved."

She said that in addition to feeling sad, that was when she first understood the limitations to her practice here. I asked if she meant medical limitations, but she shook her head.

"Social limitations, I mean . . . In Europe, in a situation like that, you do everything you can, and if a patient dies it's because you couldn't have done anything more to save him. Here, on the other hand, she died because her father thought he needed to assert his authority, or whatever, for reasons that have nothing to do with our work, with medicine. That's what I mean by my limitations."

The reassuring and terrible aspect of a doctor's life is that they are always working with the real. A writer, for example, could spend years producing on an artifact without knowing if it works. And they'll never really know; whether or not it "works" can be measured, maybe, for some, by the opinions of five or six readers; for others, by the sale of fifty or one hundred thousand copies. And, once finished, it will continue for years being that thing the writer once did. A doctor, on the other hand—a doctor working in rural poverty, in the middle of nowhere, a doctor in the middle of the storm—confronts the most extreme reality: they are good doctors if they can save that child. If they cannot save him or her, they can tell themselves it's the environment, the resources, destiny, but it doesn't make it any easier. And, if they can save that child, the good feeling of having done so quickly dissipates in the wake of so many more infants needing treatment. The doctors will once again have to work within their limitations, more severely if the doctor is female, over and over again. The reassuring and terrible aspect of the life of a doctor is that those limitations are always in your face.

Anita's husband showed up that same afternoon: the fearful lord and master, the abusive macho. He was a young man just over five feet tall, and around 120 pounds, with very dark skin, curly hair, wearing sandals that were too big for him. He was probably in his early to mid-twenties. He picked up his daughter with a rough-edged sweetness, made silly faces to her, sang her a few songs. Then he went to see Maria to tell her that he was about to travel to Delhi for work and that he needed to take his family with him. It's not true, but Maria had no way of knowing. She insisted that Kajal stay—that he should leave his daughter a few more days, Kajal needed to stay, she told him, she weighed less than six pounds so was still in danger of becoming terminally ill. The lord and master told her that he was the father and that he decided what was good or not for his daughter. As Anita began stuffing Kajal's few belongings into a green bag, Maria insisted once more to keep her here. She was pleading for Kajal's life, but her father, the lord and master, looked up at the ceiling, as if to say, the doctor can say what she likes, but I've made up my mind.

(Times like these have made me think that this book should've been a collection of minimalist stories, stories like this one, nothing more. And that each reader would read as much as he or she wanted, even if only to ask themselves why they are doing so. Instead I fell into the trap of trying to explain: to reason, to find excuses for only highlighting the intolerable. In this way, I was and still am a coward.)

4

Not far from Biraul was Mahmuda, which was not that far away from Darbhanga, which was three hours by car from Patna, which, in turn, was around six hundred miles from New Delhi. At the time I visited, Mahmuda had a population of about two thousand scattered around seven or eight streets that twisted and turned capriciously. Some days these streets were nothing but mud; others, sun-scorched dust. There was no electricity or running water or sewage. There were flies and people. There were cows.

In Mahmuda the materials used for housing indicated signs of affluence. The wealthiest families, the landowners, lived in homes constructed from brick and tiled roofing, (though many of these were only half built, as if overcome with idleness); those families who did no own land but could afford it used adobe; for the poor families who could afford nothing, reeds. At the entryway of one house, a wealthier house, was a cow. Behind, there was a dirt yard with even more bovines as well as a round bucket with fodder and a stove for cooking. The house itself was made up of a single room. Children—short, skinny, noisy—ran about. A wife walked three steps behind her husband, always three steps behind, with her head jutting forward, as if she were a buffalo being pulled by the nose with a yoke, as if she were being forced to follow him. But whenever they walked, it was the wife looking at the husband, he did not see her. The wife could veer off, escape, and her husband might not even notice. There was a fluidity to it all, too, as if the cows, if they wanted, could sleep in the house, while the family took their *katiyas*—cots made of bamboo and palm fronds—out to the yard.

In Mahmuda there were dozens of tiny shops selling grain and assorted curios, millions of incessantly buzzing flies, a tree that had watched the world go by, a crowd of very fragile trees, dust in the air, smells in the air, various birds in the air, the cows, the passing people, people passing by carrying firewood or manure or straw on their heads. The rich traveled by motorbike, the less rich by bicycle, almost everybody on foot; the women wore worn-out saris; the men wore out the women. The village was surrounded by fields of wheat and corn; the men plowed with oxen, the women tended to do everything else.

On the porch of one house sat a bored man who scowled at me but also asked me to take his picture. I must've been the fourth or fifth white man he'd ever seen. All over town, I was an event. In one shop, when I sat on the floor to write, a young clerk ran out to look for a plastic chair: I had no choice but to sit. One man with only one tooth recounted in Hindi a very long story accompanied by gestures; a very skinny man shooed away an ox so I could pass, a woman dashed out to look at me, two young mothers covered their babies and themselves with their veils; children shouted after me and trailed my walk.

Manure was everywhere. Piles of manure, balls of manure, discs of manure, bricks of manure, cylinders of manure, manure in all imaginable—and unimaginable—shapes, and I would see them carrying on their heads bundles of forest leaves, some over six feet high, to sell to the owners of a cow or, if they were lucky, to give to their own. Then they picked up the product—or waste—from these leaves. These leaves produced a kind of manure that could be used to insulate the walls of a hut or to burn as fuel for a cooking stove.

The smell of cows—cow shit, cow filth, straw used by cows—was the smell of these villages. It is also, by the way, for certain people with nostalgic memories, the smell of my country, of Argentina.

Because he spoke a little English, I hired the boy from the store to be my *maargadarshak*, my guide, during my walk. It was hotter than hell. At a large pond, people were enjoying the best part of the day's work—frolicking in the water, diving, chatting, while others used the water to bathe their buffaloes. We watched a beast being led into the water with a suspicious look on its face, a countenance shared by its owner, but after having their snouts and backs rubbed by hands and dry leaves, the buffaloes began to relax and wandered around the pond on their own accord. When one buffalo went too far out, its caretaker called to it in Maithili—the language spoken in Bihar and one of the twenty-two officially recognized languages of India—and the beast returned, swimming. Another buffalo was apparently owned by a very slouchy, very aged man who clutched a cane with his bony hand. I asked the boy to ask the old man if he was going to bathe his buffalo.

"It's not my buffalo," the old man said, looking puzzled.

In turn, he asked the boy to ask me where I was from. When I told him, via the boy, Argentina, the old man stared at the buffalo for a moment then asked my age. I told him, which prompted the old man to say something with a lot of *babu babu*, which I knew to be an address of respect for elderly people. I asked him his age, and he said he didn't know but that he wasn't as old as I was.

In Mahmuda, it's the body that worked. The equation is obvious but insidious: the poorer one is, the more energy the body exerted; the richer, the less. The bodies that work most are often fed least. In the West, to replace the work with the body, to compensate for that immobility that we've achieved, a thousand and one forms of exercise have been developed. Ways of deceiving those bodies that are still not used to being used for what they were used for: tools.

The town petered out in a few cultivated plots of land near the edge of a small forest where cows grazed. The forest also acted as a sort of barrier. Beyond it, on the outskirts of town, there was a street lined with truly filthy shacks where the Untouchables, the lowest caste, lived. The boy told me that in Indian villages the Untouchables were required to live apart from everyone else. We arrived to find a mobile MSF clinic that had been dispatched there. It was a standard practice of the MSF to treat patients remotely, monitor sanitary conditions, and, at least until it was banned, distribute Plumpy'Nut. But the team from this mobile clinic had an extracurricular mission: they had built a small school with two classrooms painted sky blue. When class wasn't in session, it was used by the *panchayat bhavan* a kind of local judge who heard and resolved neighborly disputes.

We empathize with the lives of others—the stories of others—because they are not usually dissimilar from our own. Yet so many lives—so many stories—are monotonous. Slow declines, gradual descents. An unchanging misery. The stories of misery are as common as pebbles along the road.

Sadadi, a young mother, had a daughter named Jaya who had passed away a year and a half before.

"What did you feel?"

"Nothing, I don't know. She was my daughter, she was going to be my daughter for a long time, and then suddenly she wasn't."

Jaya had started losing weight. Sadadi wasn't worried at first, they'd had some difficult days when they barely managed to eat anything, and everybody in the family was still getting by. Jaya's whimpers grew softer, then she moved her body less and less, like a flame dying out. One night, Sadadi spent hours holding her, wetting her lips, calming her down, but at dawn the girl died.

"Was her death somebody's fault?"

"No, it happened so fast, there was nothing to do."

"What did your husband say?"

"He tried to make me understand that these things happen, and if it happened it's because God wanted it to happen . . . I understood what he was saying, but I was still so sad. I didn't think I could ever be that sad."

Sadadi and her husband cremated Jaya with the little bit of firewood they had, and they tried to forget her. Sadadi thought that she would slowly forget, but she hasn't.

A year later Sadida gave birth to another girl, Amida. But before long, Amida also started losing weight. As soon as she noticed, Sadadi told me, she took Amida to the mobile clinic.

"I want to raise this girl until she's grown up. I know I can raise her well, so she grows up beautiful and healthy."

Sadadi, like the other mothers, didn't understand why her child was ill. She always fed Amida something at eat least once a day. But it couldn't always be the kind of food Sadadi would have liked to have fed her daily—rice, bread, and vegetables.

"Why not?"

"Because it's too expensive."

She looked at me pitiably as though I were a person who didn't understand the simplest things.

Nothing, actually, happens in this book. Or, better put: nothing that isn't happening all the time. The most difficult thing about this book is to capture the quantity, the scale: to understand—understand in the sense of have present, understand, as they say, to take it in—that each story could happen—and, with slight variations, does happen—to thousands and thousands of people. To think that Sadadi's little story is the grand story of hundreds of millions of Indians, for example.

But it is easy to turn these people into abstractions of hunger. A sick little girl, an anxious mother, a son-of-a-bitch father. What good does it do for us not to see these people as individuals.

Buffaloes plowing fields of rice. The rhythm of their slow, unhurried steps. Directing them was a man on a cart, toasted by the sun, peaceful. There are thousands and thousands who are not part of the global circuit, who have no idea what's going on even a couple miles from their houses. The illusion of the global is also about a concentration of wealth.

There are situations in which the simplest thing is the most difficult to understand, the most distant. They are, I suppose, the things that have kept wandering around the world.

5

"I don't know if this does any good at all. I think it does, of course, otherwise I wouldn't do it."

Luis told me. He was the coordinator of the project, around thirty, from Madrid, slender, partially bald, with an easy smile and several years of experience with MSF. In Biraul he managed a team of about seventy people: six foreigners, sixty-odd Indians.

"But that's not what made me decide to come here, to spend a year in India or in Sudan or in the Central African Republic. I do it, and I think most of us do it, because I can't not do it. Sometimes I think about the option of going back to work for a serious company in Madrid as an economist; true, I'd earn good money, I'd have a girlfriend, a pleasant life, all that, and I'd feel horrible."

Luis said he did it because he'd always wanted to make a positive change in the world, but that he didn't know how, and he didn't know either if what he was doing would make any kind of impact, but that if he didn't do anything, he'd feel worse.

"So, if you want, you can think of it this way, that in the end my motivation is purely selfish, just to avoid feeling bad. Imagine that."

They are missionaries without gods, young people who feel somewhat guilty about their First World privileges—what have I done to deserve all this?—young people sensitized by the economic crisis and their own uncertain futures, young people who want to change something but don't know how, so in the meantime . . .

MSF is the foreign legion that has passed through the fog of time and become the opposite of a military service: young people who want to leave their routines—not criminals who are forced to—and go to the most neglected countries, not to occupy them but rather to help remedy something. Like the foreign legion, they are a space of confusion and differences, where expats mingle among themselves and are different from the locals. The foreign legion à la Erasmus: a product of the new idea of Europe.

(I like the word *expat*, which is used so frequently these days. Ambrose Bierce once said that an emigrant is a poor person who goes to work in a rich country and an expat is a rich person who goes to work in a poor country. However, I'd like to think that an expat doesn't mean someone who is far away from his country but rather someone who no longer thinks about patriotism, who is far away from the concept that one's country is what matters.)

In Biraul, the volunteers of MSF lived in an unfinished apartment—like most apartments in India—without hot water, with squat toilets and rationed hours of generated electricity because public electricity is a utopic ideal that doesn't exist everywhere. Which meant not having a working refrigerator, which meant no television. Each expat had a modest room: a bed with a mosquito net, one or two plastic chairs, maybe a table, a wardrobe, a fan that stopped at eleven at night, when the power was cut for the night. They were austere but not self-sacrificing; they engaged with the community, felt passionately about why they were there, felt boredom off hours, became angry at their limitations, occasionally fell in love, almost always had their lives changed.

They would lunch and dinner together every day; people speaking English with all kinds of non-native accents. Every meal, among the chapati and the rice and the Nutella, I recalled something I'd read about the great advantage of English as a lingua franca: that one can speak it poorly and still be understood. At noon, a woman would come to prepare their evening meals; for their own safety, the team didn't go out after sunset. It was a decidedly sober life, punctuated by laughter and complications, minor conflicts, achievements, frustrations. It was underlined by one idea—one sentence—that they always kept close to their lips: "Our first mission is to save lives."

To save lives: in a world where almost nothing seemed to make any sense, where nothing seemed to matter, where everything was money or appearance, there were acts that did not require more justification.

To save lives is an act that is more real than real.

One doctor from Argentina told me she had spent many years working in the most difficult places at the most difficult moments.

"At first I didn't understand, but now I do: at MSF, we aren't trying to change the world, we're just applying Band-Aids on moments when things are at their worst, or at least trying to hold back, just a little, the disaster. That's all we do, and it's necessary even though it doesn't change the world or even the lives of these refugees, who are just going to continue in the same shit. But at that particular moment, our being there or not makes an important difference, a difference between life and death for those people."

"A proud form of humility or a humble form of pride. Don't you ever think you'd like to contribute to changing things so that this wouldn't keep happening?"

"Not for now. That requires so many things that are completely out of my hands. They are things I will never have access to, things that are dealt with on other levels, not mine. I can position myself at this level, and that's what I do."

A nurse on the emergency team was more radical: "I prefer not to think about the reasons for what's happening, if it does or doesn't have a solution. If I did, I wouldn't be able to do anything, I'd be paralyzed. To keep doing all this I have to stop thinking about what I see, its causes, its reasons."

Maria, the Greek doctor, told me she always wanted to do what she was doing.

"The world is full of things I don't like, and I want to do something to improve them. And I also want to travel, meet new people, go to new places, learn."

"Are you managing to do both?"

"The first more than the second. We work a lot here, we spend most of our time working. It's harder to pull yourself away when you know that lives depend on what you're doing. I feel good, I'm doing things, I work like crazy all day, I'm engaged, interested, I feel like I'm doing good things, but at the same time, being here you realize that the problem is so big, so serious, that everything you do is nothing, almost nothing . . ."

"So, what then?"

"So, nothing. I'm going to keep doing what I do. This is what I can do. I'm going to keep treating this individual, here, now, and at least he or she will be better. If you start thinking about everything you can't do, it's very bad for the work, very frustrating. Better to think you're going one by one. If not, you'll go crazy."

And Luis, the Spanish project coordinator, told me that the most difficult part of his work was to convince himself that he couldn't do everything. "There's always a moment, at the beginning, when you feel like shit because you have to resign yourself to the fact that you're doing something else, so you aren't going to be able to do anything for this one or the other one."

"Does that pass?"

"No, to tell you the truth, it doesn't. But you stop thinking all the time about overall change, and you understand what humanitarian intervention means; it's thinking you have to save whomever you can, whomever you have in front of you, whomever you find."

Melanie, a French woman who deals with logistics and tells more or less good jokes in her ridiculously bad English, echoed these sentiments. "What you do manage to accomplish is amazing. But the cost is high: living so far away, isolated, spending almost all your time working."

They were a well-trained team: doctors, nurses, midwives, managers. Like many MSF volunteers, their first year, they are paid seven hundred euros a month. Only after those first twelve months do they begin to earn a more reasonable salary. But the conditions remain the same: living together, far away from everything, totally absorbed in endless work.

Melanie explained, "You have to put your life on hold for those six or nine months that you spend in the field. You can do that for a while; then you have to decide if you want to have a life in a stable place, relationships, friends, or if you are going to continue to be a humanitarian nomad."

At the time, she wasn't going to decide. She would figure that out later.

I asked Maria what were the greatest difficulties of her daily life here.

"Not having electricity or television or Internet all the time, not eating what you want, having so many insects in your room . . . And, of course, seeing people in such terrible conditions, things you'd never see in Europe. Everything is very, *very* different. But at the same time, I knew it would be like this. What I don't want to do is go back to my country and think that because so many horrible things are happening here, what's happening there doesn't matter. If my brother comes and tells me that he wants to buy a house, I don't want to tell him it doesn't make any sense, children in India can't eat and there you are thinking about a house . . ."

Night in Biraul was a concert: muezzins, Hare Krishnas, celebrations of Vishnu or Durga. The night air was full of voices that seemed to have a lot to say, and, rather than trust divine powers, they put their trust in powerful loudspeakers. It was difficult to sleep surrounded by so much faith.

6

Every month, an MSF doctor would go out to do "verbal autopsies," to find out—or try to find out—what happened to certain patients who had stopped showing up and had probably died.

"Generally, they are patients who should have returned and didn't, and we hear news about problems they've had. Or, we don't get any news, which is worse."

We left at eight in the morning and arrived in our first village at ten. Bollywood music was playing on the van radio. The asphalt roads were so rundown that they were full of potholes. Still, the roads managed to carry us from village to village, from broken bridges to cows blocking the way. The further we drove away from Biraul, the more people there were; not a single spot was empty.

A herd of buffaloes accompanied an old man and a boy: Bengali herdsmen. Each year, thousands of nomadic herdsmen gathered their buffaloes and cows and traveled scores of miles to find grazing land for their cattle until the monsoon arrived and everything turned green and generous. In the meantime, it was difficult to find food.

The village was fifty houses on the banks of a wide river. We walked through a corn field to reach the hut of the first case: a two-year-old girl who was being treated for malnutrition then suddenly stopped coming to the clinic. The girl's mother was there, along with two younger girls, presumably her sisters. It was around lunchtime but the only one eating was a man the mother identified as her brother. The doctor inquired about the youngest daughter and her mother explained that the child had been doing well, but that she was complaining about pain in her belly and was whimpering; they didn't pay any attention to her. When she started crying harder, they took her to an Ayurvedic practitioner in a nearby village; the child didn't improve, and a week later they went to the hospital in Darbhanga. The doctor there hospitalized her immediately and told them that he would try to diagnose her the following day;

she died the following morning without anybody having found out what was wrong. Her mother didn't know what happened, what it could have been, and a tear rolled down her cheek. The Indian MSF doctor asked her many questions he read from a questionnaire to try to determine the cause of death. The mother barely managed to answer a few: she had a cough, she didn't think she had any fever, she was playing, yes, she was playing with her sisters. When the doctor asked if she had a death certificate, the woman picked up a cell phone with a broken screen, put it on speaker phone, and called her husband, who worked in Delhi. He said he had no idea, how was he supposed to know. The woman cried, "I wanted her to have a certificate. At least a certificate . . ."

The focus, the intensity of the oldest girl—twelve or thirteen—as she watched her uncle, the man of the house, eat—squatting on the ground, the tin plate resting on the dirt floor, rice with a little sauce in his right hand—to make sure she brought him the aluminum washing jar the moment he finished. But she was a second late; her uncle stretched out his hand without looking, and shouted; how was he supposed to wash his eating hand in the jar if it wasn't there in time. She lowered her eyes; for a moment it seemed like he was going to strike her, then he saw me observing them.

Back on the road: the shape made by a little girl asleep on the back of a buffalo, facedown, her legs around the beast's neck, her head resting on his hindquarters. And further on: the driver of a multicolored truck honking wildly at an older man who didn't scurry along or move aside as he walked down the road. Thousands were like him: Gandhian or simply absentminded.

The second village was more remote and smaller, with fewer than ten huts. The road was a path through planted fields. Before entering, we passed through a paupers' camp: pieces of black plastic stretched across bamboo sticks. Many women and a single goat took shelter under an enormous tree. The grandfather of the second case told us that he never found out what happened to his grandson. One night the boy died suddenly; he was fine, then he started getting fat and having diarrhea, his belly was swollen. Then he fainted. His family became frightened, so frightened that they thought that as soon as the sun rose, they would take him to a clinic; at night there was no way to leave the village. By morning the child was dead.

Two friends were riding their bicycles. They decided to sit down and rest in the shade of a tree next to the road—a two-lane highway, the only one in the whole district. One of them leaned the bike against the tree; the other left it on the asphalt, nearly a yard into the road. Leaving it there took exactly the same amount of effort as leaving it a yard away from the road, on the shoulder, where it wouldn't be in the way of traffic.

The house of the third case is high up on a cliff overlooking the work fields; during the monsoon, the Indian doctor told me, all these fields would flood, and the village would be accessible only by boat. The house was a partially collapsed bamboo hut; nearby were six or seven others like it and dozens of children, only half of them clothed, running around with women looking out from behind their veils and a man squatting and eating. The third case was a boy a little more than a year old, who had begun Plumpy treatment before his parents stopped it. The boy's parents weren't there. "Do you know if they are in the fields?" one of our group asked the two women neighbors.

"The fields?" They cracked up with laughter.

The man told them to shut up, that he knew where they were. The family we were looking for wasn't due to arrive till tomorrow or the next day, he told us, with a somewhat malevolent smile.

"They're not coming back today, I'm telling you."

It's improbable, but possibly true. We kept going. The fourth case lived in a village with shops, in a brick house with a motorbike parked in front: peasants with land. The little girl we were looking for died of tuberculosis almost three months before, said a skinny young male with a strained expression, sitting on a bench in the house's patio and holding a baby on his lap. He was the uncle; his brother, the baby's father, worked in Punjab; his sister-in-law, the mother, was behind him with the other women sitting on the ground a few feet away. The brother-in-law talked excitedly, almost defensively. He said that they had wanted to get her niece help, they took her to the MSF clinic because she was very thin and her arms were swollen and she was spitting up blood. Some neighbors told them that they don't deal with those things there, but he didn't listen to them and took her there, but it didn't do any good. And in the clinic, they told him that the treatment would take months to work, but he knew they were just saying that.

"Why would they do that?"

"So I'd keep going."

There were about thirty people standing around us; they looked at each other and whispered. Then a young boy brought us tea with sweet milk and lots of ginger.

"But why would they want to trick you if they weren't charging you, if they didn't have anything to gain?"

"I don't know, so we'd keep going."

There are few things worse than interrupting a course of treatment against tuberculosis; the patient relapses, worse than before. When they took her to a private doctor, they told her they would give her another treatment, but she died before it started.

I found these encounters to be strange. Visitors from the wealthy Western World, crossing a border, a coastline where the land barely mixed with the sea; meeting people who have otherwise never crossed their paths.

I wanted to know what the families we visited were thinking. They'd see our jeep carrying four people, coming from who knows where to take care of their weakest, most vulnerable children. Religions had been founded on much less than this. We returned to Biraul as the sun was setting.

These were the accidents, without exception. India was not Africa, the doctors explained; most of the hungry didn't die. But in some ways that could also be worse; the hungry got used to the hunger, adapted to it.

When I left Biraul, Gurya was still in critical condition. Rahmati was still singing her sad song. Maria kept telling her that they were doing everything possible to save her daughter. And perhaps they did.

VOICES OF THE TRIBE

How the hell do we manage to live knowing these things are happening?

Sorry to bother you, sir, I don't want to pry, but I was wondering, what are you eating right now? What did you eat this morning? And last night, and tonight? Think about it, if you feel like it, check it out, then tell me what you think.

I ask, I want to ask, but I don't know how to ask: You, dear reader, so well-intentioned though perhaps a little forgetful, can you imagine what it is like not knowing if you will be able to eat tomorrow? And this: Can you imagine a life made up of one day after another of not knowing if you will be able to eat tomorrow? A life that consists above all of this uncertainty, the anxiety of this uncertainty, and the effort of figuring out how to alleviate it, not being able to think about almost anything else because every thought is tinged with this scarcity? A life that is so constricted, so short, so frequently painful, such a struggle?

How the hell do we manage to live knowing these things?

That's all fine, brother, just fine, but you saw how I live. No, seriously, did you see or you want me to draw it for you in black and white? Nobody gives me any help, you know. I've got enough problems without going around thinking about those poor bastards in Africa or Kolkata or those places I don't even . . .

How the hell do we manage to live knowing?

Hunger is somebody else's problem par excellence. It is never directly our own. It is never *us*, those of us who worry about the ecosystem, sexual rights, freedom of expression, peace in the Middle East. Why should we care? In the name of what idea, what principal, what pain, what moral code?

How the hell do we manage to live?

"What's unacceptable is that the government doesn't deal with that. A government that doesn't have as its top priority to feed its citizens should resign, you hear that Mariano, civil servant Mariano, you should just resign."

"Always the government. This isn't a question of the government."

"Resign, Mariano. Say, sorry, I can't do it, I'm outta here, find somebody who can."

"What if the government doesn't do that?"

How the hell do we manage?

To read all this, to think about all this could, eventually, provoke a certain amount of guilt in the most susceptible souls. What good is guilt? What do we do with guilt? Is guilt the emotion that most effectively motivates us to try to do something? What if we don't try? Then what do we do with it? Or does that little dose of suffering we get from the guilt fulfill our quota and bring us peace—are we more at peace now?

The easiest thing is not to think about it.

That's almost always possible.

How the hell?

Yes, of course, of course, I realize how serious it is. If by my age I didn't realize when something was serious, it would be really sad, don't you think? But you also have to admit that things are getting better; things have already gotten much better and they continue to get better; it's true, there are still way too many people in the world who go hungry, who don't have enough to eat, but if you compare that to when we were kids, you'll see that it's not at all the same. Yes, I know it's still serious; what I'm trying to say is that you can see that democracy and development are solving the problem, and that doesn't surprise me because reason wins out, even if there is a struggle. There are people who complain because so-and-so earns too much, that such-and-such has a huge house or a yacht or whatever. Maybe they shouldn't show it off so much, maybe I agree with you there, it can be offensive and it's really stupid, but you can't forget that those guys have a fortune because they created a lot of wealth, invented something, started a company, a factory, they did something that created a lot of wealth, and yeah, they kept a big chunk of it, and that's their right, but, above all, how many jobs have they created, and how much are they paying them? How many of them wouldn't have a pot to piss in, would be begging in the streets if it wasn't for someone coming along and taking a risk and building a company and hiring them and paying them a salary? There'll always be people who are bitter and resentful and think that someone with too much money should be sentenced to life imprisonment. If those guys didn't exist, my dear friend, everything would be much worse, there'd be much more hunger, because they're the ones—

How?

CHANDIGARH

The train car must've been forty years old. It had benches and bunks in every unlikely corner, all of which needed to accommodate twice the number of people they were made for. My bench was meant for three and was seating five. But we all packed in together with a bit of tact, even a wisp of affection. Periodically, the train stopped at a station where more people boarded through the doors and windows, and what was already full, filled up even more. In the eighth century, thousands of fugitives from the Persian Empire arrived at the gates of Mumbai and asked King Maharashtra for refuge; the king didn't want them and in response sent them an overflowing bowl of milk: it was his way of telling them that he did not wish them ill but his kingdom was full. The Persians—the leader of the Persians—put sugar in the bowl and sent it back: it was his way of saying that without filling it any fuller, they would make it better, more delicious. The Persian lesson: there was always room for more. The train advanced.

At the next station, more people got on; just when it seemed not another grain of sugar would fit, more people arrived. Outside there were huts, fields, people, and always buffaloes.

It is good to prove the fallibility of your perceptions, the flexibility of the human body, and the tolerance of those women and men who have spent centuries training to accommodate. I told myself this then wondered if I preferred to adapt or fight—as if I had any possibility of doing either. But now I'd also spent some time in training to accommodate.

I was heading to Chandigarh to visit Devinder Sharma, a food and agricultural policy journalist and activist. After discovering some of his talks on YouTube, I made contact and asked to visit him. At the time he was recovering from open heart surgery, but invited me to Chandigarh nonetheless.

For hours I'd been suffering the humiliating truth of something so simple: my total incapacity to be, even for a little while. A woman had sat next to me, a white veil over her deeply lined face. It should've been easy to let this go unnoticed: she was a nobody, I was a nobody, an exchange of nobodies shouldn't bother anybody. But no, it was impossible. I would be among others and then—and this would often happen without warning—a sort of claustrophobia would set in of living an entire life reduced to oneself, not being able, never ever able, to think like any of the other seven billion thinks. I was the jailor of my own narrow prison. To write to pretend to escape.

What would we be like if we could think in somebody else's head? More understanding, compassionate, supportive? More ruthless because of the ease this would imply? More indifferent to our own foolishness? Wiser, more resigned, equally intolerant? The same old shit with new trappings?

When I got off the train at the Chandigarh station, a deafening alarm sounded. I looked around; nobody seemed to notice. On the platform, people were waiting for the train, mothers were feeding their babies, little boys did or didn't sell food and drink, men were reading or sleeping spread out on the ground, employees ran here and there as if they were doing something—and nobody seemed to notice. It took me a moment to realize that the alarm was the screeching of thousands of birds under the tin roof over the platform: deafening.

A little way farther, spread out before me, lay that most rationalized city in a country that could be at times irrational. Chandigarh was a planned city, an urban project from its very beginning. In 1949 the Indian government had declared Chandigarh the dual capital of two wealthy states: Haryana and Punjab, and had hired Swiss-French architect Le Corbusier to design it. The result was a city that was large, open, organized, spotless: not very Indian. Chandigarh is the expression of an era that believed in the cliché of redemptive modernity, a feature that would sweep away all those ancient peculiarities, not in the name of global capital but in the name of an ethic that functioned as an aesthetic.

In Chandigarh there are wide, straight boulevards, roundabouts, a lot of green, many trees, very little crowding, always sky, and the memory of the idea—at least it so often seemed obsolete—that it was possible to break from traditions and make something new.

Chandigarh was a joint project, really, planned with the best of intentions by the state, by a group of architects. This was precisely what didn't work out so well in the twentieth century: the ideas and the structures that allowed certain individuals to concentrate the power of the state in their own hands, believing in their own good intentions. They may well have had them, at first, such as: to end hunger once and for all. I always remember what the former leader of the Polish Communist Party told me when I met him in Moscow in 1991, just after the collapse: that Communism was a system for almost perfect people.

And it didn't work because we are not, and so we cast aside the search for something really good, and we accept this world that is, supposedly, the least bad, our free-market democracy, where, supposedly, the imperfections of the one with power are balanced by the imperfections of many others. Hunger shows that there is no such balance. But capitalism blurs the lines of guilt. It was always good at blurring lines. In the Soviet Union, on the other hand, a select few took on the unattainable conceit of being everything for everybody.

More than fifteen years ago I was at a meeting with the first secretary the province of Villa Clara, Cuba, and those responsible for the local and national government agencies and administration. The secretary's name was Miguel Díaz-Canel, a young man who would one day succeed Raúl Castro as Cuba's president. That day, however, that line of succession wasn't really what I was thinking. Instead I thought I was staring at a long-haired rock star. We sat around a large table while a government official recounted the progress being made on the construction of houses, another told of the fight against hepatitis, another about meat processing, energy supplies, rum production, bread distribution, ice cream production, water purity, supplies of coffins, school bus schedules, snacks for school children, among other things. As we were leaving, I mentioned to the secretary that socialism's weakness was surely its enormous and excessive ambition to be responsible for everything, for in such a system any misfortune that befalls any individual can be blamed on the state. That, in general, is the where problems flourish, in the incompetence, the reproaches.

"Under capitalism, if someone doesn't have a coffin, it's their own fault because they couldn't buy one. Here, on the other hand, it's Fidel's and socialism's fault. That's pretty difficult to maintain, isn't it?"

"Of course it is. But you can't imagine the satisfaction you get when you see things going well, see people's lives improving. You can't put a price on that, my friend, not any price."

As he talked, I started thinking about where, in the midst of all that, was the lust for power. If it is to experience that satisfaction, then the best and most generous would grab onto power like leeches so they could do good for others, so they would be able to be good. Let's just suppose— only the best. In the meantime, however, battalions of the mediocre were clinging on to power because they couldn't stand the idea of losing everything, or because they were afraid of what would happen to them when they lost it, or because they didn't have enough imagination to think in any other way. In any case, the old Jesuit motto, *Everyone for everyone else*, a readymade socialist vision, no longer applied to Soviet model which quickly became, *Everyone else for a select few*—and that meant, of course, *Everything for a select few*: the assets, the decisions, the comforts, the discourse—and under that imbalance, the whole system collapsed. Moreover, we ended up like those people who can't stand cows because they got burned by milk, and so we refuse to believe it possible to assemble something better, and we submit to mediocrity.

I arrived at Devinder Sharma's modest home. After a long journey, his warm greeting was rejuvenating. He had a gentle, calm demeanor, perhaps due in part to his sedation during recovery; he also had a very thick mustache and well-manicured nails. Like myself, Sharma had written many books, though unlike myself who had also published novels, Sharma had not wavered in his focus on agriculture, globalization, and injustice. I was surprised to hear that Sharma was from Brahmin caste—the highest caste—and that he had family obligations, which included choosing husbands and wives for the youngest members, and in turn, receiving family that was obliged to honor him; hundreds of worried relatives, some so distant as to be hardly from the same tree, had visited him during his illness. To the rest of the country, Sharma is a highly respected writer and thinker, someone who wears his passion on his sleeve. I asked him why there was so much hunger in India.

"There's no reason for there to be hunger here. In India, hunger is deliberate, it exists because we don't want to really take the bull by the horns. Hunger serves many people's purposes."

"What do you mean?"

"It can't be that a country like India has the largest number of malnourished people in the world. It doesn't make sense. Indian governments have always had public assistance programs that have been more or less generous. The problem is that most of that money ends up in the hands of bureaucrats. If there were no hunger, they'd have to earn a living some other way."

What a fantastic arrangement: hunger as a necessity of a state and its faithful servants, to keep them in their places, on the one hand, and steal a few pennies, on the other.

"Here, there's no scarcity of food. There is usually, each year, a surplus of about fifty or sixty million tons, which get exported, while two hundred and fifty million go hungry. The Indian situation is incredible: we have the hungry, we have the food, but the problem isn't being addressed. It's shameful. How can we be a major exporter of food and have the largest number of malnourished people in the world?"

I told him that what he was saying sounded familiar to me, and he was polite enough to ask me what I was talking about. I was impertinent enough to say that we often say the same thing in Argentina.

"It's a global phenomenon," he replied.

The problem everywhere: how to distribute it; who has it.

"What we need to do is revive the teachings of Mahatma."

Sharma insisted that the world prefers for there to be hunger. We spoke about the now infamous 1996 FAO World Food Summit in Rome which passed a resolution to reduce hunger by half by 2020, an effort that has since been called out for doing some numerical magic tricks to hide the fact that this number is actually going up. At that time, in 1996, there were 850 million hungry people. In 2007, there were 923 million people who qualified as undernourished. And that growth is also growing at an exponential rate. Only two years later, in 2009, that number had gone up to 963 million starving people, a number no doubt affected by the market crash of 2008, of which $20 billion "stimulus packages" were provided to save the banks and large financial institutions. At the time I had met with Sharma, in 2012, the problem was worsening. Now, things are becoming more stabilized, the number has slowly fallen to 842 million starving people. By the time you will be reading this in an English-language edition, it will be 2020. In taking twenty-four years to halve world hunger, we've hardly put a dent in it.

"It's pretty obvious that nobody is interested in ending hunger. Or, more accurately: many are interested in keeping people hungry, because a hungry person is someone you can exploit. It's more difficult to exploit someone with a full belly. But why exploit the hungry? Why not solve the problem? I don't understand why politicians don't do this, as it would give so much more power and influence if they could. If I were the prime minister of India, and I was able to solve the country's hunger problem, I would remain in power for as long as I was alive. Just imagine, 250 million people that you've alleviated from hunger. For the rest of their lives, they would remain unfailingly loyal to you."

I told him that it seemed to me, based on what I've seen, that most of those hungry people wouldn't rebel because of lack of food, that many of them didn't even understand that they lacked food, or thought that it was just par for the course, that they appeared at times to be very submissive, very resigned to this fate. Sharma disagreed: there were socialist uprisings in India, of its 650 districts, more than 200 were already being affected by guerrillas of Indian Maoists, the Naxalites. And it was agriculture that was the first to go. Either farmland would be taken over by the Naxalites, its food distributed however they wished, or the Indian government would set farmlands ablaze so that they could claim that land in the first place. Either way, the hungry poor lost out and, in many cases, left the contested area.

"When small farming is destroyed to make room for industry, and

large tracts of land are owned by big corporations and real estate investors, it provokes the displacement of people to the cities. Those who stay
often side with the Maoists. More and more people realize that the political system is not giving them what they need. And the most decisive
changes will come from the countryside, because that's where the majority live; and that's why, if you want to change things in India, you have
to deal with agriculture and the peasants," he concluded, with an almost
entryist slant in his voice.

A domestic servant brought us tea, cookies, a slice of mango, and a
banana as Sharma was discussing the peasantry. Of the 1.2 billion Indians, he told me, half lived directly from farming: peasants and their
families. Another 200 million found work based on what those others
produced. All told, 800 million people lived off the land, and the large
corporations want to replace them with more and more hi-tech production, which might be okay for the United States or Brazil, but was not
good for India. In those countries, there were large tracts of land and
little population; in India, it was the opposite. In 1947 an average farm in
the United States was one hundred and twenty acres; in 2005 it was five
hundred acres. In India, on the other hand, in 1947 the average farm was
ten acres, now it is just over three. Large agricultural operations like ones
found in the United States would leave millions of people in even greater
poverty. These are people who can't go to the cities because there is nothing for them there. So they have to be offered opportunities to be productive in the countryside, and they have to know how to make use of them.

> What's needed is not a system of mass production but rather
> production by the masses," as Gandhi said, which would allow
> them to produce food for themselves and society in a sustain-
> able fashion, so they won't be constantly pushed toward the
> urban centers, which are already totally overpopulated. In our
> current system, they say that peasants are no good at growing
> food and that's why they earn less than two thousand rupees a
> month, and they should go to the cities to work in something
> else and let the corporations produce food. In my opinion, this
> is a disaster. We need the opposite process: people should stay
> or return to their small farms, produce sustainably, without
> the need for fertilizers or chemical pesticides, and they should
> charge a fair price for their products. Our societies should be
> locally dependent not globally dependent. The big guys care
> only about what they grow (rice, wheat, soy), and the rest is
> trash. On the contrary, on a small farm, everything is grown,

because everything is food. Our model wants to create local production systems that make each region autonomous; food would be grown, stored, and distributed in areas no larger than one hundred kilometers in diameter. This is what is being tried in Haridwar, a town in Uttarakhand, by a group led by a very well-known television guru, Swami Ramdev. It's a Gandhian project of returning to the land and tradition as a way of opposing the dehumanizing growth, he says, of the food corporations. We have to encourage people to grow their own food, take charge of their own hunger. The way to combat hunger cannot be to distribute little bits of food. That's simply not the way. We don't want to give out fish; we want to teach people how to fish. Haridwar is way of showing people that it's possible, convince them they can do it.

It seemed that many people here want to convince somebody, mostly the state, of something. Sharma preached by example, the same as MSF in Biraul.

More cups of tea, more smiles, more relaxed and intelligent conversation. I asked him how it feels to be Indian at a moment when India seemed to be the great rising star, and he told me if felt good, even more so when he remembered that for a long time many looked at India with scorn.

"Now they say we are a superpower," Sharma said. "I don't know what kind of superpower we can be when we have a third of the world's hungry. It's a fairy tale: we are not a superpower now and we never will be. The economic power of the thirty wealthiest families in the country is the same as the poorest third, about 400 million people. About 77 percent of Indians can only spend twenty rupees a day, less than half a dollar. When you think about these inequalities, how can we be a superpower?"

"What should happen," he continued, he reiterated, "is that they really should return to the teachings of Mahatma Gandhi: you can't ask Monsanto or Cargill to grow food for Indians; they have to grow it for themselves. Why do we have to follow European and American models? Why can't we develop our own model? It's sad that we've forgotten our own resources and always look to the West. It's a colonial mentality, and we should rid ourselves of it and look to our own devices. Our culture is ten thousand years old. Why should we be imitating countries that are no older than five hundred?"

The modernity of culture, like the old biblical saying: pouring new wine into an old wineskin.

VRINDAVAN

Day was breaking in Vrindavan when I arrived, a breeze passed gently, a relief from the already hot morning. The streets were narrow and windy and dirty, like Indian streets can be; at dawn: the sounds of animals. It's was the hour the baboons forged for food. The cows ate the trash; the dogs ate the trash; the pigs, the goats, the rats I didn't see ate the trash, but the baboons took up and expanded their positions, on the ground and in the treetops, to claim the trash for themselves. This was their moment, though, little by little, as the heat increased, humans would recapture territory. Already that had begun: three Hare Krishnas walked by, singing into a megaphone; a motorbike buzzed by, the first horn was honked. The baboons had red bottoms, like baboons tend to have.

The smell of garbage was not that strong, not yet. Two boys with brooms made of branches pretended to sweep. A group of ten or twelve pilgrims walked by singing mournfully, as if their god had forsaken them. A man, a little farther away, was burning a small heap of trash: the smoke was black and oily. The baboons screeched, scrambled up and down the trees, shouted orders. Standing next to a kiosk, four men sitting cross-legged were beginning their day with tea and milk; the tea was boiling over a kerosene burner in a blackened pot, to his right; next to him, several smaller pots for heating, and some clay bowls. The owner was like an effigy surrounded by offerings of receptacles. A female baboon approached the tea; the owner didn't look at it. The air was lethargic.

Suddenly, something happened: a baboon had stolen a woman's purse. It was like a coup against the slow morning—quick, precision-tuned—it ran off shrieking, scurrying up a wall ten feet high, sitting on the edge, and looking down. The lady and her friends shouted up at the baboon who was clearly enjoying himself. One of the men with the tea said in halting English that the baboon wanted to negotiate: you had to give him something for him to give back the purse. Then he said, presumably the same thing, to the woman. A friend of hers handed the man a ten-rupee bill—twenty cents—which he used to buy two packages of cookies from the owner of the tea shop. He returned, threw them at the baboon sitting on the wall, who caught them listlessly, as if he could care less: the scorn of a baboon. While the baboon nibbled on a cookie, still clutching the purse very tightly in his left hand, the mother baboon with child arrived, but he refused to give her some cookie. The women watched him from below; the baboon looked at her; puffed up his chest, holding his cookies and the purse; the mother baboon offered him her red behind. He took a sniff at it, but it didn't appear to him to be worth giving up the cookie for. Instead, he opened the purse, nosed through its contents, removed some small prayer cards, probably of Krishna; he threw one out and the women shouted. They were growing desperate to get their friend's purse back. The tea man asked for another ten rupees, bought more cookies. Again, he threw them: the baboon watched the package fall beside him; he picked it up, even more scornfully than before, opened it, and crushed all the cookies into pieces. The pieces fell down to the street; sparrows gathered, a crow dispersed them. The monkey returned his attention to the purse and continued riffling through its contents, the women shouting at him from below. Then a bigger baboon showed up, with an even redder behind than the thief's; he leaped away, purse in hand. The mother baboon stayed with the newcomer, the women's shouts were now directionless, a dog barked but didn't want cookies. Chasing two sparrows was a more splendid bird, with a gray body, red head, and orange mask around its eyes. It's obvious the beautiful bird won't catch them, just as the thief baboon would never be caught. Finally, another dog arrived who began to eat the rejected crumbled cookies.

Vrindavan is one of the most sacred cities for Hindus. It is where, they say, Mr. Krishna spent his childhood preparing to be a great god. Vrindavan is in Uttar Pradesh, and has more than sixty thousand inhabitants and dozens of temples, some along its twisting streets, others in the outskirts among the fields, others next to the river with staircases that descend to the water; some are actually used as temples, others as tenement housing.

Like everywhere in India, the place was overflowing with people and animals. The dogs, for some reason, looked fat and prosperous. The city is also known for its population of widows who, without husbands, have nowhere else to go. I had come looking for a temple where they congregate, and I followed two of them, one older and the other almost young. I walked thirty yards behind them; they pretended not to notice. As the sun rose, the smells increased, intensified. When I turned a corner, a baboon leaped on me, its mouth open, showing its gums. Such an ugly sensation to have the pecking order of the food chain flipped on you. He snatched at my camera. The widows turned, having heard the shouts of the struggle. The oldest one asked me in some form of English if I needed help. I told her, muscling the camera back into my possession, that I was a journalist and I wanted to speak with them. The baboon meanwhile, withdrew in defeat.

The older woman's name was Aruthi, the younger, Moubani. Aruthi's face was bones hidden behind her faded white scarf. She had only a couple of teeth, very dark lips, and a spark of mischief in her eyes. Moubani was wearing a light whitish-gray sari, and her hands were well-manicured: one could see she had just left a very different life. But she didn't speak one word of English—the norm: we can't communicate. Aruthi did speak English, only a little, but enough to inform me that Moubani still remembered too much, that they'd come here to forget.

Aruthi and Moubani were just two of the fifteen to twenty thousand widows who wander the streets of this ancient city looking for a plate of food. Their hunger has a strange origin.

"I don't care," Aruthi said, "I'm going to die soon, so I don't care." She doesn't sound sad or frightened but rather proud. "But poor Moubani still can't be at peace. She just arrived, only a few months ago; she still remembers too much of what she has lost."

Hunger is also, often, a question of gender.

Vrindavan is the rawest expression of gender hunger.

In India, it's bad to be a widow (and a lot of other things). It was brutally so for centuries. When a man died, the Indians usually cremated his wife with him. The custom was called *sati*, and when the evil British colonizers decided not to respect their traditions, and prohibited it around 1830, there were uprisings. Until well into the twentieth century, there were still cases, more or less clandestine, of widows being burned; it's likely a few still are, here and there. But even without the flames, being a widow continues to be a sorry fate; tradition—religion—assumes it was the wife's karma that killed the husband, and the sentence is ostracism. She cannot marry again, she cannot work, she cannot do anything. Many remain alone, without resources, and others, even worse off, have relatives for whom they are an inconvenience.

It was a friend in Delhi who had informed me about the widows of Vrindavan. She told me about the widow of a poor peasant family: they lived in a shack—owned by the widow—with one room; the couple and their three sons slept there, and the widow slept outside, so as not to bother anybody, though she was still a bother. Until one day her son told her to pack up whatever she needed for a long trip because he was going to take her to visit Krishna. And he brought her to Vrindavan, because it was a privilege to die there, and so there he left her.

"Poor woman, she thought her son would take care of her until she died. You know how it was, how it still is in many cases: the mother-in-law is the real ruler of the roost, and she imposes her power on the daughter-in-law, makes her do her bidding. That's how it was for a long time. Now all that is changing; now, the daughters-in-laws are stronger and stronger."

All the stories are more or less the same: some, a few, came here on their own volition; the rest are brought here. Fifteen to twenty thousand women left to die in an old city. Fifteen to twenty thousand who wander around like lost souls with empty stomachs.

Waiting. Those who die in Vrindavan are not quite as privileged as those who die in an even more sacred city, Varanasi, but they will have made great progress in their attempt to reach *moksha*, liberation from the cycle of reincarnation, dissolution into the Divine Unity, the Hindu form of paradise: when death is final. Here, dying is a privilege; dying *here* was a privilege. They came here *to* die.

The widow Aruthi, in broken English, told me that she was from a village in the Indian state of West Bengal, she had never been to Kolkata, she had now spent thirteen or fourteen years in Vrindavan, she didn't have much time left, and now she was at peace.

"Not like Moubani, the poor thing," she said with a toothless grin.

It was Aruthi who in the end took me to the widow's temple. Who knew that a baboon's assault could be so fortunate?

Hindus worship their gods like we in Argentina cheer on our Boca, our soccer team: with shouts, hands up in the air, leaps, hops, major hullaba-loo. The Banke Bihari Temple is a hub of shouts, whistles, murmuring, clapping; people standing, people kneeling, people sitting, people lying down, people sleeping, people begging, people giving, people painting their faces, people throwing flowers, people lighting fires, fans, fires, gar-lands, lighted signs, clocks, more fires, people who leap over the podium to give the priests candies and garlands of flowers so that the god behind the curtain will bless them, more fires. The priests don't stand: they are indefatigable machines that bless each candy, zealots of holy sugar. From time to time, the curtain over the altar is opened—quickly, a kind of modest exhibitionism—and we all shout; this is when Lord Krishna scores a goal. After six or seven times, the game gets boring: they open the curtain, we see god's face, we lift our arms and shout. it's beauti-ful to watch them without all that self-satisfied virtuous stiffness of the churchgoers devoted to the cult of Rome.

We arrived at the temple. The widow Aruthi looked at me with satisfaction; I asked here where all the other widows were. Ah, you want to see that temple, our temple, she said, and off we went. There'd been a misunderstanding; she'd brought me to the wrong temple.

In the streets—we walked for a good while—hundreds of people were selling everything, the baboons were thinning out, the beggars almost always mentioned Krishna. The pedestrians touched a cow's head then their own: I imagined them sharing ideas. Then it was my tolerance for superstition that was thinning, and I feared it might bottom out.

In India almost twenty years ago, prenatal ultrasounds were outlawed because many couples were using them for, what could be called in politically correct terminology, "selective abortions": getting rid of the fetus if it was female. The law is rarely observed; there are many private clinics that still offer them. There is something that Indian progress is achieving like no other: the use of the most modern technology to carry out the most archaic customs. Selective abortions used to be infanticide within the first few days of birth; now they are nice and clean. In 1980 there were, in the entire country, 104 boys under six for every 100 girls; in 2011, 109; and in the wealthiest states, such as Punjab and Haryana, where technology is within reach of the majority, the ratio reached 125 boys to every 100 girls. This is the same worldview that makes it so that in many Indian households, when there is not enough food for everyone, only the men get to eat.

The custom even has justifications: that the men, those who supply the food with their work in the fields, need to eat to have the strength to work without which everyone would be left forever without food. The production-based logic doesn't prevent the custom from being brutal: hunger strips bare many things, placing on the table forms of violence that would remain hidden under other circumstances.

The widows of Vrindavan are the clearest, most perfect product of that society, a worthy finale for their life as Indian women. From being a possession of their own family, they went to being a possession of their husband's, never having had any autonomy or way of earning a living; when their second and last owner died, they didn't belong to anybody. Or maybe they did: to god and death—but there was no longer any point in feeding them.

It sounds brutal, but we usually believe we should respect such customs, much as we get used to accepting, in the name of diversity and tolerance, that some Muslims convince their wives that only their men should see them, so they never go out of the house without censoring even their eyes with the black cloth.

As if one should respect traditions on the doubtful merit of them being traditions.

Now, midmorning, the widows were everywhere—in every corner, on every street, begging for alms, offering water in clay jars in exchange for a rupee, trying to earn a living—while waiting for life to end. They are small women—skinny, reduced to their minimum manifestation; unremembered memories. Almost all have shaved heads, like it is believed widows are meant to have. Many wore the white saris they should wear; very few rebelled and wore something else. Some walked stiffly, wooden; others are hunched over a cane or have given up on the idea of movement entirely. Those who could lived seven or eight to a room; many resided on the streets. And every morning, thousands of them met up at the Shri Bhagwan Bhajan Ashram to sing *bhajans* to Krishna.

Thousands were sitting in a covered courtyard with dirty white tiled walls, a large altar at the back, and another in the middle; the widows sang, played cymbals, dozed off, chatted with each other about who knows what. These songs were the only thing that separated them from their final hunger. They came every morning and sang for four or five hours; in exchange they were given a plate of rice with a little *dal*, a lentil soup. Sometimes they would receive a few rupee coins. Religion, here, was stripped of its masks, naked for all to see: come, sing to God, we'll give you something to eat. Hunger was such an effective boost to believe in the power of a deity.

The ashram, upon entering, appeared small, but was quite extensive. To one side is another nave and another courtyard, and in front, another larger one; they were all full of women in white saris. The youngest also seemed the saddest; they looked around, as if still looking for some-thing. The oldest seemed beyond looking for anything. The ones sing-ing seemed the happiest; the quiet ones seemed to be scowling. One of them looked at me crossly. She was offended by my presence and said something to two others; the three of them stared at me while talking among themselves. I sat down in a corner and listened: I was the only man there. The only one who could leave and go somewhere else, any-where else in the world. Some were so skinny that it was miraculous they were still alive; others looked so lively that's it was miraculous that they would stay here until they died. It was slow, prolonged euthanasia; a state of living like the last glowing embers on a charred log—the sal-vation of dissolving.

The widow Aruthi told me, more or less, that those who complained were shameless. "Where can they go to die better than here, so close to

Lord Krishna?" In a way she was right. They were poor and they didn't always get the food they wanted, but Lord Krishna would always welcome them with open arms.

"Don't you suffer from hunger?"

The widow Aruthi shot me a glance that carried a hint of disdain. For a moment I pretended to commiserate. Then she asked me for ten rupees and I gave her fifty and walked away feeling like an asshole. An old baboon shrieked from a rooftop, but I didn't think he had anything to tell me.

DELHI

A traffic jam of pedestrians is a concept for which our language has no words, or even a notion. In our cities, walking is an individual activity: each person at their own rhythm. In Delhi on the other hand, with so many pedestrians on every street, and the cars and bicycles and motorbikes and rickshaws, one must adapt to the general rhythm. Even in this: obey. There was a broken-down traffic police jeep blocking the way of a motorcycle. The motorcycle was big and shiny but cheap, one of those Chinese deals with all the exterior details made of plastic. The motorcyclist shouted from behind; the police responded, the motorcyclist shouted again, the police again, the motorcyclist. The shouting became louder and louder. The motorcyclist moved forward, stopped next to the window of the driver of the jeep, shouted again, raised his arms, banged on the window. He was beside himself, pissed off. I've always been fascinated by those moments when some silliness suddenly turns into a possibly horrific conflict, when somebody loses any semblance of equilibrium and risks everything for something that he or she wouldn't give a damn about if they could stop and think. I've always been even more surprised by those millions of moments when the opposite occurs: when something you do care a lot about doesn't impel you to react.

The strength of ideology.

At the time I was there, Delhi was quite shaken by the story of a girl kept prisoner in her bosses' apartment. I saw it on all the TV stations, read about it in the newspapers, listened to the commentaries. The doctors Sanjay and Sumita Verma, her bosses, were around thirty, reputedly gregarious, quite orderly, with light skin. In other words, two lovely examples of the new Indian middle class: doctors with the means to spend a week vacation in Thailand, who left the maid to look after the house. The maid was thirteen, which doesn't seem particularly unusual in a country where the government says there are fifteen million children under fourteen working, and several NGOs say there are sixty million, and everybody agrees that one in five works in domestic service. Nor was it unusual, as in her case, that her bosses beat her if they didn't like something she did. Nor was it unusual for them not to pay her—the norm is that these captive girls, without any power of negotiation, work for room and board. The board is meager: two chapati and a handful of salt a day—and a video camera in the kitchen to make sure she didn't eat more.

Up to this point, everything was, all aforementioned considered, as to be expected. The problem came when the two Dr. Vermas were living it up in Thailand and decided to stay an extra week; the girl, locked inside, her provisions depleted and overcome with hunger, despaired and went out onto the balcony. After a few hours of shouting, a neighbor heard her and called the fire department. They rescued her, and she told her story, which produced a certain sense of revulsion in a country that accepts domestic service as one of their most normal prerogatives and proclaims it without flinching. "The simple idea of not having to make beds, cook dinner, clean, do laundry, or any of the rest, sounds like paradise," says the web page of an employment agency offering services to foreign residents who are presumed to be less well-informed. "Forget your guilt; remember that you are providing employment many need." Employment that paid, according to the agency itself, between two and four thousand rupees—forty to eighty dollars—a month. Or, given the relative advantage of hiring young girls, wasn't paid at all. Girls like the prisoner in New Delhi are trafficked by these agencies; this one had been sold by her uncle through an intermediary, who, in turn, sold her to the agency in Delhi, who sold her to the two Doctor Vermas. It is estimated that there are more than ten million children sold by their families to pay their debts, usually for periods of one to five years; sometimes, without an expiration date. Nothing that doesn't happen all the time, nothing that everybody doesn't know. But when the girl went out onto the balcony and shouted to the world that she was starving, something happened. Many pretended to hear her, many pretended to realize what was going on.

What do you think about them leaving her like that, locked in without food?

Well, they should have left her a few more chapati, don't you think?

The world's largest democracy—as many Indians often call their country—has 1.36 billion inhabitants. Out of this total, 680 million did not finish elementary school; 800 million don't have television sets; 950 million don't have a gas cooking stove; 980 million don't have toilets. And almost 200 million belong to the "untouchable" class.

(Not to mention—as I have done so many times—the hundreds of millions who are hungry.)

None of which puts the idea of democracy, of a free and equal people, in doubt.

Or maybe it shouldn't: in India there are more than 580 million cell phones. These are the contours of modernity in the Other World.

Ideas that will one day change all other ideas must be formulated somewhere. This is what came to mind one morning when I visited the India International Centre, a bold sixties-style building made of cement and glass and modern optimism. Surrounded by the gardens of the power zone of New Delhi, it is difficult to create a link that is not sarcastic between this large polished wood table—twenty men and women on either side, microphones, cameras, computers, air conditioning, English in Oxford accents—and any of the shacks I visited the week before.

Men and women were discussing whether Monsanto, the American agrochemical and agricultural biotechnology company, had the right to the intellectual property of seeds, and one man said no, because Monsanto is a corporation and a corporation is not a person with a mind that can produce intellectual property, and so on. The angels were growing restless on the head of their pin, I thought, recalling yet another biblical saying, and I forced myself to believe that this would lead somewhere.

The meeting was chaired by Vandana Shiva, a widely regarded Indian agricultural and environmental activist. Another journalist had told me that Shiva was a kind of Indian Hebe de Bonafini, a leading activist for mothers of those who disappeared during the Videla regime. Shiva is around sixty, has published many books, received dozens of prizes, holds an important place in the antiglobalization movement, and has a long history of ecological militancy, which began in the seventies when she hugged tress to prevent them from being chopped down. Shiva had a very pronounced Hindu dot, or *bindi*, in the middle of her forehead and was wearing a dazzling orange sari on her powerful body. Shiva ran an organization, Navdanya, that promoted traditional agriculture; she was a strong defender of traditional crops, traditional seeds, traditional culture, traditional traditions, and spoke about what worked best for India in the many centuries it existed, even up until 1991, when it was thrown aside to allow for the methods of globalization. I would have liked to agree with her, but I had the sense—I've read, they've told me—that there had always been hunger in India, that hunger had existed in India for ages, that there was never a time when it was eliminated only to have started up again. After her talk, I managed to strike up a conversation with her and brought up my issues with her claim.

"No, that's not true," Shiva responded. "Everything changed here with the arrival of the multinationals like Monsanto, with their seeds and their hunger for more and more land. Before, the government gave land to the peasants; after 1991 they started taking it away from them. And in the meantime, Monsanto was carrying out campaigns in every village in India; they'd arrive in a truck and promise record harvests, promise millions to the poor farmers if they started using their seeds. So the farmers bought them, and the whole package along with them: pesticides, fertilizers, the obligation to buy from them again for the next planting. And above all, the peasants focused on growing for the market; everything was cotton, wheat, corn . . . now even soy. Here, the most critical element was the change of mentality: from working to eat to working to sell. This places the farmers, the huge majority of small farmers, in an extremely precarious position. Before, when they had a bad stretch, they could always eat what they grew. Now, on the other hand, when the prices for their harvest drop or there's drought or debts are squeezing them, it's not just that they don't make money; they don't eat."

I told her that I believed genetically modified seeds were not, in themselves, bad: their yield was greater and this allowed for more food and possible greater income. With a higher continuous yield, I argued, peasants had a greater chance of being lifted out of poverty. She rebuked this view and told me that another speaker at the conference had just explained in English that traditional crops were easier for peasants to manage than the modified ones, which required much greater resources. I explained that I would have very much like to have understood that lecture, but that I wasn't a native English speaker and had had a hard time following it. Rather than take pity on me, the conversation was heating into an argument. We could not agree on whether the problem was modified seeds, or the large multinational corporations that controlled them. I offered that the problem was political, that a system should be put in place so that technological advances were used for the good of the majority. She shook her head.

"You are clearly not understanding what is being said at this conference."

I imagined that thousands of years ago there were men and women who complained about that new demonic tool, that stick or sharpened stone that opened up the earth in long deep lines, that would destroy the Earth, and that the harvest gods were not going to put up with it.

To spout a truism: change is not necessarily defined by being either good or bad.

Agriculture was always about trying to increase yield, since the very beginning, when men and women discovered that if they buried the seeds of that plant, they could eat one just like it in a few months' time.

A hundred centuries trying: studying plants, adapting them to diverse soils, building irrigation systems, designing better tools, discovering more effective fertilizers, fighting predators and plagues. And, modifying seeds, always, with whatever technology they had. Ten thousand years ago they began to select the best plants to use for seed; Darwinism in the hands of peasants, inventing plants that would only grow if they grew them. Three hundred years ago they began to combine the best characteristics of several varieties with grafts and cross-pollination. A good-tasting apple with little cold tolerance would be combined with a bland one with high tolerance to try to make one that was delicious and could withstand the cold—and so forth. That's what they've always done.

At the beginning of the twentieth century, the possibilities grew. Scientists from several countries tried to create hybrids that maximized resistance, yields, and results. Around 1940, American biologist and plant pathologist Norman Borlaug began to use nitrogen to fertilize wheat in order to increase its resistance to certain diseases; the experiments proved so successful that the plants, so heavily laden with grain, bent and broke. Then Borlaug discovered a gene that shrank the stalk, and this shorter, thicker stalk could hold up a heavier load of grain. Within a short time, the yield of a plot multiplied three or four times; the same idea, applied to rice, allowed for harvests ten times as large. His discoveries arrived at precisely the right moment. After the Second World War, improvements in health care and living conditions increased the population in poor countries, and there was no way to feed so many people. The new technologies made it so that billions of people survived the demographic explosion of those years. Perhaps the greatest revolution of 1968 was that India achieved the largest harvest in history, so much so that the government had to close schools so they could be used to store grain.

Shiva wrote that "in perceiving nature's limits as constraints on productivity that had to be removed, American experts spread ecologically destructive and unsustainable practices worldwide." Through some arcane means, Shiva knew what the "limits of nature" were. Norman Borlaug responded that these arguments came from the "elitists" who had enough money to not worry about where their next meal would be coming from."[18] The Green Revolution led to an unprecedented increase in agricultural productivity. Between 1950 and 2000, the population of the planet increased two and a half times; food production more than tripled.

In 1964 India produced twelve million tons of wheat on thirty-five million acres; in 1995, this rose to fifty-seven million tons on sixty million acres. A dramatic rise in the yield per acre.

Of course, everything was not coming up roses—or large ears of corn. The surge in agricultural production brought with it problems and concerns: its dependence on combustible minerals, not only to run the tractors but also to produce fertilizers and pesticides, which, in turn, led to ever-more-resistant infestations; its ability to destroy lands through overutilization, and to empty and pollute the aquifers, emptied through intensive usage; the accompanying increase in greenhouse gas emissions; the loss of crop diversity. Above all, the need to buy chemicals to increase yield forced many peasants into debt and they lost everything, while others gained—more fortunate neighbors, local chiefs, corporations, banks.

On the other hand, by increasing yield with less labor, many people were forced to emigrate to the cities, where they could be exploited in factories—extremely low salaries, piece-rate pay, and squalid living conditions—that drove the economic boom in Asia. Still, the number of people who managed to eat thanks to these technological advances is staggering. Without these increased yields, million more would have died of hunger. Without these yields—if we want to look at it from an ecological point of view—more forests would have been cut down to open up more arable land.

At the beginning of the 1980s, US and European scientists, dabbling in what we now call genetic engineering, began to recombine the genes in the DNA of certain plants in an attempt to improve certain characteristics; they were doing the same thing that had always been done only now with more knowledge and better techniques. These are what are now called genetically modified organisms, or GMOs, and they are the target of so much outrage.

Monsanto was founded in 1901 in St. Louis, Missouri, to produce saccharine to sell to Coca-Cola. For a half century it had been producing insecticides, plastics, and various chemicals, but it achieved fame in the 1960s when one of its products, Agent Orange, was used in Vietnam. A powerful defoliant, the US Army sprayed it on forests and crops to starve their enemy, torrents of the poison spread all over the country. Half a million Vietnamese died in these bombardments, and another half a million children were born with birth defects. All the while, Monsanto grew and prospered. In the seventies, it invented a powerful herbicide. Roundup, whose active ingredient is glyphosate; years later, it developed high-yield soy, corn, and wheat seeds that could tolerate large quantities of the stuff. These seeds were called "Roundup Ready."

Their seeds were sold to large agricultural producers in the United States, Canada, and Latin America. Before it was bought out by Bayer in 2018, Monsanto controlled 90 percent of the world market in transgenic seed.

Nobody disputes the fact that these genetically modified seeds produce much more than the others. Nor that they demand too much from the soil, that they depend on huge quantities of fossil-fuel based products, that they assume a model of exploitation that expels peasants from their land and requires large tracts of land and a lot of machinery. But the biggest problem is ownership. The seeds lose their fertility with each cycle and, therefore, farmers are forced to buy new ones each season; moreover, they are forced to do so by contract, because Monsanto owns the patent or intellectual property rights over these seeds.

The private ownership of reproduction is a major contemporary invention. It is a brutal form of the idea of ownership, not of the field, not of the product of that field, but rather of a natural model—the seed—that only its "owner" has the right to produce. Intellectual property rights over nature.

The whole process could be seen as a synthesis of how capitalism works. Scientists make a technological breakthrough that could benefit millions of people, but they work for a private company, so the company reaps all the benefits. And, backing them up, the state guarantees their profit by passing patent laws that make sure they get their money.

Within this system, technological progress becomes an opportunity for a select few to accumulate more wealth rather than an effort to improve lives.

(The large bioengineering corporations are also outright swindlers. They introduce small changes into the patents that are about to expire so they can extend their ownership and continue to charge. Or, they take recourse in the most ridiculous extremes. For instance, in 1997 the Texas company, RiceTec, requested and obtained the patent to basmati rice, which Indians and Pakistanis had been growing for millennia; or Monsanto itself, which patented Nap Hal wheat, which is used to make chapati—the most common bread in India—and holds the patent in the United States.)

Capitalist use of technological improvements create many other problems. Whoever controls the design of the seed also controls, in some ways, the use of the plant that will grow from that seed, that is, the fate of those foodstuffs. A corporation decides to develop the best corn seed to produce ethanol; thousands of farmers will plant it because they will make more money than if they plant food corn. Hence, that corporation has more and more control over who eats and who doesn't, at what price and under what conditions.

Moreover, farmers become dependent on those who sell them the seeds. They lose their autonomy; often, they lose their land because they cannot pay back the debts they have incurred in order to buy them. So, is the best way to avoid all this to use the old traditional seeds? Or maybe to win the right to use the new ones and adapt them and improve them? To ride a bus, one must pay a fee that not everybody has. Is the solution to obtain money or free buses, or travel by horse and cart? If we deplore the fact that Coca-Cola is bottling water, do we act against water or against Coca-Cola?

Two very different issues, then, become obfuscated: humans using available technologies in an attempt to increase the yields of the crops they plant—producing more food—and humans deciding that these improved plants are the property of those who improve them. That is where the conversation ceases to be technical and becomes political.

None of this is intended as a defense of Monsanto and its peers. They are doing their jobs as large capitalists. We need to do ours. Their big advantage is that they have no doubts about what their job is.

To counter this extreme manifestation of capitalism, many push for traditional methods of agriculture. They romanticize and extol the small farmer, who knows the truth, who remains authentic in the face of scientific falsifications.

I often wonder if the idea of returning to small-scale local organic cultivation is another effect of bewilderment: since we have no overarching plan, we take refuge in the mechanisms of an idealized past. These worked more or less well in places where three, possibly five times fewer people lived, but would never work—never did work, in fact—to feed millions and millions.

Those who advocate for such a return to the past also argue that traditional agriculture employs many more people. Or, rather: it parks them in horrible jobs that they could avoid doing by using technologies that would free them, ancient practices that disguise their true conditions by keeping them at barely subsistence levels.

There are ways to produce a lot more food with a lot less effort—fewer workers, less exploitation, more time and space to do other things. The problem is that these ways are monopolized by giant corporations; and their product is monopolized by giant corporations. As a result, some people, who don't see any way to force the distribution of those products, assume that it is better to maintain a state of shared poverty than create wealth that is appropriated by the few, as in: let's not produce because the wealthy reap the rewards. Which would be reasonable in plentiful societies but is difficult to sustain in hungry ones.

This vindication of what is traditional hides—intends to hide—their advocates' inability, their refusal, to imagine a future other than what global capital proposes. They handed over the monopoly on the future and dug in their heels for the good-old days. Archaism is based on fear, an escape backward. If we can't face the future, let's take refuge in ancient forests. In so doing, unconscionable realities are defended: brutal labor, archaic tools, low-yield plants. What is worth keeping from all that?

It's like the difference between that man who blows an incandescent ball of glass out of the end of a hollow tube in order to make, with a lot of breaths and millenary movements, a glass, and an assembly line that spits out twenty identical glasses a second in an orderly manner. Everybody knows that the handmade glass will be more beautiful, expensive, and exclusive; everybody also knows that if we want thousands of people to have glasses, they would have to be the industrial ones. Here, too, what is produced by individual effort is only within reach of a few. Sometimes beauty can also be found in quantity, in being available to all: ethics as a form of aesthetics.

There's one example—among so many—that synthesizes this idea. In a paragraph from the courageous book, *We Feed the World*, which accompanies the documentary by the same name, Erwin Wagenhofer and Max Annas say, regarding the food industry: "The two main companies active in this arena, Pioneer and Monsanto, collaborate to make disappear the certainties acquired over many thousands of years of agriculture."[19] Wagenhofer and Annas are two honest leftists, critics of the dominant cultures, who would applaud such an effort in any other field. I imagine they might write with admiration, for example, that . . . [Marx and Engels, Deleuze and Guattari, Carozo and Narizot, fill in the blanks] "collaborate to make disappear the certainties acquired over many thousands of years . . ." When it comes to agriculture, however, their admiration has turned to panic.

The problem is not the change in the paradigm of production. The problem is who is benefiting from that change. It doesn't do any good to complain about technological progress; better to fight against the ways those who control that progress are using it to increase their own power and wealth. The problem is that these technologies show up within the context of and linked to an economic model, as if they belonged to global capitalism and only global capitalism can employ them, and if you are against global capitalism, you must be against them. The quest should be to separate them, not to throw the baby out with the bathwater.

The goal, then, is to invent the way to take control of these new technologies, find the political structure to put these technologies to work to benefit the many—because without these technologies, many millions will have problems feeding themselves. It is a complicated political process, and the only thing we know lately is that we don't know what to do with political processes. We could imagine, for starters, governments that do not recognize the concept of private property when it comes to seeds. We could imagine ways those small farmers could reinvent themselves in other kinds of work, or could join together in cooperatives that would change the scale and usage of the land, or could emigrate to cities under reasonable conditions, with work and some safety net. We could imagine that, someday, every Ministry of Agriculture in every country in the Other World would have its own little Monsanto and would distribute seeds and organize farming operations. The problem is the abject failure of the political structures that might want to do any of these things. But if this makes us turn backward, we're doomed from the very start.

"Now, sickening as it must be to human feeling to witness those myriads of industrious patriarchal and inoffensive social organizations disorganized and dissolved into their units, thrown into a sea of woes, and their individual members losing at the same time their ancient form of civilization, and their hereditary means of subsistence, we must not forget that these idyllic village-communities, inoffensive though they may appear, had always been the solid foundation of Oriental despotism, that they restrained the human mind within the smallest possible compass, making it the unresisting tool of superstition, enslaving it beneath traditional rules, depriving it of all grandeur and historical energies." So wrote, in 1853, in an article published in the *New York Daily Tribune* and titled "The British Rule in India," a man named Karl Marx.

Despite our disagreement, Shiva continued talking to me, entering into something of a civil debate. She told me that more than 70 percent of the seeds used in the world were controlled by ten large agro companies, which were also owned in large part by pharmaceutical companies. I disagreed with her assessment that multinational involvement in India was designed specifically to create hunger. I didn't see a reason that anyone would deliberately create hunger, there's no profit or gain to be made by starving people. Hunger was the byproduct, not the design, of bad management. Shiva disagreed. "We are now the country with the most hungry people in the world, and this cannot be. We are not a dry arid continent like Africa; we live in a rich, fertile subcontinent. What's going on is that here we have a political and economic system designed to produce hunger."

I still didn't understand where she was coming from. So in the end I told her that in Bihar, where I had just come from, there had been malnourished people for generations.

"Well, Bihar is an exception."

I responded that, as far as I knew, it was not the only one and that it was precisely exceptions like Bihar, with its one hundred million inhabitants, that made India have so much hunger. Shiva, glaring at me with dark eyes, excused herself.

Back in the room with the polished table, a man from Maharashtra named Kishore Tiwari talked to us about the growing number of suicidal farmers. Tiwari, a large man in his fifties with a warm, friendly face, was the leader of the peasants in Vidarbha, a region in central India where twenty-five million people lived, most of whom had always grown cotton.

In Vidarbha alone, in the last ten years, more than twenty thousand farmers had committed suicide: two thousand a year, almost six a day. This was happening all over India: between 1997 and 2012 alone, an estimated 250,000 farmers took their own lives. But Vidarbha was one of the most severely affected regions, where the plague was unrelenting and spreading, as if the idea of suicide as a viable exit plan had expanded its range; something that had previously not been within the realm of possibilities became one option among others.

"It's because of progress. Progress has brought us nothing but poverty and desperation. Progress has brought us more and more death."

The word *progress*, on Tiwari's lips, sounded like a curse.

In a conversation with Tiwari after his talk, he told me that the peasants of Vidarbha have always lived difficult lives. Their plots are small and rocky, their land difficult to farm, but that they had learned to live in their poverty, that is until the genetically modified seeds from Monsanto arrived.

"Our peasants are committing suicide because they cannot pay their debts, it's true. But it is not true that they acquire these debts to pay for their sons' weddings, their daughters' dowries. Well, some do, of course, but most acquire debt in order to pay for Monsanto's seeds."

It was modernity—not tradition—that was killing them.

"The salesmen with their seeds of *Bt* cotton come and convince them to buy. They are selling them their colored glass beads."

Bt cotton is a variety that has been genetically modified through the insertion of a bacteria, *Bacillus thuringiensis*, which produces a natural pesticide against certain pests, but not others. The seed requires the addition of fertilizers and pesticides that cost a lot of money; in exchange, it grows very well with the proper irrigation; it does not always work in fields, like those in Vidarbha, that depend on rain. But the salesmen try to hide that fact and the peasants get excited about their promised yields, and they spend money they don't have on seeds and the assorted paraphernalia the seeds require. Moreover, *Bt* cotton seeds, like the majority of genetically modified ones, don't work for a second planting; each year, the peasants have to pay again—and thus they get deeper into more and more debt.

"It's what we would call an addiction, the compulsive repetition of destructive behavior. It is like smoking or drinking. Our farmers have become addicted to *Bt* cotton."

I didn't say—I was learning to say less and less—that it seemed strange to me that his farmers could be the heirs to millenary wisdom and yet so easily duped, incapable of distinguishing that lie from their own truths. It was, often, the sad task of the "vanguard" to defend the masses against themselves.

But Tiwari would consider the possibility that these seeds would work, that they would actually be beneficial, if they didn't have to hand over their profits to Monsanto. Instead he told me that some of his peasants got into debt to pay for even more basic necessities, to buy a shovel or a hoe, to rent an ox so they could plow their little piece of land. And that others couldn't even do that; often a family would plow their land with one of its own members driving the plow and two others pulling it as if they were beasts.

"Our farmers are hungry, they are often hungry. But I don't think they commit suicide because of hunger. I would say that hunger is something they can tolerate, they are used to it. Most commit suicide out of shame, the desperation of losing their land."

He told me that the farmers in Vidarbha committed suicide by drinking the very pesticide that had buried them in debt, bringing up photos on his phone to show me. In the photos, in the portraits a son or a widow held up, the eyes of the dead were wide open, as if fighting against the impulse to close them.

Tiwari accused the government of not doing anything, he accused the rich and powerful of not doing anything, he accused the press of not doing anything, though, he admitted, sometimes the press did report on this subject, and in doing so, forced the authorities into action. They usually didn't act, he said, but when there was a journalist or a TV crew, they had no choice. Otherwise the fate of the peasants was nothing more than destiny. But in this case, destiny was like crossing a street, accepting that there was traffic without actually paying attention to it. Imagine an individual, imbued with a sense of destiny, keeping his or her eyes focused on a bird or even another person's shirt while making their way across. Or, more blunderingly, he or she closing their eyes and stepping onto the pavement believing no harm will come to them. The odd part is that some of us actually make it. That's destiny.

MUMBAI

Somebody explained to me that the garbage—the infinite amount of garbage in the streets of India—was a problem of evolution. Indians throw
everything everywhere because in the past dogs and cows would've eaten
everything in a short time.

The problem is that now, with all the plastic . . .

At a sidewalk café in Mumbai, near the sea, while reading the morning newspaper and not paying attention, a crow grabbed the bread off my
plate and flew off. When animals participate in the struggle for food, it
becomes a vulgar metaphor for the state of a society.

And then there's the cliché: India lives in several centuries simultaneously. I would say it lives in this century with different classes—as it has
throughout the centuries. The difference was that the wealthy could live
both in the contemporary world, with all its benefits, and the classical
world, with all its ways of exploiting their poor. The poor on the other
hand, had no choice but to remain imprisoned by the past.

Beside the sea, Mumbai displays its colonial splendor: monumental
houses, wide avenues, old trees; a little farther away: skyscrapers, the
financial district, new and elegant neighborhoods. Mumbai is the flag
bearer of new Indian prosperity. It is a city of twenty million inhabitants
where the country's wealth is concentrated, where towers are built every
day, where shopping malls and cars and brand-name products shimmer
in the light. In Mumbai there also live more slum dwellers than anywhere else in the world. Its all-too-apparent prosperity attracts them.
Thousands arrive every day fleeing from the poverty of the countryside.

Thrown out, throwaways, so many of them ending up in Mumbai's
infamous slums. When the movie *Slumdog Millionaire* brought them
worldwide attention, earning $400 million, eight Oscars, and the drool-
ing compassion of the planet, the slums of Mumbai, particularly Dharavi,
became so famous that tour groups were formed for wealthier people to
go on a poor people safari. In truth, Dharavi is among the world's biggest
slums and the site of much misery. The poorest among the ten million
poor people of Mumbai are the "pavement dwellers," those who live right
on the street, in lean-tos built in public spaces—sidewalks, roads, ditches,
parks, dumps. From here, it is the most difficult to escape.

But some do. Geeta, a young woman around twenty, who had always lived on the street, but who, thanks to a woman's organization that promoted shared savings—*Mahila Milan*, Women Together—had escaped. Mahila Milan told each of these street women to save one rupee a day, and in a few years the group would help them build their own house. One rupee was a negligible sum to pretty much everyone else but a pavement dweller, who otherwise struggled to obtain it. But many women including Geeta made the effort and were eventually able to leave the street. When I first met Geeta, she had just moved into a small one-room apartment in a low-cost housing complex on the outskirts of Mumbai.

"What's the advantage of Mahila Milan being a group composed only of women?"

"First, if you put men and women in one group, the men will make all the decisions. But there are other things. Husbands usually beat their wives if they go out after dark. When they met at Mahila, the women began to be able to leave their houses. The men resisted at first, but when they saw that their wives were coming up with solutions to certain problems or stopping an eviction, they kept quiet. And they started viewing them differently. In the end, the women were the ones who got things done."

"Did they stop beating them?"

"Well, not completely, but they beat them less. Now, if a man beats his wife, the women in the committee go to the house and try to work things out, convince the man not to do it anymore. And they often succeed."

Geeta was atypical in that while she lived on the streets, she also attended school. She had food to eat, leftovers her mother brought from the houses she cleaned. They lived in a lean-to, which did not have a toilet or light or running water; every morning at five o'clock, Geeta and her mother had to go to a nearby automotive garage where they let them get water from the faucet—only at that hour. Her mother would also bring home old clothes her employers gave her. Geeta reached adolescence without ever having worn even a new T-shirt.

"Sometimes we had plastic to cover us, but sometimes we didn't. I liked it better when we didn't because I could read by the light of the streetlamps."

In those days Geeta would stay up late studying; it was important to her to get good grades. Some teachers treated her badly because she lived on the street; others helped her. Geeta played and studied, washed, ate almost every day. It was a peaceful life, though the threat of demolition always hung over them; from time to time, on the heels of some complaint or other, the municipal authorities would come and tear down their lean-tos. Those nights, Geeta and her family and their neighbors would wait for the authorities to leave and then build them again, in the same place or somewhere else.

"We'd return, but we were always living under threat. That wasn't so good. Some people in the buildings said the street dwellers were dirty, that we were thieves. And they'd come and insult us, or whatever. There we were, unprotected, on the street."

Now, about five years later, Geeta was living in her apartment, happy but tired. And she complained about the noise. "On the street there was so much noise that you couldn't hear the children. Here, on the other hand, my neighbors are always shouting."

I asked her if she could introduce me to a friend of hers who still lived on the street, and we arranged to meet the next day in a neighborhood not far from downtown.

That following morning, on my way to meet Geeta, I noticed an older man, a pavement dweller, sitting on the sidewalk, his dhoti rolled up around his waist; he was elegantly wetting his hands with water from a small bottle of Coca-Cola, rubbing them together, touching his bare head, his arms, his nipples—his morning ablutions. Behind him, a dozen boys were also bathing: soapy, almost naked, shouting, laughing, like they did every morning they washed on the sidewalk.

For centuries we have agreed that an important number of activities a human individual performs should take place out of sight of everybody but their family members. One might even say that the definition of family is that group of persons who are allowed to witness others performing these private activities. It didn't have to be like that; we could have lived in public—baths, for instance, were collective for a large part of history—but it so happened that we decided to live to that extent in private. Here, the people who lived on the street had recovered those previous customs.

The people who live on the street sleep on the street, wash on the street, get dressed on the street, cook on the street, eat on the street, pray on the street, get sick and die on the street, converse and meet and fuck and laugh on the street.

They are on, they are of, the street.

Geeta's friend Avani was short and skinny, with a round face and large eyes. She moved with extreme gracefulness, as if she were floating. She was wearing a thin, threadbare green and red sari; her three children between the ages of five and ten were running around us, barefoot and loud. What Avani called her house is a piece of plastic stretched between four canes. What Avani called her place is not even a slum; it's a bit farther down market.

"Nobody who hasn't experienced it can know what it's like. I've lived here for a long time, yes, but who knows how much longer I will be able to. Here, you never know. If you have to leave, if you are forced to leave, you never know if you'll have a house when you get back."

Avani was here today because she hadn't found any work for the last few days.

"Sometimes I find some work cleaning houses, but when they find out I live on the street, they often fire me; they say we're dirty, and thieves."

Avani and Geeta were friends; their parents came from the same region in southern India, they had grown up together, they told each other their secret hopes and fears. But when Avani was sixteen years old, she got pregnant with a neighbor who was a little older than her. The man had no problems marrying her without a dowry—he clearly loved her. And Avani explained that he was a good person, that he treated her well, that he also had problems finding work, but there came a moment when they believed they would be able to get off the streets, find a real place to live.

"Right then is when that night happened."

A man with a family wanted to live in the place Avani and her husband occupied. Later they found out that the man had paid the owners of the apartment about five hundred rupees to evict them. Avani described him as a thug who shouted at them to leave. Avani began gathering her things, but when the man tried to rush them out, her husband defended them, what else could he do. He fended the man off with a knife, seriously wounding him. The man disappeared to find medical help. A few days later the police arrived: the man had died.

"The police never have anything to do with us, if they come it's to throw us out of somewhere but not to protect us. But we had the bad luck that they knew that man, he did who-knows-what favors for them, and they came to find the person who'd killed him."

It had been four years since they had arrested Avani's husband, and he had still not had a trial, but it seemed he wouldn't be getting out anytime soon.

"Then everything collapsed. I was left here, alone, married but without a man, without work, the wife of a prisoner, and with three children. I don't know what to do with the children. I can't send them to school because they don't take them, they say they can't accept them if they don't have a home. So they spend all day just hanging around here . . ."

Right after they arrested her husband, Avani tried to work as a prostitute but she couldn't stand it.

"I couldn't, I just couldn't do it. Even though you do earn good money. I know a lot of girls who do it and it's fine, but it disgusted me too much, and you could tell, and it made my clients mad. It's too bad."

When she couldn't find work, Avani and her children ate whatever they could find in the garbage. Sometimes Avani begged for a few coins so she could buy a handful of rice. Almost all the pavement dwellers suffered from severe malnutrition: they ate little and badly. From time to time, Avani would find something in the garbage that she could sell; a few months ago, she said, she found a working mobile phone and sold it for four hundred rupees. Four hundred rupees are eight dollars, and the mobile was, according to her description, an iPhone that sold used for about twenty thousand rupees.

"That day I bought three pieces of chicken for my children. The little one got sick, she had a stomachache all night."

My ears perked up too when Avani described her last resort for making money.

"I'd sell my kidney."

"You would really do that?" I asked a little too loud.

"Yes, that reassures me. I know that if I'm really desperate, if we really are left with nothing at all, I can always sell a kidney. Lots of people do it. Well, I don't know if lots, but some do, for sure. My friend Darshita did it, and she's fine."

She looked at me, lowered her eyes, looked at me again. I asked her, what? and she whispered, as if she didn't want to hear herself speak.

"I'm scared. I'm very scared. I hope I can do it, if I need to, for my children. But what if it turns out I can't . . . You think I could?"

There are questions that none of us have ever asked ourselves.

When she was a girl, when she didn't eat, when she was hungry, Avani's parents always said that it was true, in the city you had to live out in the open but there was always something to eat. You could always find something, not like in the village, where sometimes days and days would pass without a bite of food, where two children of her cousin Madhu had died, and the doctor said it was from a disease, but they knew it was because he'd gone too long without food.

That's why Avani was afraid the first time they took her to the village; she thought she would die of starvation. She ate—it was her aunt's wedding, she ate a lot of rice and dal, and they all shared a lamb—but afterward, in the city, every time they didn't have food, she'd tell her mother that this was just like being back in the village.

And her mother would always say the same thing, "Did you really think we'd be able to escape it?"

Her house was made of two pieces of cardboard for walls, one on each side; the back was the wall of the house hers is leaning against. There was nothing in front, just the street and, beyond that, the city. There was a piece of black plastic for a roof and two wood cots for beds. During the day, Avani pulled off the walls and the roof so the neighbors wouldn't complain; at night she rebuilt her house. Every night.

"What are your hopes for your children?"

"I don't know, that they'll be able to get out . . ."

"Will they be able to?"

"If Geeta could . . ."

"Why could she and not you?"

Avani remained quiet.

A third of all the children in Mumbai are malnourished—and it's always the same third. Recently an NGO named Dasra said that in the slums of Mumbai, twenty-six thousand children die each year due to the effects of malnutrition—more than seventy a day. The state, here, spends 210 rupees per person per year on health care—four dollars per person per year—even less than what they spend on public media. In this city of pomp and progress, the differences are even crueler.

For now, Avani lived in what she called a slum. The English too would call it a slum; Americans, skid row; the French, *bidonville*; the Italians, *baraccopoli*, the Brazilians, *favelas*; the Germans, who merely adopted the word slum, also ghetto, a word with a charged past, to mean an area where a certain social group is crowded together, because political, religious, racial, or economic reasons prevent them from living elsewhere.

The evolution of words for slum in Spanish is an example of the linguistic dispersion of the language; the farther away a concept moves from the academy, the more chance that it will have a different word in each country. *Chabola, callampa, villa miseria, cantegril, barriada, población pueblo joven, colonia, campamento*: all the same, named in so many different ways. I've spent hours thinking about what word to use in this book. At one point I thought I would use a word from old Spanish—Arabic, of course—that is not used commonly in any of our languages, even though it has some currency in the tango dialect of Argentina: *arrabal*. An *arrabal* was, still is, the part of the city on the margin, inhabited by a population thought to be different or fallen or dangerous; it is the most Castilian word for slum. Suburb in the literal sense: a sub-urb, a city below the authentic city. I wanted to use *arrabal*, but then I realized that whether I like it or not, I write in Argentine Spanish where I would call it a *villa*. A mansion. How a pretentious word in a language became the word for something who's only pretension is to show that there are none: *villa*, *villero*: slum, slum dweller—those who live on the outskirts. All of them part of the Big Bang of Latin American Spanish.

Some also called it a *villa miseria*, a misery mansion. That seemed to be the only words that directly correlated to the well-being of those who inhabited these particular mansions. The villa miseria, or slum, is a product of the Industrial Revolution. It's not that previously there had not been poor, marginal, notorious neighborhoods, but their spread and size from the nineteenth century on was new. That is when the word *slum* came to mean those places that grew on the outskirts of London, Manchester, Dublin, Paris, Kolkata, and New York.

Already then, slums were defined as "a densely populated usually urban area marked by crowding, dirty run-down housing, poverty, and social disorganization."[20] But in the first half of the twentieth century, they became rare in the First World and—after the sixties—they flourished in the Other World, with strange momentum. For the first time in history, more people live in cities than in the countryside.

Mike Davis, in his indispensable book *Planet of Slums*, writes:

> The cities of the future, rather than being made out of glass and steel, as envisioned by earlier generations of urbanists, are instead largely constructed out of crude brick, straw, recycled plastic, cement blocks and scrap wood. Instead of cities of light soaring toward heaven, much of the twenty-first-century urban world squats in squalor, surrounded by pollution, excrement, and decay. Indeed, the one billion city-dwellers who inhabit postmodern slums might well look back with envy at the ruins of the sturdy mud homes of Catal Huyuk in Anatolia, erected at the very dawn of city life nine thousand years ago.[21]

In 1950 there were eighty-six cities in the world with more than a million inhabitants. In 2016 there were nearly four hundred and fifty. Of the thirty-five cities that now have more than eight million inhabitants, only three are in wealthy countries: New York, Tokyo, and Seoul; all the rest are in the Other World, and they are the ones with the highest growth rate. The urban population of Brazil, India, and China is now larger than the entire population of the United States and Europe combined. But in most of these cities, three-quarters of their growth is due to "informal" construction on occupied land—slums.

The slum is one of the great modern inventions—the newest, most contemporary form of habitation in the Other World. In a world that has become urban, the slum is the fastest-growing form the urban takes. According to the Slum Almanac, published annually by the UN organization Habitat, every year the amount of people living in a slum increases by twenty-five million. There are now in the world approximately 250,000 slums; with around one billion people living in them.[22] More by the time you read this. That's one in every five children in the world, and three out of every four city dwellers in the Other World.

Many of them are the ones who go hungry.

Then there is the paradox of the slum: its eventual desire to be assumed by a higher class. At some point in time, when the demographic and social pressures spill over, a group of people occupy land that nobody had ever wanted to occupy, because it was far away, or difficult to build on, or unhealthy. They have no other choice; they go there and settle. With time they manage to make the place into an inhabitable, even desirable space; then, the market decides to recuperate it, and some wealthy person, some speculator, some bank, obtains the papers and permissions that allow them to throw out the slum dwellers and sell their places.

Sometimes the process is isolated, individual, more mysterious. Someone offers the person who occupies that improved spot money they cannot afford to refuse. They hope they'll be able to buy a better shack, start a business, or even, eat more often. In other instances—so frequent—the slum dwellers are renters, and they cannot continue to pay the increased rent made possible by the improvements they themselves made.

So they have to leave, find another uninhabitable place, and start all over again.

At the time I visited India, in the late aughts, there were, according to various statistics, 160 million slum dwellers.

Peasants leave the countryside but food is still being produced there. The countryside was a way of life; it is becoming a mode of production, an exploitation, a space for an economic practice that requires fewer and fewer people.

As Mike Davis writes, "the classic mechanism in which the countryside required a lot of labor and cities required a lot of capital has been reversed."[23] Now, with the growth in the urban peripheries—no longer the result of the draw of new jobs but rather the reproduction of poverty—the Other World has a countryside full of capital and cities full of labor.

The rural population will not increase; it has reached its peak, and is decreasing. Most—75 percent—of the hungry still live in rural areas. Rather than disappearing like an ancient relic, the process of urbanization is quite effectively transferring poverty to the cities. All future demographic growth will be in cities. "Hunger will be increasingly urban," will state the manifesto that nobody is writing because it seems all too obvious, and because nobody would dare finish it off with, "or it won't be."

But, precisely because of hunger, the hungry who can, flee to the cities; Mumbai is but one example, but it is also an extreme one.

It's said that at the beginning of the last century, an English lady who was supposed to travel to an Indian village to teach there, sent a letter to another teacher who taught at the local school to ask him if there was a WC there. He didn't know, so he asked the local authorities, who didn't know that that was shorthand for water closet as the British call bathrooms, and so they debated its meaning. After much back and forth, they decided that the lady must have meant a *wayside chapel*, and they had the carpenter build one with all the hospitality of colonial obsequiousness.

> *Dear Madam,*
>
> *I take great pleasure in informing you that the WC is located nine miles from the house. It is located in the middle of a grove of pine trees, surrounded by lovely grounds. It is capable of holding 229 people and is open on Sundays and Thursdays. As there are many people expected in the summer months, I suggest you arrive early. There is, however, plenty of standing room. This is an unfortunate situation especially if you are in the habit of going regularly. It may be of some interest to you that my daughter was married in the WC, since she met her husband there. It was a wonderful event. There were ten people in every seat. It was wonderful to see the expressions on their faces. My wife, sadly, has been ill and unable to go recently. It has been almost a year since she went last, which pains her greatly. You will be pleased to know that many people bring their lunch and make a day of it. Others prefer to wait till the last minute and arrive just in time! I would recommend that your ladyship plan to go on a Thursday, as there is an organ accompaniment. The acoustics are excellent and even the most delicate sounds can be heard everywhere. The newest addition is a bell which rings every time a person enters. We are holding a bazaar to provide plush seats*

for all since many feel it is long needed. I look forward to escorting you there myself and seating you in a place where you can be seen by all.

With deepest regards.

Half the residents of Mumbai have no toilet facilities, so they shit wherever they can. A few years ago, somebody calculated that six or seven million adults shit each day in the slums of Mumbai; if each of them produces a pound, this means three thousand tons of shit every morning—which are spread around by filthy streams and pile up around the huts and the roads.

Needless to say, the lack of toilets has created extreme problems of sanitation. In the slums of Mumbai, two out of every five deaths are the result of infections and parasites due to contamination of water and lack of toilets. But it also creates other problems: women who don't want men to watch them, often go in groups before dawn, sometimes to fields far away, where they might come across rats and snakes. Or, even farther away, where men are waiting to rape them.

In the entire world, 2.5 billion people live without toilets, die without toilets. It is often believed that the phenomenal increase in life expectancy in the last 150 years is due to modern medicine and its pharmaceuticals; it is probably more directly related to the expansion of sewage systems and running water. Those who don't have it, still have shitty lives: between the years 2000 and 2010, more children died of diarrhea than soldiers in all the conflicts from the Second World War to the present.

A slum is, more than anything else, a place where the state doesn't function. There is no light, no water, no streets, no police, no schools. Until the seventies, many governments in what was then the Third World, tried to replace slums with housing projects.

Those were the policies before the British economist John Williamson proposed in 1989 what would become known as the Washington Consensus, ten policy points a country would need to follow in order to recover from economic decline. These included fiscal policy discipline, redirection of public spending toward infrastructure development, tax reform, market determined interest rates and deregulated entry, competitive exchange rates, the liberalization of trade, the liberalization of foreign investment, the privatization of state enterprises, oversight of financial institutions, and legal security for private property. Based on these points, the Urban Development Department of the World Bank proposed the following new initiative: public money should no longer be used to build housing for the poor but rather—and less of it—to invest in the infrastructure already in place. In other words, to maintain and improve the slums. The proposal came wrapped in grandiose praise of the initiatives of the poor themselves—their construction of the slums—and therefore the expediency of "helping them help themselves." It was presented as a way to "empower" the slum dwellers, and it was, in fact, a way of perpetuating extreme differences—the existence of those places of exclusion, those contemporary ghettos. And, of course, to pave the way for the withdrawal of the state, which would be carried out more fully during the eighties.

And, to oversee the state's replacement by NGOs and other charitable organizations. As Mike Davis writes:

> Their constant effort is to subvert, dis-inform and de-ideal-
> ize people so as to keep them away from class struggles. They
> adopt and propagate the practice of begging favors on sympa-
> thetic and humane grounds rather than making the oppressed
> conscious of their rights. As a matter of fact, these agencies
> and organizations systematically intervene to oppose the agi-
> tational path people take to win their demands. Their effort is
> constantly to divert people's attention from the larger politi-
> cal evils of imperialism to merely local issues and so confuse
> people in differentiating enemies from friends.[24]

Smoked salmon, ham, prosciutto, turkey breast, pomegranate salad, stuffed dates, shrimp cocktails, avocado and peaches, creamed aspara-gus, lobster tails in lobster bisque, hard-boiled eggs with caviar, cous-cous salad, papaya caprese salad, artichoke and almond salad, Mexican corn salad, salad with green apples, carpaccio of apples and pineapples, Roquefort, brie, *The Laughing Cow* cheese, Camembert, feta, Emmen-taler, edam, cheddar, red cheddar, olives with pesto, green olives, black olives filled with anchovies filled with red peppers filled with almonds, capers, raita, mango chutney, mint chutney, cold mango soup with rose-mary, cold rose-water soup, cold poppy-seed soup, rotis, papads, samosas, parathas, European bread. Sole meunière with zucchini pesto, vegetable tagine, biryani rice with vegetables, biryani rice with chicken, quiche with leek and caramelized onions, corn and asparagus stuffed potatoes, lasagna with ricotta and pumpkin, bharba dal, curry mushrooms, tikka paneer with mint, cauliflower vantalu, Hakka noodles with vegetables, tofu and chestnuts in mustard sauce, laksa vegetable soup, chicken in sake sauce, pork ribs in honey cinnamon sauce, dum ka chicken, scallops bhatti ka, chicken wings with olives cheese and sun-dried tomatoes, lamb goulash, barbecued duck breast, barbecued lamp chops, barbecued pigs' feet. Crème caramel, lemon pie, rabri, baklava, halava, pineapple cake, strawberry meringue cake, mousse au chocolat, cherry pie, fruit salad, blueberry cheesecake, praline jelly rolls, pistachio tartlets, orange parfait, strawberry ice cream, chocolate ice cream, coffee ice cream, pear strudel, cream tart with fresh fruit, almond tart, arroz con leche.

This was the buffet at the Taj Hotel, which had recovered in the few years after the Lashkar-e-Taiba, the Islamic terrorist group, had attacked it in 2009 in the name of "striking a blow against a symbol of Indian wealth and progress." Now the Taj was once again the epitome of hotel opulence, and one needed to look no further than the buffet, which included two glasses of Moët & Chandon and cost, after taxes, a little over 3,500 rupees, or fifty dollars.

A man wearing a sky-blue Lacoste polo shirt, which could've been fake (so too, possibly, his designer pants) hesitated in front of the desserts. I introduced myself. He told me his name was Karun.

"Can I ask you something?"

"Yes, of course, whatever you want."

I basically asked for his life story, from birth to buffet. He told me that he came from a middle-class background, his father worked in a bank but never rose to a managerial position, but when he saw that his eldest son might be intelligent, he did everything possible to give him a promising education. Karun studied business at an almost prestigious university, worked hard, graduated, and got a job at one of the largest advertising agencies in India. That was fifteen years ago; since then he had risen through the ranks, married a woman from a caste a little better than his, had two children—girls, but Karun added a gesture as if to indicate that he didn't really mind—bought an apartment in a convenient location, put a BMW series 1 on an installment plan. His summary was quick and full of pride; clearly Karun enjoyed listing his achievements. He was going to start his own agency in a few months, he told me; in fact, he and his wife were here to celebrate a positive response yesterday from one of the investors. Karun had gel in his hair, a glimmer in his smile, the manners and gestures of the inveterate salesman. But he looked at me strangely when I asked him if he knew that there was a lot of hunger in India.

"Yes, of course I do. I know there is, I read about it in the newspapers,

I keep informed. But it all seems so far away. My friends are much more worried about being overweight than hungry. It seems like a joke, but they're all on a diet."

Karun helped himself to a large slice of chocolate cake with cream and red fruit.

"What I don't like is for this to be India's image, that that's how you see us. That you keep talking about all those miserable poor people instead of emphasizing everything that we are achieving. It's not that I don't care, don't get that impression. I think it is our responsibility. But if we keep prospering and creating wealth, they'll end up doing well too."

I was about to ask him who *we* were—and even who *they* were—but Karun excused himself, his wife was signaling to him, he really had to return to his table. I returned to mine, so many leftovers on my plate. I wondered if all that food at the buffet would get thrown out and end up on someone like Avani's plate.

With all due respect, this country is constant proof that those who govern don't give a damn about those who don't. The filth, the decay, the state of the roads and streets, the neglect of all public spaces and services, of all sanitation—it's glaringly obvious that those who have no choice don't matter in the least to those who run things and can avoid the grime and chaos of the streets if they so choose. For instance, nestled among other towers but taller and more outlandish than the other towers is the Antilia building, the home of the richest man in India, the industrialist and financier Mukesh Ambani. Erected in 2010 on the site of a former orphanage (a controversial property sale that as of 2019, is still being challenged in court), the building has twenty-seven floors with very high ceilings, all his own; about forty thousand square meters, all his own; nine elevators, all his own; and it is, they say, the most expensive private home in the world, worth around $2 billion by most calculations. Mr. Ambani should live there with his wife, his three children, and his six hundred domestic servants. It isn't easy to build a twenty-seven-story house for five people. The house, they say, has three heliports, six floors of parking for two hundred cars, a dining room drowning in crystal chandeliers, ballrooms, gymnasium, spa, yoga studio, swimming pool, exhibition halls, interior gardens, interior trees, cinemas, a theater, a discotheque, wine cellar, industrial kitchen, snow room.

From Mr. Ambani's house you can see slums—and vice versa. But the problem, they say, is that they don't have enough windows facing east, toward the rising sun, and this contradicts the principles of *vastu shastra*, a Hindu version of *feng shui*, so it would bring bad luck. That's why perhaps it supposedly took years for them to move in, though Ambani's wife, Nita, disputed this. She also claimed that she was like any other wife, waiting for her husband to come home after a long day at work "with candles lit and supper ready . . . I like to have everything smiley and happy for my husband. Men don't want to see a grumpy face at the end of a hard day."

Mumbai is a mixture of twenty-first-century luxury, turn of the twentieth-century economic collapse, and misery of all and any year. The Che Bar & Grill is located in an expensive neighborhood; it's exterior walls are painted bright red and Guevara's face with his beret is stenciled on. There is a varied offering, in English: beer draught, absinthe on tap, two-for-one shot deals, Indian & French wines, mojitos, pizza by the slice, legendary burgers, giant hot dogs, Latin American specialties (Mexican, Brazilian, Cuban . . .), and finally: an all-you-can-eat corporate lunch for around five dollars plus tax. All these years I thought Che Guevara was dead, when he'd been hawking mojitos in Mumbai this whole time . . .

ON HUNGER: CIVILIZATION

They found a way to make the land, the humans, increase production.

By the beginning of the eighteenth century, agriculture in Europe was beginning to change. First in Flanders and soon thereafter in England, peasants found ways to avoid giving the land a rest. After the grain harvest they'd plant tubers or vegetables that fed animals that produced more food, more labor power, more fertilizer to continue planting. In England around 1830, for the first time in history, the urban population was larger than the rural; with the increase in agricultural yield, only a quarter of the English population worked in food production. "This set in motion a virtuous cycle of development . . .," wrote Paul McMahon in his book, *Feeding Frenzy: The New Politics of Food*. "Cities provided a market for food surpluses, and farmers provided a ready market for manufactured goods such as farm implements; this led to further increases in food production, allowing more rural labor to be released for jobs in factories or mines."[1]

An almost perfect circuit of exploitation.

In the meantime, hunger continued to be a constant reality and, at the same time, became the subject of those more or less new disciplines they still called philosophy. In keeping with the first attempts at the secularization of the world, hunger ceased to depend on Our Lord and passed into the sphere of the economy and its effects on society. Adam Smith, the father of neoliberalism, wrote that the scarcity of food could be the result of wars or bad harvests, but that hunger was the consequence of when "the government, in order to remedy the inconveniences of a dearth, orders all the dealers to sell their corn at what it supposes a reasonable price." He goes on to say that, "The freedom of the corn trade is almost everywhere more or less restrained, and, in many countries, is confined by such absurd regulations as frequently aggravate the unavoidable misfortune of a dearth into the dreadful calamity of a famine. The demand of such countries for corn may frequently become so great and so urgent that a small state in their neighborhood, which happened at the same time to be laboring under some degree of dearth, could not venture to supply them without exposing itself to the like dreadful calamity."[2]

Without regulatory interference, in other words, the market would find its own natural rhythm, the corn trade would balance out, and in doing so would ensure there was food for all. Such idealism had its dissenters, including notably, the English social economist and reverend Thomas Robert Malthus. The son of a lawyer, Malthus studied at Jesus College in Cambridge, taught Ethics, took orders in the Church of England, and obtained a clerical sinecure that allowed him to devote himself to his research. The reverend's work consisted of asking himself why, in spite of the optimism of the Enlightenment, the poor English— the English poor—had become such hideous scoundrels, such broken amoral drunks, such scavengers, whores, and beggars.

Malthus, so thoroughly Christian, believed that it was the poor themselves who were to blame, a premise he developed in his famous *An Essay on the Principle of Population, As It Affects the Future Improvement of Society*, published in 1798. His central thesis was that there is never enough food for everybody because our ability to reproduce ourselves is greater than our ability to produce food—because man, fool that he is, wants sex more than he wants food, that it is this reproductive drive, "this constant effort as constantly tends to subject the lower classes of the society to distress and to prevent any great permanent amelioration of their condition."[3] That if the poor are poor and die of hunger it's because they act like rabbits: because they multiply beyond their possibilities.

But there are solutions, mechanisms to avoid disaster and reinstate a certain amount of equilibrium. "Among plants and animals its effects are waste of seed, sickness, and premature death. Among mankind, misery and vice."[4]

According to Malthus, vice, hunger, and misery are the recourses of Divine Providence invented to keep things in their place. "The vices of mankind are active and able ministers of depopulation. They are the precursors in the great army of destruction; and often finish the dreadful work themselves. But should they fail in this war of extermination, sickly seasons, epidemics, pestilence, and plague, advance in terrific array, and sweep off their thousands and ten thousands. Should success be still incomplete, gigantic inevitable famine stalks in the rear, and with one mighty blow levels the population with the food of the world."[5]

And it was clever to do it that way, said the reverend. "This general law [. . .] undoubtedly produces much partial evil, but a little reflection may, perhaps, satisfy us, that it produces a great overbalance of good."[6] In other words, this law maintained the necessary balance between population and production, but also, through its example, it convinced the poorest of the poor to avoid indiscriminate fornication, improved their dubious morals, removed them from the temptation of laziness, and drove them to work. In other words, hunger wasn't only indispensable, it was incredibly useful as well.

Hunger kept the machinery functioning. In his *Dissertation on the Poor Laws* of 1786, the doctor and vicar Joseph Townsend, a colleague of Malthus, made it extremely clear: "In general it is only hunger which can spur and goad them on to labor." And, "Hunger will tame the fiercest animals, it will teach decency and civility, obedience and subjection, to the most brutish, the most obstinate, and the most perverse."[7]

According to this worldview, hunger was no longer the consequence of the problems in an economic system but rather a solution to those problems: a fundamental element of discipline.

Hunger was, once again, the fault of the hungry, the result of their vices, their moral weaknesses, their sloth. And the state had no reason to worry about their suffering, because doing so would only increase those foibles. The English word *humanitarian*—a real hit in our day—was invented then, and was used to mean a pernicious excess of concern for the poorest of the poor.

(Now, on the contrary, in the general consciousness, in "humanitarian" discourse, there is nobody more innocent than the hungry: victims of circumstances that completely overwhelm them, of an inclement geography, of the whims of the climate, of wars they did not start, of international relationships that predominate, of the injustices of a global system. Victims, always victims. In a world that fetishizes victimhood—and concomitantly produces them in such large quantities—the hungry are the ultimate victims, the purest, the most innocent. So much so, that they become nothing short of a miracle: victims without victimizers. Interpretations of hunger. Hunger on the right, hunger on the left.)

The idea that the poor are innocent, hence victims, also gained strength in England in the nineteenth century—that great testing ground of industrial modernity. In Dickens's novel *Oliver Twist*, published in 1839, it appears for the first time in great literature—great in terms of quality and popularity. The novel took up and amplified the discourse that blames the rich and powerful for the sufferings of the poorest of the poor—for their hunger. Children were the quintessence of that figure: the innocent victims of everything they cannot control and could not have had any part in creating. That is why the hunger of children has always been the stun gun of those who have tried to denounce social structures that cause such misery. That is still why.

Friedrich Engels, in his book *The Condition of the Working Class in England*, further addressed this issue:

"These workers have no property whatsoever of their own, and live wholly upon wages, which usually go from hand to mouth. Society, composed wholly of atoms, does not trouble itself about them; leaves them to care for themselves and their families, yet supplies them no means of doing this in an efficient and permanent manner. Every working-man, even the best, is therefore constantly exposed to loss of work and food, that is to death by starvation, and many perish in this way. The dwellings of the workers are everywhere badly planned, badly built, and kept in the worst condition, badly ventilated, damp, and unwholesome. [. . .] Children who are half-starved, just when they most need ample and nutritious food—and how many such there are during every crisis and even when trade is at its best—must inevitably become weak, scrofulous, and rachitic in a high degree."[8]

Then came one of the most famous and thoroughly researched famines in history.

For centuries Ireland had been a poor colony of England. A land of great feudal lords, its peasants—and later its workers—lived on one basic food: potatoes. Around the year 1840 one third of the population never ate anything else because the majority of the good land—land that produced a variety of food—had been appropriated two centuries earlier by English and Scottish nobles and was used to raise cows and sheep and grain for export to London, Manchester, and Edinburgh. Any similarity with the fate of millions of acres of African land now occupied by foreign states and companies is no mere coincidence.

That's why in 1845, when a plague—*Phytophthora infestans*—destroyed three-quarters of the potato harvest, famine gripped the country. The Irish asked for help from the English government; they sent little if any. In the meantime, meat exports continued apace, as there was no money in Ireland to buy it and the government did not forbid its sale. A country devastated by hunger exporting food. This was a very visible demonstration of how large contemporary famines are not the result of a lack of food but rather of the money to buy it.

In 1840, the population of Ireland was approximately eight million people. It is estimated that during the five years of plague, a million died of hunger and associated disease and another million emigrated to the United States. Therein another reason the Irish famine has been studied so thoroughly. Because of it, Ireland had a huge impact on the demographics and culture of the world's most powerful country.

In the meantime, in the militant texts of the left, hunger had become the incontestable proof of the failure of the system. The most resounding slogan against that system was "Arise ye prisoners of starvation / Arise ye wretched of the earth." *Hunger* was the watchword that united all who suffered it, placing them without any doubt on one side of the social war. And "bread and work" was the vindication that synthesized it all.

The *Communist Manifesto*, however, does not contain the word *hunger*.

The Condition of the Working Class in England was pure militant journalism, published almost clandestinely in Germany in 1845. But even some establishment newspapers began to print stories about the lives of workers and the unemployed: journalism was reinvented as a way of placing in front of the readers' eyes the realities they generally did not want to see.

In 1883 a militant journalist named William Stead was hired as an editor of an English evening and conservative newspaper called the *Pall Mall Gazette*. Stead transformed it thoroughly; its mission, he wrote, would be "to help on the social regeneration of the people of the world." To do this he wrote first-person vivid accounts in simple and almost violent language, and he included drawings, maps, photographs, large headlines, all of which told the stories of the most impoverished people. His greatest success was a series about child prostitution called "The Maiden Tribute of Modern Babylon."[9] There, in order to expose the sale of young girls to the brothels of London, he arranged to buy, for five pounds, a girl of thirteen to use as a prostitute. The series increased the circulation of the newspaper to 120,000 copies; as a direct result, Parliament increased the age of sexual consent from thirteen to sixteen years of age. But at the same time, Stead was tried and convicted to three months in prison for buying a minor. Stead called this *New Journalism*, in which, among other things, the journalist becomes the protagonist they still, often, intend to be.

Ten years later, in the United States, Jacob Riis published *How the Other Half Lives: Studies among the Tenements of New York*.[10] This book of photojournalism, thanks to the recent invention of magnesium flash powder, could enter the hovels and tenement houses where the poorest took refuge—and show them to the rest of the horrified city that claimed ignorance. It was a scandal, a heavy fist coming down hard on the dining room table and making the chandeliers tremble.

At that time, such stories were still scandals.

In the meantime, hunger was put to new uses. Vladimir Ulyanov, in *Imperialism, the Highest Stage of Capitalism*, quoted Cecil Rhodes, the conqueror of that part of Africa he named Rhodesia. "I was in the East

End of London yesterday and attended a meeting of the unemployed. I listened to the wild speeches, which were just a cry for 'Bread,' 'bread!' and on my way home I pondered over the scene and I became more than ever convinced of the importance of imperialism. [...] The Empire, as I have always said, is a bread and butter question. If you want to avoid civil war, you must become imperialists."[11]

Between 1875 and 1914, the colonial powers divided a quarter of the surface of the earth among them. Great Britain alone claimed almost four million square miles, more than the total area of Europe; France, three and a half. These occupied territories allowed them to kill two birds with one stone. They provided new territory where their unemployed could find occupations and land to grow cheap food to reduce the pressure of hunger. It was the perfect way to avoid that civil war. In this interpretation, hunger was neither a divine judgment nor a just punishment for sloth nor a fearful plague. It was, instead, the danger that threatened to provoke the fall of the regime.

European colonial expansion in the second half of the nineteenth century finalized, in some way, the creation of the Other World as we now know it: millions of semi-enslaved workers producing food in the Empire's territories to keep the workers in the imperial centers poorly nourished.

In few countries was there then as much hunger as there was then and now in India. Back then—at the beginning of the last century—many placed the blame on the dominant class or the colonial power. The first leaders of the Indian Independence Movement argued that in British India between the years 1860 and 1900, without counting natural disasters, there were more than ten famines that killed fifteen million people. There could be no better demonstration than these deaths, they said, of the violence of the occupiers, the result of colonial pillaging that—under the pretext of spreading the benefits of Western civilization—took over resources that would have been able to keep those Indians alive.

The mechanism was typical—and somewhat more complicated. It is assumed that the great Asian famines of the second half of the nineteenth century were the result of the integration of these regions into the world economy, their "globalization." Millions of peasants who had always lived in a subsistence economy were forced to produce for the world market—raw materials for the English factories, food for their workers—lost their lands, their way of life, their food. Their own backwardness isn't what killed them; they were killed by others' development.

These "Victorian holocausts" designed the world structure we now know. This was, wrote Mike Davis, the process that shaped the Third

World, the Other World—and created that class of rural semiproletariats without possessions, always on the verge of starvation, who also took part in many of the wars of liberation of the twentieth century.[12]

It was, in any case, an important redesign of the lives of hundreds, even thousands of millions of people. During this period there were also famines in China, Siam, Indonesia, and Korea. It's not clear how many people died; some historians cite 25 million, others 150 million. A few more, a few less.

The Industrial Revolution also revolutionized our relationship to food. There had always been conserves—salted, smoked, cured—but most food reached kitchens fresh, recently picked, recently killed, and recognizable: a carrot was a carrot with its sprinkling of dirt, a chicken was a chicken with its feathers. In the nineteenth century industrial processing allowed some food to be conserved in tins and jars for months and years, and new refrigerated transportation allowed food to be carried elsewhere, farther away. Food ceased to be what was produced in one or another season and relatively close by. Food became globalized—for those who could pay for it. And, at the same time, prices became permanently globalized. From then on, a chicken in Senegal no longer cost what a chicken in Senegal cost but what it could cost in Paris or New York, if it was worth transporting. In this system, more and more food producers all over the world began to lose the possibility of consuming what they produced; more and more consumers had to get used to paying for global food with local salaries, and eating very little.

And, more and more, we all eat food processed in faraway places, without transparency, food that reaches us in unrecognizable forms, food that is treated with products we know nothing about. More than ever, food is an act of trust in unknown entities that don't deserve it.

(Again: since the Industrial Revolution, the African who wanted to buy a pound of millet in a market in Sudan had to pay its world market price. This is one of the most successful mechanisms of hunger creation. More than ever, not eating is the consequence of a world market that manages, concentrates, neglects, excludes: starves.)

In the nineteenth century European colonists who spread out all over the world occupied territories where agriculture inverted the proportions they were used to. Instead of little space and many people, there was a lot of space and few people. This became an incentive to invent machinery that helped get the work done—and this coincided with the development of new steam and internal combustion engines. As a result, yields grew exponentially in Australia, New Zealand, Argentina, South Africa, Canada, and above all, in the United States. The first gasoline-powered tractor was used there in 1902. Fifty years later there wasn't a single farm in the United States that didn't have one. At the same time the transportation revolution made it possible for food produced in one region to be sold thousands of miles away without a significant change in its price; between 1870 and 1900 the cost of bringing American corn to Europe dropped by a third. In all of those countries, more and more land was brought into cultivation, signifying one of the greatest advances in human history in what is known as the "agricultural frontier."

Paul McMahon wrote: "The globalization of food can be seen in the nourishment of a London worker around the time of Sherlock Holmes who ate bread made from North American wheat, washed down by a pint of beer brewed from Canadian barley. The butter on his bread came from Ireland, the marmalade from Spain. On Sunday, he might tuck into roast beef, shipped from Argentina or Australia. He drank tea imported from India, sweetened with sugar grown on the former slave plantations of the Caribbean. He sat at the apex of a food system that sucked in produce from all over the world."[13]

In those years—end of the nineteenth, beginning of the twentieth centuries—usual, everyday hunger in rich countries was coming to an end because they were becoming the center of a world system. In other words, the wealthy world had ceased to depend on its own land, climate, peasants, and harvests because they had created a global order in which food is not produced but bought. And the rest of the world had to adapt.

In the meantime, hunger was not only an ordinary suffering, a slogan, and a pledge of unity; it had also become an extreme strategy. They say that the hunger strike reappeared in the West at the beginning of the twentieth century. English women asked for the right to vote, and they did so with a certain amount of violence; the sight of women fighting with the police scandalized society. From where we stand now, it sounds so strange that women had to struggle so hard to win a right that nobody now would ever question: these are the traps—the readings—of history. Another example of how everything changes, that what now seems natural did not yesterday and won't tomorrow.

The hunger strike is a form of violent action against oneself so that others in power—such as the state—have to take responsibility for the violence. The striker decides to begin, but those with power have the possibility of ending it by granting the demand. If it fails to do so, it becomes the victimizer.

A hunger strike can work only with a government the striker trusts to a certain degree. A true tyrant would respond to a hunger strike with a laugh, or not even. The striker's gamble consists of assuming that the government that values some good—democracy, justice—will not want to shoulder the weight of allowing the death of a peaceful person who asks only to be heard.

A hunger strike functions, of course, from the margins. Those English suffragettes placed it into circulation; an Indian lawyer converted it into an art and an example. Mohandas Karamchand Gandhi was an independence leader who searched for peaceful ways to intervene in a complicated and tense process full of violence. When the striking mill workers in Ahmedabad asked for his help to get more pay, Gandhi decided to support them by not eating. Gandhi was already famous and his strike became well-publicized; within a few days, the mill owners, until then quite intransigent, agreed to negotiate a raise.

In the following years Gandhi would fast in an effort to convince his compatriots to improve relations between Hindus and Muslims, to accept the "untouchables" in their temples, and, finally, several times, in opposition to the abuses of the imperial authorities. His last fast was at the end of 1947, when he was seventy eight years old and India was independent, to try to stop the violence between Hindus and Muslims, which had already caused hundreds of thousands of deaths. The confrontations stopped for a few days. Shortly thereafter, on January 30, 1948, Nathuram Godse, a militant Hinduist, joined him in evening prayers and killed him with three bullets to the chest. The following year Godse was sentenced to death. Prime Minister Jawaharlal Nehru and Gandhi's two children asked that his sentence be commuted out of respect for Gandhi's principles of nonviolence and his opposition to the death penalty, but the Indian state did not grant their request. Godse was hung on November 15, 1949.

Since Gandhi, because of Gandhi, the hunger strike is the most extreme form of pressure without violence. Or, in other words, with violence directed only at oneself. It is an extreme way to expose the fact that the state wields the power over the bodies and fates of its subjects; a way of forcing the state to face its own brutal reality.

Later, during the twentieth century, famines with a particularly terrifying characteristic increased and multiplied. The most massive and brutal were caused by man. Or, to put it more precisely, they were the result of the decisions of those in power.

2

Pitirim Aleksandrovich Sorokin was a Russian intellectual and politician who led one of the defeated factions of the 1917 revolution. The great famine that devastated Russia in those years led him to write and publish a book in 1922 called *Hunger as a Factor in Human Affairs*, in which he attempted to consider hunger from many diverse points of view. It was a book written with full and first-hand knowledge, as the author ate only a few potato peels, if that, on many of the days he spent writing it. It was also a counterrevolutionary book—it spoke of what should have remained silent—and it was quickly pulled from circulation. More than fifty years passed before his widow published it again in Miami, Florida, in 1975.

No new edition was ever issued. The copy I have in my hands from the library at Columbia University, was borrowed once in 1991, once in 1993, once in 2003, and again in 2007. It must be, nonetheless, the greatest treatise every written about hunger and its consequences, its various manifestations, its physiology, its influence over inventions, migrations, wars, social changes, crime. "For hunger, there is nothing sacred. It is blind and crushes with the same strength the great and the small, norms and convictions that are opposed to its fulfillment. When we are full, we preach 'the sanctity of property,' but when we are hungry, we can steal without the slightest hesitation. When we are full, we convince ourselves that it is impossible for us to kill, steal, rape, cheat, lie, prostitute ourselves. When we are hungry, we can do it all."[14]

There is still some disagreement about what exactly happened in the Ukraine during those years. In 1928 Joseph Stalin declared that the land must be collectivized. The kulaks—landowning peasants—were class enemies, he said, and should disappear. They were intimidated into giving up their lands and their goods. Many rebelled; in Ukraine, many sacrificed their livestock: forty million cows, sheep, and horses died in an unparalleled massacre. Between 1930 and 1931 more than a million Ukrainian peasants were deported to Siberia or Central Asia; it is not known how many were shot.

In 1932 the Ukrainian countryside was in utter chaos. Moscow decided that those who remained should provide a quota of grain, which left them with nothing to eat; in the spring of that year, some twenty-five thousand people died of hunger every day—but mentioning it would mean summary execution "for treason." Local governments asked for grain; Stalin refused. Patrols of young militants wandered throughout the countryside requisitioning what little remained; their chiefs told them that the peasants were counterrevolutionaries who wanted to destroy Communism, which meant it must be true. Hunger intensified. Cannibalism became the norm; in the villages hung signs that read, "Eating dead children is a barbarous custom," and those who did it or tried to do it were also shot.

The Ukrainians called it *Holodomor*—the hunger plague—and the histories of the Soviet Union never named it. Sixty years had to pass for the magnitude of the disaster to be revealed. This is why statistics still differ; some say five million died; others, eight or ten million.[15]

The numbers associated with hunger tend to be vague, imprecise. Those who count, prefer it that way.

Before trusting in the efficiency of the poison gas agent Zyklon B, Adolf Hitler and his deputies developed *Der Hungerplan*, which copiously utilized the power of extermination by hunger, their companion from only a few years prior, when the German populace, defeated by the First World War, nearly starved during the aftermath.

Der Hungerplan was a meticulously organized program based on a simple principle: food needed for the German army must not be wasted on the populations of the occupied countries; not giving them any would offer the Germans the added advantage—thereby completing the desired circle—of disposing of populations the Nazis considered superfluous.

True to German type, the *Hunger Plan* was punctilious and the categories it established were perfectly defined. There were four, and each corresponded to a level of nourishment that was determined by a guiding slogan from the Reich Labor Service: "An inferior race needs less room, fewer clothes, and less food than the German race." The "well-nourished" were local groups the Nazis wanted to maintain for collaboration; the "insufficiently nourished," who received a maximum of one thousand calories a day, were those the Nazis wanted neither to keep nor kill; the "starved" were the populations the Nazis had decided to reduce as much as possible, such as Jews and Gypsies; the "exterminated by hunger" were starved with intent; they were, among others, Russian prisoners of war.

Their German captors packed thousands of soldiers of the Red Army into small fenced areas, with no shelter or food, and barely a few drops of water. Even though in some instances the dying ate the dead, nobody survived more than three weeks. In one of these camps, several thousand Soviet soldiers signed and turned over to their captors one of the most brutal petitions in history, asking, please, to be shot. Not a chance.

It is estimated that during the German invasion of the USSR, approximately four million Russian civilians died of hunger. In besieged cities, such as Leningrad, the scarcity was so severe that the local authorities summarily executed anybody who didn't look like a skeleton, because only those who stole food could have any flesh at all on their bones.

The battle cry of the Soviet revolution of 1917 was "Peace, Land, and Bread." The march forward was not as simple.

On October 12, 1940, the German invaders announced the establishment of the Warsaw Ghetto. All Jews in the city were ordered confined in an area under guard and surrounded by a wall nine feet high and topped with broken glass and barbed wire. Approximately five hundred thousand people crowded into one and a half square miles: 30 percent of the population of Warsaw in 3 percent of the city.

The German bureaucracy placed the inhabitants of the ghetto in the third category of the *Hunger Plan*. Whereas the soldiers of the Reich received 2,613 calories a day, the Polish Christians, 699, the Polish Jews in the ghetto had a right to 184: a piece of bread and a plate of soup a day. "The Jews will vanish out of starvation, and the only thing that will remain of the Jewish question will be a cemetery," wrote the German governor at the time.[16] With such a diet, death would have to be quick; a system of solidarity and contraband supplemented the food supply and made it so that during the first year, only a fifth of the population—about one hundred thousand people—died of hunger and related illnesses.

Stories of heroism and infamy, of solidarity and egoism during those extraordinary days: smugglers, collaborators, beggars, thieves, resistance, thousands and thousands who did whatever they could to find a bite of food. "People dropped dead of hunger. They died on their way to work and in front of shops. They died at home and were dumped in alleys without clothes or identification, so that family members could keep the ration cards. The smells of death, decay, and human waste pervaded the streets," wrote Sharman Apt Russell in *Hunger: An Unnatural History*.[17]

Under these horrifying conditions, a group of doctors in the ghetto began one of those projects that every once in a while make me proud of my Jewish heritage. They had no medicines or instruments or food to treat their patients—or the slightest hope of surviving—but they were in a position to carry out an in-depth study of malnutrition and its effects, and they would do it in an attempt to contribute something to scientific knowledge, to contribute to other hungry people being treated better someday, under other conditions. "Men without future, in a final effort of will, decided to make a modest contribution to the future. While death was attacking, those who remained awaited their own death without giving up their task," wrote the anonymous writer of the prologue of *Hunger Disease: Studies by the Jewish Physicians in the Warsaw Ghetto*. The book, rich in case studies and statistics, was completed during the last days of the ghetto by the few doctors who had still not been deported. They met clandestinely in a cemetery. A nameless woman smuggled it out of the ghetto and gave it to a Polish professor, Witold Orlowski, who published it in Warsaw in 1946.

"The first symptoms of hunger were a dry mouth accompanied by the need to urinate. One man fell to the ground shouting, *My legs won't hold me up!*" The clinical descriptions, the statistical data, the experiments, the autopsies go on for pages: implacable. And the desperate attempts to treat their patients, "*Added chopped liver and cow's blood . . . gave vitamin A . . . Noted that the best results were obtained . . . the only rational therapy for hunger is food.*"[18]

I never found out how my great-grandmother Gustava, the mother of my grandfather Vicente, spent her final days in the ghetto. Nobody survived to tell us how she managed to complement her daily ration of 184 calories, if she had something to sell to buy another piece of bread or another potato on the black market, if she felt the pangs of hunger strongly, if she despaired, if she resigned herself, thought of suicide, of her son so far away, of those Argentine granddaughters she'd never met with the relief of knowing that somewhere her bloodline would carry on. They didn't give her much time; she was an older woman and they loaded her pretty quickly on the train that would take her to the gas chambers in Treblinka. There, she and 250,000 other inhabitants of the Warsaw Ghetto would be murdered within the span of a few months.

(Sometimes I think it's not really very surprising that now, every day, we let so many people die of hunger, that we don't care and are so adept at looking the other way. In the final analysis, we are the same as we were seventy years ago, the same ones who did it seventy years ago with Hitler and Stalin and Roosevelt and the camps and the bombs.)

The famine of the last war was the last great European famine. It is estimated that one-third of the fifty-six million civilians who died during those six years died of hunger: more than eighteen million people, including half the population of Belarus, for example, as well as large numbers of people in "civilized" countries, such as Holland and Norway.

In 1946 one hundred million Europeans ate fifteen hundred calories a day; they were undernourished. That year, an institution recently created to try to prevent another war like the one that had just ended initiated its first campaign against hunger. Inspiration for the United Nations came from that horror, and from ideas like the one expressed so clearly by Franklin Delano Roosevelt, one of its greatest supporters: "We have come to a clear realization of the fact that true individual freedom cannot exist without economic security and independence. 'Necessitous men are not free men.' People who are hungry and out of a job are the stuff of which dictatorships are made," he said to the Congress of the United States on January 11, 1944, in a State of the Union address.[19] The idea was clear: more hungry people than was strictly necessary could produce unfortunate consequences. In the final analysis, it was simpler and cheaper to give food to millions of people than fight against the Hitlers of this world.

On December 10, 1948, the United Nations proclaimed its Universal Declaration of Human Rights. Article one declares, "All human beings are born free and equal in dignity and rights," though the Declaration was signed, originally, only by sixty-four countries because the rest of the world was a colony of one of those. Article 25 states, "Everyone has the right to a standard of living adequate for the health and well-being of himself and of his family, including food, clothing, housing and medical care, and necessary social services . . ."[20]

The FAO was the first structure created by the United Nations with the purpose of helping to see to it that everybody ate. Its principles were based on the sophism that all human beings share something: humanity. "Humanity is an idea from when humanity didn't exist, from when there were small communities where the destiny of one somehow implicated that of the others. In other words, where it was easy to see that everyone's destiny implicated somehow the destiny of the others—and they took care of each other," wrote an anonymous though almost certainly contemporary Argentine writer. "There is no more resistant idea: behavior always contradicted the concept, but those behaviors are understood as errors, deviations. The best ideas, the most powerful ones, are those that are never verified—and their constant reality preserves and exalts them."

Among all the rights that were never granted, the right to food holds a privileged position. One assumes that a universal right is held above any other consideration; that one cannot abandon its fulfillment to the "free play of the market" nor to the luck of individuals. One assumes that nation-states should make sure that this universal right is applied universally.

Among all the rights that are never acted on, the right to food also holds a privileged position. It's odd, but when we speak of human rights we usually think they shouldn't imprison you without the usual reasons, or torture you, or kill you, or prevent you from traveling, expressing yourself and your opinions; we don't usually think about food. The right to eat is a second- or third-tier human right. When others are violated, healthy and lasting scandals arise; every day, hundreds of millions of people are unable to exercise their right to food and the indignation—from large organisms, from small citizens—tends to be discreet.

In the meantime, in the countries that produce discourse, hunger has become something that has to do with others. Its place in the political discourse has been nourished by this benevolent condescension—and perhaps by light touches of guilt.

It wasn't a question of misfortune, there were no external, unforeseeable, uncontrollable causes. The greatest famine of modern times—or, rather, the greatest famine ever recorded—happened in a country at peace and without natural catastrophes or climatic episodes that set it off. It was the incredible result of an accumulation of errors and arrogance, the combination of mistaken policy and the belief in the story that this policy told itself about itself.

In 1958 President Mao Zedong decided that China should take a Great Leap Forward so that in a decade its economy would, he said, surpass Great Britain's. To achieve this, China had to industrialize, turning millions of peasants into workers. Agriculture, which was the country's most productive sector, would maintain its current productivity thanks to certain political and technological changes.

Millions of people were set in motion. The land, which had been collectivized, was to be worked by peasant communes that were so poorly organized, they failed to function at all. Innovations were often insane: broken glass used as fertilizer, construction of mud dikes that collapsed with the first rains, piglets used for reproduction right after they'd been weaned. Production, needless to say, dramatically decreased, but local authorities preferred to hide this fact; in order to hide their failure and make their superiors happy, their reports exaggerated their yields by three, four, even ten times. This convinced the leaders that they were right, that the Leap was working; they broadcast it widely and ordered large percentages of these (false) harvests sent to granaries in the cities, reduced the amount of food imports, and doubled the export of grain—of which there was, supposedly, an excess. During those days, President Mao visited a peasant commune and, with the promise of a great harvest, he suggested, "Plant a little less and work only a half day. Use the other half to educate yourself: study science, do recreation, organize a university."

Confusion reigned. Even when they sent everything they had to the cities, the communes couldn't fill the quota their own lies had helped establish; many of those responsible were executed for treason and for obstructing the revolutionary process. Nothing remained in the towns and villages. The peasants were forced to eat in communal kitchens that lacked almost everything. Whenever some local chiefs began to ask for food, the leaders of the party came up with a right-wing conspiracy—

which they may even have believed to be true—and executed anybody who resisted. In the meantime, millions of people were left without anything to eat.

The famine lasted more than three years, a time of such great starvation that rumors of cannibalism ran rampant. One of the most popular was that in China, people were so desperate, they didn't only eat the dead; many children were sacrificed. Families attempted to honor the old taboos and not eat their own. The solution was to bring back "an old Chinese custom" in which neighbors exchanged children so as not to eat their own flesh and blood. "They stopped feeding the girls; they gave them only water. They exchanged the body of their daughter for the neighbor's daughter. They boiled the body in some kind of soup . . ." a survivor supposedly told the English journalist Jasper Becker many years later. [21] What is true is that the death toll soared. There were uprisings, of course, but these were decimated by the Red Army. Exact numbers have never been established, but it is estimated that at least thirty million people died of hunger between 1958 and 1962.

The world knew nothing of this—and it later appeared that there wasn't much to know. In 1959 Lord Boyd Orr, the first director of FAO and an eminent nutritionist, declared that "the government of Mao has ended the traditional cycle of hunger in China."[22] Even in 1961 a French journalist who went to interview Mao Zedong wrote that "the people of China were never even close to famine."[23] The journalist's name was François Mitterrand, later to be president of France.

Since the middle of the last century famines have repeatedly occurred in Africa and Asia. My image—my first image—of hunger is still those photographs from Biafra, those children with emaciated arms and legs, cadaverous faces, and bellies like blown-up balloons. Among my generation in Argentina a very thin person will still be nicknamed "Biafra." Among my generation, we still believe that hunger is something we see in photos.

The last large agricultural transformation began at the beginning of the twentieth century in Germany. There, engineers at the BASF factory invented a way to produce chemical fertilizers based on converting nitrogen and hydrogen into ammonia—and they won the Nobel Prize for it. In the thirties these fertilizers were used throughout the richest countries, liberating farmers from having to produce their own and giving way for the viability of new genetically modified seed. More demanding but much more productive, they required more pesticides and more irrigation. In 1930 there were 20 million acres of irrigated land in the world; in 2000 there were 680 million.

Only in the middle of the sixties did these conditions, thanks to what was subsequently called the Green Revolution, begin to spread to certain countries in the Other World: Mexico, China, India, Southeast Asia.

Food production increased like never before.

That so many of us manage to eat every day is a miracle; that so many don't is vile.

For centuries, there was no solution to famine. They happened when there was a drought, a flood, a war, a plague that used up all the reserves in a region. The richest, of course, always had food to eat, but the rest were left with absolutely nothing. And, in the larger, more centralized kingdoms, where there were other regions that could provide the food that was lacking, communication was so slow and transportation even more so; first the alarm and then the assistance could take weeks or months, time enough for thousands or millions to die of hunger. Saving them did not depend on anybody's decision; there was, literally, no way to do it.

Now, feeding the hungry depends only on will. If there are people who do not have enough to eat—if there are people who are becoming ill from hunger, who die of hunger—it is because those who have food don't want to give it to them; we, who have food, we don't want to give it to them. The world produces more food than its inhabitants need; we all know who doesn't have enough; sending them what they need could be a matter of hours.

This is what makes our current hunger somehow more brutal, more horrible than the hunger of a hundred or a thousand years ago.

Or at least speaks more eloquently of what we are.

BANGLADESH: THE EFFECTS OF HUNGER

Bangladesh is a very new country, "from my day" as they say. It stopped being an English colony ten years before I was born, then was East Pakistan until I was fourteen years old. In 1971 there was a brief civil war, many independence celebrations, speeches, then, suddenly a country. There is something unbelievable about a country that is younger than my father, and there is something devastating that People's Republic of Bangladesh has become, in its nearly 50-year existence, one of the most impoverished: 57,000 square miles—about the size of Illinois—for about 160 to 170 million inhabitants (Illinois falls shy of 13 million inhabitants. Per population, Bangladesh is the eighth largest in the world; per area, the ninety-fourth. With almost 2000 inhabitants per square mile, it is also one of the most densely populated countries on the planet. It is located at the mouth of two large Indian rivers, the Ganges and the Brahmaputra, and it is low. Almost nothing rises more than ten yards above sea level; the country floods continuously, and it is assumed that when the seas rise, it will turn into a swimming pool. For now, it is an ant hill—an ant hill of people who try to grow rice on not enough land. Even with so little space, Bangladesh is the fourth largest producer of rice in the world.

But it's not enough.

This was the sentiment of the head of MSF Bangladesh, an energetic Dutch woman named Vikki, whom I met with during my travels to the country. "Here, everything is difficult. Bangladesh is one of three countries with the highest levels of malnutrition in the world, and they don't even seem to realize it. They do, of course, in the countryside, when they have no food, but here in Dhaka, it's as if they don't."

I tried to concentrate on her words, but the chair I was sitting on seemed to be moving in a strange way. Then everything was moving about, as if the ground were shaking. I couldn't figure out what was causing this sensation: a problem of balance, maybe, or lack of sleep. Vikki kept talking and I was able to get distracted in her thoughts and observations.

"They don't realize how sick they are."

Vikki was bringing up something I have been hearing for a long time, something of key importance: the capacity of people to get used to the most difficult things. Or, put differently, something even worse: to assume that that's life.

Later, during lunch, everybody excitedly discussed the earthquake. Fear cannot be foolish; one needs to know what to fear. The lack of fear about that earthquake proved to me once again that fear is the most uncomfortable form of knowledge. I envy an animal's serenity, the serenity of ignorance. But supposedly animals know about earthquakes long before people do.

Dhaka is a model city: one that synthesizes how and why the form "city" has failed. Sixty years ago, Dhaka was a small provincial capital with half a million inhabitants; now it is thirty or forty times bigger, many millions crowded together without enough housing or streets or transportation or space or toilets. And they keep coming. Every day thousands of people appear in Dhaka thinking that here they will live better than in their villages. Or they woke up one day and found their village underwater, or that their plot of land belonged to their money lender, or that they didn't have enough to feed their six children.

To say "many millions" seems careless; it is, but it's not my carelessness. Nobody knows how many inhabitants there are in the city, but it's nothing personal. They don't know how many inhabitants there are in the country. In Dhaka there might be, they say, sixteen or eighteen million, or maybe even twenty-two.

It is a jungle of flesh and tin. In Dhaka, to walk is to dodge moving bodies—people, bicycles, rickshaws, motorbikes, cars, buses—that will drive right over you, and it is difficult to put aside as irrelevant one of the most basic assumptions when walking in a city: that others—those who drive something—would prefer not to kill you. Here, by choice, religion, or convenience, they don't stop for anything.

But then a man drives by on a not-so-old motorbike with two girls, six or seven years old, one in back and the other in front of him, pressed up against him, clinging on to him, dressed in school uniforms, each with two braids, and such happiness shining from the one in back, her face pressed against her father's enormous back, her father's warmth, her father's invincible power—she doesn't even know that life isn't like that. Or perhaps there is something she does know.

Dhaka or failure: in Dhaka there is no street lighting or care of public spaces or any visible public order. To go from one place to another can take hours and to return is suddenly impossible. The honking, noise, heat, dust, broken-down roads, aggressive cars, crumbling buildings, pestilent rivers and streams, mountains of garbage. The poorer a society

is, the more restricted its access to certain services; facilities that everybody has in Norway are the privilege of very few in the Other World.
Care for public spaces—the idea that it is territory that belongs to everybody and everybody should take care of it—is also particular to rich
countries. Here, the rich have their spaces and they maintain them—
closed.

Dhaka is a perfect failure, and it is, at the same time, a great example
of the success of cities. It is a magnet that attracts more and more people
and, by doing so, has become a disaster. The success of cities in the Other
World implies its own demise; they exist in a constant crisis of overproduction—of desire, of attraction, of hope: the mechanisms of the crises
of capitalism.

Here also, most of those who arrive end up in the immense slums—
villa miserias, favelas, callampas, shantytowns. Kamrangirchar, the biggest slum of all, is an island in the Buriganga River.

Mohammed Masum arrived here full of hope from his village three
months ago. Mohammed owned a plot of land where he grew rice and
a few banana and mango trees, but he had to leave it. Ever since he got
married, his brothers have been hounding him.

"I don't know why, maybe they didn't like Asma, my wife, they told me
she was poor, didn't have a dowry."

Mohammed knew her from their town, he liked her, they told him
she was a hard worker and a good person, and he decided to marry
her; finally, his brothers accepted her and everything settled down. Or
so it seemed. When his father got sick—everybody knew, he said, that
his father was going to die very soon—the fighting over the inheritance
became so fierce that he preferred to sell his part and leave.

"Is it a large inheritance?"

"Yes. Three plots of land, each about forty or fifty yards."

Mohammed didn't care; he'd been wanting to come to Dhaka for a
long time. He'd always heard that life in the city was different.

"I knew that people here had comfortable, peaceful, happy lives; that
you can make a lot of money."

"Where did you hear that?"

"From people. And once I saw it on television, in the village square.
There you see that people in Dhaka live well."

"Do you still think the same way?"

"Of course. My life is getting better, so I'm staying here"

Mohammed, Asma, and their three children lived in a two-by-four room—sheet metal and palm fronds—with no furniture at all: nothing. Mohammed was skinny, sinewy, with the eyes of an animal. Asma gazed at him with her warm, placid smile. The rooms in this tenement house— this shanty—were on either side of a narrow hallway; a family lived in each one and they shared a kitchen, a faucet, and a toilet—a hole in the ground. To pay for it, Mohammed drove a rickshaw.

"What's the worst part of your job?"

"That it's so exhausting. It's the most exhausting thing I've ever done."

"How much do you earn a day?"

"Depends on the day. It can be two hundred, even up to four hundred *takas.*"

Which is almost five dollars. But he said he almost never received that much; more often it was two hundred *takas*, about two and a half dollars, for ten or twelve hours. The city is full of rickshaws, rickshaw drivers. Nobody knows how many, somewhere between two hundred thousand and five hundred thousand, which means they have no idea. And each one pedals about thirty miles a day in this inferno of pollution and traffic. I asked him what he liked about his job.

"Nothing. But I don't have any money and I don't know anybody; for the moment, it's the only thing I can do. Anyway, I always wanted to be in Dhaka, so being here now makes me happy. But it's true, at home I almost always had something to eat."

In the city if you don't earn anything you don't eat, he explained, not like in the village, where you could always find a few mangos or do some small job or ask for a handful of rice from some relative.

"Here in the city, it's like everything belongs to other people."

He paused to think about what he had said, like someone looking at a new toy, turning it over in their hands; yes, here everything belongs to other people.

"Here, a day I can't work is a day I don't eat."

Then he corrected himself: *we* don't eat.

"Now it's been two days that I don't feel well and I can't go out, and we're out of food. That's not so nice. This afternoon, I'm going to have to go out no matter how I feel: being sick is for the rich."

The anxiety of earning a living today. The equation is very simple: what you were able to earn that day equaled what you were able to eat that day. Living day-to-day: no reserves. The idea of reserves, savings, security— the things on which cultures are based, what ours consists of—doesn't exist. Go out and take your chances and maybe yes and maybe no.

"But things are better now than they were before."

Things are better now, he told me. They have a bed—he was sitting on that bed, a platform without a mattress where all five of them had to sleep every night—and a fan. The fan was turning on the ceiling, bringing some relief from the stifling air, the odors.

"If I had a little money I could start a business, buy something and try to sell it on the street, anything. But I need some money for that and for now I haven't been able to save anything because I have to pay rent and food. But I'm going to get it."

"Have you thought of the possibility of going back to your village?"

"No, we can't because I sold my land to come here. No, now this is our lives. This is my life."

Mohammed looked decisive, like someone who had already jumped. I asked him what his happiest moment was.

"Happiness for me is when I'm not hungry. If I have food, I'm happy; if I don't, I'm not."

"Whose fault is it that sometimes you don't have food?"

"When I'm hungry I don't get mad at anybody. I think God sent me what I have and is going to take care of me, of what happens in my life. The good and the bad. And if I'm in this situation now it's because I must have committed some sin that made Him send me these things."

"Is it fair that some people are so rich and some are so poor?"

"No, I think God shouldn't have done that."

"But he does."

"Yes, because we aren't as good as He wants us to be. He's disappointed in us, and that's how He shows us. If we want to live better, we're going to have to deserve it."

Asma left the room to take one of their children to the bathroom. Mohammed said that sometimes the responsibility of keeping a family alive felt very heavy on his shoulders, knowing that if he doesn't bring in any money none of his family eats, very heavy.

"And sometimes, you know what?"

"No, what?"

"Sometimes I think it would be better to be a woman."

He raised his eyebrows, as if he were afraid of what he was saying. We looked at each other, and I didn't know what to tell him. Asma returned with the child and said that if we were talking about not having food we should be quiet, or it would be shameful.

"We don't talk about these things. Why should we? It's enough to deal with what's happening to us."

In 1980 the island of Kamrangirchar, a district of Dhaka, had under 5,000 inhabitants; the first electricity was hooked up in 1990, at a religious school. Now there are almost half a million, all migrants, people trying their luck. Kamrangirchar was situated on an alluvial plain, where space can easily become densely occupied. Buenos Aires, a big city by any measure, has about 30,000 inhabitants per square mile; Kamrangirchar has around 20,000, and that's with no tall buildings. Six out of every ten adults on the island don't know how to read or write; there are ninety-eight mosques and sixty-nine madrassas, which teach Koran, and seven elementary schools.

These are societies built out of leftovers. And the overdetermination of certain precise goals: the importance of understanding what brings people there. The hope of eating every day; the illusion that their children will have different lives; the acceptance that what they had is no longer viable; the conviction that change is necessary; and the resignation that the only change possible is this migration, this overcrowding. There's no history; history is what they left behind, what condemned them. There must be a future, that's what they came for; there is one, but it's far away, illusory. And, in the meantime, the present continuous, made up of continuing to survive. To have more than one verb tense is usually a luxury.

There were dozens of slums like this one in Dhaka. Kamrangirchar is not the poorest or the most insalubrious. It's just the biggest and one of the most depleted. Kamrangirchar is an accumulation of half-built houses, wayward streets, gutted streets, markets, market stalls, bridges, piles of garbage, cables and more cables, motorbikes, rickshaws, stinking markets, carpenters sawing, blacksmiths hammering, butchers butchering beasts, day workers making bricks, boatmen waiting for customers, children smoothing down the plastic edges of five hundred yellow buckets. Others sell fruit, trinkets, morphine, or heroin; Kamrangirchar is also the country's most renowned drug distribution center.

It looked like everything had always been here, but it had only been like that at the most for thirty years. Forty years ago this was a rosary of islands separated by water and swamps, a giant garbage dump until hordes of people started arriving from the interior of the country. It was a garbage dump and it filled up with people; here even the metaphors are second rate.

Along with the migrants, Kamrangirchar started filling up with precarious makeshift housing, where lives were spent. Some were huts with tin walls, roofs of palm leaves, uneven plank floors, all barely held up by some long bamboo canes buried in the swamp nine feet below. The inhabitants lived, moving beyond bad metaphors, in a precarious balance; when they left their hovels to cook or wash, for instance, they walked across little bridges made of three or four pieces of bamboo, under which was the black, stinking water: the stench of their lives.

Others were like apartment blocks, tenement houses, dilapidated row housing: on stable ground, twenty or thirty makeshift rooms crowded around a few courtyards with an oven and a toilet and a water pump. In each room there was a bed—no mattress—that everybody used, sometimes just a cloth over the planks, walls of chicken wire, rags hung up, a pot or two, a few torn garments. It was difficult to have—to possess, to own—less than this.

The rooms rarely had doors; at most, a curtain. Privacy: another luxury we rarely think about.

Later, in the street: the way Mohammed took off on his rickshaw carrying a mother, a father, and three children. He leaned his full body weight on his left leg then, with a strange little dance step, moved all that weight onto his right, two or three times until the creature rolled, and his sweat sparkled like diamonds.

2

Fatema made an all-or-nothing wager, she would see how long she could live without letting her husband move back in. Fatema was twenty-one years old, has a three-year-old son, a seven-year-old daughter, and a husband who has just left her. Fatema also had a wide, full face, a lively mind, and a pleasant smile—sad but warm. Her parents brought her to Dhaka when she was five years old after a flood left them homeless. They married her off when she was thirteen; she didn't want to get married, but she didn't think of it as unusual. She'd started working when she was seven, twelve hours a day in a textile factory, and getting married wouldn't be that different, after all. Another thing would have been to go to school. When she was little, Fatema watched the other girls who did go.

"I'd look at them and envy them so much. They were like enchanted princesses."

What she didn't expect was that her husband would end up being such a slacker. Sometimes he'd drive the rickshaw, or sell something on the street, or he'd stay around the house for an entire week without bringing in a single *taka*. And he treated her badly and beat her if the money she brought didn't seem like enough to him.

"Did you throw him out or did he leave on his own?"

"He left."

"Do you want him to come back?"

Fatema hesitated. After a moment, she told me that in the end it doesn't matter much to her whether he was around or not, it was up to her to earn the money to feed her children.

Her daughter had a fever and was asleep on her lap, both on the plank floor in the room.

"But doesn't it bother you to live like this, to be alone?"

"No, I prefer it this way. I almost always prefer it. A man should look after his family. If he doesn't, he's not a man," she said, then went quiet, her eyes half closed. Then she picked up the conversation. "A man who doesn't look after his family is worthless, a parasite."

I asked her if she had any good memories of her life with him, and she said, yes, at first, but very shortly thereafter, no. And she didn't want to look for another man: what for? She had to take care of her children.

Strange paradoxes. Fatema worked like a dog to not have to depend on a man, not have to put up with his aggression. She worked like a dog so she could be free.

While I was in Dhaka, a textile worker, Aminul Islam, turned up dead, tortured, by the side of a road in the outskirts of the city. Islam was forty years old, had two sons, a daughter, and had been one of the leaders of the 2010 protest movement, which succeeded in raising the minimum wage in that sector from sixteen hundred to three thousand *takas* a month. Three thousand *takas* are about thirty-five dollars. Islam had tried to organize his fellow workers at Shasha Denims, one of the many factories making clothes that would later be called Nike, Tommy Hilfiger, and other very cool names. But one of the requirements for the working conditions to remain as they were was that the victims didn't protest—the hunger of these miniscule salaries was enforced by paramilitary weapons. All Bangladesh governments agreed on shamelessly repressing any opposition from workers—and the famous "international community" looked the other way.

The existence of countries like Bangladesh, the existence of millions of workers who earn forty dollars a month, is a necessary condition of the world order, not only because these workers produce cheap merchandise that billions consume, but also because they determine the location of industries, which move from prosperous countries, where nobody works for that wage, to those where they do. In other words, it's the exploitation of labor in impoverished nations that allows wealthier nations to thrive. An American businessman was quoted in *The New York Times* as saying, "We need to bring certain types of production to the countries where we will be most profitable so that we can maintain the level of profit that allows us to invest in research and innovation." Here's another purpose served by technological progress: to justify the most violent form of capitalism. If we didn't produce it with superexploited workers, we wouldn't earn enough to continue to "innovate."

"What a shame, right? He defended us, gave his life to defend us, and I don't even know who he was."

Aminul Islam was a short, bearded, very devout Muslim man. Three years ago, a little after those strikes, he was kidnapped by a group of assassins working for the Bangladesh intelligence services. They beat him and tortured him, trying to force him to sign documents that informed against his comrades; finally, Islam managed to escape; for months he remained in hiding, but then he couldn't anymore.

A month ago, the factory workers returned to the streets. The conflict began when they asked for the afternoon off to watch the Indian Premier League (IPL), which was the city's obsession at the time. The bosses refused and the conflict escalated; hours later, thousands of workers went on strike, protesting their wages, their labor conditions, and sexual predation on women. A group of paramilitaries kidnapped Islam; they let him go the following day, but, less than two weeks later, they took him again.

In the last twenty years Bangladesh has become the second largest garment exporter in the world, after China. Garments represent three-quarters of their total exports: $20 billion worth of them each year. Of the four million workers in the sector, 90 percent are women. Fatema still works in the same textile factory; they pay her those three thousand *takas* a month to operate a machine twelve, thirteen, fourteen hours a day, seven days a week. But her work doesn't count for much. For every pair of jeans sold in New York for sixty dollars, the cost of Bangladesh labor—what Fatema brings home—is between twenty-five and thirty cents. And we progressive democratic Westerners, we who are so worried about human rights, wear those clothes.

Fatema spent half her life—half her life—at that job. I asked her what she thought about while she was sitting in front of her machine for those long hours, and she said she thought about her children, the money she needed, how she was going to raise them the way they should be raised.

"I think about those things, the problems, everything that's yet to come."

"Any thoughts you enjoy?"

"Well, sometimes I remember the happy moments with my husband."

She said, shyly, almost guiltily, that the best thing about the factory was that sometimes she could chat with her friends, tell them her problems, listen to theirs, and that's when she felt less lonely. But she didn't stay long because then she had to hurry home to cook for her children. Her room was very clean, very tidy; there were mats on the plank floor, two shelves in a corner with pots, a towel, and a thermos.

"What music do you like to listen to?"

And she, again, as if she were saying she was sorry, replied, "Well, I can't listen to music because I don't have anything to listen to it on, a radio, or something like that."

Fatema paid two thousand *takas* for a 100-square-foot-room, which left her with one thousand takas for everything else: clothes, transportation, food. Three people living on thirteen dollars a month; if they were lucky, rice twice a day. One usually thinks about hunger as a problem of those who don't have work, the marginal, the losers; not those who spend half their lives in front of a machine producing valuable merchandise.

"When there's not enough food I don't eat, but my children do. They are my only hope."

Meanwhile, I ate in Bangladesh diners and ordered dishes that always had rice, always had a lentil dal, sometimes a piece of chicken, and every once in while I finished my meal without having cried from how spicy it was. Even when I ordered everything, I ate for two dollars. The two diners I usually went to were very clean and always full of employees. Poverty was—for the less poor—the ability to buy people very cheaply, and to buy many of them.

They are societies of servants. If a woman cleans your house for five hundred *takas* a month, why clean it yourself, and if a man will drive your car for five thousand *takas* a month, why drive, and if a child will carry your groceries—he'll be happy with fifty—why carry anything. In daily life, that's what these chasms are good for.

Karl Marx thought about a society of equals in which the work that was necessary for survival—when there was no longer any need to produce surplus value for the few—would be much lighter for everybody, and where, therefore, men and women would have more time to spend on things that interested them. Here, the idea of leisure time—or, rather, of activities not directly related to meeting basic necessities—almost doesn't exist.

Fatema feared dying in a work fire. Factory fires, death by incineration, are among the highest causes for worker fatalities in Bangladesh. Her crowded, poorly ventilated workshop was full of fabrics and chemical products and was located on the fifth floor of an eight-story building—on each floor there's a small factory with hundreds of workers crowded in with their machines and dark narrow stairways between. These buildings are usually constructed on the cheap, and since the electricity goes off constantly, there are generators on the balconies, which add weight that the structures can barely—or don't—sustain. Fires and building collapses are frequent.

"But I can't not go. For every day I miss, they deduct two. And if I get there late, I have to work even though they don't pay me for the day."

In 2015 the richest man in Spain, Amancio Ortega, increased his fortune to almost $65 billion because his main business, Inditex—the parent company of the clothing brand Zara—was optimizing the group costs with a purchasing policy centered in emerging economies. Though clothing companies have long manufactured their apparel in places like India and China, in Bangladesh, the garment labor force equals around a quarter of a million people. And that number is growing.

I asked her how she saw herself in twenty years.

"That also makes me scared because now I can work, but in twenty years I'll be old and who knows if I'll be able to work, if my boss will want me to stay at the factory. Everything depends on how I raise my children. If I manage to raise them like I should, they'll have jobs and they'll be able to take care of me in twenty or thirty years, when I'm old. But if I don't, I won't have anything."

The choices: everything or almost nothing, when everything is very little. When I asked her whose fault it was, she said she didn't know or care. We could hear voices from the neighboring room, a child's cry. The only light entered through a few cracks. No air seemed to enter from anywhere.

"If I'd gain something from blaming somebody, I'd do it, but it doesn't matter. I think it's just my fate, what God decided for me. He put me here without anything so I'd have to make it on my own. Only He knows why."

"Why didn't He make the world so that everybody had what they needed?"

"I don't have the knowledge or learning to explain why things are like they are. I'd like to be able to express what I feel about all this injustice. But I don't know, I never went to school."

"But do you think it's the fault of God, the government, people themselves?"

"I have no gripe with God. He does what he does, what he wants. But I do have to say that the government works only for the rich; it never does anything for us, never looks after us, never anything."

I hate the habit—the laziness—of thinking that the Other World is doing the same as the First World, only this many years later, but sometimes—only sometimes—it seems true. Now, two centuries later, many poor cities are following that same pattern. In Asia, Africa, and Latin America, growing cities are facilitating the better exploitation of that almost free labor. And they have a level of poverty that forces that labor—those millions of people—to sell themselves for cheap. The lucky ones are those who make thousands come after them, thousands who don't get even that.

What do we do? Go naked so that we don't wear on our skin the torn, worn skin of those women? What a love-in that would be: everybody naked for the sake of universal justice. Do we tell ourselves that thanks to us they have work, and they eat? Do we keep quiet—guiltily, mightily, boringly quiet?

Somebody says that the poor people of Kamrangirchar aren't very interested in what's happening in the country, politically and in other ways. That they are too busy worrying about how they're going to eat; this, they tell me, is the authentic karma of the poor.

The authentic life sentence of the poor.

In the lobby of the most expensive hotel in Dhaka, a journalist friend of mine introduced me to N, an intermediary. They are the ones who take advantage of this whole business. They receive orders from Western brands and assign them to local factories. N was thirtysomething, with a radiant smile, an impeccably clean and ironed shirt, and a watch with a face as big as a soup bowl. N sipped a cappuccino and told me that big department stores, supermarkets, and brand-name companies rent their garments—he said "rent their garments"—in public but never refused their profit margins; they charged at least six times more than the price they paid him. And they were always trying to increase it as much as they could by paying as little as they could. And, said N, they worked things out as best they could. Then he got distracted. On the large flat screen in the lobby of the city's most expensive hotel, they were showing the IPL championship game, Bangladesh against India.

"Cricket is my true passion. That's where you really need to have balls. Cricket is where you really struggle for your life."

In the lobby of this monstrosity, with its opaque windows that is decorated like an airport, even pink marble, a chubby employee walked by with a small racket. The employee moved like a panther: stalked, attacked. When she struck—backhand—the racket crackled: another dead fly. Perhaps her job was to clean the air the customers breathed; perhaps to place the struggle for survival center stage so that nobody let down their guard and forgot, forgot and let down their guard. And that sharp, satisfied smile: who could ever describe in a few words the delight this woman derived from dead flies.

Around the time I was first assembling this manuscript, there was another building collapse in Dhaka, with more than eleven hundred dead. It was said that the day before, cracks had appeared that made them assess the eight-story building where three thousand workers were employed, but on that April 24, 2013, the bosses said that anybody who didn't come to work would lose a month's wages. So they all entered and two hours later the entire building collapsed within a few seconds. It was said that the owner was a big-shot in the governing party. It was said that in Bangladesh, one out of every five national deputies was a textile impresario, and those who weren't invested in the industry, received their bribes; nobody had the least interest in changing anything. Politics as the tool of one economic sector didn't usually show itself so blatantly.

It's difficult to think of Fatema—who despite having a boss who exploited her to the max, and whose work conditions were incredibly unsafe, had a steady job—as privileged. Mohammed didn't have a dependable job. He worked as hard as he could—for an occupation that guaranteed no rights or income—but if he couldn't find anyone to cart around on his rickshaw, he was screwed.

Which meant that to Mohammed, it was Fatema who was privileged by comparison.

It could also be said that men, by biological default, will always have one privilege over women: they don't require as much food to survive. Because, among other things, this is a book made of women the way a body is made of water. About 90 percent of the body of a mammal—person, cow, weasel—is water, and the water is what can't be seen. A body is made of water as time is made of the passing minute. But what could be seen as a women's issue, actually began to look like a family issue with women at the center: They require extra nutrition to breastfeed, they suffer when they cook, they suffer in their children, they suffer when they take them to the hospital and their men don't, they suffer when their men eat and they don't, they suffer. If I were an etymologist, I would want to know if there were common roots to these pairs of words in the Romance languages that mean *hunger* and *female*: *hambre* and *hembra*, *faim* and *femme*, *fame* and *famine*. Maybe it is a coincidence, or maybe only by going back to the root will we find the truth.

VOICES OF THE TRIBE

How?

I mean, me. What makes it possible for me to leave the battlefield tonight and stand under the shower and put on clean clothes and splash on cologne and order a delicious meal at the hotel restaurant and maybe even a bottle of good wine? What makes it possible for me to do that almost every night?

The evidence that not doing so isn't going to solve the problems in their lives and that, in the meantime, my life carries on? The ability to leave behind in the office, so to speak, what is, after all, my work?

The excuse that at least I'm working on this book?

How the hell?

"Really, I really would like to do something. I swear. Man, when I see them I have a fit, and when I think of those poor people there with their anguish at not knowing if they're going to eat or not, I can't believe we don't do anything to fix it. I saw a really good documentary, they give it to you straight, no anesthesia. Really, they didn't mince words, it was horrifying, I felt really, really bad, very moved, and since then I always remember them. Actually, I always have, because I remember my mother always saying that you have to eat that, how can we throw that away if there are children with nothing to eat in Africa, and I thought about those kids and I ate my food. Crazy, eh? To make me eat what they couldn't eat she'd tell me that they couldn't, that they had none. That really affected me, but now I realize that it was another of her manipulations, that what the hell did my eating have anything to do with them having food or not. I mean, if I didn't eat it, were they going to have even less? But that's not what matters. What matters is that I always think about them and, I'm telling you, I'd like to do something. What makes me feel a little better is that there are a lot of us who are trying to help them. And not only people like me. There's Bill Gates, Bono, the pope, powerful people. Haven't you seen how the pope always talks about the poor people and how the Church is there to help them? If it weren't for them . . . It makes me feel better that they're there, it's some comfort. Though, sometimes it also worries me; I wonder what a woman like me can do if the most powerful people in the world, if—"

How the hell do we manage?

"What I can't stand is eating all this knowing that there are so many people in the world who are dying of hunger."

"Yeah, it really is a shame."

"But, of course, if we leave it, it'll just go to waste. That would be even worse."

How the hell do we manage to live?

And there I was believing that hunger was the most unbearable thing, par excellence. (And that I'd never learn to tolerate being around it.)

How the hell do we manage to live knowing?

There's a swirl of guilt. We are all guilty, but not in that cunning way that shared guilt is the dissolution of guilt, the redistribution of guilt into pieces so tiny that none of them matter in the end. We are all guilty, but some are much more guilty than others, and in this quantitative progression there is a qualitative leap. It's true that you, that I, that those two over there, all with our food habits, we hoard food that others need. But that guilt, even though it's important, looks pretty tiny next to the guilt of Mr. Cargill or some president of a country. There's no comparison, and you know it.

How the hell do we manage to live knowing that these things?

Okay, okay, I understand, so what do you want me to do? Never eat again? Live on bread and water, eat only millet to show my solidarity and concern? That wouldn't help, either, my friend, it's pure affectation. I think that in the end we have to live our lives just as they are and keep in mind that if there's some way to help them, or, even better, if there's some way we can get involved to change this situation, we have to do it, but always asking ourselves, of course, what good it does, who it helps, if it does any good to keep getting so upset about a situation that is going to continue for who knows how long. It's a waste, my friend, pure waste. Or don't you remember poor Julio, what happened to him. No, I'm telling you that you have to dedicate yourself to what really has a chance of solving something, you know what I mean, because otherwise the only thing you accomplish is messing up your own life, feeling impotent and that's not going to help anybody if you feel like a piece of shit, so what you have to do is choose very carefully the things—

How the hell do we manage to live knowing that these things are happening?

3

To eat is to enact our belonging to a culture. Every society has rules about what to eat and how to eat it. The cricket that is a delicacy in China would be anathema in my neighborhood and a relief in this neighborhood. The Big Mac that is the food of the poor and marginal in New York City is a privilege for the rich kids in Managua or Chișinău. The pig that will end up as ham in Jabugo could unite Muslims and Jews in their total rejection of it, and so forth. But it is not only what gets eaten; it is also how it gets eaten; each culture sees the way they eat as natural. It seems to us so logical—I repeat: natural—to drink a hot, sugary infusion every morning, possibly a fruit juice, maybe a piece of bread or a cracker spread with animal fat and perhaps some sweet fruit spread, maybe even a couple of chicken eggs cooked in fat. It seems natural for us once noon arrives to eat a couple of savory dishes—maybe one cold and one hot—composed of animal proteins, carbohydrates, and some vegetable fiber accompanied by a cold drink that might even contain alcohol, finishing up with something sweet and once again a sugary hot infusion. And so forth. It seems appropriate for us to eat cold meat treated with preservatives and sliced very thin for breakfast but not fresh meat sliced thick and recently cooked, for that belongs to lunch or dinner. It seems logical to accompany that piece of hot meat—of certain animals, basically three or four—with certain raw or cooked vegetables, but we are not willing to complement it with a large bowl of strawberries and cream or a filet of hake. It seems normal to us to add to durum wheat made into noodles some animal or vegetable fat and certain vegetables and meats and little pieces of cheese, but it would surprise us if somebody added dulce de leche or honey. We spend an entire meal adding wheat flour baked into bread to what we are eating, but it seems strange for us to keep doing so when we finally reach the sweets.

Sometimes, during certain periods, we incorporate new things. Until a few years ago, the West almost never ate raw fish, for example, and now, via sushi, we eat a lot. But the big picture—the division between breakfast, lunch, and dinner, for example—are extremely resistant, and they impose themselves with the strength of what doesn't seem imposed. We don't usually think that the pattern could be very different and that it has been in other eras and is in so many different places.

People create a narrative of themselves every day through the food they eat and how they eat. One of the least considered aspects of hunger is that it makes you always eat the same thing. Food variety is a modern myth, a myth of the wealthy countries. Throughout history, most people ate more or less the same thing every day of their lives. Gastronomy—the art of varying what one eats—is a discipline that, for millennia, was as widespread as mother-of-pearl jewelry or fly-fishing.

Compared to the baroque rhetoric of the wealthy cities, where a diner can supposedly choose at any moment among a seemingly endless variety—from a mortadella sandwich to foie gras mousse passing through pizza, salad, chop suey, curry, hamburger, tortilla, taco, soup, barbeque, risotto, local dishes—the inhabitant of the Other World is faced with the reduced language of two or three sentences. Here, in Dhaka, for example, the food grammar allows one to write only *rice* so many times, with a piece of vegetable when there is one, a piece of fish for a party—hunger. It's a different kind of story: repetitive, blunt, obsessive, brutal.

It is a kind of dirty realism.

Let's assume that solidarity is something that develops over time.

Let's assume it is more difficult to develop in new, migratory societies. Let's assume that at a particular moment it appears, for some reason it appears; let's assume there are situations in which people think it is better for them— in their own interest—to ally themselves with other similar people rather than screw them over.

Let's assume that from that point on stories are told that confirm you should be nice and generous to others who live like you, that you should show solidarity to those who live the way you do.

Let's assume that this idea of "living like you" is created out of certain social and economic parameters rather than religion, race, family. This, in fact, was the most critical assumption made in modern politics: that each social sector has common interests, which make it in their interest to defend them in common.

Let's assume this will someday be the case.

I was in Kamrangirchar sitting on a stone bench, daydreaming as I watched the boats go by on the Buriganga River. Multicolored plastic wash basins, modernity at its most crass, piled into a wooden boat with a boatman using a bamboo oar. It was seven-thirty or eight in the morning; the sun was still mild. The two little girls looked at me for a moment, said they wanted a picture, and so I took a picture of them. One must have been ten years old, the other seven; one wore a black sari with white polka dots, had short hair, and a suspicious look in her eye; the other, wear-ing a yellow, slightly torn dress, had a shining smile. Then an old woman approached me with a strange expression on her face; her teeth were very red from betel leaves, though her green sari wasn't that threadbare, her nails were filthy. She started to talk, a cascade of Bengali words; I tried as hard as I could to make something out, but I couldn't understand a word. Then she forwent spoken language and switched to gestures, gesticula-tions. Pointing at the two girls, she raised two fingers, then one, and then pushed down with her hand. Then I understood: she wanted to sell me both of them for the price of one, a bargain. I didn't know if I should have believed what I thought, but I couldn't find anything else to believe. The girls kept their eyes on the ground in front of them.

Then, without warning, the woman started shouting at me, walked around me, shaking her finger at me in admonition; people began to gather. She looked at them, pointed at me again, her face expressing nothing but disdain. I think that to take revenge on me for my indiffer-ence, she was accusing me of something horrible, perhaps of wanting to buy the two girls. More and more people crowded around and closed in on me. It seemed I had to leave before I found out what would happen next. To know—as is often the case—came at too high a price.

I moved on. The calm was provincial. Or dead, or obstinate. Dogs slept soundly despite the thousands of flies surrounding them. The sun heated the earth to a hundred degrees Fahrenheit, not a touch of wind rustled the leaves on the skinny trees. Children ran, jumped, shouted: a swirl of children is always part of a neighborhood calm. Rickshaws rode down the potholed street along with a few motorbikes, a cart loaded with bricks pulled by people, people carrying pyramids of plastic buckets or aluminum pots on their heads. On one side of the street were shacks, a house or two, makeshift factories that manufactured these buckets, those pots, these big colorful cylinders. Many of the workers were children.

Abdel and his companions worked twelve hours a day taking plastic baskets out of a fairly new-looking machine in a shed with a dirt floor that had three other machines, another ten children, and a young boss with gelled hair and a hesitant smile who was counting silver prayer beads while the others labored. Abdel told me that he was lucky to have gotten this job, they didn't pay much but his father, who couldn't make ends meet alone, had told him that it was high time he started bringing home some food. He would be tired after his shift, but not tired enough for a game of cricket with his friends. Abdel told me that he had hoped to one day play on television—he didn't say play professionally or name a team, he simply said "on television." Abdel had just started a few months earlier. He took the baskets and handed them to another child who sat at the door of the shed with a pile of baskets and a little knife in his hand, which he used to cut off any burrs.

"I'd rather have his job than mine." Abdel looked at the burr cutter with a bit of envy.

"Why? Does it pay more?"

"No, but don't you see where he's sitting? He can watch people, see the street, the sun."

Out of the thirty-five million Bangladeshi children between five and fourteen years old, almost five million worked. In Kamrangirchar alone, half the children within that age bracket work. Their families didn't have enough money for them to have the luxury to allow their children not to, not to mention the money to send them to school. In Kamrangirchar, only one out of ten children attended school.

Few things rile the good Western conscience more than children working. I wanted to know why. In other words: to find out when, where, how the idea was born that children had rights that their parents didn't. How was it that at some point we assigned children the right to leisure, education, social assistance, and idleness, and not their parents; the right, or even the potential. Children deemed people who were still not what they were going to be and therefore contained the possibility of being something different. Children and their illusory right to be different whereas their parents were already living out these life sentences (children were, too, but that's the part that horrified us). I think it's horrible that children work like donkeys and that adults work like donkeys, and I'm happy that disapproval of the former is the norm, but I don't understand why not the latter. Was it that babies were innocent and defenseless and therefore all adults were obliged, based on Western logic, to sacrifice their lives to protect them? In how many cases were we just postponing their own life sentences?

Young and old, all were busy. Small factories of plastic basins where the colorful burrs collected on the ground like turds of modern art; shacks where women dressed in the most classic fabrics sorted the soda bottle tops according to color; yards where three or four children were separating out rags from mountains of garbage—serious, focused, determined not to make any mistakes; the street next to the river where dozens and dozens of rickshaw drivers awaited their customers, while a few yards further down, at the shore, dozens and dozens of boatmen—older, more fortunate—stood at the prow of their wooden boats. Big kiosks and little kiosks, big stalls and little stalls, where men and women sold—or at least tried to sell—candy, drinks, fish, donuts, hot fried food, cut fruit, all to the delight of the flies; empty lots where two eight-year-old children came and went with bamboo sticks, on each of which was hanging brightly colored lining; fabricated balloons dried in the sun; bricklayers erected houses brick by brick on frames made of thousands of bamboo canes; porters carried fifty-pound bags of rice or a dozen metal basins or a tree trunk or a pile of bricks on their heads; the factories of pots and pans; women washed in the black water river; men and women bathing in the black water river; children who idled around; haircutters shut away in their little metal caves, their walls covered with pieces of mirror; the kneaders and fryers of naan with their pans of oil always boiling; and the smell, above everything the smell, the brutal smell of ancient river filth that we from Buenos Aires call *riachuelo*—river sludge—but this black water was much worse, like one long stream of liquid shit.

A river black as tar, the Buriganga. Fish could still live in it. Not people: ecology didn't allow that. Not normally. But that rule didn't seem to apply here. On its slow flowing waters, the wooden boats rode down with the prows proudly raised past broken-down barges and ferries and pieces of plastic and an abundance of shit. The Buriganga was putrid like no other river I had ever seen, and yet here people were, using it to live.

Facing the Buriganga; on the side I was on, in front of one of the few three-story buildings on the island, a hundred small women stood in line holding babies in their arms. They were all wearing colorful saris; they were all thin and their faces looked patient; the children each had a thick black mole painted on the left side of their foreheads to protect them from the evil spirits, who, if they thought they were beautiful, would want to attack them. Spirits that were vain, conceited, jealous. A mark that made children appear ugly would also help them avoid the dangers of being beautiful. The ugliest children cried most quietly, all children were comforted by their mothers. It was eight in the morning, and at the door to the three-story office building across from the Buriganga River, women waited for the MSF professionals to see them.

"You have to let them nurse, give them all the milk you can."

"Are you sure, doctor?"

"Yes, of course I am."

"But really sure? How is it possible that with only the milk that comes out of me my baby will have everything he needs?"

Hunger was always part of their lives. Sometimes they didn't eat at some point during the day, sometimes they didn't eat all day, sometimes for two days in a row. And they knew that hunger was something they couldn't cure.

ON HUNGER: COMPETITION

1

When I was born, in 1957, I was one of 2.95 billion people on the planet. That was humbling enough, how to be a distinct, unique individual among 2,949,999,999 other inhabitants. And now anyone seeking to do so would encounter a number close to triple that, 7.7 billion as of 2019.

Two thousand years ago, at that conventional cutoff point that coincides with the demise of a prophet whose life we know less than his death, there were 300 million people in the world—and the number was increasing very slowly. It took humans more than fifteen centuries to double their numbers—then things accelerated. Around 1900 there were 1.7 billion, and in 1950, 2.5 billion. They say that on October 12, 1999, we reached 6 billion. They say that in 2050 we'll be—they'll be?—about 9 billion, and that regional balances will continue to shift. Asia will still have more than half the world's population, but Europe, with almost a quarter at the end of the last century, won't reach even 7 percent. On the other hand, the proportion of Africans in the world population will double, reaching one fifth of the total.

We are many, and we keep increasing at an exponential rate. When historians look back with the necessary perspective, they will say that the most distinctive characteristic of this era was the unprecedented proliferation of humans. (And that quote from Borges will not be allowed: "Mirrors and copulation are abominable because they multiply the numbers of men.")[1]

But they will also study with due care how a planet that for centuries could not feed its 500 million humans, could suddenly effectively feed 5 billion. It is one of the most extraordinary achievements in human history.

Hunger has many causes. The lack of food is no longer one of them.

In 1970, Aase Lionaes, the president of the Nobel committee, announced that they had awarded the peace prize to "a scientist, Dr. Norman Ernest Borlaug, because, more than any other single person of this age, he ha[d] helped to provide bread for a hungry world. We have made this choice in the hope that providing bread will also give the world peace." Lionaes went on to say that, "the world has been oscillating between fears of two catastrophes—the population explosion and the atom bomb. Both pose a mortal threat. In this intolerable situation, with the menace of doomsday hanging over us, Dr. Borlaug comes onto the stage and cuts the Gordian knot. He has given us a well-founded hope, an alternative of peace and of life—the Green Revolution."[2]

It was, they said, a source of constant concern. In 1974, Henry Kissinger, Richard Nixon's secretary of state, called a conference in Rome to discuss antihunger policies—and he closed it by saying that "within the decade, no child will go to bed hungry."[3] Then the decade passed. The year 1984 was always destined to be a problematic one.

But even prior to that date, the Malthusian alarm had been widely sounded. In 1968 Paul Ehrlich, a professor of biology at Stanford University, published a book that caused a furor. *The Population Bomb* began by stating that "The battle to feed all of humanity is over. In the seventies hundreds of millions of people will starve to death in spite of any crash programs embarked upon now. At this late date nothing can prevent a substantial increase in the world death rate . . ."[4]

Ehrlich said that the only possible course of action that would attenuate the catastrophe in the long term was to limit the rate of demographic growth to zero or less. To do so, one could, among other things, add to the food and drink in the most prolific—poor—a "temporary sterilant."[5] And that the United States should determine its foreign aid based on the capacity of each country to control its birth rate. India, for example, didn't know how, so shouldn't receive anything; it was money down the drain, better to let the population decrease—self-regulation through hunger—as much as necessary, said Dr. Ehrlich and his good wife. And, surprise, they didn't arrest him; instead, they appeared on the Johnny Carson Show, sold cartloads of books, and got rich. The end of the world has always been good business.

As it has been for certain highly distinguished institutions, like the Club of Rome. It's report, *Limits to Growth*, prepared by MIT scientists and published in 1972, sold more than thirty million copies and was read as the Holy Grail. The work explained, with a great deployment of statistics and models, that important natural resources were running out and that, therefore, humanity would enter into a catastrophic period and the population would be seriously reduced, resulting in wars, famines, and various other evils.[6]

Here we are. There's nothing sadder than the apocalypse, because it never fulfills its destiny. Malthusianism—recurrent, stubborn—is the caricature, the extreme form of a much more common mind-set: the temptation to think about the future by extrapolating from the conditions of the present. In general, Malthusians assume that if the population continues to increase, it will not be able to feed itself, according to the current conditions of food production. They do not take into account the historic evidence that, granted imbalances and periods of crisis, production tends to adapt to the increase in demand, and vice versa.

There is nothing more reactionary or more conservative than to think of the future world with the characteristics of the present and transplant to that constant context a single different variable, in this case, increased demand for food due to demographic growth.

And, of course, to be horrified by the results.

In 1970, just under a quarter of the 3.7 billion –approximately 880 million—people in the world at that time went hungry. The effects of the Green Revolution were decisive in improving the situation in Asia, especially in China and India. The number of hungry remained stable, but demographic growth decreased the proportion.

In 1980, 850 million undernourished were 21 percent of the population. In 1990, 840 million were 16 percent. In 1995, the number of hungry people reached its historical minimum. According to the FAO, they were 790 million, or 14 percent of the world population. International organizations were gushing with optimism and announced that the battle against hunger was coming to a victorious end.

We cared about this battle because it sustained the fantasy that the world at large cared about the world at large, a story the United Nations was very useful for telling. An extension of Roosevelt's original fear, however, is what really gave it its exuberance As long as there were two blocs—the Soviet one and "ours"—neither wanted sectors in their domains to be in the kind of crisis that would make them threaten to move over to the other side; it was useful, therefore, and even necessary, to feed them.

Almost nobody dared suggest that hunger—being hungry—might be a god's punishment for disobedience. But the Malthusian vulgate continues to prevail: if the poor are hungry it's because they have too many children. Which doesn't mean it's not true, in the final analysis, so final it doesn't explain anything. For starters: those who have a lot of babies still have no—medical, food— certainty that their children will survive infancy. Next: currently, if their children don't have sufficient food and medicine, it is not because they are many but because others are hoarding, leaving them with very little.

In the meantime, there were other justifications, many of which still stand even today. For decades there have been an abundance of sanctimonious papers—"international" European North American—that usually start with an intrepid truth: the principle cause of hunger in the world is poverty. Seems logical, almost a platitude. It is, however, pure rhetorical mystification. They could say, perhaps, and it would be totally different, that the poor are hungry because they don't have enough money to buy food, but poverty and hunger do not have a cause and effect relationship; in fact, they share the same cause. They are different forms of the same privation, the same plunder. The principal cause of hunger in the world is wealth: the fact that a few have what many need, even when it comes to food.

Then come the slightly more complex strands of justifications, about hunger being the result of other structural problems. "To end hunger, we must improve education," is a contemporary classic, which is also partially true. But: in the majority of poor countries the education of the poorest sectors does not train them to better earn their livings. Among those it does, many decide to cash in on this education by emigrating to wealthier countries, which receive them with open arms. For example, cheap nurses from Zimbabwe or Suriname are readily hired while the clamor for more education in Suriname or Zimbabwe continues unabated.

The most often reiterated strand insists that the governments in poor countries are corrupt and divert the aid that should go to feed their citizens. It's true: they are corrupt, and they do steal money. I am reminded of words of Sor Juana Inés de la Cruz: "Hombres necios que acusáis / a la mujer sin razón, / sin ver que sois la ocasión / de lo mismo que culpáis." [You foolish men who wrongly / accuse women / not seeing that you are to blame / for the evil you condemn.]⁷ Those corrupt governments stay in power with the support of those same Western governments and organizations that complain about their venality; they need them to obtain raw materials and military advantages, and now they are losing them to the Chinese, who complain less and offer them the same deals, though a little bit better.

Again: if those countries are poor it is mostly because they were colonies and their owners designed them for their own benefit, and they continue to occupy, albeit in a different way, that peripheral place in the global system. Because they are still the Other World.

In the midst of all these explanations, one—a near clone of an Adam Smith dictum—arose with a lot of strength in the eighties: If there were still hundreds of millions of hungry people, it was due to state interference in the economies of those countries that did not allow the market to do its job, to shower the people with its blessings.

The idea was part of the offensive against any regulation of capitalism, which began in those years. In the nineties, after the fall of the Berlin Wall and the supposed end of history, there was no longer anything standing in its way. The story is well-known: taking advantage of the debts the poor countries had contracted with the large international banks in the seventies—when the big banks had too much liquidity and convinced the poor countries to accept loans—the International Monetary Fund (IMF) and the World Bank imposed neoliberal policies on them. Their officials, with the power of coercion granted to them from the debts, turned into the new colonial administrators, disembarking in the capitals of hundreds of countries with the power to impose complete economic systems. Reagan and Bush in the United States, Thatcher in Great Britain, and Kohl in German were the political-military leaders who backed this offensive.

The majority of their measures reinforced hunger. Devaluation of national currencies raised the price of any imported or exportable food; reduction of the state apparatus left millions of unemployed in the streets; privatizations increased the costs of public services and left the poor with even less money to buy food; destruction of public health systems made it more difficult for the malnourished, subjected to more illnesses, to obtain treatment.

The spending reduction plans, in their crusade to give the market precedence over national regulations, included the lifting of controls on food imports, which forced the producers in the poor countries to compete with the subsidized prices of production in the rich ones. The IMF and the World Bank said that those controls distorted the functioning of the market, but they never considered other "distortions" that the rich states introduced into the market: the most extreme form of protectionism paid out in the billions of dollars in agricultural subsidies. At the Uruguay Round between 1986 and 1993, during the negotiations that led to the formation of the World Trade Organization (WTO), many countries were forced to lower their customs barriers and their agricultural subsidies. At the same time, the United States, Europe, and Japan increased subsidies to their farmers so they could grow food even more cheaply and take over those markets.

The integration of countries into the global marketplace, which redefined the role of each one and restructured local production so it could adapt to those markets (exchanging sustenance farming to export farming), led to many peasants losing their lands and their livelihood, and forced them to migrate to the peripheries of the cities. Those who remained could no longer grow their own food, and often had to work for the new landowners for starvation wages.

In many countries the policies of the IMF and the World Bank also included the elimination of subsidized food and regulating mechanisms for internal pricing, which their states had implemented through the maintenance of reserves of grain and other food products. In cases such as Niger, the effect was straightforward: thousands of people died from hunger, plain and simple.

The Washington Consensus. How horrible—for a man, for a city—to be inscribed in history with the name of a policy that screwed over so many millions of people.

The capitalist offensive of the eighties and nineties also produced a more generalized and significant phenomenon: basic decisions about a country's economy were made at IMF and World Bank headquarters—in Washington—wresting from national authority almost all their power. Elections held for these new democracies seemed more and more like an unnecessary farce. Without the state's mediation of social and economic conflicts, the poor were left even more defenseless and at the mercy of the decisions of the wealthy.

"The main single cause of increases in poverty and inequality during the 1980s and 1990s was the retreat of the state," states *The Challenge of Slums*, the UN organization Habitat's Global Report.[8]

However, sometimes we forget how much the lives of many people have improved. In 1851, for example, in London—the capital of the empire at that time—one-third of the women between the ages of fifteen and twenty-five worked as domestic servants, and another third were prostitutes.

That's just one example, among many. If there weren't hundreds of millions of hungry people, some would be able to say that the system has been successful, that we don't need a different one. As it is, many say it anyway.

Again, from *The Challenge of Slums*:

> "During the 1990s, trade continued to expand at an almost unprecedented rate, no-go areas opened up, and military expenditure decreased. New communications technologies, such as the internet, reduced the tyranny of distance, improved productivity and made it possible for people in developing countries or remote areas to share in knowledge and engage in types of work that would have previously been unthinkable. All the basic inputs to production became cheaper, as interest rates fell rapidly, along with the price of basic commodities.

Capital flows were increasingly unfettered by national controls and could move rapidly to the most productive areas. Under what were almost perfect economic conditions according to the dominant neoliberal economic doctrine, one might have imagined that the decade would have been one of unrivalled prosperity and social justice."[9]

Nevertheless, the report continues, "an unprecedented number of countries saw a decrease in development from the 1990s through to the second decade of this century.

But during the mid-nineties to the late aughts, hundreds of millions of Africans, Latin Americans, and South Asians not only ate less, but their entire lives changed. In the enormous slums of the Other World, men left without work turned over their place as head of the household to their wives, who found jobs as domestic servants or selling food on the street. Their children stopped attending school to help with odd jobs—or, often, to do nothing and get involved in more or less criminal activities. Jobs on the black market grew exponentially; the possibility of demanding decent working conditions became more and more utopian. Migration multiplied among those who could manage it. For those who couldn't, the possibilities of social improvements disappeared; the future—a word without much meaning—ended up looking much too similar to the present.

In their classic study, *Free Markets and Food Riots* (1994), authors John K. Walton and David Seddon note almost 150 protests against the IMF between 1976 and 1992 in these countries.[10] Most started as food riots. During the 1990s the tendency was clear: the number of hungry people started to increase again, reaching about 850 million and continuing upward. One of the worst food crises of recent times was being gestated. But behind it, almost silently, far away from the limelight, it was a market that struck first.

THE UNITED STATES: INDUSTRIES OF HUNGER

1

The Tribune Tower is an idea of the world. Home to the eponymous newspaper it rises tall and audacious above downtown Chicago. Its Gothic entryway is like standing before the doors of a cathedral; an elaborate design of stonemasonry—cobbled to resemble characters from Aesop's Fables—make up the façade. Off to the side is another display, a wall that includes a stone from notable manmade locations—the Taj Mahal, the Great Wall of China, Westminster Abbey, the Parthenon in Athens, among others—and all jutting out as if the wall had been unable to digest so many pieces of the world.

Mindless of the exquisite architecture were a kit of pigeons that flew about the spires and towers without an apparent logic to their direction. Their wings shimmered in the air, their movements were like a wave, beautiful without effort. It wasn't until one pigeon, presumably the head of the flock, appeared as if from nowhere that the others found an apparent focus to their flight. She placed herself at the head of the group who then fell behind her, following her movements as if they had become a single entity, gliding with ease through the trashing windy city.

> It's very simple, brothers and sisters, very simple. Everything is written in this book, and all you have to do is study and obey what the book says and you will have the best possible life, here and to eternity, all of eternity.

Preaching from a sidewalk was a black woman wearing blue jeans and a jacket, big glasses, and a tremendously compassionate smile on her face.

> Look, come: study and obey and you will have the best possible life . . .

In these streets, there were thousands of people, a homogenous rushing force of people, an electric current that flowed between these high-rise centers of power. They seemed to colonize the air, fragmenting it, transforming it, into symbols of American dominion. I didn't know of many places where a system—of ideas, of power, of business—had established itself so imperiously. Chicago is a celebration of the best architecture money can buy—forty, fifty corporate buildings constructed over the last hundred years, each of which would qualify as the best of Buenos Aires, two or three of which would qualify among the best of Beijing. One of the city's first designers, Daniel Burnham, proclaimed a foundational dictum: "Make no little plans; they have no magic to stir men's blood." In Chicago, the buildings retained their necessary magic, this required loquacity; they asserted, without a shadow of a doubt, who their owners were. No modest shops or buildings, no shantytowns or shops hawking knockoff items, no different order existed below them, only a solitary street preacher, sermonizing to people who would soon be elevated to the skies far above her.

She took a break; it must've been difficult to project one's voice for such a long time. A fifty- or sixty-year-old white male—dirty, unshaven, clothed in a seedy down jacket— approached her to confirm if all he needed to do was study and obey.

"If I wasn't sure, I wouldn't say so. Don't you believe?"

"Nope."

The sidewalks were impeccably clean; the display windows sparkled. Women and men walked by in uniform: for her, a skirt or pants suit, heels, and a purse; for him, a dark suit with a light-colored shirt. The white man wasn't satisfied with the black woman's answer and wandered off. I watched him make his way to a refuge, one I had not spotted though it was only ten yards away. It was a piece of cardboard on the ground, and on the cardboard, a torn bag, a brown or very dirty blanket, a blue plastic plate with a few coins in it. Next to his refuge was a sign on which he (presumably) had written: *Jobless. Homeless. Hungry. Any help goes a long way.*

And this was when I began to notice them: the beggars. Every couple of blocks, below these fortresses of capitalism, on the squeaky-clean sidewalks, there'd be one sitting with signs indicating that he or she didn't have anything to eat.

> Everything's written in the book, my friends. If you don't read
> it, if you don't do what it says, you are to blame and you will be
> condemned.

This was supposed to be one of the most successful cities in one of the most successful nations in the contemporary world. Yet as I wandered around that morning, Chicago, at least its downtown, began to make less sense to me. Chicago prided itself as a city of the people, yet it seemed to be a city that required a bit of privilege for it to open up to you. It required working so many hours a day, climbing the floors of these urban castles, until you could revel in superfluous expenditures—glitzy merchandise to toss aside after a season or two, comforting accommodations that you'd put to use but once, expensive meals to be left half-eaten and thrown out—until you were not able to live without them. I wondered if any of these beggars had once been privileged. I wondered if everyone else would one day wake up and ask, what's the point of all this?

(What is generally agreed upon to be necessary and indispensable— food, health, clothing, housing—is an increasingly minor percentage of what makes us happy. This is how to measure the success of a society, by the proportion of unnecessary goods it consumes. To bring a society more toward an egalitarian state, therefore, less emphasis would have to put on individual happiness and more would have to be put toward communal happiness. But of course, not everyone would be happy with that.)

The book will tell you everything!

I left the preacher and the Tribune Tower and made my way south toward the Chicago Board of Trade building. It was hard to miss: a massive, impenetrable block of enormous stones and tiny windows, and at the very top, a 30-foot-high statue of Ceres, the Roman goddess of agriculture, holding a bag of corn in one hand and a sheaf of wheat in the other. Down below, next to the door, carved letters read "Chicago Board of Trade." The building was inaugurated in 1930 while the United States was descending into the most severe agricultural crisis in its history. The stars and stripes, a sign of American prosperity and health, were now draped everywhere.

"Welcome to the Chicago Board of Trade."

A man I'll call Leslie—he insisted I not use his real name—greeted me in the lobby with a professional smile. He was a trader for one of the four or five largest grain companies in the world—he insisted that I not name it either—a company nonetheless that not only moved grain, but billions of dollars a year of it. We made our way to the elevators. After passing through security we were directed to the ones that would take us up to the floor of the Chicago Mercantile Exchange (CME). He was wearing a very pink jacket, which he explained, after he noticed that I kept looking at it, that the jacket's color was intentional.

"It's Breast Cancer Awareness Month, so all the traders wear pink sports coats."

I asked why and he looked at me as if the answer were obvious.

"To make people aware of breast cancer."

I didn't respond that colors didn't immediately bring to mind causes, or that Argentines were much less subtle in recognizing causes, such as putting the world's biggest condom on the huge obelisk in downtown Buenos Aires for World Aids Day. Instead, I nodded dumbly, just as we reached the floor of the exchange.

"All the activity you are about to see might seem a bit confusing," he told me, "but I'll explain it until you understand it."

It sounded like a warning. Then the doors opened and there before me was the buzzing world of the Exchange.

The CME closed in 2015 after being open for 167 years, but at the time of my visit, in 2012, it was a brain of commerce more than fifty thousand square feet, or in farming terminology, over an acre of traders and computers and electronic screens. Leslie led me onto the octagonal floor and, though I tried to keep focused on following him, my eyes were drawn up the high ceiling where a halo of lights showed thousands of numbers. Leslie explained that these marquees—green, yellow, and red diodes rising and falling in quick succession—indicated fluctuating price numbers, quantities of purchased and sold stock, things that would affect market prices everywhere in the world, numbers crunched into commercial data.

The floor of the Chicago Mercantile Exchange was divided into a honeycomb of specialized pits. There was one for corn, one for wheat, one for soy, and further divided from there into current day value, future market value, and type of product. Leslie directed me to the soy pit where three or four dozen traders, many wearing pink jackets and looking very bored, sat waiting for a change, any change, in the soy market. I watched one glance up from his paper to look at me, then up at the marquee, then back at his paper. Another fiddling with a pager-like device on his belt didn't bother to look up at all. We stood there all, inert, and I began to feel something of boredom being there as well, when from beyond the pit someone shouted something I couldn't quite understand. In an instant, papers and phones were down and everyone was on their feet. They spoke hurriedly among themselves and shouted back at the disembodied voice, hoisting up their blank ticket books, gesturing numbers with their fists and fingers, looking nervously at the devices on their waists, the numbers on the ceiling. It was like being in a cage full of pugilistic roosters, everyone trying to muscle in on a trade. And then, just as quickly as it had erupted, the movement dissolved, and everyone slipped back into catatonia.

"Here, everything means something, or at least we like to believe that," Leslie told me. He walked me through the gestures—the hand-speak used by the traders—demonstrating how the palm facing in or out, the fingers together or spread, at chest or face level indicated whether I was buying or selling, for how many and for how much.

"It seems chaotic, but everybody understands one another."

"It also seems quite boring when it is not chaotic."

"Well, because now almost everything is done on computers. Only a few years ago, there were days where you couldn't even walk, it was so full of people."

Those days were obviously over. The intermittent outbursts of the traders were like the roars of a centenarian dinosaur, a mime to honor an adventurous past. Everything seemed a little forced, a little nostalgic. It was hard to believe that the entire business of trading had once been essentially the pandemonium on the pits. As nearly all of it has been decentralized as trading became conducted on computer monitors across the globe, the CME had become obsolete.

To be sure, I asked Leslie if he thought this place, this temple of capitalism, was going to last.

"The CME has been here more than one hundred and fifty years; I've spent half my life here. I can't imagine not coming here anymore."

"So you think it's going to eventually close?"

"As difficult as it is to accept, I think the days of a physical floor where everything is bought and sold are numbered. But the CME will remain the place where the price that is paid—charged—is fixed for the entire world."

In other words, something had to determine what was a fair market price, even if it meant that some people got priced out, even if it meant that some people wouldn't eat. I suddenly remembered afternoons in Dahka, nights in Madaoua, when I thought about what "the floor" would be like, a place where so much was at stake. And I wondered if people here had ever thought about the impact these prices had for people living in places like Dahka or Madaoua. I expressed this to Leslie who was quick to defend the merits of the CME.

"The market is the best regulatory mechanism to maintain prices where they should be. Nobody can control the market, not even the most powerful speculators."

Another trader, a big man who sweated copiously, chimed in. "It's this place that keeps the cost of food low in the whole world."

I tried not to judge what he was telling me. Instead I asked him to clarify.

"Look, the CME is a transparent market, there is no secret business that determines the price. People and companies risk their money on a product such as soy, and that determines the value of soy. And from the value, we can determine a fair price. That's what we do. And, of course, we earn money doing it, otherwise we wouldn't do it."

I listened to him; I didn't pull a face.

The Chicago Mercantile Exchange, he continued, was created as a way of stabilizing prices, especially in the agricultural market. It's great innovation in the middle of the nineteenth century was futures contracts—now just "futures"—in which a producer and a dealer signed a document that committed the former to selling and the latter to buying a certain amount of wheat on a certain date for a certain amount of money, no matter if that price had risen or fell. The Exchange guaranteed that the contract would be honored. In this way, farmers knew before they harvested how much they would earn for their grain, and the dealers who processed it knew how much they'd have to pay. It was, at least early on, a very useful function.

"What is agriculture, deep down?" asked the obese trader. "It's taking a pile of money, burying it in the form of a grain, let's say soy, and then digging it up six months later. The problem is that while I may know, at the time I plant the soy, the cost of seed, labor, and fertilizer, it might change when I harvest it, which due to so many factors, might not be what I thought I'd yield, meaning I may not make much of that money back, not if there is a surplus and the price of the grain I plant drops. So it would be beneficial to have a way of insuring myself against a season that isn't in my favor. But say the season is bad, and many farmers are yielding poor results, then the price of whatever crop I have planted will suddenly soar. And so now it's the industrialist or the rancher who needs to be protected from skyrocketing prices. So, we reach an agreement, based on past and present data, on the price for my harvest. These are futures contracts: commitments to buy and sell something that doesn't yet exist. That's why they call it a 'derivatives market,' because the price of the future is derived from the current price of those same products. That's what helps me establish a price. Helps, but isn't the only determining factor. Since the market needs volume, not only I, who produce the soy, and you, who buys it, participate, but also the guy who thinks that the price we agreed on is too low or too high. That guy, who's called a speculator, he gives volume and liquidity to the market, and makes it so that the prices of those futures are reliable."

"There are new players now," Leslie said, "banks and funds that got involved in the whole thing; before it was a market for producers and consumers, and now it's turned into a place for financial games, speculation. This all began at the tail end of the Reagan years, when millions of jobs had disappeared—and millions of workers had been laid off—because giant corporations could "relocate"' their factories in other countries, when workers' salaries remained frozen even though their productivity rose by almost 50 percent, and when taxes for the wealthiest dropped by half, which among other reasons gave those rich people a lot of idle money they wanted to 'invest' in something that would make them more. I don't like it very much, but what can I do. I have to keep playing the game; it's my job. All of it can be summed up pretty easily." he said. "All these guys want to make money. What do they do to make money? Now, there are lots of ways, but you have to know what they are and be capable of manipulating them. You can short the market, take a long position, take exit and entry positions in two minutes flat. There are more and more ways to make money on this. There are countries—like this one—where you can say that there are people who do something 'only to make money.' In general, though, it's tough to say that someone makes the price of food rise only to make money. So, there are justifications: the price of grain rises because of the increase in Chinese demand, the pressure of biofuels, climatic factors, etc."

Leslie was a charming person, overflowing with good intentions. His colleagues—the traders he introduced me to on the floor of the CME—also seemed to be decent people. Some worked for large grain corporations, others for banks or investment funds, others were independent and playing with their own money, buying and selling, though they probably had the backing of some financier whom they charged commissions on every trade they made. They were people who made me wonder what good their work actually had on the world?

"Do you ever think about the cost in the real world of what you do?" I asked Leslie.

"What kind of cost do you mean? The economic cost, the social cost? What kind of cost are you talking about? There are many kinds of costs."

In a piece for *Harper's* in 2010, the journalist Frederick Kaufman wrote:

> The history of food took an ominous turn in 1991, at a time when no one was paying much attention. That was the year Goldman Sachs decided our daily bread might make an excellent investment. Agriculture, rooted as it is in the rhythms of

reaping and sowing, had not traditionally engaged the attention of Wall Street bankers, whose riches did not come from the sale of real things like wheat or bread but from the manipulation of ethereal concepts like risk and collateralized debt.

But in 1991 nearly everything else that could be recast as a financial abstraction had already been considered. Food was pretty much all that was left. And so with accustomed care and precision, Goldman's analysts went about transforming food into a concept. They selected eighteen commodifiable ingredients and contrived a financial elixir that included cattle, coffee, cocoa, corn, hogs, and a variety or two of wheat. They weighted the investment value of each Commodity Index. Then they began to offer shares.

As was usually the case, Goldman's product flourished. The prices of cattle, coffee, cocoa, corn, and wheat began to rise, slowly at first, and then rapidly. And as more people sank money into Goldman's food index, other bankers took note and created their own food indexes for their own clients. Investors were delighted to see the value of their venture increase, but the rising price of breakfast, lunch, and dinner did not align with the interests of those of us who eat. And so, the commodity index funds began to cause problems. Food became financialized. Food became an investment like oil, gold, silver, or any stock . . . And those who can't pay the price, pay with hunger.[1]

Leslie kept his promise to explain how the market worked *until I understood.* And I was beginning to understand, but perhaps not in the way he intended. I understood that options are bought and sold all the time, nonstop. I understood too that the price of soy one day, may not be the price of soy the day after tomorrow or next month, that the price of soy was just a number, but one that had to be foreseen with the greatest precision possible to be able to profit from its variances. But it seemed to me that it was as predictable as betting on what the exact temperature in St. Louis would be like every day for a year, or betting on the number of burps that would erupt from fourteen liquid silicon salesmen during an hour-long business dinner. There are so many things one could bet on that wouldn't change the lives of millions of people. But when grain is the basis for a speculation game it can become the difference between eating and not eating.

The game is to keep track of the tiny daily or hourly or by-the-minute fluctuations in its value; these tiny differences, if the quantities are

significant, produce substantial differences. And because speculated calculations of the market can easily be mistaken, those who work in the
market, those who sing the market's praises, those who live so damn well
thanks to the market, make money on the mistakes of the market. And
nobody says—over their whiskies in the bar, or in business classes at the
university, or in their *Wall Street Journal* articles—that what they like
about the market is that it always makes mistakes that can be exploited.

But the mistakes of the market are the condition of their business.
If it didn't make mistakes, if the soy future for September 1 negotiated
this morning for $500 cost $500 in September 1, this temple would be
deserted, there would be no way to make a profit. Nobody would say this,
instead they recite their Eulogies, spread the Word, and tell you that the
Market is the cure for all that ails.

Long live its mistakes.

2

It could be said that a decade ago world hunger entered a new era, a
year when food and financial shortages caused widespread pandemonium. The prices for grains and legumes, measured by the bushel, had
for decades fluctuated between $2.50 and $4.00, with outlying and brief
spikes and dips depending on surplus and scant production years. But
in late 2006, prices began to climb and showed no sign of returning to
normal levels; it wasn't until mid-2007 that the price increases went out
of control and remained at critically high levels for more than a year. To
compare, in February 1998, the price of a bushel of wheat was $3.23. Eight
years later, in February 2006, it was $3.85. The following February, it was
$4.60. The price took off after that, climbing to higher and higher levels
and by February 2008, the price for a bushel of wheat hit a record level
high at $10.28. The food market has a "low demand elasticity," meaning
that no matter what happens with the supply, the demand doesn't really
change. If the prices of computers increase, one can hold off on buying
one till those prices settle down, but you can't hold off on eating.

The increase did not, of course, have only one cause. Worsening
weather conditions, pesticide resistant bugs, nutrient depleted soil,
diminishing global grain reserves and increased demand for meat were
thought to have increased the price, but perhaps none so much as the
rising cost of oil. Oil is vital for food production, in farm equipment,

as well as in its transportation, storage, and distribution. The British political philosopher John Gray once wrote: "Intensive agriculture is the extraction of food from petroleum."[2] He was tipping his hat to the statistic that it takes about ten fossil fuel calories to produce and transport each food calorie in the average American diet. A post for the Center for Ecoliteracy broke down the calculation further: "If your daily food intake is 2,000 food calories, then it took 20,000 fossil fuel calories to grow that food and get it to you. In more familiar units, this means that growing, processing, and delivering the food consumed by a family of four requires the equivalent each year of almost 34,000 kilowatt-hours (kWh) of energy, or more than 930 gallons of gasoline (for comparison, the average US household annually consumes about 10,800 kWh of electricity, and about 1,070 gallons of gasoline)."[3]

The price of oil affects the price of everything. Oil is the blood of the earth—goes an oft-used phrase—and whatever it costs, everything follows. Which is why, among other things, there have been many attempts to ween ourselves from being dependent upon it. And perhaps no attempt has had such an impact on the food industry than the rise of ethanol. During the last half of the twentieth century, agricultural technology improved like never before, subsidies to farmers increased, and yields skyrocketed to unprecedented heights. Yet agricultural experts didn't know what to do with so much corn, so much wheat. It seems like a joke that the United States was facing problem with few antecedents in the annals of human history: the overproduction of food. And the joke twists cruelly that this would be a problem in a world where so many people go hungry.

Among other effects, overproduction kept prices very low for a long time. One of the first uses of this surplus was political: under the guise of "foreign-aid," huge quantities of grain were exported (though not given away). Surplus grain also became a way to feed livestock. In the United States, cows, pigs, and chickens still eat 70 percent of all grain, and in turn, the consumption of meat across the world reached levels never before seen.

Other uses would follow, such as corn syrup—the great sweetener of the food industry—detergents, textiles, and finally, biofuels.

In the United States, ethanol is made from corn, one of the country's main crops. The United States produces 35 percent of the world's corn, more than 350 million tons a year. A federal law called the Renewable Fuel Standard, enacted by Congress in 2005, decreed that 40 percent of that grain should be used to fill gas tanks in cars. That is roughly one-sixth of global consumption of one of the most widely consumed foods in the world. The 375 pounds of corn needed to create enough E85 (an ethanol fuel blend of 85 percent denatured ethanol fuel and 15 percent gasoline or other hydrocarbon) to fill a single tank of gas would feed a child in Zambia or Mexico or Bangladesh for an entire year. One tank, one child, one year. And every year, nine hundred million gas tanks are filled. Every year, more than three million children die of starvation.

The former special rapporteur on food, Jean Ziegler, always unequivocal, said that the production of biofuels is "a crime against humanity."[4]

The laws and resolutions that subsidize ethanol mention "energy independence" and the "fight against climate change." The carbon footprint of biofuels, however, is heavy indeed. Frédéric Lemaître, a journalist for *Le Monde*, wrote that while that corn ethanol "has reduced the emissions of CO_2 from cars between 10 and 20 percent, if we factor in emissions from the tractors and the fertilizers and the pesticides necessary to produce it and transport it, and the electrical energy needed to process it, the ecological impact begins to look devastating."[5]

Not to mention that the increase in the demand for corn produced for ethanol means that people who eat corn were finding it in shorter and shorter supply. When many farmers in the Midwest stopped growing white corn, which is not used for ethanol, and started growing yellow, which is, the price of white corn flour in Mexico rose by more than 400 percent. Corn, which is used to make tortillas, is the food staple of Mexico. Because of the North American Free Trade Agreement (NAFTA), Mexico's corn industry had been waylaid by corn exported from its northern neighbor, which sold it to Mexico at aggressively cheap prices. When those vanished, the prices for American-grown corn soared, and Mexican farmers struggled to keep up with the demand. In January 2007, only a month after Felipe Calderón had been elected president, the crisis hit a peak with an estimated 75,000 people taking to the streets to demand Calderón bring down the prices and protect them from inflating again.

In Guatemala, where corn is also a staple, and where half of the children are malnourished, there were no protests. Before the signing of NAFTA, Guatemala produced almost all the corn it consumed. But after NAFTA was passed, American surplus corn was sold at extremely cheap prices, and the local peasants couldn't compete. In a single decade local production of corn fell by one-third. As a result, many landowners had to sell their farms to companies that now grow palm trees for oil and ethanol, and sugar cane for sugar and ethanol. But like Mexico, Guatemalans were hit hard by the reduced production of American white corn. Before the corn crisis, one quetzal could buy a peasant ten tortillas. During the crisis, a quetzal could only buy him or her four. Five corn tortillas weigh about an ounce, and it takes around fifteen ounces of tortillas to live off of each day. Meaning anything below ten tortillas for one quetzal would not be enough to feed a family of four.

I don't think anybody is doing it to hurt anybody. I mean, it's not that the authorities and the lobbies and the US farmers want to starve Guatemalan children. They simply want to increase their sales and their prices, depend less on oil, take care of the environment—and that produces certain secondary effects. What can they do? Shit happens, right?

Indeed, it does. Following the rising prices of food in 2008, America received a crisis of its own: the worst financial crash in US history. Big banks suffered what many called "the perfect storm"—a crisis that affected stocks, loans, and international trade all at the same time. Everything collapsed; money was out in the harshest weather, and there was no shelter to invest it in. And then they found a cave: the Chicago Mercantile Exchange, or more specifically, food. In 2003 investments in food commodity index funds amounted to about $13 billion; in 2008 that number reached $317 billion. Around the same time, the United States had one of its best ever wheat harvests in its history. So much of it was reaped, nearly 55 million tons, that, after-market sales, the US Department of Agriculture announced that there was still nearly 18 million tons of grain in reserve. Not only was this abnormal but it was an outlier: in nearly every other corner of the world, grain production had actually decreased. Which meant not only even higher prices, but while grain was piling up in silos in the Midwest, all that excess wheat went instead to animals who would later be slaughtered and sold as meat to people who could afford to eat it. And that number was increasing as well.

"There are three hundred and fifty million people in India who are classified as middle class." said George W. Bush in May 2008, at a speech given in New Delhi. "That's bigger than America. Your middle class is larger than our entire population. And when you start getting wealth, you start demanding better nutrition and better food. And so demand is high, and that causes the price to go up."[6] In other words, the increase in the price of food was the result of the increase in the buying power of an emerging middle class in developing nations, which allowed them to eat more of the kinds of food once thought to be a privilege, such as meat, thereby increasing the demand for food to feed animals.

While this and ethanol are part of reasons for the food crisis, the full picture is much more complicated and brutal. According to a UN report, every year about 12 million hectares (almost 30 million acres) become unusable. In the seventies, in developed nations, motorized pumps were introduced, and the quantity of water being extracted multiplied. While the rain replenished some aquifers; others, deeper underground, had a finite amount. The one in Ogallala, Nebraska, for example, has provided a third of the water used on farms in the United States, and it could dry up in less than three decades. Everywhere in the world there are similar hydrospheric concerns. Though a food crisis has yet to repeat itself (as of 2019, the price of grain bushels across the world have fallen back to precrisis level), the fear is such that response of several governments has been to reduce their export quotas in order to control local prices, thereby reducing the supply of food and forcing the cost of food up even further.

At a conference in 2008, then World Bank president Robert Zoellick said that such protectionism was the cause of the price increases and "more freedom in the markets" was needed.[7] Zoellick had held important economic positions in the Reagan and both Bush administrations, and had been the managing director of Goldman Sachs. But a report issued soon after from Zoellick's former employer Goldman Sachs—the inventors of the commodities index fund—negated Zoellick's claim by stating "without a doubt, the increase of funds invested in food commodities drove up prices."

The price of food rose everywhere, yet the increases did not affect everybody equally. When the price of wheat doubles in the United States, the price of bread increases between 5 and 10 percent. In Tunisia, Managua, or Delhi, on the other hand, bread—or the grain the women use to make bread or tortillas or chapati—can double, or even triple. This disparity can also be seen in developed countries where the average consumer spends less than 10 percent of their income on food with the poor living in those countries spending up to 25 or 30 percent of their income on food. In underdeveloped countries, people may spend half or even three quarters of their income on food, an unsustainable amount. It only takes a tiny increase in the price of food to condemn someone to hunger and, as was seen in Mexico, not everyone who is condemned to hunger will go toward their fate quietly. But when further hunger protests erupted in 2008, the consequences were much more dire.

In Egypt, for instance, thousands of workers and unemployed marched on the outskirts of Cairo to protest the rising price of wheat bread—which given the US surplus of wheat, seemed ridiculous. Egypt is the largest importer of wheat in the world; it produces only half of what it needs. In less than three years the price of bread, the staple food for forty million people below or hovering just around the poverty line, had increased by fivefold. During the protest the Egyptian police cracked down a peaceful demonstration, even going so far as to shoot a small boy through the forehead. With the death of a child adding to the fire, the Mubarak government eventually stood down and lowered the cost of bread, even importing enough to distribute to the poor as a sort of penitence.

The Cairo demonstrations weren't isolated; demonstrations were erupting all over the world. In Port-au-Prince, Haiti, hunger protests forced the prime minister to resign. In Cameroon, a protest of taxi drivers led to huge demonstrations against the price of food, and more than twenty protesters were killed. In Dhaka, thousands of protestors gathered to rally against an increase in the price of rice, which was then being traded for $1,000 a ton in Chicago after jumping from $195 a ton. The protest eventually turned violent with thousands burning down government subsidized food stores and killing owners that were selling at market prices. Reports of these demonstrations kept coming—in Senegal, in Mozambique, in Yemen, in Pakistan, in Indonesia, in Tajikistan, in Brazil, thousands of people were taking their governments to task by asserting their right to eat every day. Even in Milwaukee, where a quarter of the population lives below the poverty line, thousands of people got together one June night in front of city offices, where, they had heard, food coupons were going to be handed out. Nothing materialized and a riot ensued. By the time police managed to calm things down, downtown Milwaukee looked as though a bomb had erupted in it.

"Food is the new gold," wrote Anthony Faiola in *The Washington Post*, which meant above all that food had gone from being a consumer item to being a commodity for speculation and stockpiling, and not just any: a commodity whose price had risen more than any other in recent memory.[8]

For many, this meant they had stopped eating.

3

Leslie was a throwback, a dinosaur who was likely to go as extinct as his temple. His colleague, Diego was much more aware of the present, more aware of the temple being of the past, more aware that the future would include him but not it. Rather than go to work on an exchange floor, Diego conducted trades entirely from various devices—his computer, primarily, but also on his iPhone and iPad if needed—buying and selling grains from various corners of the world at speeds on-floor trading couldn't compete with. What was once an activity circumscribed by the hours of the day, from nine in the morning to one in the afternoon, the hours of the Chicago Mercantile Exchange, now trading could be done around the clock with Asian and European markets. Because of this Diego wasn't ever disconnected. When we met at a bar to talk about his work, his iPad was face up on the counter right next to him. I watched as numbers actively jumped around like something out of the *The Matrix*.

It was Diego's job to be a fortune-teller of data, of being able to predict how markets were going to behave before anybody else did—supply of grain X, demand for grain Y—to advise on profit maximizing purchases and sell for his corporation. To do this, he needed to absorb huge amounts of information, but since it wasn't possible to keep up with every detail about what might influence prices, he focused on data that displayed behavioral patterns of the market, doing his best to glean any hint that those patterns might shift. The market staring at its own belly button, waiting for signs of lint. At other times, he focused on the news. When the Fukushima nuclear plant exploded, for example, he rightly speculated that demand for Japanese grains would drop, a prediction that earned his company a few million dollars. But just as easily, he could misinterpret the signs and lose his company just as many millions.

"You deal with frighteningly huge amounts of money, don't you?" I said, still somewhat mesmerized by the dancing data on his screen.

Diego gave me a slow nod. "Oh yeah. I can't go to bed thinking that I am sitting on two hundred thousand tons of soy, and that tomorrow I might lose fifty dollars on each ton, because then I'd never fall asleep. So in order to put myself at a distance, I think of that money as Monopoly money, funny money, numbers on a screen."

Diego had a warm and convincing smile. While we spoke, he sipped on a Diet Coke. He had a noticeably high attention span. Not once did I notice him break from our conversation to glance around the room.

"Still, you have low points when you ask yourself what the hell you're doing. Sometimes they'll say, you idiot, you told me it was going to rise and it fell. But I'm not a wizard. If I knew every time the price of something like soy was going to rise and fall, I would have been able to retire long ago and focus on something like playing piano for the rest of my life. You have to shoulder the responsibility of what you are doing, but at the same time distance yourself, and say, okay, I'm just playing Monopoly."

"But you must be impressed by the quantities you're dealing with, which would be unthinkable for a normal person."

"I don't think I'm doing anything special. But I do think that some people are born to do this job, maybe because they have a little of the suicidal instinct that says, okay, I can distance myself, and there are others who can't, they say, oh, damn, I lost a hundred dollars . . . It's like a doctor who loses a patient; nobody wants to lose a patient, the family will be really upset, but the doctor keeps on living, he has his own life. If not, you'd kill yourself."

Killing yourself because you've lost a money for your company is one thing, killing yourself because you have no means of making a living at all is another. It took the 2008 food crisis to lower the ballooning cost of food back to levels many more people could afford. But two years later, prices climbed right back up to precrisis levels causing yet another wide-spread hunger panic. Perhaps the most spectacular effect—and I mean, spectacular—of this development was the Arab Spring, and unbelievably, such a monumental event was arguably and literally sparked by one man. Mohamed Bouazizi, was known to friends as Basbousa, an epithet that referenced a North African cake made from semolina and honey. But in fact, eating Basbousa cake was likely a luxury Bouazizi could not afford. He had lost his father when he was three years old, and from the age of thirteen, he had to earn money to help feed his mother and younger siblings. After working odd jobs, he began to sell fruits and vegetables out of a small wheelbarrow on the streets of his southern Tunisian town, Sidi Bouzid. He was known for his compassion toward others, saving money to help put his sister through school and giving some produce to people much poorer than even himself.

On December 10, 2010, Bouazizi had his cart confiscated for not having a proper permit. He argued with the policewoman, Faida Hamdy, who had stopped him, that in fact, a permit was not required by the city. He also incurred a sizeable debt to acquire the food he was selling. If she took away his cart, he pleaded, he would not be able to pay it back. There are conflicting reports on what happened next, whether Hamdy required a bribe, or whether she slapped him across the face to humiliate him, but by the end of the exchange, Bouazizi no longer had a barrow of food to sell. He then went to the mayor's office to complain, but nobody would admit Boauzizi inside. There, at the door, he shouted that he was ruined, that he couldn't go on living like this. He went to a gas station, used what little money he had to purchase a couple of gallons of gas, returned to the door of the governor's office, and poured the gasoline over himself. They say he shouted, one last time, how do you expect me to make a living, and then lit himself on fire.

A few days later, on December 18, Tunisia too went up in flames fueled by large-scale protests of Bouazizi's death. No one could have foreseen how far that fire would spread, but there were people already smelling the smoke. For *Foreign Policy*, in April 2011, the analyst Lester Brown wrote: "That's why the food crisis of 2011 is for real, and why it may bring with it yet more bread riots cum political revolutions. What if the upheavals that greeted dictators Zine el-Abidine Ben Ali in Tunisia, Hosni Mubarak in Egypt, and Muammar al-Qaddafi in Libya (a country that imports 90 percent of its grain) are not the end of the story, but the beginning of it? Get ready, farmers and foreign ministers alike, for a new era in which world food scarcity increasingly shapes global politics."[9]

Other analysts were seeing and saying the same thing: As Rami Zurayk, the author of *Food, Farming and Freedom: Sowing the Arab Spring* wrote for the *Guardian* a few months after Bouazizi's death: "The first protests of the Arab Spring in Tunisia in December 2010 were quickly dismissed as another bout of bread riots. Arab regimes responded by making adjustments to food prices and offering more subsidies. Increasing the subsidy slightly relieves the popular pressure but also increases the profit margins for importers and manufacturers. But this time round, truck-loads of flour did not do the trick. Three trading giants, Cargill, ADM, and Bunge control 90 percent of the global grain trade. They are all based in the United States. We know that if we do not improve food security we will remain hostage to those in power. Already the Egyptian interim government has decided to support farmers who produce wheat instead of the importers. It is too early to tell the extent of the program but advisers to the new Egyptian agriculture minister have confirmed that it includes higher prices paid for local wheat, seed supply, agricultural extension assistance, and improved local storage and transport.

We have tasted the bread of liberty and we want more of it."[10]

Diego worked for one of the four largest corporations trading in raw food material. They're known as the ABCD group, a liberal play on their initials: Archer Daniels Midlands, Bunge, Cargill, Louis Dreyfuss. These four companies control more than 75 percent of the world grain market, or three-quarters of the grain in the world. In 2005 they did $150 billion worth of business; in 2011, $320 billion.

Bunge is the oldest and continues to be a good example of how these huge international corporations function. It was founded in Amsterdam in 1818, moved to Antwerp in 1859, then to Buenos Aires in 1884. It never had a clear national identity. From Argentina—under the name Bunge & Born, now Bunge Limited—it spread throughout the rest of the region and into the United States until, in 1974, the Montoneros guerrilla group kidnapped two of its owners—brothers Jorge and Juan Born—and received one of the largest ransoms ever paid at the time: around $60 million. The company then moved to Brazil and Bermuda until 2001, when it ended up settling in White Plains, New York—and began to be publicly traded on the New York Stock Exchange.

Cargill, on the other hand, is still a family-owned business; in fact, it is the largest private company in the world, with 152,000 employees in sixty-seven countries who speak sixty-three different languages and bring in three times more money than Disney or Coca-Cola. Behind Tyson Foods, Cargill is the second largest producer of beef and pork in the world, the second largest owner of feed lots, and the world's second largest producer of animal feed. All the eggs used in all the McDonald's restaurants in the United States are sold by Cargill—as are 25 percent of all wheat exports in the country. From a Cargill brochure: "*We are the flour in your bread, the wheat in your noodles, the salt on your fries. We are the corn in your tortillas, the chocolate in your dessert, the sweetener in your soft drink. We are the oil in your salad dressing and the beef, pork, or chicken you eat for dinner. We are the cotton in your clothing, the backing on your carpet, and the fertilizer in your field.*"[11]

The lyrics are quite clear; the music is harder to hear.

Cargill and the others have been implicated in a whole portfolio of crimes: deforestation, use of prohibited chemicals on crops and food processing and storage, planetary tax evasion. Cargill and the others try to maintain what is referred to as total control of the food chain.

Jean Ziegler, in his book *Betting on Famine: Why the World Still Goes Hungry*, wrote:

> Cargill produces phosphate-based fertilizer in Tampa, Florida. With this fertilizer, Cargill grows soy in fields in the United States and Argentina. In Cargill factories, the soybeans are transformed into flour. In ships that belong to Cargill, this soy flour is then sent to Thailand, where it is used to fatten chickens on large farms that also belong to Cargill. The chickens are then killed and gutted, in an almost entirely automated process, in factories that belong to Cargill. The Cargill fleet then carries them to Japan, the Americas, and Europe. Cargill trucks distribute the chickens to supermarkets, many of which belong to Cargill.[12]

Among the most heinous of the accusations against it has been a charge of child labor violations directed against it and Nestlé by the International Rights Advocates group, a court case that has been ongoing since 2005. As the Organized Crime and Corruption Reporting Project wrote in 2018:

The plaintiffs, the decision said, were former slaves that had been kidnapped and forced to work the fields of a cocoa farm for up to fourteen hours a day without being paid. The Ivory Coast is the world's largest cultivator of cocoa. 'While being forced to work on the cocoa farms, plaintiffs witnessed the beating and torture of other child slaves who attempted to escape,' the court said. The case stems from over ten years ago, when the former child slaves sought to hold cocoa-buying businesses responsible for their enslavement and trauma. They sued in 2005, but the case was dismissed in 2016. It eventually reached the Supreme Court which rejected an attempt by the companies to have the case tossed.[13]

Like many parent companies that invite scrutiny, the ABCD corporations don't show themselves very often in public; but when you bite into a McDonald's Egg McMuffin, or into a slice of Pizza Hut pizza, or when you slap a slice of Kraft cheese on a sandwich, or buy a bar of chocolate from Nestlé, when you eat a bowl of General Mills cereal, or munch on a Nabisco cracker, you are eating foods that have either been bought, sold, or speculated upon by the ABCD group. As buyers, they are almost monopolies, so they can fix prices much lower than producers could get if there were more competition for their products. But if global food prices rise, they have myriad of ways to maximize their benefits by having access to information before other agricultural firms; holding onto enormous stocks; buying where it is cheap and reselling at higher rates that then define global prices; creating temporary price increases and decreases; destroying local producers by setting unsustainable prices; increasing their profits with ports, flotillas, and warehouses; pressuring governments to give them better conditions and enact measures that favor them; speculating with fortunes—"to back up their operations with real merchandise."

And, because of their global reach, they are usually beyond the control of any government. Groups that control a large part of the food in the world have their own profit as their sole barometer of what and what not to do. And in a capitalist world where maximizing profits is a virtue there isn't any efficient way of controlling them. This is one more example of the mismatch between the globalized economy and national governments. It's also goes to show why traders like Leslie would be so frustrated with government interference when it does make efforts to regulate.

Traditionally, it has been large companies in the Americas—in the United States, Brazil, and Argentina—that have dominated the world agricultural market, companies based in China, Japan, and Korea are beginning to show a strong competitive force. These began to operate according to the "Americas" model, but they are also changing the rules of the game by aggressively buying land in the Other World to grow their own food and not have to depend on the fluctuations of national markets and producers back home. And, with some lag, the agricultural firms in the West have begun to imitate them. This is what is beginning to be called a "land grab": colonialism of the twenty-first century.

Like Leslie, Diego had requested I not use his name, or the name of his company because, he told me, it had a huge number of regulations about what its employees could and could not say.

"After I received permission to speak with you, I was asked by a colleague if I was afraid to speak with someone who was writing a book about hunger. I said I wasn't because my conscience was clean. I couldn't work in a business I thought contributed to anybody's hunger, even if only one person. I've asked myself this question a thousand times, and I've come to believe firmly that what I do for a living does not make people go hungry."

"How did you come to that conclusion."

"Well, it's like that joke about the shoemaker who sends two salespeople to Africa. One returns and says there's no business: Africa is a total failure, nobody wears shoes there, we're not going to sell anything. The other returns and says it's a gold mine, nobody wears shoes in Africa and we're going to wear ourselves out making so many sales. Here it's the same: the more people there are in the world that need to eat, the more we're going to sell."

I told Diego that I thought that analogy was dangerous. "If someone doesn't have something, that doesn't necessarily mean that they have the means to do business to obtain it."

I could see disappointment creep into his face.

"No, that's not what I mean. What I mean is that we're trying to reach as many markets as possible. I'm not dealing in diamonds, I'm not trying to get rich selling something that only a privileged few will be able to enjoy. No, my business has to do with volume. The best thing that can happen to me is that I can make a good living feeding the entire world, a world where everyone eats."

Diego was from Argentina and had spent a few years in his company's New York offices; he was a futures trader, what he called "financial risk management" of common products. Diego is around forty, blond, with an easy smile which he flashes when he repeats, "For me the busi-

ness is about more people eating, not fewer." I must not have been showing much enthusiasm, because Diego gave me a sad look and asked if I
agreed.

I shook my head and explained how it seemed that the wheat sold for
pigs and chickens and cows to eat to make meat made little sense on a
macro scale as a way of obtaining protein. "Ten people could have a meal
with the amount of vegetable protein a cow eats in a single sitting."

Diego considered this. The disappointment on his face was slowly disappearing. "Yes, I know, it's very inefficient. If everyone preferred to eat
quinoa or soy over steak, there'd be a lot more to eat. But man is the
only animal who doesn't eat to satisfy his nutritional needs. Man eats
because he likes to eat. I read some stories on your blog about some of
the places you visited and the starving people you encountered and, the
truth is, it did make me feel bad, it's hard for me to process that kind
of thing. It's easier for me to calculate how everyone in the world could
be fed. A child in Africa needs, let's say, fifteen hundred calories. So
for him to not be malnourished he would need two cups of soy beans
and a glass of milk a day? If the market only existed to accommodate
human nutrition, it would not be hard to make sure every child in Africa
received those fifteen hundred calories. But if the market were based on
only the human need for food, it would also be wildly different. Instead
the market accommodates other needs for food: animal and energy. I
can't say, I'm not going to sell any more soy or corn to feed animals or
to biofuel suppliers, I'm only going to sell exclusively for the benefit of
human nutrition. If I did that, the only thing I would achieve would be
raising the price of meat and ethanol fuel, which would become harder
to obtain, and because so many farm machines rely on fuel, even the
price of grains and legumes would go up as well."

He looked at me now with satisfaction.

"Maybe that would be the case, but right now there are millions more
starving children than animals."

"Maybe, but this is a logistical discussion as much as it is a philosoph-
ical one. Hunger is a business. It's also a way to subjugate a population. If
you've got a military leader who carries out a coup in an African country,
and you see him walking around with gold-plated pistols, and the people
are dying of hunger, it's obvious this guy is doing business with hunger.
Or look at Argentina, our own country, where people are malnourished
in the northern provinces of Chaco and Formosa. It's not because our
market is based on the rates determined at the Exchange. Rather, it's
because there's some motherfucking governor who is using the resources

in his province for his own benefit, using the government airplane to take Caribbean vacation. I'm just saying that there are complicated problems that have nothing to do with the market or the commoditization of food."

I had heard similar arguments before. In other books, in other contexts, I have called this idea "honestism": the supposition that the most the important factor in a society's economic situation is the honesty of its leaders—above and beyond the operations of market capitalism and the distribution of assets—or a lack thereof.

Traders like Diego and Leslie insisted that the capital they managed served the purpose of giving the markets liquidity and thereby allowing it to function. It seemed to me, however, that that the market was always operating no matter what was being invested in. There were good speculators and bad speculators, Diego told me, and a good speculator would make sure his or her company could buy or sell grain and processed food with the intent of maximizing profit. I wondered if a bad speculator did things like make sure more people got fed regardless of the impact on profits.

Of course traders have their own set of arguments of what is currently affecting food prices. There was the explosion of meat consumption in China, the growing use of grains for biofuels, and not least of all, the increasingly unreliable climate. And sometimes, the most thoughtful and guilt-ridden traders would tell you that maybe their activities did contribute a little to world hunger. But there was something else. The reasons stated above were all tangible, with real and unsolvable roots: the Chinese eat, fuel powers cars and tractors, droughts are inevitable. Investment funds, on the other hand, could cease to exist and nobody, except those people who owned them, would miss them at all.

Frederick Kaufman had already stated as much in an article for *Foreign Policy*: "Not only does the world's food supply have to contend with constricted supply and increased demand for real grain, but investment bankers have engineered an artificial upward pull on the price of grain futures. The result: Imaginary wheat dominates the price of real wheat, as speculators (traditionally one-fifth of the market) now outnumber bona-fide hedgers four-to-one. Today, bankers and traders sit at the top of the food chain—the carnivores of the system, devouring everyone and everything below."[14]

Investment funds are made up of the extra money of the wealthiest countries, what people don't need to spend in order to live—their surplus. It's money they don't actively use, and so they want to do something with it, such as buying the most coveted product, security. The ultimate luxury of wealthy countries: guarantees for a safe and prosperous future.

They could do this by hiding money under their mattresses, buying gold, buying bonds, buying a country's debt securities. But mostly people use their excess money to invest in ventures that companies like Diego's use to buy and sell at even higher numbers, to the point where they can wield considerable influence on the market. Investment is the way millions of "normal" people—retired people, pre-retired people, people with savings of ten or twenty thousand dollars, aggressive executives, corrupt inspectors, the recently laid-off who nurse their severance pay, successful doctors, elegant shoe salesmen, Siberian gas billionaires, Belgian professors, Dutch prostitutes, rock stars, and everybody else, including myself—contribute to the hunger of other millions. Without ever meaning any harm, they participate from afar in the mechanism that makes the price of food rise and more and more people unable to buy it.

Diego finished his second Coke and told me he had to get going. We paid up and walked to the door; outside, it was cold and drizzling. Diego held out his hand for a parting shake. "I hope I've convinced you that I'm not a merchant of death."

He then opened his umbrella and walked away leaving me to wonder just how much death I had been contributing to myself.

VOICES OF THE TRIBE

How the hell do we manage to live knowing these things are happening?

Thai Buddhists are not allowed to crack eggs; their religion forbids it. Rich Thai Buddhists have their servants break the eggs, whereby the masters aren't guilty because they didn't do it and the servants aren't guilty because they were only obeying their masters' orders.

Sometimes the world is an egg that somebody else is always cracking.

How the hell do we manage to live knowing these things?

Let's see, let's go one step at a time. If I said to you, come here quickly, your children's house is burning down, you'd drop everything, anything, and you'd run like a crazy person, wouldn't you? Of course. So what I'm saying is that you don't have to talk bullshit and say that everything affects you the same, ah humanity, ah the misery of one man is my misery, ah one single being can't eat so I can't eat. You know there are things that you care a lot about and others you could care less about, so it's worthwhile thinking about what you can do. Not make outlandish speeches or promises about how you alone are going to change the world, but at least put in your grain of sand, make your little difference, don't you think? Even though you know that it's not in your power to change things, and that probably things are going to continue more or less the same no matter what you do, but at least have the satisfaction of knowing that you tried, right? I think that if you manage that, it's already—

How the hell do we manage to live knowing?

Simultaneity, I mean: a multitude.

If you could—if anyone could—be conscious of a millionth of the things that are happening in the world in the time it takes to read this sentence, in this brief lapse, would you die? Would you explode from the horror, surprise, fear?

Six or seven things, at least.

Four or five.

How the hell do we manage to live?

There's solace. "Freedom's just another word for nothin' left to lose," she sang—and it sounded like it really meant something.

How the hell do we manage?

"What do you think about all this?"
  "You really want to know?"

How the hell?

But the Bible already said it, didn't it? It's written there that there will always be poor people. It makes me sad, no denying it, but if God wants it to be this way, there must be a reason. You think all of this is happening just because? He never does something for its own sake: everything He does has a reason. Sometimes He gives you tests you have to live through, you have to get through them to prove that you deserve His trust, His grace, because who are we to go against what He orders? It's not easy, don't think for a minute it is, because I know we've got to help them, a good Christian also has to help them, but we have to help them appropriately, just enough so that they feel in their hearts the warmth of charity and the love of others, but not too much to go against the work of our Lord who decided that they should suffer such privations, and who are we to contradict or even try to understand His reasons; if He wanted us to understand He would have made it clear to us.

How?

4

"If you've come here to St. Kevin's Church looking for food, don't waste your time, they're not open today."

"What do you mean they're not open?"

"What I said. Not open."

The man introduced himself as Gordon. He looked to be in his sixties, with a stained red jacket, boots without laces, a gray wool beanie with a pom-pom that said "*White Sox*," and an expression on his face that said he could give a shit what he was wearing.

I checked my phone to confirm the hours. St. Kevin's Food Pantry Open from 9:30 a.m. to 11:00 a.m. every other Wednesday. It was 10:00 a.m. and no one was around. I did some further googling and discovered on other pages what I had already begun to fear. The pantry date had been changed. They now opened every third Wednesday.

"I'm afraid they changed the day of the food pick up."

"What do you mean changed?"

"It says it's open every third Wednesday instead of every other Wednesday."

Gordon threw up his arms then shook his head. "Whatever."

"Do you not care?"

"Course I care, but what am I gonna do? Break down the door?"

The church was a solid building on the corner of a desolate avenue. It was a church like a lot of churches, pseudo-Norman or pseudo-Swiss, pseudo-something, with its little tower, its big windows, its signs inviting people to pray and instilling in them the fear of God. At least until recently, it passed out food on Thursdays, but Gordon didn't get the memo.

"You always come here?"

"Course I always come here. What, do I look to you like a tourist? This is my neighborhood, and this is where I come every other Wednesday to get my two-week supply of food. No one told me they were gonna change it."

We stood there together for a moment, looking at the locked doors.

"How am I supposed to eat this week?"

"You don't have any other options?"

At the question, he stared laughing.

"Oh, I got other options. You just don't want to hear about them."

He adjusted his pom-pom hat and walked away with laughter still in his voice.

"Nah, you don't even want to know."

Most of Chicago's food pantries and soup kitchens are supplied by the Greater Chicago Food Depository (GCFD), which is in the southwest Chicago neighborhood of Archer Heights. Founded in 1978 by Robert Strube, a local fruit and vegetable merchant, the GCFD now occupied a building that in a less wealthy country could've been the headquarters of any old multinational corporation: an expanse of glass, steel, the stars and stripes flapping from its roof right above the state and city flags. Wendy, my host, informed me that the building covered an area equivalent to five American football fields. Wendy was tall with thin blonde hair. She wore large eyeglasses and her thin lips were always ready to break into a smile. She was under thirty and had been working here for eight years. As we made our way down long corridors that emitted that omnipresent scent of chemical pine cleaner, people greeted her warmly. The GCFD appeared to be a place people were proud to work.

"Last year we distributed sixty-four million pounds of food," she said, "approximately thirty thousand tons, the equivalent of one hundred and forty thousand meals per day. Can you imagine how satisfying this work is, knowing that you are sating the hunger of so many people?"

Wendy noted that the GCFD did more than just distribute food and pointed to rooms with industrial kitchens where people could take restaurant and cooking courses. There were also rooms with oversized conference tables and lecterns where people could learn more about hunger activism. But it was the enormous warehouses filled with produce and packaged goods that most commanded my attention. These storerooms were as big as ball fields, if not bigger, the size of hangers perhaps. A flotilla of trucks left these hangars every day to distribute food to more than 650 shelters, pantries, and soup kitchens all over Cook County, which included the entire Chicago metropolitan area, and was the second largest county in the United States. The GCFD itself was responsible for feeding more than 800,000 people, 15 percent of Chicago's population, who Wendy described as being afflicted with "food insecurity."

"The worst part is that the numbers just keep increasing. Five years ago, there were half a million, now it's four-fifths of a million. But no matter how many people we need to serve, we make sure to give them quality, nutritious food."

I asked Wendy where Strube got the idea for such a vast operation.

"In a bar after having enough drinks to believe that something like this could be possible. Strube and his friends were sick of throwing out all the leftover merchandise. Using his own food stall, he and a small group of volunteers started stockpiling what market owners could no longer shelve but what was still edible, and began to distribute them to those who needed it. Demand was so high that in the first year of operation, his team distributed nearly five hundred thousand pounds of food donated by nearly one hundred agencies."

The initiative was part of a growing food bank movement that had begun in 1967, when John van Hengel, a devout Catholic and grassroots entrepreneur, opened the world's first food bank in Phoenix, Arizona. It was so successful that van Hengel began to preach across the country of the benefits of food banking. It's possible that Strube had heard one of van Hengel's talks before he convinced himself at a bar to try and start his own. What is known is that the GCFD was so successful that within three years of its founding, state legislature passed a law that limited liability for merchants willing to donate. More initiatives followed including a "food rescue" program that allowed grocers to donate produce and a mobile food truck that would post up in lower-income neighborhoods to distribute food and teach people about good nutrition.

Wendy pointed to a poster that showcased eighteen common foods and their benefits, including rice, noodles, beans, crackers, canned tuna, but also fresh fruit and vegetables, meat, eggs, and milk.

"We want our clients to have the best we can possibly give them."

I wondered if the word in English left the same bad taste as the Spanish *clientelismo*, which had by our Latin American governments been led to mean a kind of cronyism.

"No, client means something much different here. Companies exist to serve a need for their clients. Therefore, every company respects, or should respect, its clients above all."

But didn't their clients, their customers, the city's 800,000 people who lived without the security of food need them just as well? That the GCFD was given government funds and subsidies was substantial, but did the United States not have wealth to address hunger more directly than offer palliative solutions?

Up through the seventies, particularly during the Jimmy Carter years, the grand food bank experiment appeared to be working. It seemed that after decades of struggle, hunger in the United States was coming under control. But under the Reagan presidency and later the Gingrich congress, taxes were reduced on the rich, military spending ramped up, and budgets for social welfare were cut. Poverty levels in the United States reached a peak in 1993 with 15.1 percent of the population living below the poverty line. Throughout the nineties, that number fell, reaching 11.2 percent in 2000. After the financial and food crashes of 2007 and 2008, poverty jumped back to 15.1 percent in 2010, a percent at which it hovered for nearly four years before dropping down to 12.7 percent by 2017. That same year, the GDP for the United States was $14.96 trillion, the highest in the world for that year. What these statistics don't account for is how many people 12.7 percent actually is: 39.7 million people. In this there was something to the logic of the United States that has never ceased to amaze me:

The United States has the highest amount of wealth in the world.

The United States has one of the highest poverty rates in the world. In no other rich country do so many poor people live.

Even so, about 80 percent of insecure families have at least one member working. Here, marginalization does not always mean unemployment; it is, also, doing jobs that do not pay you enough to eat as you should, and that force you to be dependent on charity—both public and private—to keep going.

For many in the United States, subsidies and food distribution and soup kitchens are more than a stopgap measure: they are a survival strategy. "Most of our clients receive assistance for more than six months," Wendy told me. And the number of people receiving help increased by almost 50 percent in the last eight years. "What's changed since then is the demographic composition of hungry people. Before it was only the homeless, poor, elderly, and drug addicts. Now we have middle-class people who've lost their jobs, or people whose salaries aren't big enough to feed their children."

More than twenty million children receive free or highly subsidized food at school; these numbers are sharply increasing. The government pays $2.79 per meal, double what one out of every five people throughout the world have every day to feed themselves. But the hard truth is that $2.79 is not enough for a meal that isn't merely a heap of fat and carbohydrates.

Food stamps, which are given in monthly allotments, amount to around $3.00 a day (since raised to $4.00 as of 2019). To demonstrate just how difficult it is to live healthily on that little money, Jim McGovern, the Massachusetts congressman and cochair of the House Hunger Caucus, along with three of his colleagues, once spent a week in 2007 eating on this amount. During this time, he updated a blog describing the stress and low energy that resulted from being underfed. Speaking before Congress on this final day of his "Food Stamp Challenge" as he called it, McGovern recounted thousands of comments he received from people who faced enormous stress difficulties to make this budget work to feed their families day after day.

McGovern also makes an appearance in *A Place at the Table*, a documentary about food insecurity, where he describes the long term of having little to eat: "The loss of human potential is terrible. Some of those kids could become great scientists and leaders in our armed forces, but the impact of hunger ruins everything and, as a result, is weakening our nation."[15]

The easy joke would be, hunger weakens the might of the US military. But joking aside: this also seems to miss the point. Not feeding children won't just make them lose out on their potential as adults, it will make them suffer in childhood. If we only worry about who might be able to best serve the country later in life, then should we starve the children who might not be leaders, who want instead to live an otherwise normal life, in order to save a few bucks?

5

Amor de Dios United Methodist Church received most of its supplies from the GCFD. On the day I visited hundreds of people had lined up, all the way around the corner and up to the next one to enter the church.

"You came by car?" I asked one elderly woman.

"Yeah, in my *fee-at*. My two *fee-at*."

She cracked up at her own joke. The woman had a raspy Mexican accent that came out in her laughter. She was in line sitting in a chair, another woman was sitting next to her. The first woman told me that she never had a car, and she asked the second if she had one.

"Yeah, I do. Well, it's my husband's. Old but still working."

"The car or the husband?" asked the first woman.

The two of them burst out laughing. Two or three others in line looked at them oddly. It's raining, gently. Across the street an old, red sporty-looking car drives by slowly with two young men inside, reggaeton blasting from the subwoofers.

This was a Hispanic neighborhood: the main commercial street, Sawyer Avenue, was lined with businesses: Cuernavaca Bakery, Mexico Dollar Plus, Maria's Beauty Salon, Paletería Azteca, Cheli's Taquería. But it seemed that so many of their customers were here, waiting patiently in a slow-moving line, to receive bags of food. When they reached the door of the church, they would need to be signed in. Then they would go down to the basement where they would find tables loaded with lettuce, onions, carrots, potatoes, oranges, squash, a lot of cilantro, cans of beans, sausages, rice, bread, even some croissants just barely stale, which a bakery had sent over. There were even, until a few minutes ago, some chickens, but they were now all gone. Rather than be given premade bags, people were able to select what they wanted, and it appeared to be a bit of a frenzy. I asked the pastor, who stood by observing, why bags were not just handed out to speed things up.

"It turned out that that method wasn't helpful," he told me. "One day I helped an elderly man carry his bag home, and when he said, we're here, I saw that he lived in an empty garage, an abandoned structure without a bathroom, a kitchen, nothing. And there I saw that he had bags from before still filled with canned food and some rotting perishables because he didn't have any way to cook anything. So then we began to let people choose what they wanted. It's slower this way, but people get to select the kinds of foods they are able to eat."

Pastor Ramiro had that tidy, orderly appearance one expects from a pastor, even though he makes his living as an electrician. He has been running Amor de Dios United Methodist Church since 1997.

"I crossed over in 1982, so I've been here a while."

Ramiro was born in a village in the state of Guerrero, and when he was still young he went around the area preaching with a group of friends. But his family didn't always have enough food, so his father decided to cross the border to see if he would be able to send them something. Ramiro was nineteen at the time, and he convinced his father that it would be better for Ramiro, the oldest child, to go instead. And his father agreed and gave him his blessing.

"I thought it would take me a year to get them out of misery, but even I had yet to manage."

Ramiro spent a long time as a migrant wandering from city to city, working in construction, trying to earn money, living very frugally, sending money to his family. When he got married, he was able to apply for a green card to stay legally and permanently. The couple landed in Chicago—in North Lawndale, often referred to as "La Villita." It was 1990.

"There were still a few *güeros* [white people] here, but the demographic was already shifting heavily Hispanic. Things were okay for a while, and I started volunteering as a pastor here. Then actual construction work started drying up—companies left, factories closed. Then came the mortgage crisis, and things got even worse. That hurt everybody. My boss, for example, isn't working now at all. He buys old houses and restores them to sell. Now nothing sells, so he doesn't restore them, because if he did, they'd just break in and steal everything, copper especially, copper pipes, which are easy to sell. So, you can imagine."

What I had to imagine is that outside the church, which is strictly volunteer, Pastor Ramiro isn't gainfully employed, and will probably be taking some food home himself after everyone has left. Because nobody pays him to be a pastor and he needs to eat.

"But I do it happily. God will pay me, and He doesn't leave me with any debts."

La Villita started, almost a hundred years ago, as a neighborhood of mostly Central Europeans. That's why on the front of Amor de Dios Methodist Church, under the remains of a stained-glass window figure, was an inscription that read: "Jan Hus." He was a Czech heretic who insisted that Christians should take both bread and wine during communion, and he defended the poor against the powerful, even organizing a utopian community on Mt. Tabor until the pope ordered him to be burned in 1421. In one of those strange coincidences, he was somebody I had once studied extensively.

"How strange, to meet up with Jan Hus here, so far away."

"So far away from what?"

I told him the story and the pastor said he had no idea.

"I didn't know anything about that, but I like the window; it's our window, we want to fix it so it doesn't fall out. The problem is that I called some contractors to repair it and they told me it would cost ten thousand dollars. My God, I wouldn't qualify for that much of a loan. We'll see, God will provide. I hope we'll be able to do it before they throw us out."

Pastor Ramiro spoke with that sedate voice pastors often have, as if the entire serenity of the Heavens had settled upon their heads.

"Why are they going to throw you out?"

"Because the güeros are already eyeing this neighborhood. You can still buy cheap houses here, and we aren't that far from downtown. That's what they're like, the güeros: they return, they always return. It's like they let us use it for a while, but it still belongs to them. You think they've left, but as soon as it suits them . . . It already started. In ten years, there won't be any of us left in this neighborhood."

The woman with the *fee-at* was about to reach the church door. Her name was Ramona; she had one of those faces whose every feature looked like a parody drawn by an untalented cartoonist: a very large hooked nose, twisted ears, rolls under her chin like an accordion. She said to me, how unfair it was that she had to come here and that she even sometimes had a job—a hard job.

"I work in a bakery. Sometimes I clean, sometimes I pack, whatever they need," she told me, almost defiantly.

"So you get to take home lots of bread . . ."

"No, they don't give away nothing. You even gotta shake off the *migas* before leaving."

She was speaking to me in Spanglish, mixing English words like "shake" with Spanish words like *migas*, or crumbs. She told me work had been steady, and so she had been able to make just enough, sometimes sixty dollars a day, to pay her house and medical bills, setting aside whatever was left over to buy a little chicken, a sausage to accompany what she brought home from the church. There were days, however, when she spent hours waiting for a phone call to come in to work only to realize too late in the day that she wasn't going to get a call.

"There are a lot of mouths to feed at home. There's my husband, who can't work because he's sick, and my daughters, each one with her three kids."

"How many daughters do you have, señora?"

"Two."

"They don't work?"

"One does, but not always."

"What does she do?"

"Nothing, cleans houses. What else?"

Ramona and her family have been here for twenty years; they arrived when their daughters were very young, she said, too damn bad she didn't have them here, which would have qualified them for a green card, then everything would be easier.

"Would you say you're hungry sometimes?"

"Hungry, yeah, whatever hungry is . . . What we are is needy. Worried. This business of not knowing if tomorrow there'll be food. You know what I mean? That kind of worry."

The definition in the United States of food insecurity is "not knowing where your next meal will come from." It's another marvel of the culture of euphemism, the one that could call something like torture an "enhanced interrogation." Ramona did know where her next meal was coming from: from places like that church. But there was also some truth to that phrase *food insecurity*: people like Ramona feel they have no control over the supply. Someone who earns money from a job and uses that money to buy food feels like she has a legitimate claim on that food and can guarantee its supply because its continuation depends on her. The person holding a tray at a soup kitchen has no claim to anything; she's receiving charity that can be taken away in the same way it is given, without any warning.

In principle, US-style hunger is not not *having* food, but in not having *ownership*—the right to deal with it at will—over that food. In a country that's all about everyone having their fair share, that's a problem. But the concept becomes more precise when they tell you that a third of these people suffer from "high food insecurity," which means that at some point in the last few months they had nothing to eat.

Pastor Ramiro told me that his pantry's five-year anniversary was approaching. "When I came to this church we heard about these food banks for the needy and we said, wow, if only we could have a bank to help our people. And look at what we've done."

That it has grown is both a good and bad thing: they're feeding more and more people all the time, which means more and more people aren't able to buy their own food. The pastor knows the difference, but he insists on not paying any attention to it.

"Some come because they really don't have anything, if they didn't come here they wouldn't eat or they'd eat very little. Others have something and come here so they save a few dollars they really need. I want to try to treat everybody the same."

Sometimes the truth of the times outweighs the facts of a statistic.

On the corner across the street were three young men with baggy pants, oversized T-shirts, caps on backwards, and lots of tattoos. They were quarrelling with the pastor, among other reasons, because he threw them off the church basketball court after they trashed it; so sometimes they'd come on food distribution days and cause trouble, make fun of people. I watched one of them cross the street and get in line.

"Are you going to get some food?"

One of them mumbled something in Spanglish I couldn't understand. I smiled at him and tried again. I told him my name, he told me his was Nicky. He had two rings in his nose, his hair was styled in a kind of Mohawk with a touch of blue, the look in his eyes somewhere between curious and suspicious. His face looked like a repainted Olmec statue.

"You're here for food or to make fun of people?

"What do you think?"

"But won't your friends give you a hard time for being in line?"

"What'll they say? My mother needs it. *I'll take it a mi amá y que ella no me chinge* for a while. It's a good business."

"So you take food away from people who really need it?"

"We all need to eat, *güey*."

After Nicky left, Pastor Ramiro came up and explained that since his older brother got arrested on drug-related charges, Nicky's family—his mother, his sisters—had had a hard time making ends meet and eating every day.

After leaving Amor de Dios, I took a subway to its last stop in the far north of Chicago where a branch of Just Harvest, a grassroots organization dedicated to eliminating hunger, was located. I got out of the station and entered into a desolate neighborhood: streets lined with houses with patches of dirt in front of the porch, some with junk piled on their lawns, some with plywood nailed over their windows. I noticed empty lots, shuttered buildings, and wide deserted streets. Night had fallen by the time I reached it and there weren't many street lamps. Only passing cars and the public housing offered any source of light.

By contrast, I found Just Harvest to be a sort of beacon. It was clean and well lighted, with big windows and walls covered with a mural depicting butterflies and parrots, planets and volcanoes, children holding hands and multicolored zebras. The main space was taken up by a cafeteria, where you could grab a tray and serve yourself. There were three dozen tables for four to six people each, all shiny and orderly and covered with their impeccable plastic tablecloths. It was the most diverse group I had encountered: African-Americans, Hispanics, whites; children, elderly, men and women. Nobody asked them for anything; if they wanted to eat, it seemed all they had to do was arrive, write their names down on a piece of paper, and go get their tray. I was here to meet with David Crawford, the director of this Just Harvest location, and a man who dressed immaculate and professional: his dark-skinned arms and neck poked out of a starched, white, tight-collared shirt, he was wearing a tie and his well-groomed face was highlighted by a neatly trimmed moustache. Despite his calm demeanor, David spoke excitedly, shooting out words like a firing piston without pause.

"Many people think that the homeless are the only ones who come to these soup kitchens. The truth is, I think, those who think that, prefer to think that. It makes them feel better. They say: of course, they're homeless, people who fell out of the system, and so they themselves are to blame for their poverty. But it's not like that; many of these people you see here have a place to live, but the money simply doesn't stretch far enough; they have to pay rent, health insurance, medicine, and they've got nothing left to buy food. That's why they come here, all kinds of people, all with their own stories. What they have in common is not enough food, and that's for sure: nobody comes to a place like this if they can avoid it. Only a third of them are homeless, though, the other two-thirds are retirees who aren't making enough from their social security checks and working people who just don't make enough to make ends meet."

"Is it really possible for someone to have a job and not have enough to eat?"

"Absolutely. Someone working in a temporary job, or working for hire, or doing some menial job that pays by the hour, someone working a few hours a day for a few days a week. Those people are usually living on minimum wage, which is right now eight dollars an hour, so maybe in a week they'd make a little over a hundred dollars, two hundred if they are lucky with shifts. But then you have to factor in rent, which is not often less than five, six hundred dollars a month, and you have to factor other expenditures, bills, transportation. Even if you budget like crazy, you're still stretching dollars to pay for food."

Just Harvest had been feeding people for nearly thirty years, but since the recession, the number of people it had been serving had exponentially increased. Every afternoon they fed about two hundred people in an hour up from a few dozen only a few years prior. "Healthfully," emphasized David, "and nutritiously. We give them some meat, good protein, vegetables, salad, a piece of fruit, bread, everything you need for a good meal. What we most want to avoid is making them feel that they're getting second-class food. Here everyone and everything is first-class."

Then David looked at me and gestured to the buffet of food. "And you? Don't you want to eat?"

6

The shelves of the Family Dollar were bursting with primary colors. I wandered through a breakfast aisle where boxes of wild-eyed anthropomorphic creatures and human celebrities—tigers, leprechauns, bees, rabbits, toads, sea captains, gnomes, athletes in action—enticed children with illustrated plates of grain foods with kid-friendly names—flakes, brans, wheats, charms, loops, crunches, krispies, combs, smacks—so many of them sweetened over with frosts of sugar and honey, or accompanied by marshmallow or peanut butter bits, all of which were happily soaking in ponds of milk.

As I was examining this menagerie, a large woman with disheveled blonde hair, very blue eyes, and a bright pink sweat suit, came up beside me and pulled from a low shelf a box of *Trix*, inspected it suspiciously, then returned it to the shelf. The effort to push her not very full cart was causing the woman to pant. Her legs seemed to get in each other's way and taking items off the shelf appeared to be taking a toll on her energy.

"Excuse me, do you think you can hand me that box of cereal?"

The box should've been within reach—supermarkets don't want to make buying difficult—but the woman was unable to lift her arm that high.

I handed her a box that displayed no fantasy mascot, only phrases that listed its healthy bonafides—100 percent of the daily recommend grain intake, an excellent source of fiber, non-GMO modified power-packed nutrition. The woman thanked me as she took the box, examined it, and placed it in her cart.

"My kids also like this one."

I eyed over the contents of her cart: generic-brand noodles, eggs, sliced bread, packages of macaroni and cheese, canned food, as well as a box of cake mix bake, three pounds of sugar, a couple of tubs of vanilla ice cream, an extra-large jar of mayonnaise, three dozen hotdogs, and one dead chicken.

The woman told me her name was Mareshka, and that she was sorry for bothering me but that her body didn't always allow her to perform even the simplest of tasks. I didn't dare ask her what other things she couldn't do, but I did ask if she always shopped at Family Dollar. In an instant, Mareshka's friendly face turned to a glare of spite.

"I'm not poor, I earn my keep. I don't ask nobody for nothing. *We* never ask nobody for nothing."

Nonetheless, she allowed me to accompany her as we shopped. I would find out that "we" were Mareshka's ancestors. Her great-grandparents, she told me, had arrived from Poland a hundred years ago and settled in Binghamton because there was work here.

"If they could only see how little work there is in Binghamton now."

"Doesn't it make you mad that they picked the wrong place?"

"How can I blame them, my poor old folks. At least they died happy, before they found out. Or, at least I want to believe that."

I was driving East from Chicago to New York and had stopped in Binghamton, a small city in New York state about three hours by car northwest of Manhattan, three hours from the center of world power. Looking at Binghamton, you wouldn't know you were near any power. It's a town with history and not entirely a happy one. After the native tribes had been chased out by pioneers two centuries earlier, one rich white man named William Bingham ended up with the land and founded a town in his namesake. By the middle of the nineteenth century, it was already a promising, prosperous place, the southern terminus on a canal that connected the Susquehanna River with the much larger Erie Canal farther north. In 1850 the trains arrived, industry flourished, immigrants poured in, money flowed. In those days Binghamton was so important that it became the site of the world's first center to treat alcoholism as a disease—the New York State Inebriate Asylum—and Poles, Germans, Irish, and Italians began to arrive, all set on making it in America by making America what it is; a country of immigrants. And for a while, they succeeded.

Binghamton and the region surrounding it used to be called the "Valley of Opportunity": the city grew, pretty and pretentious houses were built, along with bridges, churches, a park here and there. But Binghamton truly came to prominence after another wealthy man, an entrepreneur named Charles R. Flint founded in Binghamton the Computing-Tabulating-Recording Company in 1911. Thirteen years later, the company would change its name to International Business Machines Corporation, universally known simply as IBM. After the Second World War, Binghamton reached its apex; here the flight simulator was developed, here Lockheed and company developed weaponry and high-tech military spy equipment. Binghamton thrived through much of the Cold War, but when standing up to Communism stopped being such good business, factories started closing and moving to more hospitable locales. In a strange expression of poetic justice, Binghamton lost its jobs, its people, its hope after helping win the Cold War; now, the city itself has fewer inhabitants than it did one hundred years ago. Together with its suburbs, it reaches a quarter of a million, with one in every four living below the poverty line.

In present-day Binghamton, the best houses have become small banks, large funeral homes, all kinds of churches; the priorities are clear. There are shopping malls on the outskirts, a deserted downtown, dilapidated streets, shuttered houses, and the pride of calling itself the "Carousel Capital of the World"—home to 6 of the 150 carousels left in the country. Once in a while, Binghamton shows up on national news, such as in April 2009, when a Vietnam veteran entered an office of the American Civic Association on Front Street and shot fourteen people, including himself, dead. Or in 2011, when a Gallup poll showed that it was one of the five most pessimistic cities in the country, and when it won first place for the cloudiest sky; or in 2012, when its obesity rate was the second highest in the nation, with more than a third of its inhabitants—37.6 percent—who could qualify as severely overweight.

Mareshka's Polish grandfather opened and operated a successful sausage factory. Her father didn't want to join him in the family business and got a manual labor job at IBM. When IBM relocated to Westchester, just outside of New York City, he took over the sausage factory, hated it, and ran it into the ground. By the time that happened, Mareshka was already thirty years old, married, and had three children. Without the factory, her family needed to make ends meet another way. She tried to make a go of it with a beauty salon, but that didn't work out. Her husband was a bus driver; they managed.

Then Mareshka and her husband bought a house and things became unmanageable.

"That woman at the bank insisted that we could buy a house for less than we were paying for rent. It wasn't true, it wasn't true at all, but we wanted to believe it. The bank even lent us sixy thousand dollars to purchase it. And it was real pretty, you bet, one of those little wooden houses with a backyard, a front porch, two stories, three bedrooms, really nice," she said, and then her face clouded over. "Not long after, my husband dropped dead of a heart attack. His doctor had told him he needed to eat better, but my husband liked to eat what he wanted. After he died, I couldn't afford the mortgage payments alone, and the bank seized the house."

Mareshka ended up working at her cousin's convenience store—selling beer, cigarettes, newspapers, lottery tickets, candy—and earning $2,000 a month. Her three kids were between thirteen and twenty-one.

"They always want to eat. It's expensive."

"Don't you qualify for some help with that income? Like, food stamps?"

"Yeah, I do, but I don't feel like getting it. I earn my own keep, I don't want anybody giving me anything. I'm American."

I'm American, she said, as if that meant almost everything.

Several years ago, the United States placed itself in the vanguard of fighting that strange epidemic of obesity.

To begin to be afraid of it was one of the most radical cultural changes in recent times. For centuries, in almost all societies, being overweight was a luxury; being able to eat excessively, waste resources in one's own body, and show that off, was a form of power.

Even a few decades ago being fat was a sure sign of prosperity. Kings, big hotshots, cardinals, plutocrats with bellies inflating their vests from which hung gold watch chains, those grand dames with grand hats, and opera stars, all carried their fat like trophies. At a time when working hard made you thin, a fat body was a body that announced its idleness; at a time when eating was a privilege, a body that could prove that it ate everything it wanted—and more than it needed—was a body that one wanted to show off. Then obesity went out of style. First, countercultural youths rejected it for being too bourgeois; then, the bourgeoisie decided they should take care of their bodies; sedentary work made you fat, exercise required money and free time; one had to cultivate a muscular, athletic body. But it wasn't until twenty-five years ago that obesity began to be thought of as an epidemic.

In general, it makes us feel bad. We see obesity as a dramatization of individual failure, of the result of not having enough self-control to keep your body thin, to have control over your own body. Slowly, however, it has become a symbol of social belonging, though at the other end of society; more and more, being fat means being poor.

Doctors blame obesity on the exponential increase in the number of deaths due to cardiovascular disease and certain cancers and that great contemporary ailment: diabetes. This made them want to define it, which they now do with a unit of measurement called Body Mass Index (BMI): a person's weight in pounds divided by their height in feet squared. If your BMI is between twenty-five and thirty, you're considered overweight; if over thirty, you're obese.

The measure is strict. At six feet tall and weighing two hundred pounds, my BMI is 26.8—slightly overweight, but also fairly average for men my height. Yet to qualify as obese, I'd only have to gain twenty-two more pounds.

With this strict measure, it's not difficult to determine that there are 2.1 billion overweight people in the world. The obese make up a third of those, or 700 million. These numbers also make it possible to establish a very marketable symmetry: that the world is so twisted, there are more or less the same number of undernourished as there are overnourished, as many hungry as there are fat. And, implicitly or explicitly, that the food these people are lacking is being eaten by those people; that the overweight people are eating what the hungry people don't.

Sounds like a good explanation of almost everything, and like almost all explanations, it doesn't tell the full truth.

"The doctors' tell us to eat healthier," said Mareskha, "But it's expensive to be healthy! You have to be rich to eat all that organic produce, or to buy the healthiest options on the shelf."

"Would you like to eat like that?"

"The truth? You want the truth?"

"Well, since we're here . . ."

"The truth is, no. I like my food. I know I should eat other things, but I also know I can't, I can't afford it. They can tell me all they want how it's bad for me, but I like it. I suffer enough in my life, I don't also have to think all the time that I shouldn't be eating what I'm eating, that I can't even enjoy eating what I like."

"Do you worry about your kids' health?"

"My kids are old enough to decide on their own food. I can't do anything about them anymore."

"Are your kids thin?"

Mareshka again gives me a look that borders on hatred.

It's not true; rather, obesity is the hunger of the wealthy countries. The obese are the malnourished—the poorest of the poor—of the more or less wealthy world. In these countries, malnourishment went from being a deficit to an excess, from a lack of food to an oversupply of junk food. The malnutrition of the poor in poor countries consists of eating very little, which stifles the development of their bodies or their minds; for the poor in the wealthy countries, it consists of eating a lot of cheap junk—fat, sugars, salt—and developing huge bodies.

They are not the other face of the hungry; they are their peers. The shape of inequality in this neck of the woods.

7

The light was like midnight at noon. It was a Thursday, a cold day at the end of fall, low-slung clouds, and the climate inside McDonald's on Main Street, downtown, was sweetly familiar. Sitting at two tables pushed together in the middle of the room were two blonde mothers with creamy white skin and red blemishes wearing stained sweatpants, trying to control a bunch of kids, all under ten, all blond, almost all overweight, three concerningly so. At the table next to them sat a large couple, in their thirties, feeding a baby sitting in a high chair: chubby, spattered, attacking pieces of hamburger as if they were her enemies from a previous life. At another table an overweight older woman wearing a plush turquoise sweatshirt with a hood and the logo of a faraway university, short badly dyed hair, glasses, tennis shoes, was eating chicken nuggets with her granddaughter and grandson, who were thin, young, and excited to be there. At another table in the middle sat an old, worn-out hippy in his fifties, hunched over and all skin and bones. Farther away, two very overweight women who with their facial whiskers resembled seals were talking to a man with a goatee, a black hat, a badly shaven face, girthy but not obese. The older woman had no teeth, the younger did, and when I began to see similarities in their features I realized that they were mother and daughter. The man looked nothing like either of them.

There are no animals in nature that are overweight by poor eating. Even in a hunter-gatherer society, people couldn't be naturally obese. It is a disease—an epidemic—created by human beings. To be obese is to accumulate excess fat unnaturally—a greed begat by anxiety of not knowing what the future will bring, and fearing it.

Around 1965 US geneticist James V. Neel, postulated that millions of years ago certain Paleolithic humans, hunter-gatherers, who could roam for days and days without finding food, developed physiological mechanisms that allowed them to "wear their calories," that is, store them in their bodies in the form of fat. And that because of this "thrifty gene" as it became popularly known, those humans survived better than the others, allowing this trait to be carried forward through evolution.[16]

For a long time, this ability offered a definite advantage. Now it is a problem. The world changed—above all, the wealthy world, where there is never a lack of food—and bodies keep storing fat reserves.

We accumulate it in the wrong place; instead of storing the potential for food and accessing it when needed, we carry it around with us. We are Paleolithic bodies lost in a postindustrial landscape, and we are poorly adapted. With civilization came tools that did what the body was not able to do before; store endless amounts of fat. We lacked the tools, however, to get rid of it just as easily.

In addition, bodies in developed countries were requiring less and less physical movement as machines were doing more and more labor: people took cars and buses instead of walking, they took elevators instead of stairs, they used washing machines instead of wash basins; then eventually came the robots for industry, manufacturing, and a host of other occupations. Manual labor used to be the most common form of work given in exchange for capital. Now in these societies labor is not usually physical. For the first time in history, profitable endeavors weren't being spurred on by the expenditure of calories—so they had to invent ways of spending that latent energy: gyms, exercise machines, pills that help to get rid of what until recently was so precious. People in the United States now use one third of the physical energy they used only sixty years ago; in that same period, the number of people suffering from obesity tripled, from 11 to 35 percent of the population.

All the TVs in the McDonald's were tuned to Fox News—the most right-wing of all right-wing channels. Seventies pop was piping from ceiling speakers. Clouds were gathering outside and people were already stooping in preparation for the rain. At the table next to mine sat an elderly Central European–looking gentleman with a white beard and glasses and a bow tie under his gray overcoat; he looked like he had just stepped out of a Lubitsch film. He was eating his cheeseburger and fries with perfect table manners; he used a fork and knife, after every bite he wiped his fingers on his white handkerchief. The only sign of his hunger was his greedy chewing. A black man in his twenties—very tall, very skinny, all red sweats with a red hood, red shoes with white shoelaces, gold earrings—ate a hamburger with sad bites. He stared out the window as if the world had disappeared; mustard dripped down his lower lip, his chin, onto his sweatshirt. A black woman in her twenties, a platoon of pound—her legs like two perfect triangles—sat down with a bottle of water and a salad; the earphones in her ears were connected to her telephone and she was smiling and nodding her head.

In the farthest corner sat a group of young people: two guys and four gals in their midteens who wore blue jeans and puffy jackets and spoke in loud voices. One of the boys was very large, the other not so much; all three of the girls were hefty; one of them, I'll call Leah, was a light-skinned black girl who must've weigh more than two hundred pounds. She had lovely, fine features that were drowning in fatty tissue.

"At school they told us that we were going to have problems later in life. But they don't understand. I don't care what'll happen to me in twenty years, when I'm an old lady. My problem is right now," she said, and wiped some ketchup off her face with a paper napkin. "I don't want to be like this, but what can I do? It's horrible to be like this. You think guys ask me out? Or even look at me?"

Leah told me she'd already tried every possible diet.

"The only thing I managed to do each time was make myself feel like a failure, like I can't do it. You know what it's like to bang your head against the same wall, over and over again? You know what it's like when you don't know what to do anymore? I'm sixteen years old."

The appearance of fast-food restaurants made it possible, in theory, for poor parents in rich countries to take their children out to eat, give them the pleasure of those flavors: salty and sweet and soda and fried and greasy, and allowed mothers to have a break from cooking every night, until many got used to never cooking, and forgot how to do it. And the children got used to this food, and the parents thought that to satisfy their hunger—their appetites—there was nothing faster, easier, or cheaper. Cheap, above all. When you have ten dollars to feed two or three kids, there's nothing better than to spend it on the calories, protein, and pleasures of one of those "combos." And nothing more fattening, or more destructive to the body.

More and more scientists are saying that the sugar, fat and salt in certain processed food produce the same type of addiction as alcohol or tobacco. And that this junk food and other kinds of fast food are filled with these three elements, and they are the most dangerous threat to the bodies that consume them. In 2012 Robert Lustig, a pediatric oncologist, published an article in *Nature* magazine that said that nature knew what it was doing when it made sugar difficult to obtain, and humans didn't when they made it so easy; he also said that the world consumption of sugar has tripled in the last fifty years.[17] Sugar went from being a luxury condiment to a cheap one—the first defense against hunger. Indians' tea, Argentines' sweet *mate*, and US Coca-Cola are ways of tricking the gut, sending it quick and non-nutritious calories to keep it busy for a while. More often than not, however, it's not even sugar but high fructose corn syrup (HFCS), a by-product of subsidized corn, which hides the flavors of almost all processed food and sodas and is, according to more and more studies, a major cause of the evils of obesity, included ever higher rates of diabetes. Eric Schlosser, the author of the book *Fast Food Nation*, wrote that our food had changed more in the last forty years than in the forty thousand previous years.[18]

Leah finished her Quarter Pounder and licked her lips. Her friend offered her a sip of her strawberry milkshake; Leah looked at me and declined.

Since the obesity epidemic in the United States began in the eighties, the prices of fruits and vegetables have gone up, in real value, by 40 percent. With three dollars you can buy 300 calories of fruits or vegetables or 4,500 calories of French fries, cookies, or soda. Anyone who wants to and can eat without stuffing themselves with calories buys fruit and vegetables. Anyone who needs to eat in order to obtain the minimum number of calories buys junk.

Junk food: when the priority is to get rid of hunger as cheaply as possible. Fill the body full of the cheapest crap you can buy.

Large food corporations, like all corporations, have one obligation above all else: to make money for their stockholders. To do this, they have to buy their raw materials as cheaply as possible, pay their employees as little as possible, and sell their products as expensively as a sufficient number of buyers will agree to pay. Then there came a time in the richest countries when their consumers—those who ate—were already eating as much as they needed, but large corporations needed them to eat more. Then, two closely related phenomena occurred: first, the waste of to of all food bought and the fact that children in rich countries ate an average of four thousand calories a day, or twice what they should. And they stuffed themselves with garbage made out of the three kings, and then they wanted more and ate more and wanted more—because the kings convinced them that they wanted more. To make all this happen, the corporations had to spend fortunes on advertising. There are few products where the proportional cost of advertising is greater than for junk food made by large corporations. Those are the rules of the business.

Second, the direct consequences of policies of agricultural subsidies. Subsidies began in the thirties during the Great Depression as an emergency measure to help farmers through the crisis, but then they didn't end. In the last few decades, US farming has changed so much, become so consolidated in so few hands, that the subsidies no longer benefit the majority of farming families but rather large agribusiness. 70 percent of the money goes to 10 percent of the beneficiaries, the huge farms of corn, wheat, and soy who have the lobbies required to guarantee they continue. Those products are, among others, the most common components of processed food, which is also why they are so much cheaper than fruits and vegetables, which don't receive the same level of subsidies. Which is how they poison people.

The questions Raj Patel asks (himself) in his book, *Stuffed and Starved*, makes clear that the food we eat is not a misfortune but rather a choice, even if we don't know who is making it.

"Who chooses the safe levels of pesticides, and how is 'safe' defined? Who chooses what should be sourced from where in making your meal? Who decides what to pay the farmers who grow the food, or the farm workers who work for farmers? Who decides that the processing techniques used in bringing the meal together are safe? Who makes money from the additives in food and decides they do more good than harm?

Who makes sure there is plenty of cheap energy to transport and assemble the ingredients from all around the world."[19]

Food that's junk, dregs for the dregs.

In the United States there are more than twenty-five million people living with diabetes and more than eighty million who are in danger of becoming diabetic. A child born in the United States in the year 2000 had one out of three chances of developing diabetes, one out of two if she was black or Hispanic. In a 2005 study, Stuart Jay Olshansky, a professor of Public Health at the University of Chicago and a specialist in ageing and longevity, wrote that if current levels of obesity persisted, life expectancy in the United States could decrease by as much as five to fifteen years in the next few decades.[20]

Though saying "life expectancy in the United States" is an abuse of language. The life expectancy of an educated white person in the United States is fourteen years more than a black person who did not finish high school. But it's not only black and white; it's also nine years more than a white person without education. It's also an issue by state. According to the report Measure for America, Hawaiians have the highest life expectancy at 81.3 years. Of the states, Mississippians rank the lowest at 75.0. If the territories of the United States were included, American Samoa would rank the lowest at 73.4 years on average. Even in New York, which has a life expectancy average of around 80.5, people living in or in proximity to the city live longer by an average of five years than people living "upstate" or outside of the city. And it seems to me, that nowhere does that feel more apparent than in Binghamton.

In a huge room full of long white tables and one or two hundred white plastic chairs; twenty or thirty people were sitting at the tables and eating off trays. On the walls were flags, banners of regiments and other military corps, photos of dead GIs and high-ranking officers. A black flag with the silhouetted profile of a face against a white background said, POW-MIA: You Are Not Forgotten. The twenty or thirty people there, divided up into five or six smaller groups, looked a little lost in the huge room. They were all white. They'd come to have Sunday morning breakfast served by the American Legion: six dollars for adults, three for children, under six were free, "all you can eat" from cafeteria counters full of eggs and sausages and potatoes and bacon and pancakes and bread and cream cheese, coffee and juice, and a couple of sad pieces of fruit.

The American Legion is an association of war veterans with three million members and fifteen thousand centers like this one all around the country. It's mission, according to its Preamble, is:

> To uphold and defend the Constitution of the United States of America;
> To maintain law and order;
> To foster and perpetuate a 100 percent Americanism;
> To preserve the memories and incidents of our associations in the great wars;
> To inculcate a sense of individual obligation to the community, state, and nation;
> To combat the autocracy of both the classes and the masses.

And to serve buffet breakfasts to the veterans who might not otherwise be able to afford it.

I was sitting with a man named Goofy. I didn't believe it at first, but he claimed "Goofy" was his name. Goofy must've been sixty and was so enormous that it is difficult for him to walk, he was unable to tuck his shirt into his gigantic pants, and his facial features were buried within pillows of skin. On his plastic plate there was a mountain of scrambled eggs, three sausages, a pile of bacon, and hash browns; next to it was coffee in a white plastic cup. His wife, Loretta, was sitting in front of him; she weighed a few pounds less than him and had the same load on her tray.

"I'm proud to contribute to what we do here in the Legion," Goofy told me. "We have a moral responsibility for our neighbors and for our community. We can't accept that there are children who don't have enough to eat. That's why we do these things."

"But all this food you have here?"

His wife who was sitting across from him, tried to say something, but he stopped her, "Wait, Bunny, let the gentleman talk," then nodded at me to continue.

"Do you think all the food you have on your plate is too much?"

"Who says this is too much? This is how we always eat. Or what, because there's some doctors blabbing on television, we have to stop eating like our grandparents did?"

I considered a different tactic of inquiry while Goofy swallowed his massive bite and wiped his mouth.

"Have you ever fought in a war?"

He lifted his head proudly as though coming to attention.

"Yes, sir, I fought in Vietnam. And I'm not going to say they were the best years of my life because Bunny here will kill me, something the

Vietcong couldn't do." He smiled the smile of a man married for thirty years. Bunny didn't smile.

"And you are not worried that all that greasy food won't kill you instead?"

"I don't know what you're so afraid of. That's what this food is here for, to be eaten. We all eat like this, we all live like this, we all die like this. What, skinny people don't die?"

I asked how many doctors had warned him about his eating habits and instead of answering, he took another bite from his plate while Bunny launched into a long talk about how Goofy had been diagnosed with type 2 diabetes, that his doctor had told him to lose weight and eat less fat and sugar and salt. Goofy let her talk as he finished his meal, periodically wiping pieces of food from his lips.

A *Telegraph* article from 2012 stated that obesity was causing three times as many deaths around the globe as malnutrition. Quoted in the article was Majid Ezzati, chair of global environmental health at Imperial College London, who was part of the team that reported on the findings, and who said, "We have gone from a world twenty years ago where people weren't getting enough to eat to a world now where too much food and unhealthy food—even in developing countries—is making us sick."[21]

While it is true that obesity is its own epidemic, it has one fundamental difference with people who do not have food: the malnourished don't have a choice in what they eat because they often do not have a choice in not being able to eat. On the other hand, food regulations are up to a government that is conflicted in how to deal with its obesity problem. It is not easy to accept that a society—the most powerful society in the world—not only has so many citizens that are severely overweight, but in terms of being the most obese nation on the planet, ranks number one. In fact, the same industries that fill both the obese with junk food, control the markets and appropriate the resources that keep the hungry from being able to eat anything at all. In this way, the overweight and the malnourished are victims of the same thing: the hunger industry.

ON HUNGER: INEQUALITY

How to look at inequality.

In his book *Feeding Frenzy: The New Politics of Food*, Paul McMahon divides more than 170 countries into five groups based on the production and consumption of calories according to their role in the global food system.[1] Though vastly simplified, it helps provide an overall view, a kind of map of inequalities.

The "established food powers" are the fourteen industrialized nations that are net exporters of calories: United States, Canada, Australia, New Zealand, and several European countries. These nations have favorable natural conditions and solid economies, which have always controlled the international markets and were the first to reap the benefits of improvements in agricultural technology.

The "emerging food exporters" are large countries that have become agricultural powerhouses more recently: Brazil, Uruguay, Paraguay, Argentina, Thailand, Vietnam, Myanmar, Russia, Ukraine, Kazakhstan. In the last three decades they have turned to intensive, technologically advanced agriculture that requires less human labor. Their grain exports have increased dramatically. They tend to accept the terms of global free trade.

The "(barely) self-sufficient" are countries with greatly increased populations that are able to grow their own food. Ivory Coast, Malawi, and Turkey are among them, but the most important ones are China, India, Pakistan, Bangladesh, and Indonesia. There are more than three billion people in those five Asian nations alone, and the status of their food supply determines that of the world. These countries took advantage of the Green Revolution of the sixties and seventies, but they use a lot of labor, with half their populations still working in agriculture. Their industrial and social development—and their urbanization—are changing things. Plus, they still have hundreds of millions of hungry people.

The "rich food importers" are countries with very little arable land and/or water but/or large populations, countries that bring in large sums of money through the export of other commodities, such as oil and minerals, and the products of their industry. These include Japan, South

Korea, Switzerland, Great Britain, and the kingdoms of the Persian Gulf. They produce a very small percentage of their own food but have a lot of money to buy what they need, which makes them particularly vulnerable to the fluctuations of the market and global politics.

The "poor and food insecure" are most of the countries in Central America, Central Asia, north Africa, and most of all, sub-Saharan Africa: the Other World. Though most of their populations are rural, infertile lands, unpredictable climate, competition from other countries, and, above all, a lack of capital and infrastructure condemn them to very low agricultural yields, which do not remotely meet their most basic needs. Nor do they have enough resources to import what they need. Many of their inhabitants go hungry.

Inequality has many layers.

We live under the reign of numbers; never have numbers carried so much weight as in our current vision of the world. Everything seems measurable; institutions, governments, universities, and businesses spend fortunes calculating the most obscure and most visible variables: populations, diseases, production, markets, audience, geography, poverty, perspective. Everything has a number. Calculating that number has never seemed easier. For centuries governments and patrons of all kinds have struggled to take more and better censuses, but only now do they have the tools to do what they want. When they want to know how we're doing, they measure; to know what works and what doesn't, they measure; to know what to do about it, they measure; to know if what was done was good or bad, they measure and measure and measure. The world has never been measured so much, and without measure. For centuries, anyone paying attention would notice that Indian children were scrawny and ate very little; now the most detailed reports will tell you that 47.2 percent are underweight—and then you can pretend you understand what's going on.

This delusion of measurability makes us believe we have all the information necessary. Numbers give any initiative, any policy, any business deal, any protest, the appearance of solidity. But numbers are, above all, a twisted legacy, a reflection of that universe in which what matters is if the company earned $34,480,415 or $34,480,475. Adapting the view to that view.

Numbers are the language we believe to be mutually intelligible; we pretend to understand each other, or at least try. Numbers are the contemporary way of apprehending a world that is approximate, imprecise, arrogant. This book is also full of numbers, something that vaguely embarrasses me, in the same way I feel embarrassed when in Spain I pronounce the "c" and the "z" differently to sound more like a Spaniard. I am speaking a language that is not wholly mine so I can make believe I'm being understood.

Inequality is defined by numbers.

Inequality is mentioned more and more by those who create it. The predominant tendency toward income parity in the United States and Europe since the thirties was reversed by the neoliberal counterattack of the eighties, and the consequences spread throughout the rest of the world, above all to the nouveau riche countries that were joining the club at the time. The global economy has changed a lot in these thirty years. New players, such as the famous BRIC countries—Brazil, Russia, India, China—have appeared, with South Africa and Indonesia trailing not far behind. Economic growth in these countries has created a class that is much wealthier than their compatriots. Together with the wealthy classes in Europe and the United States, they make up the global rich, people who live in several places at once, profit from many places at once, move their wealth freely around the cyber-global economy; a sector that is increasingly able to evade the control of political and judicial institutions that were created for national economic units.

The famous Gini coefficient, named after the Italian statistician and organicist Corrado Gini, measures the level of inequality in a society according to a scale from 0, if everybody has the same, to 1, if one person has everything, and shows that differences have increased over the last thirty years in almost every country. China is a good example. From a Gini of 0.27 in the eighties, it moved to a Gini of 0.48 today. In Brazil it has remained stable at around 0.50, but even in Sweden the coefficient went from 0.20 to 0.25, and in Germany from 0.24 to 0.32. The United States went from 0.30 to 0.38, and Great Britain from 0.26 to 0.40.[2]

The Gini coefficient of inequality worldwide—if all the incomes of all the inhabitants of the world are compared—is 0.70: so much more brutal than the index of any individual country.

A recent report from Oxfam says that 48 percent of the wealth in the world is in the hands of 1 percent of the population. Or, put slightly differently: seventy million people own the same amount of wealth as the remaining seven billion.

Or, also, according to the same report: the eighty wealthiest people in the world have more money than the 3.5 billion poorest.

This, we can say, is what is called inequality. And sometimes we worry about it.

With the candor that often characterizes this publication of the world economic establishment, Zanny Minton Beddoes, writing for the The Economist in October 2012 noted:

Many economists, too, now worry that widening income disparities may have damaging side-effects. In theory, inequality has an ambiguous relationship with prosperity. It can boost growth, because richer folk save and invest more and because people work harder in response to incentives. But big income gaps can also be inefficient, because they can bar talented poor people from access to education or feed resentment that results in growth-destroying populist policies.

But now the economics establishment has become concerned about who gets what. Research by economists at the IMF suggests that income inequality slows growth, causes financial crises and weakens demand. In a recent report the Asian Development Bank argued that if emerging Asia's income distribution had not worsened over the past twenty years, the region's rapid growth would have lifted an extra 240 million people out of extreme poverty. More controversial studies purport to link widening income gaps with all manner of ills, from obesity to suicide.

The widening gaps within many countries are beginning to worry even the plutocrats. A survey for the World Economic Forum meeting at Davos pointed to inequality as the most pressing problem of the coming decade (alongside fiscal imbalances). In all sections of society, there is growing agreement that the world is becoming more unequal, and that today's disparities and their likely trajectory are dangerous. [...] The unstable history of Latin America, long the continent with the biggest income gaps, suggests that countries run by entrenched wealthy elites do not do very well.

That same article states that, in spite of everything, some of the richest people continue to be skeptical about whether inequality is a problem in and of itself. "But even they have an interest in mitigating it, for if it continues to rise, momentum for change will build and may lead to a political outcome that serves nobody's interests. Communism may be past reviving, but there are plenty of other bad ideas out there."[3]

They're worried, but not all that much.

Not when it comes right down to it, I mean.

The luxury hotel industry—as an example of something whose nonexistence would cause no harm whatsoever—moved, according to Bain &

Company, $165 billion in 2012, a third more than in 2009. These are hotels that charge an average of seven hundred dollars a night and have one secret in common: they have more employees than guests—more servants.

It's a growing market. Knight Frank, a company that sells houses to the super rich, says that in ten years there will be 4,000 billionaires, up from the 2,200 there are now. These people also have needs that have not been met, though they aren't exactly basic. Right now, for example, for $6 million, they can reserve a Gulfstream G650, the coolest private jet of the fall-winter season, but they'll only receive it if they pay another $60 million and wait five years. The president of Gulfstream, a subsidiary of a larger company that makes tanks and submarines, said, he had "never seen so many powerful people with problems." There are other services, of course, that are not suffering from problems of supply. The market for steel doors and bulletproof glass, for example, continues to grow at uncontrollable rates.

Spending on luxuries and luxury security and luxury goods is capitalism in all its splendor. Or, sometimes, capitalism in all its stupidity. In 2012 the United States spent $170 billion on direct marketing, that is, words on paper or in bytes trying to sell something. Experts say that 3 percent of the physical and 0.1 percent of electronic letters led to a sale. "That is, one hundred and sixty-four million dollars were spent to bother people, fill landfills, and clog up spam filters," said another article from *The Economist*, exposing its most obvious function: give useless work to thousands of people, reproduce itself, make a few bosses right.

In 2011 Warren Buffett, the third richest man in the world, said that there's class warfare in his country. "There's been class warfare going on for the last twenty years, and my class has won. We're the ones that have gotten our tax rates reduced dramatically. If you look at the four hundred highest taxpayers in the United States in 1992, the first year for figures, they averaged about $40 million of [income] per person. In the most recent year, they were $227 million per person — five for one. During that period, their taxes went down from 29 percent to 21 percent of income. So, if there's class warfare, the rich class has won."[4]

(Capitalism is like an airplane: if it stops, it crashes. It must keep moving and can never land. The true miracle of an airplane is not that it can fly but that it can convert its fastest motion into the appearance of immobility, calm in the clouds, silence that makes it even more inexplicable and unbelievable that we are hanging in the air. The true miracle of capitalism is its ability to convert immobility par excellence into the appearance of frenzied movement.)

The increase in inequality in the last thirty years has been a brutal change from the general tendency throughout most of the twentieth century. In the wealthiest countries, few were paying attention as long as everybody was able to consume, and they remained indifferent until the crisis hit them in the face. In 2008 the wealthy nations spent fortunes to save their banks and their wealthiest citizens while condemning many of their own poor to even poorer lives, without savings, without houses, without jobs. Not to mention the poor in other places.

In early June 2008, when millions of people were demanding food in the streets of dozens of countries, when the malnourished of the world for the first time in history reached the banner number of one billion, the participants at a FAO conference held in Rome proclaimed that more than $30 billion a year for six years—$180 billion total—would solve the most urgent world hunger.⁵ At that same time, "dieting" was a $33 billion industry in the United States alone.

The rich countries promised $12 billion in aid. This was almost heroic, and more than a third of what was requested. They ended up giving $1 billion. In November the stock market and the banks crashed, and the governments forgot about the hungry. Within a few months, they spent $30 trillion on saving their banks.

What's odd is that it is surprising (to me) that governments spend fortunes to rescue large banks and much more modest sums to rescue the hungry, because finance is essential to the functioning of their system and the hungry aren't. They are, rather, a spoke in their wheels.

Even so, the rescue of the banks was a breaking point, the moment some people started thinking a few things over.

It's odd that, suddenly, unexpectedly, something that was obvious to a few, and oblivious to so many others, suddenly became widely visible, "revealed" by some fact, act, pact. Or perhaps it became crystallized in one fact and only then became a shared and accepted concept. The government bailouts of the largest Western banks led to one such revelation. Suddenly, generations or sectors who had for years been wholly content with their standard of living, their freedom, their levels of consumption, realized that they had no protection, or even worse, lived at the mercy of the super-powerful rich, who could use the apparatus of the state to their benefit. And they got mad as hell.

(In a way, those bailouts in the summer of 2008 were the flipside—the closure?—of the cycle that began in September 2001, seven years before. If 9/11 convinced millions of citizens in the powerful countries to entrust their governments with a duty to defend them—even if this meant being denied certain freedoms—the financial bailouts convinced them that, on the contrary, they could not trust their governments when they really needed them because those governments had already been taken over by the rich. It was a real change, the effects of which are still being felt, and are still in search of an outcome.)

The most well-known and best-marketed expression of that process was "the 99 percent."

It all started with an article published in May 2011 in *Vanity Fair* and written by the liberal and Nobel-prize winning economist Joseph Stiglitz. In the article, he pointed out how much wealth had been concentrated: "The upper 1 percent of Americans are now taking in nearly a quarter of the nation's income every year. In terms of wealth rather than income, the top 1 percent control 40 percent. Their lot in life has improved considerably. Twenty-five years ago, the corresponding figures were 12 percent and 33 percent." He continued by discussing why seeking personal gain in the financial sector could be injurious to an economy: "Far too many of our most talented young people, seeing the astronomical rewards, have gone into finance rather than into fields that would lead to a more productive and healthy economy," then went on to discuss how that concentration of money made the rich detached from the public sphere—schools, hospitals, parks: "The rich don't need to rely on government for parks or education or medical care or personal security—they can buy all these things for themselves. In the process, they become more distant from ordinary people, losing whatever empathy they may once have had." And added: "Much of today's inequality is due to manipulation of the financial system, enabled by changes in the rules that have been bought and paid for by the financial industry itself—one of its best investments ever. The government lent money to financial institutions at close to 0 percent interest and provided generous bailouts on favorable terms when all else failed. Regulators turned a blind eye to a lack of transparency and to conflicts of interest."

Stiglitz ends the article with a warning: "The top 1 percent have the best houses, the best educations, the best doctors, and the best lifestyles, but there is one thing that money doesn't seem to have bought: an understanding that their fate is bound up with how the other 99 percent live. Throughout history, this is something that the top 1 percent eventually do learn. Too late."[6]

The slogan spread quickly. In a few days, many spoke about the 99 and the 1 percent: politicians, journalists, advertisers, people. "We are the 99 percent," became the battle cry.

(In the United States, 10 percent of the population controls 76 percent of the national wealth, but what counted at that moment was that 1 percent.)[7]

Certainties were established. Suddenly the issue of inequality became a spot of common ground. The notion of inequality was established in relation to those who had accumulated too much. It was a quantitative rather than a qualitative difference. It didn't correspond to the place each person occupied in society, in the process of production, in the various iterations of a nation. In that blueprint, the owner of a small factory with only two hundred workers—the exploiter of the labor of two hundred workers— could be put in the same bag as the two hundred workers: both were part of that 99 percent who did not have dozens of millions of dollars.

This is the same mechanism that works so well for the nationalist masquerade. Nationalism manages to make the owner and the worker, the lawyer and the housemaid, the landowner and the peon, part of the same thing, the Nation, the Fatherland, which unites them against everybody else. Groups need a common enemy to believe they exist; the enemy of a nation is other nations, some more than others. In the same way, the enemy of that new and unlikely club of the rich and the poor, the marginal and the super-integrated, the oppressors and the oppressed that this 99 percent slogan proposed, was that 1 percent, the ones who've gone over the top. They are so grotesque, so excessive, that it is possible to assert that everybody else has something in common.

(Do the people in the United States who chant "We are the 99 percent" realize that they, all together, are more or less the 1 percent of the world?)

The 99 percent slogan brings up the subject of extreme wealth, not that of wealth, property, ways of appropriating wealth.

(Lately, it seems that all discussions stop at the door of private property: it's the *non plus ultra* of these times, the threshold one cannot cross. *Lasciate ogni speranza voi ch'entrate . . .* Basically, I suppose because there's no alternative on offer. Different forms of ownership have appeared for cultural production. Since forever, if someone wanted to share a sandwich, he had to split it in half; if a book, he had to give it over. Now one can share a song, a movie, an electronic book, a bicycle in certain *cool* cities, without losing anything. This is a radical change but still limited, a window onto other forms of ownership. But when we return to the clumsy materiality of the sandwich, everything is still the same, and as contested as always. And more than that, it is presented as unavoidable, "natural." Capitalism and the concept of private property are natural, hence to accept it is to be realistic. There are solutions and they are, needless to say, political, for starters, the awareness that accepting it is a choice. Not accepting it is another, contrary one, but one that doesn't guarantee anything will change; only that one would like it to.)

Within the current hegemonic discourse, the opposite of inequality is not equality. Those who criticize "inequality" do not want equality, they want moderation. They want an end to extremes. What bothers them is not that there is a mechanism through which some can take for themselves what others produce, but that they take too much for themselves.

Thereby the 99 and the 1. The 1 takes too much and we are left with too little. Capitalism is fine, but let's not exaggerate. In 2013, Oxfam, one of the NGOs that is most committed to eradicating poverty, reported: "Inequality has been linked to many different social ills, including violence, mental health, crime, and obesity. Crucially inequality has been shown to be not only bad for the poor in unequal societies but also the rich. Richer people are happier and healthier if they live in more equal societies."[8]

The truth is, nobody knows what's being talked about when one talks about inequality. Égalité, imposed by the French Revolution, was equality before the law at a time when such a thing didn't exist, when being born in one cradle rather than another meant you had different legal rights. Now, at a time when we assume that most countries offer equality before the law, equality has become, for many, "equality of opportunity," the idea that life is an obstacle course and what is needed is a guarantee that everybody can reach the starting line and enter the race; later, along the route, the strongest will end up with the trophies and the rest will have lost their opportunity. Others, finally, might be talking about a certain level of material equality. But even here, they probably mean "a certain moderation of inequality," an absence of grotesque differences, that those with the least have enough so as not to humiliate the rest. Because not many doctrines survive that posit material equality as a goal.

Or do they?

In order to promote this "moderate inequality," this "reasonable inequality," most governments and international organizations maintained, for the last several decades, that the solution was some form of the trickle-down theory: somehow the overflow caused by an increase in the wealth of the wealthiest will also benefit the poor.

Lately they've been saying this in a whisper, almost ashamed, so nobody will hear.

It's difficult to think about getting rid of material inequality in a society based on material inequality. The old saying goes that only in death is everyone equal, but in death, too, there is inequality. For most of history, people died from diseases nobody knew how to cure. Needless to say, poor people died because their food, their sanitary conditions, their lives were worse, but there was no efficient cure against gout or syphilis or breast cancer. In the final analysis, kings and slaves died of the same things.

Not anymore. Due to advances in basic medicine in the last few decades, the population in Africa tripled between 1950 and 2000. Not as many women now die in childbirth, or children in their first few years; not as many people are sick from malaria or tuberculosis. However, many still die before their time. One out of every ten African children dies before she turns five: fifteen times more than in the rich countries.

The difference is that now they don't die because there isn't treatment for their diseases but because they can't afford to buy those treatments. In Uganda, for example, the government does not have enough money to supply the required dose of malarone (atovaquone and proguanil hydrochloride) to prevent malaria in everybody, so it supplies less, and the hospitals divide it up and pass it out and everybody takes less than required. These reduced doses become a kind of vaccination against the medication, creating resistance to malarone so that when they contract the disease, they die. What kills them is having had less than the prescribed dose of the medicine, not the disease itself.

Maybe this would be, provisionally, an urgent measure of equality: that nobody should die of illnesses for which there are cures. A minimum amount of equality in the face of the great equalizer.

Rather modest.

The equality of eating every day is even more modest. As we said: in a world where there is nothing more legitimate than being a victim, hunger produces victims—many victims—without an apparent victimizer.

What is a victim without a victimizer? *An act without an agent, a deed that nobody has done, the confusion of not being able to finish a story. And, therefore, a bothersome story, which so many overlook.*

And they talk, if they talk about anything, about inequality, but perhaps not as beautifully put as by these lines by the fourteenth-century Spanish poet Jorge Manrique:

"Joined together in equality / are those who live by their labor / and wealthy men."⁹

ARGENTINA: THE WASTE OF HUNGER

1

The sun as assailant. A dirt road, an open field, a horrible stench; then a bridge. Under the bridge, the Reconquista River is a medley of brown water and foam, of putrefaction. Hundreds of people are waiting on the bridge for a barricade to open a few yards away. They sweat, they wait, they look at each other, they talk a little; many have bicycles. Some shouting is heard from under the bridge: two kids, fifteen or sixteen, chase another kid, fifteen or sixteen. On the bridge, when the barricade opens, hundreds of people take off running toward a huge mountain of garbage. Almost all are men, almost all are young, but there are a few women and old people. Under the bridge, the one who was being chased is screaming. His pursuers have caught up with him and fall upon him; he screams again. Some on the bridge look, they look even though they pretend not to look. Below, the pursuers knock him down, grab his arms and legs, swing him in the air, throw him into the river. He falls into the rotten river, no longer screaming. The people waiting wait. The sun explodes.

> The José León Suárez garbage dump is an Argentine tradition. Here, more than fifty years ago, the military government shot an unknown number of civilians who had attempted to support a Peronist military uprising. "Six months later, on a suffocating summer night with a glass of beer in front of him, a man says to me, 'One of the executed men is alive.' I don't know what it is about this vague, remote, highly unlikely story that manages to draw me in."

So wrote Rodolfo Walsh in 1957 in the opening of *Operation Massacre* and it feels natural that a story about a failed execution would begin at the José Léon Suárez garbage dump.[1]

The garbage dumps have changed a lot since then. They are now a business called Coordinación Ecológica Área Metropolitana Sociedad del Estado (CEAMSE), spread over a few hundred acres. Its origins are so clear they're turgid. In 1977 the same military forces that murdered with impunity and filled the river with dead bodies decided they had to do away with the smog that was fouling the air in Buenos Aires. It was a noble cause, and they prohibited the private burning of garbage and opened huge dumps on the outskirts of the city. Within that metaphoric system, the clearness of the downtown sky was bought with the filth in the periphery.

Right around that same time and less than a mile way, in one of the largest military bases in Argentina, Campo de Mayo, hundreds or thousands of bodies were disappeared, burned, buried.

The city of Buenos Aires produces the garbage; the surrounding areas receive it, process it, consume it. The three million people living in the city of Buenos Aires produce 6,500 tons of garbage a day; the ten million living in the thirty districts around the capital produce 10,000 tons a day. In other words, every inhabitant of the capital throws out twice as much as one inhabitant in the suburbs. Belonging has its privileges.

There have always been scavengers, people who search through garbage for things to sell. When CEAMSE opened and the amount of garbage increased exponentially, the local scavengers got busier. At the end of the nineties, when Argentina became a socially divided country, the government built a fence around the dump, and dozens of policemen stood guard. They did their job without many qualms. A scavenger caught sneaking in was beaten and his booty confiscated. CEAMSE officials claimed this was for their own good, they couldn't allow them to take and eat rotten food that might make them sick. The same government that gave them no food security made sure they didn't eat a spoiled yogurt. The scavengers began to improve their skills; they snuck in at night, one or two or three at a time, and when they saw a cop, they hid, often under the garbage.

Scavenging was a possible job in a country where jobs were scarce. And a belt of vacant land surrounding the garbage dump, land deemed uninhabitable for sanitary reasons, slowly began to be occupied.

It was 1998 and Argentina, as usual, was in the midst of an economic and social crisis. The land around the garbage dump was filling up with people who had been left unemployed, who could no longer pay even the minimum rent they'd been charged for a shack where they'd at least had a roof over their heads. Furthermore, thousands of refugees from the floods in the northeast had arrived, and the area was bursting with poverty.

"The occupation was completely spontaneous. When you first squat, it's a huge mess, full of pieces of wire everywhere to mark off the lots, and I was sitting on a rock keeping watch. I used to have a neighbor, named Coqui, and he always harassed me. 'You remember those days, when you used to be so white?' he'd say."

Lorena had arrived from Uruguay eight years earlier when she was sixteen. She came from a working-class neighborhood in Montevideo. Her father had left when she was young; her mother, a seamstress, worked hard to support her four daughters, who emigrated one by one to Argentina. Her last big effort was to throw a quinceañera for her youngest, Lorena. She was already sick, and she died of a heart attack two months later. Lorena, alone, without anything, had no choice but to go to her sister's house on the other side of the La Plata River, to the suburbs of Buenos Aires, to José León Suárez.

"I got on the bus in Montevideo and traveled all night. We reached Buenos Aires at dawn on a freeway, straight into the city center, and I looked out the window and said to myself, Hollywood, I've landed in Hollywood: lights, freeways, women from who knows where wearing boots up to their knees and short shorts. I was like a Janis Joplin type, with my Indian blouse, long braids, clogs, and those chicks were coming out of those dancehalls wearing boots and super short shorts. I looked out the window, and my eyes were popping out of my head, 'cause it was too much. 'Freeway, boots, ass,' I kept repeating. My heart was pounding and I said, where am I, what's this, where have I ended up."

She didn't understand anything in José León Suárez either. Her sisters were worried about this teenager who came from out of their past. Lorena had no papers, no education, no idea what to do with her life.

"I started working in a *choripán* sandwich shop at the train station. The owner was always grabbing my ass and I didn't want to say anything, then one day I blew up and told him to go to hell, and I never went back. And right then is when I started to scavenge for cardboard, *cartonear*. Here in Suárez everybody had their carts and I started to do drugs, a lot of drugs. I didn't even know what a joint was . . . and that whole underworld of poverty, of misery. I wanted to kill myself. Then something really beautiful happened: I met the father of my children. I spent many years with him, sixteen years with the father of my children. It was a beautiful love story."

The boy's name was César, he worked in a factory, he had a family. Together, they created another one: two biological children, an adopted daughter. In those days, 1998, they lived in a rented shack. Then he got fired from his factory job, and they couldn't pay the rent. Anyway, Lorena always wanted to have something of her own, a piece of land. But that afternoon, he didn't want to occupy.

"I was already fed up, I couldn't take it anymore. I always did things the right way, and still, everything went wrong, I never had anything. But he didn't want to break the law, he wanted to do things the right way.

And even more when he saw what it was like there, a half-flooded garbage dump, everything full of shit and mud, rats this big. It was the first time we separated."

That afternoon, everybody staked out what they could. Lorena remembered it affectionately. "I had heard people were moving in, and I was there at six with my tent. It was difficult, very difficult. It's like every barrio: one goes, then two, and by the time you look, everybody's there. Hamburger patties, tomato sauce, soup, things like that. Yes, almost everything I cook is from up here."

"What do you cook most of the time?"

"Stew. Stew with potatoes, noodles, rice. If I find any meat, meat. Depends what I find on the mountain. That's when I finally realized what it means to be poor. People helped each other: come over here, here's a place for you, what do you need. At first everybody got a thirty-by-thirty lot; then they saw there wouldn't be enough for everybody and they decided to split them in half, thirty by fifteen. They started marking out the streets, the space where one day there'd be sidewalks. Weeks of work, lots of enthusiasm. And conflict: some wanted to occupy land so they could sell it to those who came later, but their neighbors prevented that.

"When I found out that some were trying to make money off my comrades, I said, let's go there and we'll stay there until we get a family to come, and we didn't let them sell it until a family came. We all had tents, and we lived in them for about six months. For survival, those of us who were already living there had to organize ourselves into groups, so we could cook and make fires, because the police didn't let us bring in any wood, or corrugated metal. We didn't have water either; the water here was really nasty, and infected with hepatitis. We organized a soup kitchen, an *olla popular*, and began to figure out how we were going to get water. A settlement is really difficult at first. That's when I started to see things I could do.

"A while later, somebody realized that a barrio without a name wasn't a barrio. They discussed it at a neighborhood meeting. Some wanted to name it José Luis Cabezas, the name of a millionaire photographer and supporter of Menem who had been murdered the year before. But finally they decided to call it Ocho de Mayo, because that was the day, the eighth of May, when they'd dared, the day it all started."

In the following few months, many thousands more arrived; all the wasteland—the garbage dumps, the swamps—was being transformed into barrios. After a while, César agreed to come live in the occupied territories, and he and Lorena got back together. They didn't have many sources of income, and there were days they didn't have enough to eat.

They scavenged, *cartoneaban*. *Cartonear* is distinctly Argentine Spanish, a word we invented three decades ago. It is the politically correct, the decaffeinated verb that describes what those who call themselves scavengers, *cirujas*, do: searching through other people's garbage.

Lorena usually went to a fancy neighborhood in Buenos Aires, Belgrano, to dig through trash. Some of her neighbors also made the trip there, and among them were Noelia's parents.

"A long time ago, when Noelia was five or six, she used to come to a community center we set up in the neighborhood. I taught a workshop for children, and I remember we were talking about dreams, what each one dreamed of, and Noelia did a strange drawing. I didn't understand it at all, and I asked her to explain it. 'This is a McDonald's.' And I asked her, 'Is that your dream?' 'Yes, to eat, but inside.' And that made an impression on me. Because the truth is, she was used to eating from the McDonald's dumpster, but she wanted to eat inside," explained Lorena. And that McDonald's was "Saint McDonald's because the hamburgers were the prettiest. Even now, you can get the cleanest food from McDonald's," she said. But Noelia wanted to eat inside.

Most of the residents of Ocho de Mayo, at that time, ten years ago, climbed the Montaña, the mountain of garbage, to scavenge. That's what they still call it.

"You gather up your courage. If I say, hey, get your ass onto that Montaña there, you think you'll want to? I guarantee you won't. You have to steel yourself, and it'll disgust you and you'll vomit, and you'll say you can't, you can't be there."

The Montaña is about twenty feet high, and around twenty yards at the base, and it's a stinking mess, oozing, sticky remains, the stench from hell.

"But if you're really hungry, you do what you gotta do, it's hard going, and in the end you won't even notice it. It's about need . . . The only thing that mobilizes us, that gets us organized, that makes us fight to have a piece of land, is that we're hungry. I need it, so I do it. We aren't very aware, like we aren't very aware of working here. Because if we were aware, we wouldn't be here."

Here, at the foot of the Montaña, is the cooperatively run garbage processing plant that Lorena manages. "Processing plant" makes it sound quite grandiose. It's actually a shed full of garbage, piles of garbage, with several dozen men and women sorting through it to find things to sell. They're the ones who've escaped, who don't have to climb the Montaña every day, the scavengers with steady jobs. Argentina is a country where anything can become official, and currently, that includes just about everything.

"Why? If you were very aware, what would you do?"

"I don't know, something else. We don't even think about how soon we'll die if we keep working here . . . It's terrible because the lives of everybody who works with garbage, in this whole industry . . . We're disgusting, man. We're disgusting. We work with rats, just look at these conditions. But today you have to solve the problem of food today. When you're hungry, you don't have the luxury to stand back and take a look at these things," Lorena told me.

With the Argentine economic crisis of 2001, the expansion of squatting, and the lack of money, the number of scavengers suddenly increased, as well as their determination and despair. They say that the guards at the dump became more violent and would try to chase them away with bullets. So the scavengers began to attack the garbage trucks as they were arriving. Repression also increased and spread into nearby neighborhoods. There were beatings, shootings, wounded.

The scavengers say that police methods improved. Sometimes they'd let them in, then they'd catch them as they were leaving so they could take what they'd found and sell it themselves, in their own slums. Some policemen, the scavengers still say, charge them an entrance fee in cash, merchandise, or sex.

Until March 15, 2004. That night, sixteen-year-old twins Federico and Diego Duarte entered as they had many other nights before to scavenge on the Montaña. When the police arrived, they hid under some boxes. Federico saw a truck dumping a load a few feet away, right where his brother was supposed to be. When the police left and he came out of hiding, he looked for him everywhere. The next day, his sister Alicia reported it to the police, but they ignored her. Two days later, a judge ordered a search, but it was too late.

Diego Duarte's body was never found, and the case became a scandal that the national newspapers wouldn't let go of. In protest, the Camino del Buen Ayre, a road that passes through CEAMSE's property, was blocked by *piqueteros*, organizations made up of labor rights activists. A few days later, hundreds of scavengers set fire to warehouses on the grounds. Finally, the company negotiated; they agreed that every day, for one hour, around five in the afternoon, the scavengers could have access to the Montaña. It was a way of sanctioning, of making official, something that had, until then, been clandestine and marginal: the fact that thousands of Argentines picked through garbage to find food.

To possess food is a privilege, to throw food in the garbage is a gesture of power, the power to trash what others might be able to use, but the urge to find food is more powerful than the ability to get rid of it.

2

The Institution of Mechanical Engineers in Great Britain (IMechE) is a respected, level-headed organization. In January 2013 they published a report that seemed to be pure sensationalism. After years of research they had reached the conclusion that about half the food produced in the world was not eaten.

Their figures weren't that far away from those that were usually tossed about, but stating it in such clear terms had a certain impact. Their report *Global Food: Waste Not, Want Not*, concluded: "Today, we produce about four billion metric tons of food per annum. Yet due to poor practices in harvesting, storage, and transportation, as well as market and consumer wastage, it is estimated that 30–50 percent (or 1.2–2 billion tons) of all food produced never reaches a human stomach. Furthermore, this figure does not reflect the fact that large amounts of land, energy, fertilizers, and water have also been lost in the production of foodstuffs which simply end up as waste."[2]

The reasons for this vary from region to region. In the Other World, food is lost due to a lack of infrastructure. It rots in the fields because of poor harvesting equipment, it spoils in poorly built storehouses, it doesn't arrive at its destination because of the deplorable condition of roads and the vehicles, or rats or insects get to it first. This doesn't happen only in countries with the most extreme conditions. "In South-East Asian countries for example," says the report, "losses of rice can range from 37% to 80% of total production depending on development stage, which amounts to total wastage in the region of about 180 million tons annually. In China, a country experiencing rapid development, the rice loss figure is about 45%, whereas in less-developed Vietnam, rice losses between the field and the table can amount to 80% of production."[3]

In the rich countries, food spoils in coolers or on the shelves of supermarkets or in restaurants, but above all in the refrigerators of consumers. Food must be too cheap, still. And the prevalent paranoia about food allows those who can to throw it away as soon as it even approaches its sell-by date. Moreover, we are too demanding. "Major supermarkets, in meeting consumer expectations, will often reject entire crops of perfectly edible fruit and vegetables at the farm because they do not meet exacting marketing standards for their physical characteristics, such as size and appearance. For example, up to 30% of the UK's vegetable crop is never harvested as a result of such practices." In addition, the report continues, "of the produce that does appear in the supermarket, commonly used sales promotions frequently encourage customers to purchase excessive quantities which, in the case of perishable foodstuffs, inevitably generates wastage in the home. Overall between 30% and 50% of what has been bought in developed countries is thrown away by the purchaser."[4]

One year earlier, FAO had been more discreet about saying more or less the same thing. In Europe and the United States, the average consumer wastes over hundred pounds of food a year; in Asia and Africa— barely twenty.[5] And every year the citizens of the twenty wealthiest nations waste an amount of food equal to the entire agricultural yield of sub-Saharan Africa, about 220 million tons.

And then there's this: every year in Italy enough food to feed forty-four million people and worth about €37 billion is thrown away. In the United States, according to the National Resources Defense Council, 40 percent of all food is wasted.[6] A survey done by the Shelton Group says that two out of every five people in the United States feel "green guilt" for throwing away food.[7]

In other words, every day the English throw away 4 million apples. Every day the English throw away 5 million potatoes. Every day the English throw away 1.5 million bananas. Every bloody day.

Throwing away food is a clear consequence, one of the most brutal consequences, of overabundance. In 2007 the English threw away 8.3 million tons of food; in 2010, during the crisis, this dropped to 7.2 million.[8] Which makes the act of throwing away food somewhat ironic: the poorer we get the more careful we are not to waste food.

There's something wrong with these numbers. It's unbelievable that we waste half or even a third of the food we have while so many have none. But I've checked it many times, and everything confirms it.

A 2011 study by the Instituto de Ingeniería Sanitaria of the School of Engineering of the University of Buenos Aires found that the city of Buenos Aires throws away between 200 and 250 tons of food a day, the equivalent of about 550,000 meals.

Garbage—the abundance of garbage, the wastefulness of garbage— is one of the most obvious metaphors of the global system: that some throw away what others need so badly, that some lack what others have too much of.

"The winner takes the best."

A kid shouts at me, his Boca jersey full of holes.

The sun as assailant. Along the dirt road: the vacant lots, the stench, and thousands of people waiting on the bridge. They are alert, crowding in across the entire width, waiting for the signal. The sun is insistent. In front, a policeman stands guard, killing them with his indifference. Suddenly he raises his arms, twirls his arms: this is the signal they've been waiting for. A thousand people press forward without any shouting, on their way to the Montaña.

The first option is to throw extras in the garbage; the second, to throw it to third-class citizens.

When the policeman gives the signal, you have to run. You have to get there before everybody else, take advantage of those three-quarters of an hour that the Montaña is open. You have to run a whole kilometer, run and climb and push and fall and shout, and toss a joke out here and there. They run, they pedal along the road of dirt and puddles, between and around the piles of garbage and the scrub and the stagnant pools of water; everybody runs to see who can get there first to dive into the garbage, to get the best leftovers. Most are men but there are also some women and children; a thousand men and children and women running to get to the garbage first. It is a battle for survival staged by a director without a touch of talent.

"I ride my bike, if you fall they run right over you. Or they run into you, because it's a mess, and if you fall, they'll run right over you. Lots of bruises. It's like a marathon, and whoever falls, tough shit. If you don't get up right away, they'll run right over you. Everybody wants to get there first. That's what hunger does, and whoever gets there first, takes whatever he can, and whoever doesn't, doesn't. So you gotta run."

Laucha had spent ten years climbing the Montaña. He used to work in construction, but it's hard to find work, he said, there was less and less of it.

"At least for me there isn't any. So I go up the Montaña," he told me later, on the way down.

Some bring handcarts—horses are forbidden—but they're slow, too slow. Carts are good only if you work in a team so someone can ride ahead on the bike. The bicycles are old, broken down, bumping along the dangerous terrain full of obstacles and sharp objects, and a wide range of decay.

"Did you see? It's like one of those horse races, they've got all of us there and then we have to take off running, come what may, and they push you and run you down. Once I broke my shoulder, and a hip, luckily some guys dragged me out, you can't believe how much it hurt . . ."

They were dressed in filth: dirty shorts, dirty T-shirts, a dirty hat, and dirty tennis shoes; a whole filthy team to get dirty fighting for the best garbage.

"But nobody's gonna help you here, you gotta look out for yourself."

La Flaca didn't used to go up because she didn't have a bicycle.

"Without a bike, it's really hard, by the time you get there, there's nothing left."

La Flaca would go to downtown Buenos Aires with her cart to scavenge there—the Capital, she calls it, la Capital—but she'd leave after lunch and wouldn't get back till late at night. It got harder and harder to find people to look after her children, and anyway sometimes downtown she'd find things and sometimes she wouldn't.

"Here there are more opportunities, you'll always find something. Well, not always, but mostly. And anyway, it's much closer. You wouldn't believe how much I had to save up to get a bicycle. For years I've been wanting this bicycle."

La Flaca was *flaca*, skinny, in her thirties, with five children between twelve and two.

"So, finally you were able to buy one?" I asked her later, and she looked at me as if she didn't understand. "The bike," I said.

"No, what are you talking about, buy it. I found it in the Capital, in the garbage, a total mess, and we fixed it up."

The smells, the stench, the amount of bugs: an infinity of bugs.

"Before you go up there you should know that it's like jail, like living in a prison. You're just waiting for someone to kill you or for you to kill someone. It's dangerous, I'm telling you, dangerous. Not only for you, don't be getting the wrong idea. When new guys come from a different area, they also get beat up, they break their bones and take their bikes, their hats, slash their faces, it's a mess. It's a madhouse, how you've got to fight for your place. The other day they knocked out a kid, a little kid, eight, ten years old. And his mother was there, a big lady and she grabbed the bike chain and chased them off because they'd knocked out her son."

"You afraid?"

"I'm a tough woman, I can take care of myself and my family."

They kept coming, in droves, a frontal assault, and they reached the top. At the top there was a kind of plateau where policemen dressed like commandos park their jeeps and motorcycles, where the yellow excavators would come and go, where the ground was traversed by miles of piping to release the buried gases, where, finally, the Montaña peaked, the summit of the Montaña, that interminable mountain of garbage.

"Tie it up, Matute!" a twenty-year-old shouted.

Matute did what he said; some tied their bikes to a piece of fencing; others just dropped them, trustingly.

"There are a lot more men than women. Men are stronger. We women have to look for food, we can't be carrying lumber or jerry cans. You start to learn how to find things. You get an instinct," La Flaca told me later. "Anyway, there aren't many women because it's really dangerous. They crash into you, hit you. But there are some. Some even bring their children. But that can be really bad for them. The smells, the filth, all of it."

La Flaca had a husband who'd been unemployed for a long time; they received a subsidy—Asignación Universal por Hijo (Universal Child Allowance)—for one of their children, who had her last name because they were separated when he was born. But not for the other four because they had her husband's last name and her husband once had a real job, so they didn't get it for them. Now she had to go fill out some forms so they'd receive the allowance for them too.

"Isn't it bad for you?

"What?"

"The filth, I mean, the contamination."

"Thank God, no, not yet. I'm used to it."

The smell of some kind of strange gas, turkey buzzards, a few plants that stubbornly remain alive, mountains in the middle of the plain. On one of the flattest landscapes in the world, in the middle of the pampas, five or six little mountains made out of garbage. You can see far and wide from up here. First, the prison buildings: three, one next to the other. Farther away, the slums: many, interminable. Someone told me that this is a theme park of poverty, where nothing is missing: garbage, jails, shacks—somebody once put up a sign at the entrance that said "Welcome to Quemaikén, Poverty Theme Park."

"I'd rather be modest than wealthy. I'm better off with what I've got than people are who have a lot more," explained Tato.

"Why are you better off?"

"Because if you're modest, they give you more. If you're not, they won't give you anything. You get more with poverty than grandeur."

"What do you find, mostly?"

"Food, my friend, food," said Tato. He was over fifty, or maybe he was thirty-two. In the garbage, on top of the mountain of garbage, hundreds fight over the most sought-after merchandise: yogurts, sausages, patties, packages of pasta, crackers, french fries, canned goods, bottles of soda, diapers, broken wooden pallets, paper, a piece of furniture, an unusual something or other. There were myths: so-and-so found a cell phone worth so much, another found one of those really good watches, and yet another, a wallet with a wad of bills.

"What do you look for most of all?"

"Gold," Tato said, laughing.

"Have you ever found any?"

"Are you kidding?"

"Other than gold . . ."

"If there's yogurt, I take it because I know it will bring in money, I've got customers who'll buy it from me. Sausages, fresh cheese, cold cuts, cheese, everything," said Mr. Tato, his teeth quite lost, his New York Yankees cap faded to colorless. Mr. Tato paid attention to brand names; he knows one from the other.

"Everything. That *Actimel* yogurt, they throw out whole packages. Or *Beldent* gum, we take it and we package it up again, you wouldn't believe how good it looks. Or those packages of premade french fries that McDonald's throws out still frozen. That's some good stuff."

Mr. Tato asked me if I had a cigarette.

"No, I finished mine."

"Ah, just a sec," Mr. Tato said. "I'll go find some."

A few minutes later he came back with a slightly smashed pack of Marlboros, still closed; he offered me one. "From the dump."

Another man came from nowhere to bum one from Tato. He wasn't in great shape: his belly hung out over his short T-shirt, his pant legs ended at the middle of his calves, his shoes were in rags. I asked whether it was easy or not to find things like clothing that fit.

"You never know what you'll find," he said. "Maybe a perfect fitting pair of pants, maybe a body. It's happened. Many times. I never saw one, but others have. They also throw out coffins. If you start looking, you'll find all the equipment you need. If you want to die, it's easy."

"Do you ever imagine the kinds of people who would throw away a coffin?"

"What the hell for? Better not to think about it, my friend."

Some arrived late. They scavenged through what others have already foraged. An old stooped-over man carrying a burlap bag gave me a toothless smile.

"These kids miss a lot," he said, tossing an unidentifiable object into his bag.

People on the garbage mountain, hundreds of raunchy, sloshing people rummaging through garbage. The police with their guns ready. And birds, the dirtiest birds I'd ever seen in my life.

"This is the world upside down," said a man who introduced himself José Luis. "Instead of giving it to others, they throw it here, so the prices won't go down. Sons of bitches."

Here, right here, they throw ten thousand tons of garbage a day: the equivalent of two hundred train cars full of garbage a day. Everyone seemed to have a different purpose for the things they discovered. They could consume it, they could sell it, they could trade it.

I asked José Luis what he did with the things he found.

"If you can eat it, you eat it. And if you've got something of value, you sell it in your barrio or to the buyers who stand at the entrance." He waved in the general direction of the way out. "But they don't want to pay more than a few cents. But that's fine, I can sell for cheap."

"What, so as not to fight with your neighbors?"

José Luis laughed, or something like that. José Luis was almost forty. He arrived in José León Suárez when he was little, one or two years old, from Santiago del Estero. His T-shirt is pretty clean and he's wearing gloves.

"Well, more or less. And because everybody knows it came from the dump. If I find a package of six hot dogs, I sell it for three pesos; at the store they cost seven or eight. But I put a lot of sweat into it; cleaning the packaging in a tub with bleach and detergents. Then I sell them."

"Do they ever complain, afterward, that they got a stomachache, that you almost killed them?"

"No, the merchandise is fine, it's not rotten. It's fine. It's a good deal for them, if you've got a couple of kids and you need three packages of hot dogs with twelve in each. Do the math. They're not past the due date. They're fine. Can't understand why they don't donate them to the soup kitchens, to anybody. Not only do they throw them out, but they come with the bulldozer and smash everything. And when you get there, you have to dig through what's left. It's because the supermarkets throw all this out so they can get the insurance, not because it's rotten or expired. Garbage is a business, garbage is. It's all just business. But the people who come in alone get the best stuff, they come in the morning, they work it out with the police."

I spotted a kid wearing a jersey of the Chacarita Juniors, the local soccer team. The jersey and the kid were catalogues of stains, but there was a smile on his face nonetheless. Then I saw why. On his bicycle handlebars hung a huge plastic bag of very bloody meat. I asked him what he was going to do with all of it. "I'm going to make myself a finger-licking barbeque!" he told me. "I've got enough to eat, I've got enough to sell. Some days it seems like God is taking good care of you," he said, and laughed heartily.

"Why do some people have so much and others have almost nothing?" I asked another woman nearby.

"Those who have more suffer more than those who have less, that's the only explanation I can give. I'm happier with less than my neighbor is with more. People who have a lot are very unhappy."

"Why do you say that?"

"Because in my barrio, everybody envies me; she's got less, they say, but she's doing well with her kids, they say; they envy me."

"Don't you wish you had more?"

"No."

"Like always having something to eat?"

"I like having what I need for the day, each day, it's better than having a lot of food and not having the love and affection of your children."

"What about both?"

"You can never have both. When you have more, you get more health problems, and other problems."

An eight- or nine-year-old girl cut her foot on something—a can, a piece of glass, an iron stake. There were shouts, blood, two or three people started running, they carried her down in a cart.

"I fight the system, I fight corruption. I fight power. Here, ten or fifteen dudes have got it all worked out with the cops, and they take everything, fucking over the thousands who come, and when they get here they don't find anything, only scraps, garbage," Carlos explained. Seemed like he was the political point man of the Montaña, or something like that.

"I've made mistakes in my life, but for the last twelve years, nothing. Anyway, I never sold drugs, I never took money from people who have nothing. I always stole from the government."

"How did you do that?"

"The government, banks, serious shit. But twelve years ago, I changed, now I do social work. I grew up in poverty, I come from a humble family and we're eleven children. I'm illiterate."

"But now you've learned to read?"

Carlos looked at me with an expression that could've meant yes or could've meant no or exactly the opposite. He had a face that seemed to always mean yes or no or exactly the opposite: a face you never got to know. Very short hair, thin features hammered out of stone, thin tight lips, a couple of scars, a few modest tattoos. A motorbike, blue jeans, and combat boots; he told me he was illiterate with pride, like someone who said: look where I came from and look where I am. And he had just bought an ambulance so that the people in the neighborhood could get to the emergency room, and he was going to present it on Saturday night at the regional parade, and years ago he had bought another one but the mayor of San Martín, out of jealousy, took it away, accused him of all kinds of shit and put him in jail for six years.

"Six years," he said, "they had me, they trumped up three charges, finally they ruled I was innocent of all three, exonerated. But those six years, they couldn't give them back to me. They didn't even say they were sorry, the mother fucking assholes."

Up there, on the Montaña, Carlos was the lord of the rings: dozens of kids approached him, told him something, gave him a cigarette or a can of beer, asked him for work, stole a minute of his precious time. He was the one who gave me permission to go up there—he brought me up there—though at first he didn't want to.

"How am I going to get you in with that face of yours? They're going to check you out and over. Then they're going to beat the shit out of you."

I told him I didn't have another face on hand and that surely he would be able to defend me.

Carlos grumbled, then said, "Okay, I'll take you, but no guarantees. I'll say you're my cousin who just arrived from Paraguay, but keep your eyes down. Here, they'll beat you up for nothing, so be careful."

Then, a ten- or twelve-year-old kid brought him a crushed pastry he had just found. Carlos offered me some, and we ate it. Later the kid told me that he tried not to let his classmates know that he went up the Montaña.

"If they knew, they'd give me a hard time, they'd call me a scavenger."

Two boys struggled over a bag full of dried soup packages. They stopped and stared at each other: let go; no, you let go.

"You don't know who you're messing with."

"You're nobody."

One of them had a blue patch of hair and a broken nose, was only about five feet tall, but was ropy with muscle; the other rotund with a shaved head.

"I'll fuck you up, stupid."

Many carried knives, and these two were no exception. They brandished them.

Juana lived in a slum called Ciudad de Dios, because at some point it was full of drug dealers, and she'd been coming to the Montaña every day for years.

"You're a journalist?"

"I'm a writer."

"What kind of writer. No, I already know the answer, you've got to be a journalist. Find someone else to talk to, I'm not going to tell you anything, but don't you be coming and messing us up by saying that everything's rotten. A while ago some journalists came here and started saying that everything here was rotten, and it's not true. I feed my kids on this, thank God. I've got eight kids and none of them have ever gotten sick. They're nice and healthy, maybe a bit chubby."

Despite her protest, Juana kept talking to me. She was afraid that if journalists talked about how awful the dump was, someone would get it into their head to close the dump—and then she'd be left without food.

Showing me her empty gums, Juana said, defensively, "A lot of things are frozen, and when we find them, they're still frozen."

"They're still frozen? How's that possible in this heat?"

"Yeah, still frozen. Because this is the hour that they toss that stuff. They've got a schedule for throwing out the good and frozen stuff, and it's right about now."

"Do you get something every day?"

"Almost every day."

"Do you come every day?"

"I used to come with my oldest daughter, Yoli, who's seventeen, eighteen, but now she doesn't want to come, it's gotten really dangerous because they're kids who steal, who harass us. I'd rather come alone, just in case. But it's just one small group who are really bad. A lot of the people are really good."

It was individual work, each one on his or her own.

Or, rather: pure competition.

It was also an apprenticeship.

"Have you been coming here for a long time?"

"Who knows since when. When I was little I started coming here. I always tell myself I'm not going to keep coming. I used to work as a domestic servant, but I'm too old for that now. They don't want to give me work anymore, not with this face of mine. But what can I do. I've gotta eat," said someone who stopped being little a long time ago.

"There're a lot of jerks who look down on us for doing this. But what do they want us to do, steal? Truth is, they should be grateful; for every scavenger, there's one less mugger."

An elderly couple are walking down the mountain with empty bags.

"I've been coming here about twenty years. This is where life has brought me," the man said and I asked him if he often left like this, with nothing.

He winked; with all his wrinkles, the wink wrinkled his face a little more. "By now it's hard for me to get something, my wife too. But we always come, they know us here; there's always some kid who gives us something."

A very authoritative-looking fat man with a naked torso and a bursting belly said, here, some peas, and handed him a package. Hundreds are leaving, their clothes soiled with a kind of gray mud that doesn't exist in nature. Their faces, their hands, all covered in this mud.

"Did you get anything?"

"Food for the chickens, my man," a boy said. He had very skinny legs, a festival of tattoos, and he was carrying a bag full of popcorn. "There'll always be somebody to buy it, and then you've got your dinner."

Some pulled their carts using human traction, garbage rickshaws. Others walked their bicycles, the loot-filled bags on the handlebars. Here, there were also social classes, or something like them. Some were carrying one bag with some food, some had a whole stack of tubs or a bundle of wood on a cart.

"It's a lottery. Some days you find, some you don't."

The police, from behind, hurrying them out. Their three-quarters of an hour are over.

"Today there wasn't shit," someone said, his face smeared with dirt.

"No, not shit," a fat guy with his hair sticking up answered, and when the other person left, he added, "That guy can't find nothing, he doesn't know how." His pockets were full of hot dogs.

"Here, in this country, if you're hungry it's 'cause you want to be hungry."

3

The question has a classic resonance: How can a country that produces enough food for 300 million people not manage to feed its own 40 million citizens?

Argentina is the fourth largest corn producer in the world, the third largest producer of soy beans, but the country consumes very little of what it grows. Argentina grows, in good or bad years, around fifty million tons of soy, but it doesn't eat soy. It is the world's number one exporter of soy oil, number two in corn, number three in soybeans, and number four in flour, all with less arable land than Brazil, China, and the United States.

And that echo: How is there not enough?

It's just a question, but it would seem that nobody wants to get besmirched with an answer.

When General Jorge Rafael Videla took power of the country in March

1976, the fickle industries of the previous decades did not fit the new globalized world Washington wanted, and, to top it off, those industries had created a much too combative working class. At the beginning of April 1976, the US ambassador in Buenos Aires received a message from his boss, Secretary of State Henry Kissinger, which summed it all up: he ordered him to apply pressure so that the economic policies of the Military Junta would work toward "a reduction in the state's participation in the economy, the promotion of exports, attention to subsidies in the agricultural sector, and a positive attitude toward foreign investment."

It's impressive to see how, in the following decades, successive governments obeyed these orders—some more, some less—until they had turned the country into a breadbasket, plain and simple.

As a result, thousands of city dwellers, whose jobs had been necessary, discovered that they no longer were. And thousands and thousands of people in rural areas, whose farms were functioning quite well, had to abandon them, swept out of the way by the incursion of corporate soy production.

Argentina was founded on this kind of displacement. People who lived off their land began to be dispossessed of it in 1536, when the first Spaniards tried, without any success, to colonize them. Later, little by little, they made inroads, but their influence was always limited. Until the second half of the nineteenth century, most of what would later be called *Las Pampas*, was in the hands of nomadic Indians who hunted wild cows and horses. In 1870, after the nation had been established, the wealthy of Buenos Aires decided that it was time to take over that territory. The availability of refrigerated shipping, which would allow for the export of frozen meat to England instead of salted meat to Brazil and the Caribbean—for the slaves on sugar plantations—made those terrains that much more appealing. Wasteland, which had been only reserves of cheap and wild livestock, became sources of significant profits. They had to be conquered. That's when they launched their final "*Campaña del Desierto,*" the "Desert Campaign," because in Argentina they always thought that a desert had to be populated and built up. This constituted the country's first national gold rush of exports.

Now, as of a little more than twenty years ago, other comparable innovations in agricultural production have produced similar effects. The expansion of agricultural frontiers assumes the existence of land that didn't use to be arable and is now; people who depended on other activities—animal husbandry on a small scale, family farms—lived there and then they were in the way. The country that goes in circles like a merry-go-round repeats its dramas, its farces, its failures.

It happened in many places in the world almost at the same time, because the causes were the same. At the end of the Second World War, a devastated Europe was hungry. One of the top priorities of the Marshall Plan and other Western reconstruction efforts was for the West to produce enough food to feed its population. The solution—in Europe and Japan—was large state subsidies to agriculture; in the United States these had been put in place in the thirties, during the Great Depression. As a result, for fifty years farmers could sell cheap, and the price of food remained low.

Which is why nobody tried to "expand agricultural frontiers"; it simply wasn't worth it. Each poor region continued growing its traditional crops, which they consumed and exported in varying amounts. To incorporate those regions into the global economy required investment—in roads, machinery, fertilizer, irrigation, political and economic institutions—which low prices did not justify. That was both the worst problem and the best defense of that status quo.

In the final years of the twentieth century, facing pressure from citizens because of episodes such as mad cow disease and other ecological disasters, European farm subsidy policies changed. They stopped rewarding volume at the expense of quality, and they ceased to prioritize production of quantity over the preservation of some semblance of traditional rural society. Production decreased precisely at the moment when the demand from China increased; this was also when the demand for biofuels increased and, with Chicago as mediator, when speculation increased as well.

With the rise in prices, lands that had not previously been deemed profitable, became so; with more irrigation, more machinery, new seeds and fertilizers and pesticides, regions that had previously been worthless for agriculture, suddenly became desirable.

The new world food order is changing many things, my country among them.

Several years ago, in Los Juríes, a town in the province of Santiago del Estero, I talked to a member of the Peasant Movement. Among other things, they were fiercely resisting the large soy growers who were throwing them off their lands, changing their lives forever, and forcing them to emigrate to the cities.

"Soy creates desertification. They use herbicides that dry up the cotton, and anything else that's grown. They are using more and more fertilizers, all priced in dollars, all artificial. We grow organic. And anyway, you have to grow soy over large areas, with direct seeder machines, and you have to pay up front. Cotton, on the other hand, you can plant one acre and everybody in the family works, and then it's like having money in hand; then you go to the market and you buy the food you need. For soy, you need capital and a lot of land; it's for medium-sized and large farmers. It degrades the soil, depletes it within a few years. You can grow cotton for a thousand years, and it'll be fine. But thank God those smart-asses haven't figured out a way to harvest cotton mechanically. The machines get only 30 to 50 percent, so there's still need for our labor. That's how we spend our lives. As long as we can grow something, we'll keep existing. Then we'll start disappearing, one by one, and then a whole bunch of us. I'm telling you, seriously, if this keeps going, peasants, small farmers, will be finished. We'll all end up in the city as cheap labor, if we're lucky, or unemployed. The day we start getting our two hundred pesos from the city or some plan is the day everybody's really gone to the dogs."

In the meantime, their land has become more and more valuable, and those who want it, more and more violent. In the last few years, peasants in the region have been murdered by henchmen working for the new soy growers. Rodolfo González Arzac described two cases:

> Cristian Ferreyra died of blood loss after being shot. He lived in San Antonio, two and a half hours from the city of Monte Quemado, along a road that passes through a lunar-like land-scape. He was twenty-three years old, a day shy of his twenty-fourth birthday. For some time, he and other members of his family had been defending the land the peasant community had been farming for more than twenty years, which gives them the legal right of ownership according to the laws of acquisitive prescription. Ferreyra was murdered, according to the case of the prosecution, by a hired assassin, a neighbor who also worked for the businessman. A neighbor who, as is common in such small communities, knew him well; they even shared family ties.
>
> Miguel Galván died after having his throat slit. And just in case, after he was already dead, they stabbed him in the liver. The murderer was carrying a gun with two bullets that weren't fired. They killed him in the Salta region. In the hills there are no boundaries, just a few low-growing trees, animals, dust, and families that produce food and live between austerity and shortages. But the zone is known regionally as the triple fron-

tier. Galván had gone to Salta for his mother's funeral, three months earlier. And he had stayed, even though his family missed him, to help his two brothers, who worked for the owner of the soy farm.

These Spanish peasants—and almost all the others—came to this land hundreds of years ago as the indigenous population dwindled from being chased out of their land or killed when they chose to stay. The peasants and the natives interbred, of course, but their mostly Hispanic culture replaced the indigenous one. Now, curiously, those being expelled were those who took their place. The primitive—the savage—was now defined by a refusal to be "globalized," to adapt to the world economy, to be integrated into whatever modernity was currently in vogue. Above all, a modernity that couldn't find a way to make them profitable.

At that time, I had thought it reasonable for them to want to hold onto their customs, their traditions, their way of life, to not want to end up in a shack in a slum, which seemed to be their only option.

But it is also probable that their yield was much less than a field of well-planted soy. So, rethinking that first reflex of defending their right to continue to live as they had lived till then, a question arose: If we had always thought like that, wouldn't we still be living in those magnificent caves with campfires and clubs and bison?

Then I found a passage in Denis Clerc's foreword to François de Ravignan's *La faim, pourquoi?*, in which he said that "in the countries of the south, in order for everybody to eat, everybody must work, even if that goes against global efficiency. A less efficient society might be less poor than an efficient society. Think about two countries: in one, the tools and techniques of modern farming allow for 10 percent of the population to produce a million. The remaining 90 percent survive more or less well from the crumbs distributed by the state. In another country, archaic tools allow for the production of half a million, but these tools are used by everybody and require everybody's cooperation and labor; they give everybody enough to eat and live, poor but decent. Which of the two countries is poorer?"[9]

I fear my answer is not the same as Clerc's. If, in order for a population to eat, they have to be guaranteed backbreaking work within a system of primitive, inefficient production, something's wrong, and if the quest does not include a political proposition, a way to produce a lot and share it, what good is it?

Argentina has become one of the great agrarian focal points of the world, but its production is focused on the global market and, more specifically, Chinese fish and pigs. Unprocessed soy, without almost any added value, the vast majority of those fifty million tons, goes to feed animals that, in turn, feed the new Chinese middle class.

The butterfly never stops fluttering its wings. It is impossible to keep track of all the nuances of an integrated system. In Mexico, as in Guatemala, the price of corn is a serious issue. Ever since the North American Free Trade Agreement (NAFTA) was signed in 1993, US corn, massively subsidized, began to take over the Mexican market, leaving millions of farmers without a livelihood. Ten years later, a bushel of US corn was being sold at $1.74 even though it cost $2.66 to produce.[10] The difference was in the subsidies for the machines, fertilizers, credit, and transportation that the growers received.

Growing corn in Mexico was no longer profitable, so more and more land in Mexico was being used to grow cannabis.

But during those same years, US corn prices increased, because, among other reasons, more and more was being used for biofuels, provoking protests against the increase in the price of tortillas. So Mexican policies became confused, and the government authorized extraordinary expenditures to subsidize imports, which produced more demand, and as a result, the prices rose even higher. As a result, many US farmers stopped growing soy and started growing corn, which had become more profitable. So the Argentine soy growers took over the market. And because of the crisis of Mexican tortillas, there was much more money in the shopping malls in Buenos Aires and Rosario.

The consequences of these successive waves of expulsions have accumulated in the slums of Greater Buenos Aires. They are the ones—there, now, in the soy basket of the world—who manage to go hungry.

In the meantime, millions of Argentines prosper on the global market. We play the fool, we don't want to see. Millions and millions of other people pay for our prosperity. Argentina emerged from the worst of its crisis thanks to the increase in the price of grain. Because of those prices, millions in Africa, in India, all over the Other World, are dying of hunger. I'm not saying we do it on purpose. No, please. We were just walking by when the Chinese decided to start to eat and the laws of the market made the prices go up and the laws of the market made it so none of them could buy food and died, but why look at me, I'm just doing my job, defending what's mine, trying to sell it at the highest price possible because those are the laws of the market and I just happened to be there, what fault is it of mine.

It's true—let's assume it's true. But it's good to keep it in mind: every cent we spend on every spanking new Toyota Hilux, every day of fun and leisure in Punta del Este, every new apartment on the Rosario coast is possible because the demand for grain increases, the prices rise, the poorest people in Niger or Sudan can no longer pay, they don't eat, and they die.

The money fueling our prosperity in Argentina is bloody. It's not very pleasant to admit that it is paid for by the hunger of millions. It shouldn't be so comfortable, so easy, so cheap for us.

Even less so if we take into account that there are so many, right here, who are suffering too.

4

"This must seem like paradise to you."

María had asked me about my work. I told her about this book, how I'd been to India, Africa, lots of other places, and she said, right, "Right, so this must seem like paradise to you."

María was short, with a pleasant, round face, a carbohydrate belly, a green-and-black stripped T-shirt, black leggings, and plastic flip-flops. María was just shy of forty and had already had seven children. The oldest was twenty-one, the youngest is two.

"What do you mean, paradise?"

"Well, compared to those places you've been, this is paradise. I've seen on TV how it is there, in those places. I don't know why I watch because then I just cry like crazy. My husband gets angry, he says I don't understand why the hell you'd want to watch that crap if you're just going to get so upset. But I watch, I don't know why. And to think that we complain. Suddenly you see other things and you realize that here it's difficult, really difficult, but it's not that bad, there aren't those kinds of famines."

In the middle of the twenties, the great Argentine writer Macedonio Fernández said that the City of Buenos Aires should pay a really grotesque man, a real monstrosity, to walk along Calle Florida so everyone else would say: Well, I guess I'm not so bad off after all.

There are reports, chronicles that can serve the same purpose.

The floor laid with uneven tiles, the walls with no plaster, a skinny black dog lazed around, three skinny kids kicked around a ball as if they didn't have a care in the world, four fat women chatted as if they didn't have a care in the world.

"Betty didn't come this morning?"

"Nah, you know how she is. And that guy she's got now . . ."

They did have a care, many cares; they were waiting their turn to fill the empty pots they were holding. The Ocho de Mayo Soup Kitchen is in the middle of the Ocho de Mayo barrio, on a corner in front of Kiko's, the grocery store. The soup kitchen consisted of two large rooms the locals built with a huge amount of effort, with materials they found here and there, donating their own labor. In one of the rooms were the children, the dog, the women; in that room, in the back, there was a fresco painted by slightly awkward hands, black and white with a few touches of color. It depicted people digging through mountains of garbage; in one corner, a smiling man with his arms spread out exhibited his booty: a cow, some fish, a bottle, cans, bags and more bags, a TV set. Closer to me, there was a man with long hair and a sad face, the corners of his lips pointing down.

"It's 'cause he didn't find much, you see? He's leaving with nothing."

One of the women explained to me. In the next room: the kitchen, another four women talking but also running around, sweating, taking noodles out of a blackened pot, straining them, responding to requests, talking, running, sweating. The kitchen was big, and half empty: there was an industrial oven, which looked pretty new, a gas stove with a tank, a large sink basin, a tile counter, a significant amount of heat. One of the four fat women was pouring penne pasta onto a large flat serving dish and then with a large serving spoon pouring red sauce over them— tomato, onion, potato, some bone with a bit of meat on it—then stirring all of it. On the other side of the large counter, a girl handed them a plastic basin; one of the women—the least fat, the one named María—filled it with pasta. The girl looked happy; one of the fat women from the other room arrived with her pot, she gave it to María, waiting for her to fill it.

The last survey taken by the Ministry of the Health—that would be in Argentina—said that 28 percent of Argentine homes receive donated food and 12 percent eat in community soup kitchens. In the Greater Buenos Aires region there are many hundreds of these kitchens, some say two or three thousand, but nobody knows the exact number.

"When we went to live in Chaco, we really did go hungry. We were desperate, we had nothing, we'd have to go to bed with a cup of yerba *mate* tea, not even a cracker, not even a piece of bread. We came here as soon as we could."

"And here, you're never hungry.?"

"Well, I'm not saying never. But here, if you don't have any money, you can find something somehow, somebody will always give you something, lend you something, throw you a bone. That's what's good about being here."

Two thousand families live in Ocho de Mayo, more than ten thousand people. Many houses are already built with solid material; some are still assembled precariously with corrugated metal. Many of the first residents left; others arrived with a little money, three or four hundred dollars, and bought their places. The others went to occupy other sites, always farther away. But the streets are still unpaved—dirt, or mostly mud; the few cars are cadavers of cars, junk cars. The dogs are little; the trees have grown. The burnt smell never goes away.

And then there are the floods whenever a few drops fall, and the overall difficulties of living on a garbage dump that sits on a swamp. Those who live closer to the river, for example, can't dig a cesspool because they reach water too soon. And then there's the mountains of garbage, the off-gassing, the diseases, the stench: always, all the time, the stench.

There were a few shops: a butcher who sold mostly eggs, a kiosk with beer, sodas, cigarettes, and a sign that indicated they "sell drinks ice" and had every spelling error possible—VENDO VEVIDAS IELO instead of *vendo bebidas hielo*—another kiosk with notebooks and SIM cards with a sign that says BOOKSTORE. Various cumbias were playing. Three very fat women were sitting on a doorstep of a shack built with corrugated metal; the little boy who was running around was naked, but that's not the norm; two others shout, cry, run. The little dogs were dirty.

"Be careful, don't step on the shit."

A woman standing at the door to her house shouted at her barefoot kids. I looked at her; she looked back at me, as if apologizing.

"It's just that they step on it, and then they fill my house with shit."

Two bigger kids drove by on a little motorbike. A black dog picked through the garbage; there was garbage everywhere.

Slums, *villa miserias*, are nothing new in the Argentine suburban landscape. There were many before the seventies, needless to say. But there were fewer and, most importantly, they seemed to be temporary. For their inhabitants, they were a stepping stone, a place they would live until they found a better job, and with that, a little house in a proper neighborhood, and a life with new opportunities and hard work. Not now.

Now they have a destiny.

"I know how to write too," Quiara told me when she saw me writing. Quiara was five, with short, dirty-blonde, straight hair, wearing shorts, a very well-washed worn-out T-shirt, and pink plastic flip-flops. "You like my new shoes?"

I tell her they're very pretty; she smiles.

"Who taught you how to write?"

"I taught myself. But I don't have a book bag so I can't go to nursery school. When she gets paid, my mom is going to buy me a book bag."

"You want to go to nursery school?"

"Probably. But I already know what they'd teach me."

The smell, always the smell of something burning.

Every day, María reached the soup kitchen at eight in the morning, looked at what was there, and started to figure out what she would make that day with the food that she had. That was when the other three also arrived. If they could, if they had what they needed, they started peeling, cutting, and cooking. Every day at noon—whenever they could, whenever they managed—María and her colleagues passed out two hundred meals: potatoes, noodles, rice with bits of meat or vegetables; a lot of carbohydrates and very little protein. Women and children started to arrive at eleven-thirty in the morning with their pots to get a serving of the dish of the day.

"Before, we'd feed them here, but then we realized that many were ashamed to be seen and wouldn't come. So we started to make it 'to go,' to let people come and get it. Almost everybody sends their kids, as if it were only for them. But we know, and we always send an extra helping so the parents can eat too. It's not easy to come here and say, I don't have any food, I didn't find anything today. They're really embarrassed," María explained.

And there were times, like now, when they didn't have enough supplies to cook every day, and nothing depressed her more than those days when she had to stand at the door of the kitchen and tell the kids and the women arriving with their pots that there was nothing today, ma'am, nothing today, kiddo, so sorry, hopefully tomorrow.

"I'm a softie, I guess; it really upsets me to see people digging through the garbage to find something to eat," María said.

At around two they finished, cleaned up, put things away, conversed, planned. María went home and to take a nap; when she got up, she made dinner for her children and her husband, who, if he had work, arrived at about eight. Then they ate, watched a bit of television, and got to bed early, because it was not a good idea, she said, to be out on the streets.

"I like to watch something on TV that makes me laugh. Or that makes me cry, like those Mexican or Colombian soap operas. I'd like to go to Colombia one day; it looks so pretty there, the landscape, the houses. Well, truth is, I'd like to go anywhere, travel, get out of this barrio a little. But how could I ever? How could I ever get out of here?"

María said that with the kids she didn't have any time because she always had to be on top of them, every second, on top of them so that they didn't go bad, start down the wrong path, so really she'd been almost nowhere, she said, almost nowhere.

"What do I know?"

Lori was thin, in her forties, with very few teeth and five children. For years Lori didn't have a steady job but now she'd been working a few months at one of those cooperative plants that recycled garbage. She earned about 1,500 pesos a month—$140—though some months it was less and other months she never got paid or she got paid late. But since she started working, she stopped going to the soup kitchen for food. María told her to keep coming, she could still get her meals, but she said, no, thank you anyway, for now she could manage with what she earned.

"Well, you can still send one of the kids to get food; it always helps."

"Thanks, María. I like to buy my food with what I earn."

María said there are days she came full of hope and on other days, she got depressed, she thought they'd never get out of this, they'd always be scraping the bottom of the pot.

"I get depressed, I do. But I get even more depressed when they rip us off. How can they steal from here, from the Kitchen?"

A month and a half ago, she said, someone stole all their pots, the tools they used to cook for the community

"Truth is, you've gotta be a little weird to steal our pots, don't you think?"

"Weird?"

"Yeah, weird. Like how one evening, two weeks ago, someone stole the water tank from the roof of the community kitchen. Why would you steal something like that? Who does it benefit? It's just a sign of how bad things have become around here.

She couldn't let people use the kitchen for birthday parties, like they used to, because the parties always ended up in fights.

"They'll fight over anything. Over a hat, a pair of shoes, why you looking at me, anything. There are a lot of drugs around here, and very little hope. The place is full of young people who don't see any way out."

María had a son who did see one: he played soccer like a pro. Suddenly, all the family's hopes were pinned on that boy. If he could make it, everybody would be saved. But he couldn't, because they didn't have enough money to pay for the expenses: the bus to get to practice, the shoes with cleats, the special food.

"The clubs always said they would give us enough to pay the expenses, but in the end, they never gave us any because I wouldn't sign over my rights to be his custodian." María told this to me with bitterness in her voice.

A boy arrived with a pot to be filled. The boy was wearing a short-sleeved shirt, shorts, had a plethora of *tumberos*, the word in Lunfardo, the dialect of Argentine gangs, for prison tattoos.

"Poor kid. He's got two brothers in jail, but not for small offenses, for murder. He was inside, too, but not for anything that serious. Now he's out, but with those tattoos, they won't hire him anywhere. What can he do, the poor kid. No matter what he's done, his belly also growls when he gets hungry, you know what I mean? I know all about that."

There are few places where social inequality can be seen more clearly than at the table—or wherever anybody eats.

For decades, the food Argentines ate was surprisingly egalitarian. The first survey containing reliable data came from the National Development Committee in 1965 showed that rich and poor Argentines ate basically the same food: red meat and milk products, fruits and vegetables, pastas and breads, all in similar proportions; it was a symbol of that unfair Argentina that we, in all fairness, wanted to change.

"The food wasn't the same because the meat the poor ate wasn't the same as the meat the rich ate. The rear part of the animal went to the wealthy neighborhoods, the front part to the poor neighborhoods, and certain cross sections were for everybody: the ribs, the sirloin tip for breaded steak, *milanesa*, for example. But if I make a list of what was in a food basket belonging to the poor of that time and show it to a nutritionist now, they'd say it was food for the middle class. The quantity and variety of that food is not even comparable to what they eat now," Patricia Aguirre, anthropologist, explained. She had studied national nutrition more than anybody else. "There might have been differences in prices and quality, of course, but protein consumption was very similar across all sectors of the population, which is why the poor didn't have nutritional deficits."

I recall a tradition that has been lost: the construction-site barbeque, the epitome of that country, the aroma of the city of my childhood.

The model began to fall apart in 1985, and in the census of 1996 the new trend had been established: the food of the poor was radically different from the food of those who are not poor. Now, in this Argentina we seem to have resigned ourselves to, there is food for the rich and food for the poor. It's no longer even a question of quantity but of composition: the upper and middle classes eat fruit and vegetables and meat—more

white than red—that keep them thin and healthy, and the poor eat potatoes, rice, and noodles—sugar, carbohydrates, and fat—that fills them
up; very little meat, very little fruits and vegetables. It is a rational choice;
meat is too expensive, fruit and vegetables are not only that, but they fill
you up much less than flour does.

"It's not that they don't know; they just can't," Patricia Aguirre, a
health studies professor at the National University of Lanús, told me. "It's
not that they are irrational, like nutritionists sometimes accuse them
of being; it's that their rationale is different than yours. It's not that the
mother doesn't know that her kids need fruit and vegetables; it's that for
the cost of a pound of peaches you could buy a quarter pound of beef, so
the fruit isn't worth it. It's not that they don't think about a healthy and
balanced diet; it's that they are thinking about the best way for everybody to eat with the little they have."

And there's not only a difference in the products, she told me, but also
in the way they are cooked. The poorest of the poor do not use ovens to
bake and roast their food; each meal would use half a tank of gas, and it's
too expensive. So, when there's food, they fry it or stew it on the stovetop.
In the nation of barbeques, it's a return to the classic peasant cuisine, the
poorest cuisine: stewing is the way to combine leftovers, to get the most
out of cheap ingredients, to use fire most efficiently, to allow the cook to
get other things done in the meantime.

"I remember once talking to a woman in a poor neighborhood. We
talked while she was cooking her lentil stew, and her son arrived home
with four friends. Hey, Mom, can they stay to eat? Yes, son, they can stay.
What's there to eat? So the woman grabbed the kettle and poured water
into the stew: lentil soup, she said."

It reminded me of something María told me, how she had to go to La
Plata to visit a government office, and she saw all that land, she never
imagined there could be so much land.

"I saw all that land, and I thought, what's going on with those people
who have money, the government, all of them, who don't realize that there
are so many of us who need, who don't have anywhere to live, and they
keep everything, everything always for them, so much space just wasted."

"Why do they do that?"

"Because they're selfish, they want power. They must think that way, I
don't know, I imagine they must think that way."

The fact that a significant number of Argentines—one out of four,
more or less—have habitually stopped eating the national food—meat—
is so brutal, so definitive, that I am always surprised that it doesn't appear

to us, as Argentines, to be a fundamental aspect of the new country, this sustained failure, we have managed to create in the last thirty or forty years.

(It is, in a way, the perfect opposite of China, which spent years without seeing meat even in paintings and now consume more and more pigs fed on Argentine soy.)

"In Argentina today," Aguirre said, "there is almost no acute, hardcore malnutrition."

Sometimes the newspapers run stories about children dying of starvation in Misiones, Formosa, Jujuy, Tucumán. But it really isn't the norm, hence it shows up in the papers. Remember when the dead had names, a friend who lived in exile in Paris at the end of the seventies, used to ask me.

"There's help that reaches almost everywhere, except the most remote regions of the country. But what do we bring those children? Noodles, rice, potatoes. So they're not undernourished, they're chronically malnourished, children who don't grow as they should, who don't develop."

It's the story of Bengal, India, Africa; the usual story in the Other World. People who get used to eating poorly, less than they need, other than what they need, and learn how to survive poorly on it, their brains, their bodies developing poorly. To live much poorer lives, almost without knowing it.

In Spanish we say *tener hambre* "to have hunger," literally, but used like "to be hungry," and *pasar hambre* is what we use to say the equivalent of "to go hungry," in English. What's odd is that having (being, in English) is more temporary than going. I am hungry. Relax, we'll eat in a while. Oh no, she's going hungry. Yes, the poor thing, ever since she lost her job. Nor is it the only eccentricity about this strange thing we call hunger.

Or, as Tolstoy put it, "Paint your village and you will paint the world."

VOICES OF THE TRIBE

How?

Again: perplexed at how normal it seems, at how our eyes don't pop out of our heads like rabid rats, at how it doesn't prevent us from living as we live. Normal, natural, part of the order of things: immutable. Managing that requires an enormous cultural apparatus. Or, maybe the contrary, maybe every man for himself is what's natural and culture consists of doing something, coming together, thinking collectively.

How the hell do we manage?

. . . but it also wears you down. In the end you can't understand what they want. There have always been rich and poor in the world and there always will be. Look, right here, in this neighborhood: you can't tell me that the Meldani family is the same as the Salvatierra family. And this isn't something new, my friend, it's always been like this, why should it stop being like this all of a sudden? The point is, if the poor are poor it's because they don't do enough; they're stupid, lazy, violent, they have dozens of kids they know they can't support, they're bums, they are everything they shouldn't be if they want to succeed in life. And then they want us to feel sorry for them. What I'm saying is that you don't have to look so surprised, oh, how weird, how can it be that so many go hungry. Let's not pretend we don't know; if they're hungry, it's because they don't want to work, they don't make any effort, they just don't feel like it. And I'm not saying they should just go to hell; if they can be helped, they should be helped, of course, but we shouldn't be such hypocrites and pretend they're the same as us. After all, there has to be some selection process. If not, breaking your back wouldn't do anybody any good. Or what, you prefer that everything will be the same and that—

How the hell do we manage to live?

The old prophecy trick. In 2050 there might not be enough food on the planet, they tell you, because according to their catastrophic projections, in 2050 there might not be food in some of the wealthier regions of the planet—if the poor keep growing and claiming more of their share. In the rest of the world, in 2050, terrible things can also happen, similar to what is happening now.

How the hell do we manage to live knowing?

Small lives: What do I do so I can eat tomorrow?
  Epic lives: What do I do so I can eat tomorrow?

How the hell do we manage to live knowing these things are happening?

"Well, it's reality, what are we supposed to do about it?"
  "Something, we have to do something. Politics, for example."
  "You really don't understand how politics work, do you?"

How the hell do we manage to live?

Though, I don't know, I'm telling you, I don't know what to think. Yes, some people tell you that the world is full of people who don't have enough to eat, and they give you statistics and figures and other things and they even tell you that there are some right here in this very city, and more than once I've had to go into poor neighborhoods, pretty tough places, and not only don't you see people dying of hunger but they're all fat, well fed. So, I don't know, I really don't have any idea, but sometimes it seems like it might also be some kind of propaganda from who knows what interests that want to sell that line. I'm not saying it's not going on, maybe it is going on a little, but they sell it to you as if it were some kind of catastrophe so that you'll buy the whole box and you'll think you're—

How the hell do we manage?

5

"Is somebody to blame for some having so little and others having so much?"

This was the question posed to me by Paola, an unemployed mother of three.

"The government should create more jobs so people have a way out, so we can eat every day. The government doesn't care about poor people, it pushes them aside. Illness, everything, it's for the politicians because if you have a job, you eat, and if you don't, you don't."

Paola looked at me with fear in her eyes.

"What do you imagine ten years from now?"

"I don't know, because I don't know if I'll make it. I live day-to-day, how can I know what's going to happen in ten years. Why should I try to imagine ten years from now if I don't know if I'm going to sleep or if I'm going to wake up?"

Every day at noon, all days at noon, Paola brought her three children to the soup kitchen in her barrio, Gregorio de Laferrère, in the La Matanza district, about five miles from downtown Buenos Aires. Paola's children were two girls, ten and three, and a seven-year-old boy; she had two others who died.

"Both, during childbirth, poor things, they were born and died right there. When the last one died, Abi understood everything, poor girl, and she was very upset. That's why I carry her all the time."

Abi is Abigail, the three-year-old girl, who didn't get off her mother's lap. Paola rocked her, caressed her hair, comforted her.

"I don't want to lose another child. Not a single one, I don't want to."

Paola was twenty-seven years old, and wore brown Bermuda shorts and a pink T-shirt, had long straight hair, skinny legs and arms. Her father came from Tucumán, in the northeast, before she was born; they discovered much later that he had left behind a wife and several kids. In Laferrère he got a job working in a detergent factory; he met Paola's mother at a dance, courted her, then went to live with her. They had two daughters, then separated because he "drank a lot, did drugs, and beat my mother." A little later, she found another husband, a man who had just gotten out of jail—she had more children with him.

"I respected that man as if he were my father. I considered him my father until he started abusing me, from the time I was seven, more or less. I always preferred he do it with me rather than my little sisters who were even younger. That's how I lived till I was twelve."

"What did he do to you?"

"He fondled me, touched my private parts, made me look at pornographic magazines with him, made me touch his parts, and then everything that comes after that. But it happened slowly. My brother was born with a problem that makes him disabled, and he was always sick, so my mother spent a lot of time at the hospital. Or sometimes she'd say she was going to the hospital, and she went out, hung out with other men. So I had to stay with him, do the washing, cooking, like I was a wife not a daughter. I didn't go out to play like the other kids. I stayed at home. One night he grabbed me, I felt a terrible pain behind, he'd penetrated me from behind. I didn't tell my mother anything. I put up with it and spent three years like that. Everybody knew, everybody kept quiet."

Her younger sisters, finally, told their mother, who didn't believe them; now Paola suspected she preferred not to believe them because the situation was convenient for her. But one day the man thought that his wife was sleeping and began to fondle Paola; his wife woke up, saw them, and couldn't be in denial anymore. Or maybe she was jealous.

"Then my mother told me we had to keep our mouths shut. She said, just imagine what'll happen if you say something, your brothers will be put in an institution, including your disabled brother, and I could go to jail, she told me. And what will our neighbors say, she told me. With so much pressure, I had to keep quiet."

And once, many years later, Paola asked him why he did it, why her, when he said he loved her like a daughter. The man told her that it was revenge against her mother because she left, because she didn't take care of him the way a wife should take care of a man, that he had to go out and steal to support them and she didn't take care of him.

"I told him that if he went out and stole it was because he wanted to, that I'd never asked him for anything. And with so many women around who would give themselves to him for any little thing, why did he have to do it with me? 'Were you aware of how old I was?' I asked him. 'No,' he told me, 'I wasn't aware, and I don't know how to ask you to forgive me.' But I did forgive him, because I went to church and they showed me how to forgive. I forgave him. But with all that, I never had a childhood."

Nor did she have, at that time, enough food. Her mother would leave sometimes for days and Paola had to figure out how to feed her siblings. She was ten, eleven years old, and she'd go out and ask for food in the neighborhood.

"I was really ashamed to ask. But I had no choice."

Sometimes she'd find something, and then she'd prepare lunch for all the kids, a big bowl of noodles with salt and maybe a splash of oil; then, later, a cup of *mate* tea, and at night, they'd go to bed early so as not to feel hunger pangs.

"What if you didn't have noodles, what would you eat?"

"Rice, potatoes, whatever I could find, anything. Or I'd ask my grandfather, who had a cart and would bring vegetables the grocers were throwing away, and I'd take off the bad parts and cook them. Or I'd cut up the fruit, I'd remove the bad bits and we'd eat the rest."

"Did you ever eat meat?"

"Oh, very, very rarely."

"Did your situation make you angry?"

"Yes. Sometimes we even ate stuff that was spoiled. If you did that now you'd get sick, but we didn't even notice. We ate everything. Thank God we never got sick. That's how we fed ourselves."

"Did you think about whose fault it was that these things were happening to you?"

"No. I tried not to blame anybody. It's sad, but at the same time it's what teaches you about life. It taught me too much. I know too much, I don't need to know so much."

I went to meet with Agustín Salvia at café on the corner of San Juan and Boedo. Salvia is a sociologist, professor at the University of Buenos Aires, coordinator of the Social Debt Observatory at the Catholic University, where the best surveys are done on the socioeconomic situation in the country.

"There's a segment of the population that is absolute surplus in this model of accumulation and growth. The model doesn't need them, they are too many, they are expensive, they have to be taken care of. Moreover, they make demands, give speeches, say things; they denounce, pronounce, vote. All of this has a very high price for the reproduction of the system. Yes, they are surplus," Salvia told me.

"One might think, theoretically, that it would be advantageous to incorporate that labor force, which is capable of producing wealth, not only for their sakes but also for the collective good. Under a different model, not more or less capitalist, just one with a different logic, where the informal sector is integrated into the formal sector of the economy, where there is a transference from the more concentrated sectors to the less concentrated ones, there would be a process of social inclusion of these people, and small family businesses could fulfill a socially and economically productive role. That's not done now. Now they are surplus. If they disappeared, nothing would happen. On the contrary."

Paola, moreover, missed her biological father; she hadn't seen him for three years when he suddenly appeared, on her twelfth birthday. He was drunk and he told her that he was her father, he loved her, and he wanted to give her something.

"I told him that if he wanted to see me, he should come sober, it doesn't do me any good for my father to be drunk when he comes to see me. I wanted a sober father, I told him. If I want someone drunk, I've got my uncles and my grandfather. I wanted a father like most people have. And I told him that the only present I wanted was for him to be with me always, and when I was fifteen, I would go live with him."

Her father said, yes, of course, we'll see. But three days later somebody came to report that he had fallen or thrown himself into the Matanza River and they'd fished him out, dead. That year Paola started to work, babysitting a little girl, the daughter of a policeman. Whenever she could, she went to night school. It was hard on her; she would arrive home tired, and she was afraid of leaving her siblings alone. Sometimes she had no choice; other times, her mother was there. But at least she was contributing some money—some food—to the family budget. The most difficult thing was getting milk for Camila, the youngest, nine months old.

"That day I didn't go to work because Camilita had a fever. In the morning I gave my other sister milk, I prepared the bottle for Cami, I told my mother that since I wasn't going to work, I'd take care of her. I gave her the milk and later in the morning my disabled brother who slept at the end of the bed with her, woke up my mother to go to the bathroom, and my little sister was dead. She forgot to breathe. That was the worst, because I'd taken such good care of her. It was terrible. Of all the pain I've had, that was the worst," Paola said.

Hardcore unemployment in Argentina is at around 15 percent, or about three million people. They and their children, their families, live in situations that are hard to imagine, though we don't try very hard. They have no steady work, no running water or toilets or electricity, no streets, no protection; they do not always have enough food.

"It's a marginal culture that produces its own bonds of solidarity, of mobility, in which the extralegal does not constitute a problem. Everything functions through the black market, there is no need to standardize or formulize, and violence resolves economic conflicts, because there's no justice, no norms," explained Salvia.

And, above all, the barrier between those sectors and the rest of society is bigger and bigger. The possibility of crossing over is not only illusory, it's unimaginable. In Argentina there are millions of people who don't think they'll ever be integrated into conventional society, who know that this insurmountable inequality is the condition of their lives. They know that even if they prosper in some informal—either legal or illegal—activity, they will remain in that sector. In general, however, they do not prosper, they survive. They include the vast majority of that 5 percent of Argentine homes living with "acute food insecurity" and the 7 percent with "moderate food insecurity," that is, 12 percent of homes with food insecurity. And, of course, that 8 percent of children—a quarter of a million children—who are chronically malnourished.

Twelve percent of Argentine homes are five million Argentines, who don't eat what they need to eat.

When Paola was fifteen, she got desperate. Her mother was sometimes there and sometimes gone, and there was never enough money, or food. Then she discovered that there were men who were willing to give her money or goods in exchange for sex.

"I found myself with guys I never should have been with, and unfortunately I had to do it to get money. They were friends of my uncles, guys who had known me since I was little. Sometimes I didn't want new clients. There were friends who, since they had known me since I was little, didn't want to, but they gave me things anyway, but there were others who did. I just closed my eyes and kept thinking about my siblings."

When Paola was seventeen she met a boy at night school who seemed to understand her. They liked each other, they went out, Paola got pregnant. He took responsibility: whenever he had anything, he'd give her a few pesos, something to eat, some candy; she stopped having sex for money. She named her first daughter Camila, after her sister who'd forgotten to breathe. Sometimes he found some work, a gig. A while later they found a shack in the barrio and moved in together. The following year, Joel was born.

Paola was almost happy; everything seemed to be on track. She had her little house, her mattresses, her beds, her rickety table, her propane stove. But her family started waging war against her man, saying that he fondled his daughter, raped her, that he was dangerous. Paola believed them and left. She was twenty years old with two kids, no income, and her older sister proposed she work in a bar as an escort.

"In the bar they pushed me to do more so I could make more money. I said no, it wasn't for me. It's different to sleep with somebody to get a few things, and it's another to sleep with fifty, but finally I decided to do it. I talked to my brother-in-law, who was the one in charge, and started. Then my kids had everything they needed. They all had their things. They asked me for things, and I could afford them."

It was a relief: they ate every day, she could make them empanadas, buy them sodas when they wanted. But she didn't like that life, she missed her husband, she had a boyfriend, she got pregnant. Her clients took care of her, they didn't let her drink alcohol, said Paola.

"Sex costs sixty pesos for a half hour, thirty for the girl and thirty for the owner. There wasn't a bathroom to wash in after having sex. I always took care of myself. They give you condoms and force you to use them. During the week I'd start at eight at night and get home at three in the morning. I worked in Constitución, and from there I'd come here, where my siblings were taking care of my kids. The weekends were the same, but I got out later, at seven in the morning. I'd arrive home, sleep a while, then go out again. One day I ran into my husband, and he said he wanted to see the children, and I had to tell him that I was pregnant, that I worked in a brothel in order to feed them, that I didn't want to ask him for anything."

In her fourth month of pregnancy, she stopped working. Weeks later, one night, she started having cramps and she asked her brother to get a doctor, but the one in the local clinic didn't want to go to her because he didn't have an ambulance, and he said the patient should come to him. Paola couldn't. Her sister helped her; at about five o'clock, the baby was born in one push, dead.

"My brother went and shouted at everybody at the clinic, and they had no choice but to come see me. But the baby was already born, they'd wrapped her in a sheet, in a box. Nobody wanted to take me, nobody wanted to be responsible, not even the police. They had the nerve to accuse me of things, that I had given myself an abortion, because I was already in my sixth month. My soul was aching, and at the same time, it made me make a big decision. I got up, went to the church, never wanted to go back to the brothel. I wanted to live a normal life like before."

Paola got back together with her husband. Two years later she gave birth prematurely again and that baby was born dead. Now the five of them lived in their one-room shack with two small beds, one for Paola and her husband, the other for her children. A relative lent them a propane stove; when they wanted water, they had to go ask a neighbor.

"We want to save so we can get a bathroom, a toilet. In the meantime, we use the pit."

The situation was better, Paola said. Her husband got a job cleaning a factory, and they paid him a thousand pesos—about eighty dollars—a month.

"He earns more, but then they take out money, I don't understand why."

"Do you get the child allowance?

"No, because it seems that because he has a job, we don't qualify. At first they gave it to me, but then they took it away."

The myth is that here, very near here, dulce de leche was invented. The story goes that on a ranch owned by Don Juan Manuel de Rosas, the omnipotent caudillo from the first half of the nineteenth century, a servant was heating milk with sugar when one of the master's enemies, Juan Lavalle, arrived to pay her boss a visit, and she had to attend to him. When she finally remembered what was on the stove, she found her concoction thick and brown, and she was worried about what her master would say, so she brought it to him to try to explain. Rosas tried it and liked it, and he offered some to Lavalle, and they enjoyed it together. Ten years later, Rosas would chase him throughout the entire country until he hunted him down and killed him.

A few months ago, Paola took her three children to a neighborhood organization for them to be weighed and measured. They told her they were "underweight." Paola didn't understand; they explained to her that it meant they were thin, and that they were also short for their age, that she had to feed them better. At first Paola got angry, defending herself against what she took to be a reproach; then, she said, she started to cry.

"Finally, they told me that the government sends bags of food to underweight children, that I had to go fill out some forms and ask for it. And they gave it to me. Every fifteen days they give me a box with four packages of noodles, rice, oil, and *dulce de batata* [sweet potato jelly]."

Paola was happy but she still felt guilty. She cried, still, when she said, "My children are the most important thing, and I know that they are underweight because I haven't taken good care of them. Before, if we could, we would put aside a little of my husband's salary so we could wash, for example, but now we say that the most important thing is for them to eat well. There's not enough money, we just barely make it to the end of the month, but now we really try to make sure the children eat. We can't allow our children to go hungry. At noon I take them to the soup kitchen and at night I have to give them something. Even if we go without eating, they have to. Even if only a soup, some noodles."

"Whose fault is it that you don't have enough to eat?"

"I don't know, what do I know. What I like is when the president says there's no poverty. I heard her say many times that there's no poverty. She should come and see the poverty there is, the children who are starving to death. The other day on the news I saw that mother whose daughter died of starvation, that woman from Misiones Province they put in jail. You know how horrible and impotent I felt when I saw that? So many rapists, so much crime, and they put in jail a woman whose daughter dies of starvation."

As Salvia told me, "The most recalcitrant structural marginality would include up to 15 percent of all homes. That's five, six million people. Considered from the perspective of Fidel Castro in Cuba twenty years ago, who opened the floodgates and told them to go to Miami, or General Bussi who rounded up all the vagrants and took them to Catamarca, it would be a real boon for the system if they left. They're surplus."

I replied that in that case feeding them poorly was almost clever.

"Well, they have to be fed in order to avoid social upheaval, where looting will be the systematic way they settle their accounts with the state."

"No, you misunderstood. I'm not saying that it's clever to feed them but to feed them poorly. Because it's better if they aren't intelligent and strong and, anyway, it's much cheaper. In terms of profitability, why spend more money to feed people who aren't going to produce anything? And in the end, this benefits you because it produces people who don't have the initiative they might have if they were better fed."

"I agree. But I don't think there's a mind controlling this and carrying it out."

"No, neither do I, because I don't think they are that intelligent."

"But, on the other hand, I do think there's logic at work: what would be the threshold beyond which these people will loot supermarkets, cause political upheavals? Two hundred and fifty pesos? If so, that's what they're worth. That's the idea. Tomorrow, they create conflict because they don't have enough food, so I have to raise that to five hundred pesos. What is the threshold for social containment, social control? If it is too high, I'm in trouble. I can't pay that much, because then I have to take it from somewhere else. But I have to pay something, the less the better."

This isn't an Argentine trick. The ruling strategy has always been to maintain the governed at their lowest possible level. Search, empirically, for that level in each case: trial and error. The error could be that thousands die of starvation or that they rise up and make demands. The mechanism endures. When Europe and the United States decide to spend on their banks what they do not spend on their poor, they are abiding by the hypothesis that the poor will tolerate it. When they speculate with the price of food or extract raw materials or transform corn into fuel, they trust that the death of a certain number of Africans will not affect their lives. When a government gives handouts to their subjects, they hope it will be enough to maintain them oppressed and dominated, inoffensive and silent.

Because hunger is, in spite of everything, a powerful form of blackmail. Many people might be made uncomfortable for ten minutes when there's a news item about some hungry people, and the discomfort tends to be directly proportional to geographic proximity—go thirty miles out of town, let's say, and it might increase to fifteen minutes. And there is nothing a government detests more than their subjects feeling uncomfortable, in fact their job consists of making them feel so comfortable that they don't feel anything. Then acts of Christian mercy can be played out, or their contemporary version, *assistentialism*: to give the poor the bare minimum so that they survive and avoid sullying TV screens with their blood and bones.

Many survive; others don't.

6

The La Loma neighborhood, in Gregorio de Laferrère, in the La Matanza district, has dirt streets, little one- or two-room houses made of wood and corrugated metal or bare brick, a ditch on either side of the street full of stagnant black stinking water. Women sit and drink mate tea in front of their houses with their radios blasting, cumbia playing in the background, a whiff of marijuana, freshly planted trees, children running around outside. A man with a machete is pruning a tree; two skinny horses graze on the little bits of grass that grow along the dirt sidewalk. On every block there are two or three street lights. About a dozen cables are strung off each pole: neighbors stealing electricity.

At the entrance, there's an entire block of vacant lots: garbage, weeds, the remains of a bonfire, a couple of old willow trees. On one corner is a painted wood sign that says "Parque de la Memoria," Remembrance Park.

Closer to the river, the shacks get sparser and sparser because of the danger of flooding. There are reeds, mud, shoals; this used to all be swamps, which the poorest of the poor first occupied. One family raises pigs, another bakes bricks, another searches among the weeds for bottles, pieces of cardboard, rags. I was seated with Claudio, a tall, stout, man wearing cutoff jeans and a very roomy blue shirt; he was clean shaved, with a goatee, short hair, and a warm smile, and he told me that a few weeks ago the barrio was totally flooded, with water up to their necks.

One hundred yards away, the Matanza River runs darkly between banks of weeds and rubble; on this side, garbage; on the other, a forest. Claudio told me that sometimes he still went to catch eels by hand, even though it was prohibited, it was his favorite fish, and Romi made a damn good stew with a couple of eels.

"Many kids still go across to steal. There's a section that's full of trails for off-road vehicles. The kids go on raids, and you wouldn't believe the vehicles they've brought back here for the neighborhood. You wouldn't believe how many friends of mine have died there, on the other side. If the cops catch you there, they kill you and leave you there, in the forest, for the worms to eat. Who'll find you there? A few times we had to go look for the bodies. Once someone they called the Devil was found stealing, and there was a shootout, and they left him for dead. When he didn't show up, some friends went looking for him and found him there, shot through the eye, his head a mess, full of worms but alive. He couldn't see anything because it was all infected, and he was screaming, delirious. The kids brought him to the hospital, but he lost his vision in that eye because the worms ate it."

The river is treacherous:

"You look at it now, and it looks so calm, but when it's full and over-flows, it covers everything, the bastard. Those sons of bitches close the floodgates lower down the river so it doesn't flood the rich neighbor-hood, and they get all the water; I was stranded in my flooded shack with my two older sons."

The water flooded the streets. Claudio assembled a raft with scraps of wood and blow-up bags, some branches for oars, so he could get out and get provisions. But he said he had to act fast.

"Here, the kids are terrible. If you leave, they'll steal everything."

Claudio was born here thirty-six years ago, and he had lived here ever since. Until he was thirty, he said, he was lost: a bad guy, a fighter, a hooligan. He was the top honcho of a corner gang, harassing the locals, sometimes charging them tolls, he said, "If they didn't pay, they didn't pass. We were always fighting: you owe me two grams, don't you come here, this is my territory. I was a bad guy. But, also, those were different times. The other day I walked by that corner, the one I used to rule, and those guys were still there, getting high, and I don't know if I got a whiff of the smoke or what, but it was like I'd gone back ten years. All of them there talking the same bullshit, about drugs, heists, women, how last night I fucked that one, the other night I ripped off that place. I looked at them and couldn't believe it. Now they're even crazier. Those kids don't respect anything. If you don't watch out, they'll shoot you, and nobody respects you if you don't have a gun. Before, we'd resolve things with punches. Now, even they say, no, old man, this is the powder era."

Claudio said he never robbed; he hung out on the streets but he didn't steal.

"I always worked; I did drugs but I paid for them. I never could imagine being a thief. We're from a Christian family, and they always taught me about God. I'd do a lot of drugs but always bought it with the money I earned. I finished school at fifteen, and since then I was on the streets, until I was thirty. I spent fifteen years on drugs."

Claudio started off sniffing glue, then he smoked marijuana, and finally found his drug of choice: cocaine. He spent every peso he earned in construction snorting all weekend and drinking wine all week.

"That's why I know that nobody can get out of drugs without God's help. But God, when he gets you out, he gets you out forever, he cleans you up for keeps. Now, if we catch a kid stealing stuff, we counsel him, I preach to him. Sometimes they come and they tell me that they want to quit this life, but they can't, and I tell them they can, and with the help of our Lord, they can. I know, because I did it."

Claudio worked in construction in Buenos Aires, until one morning a few years ago. He was plastering the front of a house, minding his own business, when four men came and asked for the contractor. Claudio told them that he was inside, and he went back to work. A while later, they returned, thanked him, and walked away. When he saw them turn the corner and start running, he understood what had happened. Claudio ran around to the back and found his fellow workers tied up, prostrate, and his boss was convinced that he had been involved. He said he wouldn't turn him in, but he shouldn't come back. Claudio had no way to prove it wasn't true; suddenly, the people he'd worked with for years didn't believe him. Claudio was so angry he cried.

"How do you defend yourself against a false accusation? What are you going to say, if they're already convinced you aren't trustworthy? What can you tell them? I'm from Lafe, my friend: everybody'll tell you that we're all thieves."

During those years, Claudio and Romina would often scavenge but they finally stopped; they found fewer and fewer things, he said, because people threw out less, or because of the danger of malaria, or maybe because there was too much competition, a lot of kids out scavenging, so it was a real relief when he got his first "Jefes y Jefas" benefits, from the Program for Unemployed Male and Female Heads of Households.

For years, the Argentine government under the Kirchners, first Néstor then Cristina, refused to pass out money without getting something in exchange. "If you stop at welfare, people also stop at welfare," said the Minister of Social Welfare and sister of Cristina. "People tell me that they want to set up a cooperative or a garment factory. If the welfare is to help set up a family workshop, you are giving people an opportunity. But if it's just cash, and a limited amount on top of that, you're not really offering them anything. Or does anybody really think that the problem of poverty can be solved with a hundred pesos?"

But a couple of election losses convinced that same government to radically change its position, and their "General Child Allowance" turned into their great social welfare measure: they would distribute a fixed amount, equivalent to about forty dollars a month, to more than three million children. Of course, they didn't present this as a failure of the six years of the opposite policies but rather as a great step forward along who knows what path. In fact, it was the triumph of *assistentialism*, Christian charity in the hands of the state: I give you a little, the minimum necessary for you to continue exactly as you are.

And it created, needless to say, conflicting loyalties: to the government that gives the handouts, to the visible face of that government, to the local commissars, to all those who get some kind of perk for passing them out. It created a certain amount of gratitude, and at the same time it generated fear: if they gave it to me it's because they want to give it to me, and they can take it away whenever they want. Let's not rock any boats, otherwise we'll be left without that as well.

Assistentialism is a way of addressing the effects of poverty—lack of access to the most indispensable things—and not its causes. Or, to put it in other words: a way of maintaining poverty, not creating the conditions necessary for those same people to once again start to fend for themselves. *Assistentialism* keeps the poor brutally dependent on handouts from: the government, the state, NGOs, whatever church. *Assistentialism* saves people in the short term, and through the same mechanism, it sinks them deeper and deeper into their condition as people who need to be rescued. Which makes it difficult to stop thinking that it is a provision of the system, the way an unjust system maintains and perpetuates itself.

When Claudio turned thirty he heard, he said, the "call." Now he fasted, conversed with God, made Him promises, tried to fulfill them—and spent his time spreading His work throughout his community. He told me about his encounters with his god and he mentioned his own misfortunes—Evangelicals use the story of their own misfortunes—they give testimony—as a way of bringing others back to the path of righteousness.

"I'll tell you the truth: I was also raped when I was a child. I never told anybody, not my mother, not my wife, not my friends, not anybody until one day the Lord spoke to me through a prophetic pastor and told me that he knew that I had been abused as a child and that I had to forgive them in order to purify my heart. He knows everything. He scrutinizes your heart and knows everything."

Every night, Claudio asked his god to help him stay on the path of righteousness, to help young boys and girls find their way out of drugs, help them return to the path. Until one night He appeared dressed all in white while Claudio was sleeping, and He took his hand and led him, in his sleep, to a door of a house. He pointed to it, Claudio said. Come, He said, here lives my daughter, I want you to talk to her.

Claudio said that in the dream he told the girl everything that his god told him to say, and that she confessed, in the dream, to her sins: adultery, drugs, an abortion. And he said that he woke up scared to death but grateful for that opportunity, and the next day he went to find that girl and everything happened exactly as it had in the dream—because the dream wasn't a dream but his god leading him to righteousness. But he had to struggle with her.

"What happens is that the Devil doesn't want to lose the life he has taken over. So if you go to fight him for it, he appears, and he attacks you. But if you are strengthened by prayer and fasting, you can beat the Devil. It's not me who says this; it's the Bible. But it's not easy to see the Devil. My younger brother has that god-given ability: he sees him in trees, in houses, just walking around, he sees him when we are exorcising someone, and the Devil comes out of their mouth. But it's difficult, because the Devil knows everything, he knows who you are, what you do, everything, he tells you what only you are supposed to know, just to scare you."

A few months ago, Claudio went to the city to request an electricity hookup, one with a meter. It cost him 150 pesos, and he had to start paying for electricity, which seemed like a very bad deal, but in order to buy anything on credit—"a pair of shoes, a stove, anything"—they ask for his electric bill. Also, to apply for the child allowance. It's one way of being integrated into the system: if you pay for electricity, you exist as a consumer. But they still hadn't come to actually do it.

When he converted, Claudio already had two children. He had gotten his neighbor Romina pregnant when she was fifteen and he was twenty. Romina refused to have an abortion; the child was born healthy but they didn't get together: each one stayed at their parents' house, across the street from each other, and they fought a lot. Only after their second did they think about moving in together, but they didn't have any money. One day Claudio's godmother offered to sell four hundred square feet of land to him for 2,000 pesos—$180—and said he shouldn't worry, he could pay her off slowly. It was very low-lying land: prone to flooding, but lacking running water. Claudio started filling it with rubble and debris he brought from the dump, though he didn't have a cent to build four walls. For hours on end, he said, he prayed for a solution. Until a friend appeared who was going to start to build a house and offered to give him his wooden shed.

"It was just one room, kind of rotten, but it was much better than nothing. And it was a sign that the Lord had not abandoned me, that He was looking after me, listening to me."

That's how it started, very slowly, brick by brick, Claudio and Romina built two rooms with a cement floor. In one room there were two small beds where the three older kids slept, and some clothes racks, where they hung their clean clothes; in the other was a double bed for Romina and Claudio, and a twin for the two smallest girls, and more clothes racks. In the old shed was the kitchen with its propane tank and a small table. Everything was very tidy, clean, swept. Everything, said Claudio, was proof that God had not forgotten them.

"That's why I have to help others, show the Lord that I can be his instrument for doing good."

That's why, he said, he was now building a room for a girl he knew from the collective, who hired him. She had five children and a husband in jail.

"She doesn't know that the Lord told me not to charge her, to do it for free, but I won't tell her until we're finished. Just imagine what a surprise it will be for her!"

It was a very expensive luxury. There were periods when Claudio had more construction jobs but it had been months since he'd had anything.

"You have no idea how tough things have been. These last few days I've sent my wife and the littlest ones to my mother's house to get something to eat, because we've got nothing here."

Each month Claudio received a thousand pesos—about eighty dollars—from a government program that was billed as a "workers' cooperative." To get it, he had to sweep the streets on Saturdays and Sundays, for two four-hour shifts, in downtown Laferrère.

There, a sign on the bridge near the station said that in 2011 the town celebrated its one hundred year anniversary: "Gregorio de Laferrère, 100 Años de Historia . . ." where the ellipses must represent the future. Gregorio de Laferrère is a half hour by train from downtown Buenos Aires; it was founded by an Argentine politician and journalist and dramaturge, Señor Gregorio de Laferrère, who was so generous, he wanted to give it his name. He failed: now everybody calls it Lafe.

Downtown Lafe *is* the train station. Shops and business are crowded around the bridge: a *choripán* sandwich shop, one for more or less legal cell phones, two kiosks that sell cigarettes and candies, one selling Paraguayan *sopas*, a kind of frittata or quiche, and *chipás* (cheese-flavored bread rolls), *La Reina del Regalo*. A little farther away, there are a few other businesses: a McDonald's, a large delicatessen, El Porteño *panchería* or hot dog stand, two appliance shops, a loan broker. The asphalt along the avenue is pitted, like the surface of the moon; dozens of people are waiting for the bus in long, serpentine lines on the sidewalk. The faces are coppery; the landscape—the billboards, the crowds, the garbage, the shouting—are very Latin American.

Many women, children, old people, men with calloused hands. The cooler youngsters wear Bermuda shorts, moon-landing shoes, and, if they're not too hot, baseball caps. The more flirtatious girls dye their hair blonde and wear very short shorts; the most flirtatious girls are chubby. Flesh is doled out unfairly: the boys wearing Bermudas are skinny and muscular; the girls in those shorts have more fat on their bones.

"When they passed the law that gays could marry we went to the plaza to protest that this was against the word of God, because His word is for yesterday, today, and tomorrow, it is an eternal mandate. And then [Néstor] Kirchner died. Because God's word is, I am love, but it's also, I am a consuming fire: if God wants to, he smites you down, he takes your life."

At times, Claudio used "Bible-speak," that strange jargon of suburban preachers, not only using the *tú* form of the verb, like in the Bible, and in a country where nobody uses *tú*, but also using archaic words, as if his god were speaking from the depth of time and issuing the most brutal threats in the name of love and harmony. Moreover, Claudio said them in his nasal accent that seemed to skate over the words, and he dropped final consonants, like the chanting of Argentine soccer fans.

"I think that's why the president died. Because we are living in strange times, when they call the good bad and the bad good, when everything's been turned upside down."

Lafe is the land of the Ford Falcon, the purgatory where they survive, for lack of a better hell. The Falcon, launched onto the market in the fifties and imposed on Argentina a few years later, was, for many years, the favorite car in Argentina: sturdy, reasonable, solid. This, until the seventies, when Falcons—especially the green ones—carried army personnel and policemen who kidnapped and murdered thousands of people. Since then, Falcons began to disappear from the landscape of the capital; now I saw they'd gone to live in Lafe. Here, the corpses of Falcons were used as collective taxis: for two pesos, they carried as many people as could fit inside. They were rusty, dented, broken, and missing parts, but they ran; some even had license plates.

"Doesn't it bother you that God hasn't made a more just world?"

"That's not God, that's men."

"But, for example, when you have to send your children to their grandmother's house because you don't have enough food . . ."

"Yes, but this is an apprenticeship. What He wants is for you to know how to live in scarcity as well as abundance, whatever He sends you. What He wants is to teach you that you have to accept what He sends you, that you depend on Him. But my wife, Romina, she doesn't understand that. She only kind of believes, her heart shuts down to God. The Lord is banging at the doors of her heart, and she doesn't want to open for Him. That hurts me. I see other couples at church, and I'm always there alone even though I'm not a widower or a bachelor; I want to go with my family too. God tells me to wait, because He also tests your patience. Romi thinks the government should give you things. It's okay, she finds what she needs. But God wants you to depend on Him. The pastor told me again, recently: God wants you to stop going around asking for things from men and ask it from Him. He is the owner of everything; if you ask Him in prayer, He will give you what you need."

Romina told me she was lucky with her husband. It's true, there were times when he was a problem, he drank, he took drugs, he hung out on the street, but ever since he was cured—she said "cured"—he was a different man. He helped her out, like when she had to go to a protest march. He cleaned the house, washed clothes, took care of the children, put them to bed.

"He treats me well, he's good, he never raises a hand, nothing. Too bad we can never just relax. You know how much I want to just relax?"

"What would it mean to relax?"

"Nothing, just not having to go out scavenging all the time, to just have what we need to eat till the end of the month. I would be so relaxed . . ."

Romina was thirty years old and had five children. Long thin legs, black-and-white shorts, a fuchsia tank top, violet-painted toenails, short dark-red dyed hair, angular features, large and slightly crowded teeth. It was hot and she was sweating; I asked her why she didn't believe in God.

"No, I do believe. Because a lot of things have happened. When my middle son was three, my in-laws gave him a rooster and a hen. He liked to touch everything, and he wanted to touch the rooster and the rooster grabbed him with his claws and made four holes, and my son started bleeding, like a sieve. And my husband and I went running to find a taxi. He was dying on the way, the taxi driver told me to wake him up, he's dying, he was dying in my arms. And we got to the clinic, and they didn't help us, and my husband started screaming, 'Help us, our son is dying!' Finally they helped us, and the man said, here, take this, give this to him, and it was saline solution. What are you doing? I asked him. He's dying and you give this to us? There's no pediatrician on call today, he said. Just bring me a doctor, something, because if my son dies you're going to be responsible. Finally, they cleaned him up, dressed his wounds, but he didn't respond, like he'd fainted. And we thought we should take him to the children's hospital, but we didn't have a single peso. Right there next to the clinic, there was a church called Dios es Mi Salvador. And we went in there, and my husband said, we're going to pray. And the pastor came, and he also prayed, we all prayed for about two or three hours, and suddenly he woke up, he recognized us. The Lord patched him up, because if it hadn't been for Him, our son would have died, he was already dying."

"Why did you stay in the church instead of going to the hospital?"

"Because we didn't have a peso."

"The pastor didn't want to give you the fare?"

"No, well, what happened is we went in, we were praying, and he woke up. He was dying and he woke up," Romina said, but she still wasn't sold on divine largesse; she preferred what the government had to offer.

7

The word *client* comes from the Latin *cliens, clientis,* which derives from the verb *luere,* to hear or obey, and it probably refers to the most ancient of republican relationships. A citizen—the *cliens*—recognizes the power of another citizen—the patron—and agrees to do what he asks in exchange for his protection, for him employing his power—which his, the citizen's, obedience, augments—to help him.

Clientelism, that relationship between the people and the powerful, is one of the principle mechanisms used in the more or less democratic regimes of the Other World and its surroundings.

(Hence, the classic right-wing trick of discrediting state intervention by naming such intervention "big government" consists of replacing it with clientelism, that is, of claiming that the best intervention is the passing out of charity. It should consist of arbitrating, of creating the necessary condition for wealth to be distributed fairly.)

"If we give them food, they'll never work."

"We give them food because we can't give them work."

"What?"

Age-old dialogues. Those who opposed charity fifty or two hundred and fifty years ago—in the age of the good old Reverend Malthus—had solid arguments: if we get them used to receiving free food they will never want to go back to work. Hunger appeared as a market necessity, to keep workers working, to maintain the old curse of bread in exchange for sweat. But this is no longer the case: the market doesn't need those people, and the only way to keep them alive—until or unless they find a way to solve the problem—is to give them food.

For two years, Romina worked at a community soup kitchen in her neighborhood. She cooked and served, and in exchange, she earned the equivalent of about $150 a month and could bring food home for her family, sometimes even a bag of groceries. But the kitchen closed last year because of a fight among the group that ran it. "It had to do with some who were involved in politics, I don't know; I asked so many times but they didn't want to tell me anything," explained Romina—and some government official who stopped sending supplies.

"I just signed up for *Barrios de Pie*, but I've gone to other marches. I'd spend all day and they'd pay about 150 or 200 pesos, but you'd have to go, you'd have to keep going."

"Where?"

"To the Casa Rosada, places like that."

"What was the name of that group?"

"*Teresa Vive*. But now I signed up for *Barrios* and I have to go to marches."

"A long time ago?"

"No, just recently, two or three weeks ago. And I signed up my youngest brother, who also needed money. He used to work in construction, but he can't find work, so he comes with me and gets something too."

In the yard of their house—in the empty part of their lot around their house, surrounded by debris and a half-built well—there were three or four cats and a bitch who just had a litter. A very large black bird was fighting with a cat for a piece of something: it looked like meat, but it was hard to tell. They screeched, both the bird and the cat; they fought.

Romina said that now, with *Barrios*, it's better than before. They give her more or less the same amount but she doesn't have to walk as much.

"What do they give you in *Barrios*?"

"For now, groceries, and I already got a little, and my pay, which I'm still waiting for, Seven hundred and fifty. Because I get the allowance for the kids, so I told him. They said, no problem, don't worry. Those who don't get the allowance can join the cooperatives, where they get twelve hundred. But we have to go to the marches. If they don't see you at the marches, they'll drop you."

"So you go?"

"Yeah, I go."

"Where does the seven fifty they give you come from?"

"I don't know, it's some kind of salary from an organization, with three letters, I don't know if it's *p c,* or *p n l,* something like that."

Clientelism is not the exclusive territory of governments—national, provincial, municipal—or even of the most traditional political parties. Nothing, of course, compares to the charity power of a Peronist govern ment, but even groups on the so-called left function along the same lines. Each group maneuvers its influence in the state apparatus and its people in the streets to obtain the greatest possible number of subsidies and sinecures for its followers—which, in turn, allows them to sustain and increase their numbers. Or, it sometimes becomes the only reason why many of them participate in these activities at all.

"Do they give you a check?"

"No, they are supposed to give you a card. Mine is in process. The coordinator of *Barrios* here told me she already asked for it, and they'll give it to me soon."

Barrios de Pie is an organization that used to be part of the Néstor Kirchner government, who ran the country from 2003 to 2007. Although the organization is no longer, its founders obtained favors, which they still receive.

"Do you get the child allowance for all five?"

"I'm supposed to, but the truth is, these last few months they haven't been paying all of it because I haven't gotten a new ID for my ten-year-old. Same thing with my three-year-old, I went to turn in the application, and they wouldn't accept it. And the last time they didn't, I told them that I've been waiting for a year and a half, she's going to turn three and they can't reject it every time. And they told me, no, because of this, that, and the other, and I sat down and left the application there and I told them that I was not moving, because they did the same thing to me with my eight-year-old when he turned five when I took him to the nursery school in the thirty-second district, over there, and the person there, in the thirty-second district didn't want to sign it, and without the signature . . ."

Romina got all worked up, agitated, she went over and over every single bureaucratic problem she'd had to deal with to get the allowance for her children. It was a sprawling labyrinthine story of hours and hours of waiting, digging in her heels, mild humiliations, a measure of violence—it was as much work as a job.

"And then the six-year-old, who has a birthday on May first, and had to have a new ID and I didn't have the money and couldn't do it. And they rejected her application and wanted to exclude her, and I explained to them that I needed it, that without that money I can't feed them, and on that day, too, I stayed, I didn't move from that chair, and it was full of people and there was a big hullabaloo, but I didn't leave. So then I said, I want to talk to someone who can tell me what they're going to do, and they told me to leave, and my husband didn't even want to look at me, I think it made him . . . I don't know what it made him, but I stayed there till eight. I said I wanted to talk to the manager, and the man said that I couldn't file a complaint and I talked and I fought and . . ."

Romina, for now, managed to get them to pay 1,200 pesos, instead of the 1,500 that would cover all five children.

"They owe it to me. But at least this helps."

"Did you look for work?"

"Cleaning, that's mostly what I find, by the hour, because otherwise who'll look after the children. But right now I don't have any work at all, so I go to those marches. You do what you promise, I tell them, and I'll do what I promise. And if they give me a hard time, if I go and they don't give me anything, I won't go again, and that's that."

"What is it you promise to do?"

"I go to the marches. There've been three so far. We leave at seven in the morning and by two we're back. It works for me, it's easy. The marches I used to go to lasted till nighttime, I'd arrive home at midnight. Imagine that."

"Where were the last few?"

"We went to the Plaza de Mayo, to the Mercado de Abasto, in San Justo . . . oh, and also to the Obelisco."

"What are they for?"

"I don't know, to protest, they say. Or to ask for programs. The one at the Abasto was to ask for new programs. And for a Christmas bonus."

"What about the protests? What are they for?"

"So they'll pay me," Romina explained, as if she didn't understand what she didn't understand.

But it wasn't enough; often, it was not enough. Ever since the soup kitchen closed, the kids were eating less, Romina explained to me, and almost always the same thing: stew with rice, stew with noodles—sometimes with a piece of meat but mostly not—mashed potatoes.

"Sometimes when it's hot, salad, with *cornebé*, that meat pie thing [spam]. And if there's ground meat, I make them a *pastel de papa*, with potatoes. I put together whatever I find and make what I can. When we're scrounging, when we don't have enough, every peso we find is for them. We don't eat and they do. And sometimes they notice and ask: what, you guys aren't eating? No, it's okay, we already ate, now it's your turn to eat."

"What do you like to eat?"

"I have no problems eating anything," she replied, as if to like something would be risky, the consequence of rejecting something truly objectionable.

"But what do you like most of all?"

"I don't know, I like frittata with chard, vegetables," Romina answered.

Claudio and Romina are worried because their youngest daughter, the three-year-old, is "underweight." That's what they told Romina at the clinic of *Barrios de Pie*, where they were serving snacks. She took the kids there for them to have something tasty to eat and drink, and they weighed them and measured them and told them that Tuti should weigh at least forty-five pounds, and not the thirty that she did weigh. But they shouldn't worry, they told her; they would take her to see the doctor at the clinic to get her an underweight certificate. With that they would give her a box of groceries every two weeks, or even every week. Romina knew the drill: her two older children had gone through the same thing a couple of years before.

"The problem is that the doctor doesn't agree," Romina said, sighing—the world is a difficult place, full of people who make it even more difficult.

"We went there with the lady from *Barrios* and the doctor said, no, she was fine. But I didn't see when she weighed her because I waited outside because it was so full of people."

"What do you think?"

"I don't know what to think anymore. The *Barrios* woman told me that we're going to go back and fight, go to a different doctor. And I told her that maybe the other doctor won't want to, either, because there are doctors who just don't want to give you the certificate."

"Why?"

"Because you're from *Barrios de Pie* or some other organization like that, they just don't want to. They give them to the people from the government, I think. I know a nurse and she said the chief of pediatrics is like that, she doesn't want to give certificates. Maybe they ordered her not to. And I don't think that's okay, because if we go to ask for something, it's because we need it. But, well, hopefully she's right, right?" Romina said, as she eked out a sad smile.

In a way it would be great if her daughter was fine, though that would make her lose the chance of receiving the box of food that would change her diet.

"There's oil, sugar, noodles, rice, *dulce de batata*; it's really lovely. I can't complain. The problem is they give it only once a month, and that's not enough."

On the other hand, she suspected that her daughter really was malnourished, that she really needed it, and that she wasn't receiving it because of some capricious bureaucrat.

The world is a hostile place, more hostile than any other space, full of rules that are constantly changing, full of tricks others know, full of ways to get screwed.

Romina bought the few things she buys at a small store two blocks from her house, because the owner sold to her on credit. In exchange, he charged 50 percent more for everything. Romina would like to be able to buy elsewhere, somewhere she could pay for those noodles, that sugar, that oil at their real price, but she can't because then she'd need to have the cash.

"He's earning millions on us, that guy. But what can we do? We can't do anything. In the end, we can never do anything."

In today's Argentina there are five or six million surplus people. The poorest are surplus; their total exclusion—their uselessness—is relatively new and nobody really knows what to do about it, what to do with them.

There is something that sociologists, politicians, and NGO workers call, with a certain amount of involuntary cynicism, inclusion. It is a relatively new concept; until recently, the poor and the defenders of the poor asked for equality not inclusion. This belonged to times when society had the mechanisms to use their poor, and they were willing to give them something in return: the certainties of slavery, the guarantees of serfdom, the uneasiness of a steady wage. For most of the twentieth century Argentina was a country where the poor had a place: they were workers. More or less industrialized capitalism needed them to operate the machinery in their factories and workshops, to offer services, and that need made it possible for the needy to demand certain conditions, improvements—never enough—in their standard of living.

When wealthy Argentines decided to send in their military to change the system—to re-create that pastoral arcadia that had never existed, to close factories and expel peasants so they could become the soy basket of the world—they might not have foreseen that this would leave millions of people unemployed, in the strongest meaning of the word: useless, unnecessary. In this way they managed, among other things, to replace the threat of organized worker violence with the threat of inorganic slum violence: an individualized and frayed violence that can explode in completely unpredictable directions. And now they have regrets.

They should have been able to imagine it—or could have studied it—because the exclusion of millions had already happened in other Latin American countries. But wealthy Argentines are a bit thick, and they believed they could construct a country in the Other World and continue to stroll peacefully down the street. It took a long time for them to understand that they were wrong: the exclusion of the poor produced violence, crude violence without purpose, without future.

"I don't know, my little girl says she wants to be a doctor, and the boy told me he was going to be a lawyer."

"Where did they get those ideas?"

"They must have seen something on television."

"You think they'll be able to?"

"Who knows. I hope. But I don't know how."

In Argentina about 750,000 young people between the ages of eighteen and twenty-five have no job or any prospects of having one.

The peculiar thing about Argentina—what perhaps makes it an interesting case—is that this mass of people who've been shoved aside—disposable, as the Colombians would say, superfluous—is a relatively new phenomenon. Here one can reconstruct how they appeared in a country that had previously avoided it.

"The late-capitalist triage of humanity, then has already taken place." As Jan Breman, writing of India, has warned, "a point of no return is reached when a reserve army waiting to be incorporated into the labor process becomes stigmatized as a permanently redundant mass, an excessive burden that cannot be included now or in the future, in economy and society. This metamorphosis is, in my opinion at least, the real crisis of world capitalism."[11] Alternately, our habitué Mike Davis in *Planet of Slums* noted from a CIA report in 2002: "By the late 1990s a staggering one billion workers representing one-third of the world's labor force, most of them in the South, were either unemployed or underemployed."[12] And, further on: "Altogether, the global informal working class (overlapping with but nonidentical to the slum population) is about one billion strong, making it the fastest-growing, and most unprecedented, social class on earth."[13]

Men and women used to serve a purpose. India was a good example. For centuries, the poorest of the poor were the very cheap labor that, on the one hand, grew what the rich ate and, on the other, served it and served them. They were, of course, interchangeable: they were not individuals but rather species. Since nobody cared if they lived or died, the hundreds of millions functioned as a kind of useful reserve and a pressure to keep salaries at miserably low levels.

In societies that used a lot of labor, people were always a necessary resource. For example, the problems of the Roman Empire to maintain a good supply of slaves, and one of the reasons for its decline, was that once the world was theirs, they found it increasingly difficult to renew their labor force through wars of conquest. We know, for example, that the European Industrial Revolution needed millions of factory workers who came from the countryside because agricultural technology had made so much progress. They went to the cities to run those labor-hungry machines, and even the unemployed fulfilled their economic function by putting pressure on the employed to accept more work and demand less pay—they could be replaced at any moment. Agrarian societies, until a few decades ago, were based on the sustained, sweaty labor of the peasants.

There are systems that optimally exploit their human resources by assigning each individual a profitable task. The balance is unstable—and never lasts, in historical terms, very long. Or, there is no balance because there is no simultaneity between improvements in certain technologies that free up labor power and an increase in the demand for this labor power to perform other tasks.

Now, in a world where machines are so much more efficient, labor and work—people—are surplus. Wars and epidemics, which always functioned as demographic regulation mechanisms, have, in spite of everything, significantly decreased. People live longer, children die less often; there are too many of us. But we are not too many in the abstract, in general, some of us are too many.

It is a perfectly anomalous situation, one that might never have happened before with this kind of intensity, to this extent. Sometimes I think it is one of the great changes of our era, that for the first time in history, a sixth or a fifth of the population of the world is surplus. And since it wouldn't be nice if they all died without further ado, they are kept barely afloat, undernourished but not starving to death.

Argentina—as I was saying—serves as an example. It has closed thousands of factories and workshops; it has managed to replace the majority of its rural peons with increasingly efficient tractors and harvesters; it has managed to produce much more grain with many fewer people than before.

But it hasn't figured out what to do with those people. If the people in charge in Argentina—the rich and their representatives—were one day given the proper dose of sodium pentothal, it would be fun to listen to them discuss truthfully how they wanted to get rid of five or six million people. They would think of it as a true service to the nation. The rest could live comfortably, crime rates would radically decline, the Evangelical sect would lose influence, a lot of land would be freed up for cultivation and private neighborhoods, public transportation would work much better, the state would save resources—subsidies, programs, police, prison guards—it could use to improve, for example, the schools and universities and hospitals that educated people would use wisely. Perhaps they would lose a soccer player or a couple of boxing champions or two or three bad singers; perhaps Peronism would lose a few million votes and everybody would have a little more difficulty finding maids, but in general they would gain more than they would lose.

They don't do it. Perhaps they don't dare—for now—so they try to appease those millions with welfare programs. Perhaps they would rather those millions exist so that through these programs, they'd be guarantees their votes, and in exchange for this guarantee of power, they are willing to put up with the hiccups. For them, the wager also carries risks. It's really a drag not to be able to go out for a stroll without being afraid, and there's always the bigger fear that one night they'll have had enough and the whole thing will explode.

"No, when young folks start talking about stealing, about armed robbery, I always tell them, hey, guys, cool it, stay cool, it's not worth it. In the end, you'll always be the losers, it's not worth it. But they tell me not to be such a pussy, that I've gone soft, that those preachers have turned me into rubber. The young folks laugh at me, and sometimes I get hot under the collar and curse them. They just laugh at me more and tell me, oh, we thought you were the holy one, the good little Evangelical."

Argentina is a particular instance of the billion-dollar question: how did we manage to convince ourselves, after living in a country of relative inclusion and social homogeneity, that it is normal for so many citizens to be left without any possibility of a dignified life?

The same thing is happening, in one way or another, in many places. With differences, of course. The political purpose those million serve in Argentina is not the same as the economic purpose they serve in India or Bangladesh, or the lack of purpose they serve in many other places. But the fact that their function doesn't justify their existence repeats itself. The same fraction of the population that is surplus in Argentina is surplus in the world: these are the 1.4 billion people, that 20 percent of the world population, who live in extreme poverty, who live on less than $1.25 a day, who go hungry.

There are other possibilities. The textile workers in Dhaka are integrated into the world economy, exploited to make cheap clothes to be sold in the First World. Is the option to likewise "integrate" Africans, Latin Americans, Nepalese? For the moment, this does not seem possible in economic terms. Stated in a different way: they don't know how to derive surplus value from them.

The best scenario for the rich countries is that the leftovers in the Other World survive on their own. That they tend to their own animals, cultivate their own gardens. The wealthy don't like them occupying land they could use, but there are still some regions that are too difficult to make profitable. Then, when everything explodes, they can send them a bag of grain. Then there are the worst-case scenarios: that they will organize and rebel. They are, obviously, a bother:

Dead weight.

(The disposable ones also have their own "soft" version: the millions and millions who do perfectly useless jobs, defined as those jobs whose disappearance would only affect the same structure where that work is carried out. David Graeber, professor at the London School of Economics, says, "It's as if someone were out there making up pointless jobs just for the sake of keeping us all working."[14] Employees—an infinite number of employees—in all kinds of service companies, employees of state bureaucracies, all kind of managers, lawyers, public relations people, salesmen, receptionists, secretaries, journalists, and so many others of us who are there so that nobody realizes that we don't have any real place in the chain of production, that if we all occupied a real place we could all work just ten or fifteen hours a day, that we are really as disposable as the peasants in Bihar—except in some countries where things are a little more complicated. The employed disposables have the advantage that in general nobody tells them how disposable they are—and they try not to tell themselves.

And they eat whenever they want.)

The system never gives up, and from time to time it discovers fresh uses for the disposable ones, such as those Indian clinics that hire very poor Indian women as wombs. Mothers and fathers from the rich world send their embryos or their eggs and sperm to local doctors who implant them in a local girl. With her body working full time for nine months, she earns what she would have earned in twenty years of hard labor, about $4,000 or $5,000. For the same job, a woman in the United States can charge $30,000 or $40,000. The total price of a baby incubated in the United States is around $100,000, which limits its widespread use as a method that is available to the middle class. Not any longer. In India you can do it for about $15,000.

At the fancier Indian clinics, the system looks more like the classic chain of production. They no longer leave the women to gestate in their huts, where "they ate poorly and worked too much and suffered scarcity; it was better for them and for the baby to stay with us and receive healthy and controlled nourishment." In this profession, a poorly nourished worker makes for bad business, so they board them for nine months in communal houses where all they do is reproduce, peacefully and well-fed. And when they give birth, they sign a paper that says they will never try to find out the fate of their product.

Since the end of slavery, only the external parts of the body were used in production; the interior was out of bounds, spared. Now, technological advances are finding ways to use people's insides to produce people—no longer slaves. It is, of course, for a good cause.

The market is new and must struggle against certain restrictions. For now, India prohibits single people and gay couples from using rented wombs, and France and Germany, among others, forbid the procedure. The exporters of white babies—Russia, Romania, certain Argentine provinces—have not yet protested; they will soon realize that these new technologies will ruin their business. The beauty of the procedure is that the rental mother's genes do not participate in the baby produced; the Indian woman is merely a warm, moist incubator—and the child comes out blond.

There are more than a billion, and they survive. The rich counties do in Africa what the Argentine state does in Argentina: they give the extra people the minimum necessary in order to survive, so they won't horrify the do-gooders, and so they'll know that without this assistance they would be much worse off and don't burn it all down.

But a system can't squander its resources so foolishly. If it doesn't learn to use these people—or doesn't eliminate them—it will have serious problems.

In the meantime, they are an inconvenience, much like all that garbage nobody knows where to put.

ON HUNGER: CHARITY

1

They are 1.4 billion poor people, those who spend less than $1.25 a day; 1.4 billion poor people, those who have none of the things we consider so normal: house, food, clothes, light, water, perspectives, hopes, future—present.

Again: 1.4 billion poor people, those who eat less than they should; 1.4 billion poor people, those who are not necessary, disposable, men and women the globalized system doesn't need but must tolerate because quick genocides don't look good on TV, and might give nightmares to the weak of heart.

In response to their existence comes a classic sentence of triumphant neoliberalism from its best media sources, *The Economist*: "Despite two centuries of economic growth, over a billion people still live in extreme poverty."

In which all the weight is on the "despite": the assumption that the economy of those two centuries is not actually the cause of such extreme poverty.

From an address to the Board of Governors by Robert S. McNamara, President of the World Bank Group, Nairobi, Kenya, September 24, 1973: "This is absolute poverty: a condition of life so limited as to prevent realization of the potential of the genes with which one is born; a condition of life so degrading as to insult human dignity—and yet a condition of life so common as to be the lot of some 40% of the peoples of the developing countries. And are not we who tolerate such poverty, when it is within our power to reduce the number afflicted by it, failing to fulfill the fundamental obligations accepted by civilized men since the beginning of time?"[1]

Words spoken by a man widely credited for escalating the war in Vietnam during his term as Secretary of Defense.

Platitudes strike again: the world of the USA. The United States of America has been the definitive political, economic, cultural, and military world power for one hundred years, with a level of hegemony that pales anything that came before it.

Until a little over a quarter of a century ago, the United States faced a certain degree of opposition from the Soviet bloc; since then, nothing. In the year 2000, US military expenditure was equal to all other countries combined; with one-twentieth of the world's population it controls a fifth of its wealth; seven out of every ten internet pages are written in its language; its scientists win half of all Nobel prizes in Physics, Chemistry, and Medicine; its political power has been so unchallenged that the term "unipolar world" has come about.

Hence, without risking exaggeration: this is the world that US capitalism and democracy have produced. The poverty and hunger of those million is the consequence of that world—not its mistake.

The fact that we think, when we think, the opposite is one of its great achievements.

And its entire strategy consists of addressing the problem as if it were a correctible and temporary mistake.

"If you want to see what men and women really believe, look at what they do, not at what they say," said Terry Eagleton.[2]

Humanitarian assistance is, above all, the putting into action of a conventional idea: that it's not a good idea for people to starve to death. It shouldn't happen, this system shouldn't allow it—they say "allow it." If it's happening it's because there are corners the system doesn't reach, situations that spiral out of control. Humanitarian assistance is a myopic and optimistic gesture.

"Oh, dear, how could it be that in the twenty-first century there are still people who go hungry."

"Yes, poor things, how hard it is for them."

"And for us."

"For us? Oh, right, for us too."

Humanitarian assistance is, in its best iterations, the act of devoting oneself, with the best of intentions, to correcting certain mistakes and excesses of the system, thereby underpinning it. Though also, like everything, it admits to different descriptions.

"The existence of hunger in a world of plenty is not just a moral outrage; it is also short-sighted from an economic viewpoint. Hungry people make poor workers, they are bad learners (if they go to school at all), they are prone to sickness and they die young. Hunger is also transmitted across generations, as underfed mothers give birth to underweight children whose potential for mental and physical activity is impaired. The productivity of individuals and the growth of entire nations are severely compromised by widespread hunger. Hunger breeds desperation, and the hungry are an easy prey to those who seek to gain power and influence through crime, force, or terror, endangering national and global stability. It is, therefore, in everyone's self-interest—rich and poor alike—to fight hunger."[3]

So says the FAO in its *Anti-Hunger Programme*, launched in 2003 and quietly deactivated because nobody really paid much attention to it.

There have always been institutions that have helped people. In fact, it is one the principal activities of many churches: charity, the unidirectional form of mutual aid. "Doing good" through the Church of Rome—*bene facere*—was for centuries the most widespread form of humanitarian aid in the West; women—usually women—of the big and powerful concerned themselves with the fate of the small and impotent, those their husbands exploited, bringing them alms. One could say that they generously gave these poor people what the low wages their husbands paid them did not make it possible for them to acquire on their own. Alms rather than a right.

So, from time to time, and under catastrophic circumstances, people from more fortunate states would help the citizens of less fortunate states, up until the end of the Second World War, which is where the story of modern humanitarian assistance really began. The Marshall Plan enacted by the United States between 1947 and 1951 meant the sending of enormous quantities of food—among other things—to non-Soviet European countries, which had been devastated. The Marshall Plan was key to the economic recovery of Europe—and its configuration was to US interests.

All the manuals say, in one way or another, is that "humanitarian assistance is the aid and action designed to save lives, alleviate suffering, and protect human dignity in emergency situations," and can be recognized as that which is ruled by principles of "humanity, neutrality, impartiality, and operational independence."[4]

That's what the manuals say.

In July 1954 the United States Congress passed Public Law 480, the Food for Peace Act, which authorized the sale of food to "underdeveloped" countries at minimal prices.

At the time, the drumbeats of the Cold War were endless, and many countries in the Third World were tempted by the possibility of joining the Second. The United States didn't skimp on ways to prevent that from happening. A hot war was one—the army had just been fighting in Korea—and maintaining military bases wherever possible was another—from Germany to Japan, passing through South Africa, Turkey, Panama. The installation of friendly dictators was the norm—Jacobo Árbenz, president of Guatemala, had been overthrown a few weeks earlier—and food aid seemed like an excellent weapon in the ongoing struggle against the red menace.

Moreover, there was a surplus of grain. In the United States, the modernization of farmland had increased agricultural production, and the mechanization of transportation had reduced to a minimum the need for beasts of burden. The countries who had benefited from the Marshall Plan had already recovered and were growing their own. Grain farmers—and especially the large grain companies—didn't know what to do with their grain. Their lobbies pressured everybody they could to make sure the Food for Peace Act benefited them.

And it did, in several ways. For starters, the state bought from them at high prices the food they would send to poor countries at highly subsidized prices. Next, according to what President Eisenhower said at the time, the law would lay "the basis for a permanent expansion of our exports of agricultural products with lasting benefits to ourselves and peoples of other lands."[5] In other words, it would open up new markets. In cruder words, it would make them dependent on the food they were sending, for several reasons.

First, local farmers could not compete with the cheap grain and were excluded from the game, causing the ruin of millions of peasants who emigrated to urban areas. Second, these shipments changed eating habits. I saw an extreme and dramatic example in the Marshall Islands, the midpoint of the Pacific Ocean, atolls where breadfruit trees grow and fish abound, where its inhabitants lived for centuries on their own resources. Annexed by the United States after the war, they got used to pasta, pizza, hamburgers, and hot dogs. They still spend most of their meager income on such imports.

In the Marshall Islands, these imported foods are almost a caricature; in many other countries, they are one of the reasons so many go hungry.

One way to think of humanitarian assistance is as the mechanism of a global system of patronage. This must have been, at least, how the United States thought of it in the second half of the twentieth century: an extreme way of establishing dependency between a patron and his clients—in the most Roman sense of the words. I give you if you give me. I: food; you: submission and some service or other.

When the law was being debated, then-senator and later Vice President Hubert Humphrey famously said in 1957 that "before people can do anything they have got to eat. And if you are looking for a way to get people to lean on you and to be dependent on you, in terms of their cooperation with you, it seems to me that food dependence would be terrific."[6]

Empires always imported food. The American Empire was the first to export it.

(Or, rather: the Roman Empire understood that its clients were neighbors, the American one spread to all corners of the world. These are, in the final analysis, differences of scale—and forms of control.)

But assistance cannot only serve the purpose of gaining political control over the planet. It has to benefit the population in the giving country in order for them to support it. Hence, the US law stipulated that 75 percent of its food aid would be in the form of food manufactured, processed, and packaged in their country. The large grain companies that dominate the sector, such as Cargill, Bunge, and company, are those who benefit most: they get half the orders—and according to a classic study by Barrett and Maxwell, they charge receiving countries between 10 and 70 percent more than market price.[7]

The law also stipulates that 75 percent of the food be transported on US-owned ships. US merchant shipping is an unstable business; other countries with lower taxes and fewer labor rules ship at lower cost; only 3 percent of international trade to and from the United States is transported on US ships, so the transport of that food is one of the sector's main life preservers. In a recent study, it was estimated that shipping accounts for 40 percent of the US expenditure of food aid. Or, in other words: in assistance to its own shipping fleet.

The law also allows US NGOs that receive US food from the US government to sell them in the markets of the receiving countries in order to pay for their operations. They call this "monetization," or in straight talk, making a quick buck. Barrett and Maxwell reviewed the figures of the eight largest NGOs and estimated that they sold approximately half the food they received, from which they derive a third of their income. Not only does this sound slightly perverse, but all that highly subsidized food, which is unloaded in the markets of the poorest countries, does not reach those who most need it but rather those who can pay, thereby reducing local production, destroying local farming, reproducing a cycle of hunger; in other words, achieving the exact opposite of what it proposes.

This is why some people in the United States have for years been proposing that at least some food aid be bought in local or nearby markets. Buying locally has obvious advantages—and almost all other donor nations do it. For one, it would greatly speed up the arrival of food: it's faster to bring it from a neighboring town than from Iowa. For another, it's much cheaper: no long-distance and inflated costs for shipping or customs or bureaucracies. And, above all: not only do you alleviate the suffering of the country's hungry but at the same time support local farmers.

But whenever anybody, with the very best intentions, proposes change, there is always someone, with the very best intentions, who says, no, better not, that a change under current conditions would mean the loss of support from agribusiness, US shipping companies, and certain NGOs—the so-called Iron Triangle—and that it is unlikely that the United States would maintain its level of food aid without pressure from those groups, or rather: instead of improving things, change would make it worse. A very contemporary argument.

So, proposals in Congress for aid to comprise up to 25 percent cash failed every time they were proposed, such as when they were proposed by the George W. Bush administration. The then administrator of the US Agency for International Development (USAID), Andrew Natsios, told Congress that if at least a quarter of the $1.2 billion used to buy food aid were spent in situ, everything would improve: buying locally would double the amount of food reaching those who need it in four times less time.[8]

No dice.

Barrett and Maxwell studied, among other things, the large US intervention in starving Ethiopia in 2003. At the time, they sent $500 million worth of grain—produced in the United States, shipped on US ships, distributed by US NGOs—and only $5 million worth of agrarian development aid to avoid repeats of such famines.

Talk is cheap, and everybody likes it that way. In 2002 former president Bill Clinton complained to the Council of Foreign Relations in Washington that President Bush had decreased the foreign aid budget. "If you took a poll among the American people and you asked them what percentage of the budget do we spend on foreign assistance, and what percent should we spend, there's been research on this for ten years, it never changes. The biggest block always say we spend between 2 to 15 percent of the budget, and that is too much, we should spend between 3 and 5 percent. Now, I actually agree with them. Of course we spend less than 1 percent, and we're dead last among all the advanced economies of the world in what we spend on foreign assistance," said Clinton.[9] When he became president in 1993, the United States spent 0.16 percent of its gross national product (GNP) on foreign aid; when he left in 2001, that had decreased to 0.11 percent.

In 1970 at the General Assembly of the United Nations, the developed nations committed to spending a minimum of 0.7 percent of their GNP on foreign assistance to poor countries. Assistance, in general, not just food aid.

That 0.7 percent doesn't seem like much, and their actual contributions never surpassed 0.4 percent. In 2005 the same commitment was made again; the figure has been hovering around 0.3 percent—less than half—for the last few years.

In 2012 the twenty-three countries in the Organization for Economic Co-operation and Development (OECD) gave $125 billion in aid to the countries of the Other World. That sounds like a lot. Two facts make it seem less: it is 7 percent less than in 2010; it is 0.29 percent of the sum of their GNP.

The United States continues to be the main donor with $30.5 billion, 0.19 percent of its GNP. What's interesting is that its citizens are convinced—as Clinton said—that their country spends much more on foreign aid than on their own entitlement programs, Medicaid and Medicare. Between the two, the United States in 2011 spent $992 billion: more than thirty times more. The Center for Global Development, a Washington establishment think tank, estimates that less than 40 percent of foreign aid actually reaches its supposed beneficiaries; the rest is lost in diverse intermediary bureaucracies. In other words, the real amount of aid doesn't reach even 0.12 percent.

It's a trifle, but true: humanitarian workers are expensive.

Second after the United States comes Great Britain, with its 14.6 billion GBP committed to foreign aid, or 0.56 percent of its GNP. Only three Scandinavian countries and Luxemburg give more than 0.80 percent; three countries in crisis—Greece, Italy, Spain—and South Korea give less than 0.15 percent. Korea emerged from poverty in the sixties thanks to multimillion-dollar international aid, but there was an additional factor: it was one of the hottest borders in the Cold War, so a strategic point where it behooved the rich West to spend a lot and wisely. This is not the case, obviously, with most of Africa.

There is an important difference between aid in the last twenty years and previously. Until the nineties the destination of US aid, distributed mostly through its own agencies, drew a map of its geopolitical interests. In the fifties, most went to Europe and the Far East; in the sixties, to India and Southeast Asia; in the seventies, the Near and Middle East. In the nineties, Africa.

In these last twenty years, sub-Saharan Africa has accounted for more than half of all world food aid. About 80 percent of this aid has gone to emergencies, and not to medium- and long-term projects. Protracted aid for preventative programs doesn't get much press; nobody hears about it, it wins no easy applause or misled votes. On the other hand, when there's a drought, airplanes loaded with grain and a couple of boxes of antibiotics so that a few fewer children die is always a crowd-pleaser.

Until the nineties, when there was still a Second and a Third World, geopolitical variables were more determinate. The distribution of food is now used less often to compensate friends and punish enemies or rebels.

But it does serve to reproduce the client system that divides the world—or confirms the division of the world—into rich countries that give and poor countries that receive. Another possible criterion to define the Other World: countries that receive food aid.

Food that is given as aid accounts for 0.015 percent of the food consumed in the world: a great advancement along the road that leads nowhere.

Here's a stupid and deceptive number but one that is so eloquent: the United States spends $1.76 billion daily on its armed forces. That money is more than enough to give every one of the eight hundred million hungry people in the world the two dollars they need to eat so that nobody is left without food. Of course there's no point in thinking of food in terms of charity and, moreover, it would be a different world . . .

. . . And yet.

2

It was an almost concrete proposal. With its Anti-Hunger Programme of 2003, FAO wanted to offer a possibility to fulfill the 1996 Millennium Development Goal of cutting the number of hungry people by half by 2015: a little more than 800 million. They prepared a meticulous plan that promised to solve everything by spending $24 billion annually in the intervening years.

"The investment package includes, inter alia, an injection of start-up capital, averaging US$500 per family, for on-farm investment to raise the productivity and production of 4 to 5 million households in poor rural communities. It also covers targeted feeding programmes—at a cost of $30 to $40 per person per year—for up to 200 million hardcore hungry people, many of whom are school-aged children. Other components are for the development of irrigation systems and rural roads linking farmers with markets; the conservation and sustainable management of soils, forests, fisheries, and genetic resources; and agricultural research, learning, and information systems," said the Anti-Hunger Programme document, and the money should come from international donors and interested governments.[10]

The money never showed up; it will never be known if the plan would have worked. Jacques Diouf, the director of FAO, launched it again in the middle of the 2008 crisis; by then the number of hungry people was reaching one billion and the amount required had grown to $30 billion annually.

They didn't give that, either. But through the magic of mechanical reproduction, the $30 billion turned into a slogan oft repeated: it was the money needed according to the FAO, to end world hunger.

In the middle of the worst food emergency of recent decades, Jean Ziegler, the former UN Special Rapporteur on the Right to Food, complained that the budget for the UN World Food Programme (WFP) had gone from $6 billion in 2008 to $3.2 billion in 2011. Due to the financial crisis, needless to say.

The UN WFP was founded in 1961 to make up for the deficiencies of the FAO in its mission to alleviate world hunger. Now, its website defines it as "the world's largest humanitarian agency fighting hunger."

Little by little, the WFP has taken over urgent—and less urgent—interventions in famines and various other catastrophes where food is scarce. The officials of WFP often refer to themselves as "hunger fighters" as in "firefighters," as if they were volunteers putting out a fire here, a fire there, confronting a series of unfortunate accidents. Those shacks go up in flames all too often.

Famines served an important pedagogical function: they were good at making us believe that hunger was extraordinary, an emergency, and that other than them, nothing very serious is going on. Organizations that brought—bring—relief during a famine are an idea of the world to act when faced with something unusual, to correct mistakes and excesses.

But there are no longer many classic famines. In Africa, where they might occur, the US government, in the eighties, organized a prevention system called FEWS—Famine Early Warning System—run by the FAO and USAID, which analyzes data to prevent scarcity produced by droughts. When the threat is real, the WFP and other international agencies intervene, so hundreds of thousands or millions don't die in a single blow, rather than those who always do, day after day, incessantly.

These are, in any case, palliative measures; actual prevention would require investments in agriculture, in giving local resident the means to survive on their own. And then there are the cases when international organizations are unable to intervene, such as in North Korea, or Mozambique several years ago, or Darfur and Somalia more recently.

In 2007, for example, WFP school programs fed about ten million African children. Their experts estimated that another ten million were being fed by other agencies or governments. Those twenty million children ate 720,000 tons of grain. But those same experts estimate that there are still about twenty-three million children under twelve in Africa who go to school hungry and receive no food aid. And another thirty-eight million who don't go to school at all.

Now more than half the food aid from rich countries is channeled through the WFP. It is assumed that this makes them more impartial, that it avoids—or attenuates—political abuse. And that this couldn't have happened when aid was being used as reward or punishment.

The aid that comes through WFP is much more convenient for those who receive it: it brings no conditions, carries no obvious political or military strings. By the same token, governments accept it more willingly and feel less urgency to foster autonomy: they become used to it, better and more deeply committed clients.

The WFP channels aid because the United Nation—the nations in it—feel the need to do something to slightly attenuate the failure of the goals they themselves defined as Millennium Development Goals. And the first, the one that keeps increasing the number of hungry people there were in 1990, consists of reducing "extreme poverty."

(We use the term "extreme poverty." At one time we'd say "misery." But the word misery today is tinged with ideas and feelings, and politicians and bureaucrats have discarded it; now they say "extreme poverty," which is the same but a little cleaner and it seems measurable: even that dollar a day—now raised to $1.25—is poor; less is extremely poor. Bureaucrats like their measurements to be clear.)

The Millennium Development Goals became the beacon of "humanitarian" action. In the meantime, they made room for a plethora of reports and brochures, a strange kind of documentation that states pertinent truths such as, "reduction in prevalence of underweight children (under five years of age) has been included as an indicator for one of the targets to eradicate extreme poverty and hunger." If the people who spend many hours and charge a lot of money didn't make such serious faces when they wrote it, it would be a mediocre joke. The world of the large international organizations tends to be a perfect ecosystem for the self-evident, populated mostly by men and women who are clinging to their own privilege, terrified at the mere possibility of being inappropriate hence taking shelter like nobody else in cliché. Sometimes they really should pretend, at least.

Reduction by one half was the goal. Still to be discussed is whether or not a goal that consists of making sure that there are *only* several hundreds of million undernourished people is worth articulating, or if it would be better to keep silent, ashamed.

In the meantime, the WFP announce that they've reached their goal or they almost did and they show you their charts. They say, for instance, that they aren't talking about the undernourished but rather those living in extreme poverty; often they are the same; sometimes they aren't. Still, they say, in 1990, "in developing regions, the proportion of people living on less than $1.25 a day" was 47 percent. They were 1.9 billion people. In 2010, on the other hand, "the proportion of people living on less than $1.25 a day" in developing regions was 22 percent, or rather: less than half.[11]

During this period, from 1990 to 2010, about 500 million Chinese stepped over the threshold of extreme poverty due to economic development in their country. Or, rather, the majority of the population that stopped living in extreme poverty in those twenty years are in China, where the economic development of their country integrated them into an ever more unequal but much wealthier society.

Or, rather, almost the entire reduction of poverty happened in a country where the international organizations did not have any influence, where they were not allowed to carry out their policies.

Which doesn't prevent those same organizations from being the ones to boast about their achievements: the reduction of extreme poverty.

(In a globalized world, the famous flutter of a butterfly can cause earthquakes. The decrease in Chinese poverty is an example: the same forces that reduced the number of malnourished in China—the access millions of them had to the market through jobs and salaries that allowed them to buy more and better food—are the same forces that contributed to the increase in prices that made many poor Africans and Indians eat less— and many rich Argentines and Brazilians even richer, as well as many other things.

And, of course: that the country where poverty has been most effectively reduced is an iron dictatorship, a brutally authoritarian capitalist regime with unlimited power is bothersome in more than one way.

In the meantime, in 1990, when FAO began to count the Millennium Goals, there were 823 million undernourished people. In 2010, when the goals "were close to being achieved," there were, according to FAO itself, 820 million.

And China is still, in spite of everything, the country with the second largest number of hungry people in the world.

3

Humanitarianism is one of the last incarnations of the idea of humanity.

Humanity is a relatively recent concept. It assumes, on principle, that the world is a unity: first of all, that there is a round planet that defines our possibilities and our limitations.

Until very recently nobody knew what the world was—and almost nobody even thought to ask. The immense majority of men and women who have been alive knew only the landscape around their house, their village, their town: ten or twenty miles beyond their homes. For them, the idea that there was something beyond that was confusing and even unbelievable. It was highly unusual to meet a stranger, and if it happened, it was dangerous. The world, as we think of it, was an abstraction, inconceivable, and it didn't need to be conceived of.

At that time, concern for another was concern for a neighbor, an acquaintance, a compatriot, for someone more or less known and related through precise connections. Until the idea of *world* emerged and transformed that notion, as well.

The world began to exist, in broad terms, five hundred years ago, and with it the idea of worldwide, or global: that which includes everybody. Then, little by little, a path was forged for the idea that this "everybody"—the totality of men and women, the species—formed an ensemble called humanity. It seems obvious, but it wasn't. For millennia, cultures and religions had made sure to establish differences, convince their believers that others were not equal and therefore deserved whatever was inflicted upon them. Kingdoms and their kings did the same.

Christianity was one of the great promoters of the notion of humanity: it needed to establish the notion that we were all part of the same thing—creatures of the same god—to justify its missionary impulse, its wish to submit the world's inhabitants to its doctrine. Modern revolutions—the French one, for example—took up this idea: the Declaration of the Rights of Man and the Citizen, Paris 1789, is a kind of cornerstone in the assertion that humanity is a brotherhood of people with equal privileges—as long as they weren't black slaves on Caribbean plantations.

The last avatar, till now, of the notion of humanity was the revolutionary internationalism of the nineteenth century, destroyed when some of the participating cultures rose to power in Russia at the beginning of the twentieth century.

Since then, the idea has lost steam. Nationalism peaked in the twentieth century; if there were three or four worldwide movements, they were all moving toward a Reich that would take over the world. Then, at the end of the century, a series of political and technological changes created the most integrated planet we have ever known: "globalization" means a world in which money can circulate freely, and human beings try to. And, after half a century of clear centers of power, constitutes a moment of transition in which the weight of power is more widely distributed than we are used to seeing, thereby accentuating the globalizing effect: if the head now sees less clearly the body, the rest of the planet, is thrown into more equitable confusion.

To be concerned about hunger requires a certain—albeit weak—idea of internationalism or, even better, humanity, in order to postulate that all humans should be concerned that all humans have enough food. If not, in the name of what would we care about the misfortunes of the Abyssinians, the Kazakhstanis, or the Bengalis?

It's truly an extraordinary concept, a huge conceptual advance that has still not been expressed through social practice. It might spread, start to grow again. For now, the amount of "humanity" that exists is sufficient for what we now have: declarations, sniffles, crocodile tears, assistance, rescues. Humanity as a form of guilt. Send bags of grain, but don't deprive yourself of too much affluence. Not enough humanity to find a real solution to the problem.

Not enough humanity to place it on the same level as the difficulties of those close by: our compatriots.

Nations are not only foolish; they are nasty. They are a means through which the structures we call nation-states make sure that their subjects have, overall, more than others living under other similar structures, and make sure that at the same time some of their subjects have much more than the rest.

There's no more resigned way of thinking about the world than in terms of nations, hence of one's own country as more important than others. There is no reason to think that this recent invention of nation states, which in some cases is two hundred years old, in others five hundred, and others fifty, is the way the world "should" be organized.

Nationalism is a reduction of humanity: a legitimization of a certain kind of selfishness. If it's acceptable for me to feel more solidarity with the group of people who carry the same documents I do, the principle of exclusion has already been established. Whoever excludes people of a different country can, through the same process, exclude without much difficulty those from a different province, another religion, a different sexual orientation, another race, another notion about drinking soda for breakfast.

Humanitarianism may be, then, of all the notions of humanity, the one most poorly expressed.

The WFP is present in more than eighty countries and does notable work augmenting the nutrition of millions of people. It has thousands of employees who arrive in the most remote places, risking their own lives to fulfill their mission. Whenever possible, it buys food in those countries or from neighboring countries. It also uses a lot of its resources to conduct consciousness-raising campaigns. "One in nine people go to bed hungry every night," an institutional video showing naïf drawings begins. And it continues to explain with the following captions:

> Currently we throw away one-third of all the food we produce!
> Over three million children a year die from under nutrition.
> It's a global disaster.
> And social media is fueling it.
> By heightening our expectation of what food should look like.
> Just because a banana is no longer "instaworthy."
> Doesn't mean it should end up in the trash.
> So before you condemn food to the landfill, first imagine what it could become.
> It could become part of the most powerful recipe in the world.
> A dish made from food that would have otherwise gone to waste.[12]

It goes on to give instructions on how to share meals prepared using ingredients that are about to expire before unveiling the campaigns greater purpose to donate to the WFP to reach their new slogan: Zero Hunger By 2030. At no time do they mention the causes, the order that produces hunger, what should be changed so that it wouldn't be necessary to carry emergency grain supplies on airplanes to a hundred million people. Hunger, for the World Food Program, is not a political problem, it is a social media one.

Capitalism: the greatest solvable problem in the world. The humanitarian temptation consists of not thinking about what one can do with the other in order to ask oneself what one can do for the other.

Hunger, according to this perspective, is not a political problem but can produce political problems. A few years ago, when I began to prepare this book, a high official of the WFP's office in Rome told me that to "solve hunger" they should allow large capitalist enterprises to get involved in humanitarian aid, convince them that they could do good business and at the same time help feed millions of people: a win-win situation, he said, and smiled.

"We're doing that in Bangladesh, for example."

Then he explained how it would work, and how his work was fundamental to making the world a safer place, how too often citizens of rich countries didn't understand that hunger threatened their peace, produced terrorists, forced millions to emigrate and drop anchor in their countries, producing complicated situations, and nothing would help them live peaceful lives more than moderating or putting an end to it.

If we accept this discursive strategy, we would have to admit that nothing contributed more toward feeding the poor in Africa than the attacks of September 11, which placed that danger front and center. In that case, attacks like those were useful and should take place frequently. On second thought, it might be better to find other discourses.

But they held onto it. It seems cynical, but it was policy:

"All political leaders know that hunger can lead to civil unrest and conflict. The old saying 'a hungry man is an angry man' has been demonstrated time and again.

"One of history's most famous examples is the spate of food riots that ignited the French Revolution in 1789. But there are much more recent examples too. The overthrow of the Haitian government in 2008 followed street protests over high food prices.

"In fact, from 2007–2009 the US State Department estimates more than sixty food-related riots happened worldwide as a result of higher food prices and food insecurity. Food prices were also one of the sources of unrest which formed the backdrop to the 'Arab Spring' of 2011.

"The flipside of the 'hunger-instability' equation is that, in times of trouble, food assistance helps to promote peace and stability. In the face of volatility, meeting a fundamental human need brings calm," states an article on the WFP website.[13]

According to Miguel Ángel Moratinos, Spanish social-democrat and ex-minister of foreign affairs, "We must understand that if we could solve the problem of hunger and food security there would be many fewer terrorists because they would spend their time with their families and cultivating their land . . ."

The idea, obviously, is for them to stay quiet, not go anywhere, not get upset, so they can continue to be what they are in their proper places: poor, yes, but not so poor that they throw themselves into something desperate.

In play here is not the interest of a particular nation, or even of an empire; these are general political interests—or even what we often call ideology.

That's why the WFP launches programs like P4P—Purchase for Progress—which tries to bring the benefits of the market to small farmers by integrating them into the global market of food speculation. This is done with the participation of the foundations of Bill Gates, Warren Buffett, Rockefeller, some of the most powerful capitalists. Seems they have recently decided that they can hand over a few billion dollars, the product of their domination of world markets, their speculations, to alleviate the poverty that market creates.

For most of the nineteenth and twentieth centuries the rich were portrayed as caricatures, target practice, tremble oh plutocrats tremble, the greedy monster who gobbles up everything, the dirty old man who spends his money getting Lulu drunk on his champagne today and refuses to raise the wages of a poor worker who asked him for an extra piece of bread. Now they are magicians and kings who donate, save the world. As for their own assets, they still say: I screw over everybody and keep the money of millions; I throw them a bone, here and there, because I care, because I'm worried about them. And now they're the ones to decide which diseases are worth curing, what miseries to alleviate—and which not.

The trick is to present the disease as the cure.

(It is a stance that is having its day, and many are picking up on it. In 1985 Ethiopia suffered from one of the last modern famines, and the cause of it was, once again, perfectly political. Its president, Mengistu Haile Mariam, considered that the drought in the north of his country would debilitate the rebels fighting in the region; moreover, news about the hunger of his subjects would damage his image. So he didn't say anything—and he rejected aid being offered to him by organizations and NGOs, insisting it wasn't necessary. When there was no longer any choice but to admit what was happening, a million people had already died. There were campaigns, festivals, collections for Ethiopia. A new personality then joined these campaigns: Bob Geldof, Bono, and Live Aid; that's when the conscientious rock star was invented, our current version of a Voltairean intellectual, a person who takes advantage of the fame they have achieved through a cultural endeavor to help the disadvantaged. And, in this case, a person who doesn't propose to change the global system but rather to use their access to it, a person who hangs out with the nice powerful people in the world to support his cause—because his cause doesn't question those powerful. They are one of the most visible manifestations of this global conscience that worries about a problem for a certain amount of time, and for that time, it seems intolerable to him—but he doesn't put the rest of his life in question. And he makes it so that when we are talking about hunger, we are talking about hunger. This is what Bill Gates, Warren Buffett, the WFP, and so many other representatives of the business do: they are horrified by something so brutal, too loud—and, on the other side, something that could be dangerous, provoke reactions. So they guarantee that those who have nothing can eat—but don't cause problems. What are we talking about when we're talking about hunger?)

Oscar Wilde summed it up with his usual brilliance in his *The Soul of Man Under Socialism,* in 1891:

"They find themselves surrounded by hideous poverty, by hideous ugliness, by hideous starvation. It is inevitable that they should be strongly moved by all this. The emotions of man are stirred more quickly than man's intelligence; and, as I pointed out some time ago in an article on the function of criticism, it is much more easy to have sympathy with suffering than it is to have sympathy with thought. Accordingly, with admirable, though misdirected intentions, they very seriously and very sentimentally set themselves to the task of remedying the evils that they see. But their remedies do not cure the disease: they merely prolong it. Indeed, their remedies are part of the disease. They try to solve the problem of poverty, for instance, by keeping the poor alive; or, in the case of a very advanced school, by amusing the poor. But this is not a solution: it is an aggravation of the difficulty. The proper aim is to try and reconstruct society on such a basis that poverty will be impossible. And the altruistic virtues have really prevented the carrying out of this aim. Just as the worst slave-owners were those who were kind to their slaves, and so prevented the horror of the system being realized by those who suffered from it, and understood by those who contemplated it, so, in the present state of things in England, the people who do most harm are the people who try to do most good . . . It is immoral to use private property in order to alleviate the horrible evils that result from the institution of private property. It is both immoral and unfair."[14]

True "aid"—or the transfer of resources—from the rich countries to the poor ones is the remittances migrants send home. The World Bank estimates that in 2013, through institutional channels such as banks and agencies alone, more than $400 billion were transferred. As many migrants send their money through informal channels, the amount is generally assumed to be 50 percent higher. Among the countries that receive the most are India and China, and after that, the Philippines, Mexico, and Nigeria.

One of many possible caricatures of the "fight against hunger"—or better, "food insecurity"—waged by the owners of the world was the appointment of soccer great Cristiano Ronaldo as new Global Artist Ambassador of Save the Children to fight "child hunger and obesity" in 2013. Ronaldo told *El País* that "when I found out that one of every seven children in the world goes to bed hungry every night I knew I had to get involved," and they allowed him to and they celebrated.[15]

And we manage to think of it as reasonable—and even praiseworthy—that a man who earns a significant amount more than $100,000 a day should worry about the hungry. As if there were no relationship, as if the fact that every day that man keeps money that would allow fifty thousand people to eat had no relationship to the fact that they don't eat—that they are hungry.

There are rich people like that. Surely they do it because they are good people, authentically concerned about the poor, willing to give up a few crumbs. But one also has to listen when they say how much their activities help them. In his book *Enough*, Roger Thurow quotes Peter Bakker, president of the huge Dutch express delivery company, TNT, who explained to the World Economic Forum in Davos, in front of his colleagues, how he gained through his collaboration with the World Food Program. "The skeptics want to know how much the share price has grown, or how much revenue is up . . . In 2001, we were number twenty-six. In 2008, we were number four."[16] The period corresponded to the beginning of his humanitarian activities. Bakker said that 78 percent of his 160,000 employees were proud to be helping WFP, and that it made them feel more comfortable with the company and work harder.

It's called: a company's social responsibility.

Peter Bakker runs a transport company, and subscribes to the hypothesis that the problem is that food is not where it should be. That's why they later hired a team from Vodafone, in order to communicate better among the different points of the network. Everything is about channeling charity with the greatest efficacy. And improving the image of the company and going to sleep peacefully that night and having, at least, an answer to the stupid question: "How can I stand to live in a world where millions of people go hungry—and keep for myself millions of dollars each day?

Send them alms.

David Novak, owner of Yum, a huge global fast-food corporation, which includes KFC, Taco Bell, Pizza Hut, and several others, runs 35,000 soup kitchens in 112 countries all over the world. "We've never saved a life. I never have," he said not long after he started the program. "We can save a lot of lives."[17] He was talking about the pleasure of thinking you are solving problems, that what you want to solve is solvable without changing the mechanisms that puts them in the position where they can believe that with their millions they can solve anything. Or as the Brazilian Archbishop Hélder Câmara wrote half a century ago: "When I give food to the poor, they call me a saint. When I ask why the poor have no food they call me a communist."[18]

Sometimes I ask myself what the difference is between charity and clientelism, or if there is one. Let's assume that clientelism has a political component—the expectation of a certain amount of submission in exchange for the donations- that charity shouldn't have, or rather, with charity it is measured by ideology: religion, humanitarianism. But in the final analysis when a volunteer for a charity or an official of the WFP intervene they also expect something, though perhaps less immediate, in exchange. On principle, to maintain the status quo: because they create bonds of gratitude, because they prevent the uprising of the desperate.

Jean-Hervé Bradol, former president of MSF: "According to the law of the free market, the hungry should take responsibility for themselves. If they are not able to supply their own necessities, it is their own behavior that should change not the way society distributes food. Often, national and international public action can be described as a proposal for behavioral change — have fewer children, change eating habits—more than offers of help. The free distribution of food is reserved for the poor in the rich countries."

But not only the rich countries. When an NGO assaults you with horrible images of emaciated children and sobbing mothers, it is also offering you a solution—it assaults you in order to offer you a solution that might interest you—to the problem of what to do about it: donate, get involved, give. The guilt recedes and the problem of what to do remains, for the moment, surmounted, relegated, filed away in its proper drawer.

These are small individual efforts arising from guilt. But, at the same time, they save children. So? By doing only that, the system is allowed to continue to function. By not doing it, one denies someone the chance to eat. Do it and denounce it at the same time?

I always remember the day I fell into that trap.

It was a couple of years ago. Saratou was telling me about her life; I listened to her and looked at the wood plank. In her hut there wasn't much else: a faded hemp tapestry, mud walls, a fireplace against the back wall, two blackened pots. She talked and talked; every once in a while, I asked her a question, all with that languid cadence interviews with interpreters have: a lot of time not understanding anything while you wait for the translation, take pictures, think about things. I thought, above all, about that plank and Saratou describing, in Hausa, her second birth. They had married her off before she turned twelve, and her first child was born dead; a year later. the second arrived: "When I felt it coming I locked myself in a little room, knelt down, grabbed onto a leg of the bed, prayed, I prayed a lot, and finally the baby fell onto the mat I'd put on the floor."

Saratou, subsequently, had eleven more children and, finally, an obstetric fistula, one of the most horrible, most classist diseases on a continent where a lot is classist and horrible. We were in Dakwari, a village like hundreds of Nigerien villages: adobe houses, no electricity or running water, lives that haven't changed in centuries. I was interviewing Saratou for a project of the United Nations Population Fund (UNPF). Her story was very moving, and I couldn't stop looking at that floorboard. For moments, I felt like a bastard.

"Then the midwife came, she cut the cord and put the baby's head on a broom so it wouldn't get dirty in the sand, and then I sat there looking toward Mecca and the midwife handed me the baby wrapped in a cloth . . ."

The plank was what Muslims call *alluha*, a wood plank where madrassa students write the *suras* from the Qur'an with a reed to memorize them. Then they wash them off, and write another *sura*: a notebook with only one page. And I asked myself what it was that fascinated me so much about it: if it was its aura of much more ancient times, if it was the shapes of the letters, if it was the wood like ancient paper, the palimpsest.

We talked—I listened to her, asked questions—for two or three hours. At a certain point, Saratou noticed that I was staring a lot at the plank, and she asked me—through the interpreter—why. She smiled: asking me a question was to invert the roles, an audacious gesture that made her nervous. I tried to be friendly: I told her that it was beautiful, I congratulated her. There was my mistake: afterward they explained to me that praise like that in her culture, is a request that cannot be rejected.

"I want to give it to you. Please, take it."

Saratou told me, through the interpreter, and I, through the interpreter, said no, thank you very much, and she said, yes, please, and I thanked her deeply, and she, her face looking more and more serious, said that if I didn't take it I would offend her. The interpreter explained to me that my rejection was violent, as if I were saying that the plank wasn't good enough for me, that she wasn't good enough for me, that I scorned them both the way only white people can scorn. I was in trouble—and I smiled.

Smiling, when you can't talk, buys you time. We smiled at each other, Saratou and I, for a moment, while I thought of a response. She had told me that when she got sick she couldn't look after her flock and she had only two she-goats left, and no he-goat, so they couldn't reproduce; now, without a flock, she wouldn't be able to make *puff-puffs* to sell in the village square and there were days when she didn't have anything to eat, that hunger was more difficult than the fistula. So I told her I wanted to give her a he-goat, and I would feel very bad if she rejected it.

Saratou smiled differently, this time with a kind of happiness. It wasn't easy to get the animal: I had to buy it in a town that was five miles away that had a market on Thursdays—and it was Tuesday. We agreed that I would give her the money and she would buy it; that's when I had that stupid idea. I would also give her money to feed it for one year, on one condition: she would call it Martín. Saratou cracked up. Then she told me that the he-goat was going to change her life and she would always remember me. I was happy to have the plank and so happy to have been able to help her: satisfied, honorable.

"If I can have my flock again I'm going to be able to eat every day."

She told me and we said goodbye. It wasn't easy to go through the airports with my *alluha*: it stuck out of my bag and was visibly Arabic. For a few days I was a shameless terrorist, resigned to being clandestine. Finally, I arrived in Paris early one morning; before going to my cousin Sebastián's house, I bought a couple of croissants at the bakery. While we were having breakfast, I told him the story of my *alluha* and the goat named Martín; we laughed and Laurence, his wife, asked me how much the animal had cost. Only then did I discover, to my horror, that it was the same amount as those croissants.

Oh, the illusion, every once in a while, that we understand something.

And the relief—deaf, disgraceful—that suffering for others can offer.

A good conscience can be bought for a few dollars or euros: loose change. But is sold for a lot. A bad conscience is the basis of huge businesses in the rich countries. As Zizek says: in the coolest, most contemporary businesses, the very selfish act of consuming already includes in its price its opposite: the satisfaction of the need to feel generous, to feel that one is doing something for Mother Earth or the dispossessed of Somalia or the starving children in Guatemala.[19]

To buy organic, fair trade, ecologically conscious and all the other labels is to buy a few inches of a good conscience—so cheap it's never unwelcome. Though it's odd that a society that is so well organized in ways that so deeply disturb that conscience has had to negotiate with itself and include these homeopathies of redemption in the marketing of its products. The current "progressive" form of the classic religious redemption: they pass you the box, you drop in a coin.

(Or, if not, you write this book.)

Though, of course, it does produce results. The rich ease their conscience and gain a certain geopolitical calm, but not much of either. The poor get food for the following day, and a growing dependence on that food. Food aid from the richest countries, international organizations, and huge foundations maintains, consolidates—just barely above sea level—this order where there are a billion surplus people.

Charitable efforts against hunger are the result of the idea that we all have the right to live . . . or survive. It is a modern, innovative idea that nobody would have mentioned two centuries ago—and that many still mention because of media pressure.

But it now forms part of the cultural package. One of its consequences is this aid, and so many different people practice it because it does not question inequality and its mechanisms, only extreme want. Better: it allows us to posit that the problem in these societies is not inequality of ownership but rather the extreme form of inequality that can produce hunger. That inequality is fine, it is invigorating, and is capable of self-correcting. The problem is not that the famous 1 percent has so much; the problem is that sometimes some people don't manage to eat. If they can be fed, everything will be better. And if that 1 percent gives, all the better: see how good they are, they who produce wealth for all?

Against the idea of food security understood as the guarantee that everybody will receive—receive being the key word here—enough food, an international organization, La Vía Campesina coined the idea of food sovereignty. In their Declaration of Nyéléni in Mali in 2007, they defined this as, "the right of peoples to healthy and culturally appropriate food produced through ecologically sound and sustainable methods, and their right to define their own food and agriculture systems. It puts those who produce, distribute and consume food at the heart of food systems and policies rather than the demands of markets and corporations. It defends the interests and inclusion of the next generation. It offers a strategy to resist and dismantle the current corporate trade and food regime, and directions for food, farming, pastoral and fisheries systems determined by local producers. Food sovereignty prioritizes local and national economies and markets and empowers peasant and family farmer-driven agriculture, artisanal fishing, pastoralist-led grazing, and food production, distribution, and consumption based on environmental, social, and economic sustainability. Food sovereignty promotes transparent trade that guarantees just income to all peoples and the rights of consumers to control their food and nutrition. It ensures that the rights to use and manage our lands, territories, waters, seeds, livestock, and biodiversity are in the hands of those of us who produce food. Food sovereignty implies new social relations free of oppression and inequality between men and women, peoples, racial groups, social classes, and generations."[20]

What would happen if we all ate, if nobody died of hunger? Would it then be fair that some had billions and others just enough to eat. It's not going to happen anytime soon, but if hunger one day ends, we should think through a few of these things.

SOUTH SUDAN: DEVELOPMENTS OF HUNGER

1

NEW COUNTRY. NEW BEGINNING. TAKE AN HIV TEST TODAY, says the large billboard on a street in Juba: here, still, everything is pierced through with the emotion of a new beginning.

It must be strange to start a country: most of us will never know how such a change feels, even when afterward, the days follow one another in much the same way as they did before. They say that the parties went on all night, the dancing, the food, the singing, the shots fired into the air, the children born nine months later, the name of their new nation branded on their buttocks. Still, in every conversation, on every street corner, there's someone who wants to believe in something.

"They're still excited, the excitement lasts, as you can imagine, after wanting this for so long," an expat humanitarian veteran told me. "But they also want the basics: hospitals, roads, schools so their children can live better lives. They are at that moment when they believe that everything is possible."

There are likely billions of people who don't know that South Sudan exists. It's likely they also don't know that Gambia or Swaziland or Bhutan or Belize exist, but in the case of South Sudan it's more understandable. A few years ago, South Sudan didn't exist.

Sudan was yet another invention of the British. It was a combination of an Arab, Islamic, semi-desert nation in the north, and another, more African, greener, Christian, and Animist one in the south. Since the end of the occupation, the people of the south fought to break with the power of the north; the first civil war lasted from 1955 to 1972; the second, from 1983 to 2005. The few people who talked about it said that it was the longest civil war of the century. Almost nobody mentioned that the war probably wouldn't have started up again in 1983 if Chevron—formerly Rockefeller's Standard Oil—hadn't found, three years earlier, important oil deposits in the zone that the South Sudanese considered their own. As is often the case, the discovery of a new asset brings new misery and sufferings.

South Sudan is a by-product of oil, among other things. Without oil the South Sudanese would never had had the support they finally received from the United States. But history is long; at the beginning, Chevron and US diplomacy placed their bets on Khartoum's government—the country's central government—which tried to compensate them by clearing out the areas in the south where there was oil. The rebels of the Sudan People's Liberation Army, considered leftists, did not enjoy any US sympathy until 1991, when Sudanese president Al-Bashir joined Saddam Hussein's side in the first Gulf War. The United States blacklisted him and transferred its support to the rebels in the south, sending weapons through the government of Uganda and defending them in international venues. Without US help, it's unlikely the rebels could have confronted the regular Sudanese army, equipped by the Chinese and, above all, by the profits from the oil wells. A virtuous circle: defending the oil wells makes it possible to buy more weapons to defend, among other things, the oil wells. Khartoum didn't want to let go: the oil in the south accounted for half the country's income. But the circle broke when the Sudanese in Khartoum understood they could not override the United States, and they signed a peace treaty.

It was, in any case, a bloody war the world heard relatively little about. During those twenty-two years, two million people died, about two hundred thousand of which were soldiers killed in battle, and the rest, civilians killed by violence and hunger and the diseases those two weapons produce.

The war was considered over with the signing of the treaties in 2005. The agreement called for the installation of a provisional government in Juba, the capital of South Sudan, under the jurisdiction of the national Sudanese authorities, and a popular referendum that would finalize the accords. The referendum was held in January 2011; 98.8 percent of the South Sudanese voted for independence. On July 9 of that year, South Sudan became the youngest nation on earth, and one of the poorest.

In the meantime, the war continued on other fronts.

July 9, I said: a difficult start.

When I first visited Juba just after South Sudan achieved its independence, it was not yet a city: it was then a conglomeration of houses and compounds and huts and stands and two dozen ministries, which are very large houses, and a presidential palace, which is an enormous house, and trees and a couple of roads and very black very tall people walking along the unpaved streets, but not that many, and construction sites and dust and garbage.

Before it became the capital of a nation, Juba was quite different: a sleepy town with one-story houses and a few cars; a provincial backwater where a variety of humanitarian workers were the most dynamic element—an "NGO" town, as some call it—but now there are embassies and construction companies and opportunists and more or less serious entrepreneurs looking to turn a dime.

There's money in circulation, everything that used to be taken to Khartoum, they say here, but the truth is that the country hasn't produced anything for months and construction is booming. There is foreign investment, drawn to the possibilities of quick and profitable deals; in oil, of course, and in the buying of land and exploitation of minerals and wood, but also in real estate. None of those large and ugly houses the international agencies rent to house their offices and their people costs less than ten thousand dollars a month, and many cost a lot more.

"There are people here who earn a lot of money on humanitarian aid. They rent them houses, sell them services, all at ridiculously high prices, because they control the market. And the people in construction want to get their money back as soon as possible. Who knows what will become of all this in a few months, or a year," one expat told me.

Others are South Sudanese and the provenance of their wealth is always somewhat suspect. Most, they say, are relatives or front men for members of the government, who are getting wealthy hand over foot. There are some ten buildings with more than five stories, and several more under construction. Under construction is, among other things, a quite grandiose hotel. These are the advantages of unequal development: in order to extract raw materials that some countries have and others want, certain conveniences are needed. That is why, for example, in all impoverished countries, there are a couple of five-star hotels. The plunderers—of oil, diamonds, uranium, rice, soy—want to sleep in beds that meet their standards. Not to mention the international officials who come bearing Western guilt turned into cash.

In the meantime, Juba is filling up. In 2005 there were 150,000 inhabitants and as of 2019 there are 500,000. Most are desperate peasants drawn here by the illusion of guaranteed food, people who end up living in miserable shacks scattered around the city, without electricity or running water, like in the countryside but with no land to farm. But also so different. In the overflowing marketplace, hundreds of men and women and children crowd into a barracks building made of corrugated metal with wooden benches facing two TV sets. In one, they're playing a romantic comedy; in the other, a soccer game with an English league. Both have their volumes turned way up; the audience is also shouting a lot.

There's a point in the evolution of places like this when all small-town, folksy charm has been lost and the structures or attractions of a city haven't emerged. That's Juba: everything halfway there, promising and broken.

South Sudan is the size of France and has a population of 12.5 million as of 2017. South Sudan, for now, has no numbers of its own, but by extrapolating from the whole of Sudan, one can estimate that more than a third of the men and two-thirds of the women don't know how to read or write and four out of five have less than a dollar a day to spend.

"I always say that I visited the future and now I've come back."

Agy, a tall South Sudanese young woman, told me a few days later. Smiling, educated, in her twenties, she lived her whole live in Kenya, Uganda, and Spain because her father was an exile with status and is now a minister.

"I think two generations will have to make sacrifices so that our grandchildren, in fifty years, can live in a real, just, and egalitarian country."

She said while sitting on the terrace of the best hotel in Juba, the new capital, eating a hamburger. And that's why she came here to get to know her country a few years ago and now had come back to stay and was willing to do whatever she could to help it succeed. But she knew it was going to be very difficult.

"The World Bank is saying that our economy could collapse. What economy? Everything now is a problem, but we couldn't keep feeding that one who abused us for so many years; at some point we had to free ourselves from our torturer," she said, because it had been several months since the South Sudanese government had made a very drastic decision about a decisive issue. South Sudan has oil. South Sudan is oil. But South Sudan does not have pipelines, or rather, the pipelines that carry its oil to the Red Sea pass through Sudan. So the Sudanese wanted to charge 30 percent of the oil for its use; the South Sudanese offered them 2 percent at the most—more like 1 percent.

That was the conflict. The discussion was long and vociferous until Juba, sick and tired of Khartoum taking its oil out of the pipes to charge its abusive commissions, decided to turn off the tap in January 2012.

Since then, for more than a year, until April 2013, a country that extracted 98 percent of its exports from oil no longer extracted oil. The declaration was supported, celebrated, and backed up by many as a grandiose gesture. Now they'd show those Sudanese what the people of the south could do. And if they had to make sacrifices, they would, happily, because the newborn nation deserved this and a whole lot more.

I was there for the first time in June 2012. The sacrifices being made were more and more obvious: South Sudan was being left without dollars, loans from China and Qatar—about $4 billion worth—had already been spent and debts remained; Kenya and Uganda—their main providers of food—were unwilling to keep giving them credit, many goods were scarce, inflation was soaring, the South Sudanese pound was sliding on the black market. The population was worried, the government was worried about the general worry; national proclamations never ceased and became more and more inflammatory, more and more expensive.

I heard people defending the measure and, somehow, I found myself respecting them. One thing is melodramatic nationalism, the "if you don't give me back those despicable pirate islands, I'll be insulted," the nationalism of "touch me and I'll kill you," and something quite different is this battle between life and death, when hunger's in play. I don't know if I want to say that one is better than another; but I respect this one.

South Sudan is a country that, for now, has no more than a hundred miles of asphalt, no power lines, no running water or toilets, and doesn't produce anything that isn't black and sticky. All the rest—including food staples, eggs, fruit, vegetables, soap, oil, matches—is imported and paid for with foreign currency from oil.

"South Sudan is like an infant. It was just born, and still has to learn to walk. You can't make a country if you don't even have roads," a veteran humanitarian said.

A territory, a town, a flag, and an army don't seem to be enough, not even when they are sitting on a plush mattress of oil. One out of every ten babies born alive dies and one mother out of every fifty doesn't survive childbirth, and 85 percent of public health services are being provided by international organizations. In 2013 the government put out a call to international donors for $1 billion and halfway through the year they had received half, at which point they revised their estimates and determined that, instead of 4.5 million Sudanese without enough to eat, there would be only 4 million.

In Sudan a Sudanese man takes his ease in the breeze, my father used to sing while shaving.

I had to get here to realize it wasn't true.

2

Bentiu is the capital of Unity, one of ten states in South Sudan on the border with Sudan: dust, sweat, oil, and war. There are very wide and empty dirt streets, every so often a tree, one-story houses scattered about, straw huts, straw fences, straw roofs on churches with their little crosses, straw stalls where they sell tea with *shisha*, the tower of a mosque over there. There's a broken-down bridge over a river and craters left by the April 2012 bombing. There's a dirt runway and cement pylons holding up electric cables that haven't been live for more than a year; nobody can pay those hundred barrels of diesel a day that's needed to run the small electric generator. There are a few shops made out of bricks, two banks, three elementary and two high schools, a soccer field, a hospital, two dozen international agencies. There are birds, a few dogs, sun.

"Really, you've never been here?"

"No, really, never."

"Oh, how strange."

Bentiu has ten thousand inhabitants but you never really know; inhabitants come and go, change, move elsewhere with their cattle and their hunger.

Though now here, close by, they have a border.

The border, of course, is a line, more or less straight, more or less unimaginable: another invention by a pale-faced cartographer.

The map of Africa abounds with straight lines. There's no continent with so many straight lines for borders, lines some bureaucrats of the colonial powers drew while sitting at their desks to divide the continent into countries according to the whims of compass and ruler. In twenty years, between 1878 and 1898, the European empires created more than thirty African states, most of which lasted past the official end of colonization in 1960. The British, French, Belgian, German, and even Italian and Portuguese proclaimed that their mission was to bestow upon the continent the three Cs: Christianity, Civilization, and Commerce, though not necessarily in that order. In exchange they had bestowed upon them gold, ivory, peanuts, cotton, palm oil, exotic wood, cheap labor, and cannon fodder—and one or another venereal disease.

Hence, primitive accumulation in those countries occurred in London, Paris, Berlin—and of course, never went back. Hence, Africa abounds in fake, capricious, unviable countries composed of ethnic groups in conflict with each other for centuries, with systems organized principally around the export of goods to the metropolis. Roads—few— or train tracks that lead to the ports but don't connect the country; poor uneducated populations; pathetically weak infrastructure; vanished industry. And the tradition of a rich and exclusive ruling class: if the colonial powers had to offer their administrators a generous lifestyle so they'd agree to be buried away in these remote regions, the newly empowered nationals found no good reason to renounce the privileges of their predecessors—large mansions, servants, discretionary power. All of which was maintained and supported by the old colonial powers, now converted into "preferential business associates," all of this with a little charity attached. Add to that the help of large international organizations such as the IMF and World Bank, who decided that the Market would be the solution to all the problems—and who killed, with their imposed policies, more people than all the colonial expeditions together.

(The newest trend, which occupies the same media space that eulogies to austerity and the dynamism of the IMF occupied in the nineties— consists of celebrating Africa's sustained rates of development, which, when looked at them up close, are actually the effect of the international increase in the prices of the raw materials many of these countries export, without any benefit to the majority of the population. In fact, a recent report from the International Labor Organization says that in black Africa only 7 percent of young people have a formal job: that's one in fourteen. The rest have nothing; they cultivate their parents' land or try to make ends meet by squeaking by with some little business or other. The same report insists on the responsibility of (bad) education: it says that in countries with more developed infrastructures, such as Egypt and South Africa, there are hundreds of thousands of young people without jobs and, at the same time, hundreds of thousands of open jobs that those young people, without the necessary qualifications, cannot do.)

It was almost noon: more and more people were walking by, the sun was viscous. They walked as if with forgiveness, their majesty impressed me; they were, as my grandfather Antonio would say, long like a day without bread, and they walked with the heads thrown back, their foreheads high, so that the air would part before them. Every step they took was like a sign. They were all tall, thin—the excesses of a photoshopping session gone mad—and many of their faces were sculpted with artistic carvings: drawings that attached them to their tribe, that said who they were.

More and more people walked by, but none were old. They were all young; every once in a while, someone in their fifties. They said—nobody really knew—that life expectancy hovered around fifty-five, but I had been in other countries with similar statistics and never saw such uniformity, such short lives. A barefoot man walked by carrying his shoes: they were very well shined.

Dozens and dozens of donkeys also went past; they were barely larger than Great Danes, pulling carts made of pipes with two rubber wheels and two water-filled drums; they were led by children who walked alongside and sold the water, river water, dark and thick. No cars drove by, other than a white four-wheel-drive vehicle every so often that belonged to an international agency or the government, and maybe a scooter or two.

Every once in a while, a woman laden down with very heavy burdens. They carried their belongings on their heads: a plastic chair, the wash basin, a pot, a cot, a garbage bag full of clothes. A few miles ahead were the men and the cows; the women stayed behind. As night fell, when the cows stopped, the women would too.

Here wealth, whenever there was any, was measured in cows: nine out of ten people didn't have even a dollar a day. With cows, deals were made; with cows, violations were paid; with cows, wives were bought and sold. Every herd of cows—skinny with long and crooked horns—was tended by two or three herdsmen: many young, tall, agile men wearing tight shorts and feather bracelets on their left knees. They held a cane in their right hand, a handful of spears in their left.

"What are the spears for?"

"To fight against other men."

"Why?"

"To fight. We fight. If you walk down the road and cross paths with other men, from another tribe, you might fight."

And then they speared each other and hurt each other and killed each other, and that was what men were for, he said, and, finally, as if thinking twice, "Or, we also use them against animals."

Spears, he said, because men also kill animals.

But the day before yesterday in the market a woman had split another woman's head open with an axe.

"Why?"

"Who knows, women fight."

It wasn't clear why Justin thought this would be a good place to find a wife, but he was wandering around the towns near Ler looking for a woman to marry. Ler is thrity miles south of Bentui, a distance that could be covered in three hours by bus or two days by foot during the dry season and by someone who knew when the rains would come. The road had its quirks: every so often a mine exploded, a relic from the years of war.

Nyankuma is sixteen years old, nearly six and a half feet tall with a dark and dangerous look in her eyes. When that slightly older man told her that he wanted to marry her, she laughed, then she looked at him again and saw that he wasn't laughing. She told him he was too old to be looking for a wife; then he smiled and told her that he could see she was no fool.

The next day, Justin met with Nyankuma's father and uncles and came to an agreement: thirty cows. (I asked many how they measured a woman's worth in cows and couldn't get a consistent answer; the price of a cow is obvious, but nobody knew how much a woman was really worth.)

Nyankuma had her day, her wedding, and finally, when she arrived at her husband's house, she met the rest of the story: Justin had a wife who had already given him five children; the eldest had just gotten married, and her husband had paid thirty cows for her. With those cows, his daughter's bride price, Justin had gone out to find himself a second wife, a younger one.

"Were you angry?"

"No, why would I be angry?" Nyankuma said. "They lived well like that."

Nyankuma had broad shoulders, a thin, sweet voice, evasive eyes; she said she had no reason to get angry, Justin was both of their husbands and they were both happy, each one with her *tukul* and her children, and if this was what her husband wanted, it was what she wanted too.

"What if he gets another one?"

"Whatever he wants. I would be happy, because if he has another one, it means we have enough food."

"And if you don't have food?"

"Sometimes we have, other times we don't."

Nyankuma lisped in a strange way; like many women, she had a big hole where her four front bottom teeth used to be. It is a rite of passage for the women in the Nuer tribe, but nobody could explain to me why those teeth, why that strange hole just under the tongue.

"Because it looks beautiful," Nyankuma said, and the hole smiled at me.

For women, it's the teeth; for men, stripes carved on the face. The scars are a way of showing who is who forever, to which tribe they owe their loyalty. Years ago, a Salvadoran gang member explained to me why his face and neck were covered in tattoos. "It's 'cause at some point you might be surrounded by your enemies, and you might be tempted to turn on your people. But if I have those marks, you can't. That way you're sure you won't betray them."

The marks are, among other things, an insurance the community offers the individual against the temptation of abandoning their community. Getting marked is a very painful process, a rite of passage: they do it to every man to make him a man—with a lot of pain, blood, and the sacrifice of a few oxen.

The best man, the manliest man—they explain to me—is the one who tolerates the most pain, without complaining or crying no matter how much flesh they cut. If you can't beat it, join it: pain—suffering—is the most surprising, the most tragic thing that can happen to a man It's not impossible to imagine a world without suffering: there is nothing that makes it necessary. But there it is, it exists, it reigns, and one has to do something with it, integrate it into a system.

In a system with gods—beings that created all of this—there is even more reason to turn pain into a system. One must explain its existence, the insistence of what's unjustifiable. The justification for evil—for suffering, for pain—is one of the most fascinating regions of those grand fictions: authors recounting how and why their characters do something that radically denies the goodness attributed to them. To achieve this, they invented a lot of things, among which was the redeeming value of suffering—*blessed are the poor because theirs is the kingdom*—thereby giving them a purpose, a usefulness. God sends it to you to test you and improve you. Suffering is not gratuitous, not all loss. Suffering is a way of saving up, a nest egg to spend in some heaven; suffering is a blessing if—and only if—you believe in that heaven. Others are more daring; like the Nuer, they decided that pain—the ability to suffer pain—is a privilege and a way of measuring the value of a man. Whoever suffers better and more is better and more now, not elsewhere and in some always doubtful future.

So, the boy so recently become a man suffers, grows scars, and, finally, gains his rights: he can give orders to any woman—including his mother—can carry a spear, can fight, and should never milk a cow. The Nuer make six lines on their foreheads: each line is one of these rules—you must not fear, you must not steal, you must not commit adultery or fuck your cousin—that a man must follow to be a man.

Nyankuma had three children: a girl, who was six; a boy, four; and another girl, one. When Nyankuma was in Ler, she lived in her *tukul* with her three children; her husband often slept with her, sometimes with his first wife, and sometimes in his own *tukul*. *Tukuls* are those huts with dirt floors, walls of adobe or straw held together with mud, thatched hipped roofs with ruffled edges, and that charming point on top. Inside the *tukul* there is usually a cot without a mattress, a corner for utensils, another corner for clothes, sometimes a plastic chair, sometimes a kerosene lantern, a decoration hanging on the wall. When a family has two or three *tukuls* they surround them with a reed fence; the enclosed area comprises the compound, the open air where the family really lives, cooks, talks, plays, grows a few rows of okra. The *tukul* of the cows—when there are cows—is similar to that of the people but much larger.

Nyankuma got up every day at five in the morning; if it was the growing season she'd pick up her stick with its metal tip and go to turn the soil or plant or tend to what had been planted. Then she would go into the small forest to look for firewood, grind the sorghum in a wooden mortar, start the fire, and begin to cook the *walwal*. *Walwal* is the Sudanese equivalent of Nigerien *woura*, a kind of porridge made of mixing ground sorghum with boiling water; if there's milk, they add some, as well as salt, if there is any. At ten in the morning they ate: everybody was hungry. They ate next to the *tukul*, sitting on the ground; at that time of day the sun was strong and lunch was fast: never more than five or ten minutes. Then Nyankuma took the plates and the pot to the pond two hundred yards away and washed them; this was a pleasant moment of the day when she met up with the other women, and they chatted and gossiped. The children played together, jumped into the water if there was enough. Until June, when the rains started, the pond was a swampy mudflat. If she had dirty clothes, Nyankuma also washed them; when she was finished she would back to her *tukul*. Her eldest daughter helped her carry the water drum from the pond for the rest of the day. Justin usually wasn't around; depending on the season, he might be working the little plot of land they had; if not, he'd be chatting with a friend or maybe in his first wife's hut. Nyankuma played with the children for a while, chatted with a neighbor, took a nap. Around seven, they ate again, the leftover *walwal*, and sometimes some soup made of a few leaves, or, with luck, some okra. Then the sun set, darkness spread, and the day ended.

"Do you eat anything else on other days?"

"No, every day *walwal*."

"Would you like a change once in a while?"

"I don't know. We grow only sorghum."

"Could you grow something else?"

"I don't know. I don't think it grows."

"Do you ever eat beef?"

"Yes, sometimes, not always."

Nyankuma was wearing a necklace of shiny plastic beads. When she was nervous, she touched them, turned them around in her fingers.

"When did you last eat meat?"

"Once, last year."

At other times they had nothing to eat and they didn't eat, Nyankuma said. And when she was hungry, all she could do was think about food, how she'd get food, where she'd go to find food; what she didn't like about hunger, she said, was that it made her think about food all the time.

"I'd like not to think about food so much."

Now she was thinking about it. Her youngest daughter, Nyapini, had been admitted to the small MSF hospital in Bentui, where they treat childhood malnutrition. Nyankuma, Justin, and their children had come—without the other wife—from Ler to Bentiu to "spend the summer": the driest season that lasts from January through May. Sudanese move around; a culture of nomadic herdsmen—people who walk to find their food—they always did, but now with the threats of conflict, they do it that much more.

And they plant less. The fear that keeps them on the move prevents them from taking full advantage of this difficult soil. Four months ago, for example, the South Sudanese army occupied Heglig, an oilfield about twenty-five miles from here across the border; it is disputed territory, which the maps of each country include as their own. A few days later, the North Sudanese returned, threw out the aggressors, and increased their cross-border attacks. Both sides speak of wounded pride, blood redemption, and imperishable nationhood, but when they're serious, they speak about oil.

"Did you come here to get away from the violence?"

"No, in Ler there's less than here. Anyway, there's no place safe where you can go and say, ah, here I'm sure I'm safe." Nyankuma looked at me as if I could give her that place.

"Why did you come, then?"

"The soil isn't very fertile, we can't grow enough to eat all year. So we came to see if we could find some work here, so we could get something to eat."

They looked for wood to make coal and sell it; they distilled alcohol from sorghum. But Nyapini got terrible diarrhea, was weaker and weaker every minute, and they brought her to the hospital. Here they told them she was severely malnourished, and they would have to keep her here for a few weeks. They had to delay their return to Ler and now they didn't know what to do.

"We're very hungry," Nyankuma said, so large, so emphatic, it's difficult to imagine her so helpless. But she insisted that she just wanted her *walwal* every day, that she didn't want anything more than her *walwal* every day, and I asked her whose fault it was that she didn't have it.

"My husband's."

"Your husband's?"

"Of course, he's responsible for feeding me and my children. That's why we got married."

"But he's also hungry. Is that his fault?"

"I don't care about that. He's the one who's supposed to feed us."

There were cries and screams and three dozen children, their cots, and their mothers in a sort of round cabana with a thatched roof, mosquito nets over the windows. It's the ward for the most gravely ill.

Nyankuma had Nyapini in her arms; Nyapini didn't want to nurse anymore and just cried. Nyankuma had an iridescent fly standing on her very long nipple. Nyankuma said that the problem was that the less they had to eat, the more they had to go look for something, but then they didn't have enough strength to keep looking. She didn't say so, but she meant that hunger was a trap, a vicious circle like few others.

"What do you look for when you go out looking?"

"Anything. Insects in the fields, crickets, some leaves we know about. Anything. And sometimes God leads you and then you get to where there's a small job, something."

"Do you always find something?"

"No. Sometimes we've gone four, five, six days without food."

"How do you feel?"

"Like I'm dying. I feel like I'm dying, like I don't have any strength left for anything. I don't even have the strength to die."

"Do you know people who have actually died because they didn't have anything to eat?"

Nyankuma looked at me as if I'd said something extraordinarily stupid. I probably did say something extraordinarily stupid. The look she gave me, in any case, was a compendium of scorn.

I tried again, "Does that possibility scare you?"

"Yes, it scares me. I'm always scared of that."

"What can you do to avoid it?"

"I don't know, I don't know what I can do. I try to find food here or there, and sometimes I get some and sometimes I don't. That's why the fear is always with me."

Misery is the condition in which when something, anything, fails, everything falls apart. Such a precarious balance.

This time, Nyapini would be cured. And Nyankuma and Justin's family would return to Ler and the *tukuls*, where Justin's first wife and the rest of his children were also waiting—if she was still there. Nyankuma was impatient to return and was optimistic.

"Life will change now that we are independent, now that the Arabs no longer rule over us. Before, we weren't free, the Arabs would tell us what to do, where to go. But now we can make our own lives, nobody can tell us what to do. We're free."

"Will that freedom give you food?"

"Yes. Not yet, but in time, of course, it will give me food. Now that the Arabs don't own everything, and once they stop bombing, we're going to be able to farm much more land, so we'll have much more food."

The war continued: it'd been more than a year since I saw Nyankuma in Bentiu and the war continued, settled down for moments, paused, then raged again.

For the last twenty or thirty years, most wars are like this: they happen in poor countries between poor armies—or at least one poor army—and they last, stretch out, start and stop, calm alternates with explosions. They call them low-intensity warfare because not so many soldiers die; instead women, children, and some men die. They are raped, expelled, pillaged, starved: they kill more often with hunger and illness than with bullets.

(I wrote these pages in the middle of 2013 while still in South Sudan. Back in Barcelona the following year, correcting the proofs of these same pages, I came across a report from Yuba describing the fallout from ethnic conflicts, including attack on an MSF hospital in Bentiu. Members of the White Army, a Nuer "rebel" group, had massacred over thirty Dinka people taking refuge there. Buried within the article too was news that the conflict had caused a food shortage in the region leading to mass starvation. It was strange to reread my impressions of a country that seemed to be at a precarious peace while I was there, that would descend into civil war shortly after I departed. It wouldn't be until many years later, looking over the proofs of the English language edition in 2019, that conditions in South Sudan would finally declared as "improving.")

3

The house and offices of MSF-Holland in Bentiu are in an open field, like most of them; it is a rather awkward, homely building, surrounded by a wall that leaves only about nine feet of yard around it.

The house was small, so I stayed at the Grand Hotel Bentiu: three rows of prefabricated rooms with corrugated metal, a tin roof, a tiny window in a corner, a narrow bed with mosquito netting, and a plastic chair. The washroom, outside, far away, was a water barrel and a washbasin; you could find the toilet, a few steps farther away, from the smell. The flies knew everything.

In Bentiu there was no internet. Sometimes there was, but it was not

working those days. In most places it was difficult to have the experience of being out of touch; here it was easy. In the world—at least in my
world—anything could be happening, but rather than know instantly, I
wouldn't find out for days. We have lost the habit of that lack of simultaneity that was, until a very short time ago, our way of knowing things.
Something would happen, but it wouldn't happen for many others until
much later. María Guadalupe Cuenca, the widow of Mariano Moreno, an
eighteenth-century Argentine politician, wrote him letters two months
after he died on the high seas, because she didn't know. For her he was
just as alive as ever; she told him about the house, his son, the slaves.

I'm surprised: instead of anxiety, I felt very calm. It was like that time
I was in a car accident. I had just split my face open on the steering wheel
and I was about to enter the operating room. Instead of the terror I imagined I'd feel, I was detached, I knew there was nothing I could do. Now,
in the depths of South Sudan, without any possibility for an internet
connection, instead of frantically trying to find some way, I had a similar
sensation: my world, for now, wasn't mine.

For many here, this was still the way of knowing; Justin, for example,
had spent months without any word from his other wife and children.
And that was completely normal. Suddenly, this need—our habit—to
know everything immediately seemed slightly monstrous.

Like trying to pretend that space isn't time.

It was a struggle. At the office of the World Food Program, I attended
a meeting between the agencies that dealt with "nutritional issues," a
meeting which then happened weekly, and when I went quite convivially.
A. said that his organization had done a survey of several districts in
Rubkona and had detected an increase in malnourishment in children,
up to 18 percent, and then B. asked him which districts were the most
affected, and A. told him that he didn't know that detail, and B. said that
he needed that information to be able to intervene because the treatment
team he wanted to send would be much more efficient if they knew where
to focus their efforts, and A. said, of course, if you drop by the office later
I'll give it to you, and B., how about two thirty? And then C. said that if
B. continued having problems with his supply of Plumpy'Nut, he could
divert some to his supply for a few weeks, and so forth for another hour.

I didn't mean to imply that all was idyllic, or even close. There were
quarrels, conflicting agendas, pride, personal and political interests at
play, but I was impressed at how these men and women, in spite of everything, had decided that their job was to make sure that fewer children
in this corner of the world died of hunger and they took that job very

seriously, and they spent the days of their lives seeing what they could do—for better or worse—to achieve that. They knew it was a Band-Aid and had no illusion that they were going to change anything structurally, but all the same. They were neither internet trolls for their fatherlands nor provincial officials nor well-placed bureaucrats nor daring journalists; they were some Joe Blows and Jane Does who stuck it out for months at a time in the middle of nowhere just to see if they could save a few children.

For several centuries, a white person in this part of the world was somebody who came to get something. Now one assumes that in most cases it is someone who comes to give. And, in spite of everything, above and beyond the reasons, the logic that led them to do it, there is something moving about all their effort.

They told me that in the last few days a hundred thousand half-starved refugees had been fleeing from some battles in a part of the world most of them had not even heard of: Maban, in the Upper Nile state, almost two hundred miles—and several days by foot—from here. There were thousands running away because the enemy soldiers poisoned their wells, burned their houses, killed hundreds of them. So here and in Juba they were setting in motion—on different schedules, with different levels of efficiency—a huge operation designed to get food to them. There were no roads, so they'd need to send airplanes with food and medicine. There was no water on the ground, so they were spending a fortune exploring for new wells—without much luck so far. There was no health care, so they sent doctors, nurses, logistical personnel. There, they told me, people took refuge under plastic tarps, drank water from puddles, and ate the bark of trees. Suddenly, the survival of those hundred thousand lost people—difficult, improbable—became the fifteen-hour-a-day task of a frenzied group of people who fought, pointed fingers, hounded each other, and, finally, would save a few hundred, maybe a thousand. And they wouldn't be able to save the rest.

"I'll never be able to get out of my head that memory of Liben. I think that was the worst thing I ever experienced in my life," Carolina would tell me later, in the quiet of the night, on the patio of the MSF house in Yuba, the mosquitoes like trains, shouting and shots heard in the distance. Carolina is an Argentine doctor in her thirties, a veteran of wars and famines. Now she was waiting to leave with the emergency team to Maban. I was also waiting; the people in charge at MSF had said they could take me but the day before, the head of MSF-Holland told me they couldn't because there was no room on the airplanes, everything was filled with emergency equipment—and if there happened to be any free space they would give it to somebody from Reuters or BBC or Al Jazeera, they hoped I would understand that they had priority.

"That year, 2011, things were very complicated in the whole Horn of Africa, the harvest was very poor, and there were emergencies everywhere, but especially in Somalia, where the situation was particularly chaotic and violent, though we didn't really know what was going on because we had no access . . ."

What they did know, Carolina explained, was that the refugees were arriving in unstoppable waves. In June, Liben, a district in the southern part of Ethiopia, near the Somali frontier, was receiving two thousand people a day.

"They were arriving in a deplorable state, after months of very little food, weeks of walking under the sun, without water, without anything. Normally the proportion of those suffering from moderate malnutrition is at least five times those with severe malnutrition, but there were hardly any moderate, most were severe, extremely severe. We were all overwhelmed, we couldn't manage; there were too many, there was like a bottleneck in the arrival areas to the camps. Poor things, they arrived in such a deplorable condition and instead of waiting one or two days, they had to wait two or three weeks. It was horrible."

"The people arriving, were they very angry?"

"They were amazing . . . They were quiet and they died, sometimes they complained a little, of course, but what amazes me the most is that in the middle of such a disaster, they were thanking god."

"What were they thanking him for?"

"That's what I thought, what can they thank him for. But they thanked him that they died one by one, not all at once, that at least some were saved, that kind of thing. I think that it's because they don't know anything else, they have no idea that the world could be fairer. And since they don't know, they don't suffer that much. What I'm saying is horrible, but . . ."

In Liben there were not enough tents or medicines or water or food. There were two camps, both at double their capacity, so they opened two more, and in very little time there were 180,000 people. More and more children died, at an infernal rate.

"I had never seen anything like it, and I hope never to again. And that time I was very angry because it was something that could have been foreseen and it wasn't, the international community didn't take responsibility. It was the anger of seeing more children dying every day . . . it's despairing. I despaired. I didn't know what to do. I didn't stop a single minute all day every day, and the children kept dying—fifty, a hundred children a day. I asked myself what I was doing there if anyway they're dying . . ."

The world never knew what was going on in Liben. Its story went unreported. From time to time there's room for only one place, and at that moment it was Dadaab, a collection of camps full of Somali refugees in the north of Kenya. Dadaab had its few minutes of fame—two or three—on some news report in the rich countries, on the fourth page of some important newspapers. For a few days it seemed like it was going to become one of those places whose names suddenly carry weight, like Darfur, Auschwitz, Hiroshima. Dadaab was, at the time, a very brutal form of failure. The encampment was built around 1990 for about twenty thousand people, where there were already four hundred thousand refugees and thousands more arriving every day, fleeing starvation in Somalia. They arrived malnourished, they died, the situation was desperate.

Then, the public got bored—nothing new, nothing different was happening—and finally, the situation calmed down. The emergency passed, and four hundred thousand remain: people without a country and without prospects, who live in an enclave they can't leave because they don't have documents, where they've carried on living a life of resignation: inhabitants of nowhere, captives of humanitarian aid.

Just like Dadaab, Liben had a moment, only to be left behind. MSF veterans, now, name it like a mantra, a code: the pride of having reached the edge of hell.

Carolina told me, "I'll never be able to forget those months in Liben. It was horrific and frustrating and I was exhausted and I cried every day, but every day I thought that there was no place else in the world I would want to be. I was where I was most needed; I knew that being able to be there, doing that, was the best thing I could do with my life. Of course there's a certain quota of egotism, you feel good doing it. I know it's good for them, but I am happy to be able to do it."

"Sometimes you have the temptation to think about all those people who are living peacefully in their houses while here people are dying of hunger and you are here, too, and there's the temptation to think that you are one of the good ones, one of the few good ones. Sometimes I think like that, but I fight against it," Carmack, an Irish doctor, told me in Bentiu. And he wasn't in Liben or Dadaab but he could imagine it, and the worst thing that happened to him in his life was once in Darfur, where he had to do triage several days in a row.

"Many children were arriving, very malnourished, and wounded, we were overwhelmed and we couldn't handle it all."

Triage comes from the French and means "selection" and is used in medicine in a lot of languages; it is the moment during an emergency when a doctor or a paramedic receives a group of patients and, faced with the reality that they don't have the means to treat everybody, they must decide who has the best possibility for survival—and they abandon the others to their fate.

Cormack whispered, "I can't imagine anything worse."

VOICES OF THE TRIBE

How the hell do we manage to live knowing these things are happening?

It is a moment.

   When was the last time somebody talked about some form of universal sharing? How hard did they laugh? Who looked down, as if to hide something, who at an accomplice to share a smile of complicity. Who really laughed?

How the hell do we manage to live knowing these things?

. . . the problem is that they want to fix everything with charity, they think that will be enough. Enough for what? It's not enough for anything, and on top of it, they get used to receiving, and, obviously, they always want more and more and more, and finally nothing's enough. What has to happen is that they themselves have to be able to produce it, they have to manage to supply themselves with what they need, because otherwise the world won't work, because this really doesn't work; if this goes on, they're going to come after us. Have you seen the number of Africans who come to Europe every year? Or, even worse: if this keeps going like this they're going to hate us more and more, and you've already seen what happens when those types of people hate. So, let's not act like fools, and let's give them the means to feed themselves; not give them food: give them the means, teach them how to fish, it's the only way to convince them to stay at home once and for all. Don't you think? I'm not saying they're a huge threat; not even, because, poor things, they don't even have the means to be a big threat, but that's now, and if this keeps going, who knows, one day they'll—

How the hell do we manage to live knowing?

And maybe not remembering who it was who said it, that seen one by one, individuals can be tragic, but in a group they're pathetic, or who said that the story of one person moves you, the story of a million bores you, because it doesn't allow you to exercise that scarce faculty of imagination.

How the hell do we manage to live?

Sentences that turn into silence. Sentences that, said so often, nobody hears; there are 800 million people who don't eat what they should eat; every five seconds a child dies of hunger. I have read it, I have written it, I have heard it and said it I don't know how many times, like someone who says it's raining—even when it is raining.

How the hell do we manage?

Such sibylline forms of silence.

How the hell?

. . . well, man, you don't have to take it like that, straight to the heart, you gotta use your head. I mean, I'm telling you: if there's hunger in the world, it's not an accident, it's not because god is a son of a bitch or because of climate change or because black people are idiots or because your grandmother doesn't have wheels but because there's a gang of assholes who take everything, who've been exploiting them for centuries and so what are you going to do, how do you want to solve the problem of hunger of all those people without changing the system. You can't, man, you can't, and if you try, in the end what you're doing is helping the system perpetuate itself, stay in power, you understand? Instead of doing something that will end this once and for all, what you're doing—

How?

4

Angelina, a woman from the South Sudanese village of Moya, had spent several months in fear, in a lot of fear. "They've been treating us worse and worse," she said, "insulting us, telling us they're going to kill us." In Khartoum, the capital of Sudan, the life of people from the south had become impossible since independence.

"Even the people I've been working for twenty years told me to leave; they said I had become a strange enemy."

"A strange enemy?" I ask, to see if this was an error in translation.

"Yes, that's what they said: a strange enemy. And I should leave, and never come back."

Angelina may now be South Sudanese., but when she was born, thirty years ago, her village was in Sudan, a single Sudan. That's why, when her mother was left with nothing, she took her five children and went to Khartoum.

"Do you know what it's like?" She asked, and I didn't understand the question. Angelina explained, if I knew what it was like to have and then suddenly not to have. Because there was a time when she had, said Angelina; her family could manage until her father lost all his cows— Angelina didn't know how many he had, maybe fifty, she said, maybe a hundred—in a raid by another tribe.

"You didn't try to get them back?"

"When they steal your cows, if you don't catch them immediately, it's very difficult to find them. If you're strong, you can go and steal cows from that tribe, but you'll never get yours back."

In South Sudan there are hundreds of registered tribes, but some have only a thousand or two thousand members. The Dinka—in all their variations—account for more than half of the South Sudanese and are at the center of power, including President Salva Kiir; the Nuer are the second largest group; then come the Murle. The civil war, which managed to unite them against a common enemy, ended, and they were left free to pursue the conflicts between themselves. And, the gentle and sustained form between themselves is cattle rustling.

For centuries, most Sudanese were nomadic herdsmen who had nothing but cows, and a good part of economic circulation was carried through theft. Rustling is a secular custom, with its rites and traditions. A while back an ex-head of the MSF told me that from time to time a local employee would ask him for a few days off to go cattle rustling— and he'd say it as if it were the most natural thing in the world. It was the most natural: it was their culture. In certain tribes, like the Murle, a boy only becomes a man when he goes out to steal cows.

The problem is, again, the means and the scale. They used to do it with spears, bows and arrows; lately they've been doing it with Kalashnikovs, and their power over life and death, that had remained more or less contained, has run riot. In this area there are Murle groups—militias who've split off from the rebel army—who not only take cattle but also kill women and children, burn houses, plunder. So the old hatred of the Nuer for the Murle becomes more violent and picks up on age-old arguments: the Murle are sterile and steal children from other tribes, the Murle are violent—and that's why you have to attack them and kill them, they say, and that's why they arm small militias who can do just that.

Kwia, my translator, was Nuer. He told me that sometimes he thought that his friends were right when they said that they should invade the land of the Murle and wipe them off the face of the earth. Other times, he said, he thought they were all Sudanese—he meant, South Sudanese— and they had to take care of each other. But he didn't sound convinced.

Oxfam calculates that there are three million unregistered weapons hanging around South Sudan, the result of decades of war. If the figures are right, very few men don't have one. It makes sense in a country where the state is in no condition to offer even a minimum guarantee of safety. It makes sense on a continent where there are tens of millions of Kalashnikovs. And that's not counting all the rest.

Angelina's father never got his cows back, and he died only a few months after they were stolen. Angelina said that she was very young, and she wasn't sure, but she thought many people died of hunger during those months.

"I think my father did too. Unless he died from the sadness of losing his cows. But I don't think so because during that same period many other relatives died who hadn't lost anything."

That was during the famous famine of 1988: first drought, then heavy rains that drowned the little bit that had managed to grow. Thousands and thousands took off walking—Sudanese, after all—in search of food. Her mother was lucky: a brother was able to sell a bull and pay for them to get a ride in a truck—she and her five children—for the three- or four-day journey to Khartoum.

Angelina was the oldest. Actually, there'd been another sibling but he died when he was very young. So when they reached the city, Angelina, seven or eight years old at the time, began to help her mother with her job as a domestic servant in the house of a rich merchant; she cleaned, washed, ironed, cooked. That's what she would do for twenty years.

When she grew up, Angelina married a man from Bentui who was also working in Khartoum. But the payment for her, the cows couldn't be given in Khartoum but rather far away, in South Sudan, and to the mother's brother, the owner of the bull. A few years later, Angelina's husband went to Nairobi to look for work and was accepted into a nursing school run by a Christian group; when he returned, he got a job in a hospital but he had too strong a liking for wine. A short time later, said Angelina, he became an alcoholic, lost his job, and stopped showing any interest in her or the children; it'd been several years since he'd given any signs of life. But his son, Tunguar, was only a year and a half, and when I asked, Kwia, the translator, about that, he said that he was the son of that husband who wasn't here.

"Why, because he comes to see her every once in a while?"

"No, she says he doesn't."

"So he couldn't be the father."

Kwia got lost in the sinuous paths of the marriage customs of the Nuer and the number of cows that are paid depending on the candidate and how they make the arrangements they make and how they are broken if they are broken and when the brothers of the father and the sisters of the wife intervene and so forth for a while. Until I lost patience.

"The question is simple: who is the father of that boy?"

"Angelina's husband, I already told you. It might not have been him who sired him, but he's the father. Among us, it doesn't matter who sires the child; the father is the one who pays with the cows, the husband. As long as they don't return his cows, he's still the father."

Tunguar was very skinny and dozing off; he couldn't care less.

Angelina said again that she believed very strongly in god; obviously, the feeling was not mutual.

Angelina fled Khartoum because life had become impossible, her employers of so many years had thrown her out, she earned her livelihood making wine, but it was illegal, and if they caught her, she said, who knows what would have happened to her. She'd heard stories about people from the south who were arrested for committing even less serious crimes and they did really horrible things to them.

"What horrible things?"

"It doesn't matter. Horrible things," Angelina said, and she said that nothing serious happened to her, her voice very low, like someone who wasn't really saying what she was saying. Later she would say that her friend Tombek was arrested for making wine and she was in jail for months until her brothers managed to collect some money to pay a bribe to get her out—and that horrible things happened to her during those months. The bones in Angelina's face were very noticeable, and the look in her eyes was of someone who didn't want to look anymore.

"It doesn't matter, it doesn't matter, it's over," she said, more to herself than to us, and there was something extraordinary in her story, something silenced—and her thin face shut down as if she didn't want any memory to filter through.

Then one day she grabbed her four children and with the money she'd saved from selling two pots and the wash basin and an old radio, she was able to pay the bus to a town from which she took a boat, one of those barges that go up the Nile, and there the owner gave her a good price because they were from the same tribe. But the trip took more than ten days and after six or seven she had only a pound of sorghum left to give her children to eat and she was desperate.

"On the boat, can you imagine, what could I do to get food."

Angelina had an idea: she kept a T-shirt for each of her children and a blouse for herself and she sold the other two or three each had to a man from the town where the boat stopped. With that, she said, she was able to buy some fish from some fishermen along the river and eat until she got here, to Bentiu, where she had relatives.

"Did they feed you?"

"Well, yes, it's not like they have a lot, but they gave me something."

But Tunguar was already so skinny that they told her to bring him to the clinic.

"Poor thing, he's really hungry. Nothing happens to me if I go hungry, I already know how. But him, poor thing," said Angelina and she repeated, "I already know how."

"What do you mean, you know how?"

"It's doesn't do me harm. When there's food, I eat; if there's a little, I eat less; if there's nothing one day, I don't eat. In the end, there will always be something," Angelina explained, and then she told me that her first son was sick like Tunguar and then he died, and that's why she was pretty worried.

"It started the same, with a bad diarrhea, but that was more than ten years ago, and I didn't know where to go. Finally, I took him to the hospital, there in Khartoum, and he died two days later, the poor thing. The place was full of doctors, but he died anyway. Obviously God wanted to take him."

Angelina was a very devout Christian and she said that was also a problem for her in Khartoum, where everybody is Muslim. She wanted to go back to Moyam, to see if she could find her family, but she didn't know if the roads were still passable now with the rains. "If they aren't, I'll have to see what I can do," she said. The next time she'd tell me all about it.

5

Bimruok is about ten kilometers from Bentiu, but it feels like a different world—within the Other World. In Bimrouk, that morning, the people from MSF were setting up a "mobile clinic": several tables under a large mango tree with a health worker—a local—at each one; sitting, standing, lying on the wet ground all around were about a hundred women with their children. They were mothers and their malnourished children who come for their weekly dose of Plumpy'Nut and to check their progress; a little ways away, under a tent, another hundred waited their turn for a first check-up: the taking of necessary measurements—mid-upper arm circumference, weight, height—to know if their children needed treatment. There was a lot of crying and a lot of flies.

There was mud: the previous night the first strong rain of the season had fallen and there would soon be rain storms that would make most of the region inaccessible. International agencies and organizations tried to store tons of grain in the zones their trucks would not be able to reach. The population migrated so as not to be isolated and without food.

The First World doesn't remember a time when rain could leave us in dire straits. Civilization—this form of civilization—made it possible to stop adapting every detail of our lives to the rhythms of the seasons and the climate. Here, no.

"But I give him his *walwal* every day!"

"Sometimes that's not enough, ma'am, it's not enough."

"What do you mean, it's not enough?"

Bimrouk is a cluster of *tukul* huts spread around without any apparent order and here and there a few rows of sorghum, okra, and corn. This was the season: there were men and women with hoes, digging furrows, planting seeds. The plantings were always very small, with lots of uncultivated land around them, as if they could plant more but they didn't want to. Seed was expensive.

In the middle of the village, a vacant lot acted as the town square; the school was seven groups of benches under some trees in different corners of that large vacant lot. In each corner a young and tall teacher stood in front of a blackboard and fifteen or twenty children; obviously, class got cancelled when it rained.

"So, what can I do?"

"You have to bring him to the hospital in Bentiu."

"But my son isn't sick!"

So far this morning, the MSF team found twenty-eight malnourished children. I mean: in a few hours, in one village, twenty-eight undernourished children.

"He's not sick, ma'am, but he needs treatment."

"I can't give him treatment. It's hard enough to feed him."

Two hundred yards away, men were working their plots of land: making fences out of reeds to mark off what was theirs. They moved slowly: every step, every movement seemed like an independent decision, something that could or could not happen, a series of chance occurrences. Inside the fenced off areas, there was still nothing growing; I asked Kwia if these were new plots; he said, yes, that many people were building fences now because the government was finally selling them land.

"Selling it?"

"Yes, but very cheaply. One of these plots, the ones that are twenty by thirty, costs six hundred and sixty pounds."

"That's less than a bag of sorghum," Kwia gloated. Those 660 pounds were worth about $150, and Kwia was in his early twenties, a poor clone of Stringer Bell, the elegant drug kingpin of *The Wire*. Kwia had the same goatee and wore loudly colorful shirts; he was also a fervent patriot.

"Yes, because in the market, things are different. In the market there's somebody who wants to make a profit and so they set their price. The government, on the other hand, doesn't have to make a profit because the land belongs to the community, so they can't charge the community for land that's theirs. The only thing they do is put a low price on it in order to keep the distribution organized, so nobody goes without land."

"What happens if somebody wants to buy a few extra yards?"

"Then the price changes completely," Kwia replied, and explained that anybody who wanted more than the basic plot of land had to pay twenty pounds per square yard, so a decent-sized plot ended up being expensive. But also you could buy land from somebody who had received it and wants to go somewhere else or try their luck with that money, and he'd probably sell a thousand square feet for 2,500 or 3,000 pounds. And that in fact there were people who got more than one plot from the government and then sold them; a friend of his already had three or four.

"How do they do that?"

"It's easy, they ask for plots in different places. They can also ask for them under different names, the name of a sister, things like that."

"Why does your friend want them?"

"Well, maybe one day I'll have a big family," he said, and smiled when he realized that without meaning to he had switched from the third to the first person.

"Many wives, or something."

"But that's not legal, is it?"

"It's somewhere between legal and illegal, right in the middle," Kwia said and stopped. He was thinking, and it looked like he was going to stop talking. Finally, he got sententious: "You can do anything if you have a friend in the right place."

"We fought for freedom, justice and equality. Many of our friends died to achieve these objectives. Yet, once we got to power, we forgot what we fought for and began to enrich ourselves at the expense of our people," wrote Salva Kiir Mayadit, the former leader of the Sudan People's Liberation Army who became the first and current president of South Sudan, in May 2012, in a "Letter to corrupt government officials, current and former," published in the local media.[1] In his letter, Kiir asked his fellow government officials to return the $4 billion they stole; in exchange, he offered amnesty. The first month, a few returned $70 million; $3.93 billion remained lost in the fog. It's nothing new: everybody talks about the corruption of the South Sudanese government, but there is something hypocritical about the president of that same government doing it.

They say that Salva Kiir published his letter because the United States demanded he do so as a condition for the continuation of humanitarian aid. Who knows. A local journalist is surprised—says he is surprised—that people who sacrificed so much for so many years, who fought under the worst conditions, and risked their lives to have an independent country, now devote themselves to snatching any money their position allows them to. "I thought that once they were in the government, they were going to behave as they had been until then. But it's almost as if they were getting paid back for all their sacrifice in thousands, millions of dollars."

They are often accused of corruption, and it's true that most African government steal part of the international aid that comes into their countries. It is, in fact, one of the main arguments used by those who say that African governments are to blame for hunger in Africa.

"Why keep sending them anything if they steal everything."

Because of this corruption—say organizations such as the World Bank—aid doesn't get to where it should get, it stops halfway, and doesn't resolve the problems it should resolve, and that's why so many people are still suffering from hunger. It's true that most African governments are more than corrupt: they're ultra-corrupt. But what they steal is nothing compared to what their countries and their citizens lose as a result of the international order into which they've been recruited for a century and a half. International organizations use the corruption of the governments in the same way that the national governments use the rapaciousness of international power: it's easy to say that millions of Africans go hungry because their governments are corrupt and thieves; it's easy to say that millions of Africans go hungry because the global capital is rapacious and insatiable. Both are true—and both of them are less right when presented as the only reason.

And both avoid the problem of private property and the distribution of wealth, little things like that.

"The rawest kind of corruption appears when governments take money or resources from international aid. The problem, in the first place, is a system that requires that kind of aid. So, who is making the necessary investment to make sure that the land yields enough? In Sudan, for example, what percentage of the oil profits are taken by each party? Though, of course, that oil could not be exploited without the technology and investment only the major powers have," a high-level official of an important NGO said to me. He was someone who didn't say such things—so he said them only if I assured him I wouldn't say who said them.

"It would be much better if the state and the international donors invested in the creation of an infrastructure (wells, a small dyke, solar energy installations, a road) so that people could then take care of themselves. But of course, that would make them autonomous, and that wouldn't be convenient for our governments or the donors. So they prefer to keep sending bags of food. The more I put you in a position of having to spend twenty-four hours a day trying to get a bowl of grain for your family, the better for me, because you won't have time to look at what I do."

If these countries didn't have appealing assets and if there weren't men whom they appealed to, there would be much less corruption. Corruption grows when there are businessmen who want a resource whose access can be guaranteed by a corruptible official. So: what difference is there between a Texas oilman who is given Sudanese land and exploits it and a government official who benefits from it? The way the wealth is acquired? Because we assume that owning property or the license to the land allows you to keep what is there, but not to manage it in the name of a state. It's logical that managing something in the name of a state doesn't legitimize you cashing in on it. But, is it logical that owning that same thing legitimizes it?

6

"I don't want to build myself a house. I had a house and I had to leave it, because of the war. If I build a house now, how do I know I'll be able to stay? It's really hard to have a house and have to leave it. I prefer not to have one."

"Where will you live?"

"I don't know, we'll see."

Beyond the beyond, a mile past Bimrouk is Manquay, a hundred huts in the middle of nowhere and a dark river where the water comes from. Here, the rain didn't have any effect; the ground was still dry, ochre, cracked. Here the huts were even poorer: six by six feet, squares with reed walls, roofs made of black plastic bags, maybe a brown plastic chair and a wood cot inside, a pile of clothes on the dirt floor. The huts were scattered around a large area next to the river; every so often there was a square field of okra or corn, a single tree, women cutting branches or making fires or sweeping with a straw broom or grinding grain with a mortar or walking by with water containers on their heads or washing in brightly colored plastic basins. On the edge of a basin was written, half erased: Made in Bangladesh; I assumed, in Kamrangirchar. A woman told me this was the soldiers' neighborhood, these were all families of soldiers conscripted to serve for six or seven years in Bentiu, and almost all of them brought their families—those who have family, the woman said, looking at me as if we were accomplices in something. The woman was wearing a yellow T-shirt and the gap in her teeth and her cheeks were like black apples; she was sitting on a plastic chair next to two other skinny women wearing yellow T-shirts sitting in plastic chairs; the three were cleaning and separating leaves—round, very green—from the branches. They said they were from that tree there and that they couldn't be eaten like that but they were going to make a soup.

"What are you going to eat it with?"

"Just soup."

Their husbands earned about 800 pounds a month—$180 on the

almost black market—and that's what they were charging in the market for a couple hundred pounds of sorghum, which is enough for a family to eat *walwal* for three weeks. There were days, like today, that they ate the leaves from the trees, said one of the women with a yellow T-shirt, and I saw that the other two were looking past me as if something were happening there.

"Good day to you, sir, and welcome."

A tall man with shoulders broader than most, around forty, well preserved, strong, clean clothes, his head held high. The man said to me in intelligible English that he was a lieutenant colonel, and could we please move a few steps away. The lieutenant colonel acted like somebody who was used to giving orders.

"Welcome to our neighborhood. We are here to defend our new country. Now, finally, we are all the children of one mother," said the lieutenant colonel, and I didn't understand the metaphor but I couldn't get him to explain. So I asked him about his role and he told me that his job was in "MO," Moral Orientation, which was very important because a town that had no moral orientation could not stay on track and that only with good morals and a straight track could they finish this war against the Arabs once and for all and live as a free people, or something like that. Then I tried to ask him carefully about those poor women who were preparing leaves from the trees, and he gave me a broad smile.

"Yes, I see them. The fattest one, wearing yellow, she's mine."

The lieutenant colonel said proudly, and I said that all three were thin and all three were wearing yellow. We kept walking in between the huts; two dozen kids were running around, following us, shouting, touching me with caution. The bigger ones barely paid attention to us; three played with an empty bottle tied to a rope tied to the end of a stick stuck in the ground. The game consisted of kicking the bottle as hard as possible to make it turn upside down. Four others were shooting with clay guns; one had a Kalashnikov and mowed them all down. I asked him if he told them to play war and the lieutenant colonel said, no, they do it on their own. The girls played less: almost all of them were carrying babies on their backs.

"I thought officers lived elsewhere," I said, so as not to say that I thought they didn't live in such misery.

"An officer has to be with his soldiers. Also, you are seeing us this poor because we just came out of a long war. Soon, this will all be very different," he said, like someone resolving the conversation before it began. But he continued: "What kind of encouragement and direction can I give them if they don't see me with them? Maybe others don't agree, but that's what my father taught me."

"It's a difficult life."

"Who said it's easy to make a new country?" he said, adding that he agreed with everything his father taught him, that's why his father died fighting against the enemy. "My father, and so many others. You have no idea how many dead are here in our *tukuls*," he said sternly, and stretched out his arm, pointing to the *tukuls* and the dead. The lieutenant colonel for moral orientation had the six parallel lines across his forehead from temple to temple: the marks of his tribe, of his manhood.

"And now, if you will forgive me, I have to go. I have to deal with some very important issues."

The lieutenant colonel gave me his hand and left. A few huts away was a gathering of women. They were sitting on the ground around a charcoal fire, where coffee beans were roasting and a kettle with water was heating up. They told me they didn't have money to buy sorghum and make wine, so they'd have to make do with coffee—and a water pipe they were passing around. They smoked with pleasure, lusty pleasure. They had children hanging off their teats and they laughed and were all talking at once, just as if they were having a great time. Then one of them asked me if I thought that the war was really going to end, like they said, and I told her that I didn't know, hopefully, that's what everybody hoped for. And she said, of course, that's what we hope for, but can she ask me a question.

"Yes, of course."

"When the war ends and they don't need soldiers anymore, what will become of us?"

It would have been despicable of me to tell her not to worry, that around here they'll always need soldiers and you will be able to carry on chewing your leaves; it would have been despicable of me to say, you're right, what will become of you poor women; it would have been despicable of me to ask her if she's sure she would want to continue like this for the rest of her life. The other women laughed halfheartedly; I did the same: despicable.

There were no old people here: another triumph of the ecosystem.

We all feel a little lost when facing certain technological innovations. Old age is one of them that we still don't know how to handle. It always surprised me that getting old meant deterioration: nothing about a person's physical functioning improves with age; time is pure decadence. For centuries, many societies attempted to compensate for this loss with the idea that knowing belonged to the old, or as the saying goes, "the devil's wise because he's the devil, but wiser still because he's old"; now, ever since we assume that the more valuable knowledge is the most recent, even that symbolic value has gone over to the youth camp.

I've always wondered why nature, that usually does things well, forces us to undergo that process of degradation. Until I understood, fool that I am, that contemporary old age is not an absolute of nature; it is one of the great inventions of human culture. In their "natural" state, humans lived no more than twenty-five or thirty years, and they died before they had a chance to degrade. Until recently median life expectancy in rich countries didn't go past sixty. Now, this average has risen to more than eighty, and continues to rise. A huge amount of technology achieved this, but we are in the midst of a transition, a mixed moment: we have learned to prolong old age but not avoid the toll it takes.

But it's not nature's fault. We have invented an antinatural state—extreme old age—but we've still got a long ways to go: we are halfway there, still full of mistakes.

At a time without future, old age doesn't offer anything but melancholy. Before, the issue was clear: work hard to build, reach a certain age, behind you is the career that made you an honorable and fulfilled person. Now it's all loss: the symbolic owners of the world are young—and leaving that condition offers no compensation.

But here, youth isn't a symbol of anything, but rather the only possible condition: nature in all its splendor.

It was easier to talk to Peter: he was less commanding. So I asked him if it bothered him to fight for his country when his family didn't have enough to eat. Peter, a soldier, was tall and thin, wearing new camouflage, flip-flops, and he carried a fairly shiny Kalashnikov.

"No, on the contrary. It gives me even more reason to fight. I know that when we finally win this war, we're going to have all the food we want."

They tell you that the war of independence is over, but it's not true. There are constant skirmishes, militias supported by one country or the other operating in enemy territory, and, from time to time, a real assault. The war continues, and continues. Bombings, different kinds of confrontations. It continues enough for South Sudan to have to maintain a large army, which in turn is the power base for the party in government. And this works well for both governments, their critics say: a war that keeps their people united, pushes away other problems, solidifies their own control.

A few years ago, former executive director of the World Food Program, James Morris, said that Africans at war get a lot more attention than Africans at peace. "I have thought the worst place for a hungry child to live in Africa today is a country that is at peace with its neighbors and relatively stable."[2]

A few miles to the north, in the Nuba Mountains, which in ancient times was called Nubia, thousands and thousands of people have had to leave their homes and go to live in caves that offer some protection from the Sudanese Air Force's bombs, dropped with full impunity. The airplanes are old Antonov from the USSR, and they drop three or four bombs at a time and rarely hit their targets, but sometimes do. They throw them on towns, on civilians. Those children, women, old people are the families of the rebels of the Sudanese People's Liberation Army (SPLA-N), fighting against the Bashir regime in Khartoum. Bombing them, Bashir's people say, worries the rebels and complicates things for them behind the lines.

But Khartoum had another more efficient weapon: because of the bombs and the lack of security, the Nubians were not able to plant that year, and the Sudanese government had forbidden international agencies from bringing them food; the stories coming out of there talk about sustained hunger, large numbers of people living on roots, leaves, insects. The stories spoke without saying so of one of the oldest uses of hunger: as a weapon of war.

In any case, the border was closed and the food that used to reach Sudan didn't anymore. Yuba was over four hundred miles away, on dirt roads that were becoming impassable because of the rain.

For globalized citizens the world is one big supermarket: we push those carts around buying food, memories, blue jeans, a job, various sensations, beaches—even stories, illusions of business deals and great changes.

This is not the least of all inequalities; it is, in any case, the one that makes the word "world" mean different things to different people.

Bimrouk existed in a world as well, a world of pure misery.

The smell was a mixture of filth, dust, and persimmons. The stalls were built out of reeds and tin: two dozen around an empty field. The biggest one sold candles, detergent, razor blades, crackers, packets of juice concentrate, local cigarettes, a few cans of mackerel, and a large quantity of soap slabs: where there's crises and poverty, soap is always the last thing left. There were smaller stalls that sold pound bags of coal; round flat bread; old donated T-shirts from the West; used and new flip-flops; bags of sugar and straw brooms; no fruits or vegetables or animals except for one stall that was selling three onions, exactly three. I had been to markets like this all over the world, and this was the first time I saw one without fresh food whatsoever. A chicken walked by—powerful, unique; then, a small burro carrying water. I tripped over a dead rat—very small and silvery grey.

A bit further on, a stall made of corrugated metal said CENTER PHONE CHARGING, so that people without electricity could have cell phones; later, I'd find out that this was the latest big business. Telephones that were cutting-edge technology ten years ago were now here, and thousands of people wanted to use them. Hence this service, which would be unnecessary in so many other places: a young man, a boy, a couple of car batteries, three dozen plugs, various kinds of chargers, a pair of speakers to deafen with music and ambiance, and a certain entrepreneurial spirit, were set up in the middle of the market selling electricity in homeopathic doses. Like everything here, it was pretty expensive—about half a dollar—per charge.

At the far end was a hut that offered the other service at the market: the grinding of grain with a small electric grinder. The prices, the man said, had gone up a lot, and he had less and less work. Over and above the sound of the generator, loud music was playing, a king of reggaeton at top speed; next door was a *tukul* that served as a bar. Seven men, including four soldiers, were sitting on brown plastic chairs, the kind you saw everywhere; they were drinking tea and smoking water pipes.

A hundred years ago, vanguard artists, disenchanted with modernity, came to towns like these that were supposedly closer in touch with true human essence for their inspiration. That idea of "essence" was pure foolishness but it placed them: people who lived "in a natural state" as opposed to civilized white people who lived under social and religious rules that denaturalized them. Now their image was quite different: they were a stupid form of ourselves, our failed selves, ourselves who didn't know how to do what we should do. Now we saw them as the missionaries did, men and women ignored by god, whom we must rescue so that they didn't die from hunger.

Mariya asked me if I was going to drink my tea with milk. I said, no, and asked her to tell me her story. Mariya was long, elastic, sumptuous, with lips and cheekbones and almond-shaped eyes; when she moved, it looked like she was floating. I discovered in myself the worst possible prejudice: that she was too beautiful to be so poor.

"Come on, drink it with milk. With milk it's two pounds," she said, and pulled a face, and explained that when she didn't have anything to eat, which was often, she came to this *tukul* to make tea, the owner rented her this corner for ten pounds a day. She bought a pound of tea and one of milk, and sold it. There were days she broke even, days she lost, and days she won. But it's her only option, she said, because there were no others left.

Mariya had her first son, she said, when she was fifteen, because a soldier got her pregnant—and I didn't dare ask her how. I thought about different ways: to ask her, for example, which army. I didn't dare. But afterward she got married to a boy from her village who didn't have very many cows, and then they had another child, who was eleven months old now, but he went to Yuba and it seemed like from there he went to Kenya, and he'd been gone and lost for a while: who knew if he'd ever come back. Mariya was wearing a long green-and-blue cloth tied around her waist, a faded pink T-shirt with a hole on the left side. She said she was still living with her mother because her father died a while ago and that there were many days—half the days, she said, or more than half—she didn't have any food.

"Are you afraid of hunger?"

"I never think about it. If I eat, I eat; if I don't, what can I do about it."

When they ate, she said, they ate *walwal* once or twice a day; sometimes at night they ate *yodyod*, which was made from *walwal* leftovers. And every once in a while, okra soup.

"If you could eat anything you wanted, what would it be?"

"*Walwal*. With a lot of milk. *Walwal*."

"But I mean anything: chicken, beef, fish, anything."

"I don't have money for anything, so I prefer *walwal*."

And that's not the problem: if she had *walwal*, then she was not hungry. The problem she said, was the children. Those doctors from MSF came a while ago and told her that they were malnourished. Mariya said that as soon as she could, she'd go to the clinic to have them treated.

Later they told me that Mariya's husband didn't go to Kenya; he died from stepping on a mine; he was plowing a field when it blew to pieces. But Mariya was afraid to say it, they explained, so she made up stories.

7

Nyayiyi squinted to see, she said she didn't see much. She asked me if I saw those things far away, she thought they might be cows. In those suburbs of the world, there are no eyeglasses: everybody sees what they see. For some, the world is sharp and colorful, for others it's bland, for others illegible. Remnants of the old variety of vision; now, in rich countries—in the countries with eyeglasses—we convinced ourselves that there is only one way to see and that we have to aspire to that, use whatever we have to achieve it. Because the functions are also uniform: to read, for example, which requires a certain precision of vision, is a new phenomenon for three-quarters of the world's population. For centuries, millennium, most people's lives did not require such definition.

Here, like then, things can be left very undefined.

Another common story: another fourteen- or seventeen-year-old girl gets pregnant one night next to the river, over there past the houses; another girl realizes too late, tells the boy to take responsibility, listens horrified to his response. Another girl now, three years later, with a two-year-old child in her arms, tells me that the problem was that her father wasn't there to force the boy to fulfill his responsibilities, to pay the necessary two cows and marry her. Nyayiyi spoke slowly, her voice wearily dramatic, like someone who was bored with her own story.

"My father is in jail. He shouldn't be, but he is," Nyayiyi said.

Her father was a soldier, a truck driver in the army and at the end of last year he had an accident and two people died and they put him in jail, as if it were his fault, she said, and that's why he couldn't force that boy to take responsibility.

"My father should have come and caught that boy and threatened him so that he would take responsibility, pay his cows, take care of his wife and child."

The father didn't do it, the boy didn't do it. Nyayiyi said she was twenty, but she wasn't sure, and she looked fourteen. Her eyes were wide and look frightened, she was wearing a blue-and-black dress, a snail shell as a necklace, and her scalp almost shaved clean. Here, almost all the women wore their hair closely shaved and some, the most elegant ones, those who could, wore wigs. The wig might have curls—blonde, brownish or reddish or purple, all kinds of follicle fantasies.

"My father was so angry at me that he threw me out of his house. He told me that with a daughter, who is going to want me, that if someone shows up he's not going to want to pay any cows and that I should leave. I had to go live with an uncle of my mother's," she said, and she wrung her hands, pressed her lips together. Nyarier, her daughter, opened her eyes and looked at her, as if surprised.

Yet another common story of unrequited love, of little mistakes that cost you half a life. But hunger plays a role. Hunger is nothing, really, just the norm in lives that cannot be different; but they share that norm: eating is one possibility among others, the shape of a constant threat. Here, hunger makes a story of normal sadness one of life or death.

A few weeks earlier, Nyarier, the little girl, started coughing and sleeping a lot, too much. A few days earlier Nyayiyi finally took her to an MSF mobile clinic, and they told her that she was severely malnourished. So she was now hospitalized with a feeding tube to stabilize her. Nyayiyi was holding her, rocking her, cuddling her. Nyarier was very skinny, her bones brittle, coughing constantly.

"What do you plan to do when she gets better so she won't get sick again from being hungry?"

"I don't have any option. There's nothing I can do so that my daughter doesn't get sick again. I can't find work because I don't have any education and I don't know how to do anything. If I knew how to do something I could feed my daughter, but I don't, and my father doesn't want to give me anything and my daughter's father doesn't even know."

"Would you like to get married?"

"Yes, of course. I want somebody to look after us."

"Do you have someone?"

"That's a secret," she said, blushing. She couldn't talk about that, she said again. We were quiet. Then she said, yes, there was a man who came to her and wanted to give her money and take care of her, and maybe he would marry her. "But my father had me beaten and he sent somebody to tell him that if he found out that he was anywhere near me, he'd have him killed."

"How will he do that from jail?"

"My father has brothers, cousins. He can do it," Nyayiyi said.

I asked her what solution there was, then, for her daughter.

"Maybe she'll die," she replied, without barely moving her lips. That she'll die.

But that's not a solution, I said, without knowing how to say it.

And she continues, apathetic, "No, it's not a solution. But if fathers don't take responsibility, I don't have another one."

And I ask her again and then she said that it was not that she wanted her to die, no, how could she, she said, and she wiped her nose and shooed away the flies. Nyarier was crying very quietly.

"I don't want her to, how could I? But I don't know how to get her fed. And if she isn't fed . . ."

Something—a couple of thousands of years of culture—interfere with me: I couldn't stand hearing this woman say that her daughter would most likely die, and she didn't think that there was anything she could do.

"But, do you think your daughter will survive?"

"If she doesn't get malnourished again, yes, I think so. But if she does get malnourished again, I don't know."

"Again: what can you do so that she doesn't get malnourished?"

Nyayiyi had that tranquility that is more terrifying than any rage. She listened patiently to the translator, looked at him, looked at me, and said,

"Nothing." She said she couldn't do anything. And she looked at her, straightened out her little red-and-white T-shirt, caressed her: nothing.

Sudanese hunger, like all hunger, has very complex causes. The land is not very fertile, and little of it is farmed. It's ugly to say so: even near villages one sees a lot of land not being farmed. Political correctness tells us not to include among the causes of hunger and poverty a lack of desire to work, though it also plays a part, but only a part. It's also the case that the land is being constantly disputed in one of the oldest conflicts in history: more or less nomadic pastors against more or less sedentary farmers. Along with its cultural and social translation: facing the prestige of the armed, upright herdsmen is the bent-over and dirty farmer, who was always considered inferior. Seems like here that image still carries weight—and that the farmers farm little because they hold onto that prejudice in spite of everything.

Or because any day whatsoever, a herd of cows or boys with spears or guns are going to destroy their farm.

Nomadic animal husbandry is one of the most ancient forms of production: they are hunter-gathers with cows. Their cows do the gathering for them, and they don't work the land, they don't gather anything. I am not trying to disqualify "the ancient" in opposition to "the modern." I say ancient in order to say: capable of functioning in a world that, for the last two centuries, had seven times fewer inhabitants, where each of them could live off what seven times more space provided. That's why I say ancient—and I think that in this overcrowded world, it also means unsustainable.

And though it's true that the soil is not very fertile, it's not necessary to be limited to only corn and sorghum; fruit and vegetables could be grown, and they don't, they never did. And it's true that the tools are few and expensive, the seed poor and expensive, the technology archaic. Sudanese agriculture hasn't changed at all in the last several centuries. Recently a newspaper, the *New Nation*, said that the government chose 180 "model farmers" capable of farming a minimum of six *feddans*— about five acres—to give them metal plows that can be pulled by oxen. The plows were green, simple, with a single glade to plow a furrow. The Minister of Agriculture, Mr. Bol, said that it was "important to leave behind the hoe that doesn't allow for the cultivation of more land."

In the entire world—in the Other World—there are more than a billion peasants without tractors or oxen to help them work their land; they have to do what they can with their hands, their bodies. They have no irrigation no special seeds no fertilizers or pesticide; they depend on the rain and their hands, as they did at the time of Christ.

And on top of that they have to deal with the weight of protectionism and agricultural subsidies in the rich countries.

In 2012, the rich countries paid $275 billion on various subsidies for agricultural products in the form of incentives to export or protectionist tariffs on imports, purchase of their products, incentives to grow biofuels, or direct payments. In most of those countries, farming is a guaranteed activity: if a farmer does not manage what is considered a normal harvest—due to drought, pests, or whatever—the government compensates them for what they didn't earn.

In many poor countries where they live poorly from agriculture, the state doesn't intervene almost at all. Or, often, they intervene on the contrary: they lower the market price of food so their urban population can buy it—but their peasants lose.

Globalization has amplified social differences. A few centuries ago, whatever food that was grown in places like Kenya or Cambodia or Peru was mostly eaten by the rich, as things were exported on slow or small boats, and the rest—that couldn't be exported or consumed because there weren't that many rich people and means of transportation were not very efficient—was left for the poor. Now that almost everything can be exported easily and quickly, the poorest in every place don't receive those remnants: the quantity of potential consumers is multiplied by the inhabitants of the world, and the possibility of distributing their products among those who can pay for them far away leaves nothing for those who can't pay for them there at home.

Said in other terms: now they don't have to compete for their food only with thousands of people much richer than they are, but with two or three billion.

Globalization has increased social differences on a global scale. A few centuries ago, in Kenya or Cambodia or Peru, people grew what they could, the wealthy ate most of it, a little was exported on slow and small boats, and the rest—whatever could not be exported or consumed because there were not enough people and the means of transportation were not efficient—were left for the poorest of the poor. Now that almost everything can be easily and quickly exported, the poorest of the poor in every place no longer receive the extras: the quantity of potential consumers is multiplied to equal all the world's inhabitants, and this possibility of getting those products to those who can pay for them far away means that nothing is left for those who cannot pay for them where they are grown.

In other words: the poor no longer have to compete for their food with a few thousand people who are richer than them but rather with two or three billion.

Subsidies allow farmers in wealthy countries to sell cheap—because anyway their governments already gave them enough money—and in this way, they break the markets. The classic example is the case of cotton, which has been extensively researched. If the United States did not subsidize its own cotton farmers, says Oxfam, the international price would rise from between 10 and 14 percent, making the income of every home in eight countries in West Africa—poor cotton growers—increase by 6 percent.[3] That might not seem like a lot, but it often makes the difference between eating and not eating.

And there are more old but good statistics to help us understand how this works. In 2001, the thirty members of the Organization for Economic Co-operation and Development (OECD)—the wealthiest countries—gave approximately $52 billion in assistance to the world's poorest countries. That same year, they gave their farmers subsidies to the tune of $311 billion, or six times more. A United Nations report says that, due to those subsidies, the poorest countries lost approximately $50 billion in unsuccessful exports. It's easy to give with one hand what I take back with the other. Roger Thurow, in *Enough*, said that the USAID official in Bamako told him that, yes, it would be better for them to spend their aide dollars to stimulate cotton farming in Mali, which has been so adversely affected by the subsidies, but that they couldn't because of Bumpers. "Dale Bumpers was a senator from Arkansas who authored an amendment to legislation in 1986 stipulating that no foreign assistance funds be used for 'any testing or breeding, feasibility study, variety improvement or introduction, consultancy, publication, or training in connection with the growth or production in a foreign country for export if such export would compete in world markets with a similar commodity grown or produced in the United States."[4] Resounding clarity: I'll help you as long as you hand over the business to me.

Be that as it may, farm subsidies produced statistics that became famous, some from that study in 2002 by the Catholic Agency for Overseas Development (CAOD), which showed that a European cow received from the European Union about $2.20 a day, or $800 a year. That is: each of those cows was wealthier than 3.5 billion people, just under half the world population.

In a dry vacant lot with four or five trees on the way out of Bentui, a hundred or so poor cows mooed softly. They were tied to stakes nailed into the ground, grazing on illusive grasses. It was a cow market: here their owners brought them so they could stop owning them. It smelled of manure, the perfume of life.

"Nobody's here yet," said a skinny young man with his face full of drawings; he was wearing a striped tank top, worn-out jeans, a bright red cell phone.

"It's already noon. Seems nobody's got any money."

The young man wanted to sell his six cows; I asked him why and he said so that he could buy sorghum to feed his family. An average cow could sell for eight hundred pounds. Never before, he told me, had a cow been worth the same as a bag of grain.

"So with six cows you can buy six or seven bags of sorghum."

"I have a big family," he said, and laughed with mischief, and then he said, no, he's going to buy two bags for his family and he's going to save the rest: then he'll sell them in the market in a few months because they told him the price was going to go way up.

"But in two months you won't have any sorghum left to eat, you'll have to buy it for the same price you sell it." I told him, and he gave me a strange look, and thought. And the other young man with more lines across his forehead, skinnier, with even more worn-out clothes, told me that he was selling that cow there, why didn't I buy it. The cow was brownish gray, crooked horns, a lot of bone.

"Do you have others?"

"No, that's all I have."

"Why are you selling it?"

"Because I have no more food to feed my family."

"But if it's your only one, what will you do once you've sold it?"

"Sleep. I'm going to sleep for a long time," he said, and laughed and scratched his nose full of flies.

And I laughed and said, of course, and then asked him, "And after you sleep, when you no longer are sleepy or have any cows?"

"I don't know. We'll see."

Nomadic herdsmen, sustenance agriculture. They are, in any case, the perfect example of a useless, disposable population; to the globalized economy, the big markets, none of this is worth anything to them. What is worth something to them is the oil that appeared below ground. But they can't, as they'd like to, eliminate the herdsmen and do away with the bother of them being alive and demanding and the bother that, in addition, they wage wars, and then, without all those bothers, they could send a few more or less qualified workers to get the stuff.

Or at least they can't do it all at once; they do it little by little, with charity and supposed respect.

Quite different would be to create the conditions for them to be self-sufficient: infrastructures, tools, various sets of knowledge. Here, the lack of roads and transportation is a serious problem: and there's less and less. Trading with the north, which used to fill the markets in the region, ended when the borders closed, and bringing things from the south is much too expensive and for much of the year impossible. The scarcity of fuel makes it even worse: very little food arrives and the little that does is sold at prices that put it out of reach of the majority.

The price of sorghum doubled in less than a year. To which, of course, the price of grain on faraway markets, like Chicago, for example, contributes.

Sometimes conflicts and wars produce hunger in the most indirect ways. In Syria, the civil war made it impossible for the peasants to farm, the merchants to buy and sell, the producers to transport things like flour for bread. These are the moments one must recognize the cleverness of certain cultures that are more used to war, who agreed to truces and gave their soldiers leave when the harvest was ready because they knew that if they didn't hunger would defeat both sides.

Here, now, the war is not so brutal—they say it had ended, but it continues, sibylline, simmering—but even so, it is the most immediate cause of hunger. War assumes horrible slaughters, constant migrations, sustained fear, and the idea that it isn't worth sowing because one doesn't know if one will be able to harvest. For twenty years it was very difficult to produce food in South Sudan, and the country became completely dependent on foreign aid. Now, when the war should have ended, there are still fights over oil, border conflicts, tribal warfare, random militias still fighting on their own, sporadic bombings, fear, destruction of precarious infrastructure, two million buried mines.

Violence is still creating consequences: roads are blocked, it's more difficult to farm, men and women are afraid to remain in their homes, so they run away, are attacked, are killed.

The violence in South Sudan is the poorest, the shabbiest, the quietest oil war—a genre that was always there but became more important after the Cold War: the Black War is the main conflict these days, while we wait at last for the China War.

During the Cold War, the balance of the two great powers forced the United States to use its "intelligence" to maintain control over the oil states. The CIA and its minions planned coup d'états any time a fickle government threatened US control over local oil: Iran in 1953, Indonesia in 1965, Ghana in 1966, and so on. When the United States no longer needed to hide its actions behind local actors—and was handed the horror of Islamic terrorism to justify any intervention—the secret oil wars became much less secret.

The United States maintains 737 military bases in 120 countries in the world on the pretext of carrying on a "war against terror." Its central aim is to defend its economic interests, especially its access to oil. An ex-candidate for vice president from the Democratic party, Joe Lieberman, said in 2005 that the efforts of the United States and China to guarantee imports that satisfy their demand could lead to a "race for oil [that] becomes as hot and dangerous as the nuclear arms race between the United States and the Soviet Union did in the last century."[5]

On the same subject and in 2002, US Vice President Dick Cheney launched an initiative that would have a large influence over the lives of Nyankuma, Justin, Angelina, Mariya, Kwai, Peter the soldier, the lieutenant colonel of moral orientation, and all the others: the Middle East is so unstable, he said, that the United States should improve its supplies of oil by "deepen[ing] bilateral and multilateral engagement to promote a more receptive environment for U.S. oil and gas trade, investment, and operations" in Africa.[6]

So, in 2007, one of the last measures taken by the Bush administration was the creation of Africom, a unified military command for Africa, devoted to increasing the armed US presence on the continent, and its first important deployment was the NATO intervention in Libya, another country full of oil, in 2011. Africom is a military organization with one goal: already in 2008 its sub-commander, Admiral Robert Moeller, defined its mission as "guaranteeing the free flow of African natural resources for the global market."[7]

African oil has one advantage and one disadvantage: it is not owned by one or two strong states to which one must make concessions but rather a dozen small and weak states, which are easier to manage. There's Nigeria, of course, but also Libya, Algeria, Egypt, Angola, Guinea, Ghana, and Chad, and new fields are constantly being discovered. Africa is, also in this, one of the last unexplored territories on the planet. Not long ago, for example, on the border between the Democratic Republic of the Congo and Uganda, they found one of the largest deposits on the continent.

Obviously, oil is an ugly, dirty evil that pollutes the Earth and causes war. But the fact that its energy has replaced the backs of oxen and bodies of men is an extraordinary improvement, one of the great inventions in the world.

Another contradiction, another paradox.

The Sudanese civil war was like a preview of something that will surely repeat itself many times over the next few years: the Africa chapter of the Black War, especially between China and the United States, the two major importers of oil in the world, with cameos in Korea, India, Russia. South Sudan was, deep down, a battle in that war, which, as is fitting, was fought by the poor natives rather than the interested parties. With two million dead, this country's hungry inhabitants were collateral damage.

Nothing more.

ON HUNGER: METAPHORS

1

Thirty years ago, the Oxford University Press published a book by the economist and philosopher Amartya Sen that would have an impact on the issue of hunger as strongly as Upton Sinclair's *The Jungle* had on the issue of labor. *Poverty and Famines: An Essay on Entitlement and Deprivation*, brought world hunger to the forefront of world crisis, and took much from Sen's own upbringing. While Sen was a product of Empire, an Indian who had spent most of his life at the best English universities. as a youth he had lived in Dhaka in the forties, a period that saw the worst famine of the century, one that killed three million people. The hunger in Bengal was a result of the export of thousands of tons of grain to the colonial metropolis, England, to make up for what the war had made impossible to harvest. There was still food, but prices had increased so much that the poor couldn't buy it, and they were made to perish like rats. Winston Churchill, the British prime minister, however, was not worried. He said, during a meeting of his cabinet, that it wasn't serious because "Indians reproduce like rabbits."[1]

Sen would later say that this experience marked him for life and was the reason he wrote *Poverty and Famine*, which appeared in 1981 when Sen was a prestigious professor at Cambridge and Harvard. None of this would hold any interest if it weren't that Sen's texts are endlessly quoted as a moment of revelation, the moment we understood the mystery: that people who don't eat are those who cannot buy food. The issue intrigued me: why so much enthusiasm for what is so obvious? It wasn't until I realized that the international establishment had yet to realize this, did I understand the importance of Sen's work.

Among its oft-quoted lines: "Starvation is the characteristic of some people not *having* food to eat. It is not the characteristic of there *being* not enough food to eat."[2]

And further on: "There has been a good deal of discussion recently about the prospect of food supply falling significantly behind the world population. There is, however, little empirical support for such a diagnosis of recent trends. Indeed, for most areas in the world—with the exception of parts of Africa—the increase in food supply has been comparable to, or faster than, the expansion of population. But this does not indicate that starvation is being systematically eliminated, since starvation—as discussed—is a function of some entitlements and not of food availability as such. Indeed, some of the worst famines have taken place with no significant decline in food availability per head."

And: "To say that starvation depends 'not merely' on food supply but also on its 'distribution' would be correct enough, though not remarkably helpful. The important question then would be: what determines distribution of food between different sections of the community? The entitlement approach directs one to questions dealing with ownership patterns . . ."[3]

Which brings me invariably to a sentence that no longer means anything, that has been out of use for decades but had its moment of glory at a time when I started paying attention to such sentences: "People who don't have any money are the ones who go hungry."

(Blinders are curious instruments: you learn certain things and they seem so clear that you assume that everybody knows the same things, and it is sometimes a brutal awakening when you realize that this is not the case. You might live convinced that everybody is convinced of what they believe. It never occurred to me to think that access to food—like any other good—depended on anything other than the forms of ownership in each society. Nevertheless, millions and many in power think otherwise.)

But, as often happens: anybody who wanted to know, knew. Those who didn't know didn't want to know for various reasons. For many millions of well-fed citizens, it was much better to think of access to food in terms of distribution; for those suffering from savior complexes, it was easier to imagine the problem as one of scarcity and plunder. If the Ethiopians or the Indians or the Irish died of starvation, it was because there was nothing to eat, because problems with the climate or war or cataclysms or who knows what acted together to produce "that tragedy." They didn't have to admit that if some didn't have, it was because others had too much, thereby avoiding their own real role in the matter and returning them to the problem: how do I live with that idea?

For those who rule over those millions of citizens, the question is: how do I help others live with that idea? The easiest answer: make it so that you don't have it.

The discourse of "the struggle against hunger" used by governments and international organizations during the Cold War was based on the idea of scarcity. For this reason, FAO and its members insisted that the solution was to increase production. They did it, and of course, it didn't solve anything.

For them, Amartya Sen's discourse was a problem. Or maybe it was, on the contrary, the way to legitimize what they could no longer deny. A concept often spreads when a simpler version of what somebody else said is distilled from a denser version, when it is tamed and its most threatening, critical contents polished away. In Sen's discourse the solution to hunger is linked to a particular distribution of wealth; it is nothing more than a moral critique of the fact that an excess of concentration of wealth kills while a minimum of distribution is the solution. That is, Sen was less interested in questioning the idea of property than he was tempering its mistakes and excesses.

And, as a bonus, Sen offers the exercise of western-style democracy as one condition to resolve the problems: "[Famines] have never materialized in any country that is independent, that goes to elections regularly, that has opposition parties to voice criticisms and that permits newspapers to report freely and question the wisdom of government policies without extensive censorship," he wrote later, because supposedly the press would warn against the phenomenon while there's still time to intervene and the voters could then punish any flaws in that intervention.[4] Clearly he did not take into account his own country—without going too far afield—where what kills isn't famine but rather silent, sustained, seditious hunger, which rarely make its appearance in the 13,520 registered newspapers published every day in the largest democracy in the world.

(For this book, I went in search of different forms of hunger and their effects in a dozen countries on three continents. All of them except Madagascar boasted what is called democracy; everywhere except Madagascar there had been elections within the three previous years.)

Amartya Sen is another of the numerous phenomena I'm unable to understand. As late as 1999, a year after he received the Nobel Prize, and the media were calling him the "Mother Teresa of Economics," he could write things like this, and other experts and scholars quoted him:

"Hunger relates not only to food production and agricultural expansion, but also to the functioning of the entire economy and—even more broadly—the operation of the political and social arrangements that can, directly or indirectly, influence people's ability to acquire food and to achieve health and nourishment," he wrote in his book *Development as Freedom*.[5]

"The Mother Teresa of Economics"; that explains almost everything.

A few years ago, I had a friend in politics, and I had a plan. The plan seemed so good to me that I assumed it would be a no-brainer: summon a large national movement to end hunger in Argentina. In a country so vast, and so without purpose, the effort would give us a clear purpose; in the face of so many vague promises, a clear objective; after so much frustration, a goal we could achieve.

It would happen in stages: to start, thousands of volunteers would carry out a national census to determine the reality of the situation. For months, Argentines would talk to Argentines, meet up, exchange stories of their lives. Once the necessary data had been collected, meetings and assemblies would be planned and programs aired to discuss among a broad swathe of the population what should be done. Experts would present their plans, politicians theirs, people—many people—would join the debate. Finally, after reaching some kind of consensus, thousands upon thousands of people would be set in motion to put an end to hunger in the soy basket of the world. It was a way of giving ourselves a goal and, at the same time, the possibility of creating something together, that could grow and expand. It was the possibility of aiming for something we could reach, to recover confidence in our own strength.

I went over the details: everything fell into place, everything complemented everything else. Excited, I told my friend; he, with his prestige and popularity, would lead it. It would, moreover, be his great cause, which would carry him who knows where to the top.

My friend listened, was interested, thought about it, and finally told me that the underlying idea was "too generous," that millions of Argentines never were and never would be hungry nor did they see hunger as something that had anything to do with them; it would feel absolutely foreign to them. Unfortunately, he said, he didn't think it would work.

Hunger—for us, Western middle-class readers—is a chimera. Hunger is a reality for Aisha, Hussena, Kadi, Mohamed. For us it is the least debatable, most easily seen—and so unseen—way the world works.

Or, in other words: hunger, for us, is a metaphor that can sometimes be efficient.

And at the same time, a difficult metaphor.

For starters, it's overused. There's nothing stupider, nothing more late-night bleeding-heart than to hear a man or woman lamenting hunger in the world while drinking tea, or even if not.

Again, for starters, it's dangerous to talk about it: always on the edge of jerking that tear, of sentimentality. Always approaching cheap sensationalism.

Next, it's complicated to talk about; they are slow, complicated situations. There's no single event: there's a state. We are used to thinking about hunger as a crisis. But we live in a much more controlled world where hunger is not an event but rather a dull persistence, the way of life of one in seven people—always other people.

And, finally, its various causes, mixed up, difficult to untangle. Because generally there are two levels of explanation: one is complex, subtle, full of interrelationships including the prices blahblahblah the subsidies blingblingbling the infrastructure lah-di-dah, and so forth. Another is the basic one, the brutal one, where one part of the world decides that in order to live better, it can or should or is in their interest to maintain misery in other parts—and puts in place all the mechanisms to do so.

Also, finally, there is the constantly renewed risk of being moralistic.

The problem is to be moralistic.

The problem is to not be moralistic.

How to talk about something that we all condemn and all condone? Lovely word, *condone*.

(A proposal: let's call hunger not only the impossibility of eating what one needs, but also the impossibility of defending oneself against those who have more of something: money, offices, weapons.)

More than once over the last two or three years I have thought that writing a book about hunger was a fool's errand: giving in to the metaphor.

One can say that hunger is a metaphor because it is not a subject for debate: it does not produce any reflection because there is no opposition. To speak against hunger is a fool's errand because nobody is in favor of it; nobody says they are in favor of it, no matter how big a part they play in maintaining it. Victims without victimizers. Hunger produces the illusion that shared causes are possible, that we will be unanimous, that we are all in this together, everybody against hunger.

Metaphor of an illusion. Everybody deplores hunger, but in the discussion about what to do to fight it, one begins to see the insurmountable differences. Let's introduce the Tobin Tax on financial transactions; open up more markets; forbid speculation on food; send experts to explain how to plant a particular seed; collect bags of food; take power; keep ourselves in power; send bags of food.

Then we could say that hunger is the ultimate metaphor for poverty: its most indisputable expression. Poverty, as we have seen, is relative. Poverty is something that would be a relief for some and absolute misery for others. Hunger, on the other hand, is not open to opinions. Hunger is the most indisputable expression of poverty, the point at which all debates cease. One can dispute this or that, but nobody disputes that eating less than 2,100 calories a day destroys you; nobody disputes that going hungry is the worst thing that can happen to you.

Hunger is poverty that does not brook opinions.

One could say that hunger is a metaphor of division: a categorical barrier between them and us, those who have and those who don't have, those who have and that's why others don't have, those who don't therefore do. If ecology prospers because it always gives the sensation that it effects all of us equally, that when the temperatures rise, we are all going to fry—even if it's not true; if ecology is the most egalitarian of threats—and that's why it has garnered so much support—hunger is the exact opposite: it is the most classist threat of all. There are many of us who know it is not our problem. So, why should it be our problem?

Ethics, guilt, shame?

Somebody said there are two kinds of culture, ones based on guilt—Judeo-Christian, for example—and ones based on shame—Japanese. When faced with hunger, are we Christian or Japanese? Do our own consciences hurt or the other's gaze?

Neither? Nothing?

(Proposal: let's call hunger not only the impossibility of eating what one needs, but also the powerlessness of those who have to accept jobs that are so exhausting, disgusting, demeaning, that the rest of us would reject them out of hand; lives that would destroy us if they were ours.)

Max Weber defined wealth, for Protestants, as the sign of the grace of their god, and therefore, poverty was the lack of that grace. The poor were those who did not deserve it for some reason: because they had not done enough, because they had not earned, with their dedication or hard work, the divine favor needed to not be poor. Those half-savage Indians and Africans deserve it: they are as they are because they are brutish, violent, lazy. If they worked, it wouldn't happen to them.

Of all the stories created by capitalism to justify itself, none is better or more effective than the one that proposes that those who earn more are those who deserve more because they are the most intelligent, the hardest workers, the most tenacious. Earning money is the result of merit—and the meritocracy justifies all differences.

A metaphor: the most brutal, the most immediately understandable of the contempt some have for others, of the disdain for their fate, the disgrace and injustice to not be able to do the most basic things. For us, readers, well-fed Westerners, hunger is a metaphor for I don't give two hoots about others. Or I don't give one hoot and forty-eight mini-hoots because, even though you wouldn't believe it, I give to those who go there and help. Which is a valid position with very solid theoretical backup, but you still have to be bold enough to actually say it.

And, at the same time, it is a brutal metaphor for some who suffer it: they don't give a shit about me, I'm going to die anyway, I don't exist—for them. I wish they didn't exist for me.

(Proposal: let's call hunger not only the impossibility of eating what one needs, but also the possibility of living in homes the rest of us wouldn't call homes.)

In rich countries, hunger has always been the banner of the left, which used it as an argument to legitimize their desire to change the social order. Now it sounds more like a decoy for all those well-intentioned types, groups that reject a definition or political representation: international organizations, NGOs, all kind of churches.

In rich countries, fighting for bread is an archaic act: the struggle of our ancestors. Now, their objectives are many and more varied. Perhaps also that's why for them hunger has lost its political weight and turned into a cliché, a half-dead word, an image on a postcard for a different kind of tourism.

That's why, in those countries, hunger is not only a metaphor for others' poverty; it also says the past.

Or the threat of falling: hunger returns, we can always go over the cliff.

Hunger also fills another inestimable social function. The world's hungry are there to show us how much better we Westerners are than those brutes who don't have our history, our culture, our institutions.

They are the absolute Other: the ones that remind us, with their interminable suffering, how good we are for being us—and the dangers of being otherwise.

(Proposal: let's call hunger not only the impossibility of eating what one needs, but also the possibility of dying from diseases that can be cured with twenty dollars at the right time.)

Then it would be possible to say that hunger is the most extreme way of saying poverty—which says so many other things: disease, sadness, loss, illusions, broken illusions, illusions achieved, non-potable water, anxious mornings, one blow another blow another blow, twelve hours of work, fifteen hours of work, the joy of children, the illness of a child, encounters, missed encounters, violence, hope, other.

(Proposal: let's call hunger not only the impossibility of eating what one needs, but also the impossibility of imagining another course of action, improvements in life, a different future.

blows
and more blows
While calling hunger a metaphor.
Go tell those kids who are skin and bones that it's a metaphor.)

MADAGASCAR: FORCES OF HUNGER

1

They looked at me and laughed. Fifteen Malagasy journalists, twelve men and three women, sitting on both sides of some Formica tables arranged in a U-shape in a dreary room, and cracking up at my presence. I arranged my face, smiled, shrugged my shoulders. Through my interpreter I explained that I was here to report on the Malagasy issue of land grabbing, and this sent them into whoops of laughter. *It's so bad that even journalists coming from Europe want to report on it? Can you believe that?* I was the journalist from Europe, the stranger who came from so far away, and they laughed because they didn't quite know what else to do.

The room we were in was a large building, a little run down, which belongs to an order of nuns and which houses a Malagasy humanitarian organization called Tokovato, where a group of journalists from all over the country had come to take a course for two days to learn how to better report about land grabbing by foreign companies.

Ain, the organizer of the conference was in charge of research and communications for Solidarité des Intervenants sur le Foncier (SIF), the Malagasy branch of the International Land Coalition. Ain spoke with contagious enthusiasm; he was a young agricultural engineer who wore sports shoes, with a small beard, and glasses, and very shiny teeth. He was convinced that he was doing what he should be doing even though it's never enough. I later learned that his full name was Hieriniaina Rakotomalamala, and that his was among many names around here that were shortened.

Sitting around the U-shaped tables, identified by handwritten signs, the fifteen journalists were all in their thirties, except for one very thin, almost old man wearing a dirty white visor, and a woman with peeling fingernail polish whose face looked as though it had suffered quite a lot. It was cold and the journalists zipped up their jackets, but Ain talked and talked and sweated.

". . . these things have to be verified, the conditions in every case. Like the Indian company Varun, which gives its workers, who used to own that land, thirty percent of the harvest, but of that thiry percent they are forced to sell seventy percent to the company at a price the company sets."

The journalists laughed, they gave each other complicit glances. It's good when the bad guys are so obvious. Quoting Louis Pasteur, he told the journalists, "The facts only speak to you when you are ready to understand them." He explained Pasteur was a chemist who found some incredible things in his microscope because he knew what to look for.

He continued, "The important thing is to understand how the land grabs work, so you can recognize the facts they bring us, those we manage to obtain."

He told them the goal of this meeting was to put in place a system of information sharing about the land, set up a large network so we could know what was going on. This was something that would benefit everybody. "Madagascar would stop losing its land to foreigners; journalists— you journalists," he said pointing at me, "would have new and hot topics to report. SIF—we in SIF could continue to do the work of tracking and denouncing."

A man with manicured hands, who wore a blue French jacket with padded shoulders argued that this might cause them problems with their bosses: "In my region, there's a Chinese company that is harvesting trees. Every day they take away truckloads of wood, and I know they are giving money to the owner of my newspaper so we don't write about it. What am I supposed to do about it?"

Others looked at him, made gestures that indicated that this was happening to them as well. A very young journalist with straightened hair stood up and told him that if he wanted to be called a journalist, then he had to be a journalist. There was giggling, people moving in their chairs Ain tried to avoid the conflict. He told them that their work was fundamental, that a good information network could do a lot to save thousands of peasants from poverty; the most important thing was to find out about things before it was too late. We often find out when it's already too late, he said. And they know that, and that's why they are doing everything they can to make sure we don't know. A skinny journalist to my right asked who "they" were.

He asked, very seriously, and took a sip of water. "There are many of them; the ones who buy the land, the businessmen and politicians who sell it to them, the bureaucrats who receive their cut, the journalists who receive theirs," explained Ain.

Fifteen journalists laughed, uncomfortable, nervous, very Malagasy.

"But there are also many people who want to know, because knowing allows us to do something. Or do you think that if people hadn't found out, Daewoo wouldn't be exploiting our land?"

When he said Daewoo, everyone stopped laughing.

Throughout 2008, there were rumors, suspicions, bits and pieces of certainties that the government under President Marc Ravalomanana was handing over huge amounts of land to foreign companies, but nobody had precise information.

Ravalomanana had come to power after several contretemps. In 2001, when he was mayor of Antananarivo, he fought over elections with the president at the time, Admiral Didier Ratsiraka. Both claimed victory; Ravalomanana had strong support in the capital, Ratsiraka in the coastal city of Toamasina. A confrontation seemed unavoidable, but it was. The United States, most of Europe, the World Bank, and the IMF intervened in favor of Ravalomanana and made him president; then they collaborated by giving subsidies and making investments during his reign, which lasted seven years. With his successor as mayor and a businessman in his thirties, Andry Rajoelina, started a more or less popular rebellion against him. The discontent began with the increase in the price of rice and other basic foods, but the first large demonstrations were provoked by the closure of a very popular radio station owned by Rajoelina, and the hijacking of a loan from the World Bank to buy a second presidential airplane. The final blow was his proposal to give land to the Korean company Daewoo.

"It all started," Ain explained, "when an agricultural engineer working in the capital, and the chief of his town in the eastern part of the island, found out from friends that there was an ongoing process in the government to hand over more than a million acres of Malagasy land to a foreign company. And he found out because the land was spread around the country, but many thousands of those acres were in his region."

I heard this in the XI arrondissement in Paris—in a mansion where so many exiles, ecologists, alterglobalizationists, and other contemporaries met—from Mamy Rakotondrainibe, the president of the Collective for the Defense of Malagasy Lands (TANY).

In 2008 the engineer dug around and found out what he could. A few weeks later, he called a press conference to denounce the plan. He didn't have many details, but he could confirm that it was a handover of land on an unprecedented scale. There were many journalists at the news conference, but few media outlets published anything. The engineer and some of his friends did not admit defeat. They obtained more information, talked with everybody, distributed photocopies of the paperwork they found, until the police led them to understand in no uncertain terms that if they didn't stop, things were not going to go well for them. He traveled to Germany and, most importantly, France, the former metropolis where the Malagasy colony was pretty big, to tell them what was happening and ask for their help. That's when he met Mamy.

Mamy was about sixty, had a gentle smile, and spoke with a sweet voice, implacable words:

"We were already doing everything we could for our country, collecting money and sending food, medicine, basic goods, those kinds of things, but when he told us about this, we thought that we had to get involved. So, we founded the Collective. What's going on in Madagascar is that many people are afraid to talk about these things. Especially after what happened in Ankorondrano."

Ankorondrano is a small town about sixty miles west of the capital, where a wealthy landowner had the police evict several dozen peasant families who had been living for decades on a piece of land that he claimed was his.

When France occupied Madagascar in 1883, the law stated that most of the land belonged to the colonial state, and that they could assign ownership to whomever they wanted. The same thing happened in many other African colonies. In many of them, the system was kept after independence: land appropriated from the colonial power remained in the hands of the new state, which allowed the peasants to use it.

Little by little ways to register ownership of ancestral lands emerged, but they were complicated and expensive, and there didn't seem to be much reason to do it; most of the inhabitants continued living on the land where they'd always lived, without thinking about having any papers. Still, half the peasants in Madagascar live and work on land that they and their ancestors have occupied for centuries, land that formed part of the communal property of their towns but that didn't belong to them legally.

(Moreover, since independence, there has been a law that prohibited the sale of Malagasy land to foreign citizens or companies. In 2003, under pressure from the IMF and the World Bank—in the name, of course, of economic development—selling land became legal to anybody with money, and a deed of ownership gained importance.)

Now, for many, not having that deed has become an extreme hardship: the awareness that at any moment some lawyer or politician can throw you out of your house so they can keep your land, so they can give it to who knows what *vazaha*—what the Malagasy call foreigners. The awareness that the various forms of property use and ownership—communal, collective—are no longer valid, having been defeated by the hegemony of the market and the monopoly of private property is . . . terrifying.

In August 2006, hundreds of Ankorondrano peasants refused to give their land to the wealthy landowner; the police insisted and an old woman died in the ensuing conflict. More anger, more confrontations:

two policemen killed. One year later, a court found ninety-three peasants guilty of the uprising and the deaths. Six of them were sentenced to twelve years of forced labor, thirteen were given the death penalty. In Madagascar, capital punishment is rarely carried out, usually commuted to life imprisonment. But the judgment worked to scare the restless: very few dared, in 2008, to discuss the issue of land. Many local wealthy people took advantage of it to expropriate more and more; many of them were, in addition, front men for foreign companies.

From the relative security of Paris, Mamy and the others, indignant about the Daewoo project, insisted. They circulated a petition on the internet to stop the handover, which got thousands of signatures in Europe. In Madagascar, Mamy said, many people answered privately, encouraged them to continue, but said they were afraid to sign. They did, however, agree to continue to spread the word.

That was when an article appeared that finally put the Daewoo affair on the world stage. Curiously, it was published in the *Financial Times*, a publication that has never been famous for its defense of the poor people of the world. The article was titled, "Daewoo to Cultivate Madagascar Land for Free" and began by saying, "Daewoo Logistics of South Korea said it expected to pay nothing to farm maize and palm oil in an area of Madagascar half the size of Belgium, increasing concerns about the largest farmland investment of this kind." It then said that sources in the company will sign a ninety-nine-year lease for 250 million acres of Malagasy land. "'We want to plant corn there to ensure our food security. Food can be a weapon in this world,' said Hong Jong-wan, a manager at Daewoo. 'We can either export the harvests to other countries or ship them back to Korea in case of a food crisis.'" At the end, the article said that the contract hadn't yet been signed, that Daewoo wouldn't pay anything but would create jobs and build infrastructure that would benefit the country, and that the 250 million acres represented half the arable land on the island. Further on, in a strange boast, the article explained that the World Food Program of the United Nations said that more than 70 percent of the population of Madagascar lived below the poverty line, quoting the WFP, that "some 50 percent of children under three years of age suffer retarded growth due to a chronically inadequate diet."[1]

The rumor had turned into precise information, in words and numbers, but it still didn't make very big waves in Madagascar. In the middle of December 2008, a rebellion started because of the increase in the price of food, the closure of the radio station, and the purchase of the airplane. Only in January did the clamor for the land of their ancestors increase. In Madagascar, land is the synthesis of nationality; the word also means "fatherland": *tanindrazan* first meant land of our ancestors. The national anthem, in a single verse, insists with devotion: *Oh, beloved land of our ancestors / Oh good Madagascar. / Our love for you will not leave, / For you, for you forever.*

It was like throwing a can of gasoline on the fire. In a couple of weeks, after confrontations between protesters and the army had left more than one hundred people dead, Ravalomanana's government fell. A few days later, under popular pressure, the new president, Rajoelina, declared that the contract with Daewoo had been annulled. In the Daewoo case, Madagascar remained engraved in the memory of the few who have memories of these things as the clearest example of land appropriations—and the possibility of fighting against them.

The idea of using Malagasy land to solve problems elsewhere has several precedents. The most brutal is the Madagaskarplan of the Reich Main Security Office (RSHA) whose chief was Reinhard Heydrich. The project, designed by Franz Rademacher and pushed forward by Adolf Eichmann in 1940, called for a "resettlement" of European Jews at the rate of a million a year to the island. The plan was complicated. France, recently occupied, would hand over Madagascar, which would remain under the control of the SS; the funds requisitioned from Jews throughout Europe would pay for the operation; Jews would be transported on English merchant marine ships, once England had been occupied.

The plan didn't work because the British air defense prevented the Germans from invading. As usual, the triumph of some was a disaster for others. Without the possibility of sending the European Jewish population to Madagascar, the German government decided to send them to camps, and eventually to eliminate them altogether. A final solution when others had been considered.

2

The Malagasy people live on an island that different people have occupied before. It is an island that belongs to Africa but is not very African. In that classical outline of Africa that is used like a brand right in the middle of the signs for half the businesses and governments in all African cities, Madagascar is not there. There's the big fat continent, it's almost South American tip, its head with thick jowls, but never the large island on its lower right. For Africa, Madagascar isn't part of Africa, but it is.

For Madagascar, there's also some doubt, because in many ways it is different from Africa or, at least, from the mainland. Unlike so many other African cities, which stay warm year round, Antananarivo, the capital of Madagascar—is perhaps the coldest African city (fifty degrees Fahrenheit on August days.), a city where you don't see traditional clothes, a city without buildings made with different materials or in different styles, a city where the population has Polynesian, African, Chinese, Indian, and European features—all dressed in the scraps of modernity, without anything that inscribes them in their own past. In Antananarivo—which is often referred to as simply Taná—there are none of those colors, fabrics, flights of difference that are typical in what we usually call Africa. There's a reason the guides who sell Madagascar always talk about the baobabs, the lemurs, the forests. In spite of everything, nature in Madagascar, saved from man's destructive hand, has become its largest tourist draw.

Madagascar rose to global cultural fame through the animated movies that share its name. In *Madagascar*, the first in the franchise, animals held captive in New York's Central Park Zoo are shipwrecked on the coast of a tropical island which is also called Madagascar. It is, says the animals, the real version of what they always saw on post cards. There, multitudes of locals with accents—the lemurs—take care of them, pamper them, look after them so that they will in turn protect them from the bad guys who want to eat them. So, the lion—who until then was just a North American farce—discovers the nature of his species, and thus, what all the others are in relation to him. For the king of the jungle, the others are food.

But since *Madagascar* is a movie for children, the king of the jungle ends up eating sushi instead of his friends, and the white people come here to see what they already saw on Disney channel, or National Geographic before. They spend eight days on those beaches that don't belong to any country in particular because they all of them have the same cabañas, hammocks, mojitos, margaritas, fast-fucking, slow-burning white sands, turquoise waters like in the postcards. The postcard as a modern Mecca, a must-have, a stamp of success.

The postcard as manifest destiny.

In the meantime, Taná is a series of wide unpaved avenues that go past blocks of shacks made only from wood or stone, incredibly narrow alleyways, garbage dumps and stagnant water. Taná is urban poverty without any concession to folklore. A city without trees: pure cement, asphalt, tin, and filth. A city that is so poor there aren't even people to shine your shoes. Here the minimum salary—which a large portion of the population doesn't get—is ninety thousand ariary, or forty dollars. It costs about fifty thousand ariary for one hundred pound bag of rice, an amount that can feed a family of four for one month.

It was cold the next morning, and people covered themselves as best they could—a blanket, a worn-out robe, a colorful towel, all kinds of hats, but many went barefoot. On the streets leading to the market there was a girl herding two geese, an old man on foot pulling a heavily laden cart, two children with garbage bags over their heads, six women selling beignets. The market was a hub of activity: chickens, tomatoes, pumpkins, strawberries, guava, beets, lettuce, more lettuce, tea, French bread, vanilla pods, cassava, potatoes, strings of sausages, newspapers, oysters, bags of Indian rice, handmade rope, peanuts, more peanuts, plastic buckets, cell phone chargers, cell phone unlocking booths, cell phone calling stations, bags of coal, black, green, yellow bananas, pirated DVDs, pencils and notebooks, globes that show almost all the countries in the world, and very long zebu ribs with their black-red meat. I walked, they pushed me, I pushed back, I bought some vanilla cookies from a stand on the street, I didn't like them, I gave them to a child sitting on the curb. When he understood I was giving them to him, his face lit up with a smile. My pleasure at that smile turned to disgust at myself for having bought a generous moment with my leftovers.

And, everywhere, those piles, those mountains of eighth-hand suits and skirts and pants and blouses, wrinkled to a point of no return: the clothes of the dead, the scraps the rich West sends to Africa.

"Hey, boss, you want to buy something?"

"No, thank you."

"Yes, you do, I know you want to buy something."

Taná is a junkyard: the resting place for dead Western objects. Used Renault 4s and Citroën 2CVs, for example, which disappeared decades ago from the rest of the world, are here in these streets, painted beige, working as taxis. We assumed they had been lost in time, but they only changed space and ended up here. Taná would be—if such a thing existed—poverty in its purest state, without the help of a distinctive tradition or demeanor or space: thousands and thousands of people using a very decayed Western city, dead objects, old clothes.

Civilization of garbage and its discontents.

"I know, boss, I know you want. White people always want to buy something."

A child wearing a red cap was begging; I thought he was going to drop all his coins, or maybe he didn't care about the coins they gave him. He just wanted to be there, see that they gave him something, or whatever. But nobody understands until they understand: in Madagascar there are no coins. The smallest bill is worth one hundred ariary, about four cents to the US dollar. The kid with the cap was eight or nine years old, his hair was stiff and spiky, he was barefoot in the cold, and standing outside the school.

Inside the school with cracked walls, on the other side of the door, the children were arriving; the teacher greeted them by name, pat their heads. She said it was hard to believe:

"Hard to believe, but we didn't realize how bad it was," Sylviane, the first-grade teacher, told me. She was in her twenties, short, with thick lips, and was wearing a thick dark-blue pullover with holes at the elbows.

"A year ago, an NGO started bringing us breakfast. You can't believe how much better the students started to do. We'd gotten so used to them doing poorly that we hadn't realized that the problem was that they were so hungry they couldn't even think."

And later, she told me they explained that all of them weren't short because the Malagasies are short, but because they eat less than they need to eat. She said a woman from that NGO told her those same children, well-fed, would be five to ten inches taller.

"You have no idea how sad that made me." Sylviane added, "They don't grow anymore, they stay like that, short forever."

In Taná, like in the rest of the country, half the children are chronically malnourished. Most of this is due to the fact that they simply don't eat enough to satisfy their hunger; the rest of the time, it is because they eat only rice and this doesn't meet their nutritional needs for growth potential. Perrine Burnod, a researcher with the French Centre de Coopération Internationale en Recherche agronomique pour le Développement (CIRAD) explained that 80 percent of the population lives on rice and that Madagascar no longer produces the rice its people consume like it once did. "Now they import a large percentage, and there is no more important political or economic discussion each year than the quotas on the price of imported rice. If the importers bring too much rice and this lowers the prices, local producers are ruined, unable to sell what they grow at a price that compensates them for their work. But, if they bring less, they earn less money, and the country runs the risk of not having enough," Burnod explains. The big importers have taken over political power in Madagascar and control the business too. With the hundred pound bag of rice at fifty thousand ariary, they are right on the edge, with a large portion of the population unable to pay.

"So sad. And I thought we were like this because that's how we were."

Madagascar has twenty-two million inhabitants: three out of every four live below the poverty line drawn quite modestly at 470,000 ariary or $234 (or ten hundred pound bags of rice each year.) So, the average Malagasy spends more than three-quarters of their money on food. The situation had been improving during the first years of this century, but after 2008 it started getting worse again.

According to the report by the UN special rapporteur on the right to food, Olivier de Schutter, "35 percent of the rural population experiences hunger, a figure that rises to 47 percent among small farmers and 43 percent among agricultural day laborers."[2]

During the 2009 political crisis, development and humanitarian aid programs decreased sharply when Western powers decided to withdraw much of it in order to apply pressure for a return to democracy. This aid comprised half of the state budget, and it vanished. The health budget decreased by 45 percent, and for education only a bit less. The United States eliminated a trade treaty that had favored the building of small textile factories whose products could enter the United States without tariffs; the factories closed, and thousands of workers were laid off. Large numbers of government employees—teachers, doctors, paramedics— lost part of their wages due to decreases in foreign aid, and they went on strike. There are at least a few paradoxes here: thousands and thousands of people, poor people, workers, suffer because Western democracies decided to defend their democracy instead of defending them.

People smoke in the cafés in Taná. White people, mostly, smoke. One of the advantages of life in the Other World is that there are not as many rules, and moreover, you don't have to follow them if you are white. Sitting in a café in Taná, French in a passé, Sophie Cazade, director of Action Against Hunger in Madagascar, tells me about the fine tuning on a development project in the arid south of the country, and all the time they spent studying the population in the region to find out how best to intervene.

They want to improve access to potable water because not having any is one of the main causes of very avoidable diseases that kill millions. But, they ask themselves, once they help dig a well or build canals, who will manage the water and how? The natural tendency of a NGO like this one would be to set up a democratic and participatory structure, she says, but the locals don't function that way. So, shouldn't they adapt to their ways in order to guarantee that the water gets to where it needs to go? And in that case, is it okay to accept and support those traditional, authoritarian forms? Or is it better to go against them even at the risk of them not understanding and also, of losing the water?

They also want to improve agricultural yield by introducing new technologies, and eventually tools. It would be important for them to produce more and to diversify their crops. Sophie says that if they grow more fruits and vegetables, their diet would improve and they could sell their extras. But, how to be sure that instead of using that extra money to improve their nutrition and health, which is the NGO's goal, the head of the household uses it to buy zebus? Sophie explains the role of the zebu in this culture: they rarely use them to work the land, and they only drink their milk for a few months because during the long dry season, they don't have milk; they don't use their manure for heating or fertilizer because the zebus are the measure of their wealth and what they produce is also, so they store two feet of shit in their stables to show their power. More than a source of labor and nutrition, zebus are a way of establishing the social status of their owner. Zebus are their assets, something they can sell at a moment of crisis, give in exchange for a wife or to obtain the materials needed to build a family tomb, or to sacrifice at a wedding or funeral. So, what can they do to make sure their efforts to help them earn more money and have more food doesn't end up producing more zebus, which doesn't improve their nutrition? Sophie wondered, and she said that one option was to help the women, who were excluded from handling zebus, manage that extra income—and they were studying how they could arrange that, perhaps by incentivizing their activities, such as selling extra fruit in the market or weaving those rattan baskets, so that the money didn't end up buying more zebus but rather "objectively" improving their lives.

"What if for them improvement means having more zebus?"

"I don't know. It's always the same problem. But we aren't called Action for Zebus, but rather Action Against Hunger," Sophie replied and offered me a strange smile.

They also aimed to prolong the length of time women nurse their babies, which improves the health of those under two because more than half of those children suffer from chronic malnutrition. But they thought it would be very difficult to convince them because the population was so resistant to change, feared any change because it could displease their ancestors, who want their descendants to do the same as them and if they didn't, they might seek revenge. And, because they lived so close to the edge, she said, they thought that any change would push them into the abyss.

Another thing: for every solution there's a new problem. But they are fascinating problems. The attempt, both modest and disproportionate, to produce important changes in the life of the inhabitants in one small area of one small province in one small country; the pride of thinking they can, that those hundred thousand people can live better lives as a result; the resignation of knowing they are a hundred thousand among twentysomething million.

Nuro was leaning against a cracked blue wall, with his wide nose, his pimples, his smile, his dirty shirt. His face and body said fifteen years old and, down below, his tiny legs were like dried up branches. When Nuro walked, he walked on his hands. Nuro said that he was sick as a child and that his mother returned him to the village, leaving him in the care of others. He said that his mother had several children and probably couldn't take care of all of them including him. It's all the same; he lived with his friends on the street and didn't need her.

Nuro's eyes were lively, and he had an easy smile. His dirty feet were full of sores, the palms of his hands were like hardened shells, and I wanted to ask him what it was like to live with those legs, without legs, on the street, but I didn't dare, it was too painful.

"How do you eat?"

Little, Nuro said he ate little. Whatever somebody in the neighborhood gave him, whatever his friends found for him, whatever he begged for he ate. Sometimes they gave and sometimes they didn't. He told his friends stories.

"I tell them stories; I know stories."

He told them what was going on in the street, who came when, who had what, who brought what, because he could see everything, because nobody saw him, it was as if he weren't there. And he told it all to his friends in the street, and if they got something, they shared it with him and that was how he ate. And then, in the end, he told me that what he had always wanted was a bicycle; his life would be so much different if he had a bicycle.

3

"Buy land, they're not making it anymore," said Mark Twain.

For decades, agriculture carried no weight in the global economy. It was a necessary evil, everyone had to eat. But, it never produced great fortunes, proffered prestige, allowed for innovations or earth-shattering inventions. It never seemed modern enough, just a bothersome survival mechanism from the old days. It stayed this way until the price of commodities began to rise, bringing with it an increased fear of scarcity. Countries that produced a lot started earning a lot more and those who produced little started worrying more than a little. And the great powers realized that land and water, which there had always been plenty of were becoming scarce and therefore more and more valuable. Technology was then created to maximize upon that value.

That was the change: technology allowed agriculture to become profitable. We are talking here, admittedly, about a different kind of agriculture, one that was dependent on machines to make the land work in ways it had never done before. But no matter how far technology has come, land can't be stretched, and water doesn't come out of stones.

Land grabbing is a relatively new way of doing something very old. It used to be called colonialism where the occupying powers would plant their flags; now they plant their corporate banners in the name of globalization and free trade—not to mention, helping the poor.

The first colonizers conquered land in the name of the Bible and civilization with a promise of education in exchange for conversion. Now, in the name of humanitarian capitalism, we have to teach those being conquered to produce more so they can be integrated into the markets, buy more things, and maybe even eat more often.

"Acquisition of rural land for commercial production is not a new phenomenon in Africa," Michael Ochieng Odhiambo stated in his report *Commercial Pressures on Land in Africa* of the International Land Coalition. "Nor is the fact that in such acquisitions there exist power disparities between those acquiring the land and their interests on the one hand and the indigenous rural peasants who traditionally own and use the land for their livelihoods on the other."[3]

When they can, rich countries with little land, advanced countries with cutting-edge industry, and fortunate countries with oil-soaked subsoils send explorers to the Other World to look for things to buy. Large corporations and capital adventurers are also looking, and they find what they're searching for. Within the logic of global capitalism, they have the right. There are no laws that prevent a gentleman with money, or contacts, or strength, or the gift of gab to take whatever land he can and send his harvest to his cousin's house—even if the peasants who live on those lands, or the inhabitants of the surrounding towns and cities, are left without food.

Countries and large corporations grab land because they do not want to depend on international trade to obtain the food they need. They are looking for more direct supplies because they do not trust the mechanisms of the market: the biggest players in the market don't trust their own game. Others try because it is good business.

"We who produce say that the only solution to high prices is high prices.

The only way for grain to be worth less is, eventually, for the agricultural frontiers of Brazil to reach their limit and for us to begin to expand in Africa. That expansion requires a lot of money. And for that money to have a return on investment, the grain has to be worth a lot. If every year, twenty million Chinese move from the countryside to the city, these are Chinese who are not returning to the countryside and they need to buy their food. That demand is not turning back. So, either the world gets used to producing more food, or food will become even more expensive." Iván Ordóñez, an economist at a large Argentine soy company at the time, explained this to me months before in a bar in downtown Buenos Aires.

"Let's see. You say that for African land to begin to be fully utilized, the price of grain has to rise. When that happens, those lands will be easier to exploit because there will be fewer people on them, because with the rise in prices, many will have died of starvation . . ."

"Yes, that's possible. I'm not saying my equation is a good one; I'm just saying that's what happens. That's capitalism. You might be modern; I'm postmodern. There are already investment funds in Africa because, among other reasons, the land there isn't worth a red cent. But they still have to prove to the investor they'll be profitable."

The circle is more than vicious. Small African farmers barely survive on their land because they have no tools or capital or infrastructure to increase their yield, but the increase in global food prices makes their land more profitable and for large capital, more urgent to exploit. Thus, the peasants are expelled and end up in the cities where they have to buy much more expensive food, because those who produce it want to make a profit on their investments or because, even more brutally, they export it and sell it on the world market.

And for a change, they eat less.

The land grabbing movement in the Other World took off at the beginning of the century, but the increase in food prices since 2007 gave it significant impetus.

In the ensuing years various state and private corporations have bought or rented or obtained enormous tracts of land. It would be good to be able to write "enormous tracts" and not have to specify, because it's nearly impossible to know the amounts. Many operations go unreported, others are reported but are never finalized, others are finalized for amounts different from what were announced, and in many cases, the lands turned over are not measured or registered with any precision.

In any case, the figures vary too much. One report published in 2010 by the World Bank, which is not usually aggressively anticapitalist, said that some 140 million acres of land had already been appropriated, more than the total area of Spain. But that there is "an astonishing lack of awareness of what is happening on the ground even by the public sector institutions mandated to control this phenomenon," which happens mostly in countries where "state capacity is weak, property rights ill-defined, and regulatory institutions starved of resources could lead to projects that fail to provide benefits, for example, because they are socially, technically, or financially nonviable."[4]

On the other hand, a report by the National Academy of Sciences in the United States says that appropriations already reached 250 million acres, an area equal to that of France and Germany combined.

"But, finally, how much land has been grabbed?" Fred Pearce, the English author of *The Landgrabbers*, the most comprehensive book on the subject, was asked in 2012. "No one really knows. A lot of reported deals never happen and a lot of the largest are done secretly. Oxfam has stated that more than 750 thousand square miles in the last decade have been grabbed, two-thirds of them in Africa."[5]

But we do know that most of it occurs in countries where the land is very cheap and can be obtained almost for free, and where there are many people who do not eat enough. In July 2015, the Land Matrix database, using only verified information, named the ten countries where foreigners have grabbed the most land:

Papua New Guinea (8.9 million acres of farmland), Indonesia (8.8), South Sudan (8.6) Democratic Republic of Congo (6.9), Mozambique (6.4), Congo (6.3), Russia (4.4), Ukraine (4.2), Liberia (4.1), Sudan (4.1).

These are followed closely by land grabs in Sierra Leone, Brazil, Uruguay, Ethiopia, Ghana, Cambodia, Morocco, Argentina, and finally Madagascar, where the 1.5 million acres sold could have been greater, were it not for activist pressure that prevented several deals from being completed.

The number of displaced peasants is even more confusing, and usually doesn't appear in any reports.

About one-third of this land is used to grow food, another third for agrofuels, though the distinction is not always that clear. Some land is used to grow what is now called "flex crops," which have multiple uses, such as for human or animal consumption, industrial raw materials, or fuel. Those that offer the most options are soy, sugar cane, corn, and palm.

The remaining third is split among lumber and flowers for that strange contemporary perversion that consists of preserving more or less virgin forests to generate carbon credits, or rather, to set aside green swaths of unused terrain to compensate for the greenhouse gas emissions produced by the factories in the wealthy countries. These regions remain perfectly poor, unproductive, unusable for their inhabitants other than to pay for the environmental waste of those who are earning more and more money.

"African land has been shown to be a cheap solution for others' problems," wrote Oxford professor, David Anderson. "Africa has become the place where other parts of the world can produce what they need at low cost."

For now, the most sought-after region is the Guinea Savanna mosaic, a territory of one and a half million square miles—almost twice as big as Argentina—that stretches from the Atlantic to the Indian oceans, just below the Sahel, and through twenty countries—Guinea, Senegal, Sierra Leon, Malawi, Tanzania, and Mozambique, passing through Mali, Burkina Faso, Central African Republic, Kenya, Uganda, Zambia, and Angola, among others. The World Bank called this region "one of the largest underused agricultural land reserves in the world."⁶ It is where the colonists who occupied Africa in the nineteenth century or the armies that took the Argentine Pampa and Patagonia at that time waged what they called "desert campaigns." In the Guinea Savanna there live and work more than 600 million Africans—almost one-tenth of the world population—who are among the poorest and most poorly nourished people on the planet.

The model many of these new African exploitations would like to emulate are the *fazendas* in the Brazilian *Cerrado*, or savanna. The Cerrado is a region of 750 thousand square miles, almost the entire territory of Brazil minus the Amazon, the coast, and the far south. The Cerrado is made up of huge fertile savannas, well-watered but with one problem: most of the land is too acidic for crops. For many years it was used for livestock until, in the middle of the seventies, scientists hired by the government found a solution. If treated with large amounts of lime, the soil becomes productive—and that's when the invasion started.

The cultivated areas tend to be enormous, very well guarded—hundreds of thousands of acres patrolled by security—and very high tech. They harbor genetically modified seeds, a lot of machinery, and very little labor (barely one worker for every four hundred acres.) The local governments—controlled by the large soy, corn, and cotton growers—build the necessary roads to carry their product to the ports.

Thanks to the Cerrado, Brazil has become the number one exporter of soy, meat, chicken, tobacco, sugar, and orange juice in the world. The Cerrado attracted large investors from all over: Soros, Rothschild, Cargill, Bunge, Mitsui, Chongqing, Qatar. At least a quarter of the land was in the hands of foreigners, and a much larger percentage of the products end up outside of Brazil. Most of the inhabitants in the region continue to live in extreme poverty. The Cerrado is the first example of this form of land grabbing that is now spreading around the world.

"Or, perhaps only the most recent."

Fred Pearce said to a Brazilian agricultural producer in whose region the farms are called Bonanza, Chaparral.

"Or doesn't anybody remember how the cowboys occupied the American West?"

National governments in many poor countries tend to be more than willing to collaborate with these appropriations. In general, they gain more than political returns, and some, perhaps, even hope to improve the living conditions of their citizens. The Ethiopian regime of the ex-Communist guerrilla Meles Zenawi and his successor, for example, enacted very aggressive policies to attract "investment" with public relations offices and campaigns to lease their land for largely symbolic fees to foreigners who wanted to exploit them. They were able to do so without any legal problems because in the seventies, when they were socialists, they nationalized all the farmland in the country.

If land grabbing is a form of colonialism, it is, like all forms, taking advantage of the weakness of the states they are colonizing. No corporation, public or private, could obtain thousands of acres of land in a country whose government had the means and the will to keep it for their citizens. The land grab is, in this sense, another consequence of this strange world, where the people are represented by national institutions such as governments whose power is much less than that of supranational institutions and corporations that define our lives.

It is also the case that foreigners grabbing land in Other World countries awaken, among those who find out, appropriate outrage. These are the delights of nationalism—manifest or latent—that rich locals also concentrate ownership of important amounts of land, but nobody is outraged, as this seems to simply be part of the rules of the game. What seems intolerable is that a company or a foreign state controls those land; that a man of the same nationality does the same thing remains within the logic we supposedly accept, and we don't even ask ourselves why?

I am not in favor of staunchly maintaining land in the hands of its ancient inhabitants. To begin with, the idea that having spent centuries in a place gives you the right to spend more centuries in that place is arguable. According to that idea, the King of Arabia has the right to be king because his ancestors were. Or rather, it is a conservative idea, a form of historical ecological conservation, which is worth discussing. Nor do I stand by the argument that says we have to preserve culture at all cost. Cultures evolve. We have made disproportionate efforts to leave behind the Western and Christian culture that said that sex was a sin and pleasure a miracle and that whoever said to hell with God would be burned in never-ending flames. So, would it look good if we mourned the irreparable loss of slavery in our countries in the last two hundred years? Nevertheless, we become paternalistic and demand that we "preserve" cultures that functioned in other times, under other conditions.

Why do we insist on believing that there are "traditional" societies that should forever preserve their way of life, and that the "progressive" approach consists of helping them continue to live like their ancestors? Is it because we moderns keep wearing crinolines and gaiters, marrying virgins, traveling on horseback with swords in our hands, writing words like these with a goose feather, worshipping our king, lighting our way with an oil lamp that some frightened little black boy carries?

Tradition, purity, authenticity. This is a conservative idea of freezing evolution at some point in the past, an idea that the left shares with the right, though they apply it to different objects. The issue isn't traditions; the issue is the right to live with dignity.

And for this reason, it will sometimes be necessary to stop using old subsistence technologies—gathering, extensive animal husbandry, slow crop and land rotations—that require more space. One can even play with the idea that it is not fair that a relatively small number of people occupy space that so many need, that it would be legitimate to use those lands to produce more—and relocate their ancient inhabitants. But that would require that the products were distributed among those who need it; the entire legitimacy of that move is lost when those who farm the lands do so to increase the profits of the owners or investors. The differences between land grabbing and land acquisition are not always clear. But, to sum it up: one thing is to buy from a person or a business a farm that they owned and used—or not; another is to take, with the complicity of government officials, land that a community or certain people were using to farm, pasture animals, or provide themselves with materials necessary to survive.

All of this would be much more difficult if it weren't for an important cultural discrepancy: advanced capitalism and its idea of private property as opposed to other ways of thinking about the use of resources. About 90 percent of African land has no legally recorded owner because the ways of thinking about and registering ownership were always different. Now, national officials and foreign buyers invoke the Western idea of ownership and intervene violently, taking advantage of this discrepancy to pretend that the land doesn't belong to anybody and is therefore available for their use.

Governments then make sure to vacate the land they are giving over to their new benefactors, thereby displacing entire populations; sometimes this is done under the guise of improving living conditions. But, to cite just one example, the multimillion dollar contract the Ethiopian government signed with Sai Ramakrishna Karuturi, an Indian mogul, says very clearly that the land must be turned over empty, and that the government "shall ensure during the period of the lease, the lessee shall enjoy peaceful and trouble-free possession of the premises [with] adequate security free of cost . . . against any riot, disturbance or other turbulent time as and when requested by the lessee."[7]

These are the condition demanded by the investors: "The potential risks associated with these deals include cash-strapped local people losing not only their homes but also their source of food and future income as buyers secure the full rights to crops and land," says a report by Jacques Taylor and Karin Ireton, directors of Standard Bank Africa. And it is usual for investors to have in their "contracts with any government the guarantee that they will have the ability to operate their investments according to their needs."[8]

In April 2012, Saudi authorities announced that the Sudanese government had turned over to them nearly two million acres of farmland, where Sudanese laws and taxes would not apply, for them to use as they please—to produce food for their citizens.

Here, the word "colony" is literal.

The new colonists usually arrive with their arms full of promises and justifications. They are going to build infrastructure—roads, canals, schools, hospitals—they are going to give jobs to the locals, they are going to help feed the world; the land they are farming was empty or underutilized, and they are going to greatly increase its yield.

They don't say that this increase, on principle, will only benefit their investors, that the infrastructure projects are, without exception, those needed to extract and transport their products, that there are never enough jobs for all the peasants forced to move, that they pay pathetic wages, and that, in the final analysis, all of this is based on a strange logic whereby one must be grateful to the big capitalists who have for centuries kept for themselves the profit produced by millions of workers and are now the only ones who can invest money in order to continue to do so.

Kyung wook Hong, the deputy general manager of Daewoo, said as much to justify his 2.5 million odd acres: "It is land that is totally not developed and uncontaminated. And we will provide work and make it cultivatable, and this is good for Madagascar."⁹

Again: they boast that they are creating jobs, as if by doing so they become benefactors of humanity, or at least that piece of humanity that is working in their fields. All this means is profit. If they hire people, it is because they know they can keep a large part of the value their work produces; if they hire those people—the inhabitants of that particular place—it is because they can pay them infinitely less than back home. But they assume, and they are not the only ones, that those workers should be grateful that they are being exploited.

The other most common argument made by people committing land appropriation is that the introduction of modern technology will increase yield and they will therefore be able to feed many more people. Once more, the excuse of "civilization": at the end of the nineteenth century, when the Europeans divided up Africa, the justification was that they came to bring the benefits of the latest technologies—to civilize.

Now they say that African countries don't have the resources or sufficient knowledge to fully utilize their potential, their raw materials. So, the business is clear: I invest my money so that your country can grow, and, in exchange, I take with me the product of that growth. Just like they did before, for a century and a half, during the time when they were called colonies. And, because those countries couldn't accumulate the fruits of that wealth, which ended up in Paris or London, they are the way they are now. The solution they propose is to do the same thing all over again.

Africa has 1.85 billion acres of farmland that could be better utilized—equal half the arable land in the world today. I don't want to say they are not utilized now, just that they are utilized in a different way. The question is, as usual, political: who is going to use those lands, how, and to what end. It seems true that if they remain small, not very productive plots, hunger will increase in a region where the number of inhabitants is predicted to rise from the current billion to two billion by the year 2050. The only issue turns on knowing if the technological changes that seem necessary are going to be implemented by the grabbers who want to "integrate them into the world market" or by societies that acquire the political means to guarantee life to their members. What is that political form? That's the question.

The argument for efficiency takes the Monsanto line, which presents itself as a benefactor of humanity when it says on its website: "In order to feed the world's growing population, farmers must produce more food in the next fifty years than they have in the past ten thousand years combined. We're working to double the yields of corn, soybeans, cotton, and spring-planted canola between 2000 and 2030." [10]

What neither Monsanto nor the other land grabbers in the Other World say is that the planet is already producing enough food to feed twelve billion people, and even so, one billion don't have enough to eat. That with only the grain now being grown in the world—without counting vegetables, legumes, roots, fruit, meat, and fish—there would be enough for every man, woman, and child to eat 3,200 calories a day—50 percent more than they need. That it is always good to produce more food—it would be easier, cheaper, more accessible—but that the problem, in synthesis, is not that there is not enough food but that some take it all, and that those new farmlands don't solve anything, and on the contrary, only increase the unfairness of distribution.

The colonial movement that we call land grabbing is the most grotesque, most brutal manifestation of the inequality between countries, wherein some use the land that belongs to others to produce food that everybody needs; some take it away, others are left without. Two thirds of that land is in regions where many people go hungry. That land is there, the products are there, but the people who have the power and the money take them away where they can earn even more money. Or, even, they keep those lands unfarmed in order to speculate on the increase in price—because, in the end, the less food produced the greater the demand, and the higher the price.

The question, for once, really is not that complicated.

In the meantime, an important percentage of the land grabs fail due to the inexperience of the investors. Their total lack of knowledge about local conditions, the opposition of the population, and changes in the global marketplace all combine to make their projects fail, or almost fail. The land remains in a strange kind of limbo: given to foreigners who are more or less fugitives, the locals can't use it and the foreigners don't want it. "Sometimes, the only thing worse than a land grab is a failed land grab," wrote Paul McMahon in *Feeding Frenzy*. [11]

Since the Daewoo affair, Madagascar has become the most brutal example of land grabs, how they can fail when many oppose them, but also how they can carry on.

VOICES OF THE TRIBE

How?

Please, repeat after me:
    It is not my problem, I don't care.
    I don't either.
    I can live with it.
    It worries me. It's sad that it worries me.
    There's nothing to.
    It's a disaster but what can we do, a real shame.

How the hell?

I agree, it shouldn't be like this. Yes, of course, like everybody else, we all know it shouldn't be like this. The problem is that the impoverished who are affected don't know much about this. They have to be taught; maybe it's true that they don't have quite enough food, but above all what they lack is education, and without education they'll never get anywhere. What we have to do is educate them, teach the mothers that they have to take care of themselves when they're pregnant, they have to eat because if they don't their children won't develop properly. But most of all, what we have to teach them is to elect different governments, other politicians than those who have been governing them. If they keep electing those same henchmen, nobody will be able to help them. Because they're the scourge, they who have absolutely no excuse, those corrupt politicians who fill their own pockets while their people starve to death. That really makes me despair. If it weren't for them, everything would be different. And it's a good thing that we can still help them; if not they'd be up shit creek without a paddle. But they're going to have to do something, because maybe we won't be able to help much considering the crisis and so many other complications.

How the hell do we manage?

Not to forget that the most common response is to forget. Ways of forgetting that include a cascade of words.

How the hell do we manage to live?

The whole apparatus is held up by two or three pillars. It wouldn't work, for example, without the presumption of autonomy: the fact that that man in Madaoua is so poor that he doesn't have anything to eat has nothing to do with the fact that I—in Buenos Aires, Chicago, or Barcelona—have a peaceful, relaxed life. Establishing the relationships is an act of rebellion. Or, at least, a tiny step.

How do we manage to live knowing these things?

Though, you have to think that they aren't really aware of it. It's not like that for you, you're used to living like you live, to eating every day, eating different things, not worrying about such things. For you it would be terrible, but for them hunger is the only thing they've ever known. It's not such horrible anguish, right? Because their lives have always been like that, so, yeah, it's fucked, it's hard, but you're wrong if you think that it's the same as if it were happening to you. Do you know what I'm saying? You have to put things in perspective, because if not things can really go wrong.

How do we manage to live knowing these things are happening?

4

They are humps, rumps, horns, damp backs, wooden yokes, manure sliding down their legs, flies in pursuit, dust rising; the image is exotic and monotonous, two qualities that aren't usually found together. The oxcart advanced slowly along the uneven dirt road, shaking me with every step.

Nyatanasoa is in the Marovoay district in the northern part of the island, more than three hundred miles from Antananarivo, near the big port called Mahajanga. Near is a figure of speech: twenty miles of paved road, without too many potholes, and then a road that starts to pass through grass, scrublands, trees, and for stretches turns into a cart path that passes through dry grass, small cassava and rice farms, a lot of burned land, a few palm trees.

Here, a cart is the only possible means of transportation, or walking for hours and hours. We are used to thinking about modern travel—train, bus, airplane—as a time when one is not in motion though moving, a time when one tries to get distracted to make it all go by as quickly as possible. In the cart, there is no possible form of distraction. You have to pay attention to every bump, every shake. It takes hours. The oxen are slow, the sun weighs down like lead. Suddenly, in the middle of nowhere, a rusty sign says: TONGA SOA, BIENVENUE, WELCOME FUELSTOCK. And, a few miles farther on: NYATANASOA. None of these towns appear on Google Maps; they are not included in the image of the world.

From a distance, the Fuelstock project is an example of how wealthy foreigners are obtaining land that the locals need to feed themselves. From a distance, but not so far away, it is the story of how an Irish banker obtained over sixty thousand acres of Malagasy land for his business venture. From close up, any story is a lot of stories. There are advances, retreats, contradictions, all more complicated, more impassioned, and more difficult to understand and interpret.

Everything began four years ago during a summit on agrofuels organized in South Africa, where an Irish banker in his fifties, who was starting to get restless, met a rich Malagasy who talked to him about the land on his island, about how there was a lot of it that nobody was farming, that it belonged to the state, that he knew the officials you had to know to obtain a lot of it at a very good price. The Irishman and the Malagasy began to make plans, crunch numbers, castles in the air: they would start a farm in the north of Madagascar, they would grow *Jatropha curcas*, the new miracle plant, the latest sensation, to make agrofuels, to make fortunes.

According to Simon Nambena, the local agricultural engineer Fuelstock hired to manage the project, owners of land were better at turning a profit than knowing how to grow anything: "The owner is very good at finding money, but the truth is he doesn't know very much about agriculture. And whenever anyone tries to explain anything to him, he gets a headache."

Nambena is also a product of these times. He is in his fifties and worked for years in a reforestation project of a German cooperative; when the political crisis caused the withdrawal of a lot of the development programs, he was left unemployed. So, he was delighted to accept Fuelstock's offer to manage the plantation.

"One of the things the owner didn't know is that Jatropha requires a lot of care until it begins to offer good yields, a lot of labor, a lot of fertilizer; in other words, a lot of money he hadn't counted on. He didn't even know that in this zone, the soil is so hard that it breaks all the equipment and tools, that it is almost impossible to work it with tractors; it requires hours and hours of preparation before you can plant anything, and 30 percent of the slopes are inaccessible. On 30 percent of the peaks the soil is sand. Nobody had thought about any of that."

This often happens. When the occupiers start, they find more difficulties—and fewer roads, less electricity, less machinery, fewer mechanics—than they had imagined, and this makes their dreams of easy money problematic. Often, they don't realize that the land that seemed half empty is half full. The initial plans for the sixty thousand acres included the rice paddies of the inhabitants in the local villages who would be left without food. The mayor protested, and the locals nearly revolted.

"In any case, you can't grow Jatropha where you grow rice, not in lowland areas between the hills where all the water goes. It was a mistake, something they didn't think."

The company fixed its "mistake." And they had the bright idea that to win over the locals, they would join with them against their traditional enemies. In other words, play Cortés's game.

When Hernán Cortés landed in Veracruz with five hundred men, ten cannons, sixteen horses, and no women, its forces were miniscule in comparison to those of the Aztec empire. Quickly Cortés understood that the only way to defeat them was by gaining the support of the other peoples who could no longer stand Aztec rule.

Here, more modestly, Fuelstock personnel met with the mayor of Marovoay and peasant leaders. They told them that their presence and new plantations would prevent the Sakalava herdsmen's zebus from continuing to invade their rice fields as they always had before. It seemed almost like a pejorative to herdsmen who seemed to be managing just fine. While I was in Nyatanasoa everything seemed to exist in a natural din: birds, hens, a dog or two, children's shouts, children's cries, women's conversations, a whistle over there, the continuous drone of the pestles grinding grain in the mortars, almost always the wind, a rooster crowing, the hard work of spitting out phlegm, some bellowing, two men speaking loudly.

What I did not hear: the sound of farm equipment.

Nyatanasoa has about four or five hundred inhabitants living in their adobe huts with pitched thatch roofs. The streets have spaces between them occupied by small hens, a zebu or two, a few goats, women sitting at the doors to their huts, men sitting in a kind of empty area between three huts that might be something like a main square.

"The first time, when the mayor called a meeting to tell us that a big company was coming to settle here, we were very happy. The mayor told us that they would build schools, a medical clinic, roads, they were going to bring electricity, and give us jobs, and they were going to protect us from the Sakalava. We were almost ashamed; I thought, why are we so lucky, we don't deserve it."

I was speaking with a man named Funrasa. He was wearing an old white shirt, multicolored Bermuda shorts, a straw hat with a band that used to be red, and no shoes. In the sort of square there were two men, four boys, a woman, and seven or eight kids. The boys are wearing very worn-out soccer jerseys: one of Madrid, one of Messi in Barcelona, different ones from Brazil, and they were sitting on the ground. They'd left me the best trunk, one that is twisted into the shape of a chair.

"Is there a school?"

"Yes, but it's the school that was here before. It's open."

"Are there classes now?"

"No, not now."

"Why not?"

"Because the teachers are on strike. They've been on strike for five months, trying to get a raise," explained one of the boys.

It's true that the company helped them keep the school open. Last year they even painted the outside of it. They didn't build a health clinic, but they let the locals visit the company doctor who came a couple times a week. But, they didn't bring electricity, and they dug a well on the company land, which used to be their land, and they charged them five hundred ariary—$0.20—every time they went to get water.

"They sell you your own water?"

"Well, they don't sell it to us because we don't buy it. We went twice or three times, then we stopped going. If we have to pay them every time we need a barrel of water . . ."

So, the women in the village, after being so hopeful at first, went back to their old routine: to the pond, a quarter of a mile downhill, with their yellow plastic containers.

"Do you complain to them about what they said they would do?"

"No, not yet. Their chief told us that they haven't been able to do those things because the materials hadn't yet arrived."

"But it's been three years."

"Well, two and a half."

"Are you worried that they won't do anything?"

Another man sitting nearby, wearing an old pair of trousers with the cuffs rolled up, a jacket from a different old suit, a hat that could be called a Borsalino, chimed in, "No, they will one day. If they said they would, they will."

He was also barefoot.

"What will they do?" a woman asked. "What will they do if they haven't done anything they said they were going to do? They have their generator, their well," she added," they did things for themselves."

Everybody else gave her strange, uncomfortable looks.

"It's time we stopped kidding ourselves," concluded the woman.

Her name was Rina, and she had a green-and-red cloth wrapped around her body. She must have been in her twenties, early thirties, with fat arms, her face covered in gold-colored dust, her skin cracked: the face of dried earth.

"They want to keep everything, and it looks like we just don't want to admit it."

The others—the men, the boys—gave her looks as if to shut her up with their eyes.

Life in Nyatanasoa changed with the arrival of Fuelstock and its plantation. Several dozen locals got jobs with the company; they were paid 3,500 ariary—$1.50—for a long days' work. But there weren't enough locals to fill all the positions, so the company brought in a dozen men and women from other villages; some settled here, others came and went from their own villages. Some seasons, there weren't very many; during the sowing and harvesting there could be more than a hundred. The women in town made beignets or rice to sell to them; a small market developed in a place where there had previously been no trade at all

"Are you afraid that the new people will end up taking over your village?"

"They can't take anything. They're from another village, they come when there's work and then they leave," Albert said, and the others agreed.

Rina looked at them with mistrust and was about to say something, then didn't.

"Would you like to live in Taná?"

"Yeah, but it scares me."

"Why?"

"Because there are a lot of thieves."

"Aren't there any here?"

"Here it's different, here we know them better."

Rina told me to come with her and led me to a house a few yards away. There were two women sitting on the ground in front of the door and breastfeeding; ten or twelve children were playing around them. They looked cheerful, almost chubby, barefoot, tolerably dirty. The face of one of the women, like Rina, was covered in that golden dust. I asked her, she told me it was made from a tree bark: they grate it, mix it with water, and apply it.

"Why?"

"It protects you from the sun."

"What happens if you don't use it?"

"I turn black."

Her name was Shena. She looked like she was in her thirties and sat there telling me this, holding her baby girl to her chest. The baby was a little under a year old, she told me; another, hardly any older, crawled into her arms; the one nursing, she said, was her daughter, the other, her granddaughter—the daughter of her daughter, who must be fifteen, she said, maybe sixteen. She took care of her often, today because her daughter went to the market. She left early, and on foot. Shena said it took about five hours there, five back. It took a man four, but men didn't want to go to the market, they said they didn't know anything about it, they didn't have time, so they sent the women.

"Who works more here, the men or the women?"

"The men, because in the fields they're the ones who hold the plow. Women water, spread fertilizer . . ."

"At home, what do the men do?"

"Nothing, they don't do anything. Sometimes they go get the zebus, but that's all. We do everything in the house, the house is ours, the children, the food, the cleaning, the clothes, everything."

"So, who works more?"

"The men." Shena said, tired of explaining.

The other woman, also with a baby nursing, was called Soasara and said she needs to go cook. I asked her what, and she looked at me with a little bit of pity.

"Rice, what else."

So, I asked her when they ate and Soasara told me three times a day: in the morning, at noon, and at night.

"What do you eat in the morning, what do you eat at noon, and what do you eat at night?"

"Rice," she said, as if it were obvious.

"Do you prepare it differently each time, or is it always the same."

"No, what do you mean. We cook it."

"Do you eat it with anything?"

"Sometimes, when we have something. A little vegetables. A fish. But not much."

"How often?"

"Maybe once a month, once every two months."

Except, they said, during the *soudure*. That's between November and March, when nine out of ten families experience hunger because they have neither corn nor rice, when half of all families spend whole days without eating; that's when their very scarce food is more varied. They find whatever they find: yams, a wild potato they call *moky*, tamarind mixed with ash, wild fruit, crickets and other insects, small birds. They don't like it. I asked them, don't they prefer to eat different things.

"No! Rice is the food of the Malagasy people!" Soasara replied, with grandiosity.

"But you like it?"

"Of course I like it, I like it best of all."

They were afraid of some of the foods they scrounged, and taboos had arisen. For example: if you give an egg to a child who hasn't started talking, they'll never talk.

"But if you could choose any food, any dish you wanted, what would you choose?"

"Rice," Shena said.

Soasra agreed.

And Rina explained to me that bread doesn't fill you up, it's no good to eat; the only thing that appeased hunger was rice. "The problem is when we don't have any. The problem is that we have less and less land to grow it on, and now with the company . . ."

"What's going on with the company?"

"Didn't you hear? They keep all the water for themselves and nobody says anything."

The World Health Organization (WHO) says that the main cause of death from environmental reasons is "primitive household cooking fires." In most houses in the Other World, women cook the little they cook on wood or coal or manure fires inside their homes. They inhale the smoke, it turns them black, they get sick; WHO says that a million and a half people die each year from respiratory diseases—bronchitis, asthma, lung cancer—caused by these fires; women, mostly, and very young children.[12]

The peasant farmers of Nyatanasoa—farmers in the entire Marovoay region—live off their tiny rice farms, which they complement with a little cassava, and sometimes, as day laborers on other people's land.

"When we harvest the rice, we have to sell a lot of it to buy salt, sugar, oil, soap. And we have to keep some for seed. Then it doesn't last, and when December or January comes, it's gone, we have to buy in the market," said Soló, a fifty-one-year-old farmer.

Soló and his wife, Blondine, had four acres of rice and three zebus. Every acre yielded almost two tons with the husk, but when they peeled it, they were left with just over a ton. Soló and Blondine don't know that the average yield of an acre of rice in China or Vietnam is six or seven tons.

"Wouldn't it be better for you to keep all the rice so you don't have to buy any later?"

"Of course, but if we keep all of it we won't have any money to buy anything. We keep half, to eat and sow, and we sell the rest."

"But after the *soudure* you have to buy."

"Yup. And they charge you a lot more."

"That's what I'm saying, wouldn't it be better to keep all of it?"

"Don't you understand? We can't keep all of it, we need that money to buy things. To live, to be able to eat."

Soló explained what it was like to spend all day with his feet in the water, the mud of the rice paddies. Then he showed me his feet, like an old tortoise's neck, skin that was no longer skin but rather a map of wrinkles. Soló told me that sometimes they didn't have any food, they'd spend a day or two without eating, but he'd never experienced real hunger, what they call starvation.

"What is it to go hungry?

"I don't know, to not eat anything."

Soló was wearing blue jeans cut off at the knee and a clean but torn white shirt. Blondine was wrapped in a lilac-colored cloth. They were sitting in front of the door to their house: tamped-down earth, adobe walls painted pink, a large number of children coming and going and playing around us.

"Are they all your children?"

"No . . . nieces, nephews, neighbors. We had only two children. We had a twelve-year-old girl and a six-year-old boy who lived with us but last month they went to live with their ancestors." Soló said. Tatá, my interpreter, explained to go live with your ancestors meant to die.

"Fidy wasn't well, he looked very skinny. We gave him all the rice we could, but he didn't get any better, he was tired, didn't want to do anything," Soló explained, and one day they heard a man on the radio say that if child was like that, you should take him to the hospital. They went all the way to Antanambazaha on an oxcart; poor Fidy almost couldn't talk. He was in the hospital for two days and died the third.

Blondine said that sometimes she thought it was the hospital's fault; they told them the child was malnourished and that's why he couldn't be cured of his disease—a word she couldn't remember—but she didn't believe them. Fidy ate his rice every day, he almost always ate his rice. Soló had two or three very crooked teeth and looked at her, wanting her to keep quiet. But Blondine continued: "I think they killed him."

"Why would they want to kill him?"

"I don't know. If I knew things like that, I wouldn't be so poor."

Soló and Blondine borrowed money to buy the zebu they had to kill at the funeral, but they couldn't bury him here.

"We've lived here for fifty years, and before that my father and my grandfather lived here, but this isn't our land. Our land is in the south, pretty far away, that's the land of our ancestors, so we went to bury him there, in our land. That was also very expensive."

"Did you bury him there because you wanted to or because they wouldn't let you bury him here?"

Soló looked at me and smiled; suddenly he was very busy rolling his cigarette with tobacco from a little blue plastic bag and paper from an old notebook, thick sheets of paper with writing on them that he cut carefully, delicately. Then he said it was the Sakalavas, that the Sakalavas always tell them that they are still foreigners. And now the white people protect them, with their farms they prevent the zebus of the Sakalavas from ruining their farms, but he knows how white people are. They'll end up with everything and he'll end up being even more of a foreigner than ever; hopefully, by then, he'll be resting with his ancestors, in his own land.

"Do you think the company will keep our land?" he asked me, hoping I'd say no, no way. I couldn't.

For centuries, the Sakalavas were the owners of this land, herdsmen who took their zebus from there to here in search of the best pasture; they controlled vast tracts of territory, and were known as a violent, domineering, ruthless people.

And almost all the farmers in the Marovoay region were "foreigners," even though most of them had arrived two or three generations before and obtained permission from the Sakalavas to farm if they didn't interfere with their herds, and, as long as they tolerated those herds' frequent incursions into their rice fields, which they would trample and eat. These were the conditions the owners imposed.

That's why the owners of Fuelstock thought that their best strategy would be to ally themselves with the farmers against the herdsmen. So, they planted their fields and set up their fences between the pastures most used by the Sakalavas and the farms of the "foreigners." It was, or at first it seemed like, a good way to win the good will of the farmers; it was also the best way to set off hostilities with the Sakalavas.

"Do you think the farmers are happy you are here?"

"That's difficult to say. I don't know, but they say that all that money we give the municipality in taxes never ends up in their coffers, though we have all the receipts signed by the mayor. And, of course, there are people who get angry because they say that Madagascar shouldn't give its land to the *vazaha*, the white people. But those who are working with us, I think they're happy we're here," replied Nambena; he's an agronomist with Fuelstock.

"But they complain that you pay them very little."

"Well, they always complain. The fact is there was a lot of available land and now we are starting to use it."

"Why was there so much available land?"

"That's a good question; because it was a livestock region, the herdsmen used it for the zebus, so they didn't plant anything."

"But they were using it."

"In a very primitive way, very irrational."

The conflict exploded when the company began to plant their fields. The Sakalava chief showed up and told them that this was their land, that they had no right to it; they said that this was their land, that they had full rights to it. Herein a confrontation between two concepts of land ownership: the papers the Madagascar state had given Fuelstock against the tradition of centuries of use. The negotiations were tense, and they still are.

"The herdsmen are always going to be against us."

"Why?"

"Because they think the land is theirs, they're used to letting their animals graze there, they burn the grass so that it grows again and they let their animals be there, that's all they do. Those herdsmen don't know how to use land."

5

Outside of Nyatanasoa the trail widens and turns into a cart road. Several carts pass by on their way to market, each pulled by two zebus with a long yoke, the driver wielding a mean whip. Suddenly, a racket, galloping: two carts at full speed, pretending to race; dust and a stampede, then nothing. I spoke with Norbert, the "president" of the Fokontany, the village of Besonjo, a couple miles from Nyatanasoa.

"When the company *vazahas* first arrived, they told us that they were going to improve everything about the way we live. Everything. They told us that once they started farming here we'd no longer have problems with the herdsmen because they were going to put their fields between us and them so that their zebus couldn't get in."

"Did they do that?"

"No. Well, more or less. They took over that part, but sometimes the zebus come anyway. Other times they don't."

Norbest added, skeptically, "I don't think we've gained anything in the end."

Besonjo is very similar to Nyatanasoa, except that at the entrance there are about a dozen blackened houses—burned. Norbert was elected four years ago when a man arrived from the capital and said that they had to elect a village president, that they would vote. That same day three candidates ran and Norbert won by a landslide

"Why did they elect you?"

"Because they didn't know me so well," he said and laughed, and then he worried I didn't understand his sense of humor: "Because they like me, my neighbors like me."

"Do you like to be president?"

"I used to like it, I used to like it a lot, but not anymore. Between the attack last year and how behind the company is with their payments, I've got a lot of problems. And I have to do a lot, lots of bureaucracy, and nobody pays me anything, and I don't get the things I should be getting. And the company doesn't pay salaries when they should, and they didn't do much of what they promised, and everything's just the same. A few months ago they got so angry that a bunch of workers with machetes gathered in front of the company house to demand their money. Those poor employees, they got scared, thought they were going to kill them."

"Were they going to kill them?"

"I don't think so. But you should have seen how quickly they paid us that day," he said, and laughed again. Norbert was almost sixty; he was wearing a T-shirt from a music festival that took place long ago and far away, and he had very black hair and an easygoing smile. His grandfather arrived here one hundred years ago, his father was born eighty years ago, but this land was still not his land. It was not the land where he buried his dead because it was not the land where his dead were buried. I asked him if one day it would become his land, but he didn't understand the question.

"My land is in the south, that's where my ancestors are."

"Sometimes they have to bury relatives here because they don't have the money to take them to their land, but as soon as they can, they dig them up and take them there, and only then is he really dead and reunited with his ancestors," his wife, Marceline, looked at him and nodded, repeating his words. She worked for Fuelstock growing bell peppers, and the president said that was why they accused him of having sold out to the *vazaha*.

He said that if she could, she'd quit in a second. She worked long hours and they paid her miserable wages, but they needed that money

Besonjo seemed to be an oasis of tranquility, so I asked him about the burned houses at the entrance. I asked two or three times, and finally Norbert told me, "That was the attack."

"The attack?"

"Yes, the attack. I thought you came here because of that."

A few months before, seven or eight men attacked the village. It was a Monday afternoon. They appeared out of nowhere, shouting, blowing whistles, and pounding drums, banging together sticks and machetes. One had a rifle, and they all started shouting and running toward Norbert's house. Marceline saw them coming from the neighbor's house.

"They started shooting at the door, opened it, and shouted that they wanted my husband. My husband wasn't here, luckily. Then they entered and took things out of the house, took his rifle, the paperwork for registering the land, the official seals; they were shouting and breaking everything. I came running out and shouting that they were bandits, and the people in the village started running into the fields."

President Norbert, who was just then arriving, also ran away and hid beyond the trees. The attackers went to look for the village's vice president, but couldn't find him either. So, they ran toward the houses more to the east—fifteen or twenty huts belonging to new settlers, company workers—and set them on fire. Burning down houses seemed to be a Malagasy tradition. In 1972 they burned down the city government buildings in Antananarivo, in 1976 the palace of the prime minister, in 1995 the old palace of the queen, the most famous building on the island.

"They didn't kill anybody?"

"No, they couldn't get anybody because we all fled."

"Could you have defended yourselves?"

"They caught us off guard, we didn't know what was going on, we were afraid, and we ran."

"Who were they?"

"I don't know, we don't know."

He hesitated. He said he didn't know to say he knew, but he didn't know if he wanted to say it or not—and he gave me a very strange look. I insisted; he told me that, based on what they said, it seemed they were from around here, they knew the village, they knew the names of the people.

"Some say the Sakalavas sent them. But I don't know, how could I know."

6

"Life was better before. There used to be respect. Now there's nothing, just fighting."

"What changed?"

"There used to be respect. Our neighbors knew that we let them live on this land, and they respected us, they treated us properly. But since the company arrived, everything's been lost . . ."

I expected something different. I was surprised to see that Mangadé, the Sakalava village, was as poor as the others and even smaller: a dozen very precarious huts, an old man and another who was almost, but not quite as old. The old man's name was Adaniangy, and he is the son of the village's chief. He was barefoot, his nails like Neolithic carvings. The other man was his cousin, Gérard. He never let go of his machete; with it he drew in the dirt, collected twigs, cut leaves, sharpened a branch. "The company *vazahas* were wrong; they thought that to come here all they had to do was talk to the farmers in the villages below. They are the foreigners, we let them live here but they're the foreigners. They should have talked to us, and they didn't. They were wrong. Then they said they were sorry, but they were wrong."

"They think you sent the bandits to burn down Besonjo."

"Well, that's what some say, but maybe they say that because they envy us, who knows. Who knows what's true and what isn't. There's been a lot of resentment here, a lot of confrontations since the company came and changed things. It's not like before, when we lived peacefully with our zebus, nobody bothered us, we were at peace."

"Are you afraid the company will keep all the land?"

"Yes, we're afraid. The company has already taken over part of our land, we have less and less land to graze our zebus."

"What can you do to stop them?"

"We asked the governor, everybody; sometimes they do something, sometimes they don't. The company tells them what to do and what not to do. They don't have to ask for our permission, and we're the real owners of these lands. Our dead are buried here. If this carries on, they're going to leave us without the two most important things on this earth: the ancestors below and the zebus above."

We were sitting on the dirt in the shade of a fairly small tree; the cousins were leaning against the trunk. Around us, there were the four or five huts that made up the family compound. The ducks, a rooster, a dog with three legs also sat nearby. A little ways away, a couple of cows. The children didn't approach; they watched us from a distance. The women stayed farther away, under a palm roof eave.

"The farmers don't care because it's not the land of their ancestors. That's why they don't care."

"But they live off that land, they eat off that land."

"Yes, of course. But it's not the same."

Adaniangy, or rather the centenarian father of Adaniangy, had about four hundred zebus. An average zebu costs eight hundred thousand *ariary*, or four hundred dollars. A nicely fattened castrated one can cost twice that much. Adaniangy's father, the family, had hundreds of thousands of dollars in zebus, but this was a very different concept of wealth. Anybody who looked at them could see that they were poor; they knew they were rich—and their neighbors knew it too. It was a kind of wealth that did not translate into what it usually translates into in our countries. It was not about objects, it did not mean a lifestyle, there was nothing at all like what we call luxury or comfort; it was prestige, power, security.

"So, you are rich," I said, and they both laughed.

"It's just that this is our land, we've spent generations and generations here. That's why our ancestors are here, in their stone tombs. And that's why the chief of the village is my father, and then it will be me, and then it will be another one of us," Adaniangy said. He told me he wanted to show me the tomb of his parents, his ancestors; because I saw these houses where they lived and they looked to me—he said, they looked to me—poor, but the tombs were bigger, more beautiful, I should see them.

"Really, you make the tombs better than the houses?"

"Yes, of course," he replied, not quite understanding my question. He looked at me and explained, "That's the way it is, the way it has to be. Where do you think you'll spend more time?"

Zebus are the best form of savings in this society. They don't raise them to sell them and for others to consume. They raise them as backup for when there's no choice: three or four heads a year if there's a problem, if they don't have rice, if they have to celebrate something. They don't raise animals for sale; they are, more than anything, a form of accumulation. And like all kinds of accumulation, they don't do much good for anybody else.

"What's good about having zebus?"

"Zebus are very important. When a relative is born and circumcised, we kill a zebu; when a relative gets married, we kill a zebu; when a relative dies, and we bury him, we kill a zebu. They're also good for trampling the rice fields before planting the seed, because if you have to do it with feet it's a lot of work. And if something happens, if there's some need, we can sell a zebu and solve the problem. If we want a rice field, we can buy it because we have zebus. It's our wealth, our savings."

"Do you often eat zebu meat?"

"Yes, on New Year's, at circumcisions, funerals, parties."

"What do you eat every day?"

"Rice. And once in a while fish from the river."

"Why don't you eat more zebus?"

"We can't kill them because they're too big. There would be too much meat, and we'd have to throw it out. Our ancestors would be angry."

Owners of four hundred head of cattle told me that they ate meat only once in a while; I asked myself again what it be like if we all—all humans, I mean, even in wealthy societies—ate like that, like before: meat on important occasions; if the era of meat—of meat several times a week—would have been a brief and very localized interval in the history of humanity.

Two centuries ago only the richest people in the richest countries ate meat frequently; now, only the inhabitants of the richest countries. If the population continues to grow, if there is no way to produce animal protein using fewer resources, it's probable that in a few decades, meat will once again become the luxury article it almost always was.

"Do you think your children, your grandchildren, will be able to continue to raise zebus?"

"Who knows. If the company takes over everything there won't be any place left to graze them. And then the zebus will die."

"And what will you do?"

"We'll be poor. We don't know how to live without the zebus. We will be poor, and we will be hungry."

7

In principle, when one talks about land grabs, one is always talking about the same actors: China, South Korea, and Saudi Arabia and the surrounding emirates. China, which used to supply its own grain, became the world's largest importer of soy and corn for their pigs. When its inhabitants started to really, seriously eat, the land was depleted and they could no longer guarantee food for everybody. Korea is a small, mountainous country which experienced hunger for centuries. It accumulated wealth with cutting-edge industry and its arable land taken more and more by urban development; it needed to import 70 percent of food supply. They fear price increases or blockades will leave them with nothing on their plates in the future. Saudi Arabia, extremely rich with oil, spent fortunes drilling to irrigate its deserts and transform them into orchards and farms. At the turn of the century, it managed to produce the grain their twenty-six million inhabitants needed, and even more for export, but its aquifers began to deplete along with their agriculture and water supply. So its government decided to stop producing wheat.

When it comes to land grabs, China, Korea, Saudi Arabia, and its neighbors are the usual suspects, however, new players are entering the game.

In 2010, a US journalist working for *Rolling Stone* magazine, McKenzie Funk, accompanied a fat, foul-mouthed US capitalist on a trip to Yuba (not yet the capital of South Sudan) to hear about his attempts to acquire two and a half million acres with the help of a Sudanese general of Nuer extraction, Paulino Matip. It is estimated that more than four million acres of South Sudan are occupied by or promised to foreigners. The story Funk told was charming: Philip Heilberg, former partner of AIG explained to him that Africa "is like one big mafia and I'm like the mafia head." And "I want a country that's weaker. There's a cost to dealing with strong countries: resource nationalism. People forget that." Funk described the process of grabbing land: "All are betting that population growth and climate change—with its accompanying droughts and desertification and flooding—will soon make food as valuable as oil. On a planet of melting glaciers, overcrowded cities and millions of climate refugees, those who control the food will control the world . . . Rising powers like China, India, and South Korea have snapped up millions of acres from Cameroon to Kazakhstan, competing against oil-rich states like Saudi Arabia and Kuwait, and Wall Street banks like Goldman Sachs and Morgan Stanley."[13] The sentence, perhaps inadvertent, is a full-fledged declaration: those who have the land are China, India, or Saudi Arabia; and, instead of the United States, there's also Wall Street and a few banks.

According to a specialist at GRAIN, an international nonprofit that has become quite expert on the issue of land grabs, the companies that control the largest amount of foreign land are in Great Britain and the United States.

Then come public and private companies in China, Saudi Arabia, France, Italy, India, Korea, Singapore, and South Africa.

In general, those who obtain these lands are people who don't need them. They are people who have enough money to live perfectly at ease as they are, but devote their lives to earning more money because without doing so they would lose power.

One example of this is a London-based fund that controls most African land called Emergent. It is directed by an ex-executive of Goldman Sachs and another of J.P. Morgan. In an interview with Reuters, its CEO, David Murrin, refused to say how much money they controlled, but that it was "the largest agricultural fund in Africa."[14] Available financial information says they have, at their disposal, $3 to $4 billion to carry out profitable business with "the volatility of the geopolitical situation," and that their annual performance should be around 25 percent. On their impressive web page, they grandiloquently proclaim their system for making fortunes.

The Oakland Institute in California, says that "corporations, banks, and nation-states eager to guarantee their own future food security have been looking at and obtaining large tracts of foreign land for production or speculation. More and more, investors consider arable land to be a safe and profitable place to put their capital."[15]

Why do they think it is a safe investment?

They don't always believe it. As Lester Brown wrote in *Foreign Policy*: "Foreign investors producing food in a country full of hungry people face another political question of how to get the grain out. Will villagers permit trucks laden with grain headed for port cities to proceed when they themselves may be on the verge of starvation? The potential for political instability in countries where villagers have lost their land and their livelihoods is high. Conflicts could easily develop between investor and host countries."[16]

There is a certain kind of logic at play here. Although the saying goes you shouldn't count money in front of the poor, there isn't one that says it's not okay to show hungry people that you are taking away their food.

The surprising fact is that, in general, owners do not need to use violence to prevent somebody who really needs something and sees it there in front of their noses from simply taking it.

One hundred and fifty years ago, one of Madagascar's main resources was providing slaves to the neighboring islands of Comoros and Réunion. Few businesses have operated so constantly throughout history. There is no culture that hasn't at some moment traded merchandise that is so accessible. To keep it going, one needed only a little strength and a lot of ideology: the general conviction that people who fulfilled certain requirements—lost a war, didn't pay debts, stole a piece of bread, was born to a slave mother—could belong to another person. One of the most extraordinary changes brought by modernity is the abolition of that idea; what is now so abhorrent seemed so normal two centuries ago. This should be a warning, an invitation to entertain systematic doubt: how many of the mechanisms that now seem indisputable will appear horrific and intolerable in a certain amount of time?

Or, as Terry Eagleton says, "After all, if you do not resist the apparently inevitable, you will never know how inevitable the inevitable was."[17]

We no longer think it reasonable for a man who fulfills certain requirements to belong to another man. But we do believe that if a man fulfills certain requirements—basically, to not possess enough assets— it's acceptable for him to work for others who will profit from his labor. Who knows if in a hundred or two hundred years, millions will consider that as strange and repugnant as owning slaves?

Maybe not, but it's worth thinking about.

As said previously, a successful part of the US story is the "it's not us, it's them, they are the bad ones" mentality. Propaganda functions without cracks and when one thinks about land appropriation, one thinks mostly about China.

China is one of the key points of world hunger. On one hand, no country has managed to reduce the number of hungry citizens in the last few decades like China. On the other, one out of every six malnourished people in the world is Chinese: more than 150 million Chinese don't have enough to eat. It continues to be, after India, the country with the hungriest population in the world.

It is either a deficit or an injustice that this book does not talk more about China, but I don't know how to work in China. I had to, a couple of times; each time I ended up with the sensation that the barriers erected by the authorities had managed to keep me away from what I was trying to tell. Or, even worse: I ended up telling what a couple of bureaucrats had cobbled together for my consumption. Though, every once in a while, something leaked through.

Five or six years ago I went there to write a story for a publication of the United Nations Population Fund (UNFPA) about a young Chinese who had immigrated from the countryside to the city. The official guide took me to a factory where a dozen and a half young workers repeated one after the other the same rose-tinted tale, carefully memorized. But that night, due to a momentary lapse by my guide, I crossed paths with Bing.

"I admire President Mao more and more," Bing told me as soon as we sat down to drink a beer.

I asked him why.

"I admire him for two reasons: his authority, because he was a man who knew how to use power, to make decisions, and because he knew how to fight, how to wage war. In my spare time I always study the great wars waged by President Mao and the others to learn how to command my workers, to learn what to do when I start my own company. I still have a lot to learn from President Mao."

At that time, Bing was twenty-six years old and worked in a karaoke club in Tianjin, a port city seventy-five miles north of Beijing with ten million inhabitants. The Oriental Pearl was a glitzy monster with many floors and a hundred or so rooms where customers drank, sang, and relaxed with few restrictions. He had arrived from his province when he was eighteen to study management. He completed his studies and tried to open a business, failed, then got a job as a waiter. Intelligent and persevering, he rose in the ranks and finally became lobby manager with several employees under him. Bing earned about five hundred dollars a month, and he saved two-thirds of it. He told me he had about one hundred thousand yuan—thirteen thousand dollars—invested in stocks, ready for when he decided to start his own business. Bing wanted to be like his boss, who had started with nothing and was now rich and successful.

"The city is where things happen. The city is the future, it's where everything is possible." He told me.

Bing was born in Fuping, in Hebei province, but he was a little over a year old when his parents decided to leave their native village and try their luck in Zalantun, in Inner Mongolia. His parents were very poor and they hoped that there, in that remote region, they could prosper. In Mongolia, Bing's parents herded sheep at first; then they raised chickens.

Bing was one of the last Chinese with siblings. He was born in 1980, just before China launched its one-child policy, which turned it into a country of only children. Bing had three sisters; the oldest, fifteen years his senior, took care of him like a mother when his mother went out to work in the fields with his father.

The family economy depended on the weather. If it was favorable and the harvest or the animals did well, the family ate; if not, they went hungry. Bing still remembered that time, when he was nine or ten, when he stole a sweet from a classmate, because he never had money for sweets. They caught him and chased him. At home he had other privileges.

"At home they gave me everything they could. I was the only boy and the youngest."

In traditional Chinese families, mother, father, and sisters will go hungry so that the son doesn't.

"Your sisters didn't hate you for that?"

"No, they respected the tradition, and they always loved me."

I couldn't grasp the image of women fasting happily, or at least with resignation, as a result of the empire of ideology. It was the first time that I had come across gender hunger, which is rarely discussed in the literature.

China has achieved an extraordinary reduction in the number of hungry people, which in itself, has become a threat to everybody else. If development continues at its current rate, China will control 70 percent of the world production of wheat and 75 percent of the world production of meat by 2030. China already imports a fourth of the soy grown in the world to feed its five hundred million pigs and its five billion chickens. Here, meat rules.

China is also the world's largest consumer of grain, meat, rubber, steel, coal, copper, nickel, and many other minerals. Only in oil do the 350 million people in the United States continue to consume more than the 1.4 billion Chinese.

But China's food needs are running riot. China needs to feed 20 percent of the world's population with 8 percent of the arable land on the planet, which is shrinking. With the growth of industry and the intensive farming techniques being used, China loses millions of acres of farmland every year and an incalculable amount of water.

The Chinese plan ahead. Knowing that their farmland is becoming more and more scarce, they have decided to use it to intensively grow the most profitable crops. For example: tomatoes. China never used to grow tomatoes; in 2007 it became the first and second exporter of tomatoes in the world, with five million tons a year. Chinese tomatoes are sold everywhere except China. The Chinese barely eat tomatoes, around a pound per year against fifty pounds in the United States. They sell their tomatoes to buy the grain that they are growing less and less. In 1995 grain was grown on three-quarters of their farmland; it has since fallen down to two-thirds, and the proportion continues to drop.

The state investment company, China Investment Corporation, is one of the largest investment funds on the planet, with more than $350 billion in capital to move around the world. Much of this money is US debt.

China has become the banker—the creditor of the United States and the debt is growing due to US consumption of Chinese exports. The rise of China is one more proof of the foolishness of thinking that historical processes repeat themselves, that the equation "more market equals more representative democracy" is only one of many possible scenarios. In the seventies, US strategy—Kissinger and Co.—assumed that economic development would convert the great yellow peril into an ally; that the growth of capitalist industry and markets would put an end to Communist rule and that the process would integrate the Chinese into the global system controlled by the United States and its corporations. That's why they decided to help it happen. What happened afterward surprised them, even though capitalism with a single party, after all, isn't that new. Chinese development was supposed to be complementary and subordinate; instead, it is competitive and defiant.

And it has started its own capitalistic invasion of America. In May 2013, for example, Shuanghui International (now known as WH Group), one of the largest Chinese meat factories, bought Smithfield Foods, one of the oldest producers of pork in the United States, for $4.7 billion. In protest, questions about food safety practices of Chinese food manufacturers have been raised, with accusations that the Chinese do not clean their pigs as well as Americans do. Only when inspectors confirm that Shuangui is up to code, can the USDA breathe a sigh of relief. After all a "pig grab" is better than a "land grab."

Marvelous difference between two words that should mean more or less the same: *food safety* means that the food you eat causes you no health problems; *food security* means that you eat enough food so as not to have health problems.

With an ever-growing note, the Chinese have more money than they will need in a long time. In 2001, when they joined the World Trade Organization (WTO), they announced an economic strategy they called *Zou chuqu*—translated as "going out" or "swarming out"—which basically consists of making investments that will improve their relationships with countries that produce raw materials in order to guarantee supply.

Then they set out to occupy—buy, obtain, take over—everything they could, wherever they could.

In Africa, it seems that the Chinese can claim whatever land they want, and of course, many African leaders want them to do so. "The twenty-first century is the century for China to lead the world. And when you are leading the world, we want to be close behind you. When you are going to the moon, we don't want to be left behind," said then president of Nigeria, Olusegun Obansanjo during the Chinese president's famous tour of Africa in 2006.[18] For many African leaders, Chinese investments are a lifeline, and they encourage competition. Other countries look at them with concern and attempt to match them, and African governments enjoy a certain amount of relief from their dependence on Western countries, the IMF, and the World Bank. China, on the other hand, has never been a colonial power and maintains its "Third World" discourse of solidarity and alliance with the old colonies of others.

Moreover, the Chinese offer more complex package deals. Instead of the typical Western investment that's limited to its own profit—oil fields, lumber towns, mines—China builds roads, railways, ports, which also serve to carry the raw materials they extract and leave behind debts of gratitude and millions.

And, to sweeten the deals, the Chinese show no moral political-economic qualms; their money doesn't require any guarantees of democracy or human rights nor does it impose any precise economic models. That afternoon, standing with the president of Nigeria, Hu Jintao solemnly declared that "China steadfastly supports the wish of the African countries to safeguard their independence and sovereignty and choose their roads of development according to their national conditions."[19] The Chinese suffered those kinds of impositions for too long to fall into the mistake of trying to impose them. They have no model to sell.

There is a lot of talk about the Chinese presence in Africa. The fact that it's new makes it more visible; that it is planned by a centralized state, makes it more impressive. Western capitalist interventions are many but distinct: one establishment here, fourteen there, three somewhere else. The Chinese ones, on the other hand, are coordinated.

(In Europe and the United States, the central state exists so that large companies can keep being large companies; in China, somehow, the large companies exist so that the central state can continue being the central state.)

Africa is a Chinese objective, as is the rest of the world. China is already the second largest economy in the world, poised to become the first. Their African investments have increased, but they have still not reached even 10 percent of foreign investment in Africa. Trade between the big country and the continent has increased fortyfold over the past two decades but continues to lag far behind Europe.[20] For now, they are mostly interested in oil: more than half the trade involves importing it. Another quarter involves minerals; agricultural products do not account for even 15 percent of African exports to China.

For now, as far as land grabbing, they have preferred Southeast Asia. Which doesn't mean China isn't occupying more space, taking over land, mining operations, and other kinds of exploitation. For now, its capacity to extract raw materials remains much less than those—the usual suspects previously mentioned—who present China as the great new danger.

A very detailed report from GRAIN issued in February 2012 presents a census of all land being used to produce agrofuel in the entire Other World. In Africa, they specify appropriations of 18.5 million acres; out of this total, says the report, Chinese companies have 550,000 acres. The majority of the land is in European hands.

Here in Madagascar, the Chinese presence is never completely clear. Mamy, the Malagsy Parisian activist, told me about her efforts to understand it: "Many people tell me that there's a rich rice-growing area between Taná and Majunga that's full of Chinese, who must be investing in something there."

And a peasant activist told her that women in the area have suffered abuse at the hands of their new Chinese bosses, and government officials from that region are often invited to China, supposedly for courses and conferences. Someone she knows who works in the Ministry of Economy told them that there are a series of agreements between the government and a Chinese holding company for the use of farmlands, but they don't quite know what they are. And, the Chinese are very interested in Madagascar because in other African countries they have to create rice farms that never existed, and on the island, they've been growing rice for centuries.

"It's just that all of it is so opaque, so difficult to find out about. The territory is huge, there are regions with very little population, only the peasants in each place know what is happening in their area . . ." Mamy explained, and I felt moved by the efforts of these exiles to follow the paths, interpret the hidden meanings, discover the movements that the government of their country wants, and manages, to keep confused, secret.

Other governments also play a role. The Japanese and the Brazilian governments, for example, are behind the push for the next big scandal, or land appropriation, in Africa.

ProSavana is a program organized by Mozambique, Brazil, and Japan to farm approximately twenty-five million acres in the north of Mozambique. The region, called Corredor de Nacala, or the Nacala Development Corridor, includes three province: Nampula, Niassa, and Zambezia.

The plan counts on Brazilian companies growing soy, corn, sunflower, and other grains on this land for export principally to Japan. They would lease land from the Mozambique government at forty cents per acre per year; the companies would also receive large tax exemptions. A big portion of the initial investment would come out of the "Nacala Fund," consisting of public and private money from Japan and Brazil. Also, public money from Japan would pay for the roads and railroads and ports they plan to build in Nacala to export their products.

According to local organizations that are opposing the plan, some Mozambicans are poised to take advantage of ProSavana. There are rumors, for example, about a national company controlled by the president's family that set up a joint venture company with the richest family in Portugal and one of the largest Brazilian agricultural companies to buy and farm land in the region.

It is difficult to find any information about the four million peasants who live there that will be affected.

The use of land in the Other World to produce food and agrofuels or for speculation by rich countries is one of those phenomena we usually don't look at. But anybody who saves money in Europe or the United States might "own" an acre of Ethiopian or Cambodian land; it is not improbable that their bank or pension fund has invested in this prosperous business, which promises a 25 percent annual return.

Again: those who are buying African land are, in many cases, US and European pension funds: men and women who never hurt a fly, people of good faith who worked all their lives and saved a little every month so as not to suffer in their old age; people who, if they saw on television a skinny Malagasy rancher going hungry because some white people threw him off his land so they could grow Jatropha, would say, poor man what an injustice. Because everything is part of everything, and everything is political, and therein the beauty of the system: you don't have to do anything horrible to benefit from others' suffering.

8

The metallic sound in the left wheel, the banging of poorly joined wood, the oxen's snorts, the oxen's farts, the shouting and joshing and whipping by the oxcart driver, a boy, the slapping of the reins against the oxen's backs: a world of sounds I'd never met before.

On the road, the boy and his chunky friend talk and talk, hours of talking. Tatá, my interpreter, tells me that they are talking about the farms we pass, whose rice field is whose, how it's farmed, whose zebus are those skinny ones over there, why did they burn that parcel, why did so-and-so plant cassava right there. Night is falling and now they sound strange, their voices more excited. Tatá whispers to me that they are scared, wondering why they agreed to take me, afraid I'll kidnap them because sometimes white men kidnap a man, a woman, a child, and they disappear forever.

"What?"

"Yeah, everybody here knows that white people sometimes take somebody for their organs, to sacrifice him. Last year in Nyatanasoa, Fuelstock had to sacrifice somebody. Or several people, nobody knows. You know, every time you start to farm some land, you have to kill a zebu to make sure that you get a good harvest. Well, the company did that when they started, two years ago, but things didn't go well for them; so they sacrificed another zebu, hoping that would help, but it didn't, not very much. And that's when they decided to sacrifice people, which is much more powerful."

"How did they do it? Secretly?"

Secretly, Tatá told me, of course, and I asked him how he knows.

Tatá tended to speak softly, but now he was whispering: "Everything is known here. They're talking about that, they're very frightened."

Now it's my turn to be frightened. I tell him so: "I hope they don't take it too seriously and do something preemptively."

"Don't worry," Tatá replied. Then he added, "They think you have some kind of special power that makes you invincible. They just hope you don't want to eat them, that you're really here for the reasons you say you are."

(Days later, in Paris, Mamy would explain to me that when the first Christian missionaries arrived on the island, they talked about "conquering the hearts of the Malagasy," and this declaration of supposed Christian love was used by the local priests to convince their people that those men would steal, along with everything else, their insides. And that since then the idea persists that white people steal organs and Malagasy women threaten their badly behaved children with sending them to the whites for them to take out a kidney or some other part. A clash of cultures. Or, confusion that assists the plunder.)

I was scared; it was a long way. I just hoped that the illusion of my power survived till we got there, that one myth would protect me from another.

Moments when I ask myself what the hell am I doing so far from home: why, what for? Recently I reassure myself with the supposed utility of what's different: knowing what's different allows you to avoid the trap of what's "natural." Someone who doesn't know anything different thinks that what she sees is because it has to be that way, because it's natural, because there is no other way for it to be. She might think, for example, that it is logical that a car about to run you over will stop; that isn't natural but rather the result of centuries of trial and error, what we usually call culture.

Or that thinking that what is cultural—transitory—is *natural, which* is the worst trap: to resign oneself to not thinking of other options. So, these ridiculous trips—and even the stories they tell—are a way of saying that everything can change because everything always changes.

Night was falling, the light made you want to cry. There are moments that should be unforgettable.

And the noise was a rustling that kept increasing, getting closer: like a hidden trembling, a slow explosion that never ended. Tatá looked at me

and told me not to worry; it was the sound of a burning field. A few minutes later we saw it in the half-light of the coming night, flames already
waning over the black ground.

"If we don't do it, we won't have enough food," explained the boy,
looking at me as if it were my fault.

"Here we burn about one hundred thousand acres a year."

Engineers would later tell me the official numbers, though they
thought they were too low.

"It has to be done, it's necessary, but you have to know how to do it.
When you burn a slope, for example, the first rains carry away the top
soil and then you can't grow anything. Then you have to get a different
field, and all you did was destroy a forest."

The kid shouted a lot, whipped the oxen's backs. He said we had to
arrive before it got completely dark, night was when the bandits came
out. There were a lot of them, and they were very dangerous.

"Especially for the *vazahas*," he said, and smiled, as if enjoying it.

"Don't they get arrested?"

"Who'd arrest them?"

"I don't know, the police."

The kid laughed and told his partner what I was saying so he could
laugh too. Later, in Taná, somebody would tell me that the country was
full of small runways where airplanes filled with who knows what came
and went, he said, bringing his hand to his nose to tell me without telling
me: drugs. Another said there was no government in Madagascar. Or
that there was one, and its business was to not control certain things.

They would also tell me that there were fewer zebus than there were ten
years ago because "wild exports" increased. Thousands and thousands of
zebus were stolen, and instead of unloading them on the internal market,
they shipped them out of the country with the full complicity of officials,
who were probably running the whole operation. Many of them went
first to the Comoros Islands, which had become, without having a single
cow, an important exporter of zebu meat to Europe.

And because of this absence of an effective state, ever more radical
solutions cropped up. Local chiefs, for example, armed militias to stop
the stealing, especially of zebus; in some regions, these militias had
established some semblance of safety and had the support of the population, which participated in the judgments of the thieves. Some had
been condemned to death in those peoples' courts, and executed. And in
those regions, life was now much more peaceful.

More whipping, shouting, groaning of the oxen. It was night; the child
driver said that we were almost there:

"Almost. Just a little ways to go."

The following day we can't find any oxen. Tatá and I return to Nyata-nasoa on foot: three hours of walking, sweating, along a path between rice fields. I listen to Mozart's "Turkish March" on my iPhone—there are mornings when my iPhone is my homeland—and I can't avoid the stupid question of the day: what would have become of Mozart if he'd been born in these fields. Perhaps his grandchildren would remember that their grandfather played the drums beautifully, or maybe not. How many Mozarts, or even how many Maradonas, Pasteurs, or Stendhals lost in the folds of the Other World, in the illiteracy of these lands.

Though, who knows, maybe that mania for writing everything down, for making the ephemeral last, is one of the plagues of the West.

The vipers were small, and Tatá said they weren't poisonous. Along the side of the road, a lagoon. Two boys were in a canoe made from a hollowed-out trunk of a tree; one was sitting and holding an oar; the other was standing and fishing with a short spear. He stabbed it into the water; every so often, he speared a tilapia. Tatá told me that he'd heard that here and at another lake a couple miles to the south they might build a park: that there were people pressuring to make a park.

"Haven't you heard about the *green grab*?"

Madagascar is also a paradise for the green grab. There are always new words and for now, most are invented in the United States. They are calling *green grab* what those powerful NGOs and millionaires—Tomkins, Branson, Getty—do when they manage, through lobbying or money, to close off huge extensions of land in order to save plant and animal species, to protect them from the evil effects of peasants who never stop destroying the native flora and fauna with their obstinate need to eat them. I mean: the green grabbers are those who are converting the Other World into parks, who think them up with smug satisfaction from their offices in cities made of glass, asphalt, and steel.

Or, even, those who, in the name of conservation, build very expensive lodges and hotels in the middle of the most exotic places and make a lot of money receiving other men and women who are as conservationist as they are, and every bit as rich.

In Nyatanasoa nothing had changed: the same men, the same children, the same children and women in the square. Only Rina was different. Her face was without dust, her very dark eyes were bloodshot, like she'd been crying. Without her dust, Rina looked younger, more vulnerable—and she was sitting off to one side. I asked nobody in particular, the air, if they were afraid the company would keep their land, and nobody answered.

Finally, Rina came up to me and said, "We don't know. How are we supposed to know?" and the rest laughed nervously. "We don't know what the government wants to do with them. The government put them here, and they'll do what they want."

"But you and your people have the deeds to the land?"

"Yes, we do. Some of us do."

"If you have deeds, the government can't give that land to the company."

They looked at each other and laughed again. Albert took off his Borsalino hat and said that actually they didn't.

"We know the land is ours, we've been here since our grandparents came, but deeds, official deeds . . ."

"If the government gives your land to the company, what can you do?"

"Well, the government told us that the company isn't going to be here forever. They leased the land to them. The important thing is that they don't sell it. As long as it's leased it's still ours."

"How long is it leased for?"

"We don't know. They say for forty-nine years."

"Leased for forty-nine years is the same as sold." Rina said, nervously.

Albert tried to be patient. "No, it's not the same. Sold, it's not ours anymore. Leased, it is. It's only for a certain period of time."

"A period of time, right. Forty-nine years. In forty-nine years, we'll all be dead."

"But my kids might not be, and my grandkids. What matters is that the land doesn't belong to them forever."

"That's what the people in the government say. But we need the land now, to live, to eat."

"Nothing'll happen. We'll ask for some land so we can keep growing our rice and we'll carry on as we have till now," Albert answered, and Rina looked at him as if she couldn't believe what he was saying.

"Don't you people realize that we're not going to have any water. We can't grow rice without water," Rina said, then went quiet.

Later she'd explain: it's true that the company plants the Jatropha on higher ground, where rice doesn't grow, that the Sakalavas used it and they didn't, but they irrigated it with water the rice needs. And soon they were going to need that water and less and less would flow down, and she kept telling everybody but nobody paid any attention, then added, "They just laugh at me. They tell me that the water always reached where it had to reach. I tell them that they want to keep all of it, and they say no, not all of it, it's just a lease for a certain period of time, don't exaggerate. And the water is there, they can't take it away, they tell me. There's no way to explain it to them. It's as if they were under a spell."

(There was a lot of talk about water: they come for the water, we must defend our water, were the battle cries of the day. But nobody is going to take away water in supertankers or liter bottles; that would be expensive, heavy, unproductive. Water is extracted in this way: incorporated into the harvest, the products that need it. That's what taking out the water means—and the soil and the nutrients, and the forests they burn to plant, and the lives of those who live there.)

Rina tells me she is very worried, that she is losing hope.

"What hope?"

"The hope that someone will understand me, that they'll realize that in a few years there won't be a drop of water left for us, we won't be able to plant our rice, we are going to be left without food, we are all going to have to leave."

"Why do you think that?"

"Because it's the truth. I see it, it's not difficult to see it. I can look at what's happening and see it, not like them who are chained to the video room and can't see past their own noses."

The seventy-five thousand acres of Fuelstock in Marovoay are, after all, a relatively small plantation: just a sample.

Days later, in a market in Antananarivo, a woman would tell me that they were unforgivable: they had done something that was unforgiveable.

"They were the lands of our ancestors."

The woman must have been more than sixty years old, with a very wrinkled face and straight hair; she sold, or tried to sell, combs at the exit to the market.

"Can you imagine what our ancestors will do when they realize we have given over our land to the *vazaha*?"

Later, the woman would tell me that she and her husband had seven and a half acres, they grew rice, they always had, their ancestors had also done so before them, but that a few years ago—"I don't know how many," she'd say, "ten, many"—some men from the government had come and told them that the land wasn't theirs and that they had to leave. And her husband had wanted to put up a fight but he got sick and died, and she couldn't do anything, so she had to leave and now, they told her, there were some *vazahas* who were farming it. And she moved to the capital to live with a daughter but they barely managed to eat every day. There was not a single day she didn't cry, remembering her village, her life before, her rice fields.

Millions have gone through the same thing, and it continues.

In Dhaka, Bihar, Bentiu, José León Suárez, even here, it seems that the only things I can describe are those that are obvious: abundant, normal, self-evident. And then I return to the world where I live and again I slip away: how easy it is to live there and ignore all this and how well things go for us.

Mamy thinks that in Madagascar, ten million acres of land has changed hands in the last few years, none of them to Malagasy. She is certain that much of it goes uncounted, she says, and it's also true that among those acres are many farms that still haven't started up or whose status was never finalized.

"The more land that stops being farmed by the Malagasy peasants for their subsistence, the more land that falls into the hands of foreign companies, the more land that is set aside for growing palm or Jatropha— used to make oils or fuel, or even to grow food to be consumed in other countries—the more land that stops feeding the Malagasy people, the more hunger there will be in a country where there is already a lot of hunger."

Mamy takes off her thick glasses and rubs her eyes. The appropriation of African, Asian, and Latin American land, land in the Other World, is the construction of the hunger of the future. The careful, arrogant, violent construction of the hunger of the future.

FINAL THOUGHTS

1

Meanwhile, the world carries on, just as brutal, grotesque, and disgusting as ever. Sometimes I think that all of this is, mostly, just plain ugly. The modes of perception the monstrosities of the people who possess, the shameless waste of what others so desperately need: all revolting. It is no longer a question of justice or ethics but rather aesthetics. I mean, to try to make the world we create a little less horrible. Based on what it's done with itself, humanity should have that chagrin a creator has when they take a step back, examine their work, and see a piece of shit. I know the feeling well.

This is a book about ugliness, the most extreme ugliness I can possibly conceive. This is a book about revulsion, which is what we should have for what we've done, what we should have if we don't have for not having.

In silence, revulsion accumulates.

We are nothing, a mere trifle, a collection of sighs over a short life on a lost rock in a tiny solar system in a galaxy that is the same as thousands and millions of other galaxies. When we realize that—when we inadvertently start to think—the most reasonable response is perhaps to accept our destiny and focus on the small stuff: ourselves, our lives, the little we can choose and accept to have around us. It is one possibility and it appears to be reasonable. But perhaps the best reply to so such smallness is to act the fool and forget about it—and think in the grandest terms our tiny size allows us.

Knowing how useless it can be.

And that, in general, there is nothing more useless than what's useful.

As has been said: there are hundreds of millions of people who do not eat what they need to eat.

Over and over: a few years ago, Ban Ki-moon, general secretary of the United Nations, cited some numbers that were repeated then ignored: less than every four seconds a person dies of starvation, malnutrition, and related diseases. Seventeen every minute, twenty-five thousand every day, more than nine million every year. The equivalent to a holocaust and a half every year.

So what? Turn off the lights and leave? Bury ourselves in that darkness? Declare wars? Declare that those who eat more than their reasonable share are the guilty parties? Declare ourselves the guilty parties? Condemn ourselves? That even sounds reasonable. And then what?

When they should be naming the causes of hunger, governments and experts and smiling politicians and international organizations and foundations belonging to millionaires repeat five or six mantras:

Natural disasters: floods, storms, plagues. And especially droughts: "Drought is one of the most common causes of food shortages in the world," says the web page of the World Food Program.

The environment: overused by abusive agricultural practices, excess of harvests and fertilizers, deforestation, erosion, salinization, and desertification.

Climate change: "exacerbating natural conditions that were already adverse," and will worsen in the coming decades.

Conflict among humans, wars: mass displacements have doubled in the last twenty years and provoke serious food crises due to the difficulty of growing food or pasturing animals, and more directly because some of the sides in the conflicts use the destructions of crops and livestock and markets as a weapon.

Corrupt governments in poor countries: they swallow up most of the aid the good people of the First World offer over and over again.

(The ones with the most chutzpah even talk about financial speculation that made the price of foods shoot up and produced scarcity and revolts.)

And then there is something they call "the poverty trap." WFP's site describes this shallowly: "People living in poverty cannot afford nutritious food for themselves and their families. This makes them weaker and less able to earn the money that would help them escape poverty and hunger. This is not just a day-to-day problem: when children are chronically malnourished, or 'stunted', it can affect their future income, condemning them to a life of poverty and hunger. In developing countries, farmers often cannot afford seeds, so they cannot plant the crops that would provide for their families. They may have to cultivate crops without the tools and fertilizers they need. Others have no land or water or education. In short, the poor are hungry and their hunger traps them in poverty."[1]

In this story—in these official stories—only hunger has causes. Only poverty has effects.

At the same time, all the organizations, scholars, and governments who are interested in the subject agree on one fact: Earth produces enough food to feed all its inhabitants—and even four or five billion more.

The failure of a civilization.

The insistent, brutal, shameless failure of a civilization.

Malnourished, disposable, wasted.

As I was saying: the capitalist machine doesn't know what to do with hundreds of millions of people. They are surplus.

And their exclusion will not decrease, as the World Bank claims, with development. In the current context, technological development leaves more people unemployed, leaves more along the side of the road. Which doesn't necessarily mean new technologies are bad, but it should force us to question the way those in control are using them.

With those same technologies very different things could be achieved; under the current system, increased profits are the first option. And then, eventually, a slight increase in the alms those who are disposable receive. But the whole thing could also function with a different economic goal: instead of producing for the immeasurable consumption of some, to provide what's necessary for everybody. The problem, once again, is not development but who controls it.

The problem is political.

For now, highly concentrated and technified agriculture has left the world full of people global commerce doesn't need, not only peasants displaced through the use of powerful machinery in the fields of Argentina, Brazil, Ukraine, but also those who despair in the fields of the Ivory Coast, India, or Ethiopia because their products can no longer compete with those grown elsewhere.

Many survive by farming their lands poorly and producing yields more fitting to the era of Christ. It is difficult to deny that there are better ways to use that land. Between 1700 and 1960 the world population increased fivefold, as did the amount of land under cultivation. But in the following thirty years—during the Green Revolution—the population increased by 80 percent and land under cultivation by only 8 percent: the amount of available food increased because those same lands were producing so much more.

But now the rich countries have reached—or are reaching—their limit and are looking for new places beyond their borders. The problem is that those places—as always—are occupied. That population is in the way; they are too many and they cause problems. In order for the world to produce more food—food whose scraps those people could eat—the disposable ones have to disappear. They have no place in this scheme of concentrated development.

The same is happening in industry. Besides the few that still require a lot of labor power, most are using less and less. Those displaced or discouraged peasants arrive in cities and join those who arrived before, and there is no place for them within the productive apparatus.

In a society where individuals define themselves based on their place in production—on their work—not being employed is one of the most immediate ways of not having a functional identity. Or, perhaps, having an identity defined by a lack, to be one of those who has no place, function or purpose.

Another criterion: countries should qualify as Other World when a quarter or more of the population is disposable.

They are not proletarians—cogs necessary for the machine to function; they are refuse.

They are refuse that nobody knows what to do with.

Or they know, but they don't dare.

Perfecting the machine means having a use for everybody, not wasting, not sinking resources into what is useless. Throughout history, this has never been attained, so corrective mechanisms came into play, escape valves that would restore the balance. Wars, plagues, droughts, and famines all functioned to regulate the excess population. It was not precise—not surgical—but it worked in broad terms, rearranging society so that those who remained had a place. Now, this is more difficult. The development of certain technologies—medicine, transportation, communication—has decreased the effectiveness of such regulatory mechanisms. And "world public opinion" tends to apply a certain pressure so that within a particular system they are less effective.

The disposable ones, then, are not disposed of but rather kept in a pitiful state of limbo. And at the same time, they inspire fear. A little fear. They are too many millions and they move around, get stirred up. When? How? How many will come, what difficulties will the rich have to suffer, how many financial problems will they tolerate before they begin to think seriously that they cannot give themselves the luxury of maintaining this useless population? Already, much of the money spent on "aid" and "cooperation" has been cut. That's just the beginning. And, if it continues, if it spreads, how much weight will this "humanitarian public opinion" carry? How complicated will it be to transform the disposable ones into terrorists, a threat to all those do-gooders, and begin to do away with them?

I mean: begin to do away with them deliberately, systematically. Not like now, in such a disorderly fashion.

The hungry are the most obviously disposable ones and the elimination of surplus is the logical consequence of this model of development. Which doesn't mean it has to happen. Only if we don't know how to stop it.

The recent reappearance of Malthus is paving the way for such an eventuality. The threat of hunger for everybody has returned—via the specter of ecological disaster—along with the reverend's argument: we are too many and we have mistreated, worn out, the planet.

The Malthusian prophets hope the population will decrease and some even specify that enough will die so that the Earth won't have to feed nine billion people in 2050. The real message is that the Earth will not be able to continue to give happily to those who now eat all they want, and throw out half of it. The problem is not that we are too many; it is that there are so many who live as if we were few.

Proudhon was an optimist: "There is only one man too many on earth, and that is Mr. Malthus." Now there are more than a billion too many men and women.

(Or, maybe not: someone would have to figure out what would happen, in terms of nutrition and the use of the Earth, if we disappeared. If our 10 percent disappeared—the seven hundred million who concentrate 80 percent of the wealth of the world—the rest would eat well. Or perhaps it would be more economical to make disappear the famous 1 percent, the seventy million who concentrate 40 percent of the world's wealth. In any case, those who were left would have a lot and could start to fight among themselves for the leftovers, then there would arise a new group of privileged people who, in the medium term, would have enough, thereby again creating a sector that wouldn't eat enough. It's not enough for us to disappear.)

In the meantime, the consolidation of that legion of disposable people was, in part, the consequence of the weakness of governments that do not govern, governments that represent less and less of the real power in the globalized world. When large Western corporations imposed the Washington Consensus, they took over, among other things, the containment networks the governments in poor countries had offered to their poorest citizens.

Business is globalized, but governments aren't; business overrides national rules, and small governments have no way to control them. The world food system is a product and a reflection of this new world where companies are global and do whatever works for them in each and every place, whereas countries are local and limited by their borders and other weaknesses. Nationalism contributes to maintaining and perfecting this.

Together with the appearance of this disposable population, that notion called "nation" is coming unraveled, a notion that functioned, albeit with many problems, for a couple of centuries. Global capitalism still has not created its political form; nations carry on but decide little. They do fulfill the function, however, of allowing us to think that the bad guys are always the foreigners, thereby letting the national wealthy off easy. They also serve the purpose—inversely and complementarily—of allowing us to believe that the hunger of the people of Ghana is the fault of the government of Ghana, just to give one example.

Hunger, then, would be the most extreme metaphor of a civilization that has disposable people. But metaphors have their own way of having a life of their own: they can vary without varying what they represent. That is: one could put an end to hunger without putting an end to poverty, exploitation, extreme injustice, without putting an end to the millions and millions of extras.

The idea that the poorest countries are going to stop being hungry like the poor in the rich countries stopped being hungry is the last operative remnant of the theory of development that did such a good job of confusing things throughout the sixties. Though nobody really believes any longer that the citizens of Niger will one day live like the Swedes, still many unwittingly believe that one day the Nigeriens will eat as much as they need.

It's not very likely. We know that the world already produces enough food to feed everybody, but a third of us have a rhythm of consumption that doesn't leave enough for the rest. And all analysts predict that, now that the price of food continues to rise, now that the raw materials have returned to a critical place in the world economy, now that the huge agricultural enterprises are the meat of financial speculation, the differences of supplies will also increase: the countries that have food will sell it at higher and higher prices, so those who can pay will have it and others won't.

So, no, it isn't likely. If it did happen—it never has, but if it does—if we had a world in which nobody was hungry but some have fortunes and others the bare minimum needed for survival, would we be satisfied?

There would be ways of achieving this. Let's take, for example, the Tobin tax. The Tobin Tax is an old invention. In 1971 James Tobin, a Princeton economist, proposed a minimum tax—about 0.1 percent—on financial transactions as a way of putting a brake on speculation that was distorting currency values. At the time, few paid any attention. At the end of the nineties the antiglobalization movement revived the idea and again proposed it as a way of collecting money to help the poorest of the poor. Mr. Tobin, poor man, said that he had nothing to do with that, that he was a serious economist who supported the World Bank and the International Monetary Fund.[2] But the campaigns continued. Now, with the increase in speculative transactions—with the millions of transactions that computers now carry out—the Tobin tax would collect a fortune.

There are other possibilities. In 2013, 310 million personal computers, 250 million tablets, and 970 million smart phones were sold: about 1.5

billion devices that cost a minimum of two hundred dollars each. Nobody buys one of these devices if they don't already have their basic needs covered, so it would be perfectly fair to apply a five-dollar flat tax on the sale of each device for a food fund. That would raise $7.5 billion per year.

In 2013, 83.5 million new cars that cost an average of $31,200 each were also sold. If every buyer contributed a 1 percent tax to that fund, it would add up to $26 billion. Between cars and computers, and without sending anybody into bankruptcy, the $30 billion FAO wanted would be collected and there would even be several thousand extra.

To begin with, such proposals are illusory. When they say that the Tobin tax, for example, properly applied and well administered, could end world hunger, they don't say that the Tobin tax—or any other similar tax—could not be levied because no political power exists that would be capable of doing so. And, even if there was one or more, it would have to be capable of imposing, also, the obligation to use that money to fight hunger.

In addition, the proposal is so tiny, it is not even redistribution but rather compulsive charity.

Achieving zero hunger, a world without malnutrition, would be a great civilizing leap. It has never been achieved. And, above all, it's important to note how it is achieved, who achieves it, and the degree of equality it assumes.

One thing is for nobody to be hungry. Another very different one is that everybody has what they need and that nobody gives it to them, that they have it by their own right.

Not that the hungry receive charity but that no one has so much that they can give, while others have so little that they need. That everybody has the same, more or less. Sounds so old fashioned, and it is; at the same time, it is the only goal that seems worth fighting for at all.

A much too simple idea, they'll tell me.

Some simple, direct, basic discourses fell away along with the Berlin Wall. Let's think for a moment about the word *basic*. It should be praise, but it is an insult. Something similar happens with the idea of a society of equals: the most ambitious aspiration of humanity seems like old-fashioned nonsense, an archaism.

Hence, so many political harangues—so many so-called answers—condensed into that idiotic formula about how we're looking for "a better world," "a better society," as if someone—a politician, an intellectual, my Aunt Beany—would ever announce that they wanted a worse one. The formula is one of the peaks of contemporary idiocy, the synthesis of an era that doesn't know what to say and keeps saying it.

Now, mostly, the "struggle against hunger" consists of improving the efficiency of charity. Or, in the best case, in thinking about how to help those poor peasants farm their little pieces of land so that they can just barely survive.

It is what Fred Pearce summed up in his book *The Land Grabbers*: "This is not about ideology. It's about seeing what works. What will feed the world and what will feed the world's poorest."[3]

For me, it's about ideology: about knowing what to do so that there are no more *poor people in the world*. It's not about giving them a few extra crumbs, or even enough crumbs. And there's no question that this is an ideology. Hence the enormous campaign waged to discredit ideologies, because to carry out change you have to want to have one, have ideas—"ideology."

In part because ideology is the only reason there is hunger in the world that produces enough food. It is the ideology that claims not to be one, that presents itself as nature itself, the one that affirms that what is mine is mine—and we'll see about what's yours.

For a child of the sixties—for an adult of the first half of this twenty-first century—it is strange to me that so many people believe this to be the only option. Even if it were, it would be good to consider that it wasn't, just to put it to the test.

The problem is that we are living in a time without future.

(Or worse: when the future is a threat.)

2

I am reading some texts about biology and, as always happens, I run the risk of turning into a mystic. Is it not unbelievable that so much complexity and perfection has led to engendering lives that are so incomplete and banal? Shouldn't the sophistication with which millions of cells produce infinite reactions that are coordinated in such a way to allow a human to open her mouth correspond to splendid delights entering that mouth? Shouldn't the fine tuning necessary for an eardrum to perceive vibrations in the air and transmit them to the tiny bone in the middle ear so that they reach the hairy cells in the cochlea that converts them into electricity, which nerves carry to the brain, which assembles them in a way that offers us information, doesn't that deserve that the words heard always be musical? Shouldn't the degree of evolution of the natural mechanisms—herein the mysticism—lead us to believe in a similar degree of social evolution? Or, to put it less lyrically, does it make sense for such complex organisms to lead such horrible lives? Unless we are now in era of trilobites. Surely trilobites thought they were really something, were really satisfied with themselves, in some irrational way that we aren't able to understand.

The world is ludicrous. We spend our lives eating, fucking, consuming, using up time to use up time. But even so, the difference between a street in any city whatsoever and a forest or a meadow is so extraordinary that I cannot believe that we haven't done all this for something. We invent too much not to aspire to something more: meaning, intrinsic beauty, a certain amount of perfection . . . that would end up justifying so much effort.

Though we have reasons to feel satisfied.

For us, the more or less wealthy inhabitants of the more or less wealthy countries, life has never been so good. No matter how stubbornly the myth of the golden age persists, our lives are clearly so much better than those of our great-great-great-grandparents.

There are basic measures: we live, on average, thirty years more than one century ago, that is an indisputable proof; many diseases that used to kill us, no longer do; so many places that used to be inaccessible to us, so many things we didn't know, no longer are; there is no longer hunger due to scarcity, only greed.

Also, as a species: the fact that we have managed to grow to seven billion individuals. It is usually announced as something horrific, the sine qua non of all dangers.

(But those who criticize this do so from the more than optimistic supposition that if there were fewer people they would be among those that remain not those that don't. Here something certain: for those that wouldn't be if we weren't so many, it's a lot better that we are. Unless we want to debate whether being can be worse than not being and other such fascinating questions.)

As far as the species goes: the fact that there are more individuals and that they live more years is an indisputable sign of improvement. If there were fewer in the past it was not due to some kind of bucolic fervor that preferred not to overcrowd the natural scenery; it was because when more started being born, they died in epidemics, from hunger, or in wars that were fought for resources.

Now, there's less of all that, and this also is a clear sign of progress.

It is quite bold to say "progress."

Almost foolish.

It even sounds strange at first sight, but if you look back on history you will see that we are living through one of the freest and most peace-ful times, if not *the* most. There has been no great war for seventy years. There are no large concentration camps or efforts at mass racial or political extermination. There are not entire populations subjected to direct slavery. The level of legal discrimination against the least powerful in every soci-ety—blacks, women, homosexuals, the unemployed, randomly impov-erished, castes—is less than ever. There is, of course, extreme inequality, exploitation, and misery, but less than there was one hundred years ago.

(For all these reasons—and many more—I have returned to believing in progress; for all these reasons, I am not a progressive. Progressives believe that society is going to continue more or less the same for a long time, so they work to improve the details. I am not a progressive because I believe in general progress—more and better lives, more quality, less power, less stupidity—because I don't think it can be achieved, as pro-gressives do, through some kind of almost natural, gentle evolution. I believe—based on what I see in history—that this general progress is the result of struggles, ruptures, renewals, more ruptures.)

And so, in the midst of some modicum of optimism, hunger—the hunger of millions—is the way of saying that best is not always good, a way of calling attention to the stain that . . .

As if to say—with a certain amount of brutality, almost simplicity—that the world is better but can't be good if hundreds of millions go hungry.

Again: the strength of metaphor, for those who are looking in from the outside.

(To assemble this comparison there is also the need for an important decision: do we compare what was or what could be.)

We have never lived better. One would think that this well-being would inspire us to want more because it shows that it is possible to achieve.

But that doesn't usually happen. For many, the evidence of improve-ment discourages the search for improvements, allows one to think that the world has improved so much that it is going to end up more or less like this. As if through some strange twist, by means of a thundering ideology, this were the real end of history, and the reading of history as a long process of change no longer proves that everything always changes, as if all this has brought us to believing that everything changed in order to become what it is now.

What it is now: miserable, hungry, miserable, hopeless, miserable, unjust, miserable—the plan being to write miserable several times and each time have it mean something different.

Miserable.

So much better and miserable nonetheless.

I remember when men didn't kiss each other. I remember when there were four channels on television in black and white. I remember when a joint was a terrifying novelty. I remember when a computer was the mad fantasy of science fiction. I remember when the world was going to be better. I remember when the slums were full of workers. I remember when women didn't wear pants. I remember when blue jeans were a sign of almost intolerable rebellion. I remember when nobody knew what the hell soy was. I remember when cars had the gear shift on the steering wheel. I remember when the Soviet Union ruled over half the world and sent dogs into space. I remember when they'd come to the airport to see you off. I remember when old men wore hats. I remember when many tags said Made in Argentina. I remember when priests said mass in Latin. I remember when there were women who were virgins. I remember when boys lost their virginity with whores. I remember when Perón was a general defeated in Madrid and Guevara a guerrilla fighter who was going to win a revolution elsewhere. I remember when having long hair—over the shirt collar—was a reason to be suspended from school. I remember traveling by train to Mendoza, to Zapala, to Jujuy. I remember when gay meant faggot and they hid. I remember when it was more common to see a horse in the street than a breast in a movie. I remember when the term fart face didn't exist, or CD or DVD or digital and mouse was the last name of someone named Mickey. I remember when hamburgers were cool and that exotic English word *cool* also didn't exist in Spanish. I remember when the past was a disaster.

To say I remember is to say, of course, that I am old, but it is also to say that the world was not always the way it is. It is to say that things—objects, behavior, societies—happen in history, are dynamic, change, always change; that nothing lasts forever.

It seems so stupid, but the strongest myth of our era of incessant change is that change is not possible in the most basic things, in the order that orders our lives. Nor is that new; it's happened many times before. Many doctrines, religions, systems of government have been built on the idea that nothing changes, and then they'd try to prove that.

A religion—any religion—is a way of reassuring oneself and thinking that what there is now will always be, that everything is designed and controlled from here till the end of time, and that the power—a god, many gods—always has and always will be the same. If a believer believed that universal powers could change, who or what could promise eternal life? So power—kings, emperors—latched onto this idea: our power won't change because it is based on the Great Power that will never change, divine right.

A religion needs the immutable; that is why, for example, the extremely violent reaction of the Catholic Church when certain people a few centuries ago began to dig up geological remnants, caves, bones, and showed that the world is much older than the Bible says it is, and that it had not always been the way it is, that there were strange animals, that cows and fleas were not created by the Lord but rather through the evolution of species, that humans used to be fairly idle monkeys. Nothing could be more subversive, and it did subvert.

Is it just a coincidence that among the dozens and dozens of people I interviewed there were practically no atheists? That they (almost) all believed in some religion, some god that explained and justified the shit life they were leading?

We used to believe that we had freed ourselves of religion. Its return is one of the biggest blows of our time. If there are no more happy futures on Earth, let's return to the heavens. By so doing, we return to the most ancient future, the one that never changes.

(In July 1936 a band of semifascist generals rose up in Spain to the cry of *Viva la Muerte y/o Cristo Rey* (Long Live Death and/or Jesus Christ). Volunteers arrived from many countries in the world—mostly Western—to fight against those fundamentalist Catholic generals.

Now the only remotely comparable situation is Islamic Jihad, the religious fundamentalists who ignite a similar excitement and call on young people to leave everything and volunteer to die.

I have never met a starving atheist.

What would happen if I did?

A strange twist.

The present is always somehow a disappointment. That is why, throughout time, we have always found ways of living in other times: in the comfort of an edited past, in the hope for a better future.

For centuries, the monotheistic tradition offered a possible, reassuring future: the kingdom of heaven, in any of its forms, was compensation for shitty lives. We moderns could kill god because we have something to replace it with: that brilliant future we promised ourselves under the guise of history and science.

Modern rationalism was able to fulfill the function of that great promise. Except that the future it offered was in this world and would arrive thanks to the combined action of social forces and technological development, which in turn strengthened those social forces, which in turn produced more technological advances.

The futures of modernity took political forms; at one moment it would be liberty, equality, fraternity, then, later, once the bourgeois revolutions had done their work, a classless society. Throughout those two subversive centuries, the idea of change remained central: if society didn't function, its mechanisms should be replaced. Replacement systems were invented and, for the most part, also didn't work. In the last few decades the defeat of the "socialist" option to a large extent took with it the idea that there are other options. Now, for most Western citizens—for us, readers of these books—the future is a perpetual present with minor techno-ecological touch-ups: a more clever computer, a less threatened forest, a good job, a family, a new car every two or three years, two or three vacations a year, a hundred years instead of eighty, guaranteed tranquility, all thanks to the power of the market.

Nothing that can really be called a future.

Nothing, I mean, that functions in the way that goal does, the one that has to be reached no matter what.

Nothing that guides our steps, sets out pathways, determines lives, justifies death or its risk.

Nothing that justifies investments beyond the little tiny personal: the future as something personal

or as a threat.

The dominant myth: that our societies are never going to be very different because there are no other possibilities, that market capitalism, with elected and delegated governments, is the only possible form of organization and will last forever.

To believe that, we had to learn more than anything not to think of ourselves in historic terms, to forget that this moment is a moment.

We are living one of those boring moments in history when nobody has a very clear idea about what to hope for in the future, so we dedicate ourselves to being afraid of it. Threats like climate change are inscribed on the spirit of the era and perfect it. That's why it's logical that ecology appears as such a strong sign in these times: a time without a future project. We live in a bland era, terrified by the disasters produced by the most recent versions of a different future—the program of Marxist-Leninist revolutions—and decided not to think about different futures, imagining that our societies are going to continue more or less the same *per secula seculorum* amen. The present always guaranteed to be unsatisfactory. Why, then, do certain presents produce futures of hope and others futures of terrors? Someone might think that the history of the world rather than the world can be read from the perspective of this dichotomy: the eras that desire a future and those that look upon it with terror.

God has taken his revenge: we are out in the storm, alone with the present and without any refuge.

The future as a continuous present or as a threat, the future without promise, the indistinct future, is one of the axes, the wealthy version of the world without future.

The poor version is one of scarcity: in general, the inhabitants of the Other World don't think about the future because they don't have the tools to do so.

Aisha and her two cows.

Because the most extreme poverty of extreme poverty is that poverty of a future.

There is no greater waste, miserable.

What is a present without a future? What does a present that doesn't have a future consist of? How can one live in a present without a future? In a present where the horrible things that happen all the time are not counterbalanced with any belief that they won't continue to happen?

Aisha wanted two cows. When I offered her the world, she asked for two cows. I know I don't have the qualifications to offer worlds, but it was a game and even so: not even three or four cows.

I have spent—I spend—a lot of time in poor places, with very poor people. What surprises me most, every time, over and over again, is that they don't react; that each one of them, that so many millions allow themselves to be starved or be abused or lied to or mistreated in the most diverse ways and they don't react as I believe, some believe, they should. Or rather, as they could.

That's what worlds without futures are, without any horizons than their own: those two cows.

It used to be called ideology. Ideology is Aisha's two cows: the forms of desire, the limits of desire. At the end of the eighteenth century that great ideologue of modernity, Emanuel Kant, signed off on a short text, *Sapere aude!*, where he said: "*Dare to Know*. Knowing is little, or has become the opposite: the ballast of a reality seen as the only truth, one that prevents dreams or desires."

Somniare aude Desiderare aude.

I grew up believing that everything was about to change. Or, better yet, that time meant constant change. I managed—almost unable to catch my breath—to grab onto one of the last wagons of a generation that believed that after us nothing would be the same. It didn't even matter how; the hows come one after the other, vary, seek each other out in the conviction that they are happenstance, that one way or another the new society—new culture, new machines, new sexuality, new languages, new power relationships, completely new politics—was just around the corner. And new things were happening all the time.

It is true that much of what we did ended up disastrously, not only in obvious ways, such as the armed struggle. But also in these: the idea that drugs gave us access to new perceptions led to narco-trafficking, the return to nature led to ecological conservatism, free sex led to AIDS and loneliness, the perfect society into the world we live in now.

But even so, I vindicate that faith: the delirious idea that the world can be changed if there is enough will.

(And that it is always changing anyway.)

The rest of my life I've had to learn that a society can think of itself as immutable, permanent. Now neither the will nor the confidence exist. We don't think we are capable, and therein a strong cultural retreat. The human race has fallen far. Whether we were right or not, fifty years ago we thought we were able to do great things. Now, we don't, and it's sad.

Little things determine a lot more than we usually want to admit, and a few little things were more than efficient. They convinced us that being on the left—wanting to change the world—was an anachronism, an archaism. On a globe ruled by the modern idea of fashion, the most powerful idea of modernity went radically out of fashion. It was no longer a question of confronting certain powers, certain entrenchment; one also had to deal with the condescending, pitying looks of friends and relatives who were worried about this fool who said he thought what was no longer thought, who did what was no longer done.

I still haven't learned. It's hard for me to live with this life as the only recourse. I learned to live in a happy future: the present was the certainty of that happy future; it was colored by that future, stroked by it. To live in this pure continuous present seems like a swindle; I admire and scorn and envy and scorn those who can do it.

Because selfishness shimmers just behind the generosity attributed to those who struggle. There is a well-known secret: to sign up for some more or less grandiose goal is one of the few known antidotes against the banality of life.

It is likely that our posture in the face of the gigantic, in the face of what appears to be inalterable, determines very little. But it does at least determine a more minor question: Who the hell I am.

Who am I, who would I be when it counts? Who is that person who was born, learned, worked, played, loved, reproduced, aged, and died like millions every day? Or will I have been also one who did the little he could so that the world would be another? Is it not easier to live and die with the relief of having tried?

Maybe I can't wait much longer, but no day passes without me asking myself when the future will return.

And try again, and fail again, and fail better.

Sometimes I'd like to know something in the way I knew things when I was twelve, when one learns or understands something about something for the first time, with that astonishment of understanding, not yet knowing that one could know many other things that would contradict it, without the ballast of knowing that the same thing had happened to you so many other times, and that you again had to confront everything that contradicts it.

It is almost a cliché that youth is the time for utopias, which are abandoned as one grows into adulthood, and it is often believed that this happens because people calm down, settle down, take on responsibilities. I think one tends to lose utopia when one begins to understand brevity, finitude. When young, we think of time as endless, that there's time for everything to happen. As older people we know that twenty years pass very quickly without anything happening or with everything happening or better yet: that everything happens the same as always. All my efforts go against that supposition.

To grow old—do I have to say grow old?—is to know that there are things one will never know. That is, to forget the hope that one day everything will come to pass.

I'd like to know, of course I would. Now I know that I probably won't, but that's not what is going to distance me from the question. It is difficult to ask questions whose answers one knows to be unattainable; it's sad not to ask them.

And wanting to again, and again being wrong.

I think I am angry with the times and hunger is the synthesis of everything that makes me angry.

I think that anger is the only interesting relationship that one can have with one's times.

3

And if there weren't any more hunger? If nobody was ever hungry again? Hunger is a hyperbole. Hunger is the most awkward, the most extreme form: a shout at the deaf, a metaphor for those who play dumb.

As we said: a choice, an ideology. If Aisha gets her ball of millet every day, even her milk, her little piece of meat every once in a while, will we be satisfied?

Well fed?

We are the others. It's unlikely, very unlikely, that any reader of this book is one of the millions who don't eat enough and, at the same time, that any of those million will ever read this book.

It's clear that the world moves at different velocities. It always has. In the last few decades, the economic and technological acceleration also sped up the difference in goals and necessities. The societies of rich countries—or the rich sectors of the more or less rich countries—have guaranteed their survival and are busy deepening their civil rights. Hence the distinction between what is called the left and what is called the right, which in our societies mostly consists of supporting abortion, gay marriage, tolerance, various freedoms, or not.

While some want to marry whomever they want, others want to eat every day. Where do such different purposes meet or intersect? When there was a general theory of change, could one think about this particular change, that this radically different society would give each person what each person needed? Now there isn't one.

We are the others. For a couple of decades, the big goals seemed too big, so we accepted the little ones: to live better, improve our neighborhoods, take care of our environment, respect minorities, contribute to good causes. Everything very lovely and valid; we were happy living a small era. Perhaps that made it more reasonable, more realistic; it undoubtedly made it smaller.

Until 2008, when a break came. The crisis, the lost jobs, the lost guarantees, the bailouts of the banks, the barbarity of capitalism when it defends itself when wounded, all created, in the most wealthy countries, a kind of shiver: how could it be that the wealthiest nations spent that kind of fortune saving the richest among them?

The reaction has held aloft one word that defines the period: indignation, the indignant.

"It is true that the reasons for outrage today may seem less clear or the world more complicated. Who runs things? Who decides? [...] But some things in this world are unacceptable. To see this, you have only to open your eyes. I tell the young: just look, and you'll find something. The worst possible outlook is indifference that says, 'I can't do anything about it; I'll just get by.' Behaving like that deprives you of one of the essentials of being human: the capacity and the freedom to feel outraged," said *Indignez-vous*, the pamphlet by Stéphane Hessel that gave name to the movement.[4] And he defined his reasons for indignation: the difference between the rich and the poor, the mistreatment of immigrants, the deterioration of the environment.

I don't like the idea of indignation. It seems to me, somehow, an elegant feeling, controlled, of someone who has the benefit of entitlement: oh, dear, I'm so indignant. Desperation is what one feels when there is something that cannot wait. I believe in fury. I tend to believe that things that cannot be discussed calmly, without passion, without fury, are those that are important. That the only things with meaning are those that lead you to detest, even if only for a moment, someone who says the opposite.

The problem is what to do with anger. They will tell you: if you have no choice, better to avoid it. This ideology (?) is not stupid: it pushes us to do what we do and it provides us with discourses to justify it. It says that anger is foolish because it cannot lead to effective change and that little by little things will get better and we should limit ourselves to worrying about what we can change.

Or, if not, get indignant. The movement of the indignant is the quintessence of the most current form of well-meaning political participation: the defensive reaction.

We are indignant because inequality is more brutal than ever, because they are killing people in Syria or Sudan or on the Mexican border, because they're destroying nature, because the globalized corporations manage (the wealth of) the world, because nations shirk their responsibility to offer health care or education, because the armies of the wealthy send off drones, because hundreds of millions of men, women, and children in the world go hungry.

We react: we defend ourselves—we try to defend ourselves—against it. But we have no alternatives to offer in their place.

How long has it been since there's been a great cause *for*?

How long has it been since there has been a movement with its own name? I mean, its own, one that doesn't remit to what it is against: that isn't *anti*globalization, that isn't *resisting* some dictator, that doesn't go *against* this or that, that isn't *indignant* about what others do, that does not deny and denounce and endure.

One that proposes, that has something to propose and proposes it.

(We are, we say we are, talking about hunger. The problem of hunger tends to be the synthesis of this defensive posture: it can't be that hundreds of millions don't eat enough, it makes us indignant that hundreds of millions don't eat enough, we try to do things so those hundreds of millions will eat enough, so they'll get at least some food, so they'll have a plow with two cows, so they don't suffer quite so much.

How to transform a defense into an attack?)

Hunger has often been the point of departure for revolutions: it shows beyond any shadow of a doubt that the state of things wasn't working, wasn't fulfilling the basic necessities. And, moreover, it placed life in relative terms: since I am hungry and I am going to die, I might as well die fighting, at least then I'll die with hope. That's why hunger is frightening; that's why they send their bags of grain.

But that doesn't mean that hunger is still a point of departure. More than desperation, what is indispensable for serious change—a revolution?—is an idea.

All are, at a certain moment, defensive: forms of being fed up. Out with that king who is starving us; enough with these czars who keep us in poverty; we will no longer tolerate that dictator. Those things that have always fed us up still exist. But lately they are movements with no exit, no purpose—defensive movements. They get rid of one government and put in the next: from the Wall to Putin, from Tahrir to Al-Sisi.

Having a project is what makes a difference.

One thing is to devise policy, another very different thing is to devise desire. But if policies are not imagined as a way of concretizing those desires, they are only the administration of sadness, of mediocrity.

What I mean is that I don't believe that hunger will ever end within this social model. Ending hunger means changing the model. We just don't know how.

Above all: we don't know what to propose. For a century and a half, revolutionary movements were too clear about what they were proposing. They sinned—we sinned—by assuming we knew everything, by believing.

Because trying for a revolution, any revolution, usually meant putting your life on the line and, as I wrote almost thirty years ago, "Nobody puts their life on the line shouting 'maybe.' To do that, to withstand the pressure and the risk, humans always needed the guarantee of a guaranteed future: an undeniable truth. They needed to believe that what they wanted was guaranteed by some external instance: the word of god, the ineluctable march of history."

And, then, all the pitfalls of belief, and the worst of all, the concentration of power in the hands of a few priests. Those iron convictions, those absolute truths served to construct evil apparatuses of ravenous power—the power of Marxism, Leninism, Stalinism, Maosim, Castrism, and so many other *isms*. So now I propose we find a way to stop proposing a defense and start proposing something that avoids certainties, that accepts fallibilities, that is capable of saying: this is what I want, not what I believe; and that's why it's worth fighting for, even if I don't achieve it.

Organize projects without belief.

We don't know how. It's obvious that we don't know how. For starters, every revolutionary project is stained and under suspicion: they were at the root of those disastrous processes.

The attempts at equality ended up producing a concentration and abuse of power that had rarely been seen. So? Should we stop trying? Should we just forget that stupid idea that the world wasn't worthwhile if we weren't all equal? Do we make our peace with the more or less modest injustice in the wealthy nations and the brutal injustice in the poor ones? Do we make do with the new French revolution and keep shouting security, sexuality, longevity?

We are at one of those moments without projects, in one of those eras when the previous paradigm has broken down and another one has yet to appear. They happen, and are more frequent and longer than somebody born in the middle of the twentieth century, in full splendor of a paradigm, can imagine.

They are difficult times, somewhat orphaned. It was easier to know without doubts. But they are also fascinating times, times of seeking. There is nothing more exciting and more anguishing than seeking.

Nor does anybody know how to put together a new paradigm. The last great example was constructed by a man with a beard who shut himself away in the best library of his day, reading, writing, thinking, alone, coming out of his enclosure very rarely: the power of an extraordinary mind. Now, smack in the middle of the wiki era, it's probable that the model will be quite different, likely it will be the collaborations, confrontations, reformulations, the seeking of thousands, which somehow—still embryonic, still hesitant—is happening.

(One must think through, among other things, that old trick of the vanguard: those who assume they understand what others need, a trick that worked mostly to create the most brutal most autocratic power of recent history.

A vanguard is, by definition, a group that does or thinks what others don't, and ends up assuming that this gives them rights. We agree that they are damaging, history shows us as much. But, without them, how to change thinking? Who is going to think what nobody else thought, if the entire cultural apparatus—the ideology—is thought out so that we all think what has already been thought?

The emergence of something different is the result of trouble, anger, the poor adaptation of a few, those who don't conform. But, if we accept that there will always be some who imagine something different, how can they be prevented from assuming that this knowledge gives them rights? How to construct a nonauthoritarian vanguard? How to construct a vanguard that doubts?)

The difficult part is not to attain what seems impossible; the difficult part is defining what that is. In France some philosophers began to think about the unthinkable possibility of a government without a king; in America some businessmen and lawyers began to think about how they could govern themselves; in England some women imagined that they were persons like their husbands and like them could decide who governed them; in India some young men educated in English began to think that they didn't need weapons to overcome a huge army—and so forth. In each case, the impossible was very clear: not having a king, governing oneself, the vote, fighting without killing. Even so, in each case, they led to processes that lasted decades and met obstacles and retreated and had doubts and more decades.

I am in favor of the unthinkable because it has been achieved so many times. It's only a matter of thinking which unthinkable we want and betting on it in any way we can.

A new paradigm is the unthinkable. That is what makes it difficult and attractive and difficult. It is what makes it worth thinking of.

In short, to find a way of forcing us to share: of forcing goods to be fairly distributed, of forcing power to be fairly distributed. To find the political form that corresponds to a moral idea of the economy rather than the form of the economy that corresponds to a moralistic idea of politics. Said like that, it seems simplistic, but we don't know what that is.

It's not clear who could think it up; less so, who can do it. One of the most ingenious things about Marxism was defining a social sector as the carriers of revolutionary legitimacy: the proletarians of the world united were those designated to carry forward with definitive change. They were the dispossessed, those who had nothing to lose—and therefore, everything to gain.

However, they weren't the ones who imagined this. Perhaps that was the origin of the disaster; perhaps not.

Once again, I say that the hungry are a synthesis of the most dispossessed, those who are dispossessed every single day of the possibility of eating enough. Those who are not even proletarians. The disposables, the surplus.

I spent years listening to them. I think I was hoping to find some intimate, intrinsic knowledge, and I was wrong; living certain things doesn't guarantee you know the why but only, possibly, the how. They can talk about what it is like to be hungry; they have no idea why they are. Most speak about god, about injustice, about god, about a misfortune and a wrong turn, about god.

I mean, and I disgust myself a little: most of the people I describe in this book would be surprised by the majority of the facts and mechanisms that this book discusses. And the obvious but insistent question: How different would it be if they knew? What would change if they knew?

It's difficult to say, it's ugly to say: they don't seem to have many possibilities to influence the mechanisms that make them hungry. They are on the margin, and they don't have the strength.

So, who does?

So, how will they?

There is, in any case, a tradition of "thinking for the other," the result of concern for the other, which begins to be concern for oneself; personally I, who talk to them as far as I'm concerned, I feel disgusted by a world where hundreds of millions go hungry every day. As far as I'm concerned, a world like this seems to me to be a horrifying machine in which non-conformance does not compute.

How can you stand to live knowing that?

Well, let me explain.

Facing such an ugly world, the only possible aesthetic is rebellion—in any, in all its forms.

I have traveled the world and I am more and more in despair. But I believe more and more in desperation and despair.

I think it would be good to separate the action from the results of the action. Not do what I want to do for the possibility of a result but rather for the necessity to act: because I can't stand myself if I don't.

And I think that nothing is completely true if I don't do it out of some form of selfishness. And that the great moments in culture were produced when the selfishness of thousands consisted of deciding that they should do something for others: that this is the way of doing something for themselves, selfishly.

To think about what a world that didn't make us ashamed or guilty or discouraged would be like—and begin to imagine how to find that world.

It could take years, decades, so many mistakes and disasters and still who knows.

It could take lives and more lives.

It could take the return of history.

ACKNOWLEDGMENTS

Above all, I would like to thank my friend Carlos Alberdi, who did everything in his power to make this book a reality: to your well-being. And, while we're at it, Miguel Albero, the poet and ambassador of Spain; Jordi Carrión, my Catalan family doctor, whom I still love, for reading, for thinking, for his suggestions; and Lucía Álvarez, who led me through the Argentine suburbs.

I would like to thank Fernando García Calero from Doctors Without Borders, who persistently searched for stories with me, and all of his colleagues—especially Silvia Fernández, Juan Carlos Tomasi and Luis Ponte—because they also made the project their own.

Thanks to the intrepid correspondent Ana Gabriela Rojas—for India—Mercedes Casanovas and María Lynch, Laura Mahler and Laura Laski because they helped me get started, and Margarita García because she built me up when I lost heart.

Juan Caparrós, porque quiero.

NOTES

INTRODUCTION

1   Ziegler, Jean (2011). *Destruction Massive: géopolitique de la faim*, p. 13, Éditions du Seuil, France.

NIGER: FORMS OF HUNGER

1   Food and Agriculture Organization of the United Nations (2008), *An introduction to the basic concepts of food security*, EC-FAO Food Security Programme.

2   Ziegler, Jean. *Betting on Famine: Why The World Still Goes Hungry.* New York: The New Press, 2013.

3   Hurt, Stephen R. (2016), Washington Consensus, Encyclopædia Britannica, Inc.

4   Roberts, Paul. *The End of Food.* New York: Houghton Mifflin Company, 2008.

5   Ziegler, Jean. *Betting on Famine: Why The World Still Goes Hungry.* New York: The New Press, 2013. p. 32.

6   Roger Thurow and Scott Kilman. *ENOUGH: Why the World's Poorest Starve in an Age of Plenty.* New York: Public Affairs, 2009. p. 74.

7   Whitlock, Craig. "Drone Base in Niger Gives U.S. a Strategic Foothold in West Africa." *Washington Post.* 21 March 2013.

8   Rossi, B., "The Paradox of Chronic Aid," in X. Crombé and J.II. Jézéquel (eds.). *A Not-So Natural Disaster: Niger 2005.* London: Hurst, 2009 (English translation of original French volume). pp. 105-124.

9   Crombé, Xavier. "Building the Case for Emergency: MSF and the Malnutrition Factor." *A Not-So Natural Disaster: Niger 2005.* London: Hurst, 2009 (English translation of original French volume).

10 Prahalad, C. K. *The Fortune at the Bottom of the Pyramid*. Upper Saddle River: Wharton School Publishing, 2006.

11 Rice, Andrew. "The Peanut Solution." *The New York Times Magazine*. 2 Sept. 2010.

ON HUNGER: ORIGINS

1 Cordón Bonet, Faustino. Cocinar hizo al hombre. Barcelona: Tusquets Editores, 2002.

2 King James, Exodus 16:3, 16:4.

3 Russell, Sharman Apt. *Hunger: An Unnatural History*. New York: Basic Books, 2002.

4 Gregory of Tours. *History of the Franks Books I–X*. New York: Fordham University Internet Medieval Source Book, 1997.

5 Quevedo, Francisco de. Historia de la vida del Buscón. Tr. Katherine Silver. Biblioteca Virtual Universal, 2006.

6 Swift, Jonathan. *A Modest Proposal*. Project Gutenberg, 2008. Web.

7 Blanc, Louis. Histoire de la Révolution Française. Brussels, 1850.

INDIA: TRADITIONS OF HUNGER

1 Satapatha Brahmana, Part II, 3.1.2.21.

2 Valluvar. Thirukkural. Book 1, ch. 26.

3 Parmentier, Bruno. Nourrir l'humanité: Les grandes problèmes de l'agriculture mondiale au XXIeme siècle. La Découverte, 2009.

4 Harris, Marvin. *Cannibals and Kings: Origins of Cultures*. New York: Vintage, 1991 (reissue).

5 Brown, Lester. *Plan B 4.0: Mobilizing to Save Civilization*. New York: W. W. Norton & Company, 2009, pp. 233–234.

6 Hitchens, Christopher. *The Missionary Position: Mother Teresa in Theory and Practice*. London: Verso Books, 1995, p. 11.

7 Ibid.

8 Mother Teresa. "Acceptance Speech." NobelPrize.org. Nobel Media AB, 2019.

9 Niebuhr, Gustav. "Abortion, Contraception Commended." *Washington Post*. February 4, 1994.

10 United Nations. "Millennium Summit (6–8 September 2000)." Un.org.

11 United Nations. "Goal 1: Eradicate Extreme Poverty and Hunger." Un.org.

12 Truman, Harry S. "Inaugural Address." Speech. Washington, DC, January 20, 1949. Harry S. Truman Presidential Library and Museum.

13 United Nations Development Programme. "Human Rights Report. Table 2. Human Development Index Trends, 1990–2017." United Nations Development Program. <http://hdr.undp.org/en/composite/trends>

14 Chu, Henry. "India's Gnawing Pain." *Los Angeles Times*. August 24, 2008.

15 Singh, Manmohan. "Independence Day Speech." Speech, New Delhi, August 15, 2008. Embassy of India Embassy Archives.

16 Rossi, B. "The Paradox of Chronic Aid," in X. Crombé and J. H. Jézéquel (eds.). *A Not-So Natural Disaster: Niger 2005*. London: Hurst, 2009 (English translation of original French volume), pp. 105-124.

17 Patil, Pratibha. "Address by the Hon'ble President of India, Shrimati Pratibha Devisingh Patil, to Parliament." Speech, New Delhi, June 4, 2009. Pratibhapatil.nic.in.

18 Gillis, Justin. "Norman Borlaug, Plant Scientist Who Fought Famine, Dead at 95." *New York Times*. September 13, 2009.

19 Wagenhofer, Erwin and Max Annas. We Feed the World: Was uns das Essen wirklich kostet. Berlin: Orange Press, 2006.

20 "Slum" in Merriam Webster's Collegiate Dictionary, 11 ed., 2003.

21 Davis, Mike. *Planet of Slums*. London: Verso Books, 2006, p. 19.

22 UN Habitat. "Slum Almanac 2015–2016."

23 Davis, Mike. *Planet of Slums*. London: Verso Books, 2006, p. 16.

24 Davis, Mike. *Planet of Slums*, p. 78, citing P. K. Das, "Manifesto of a Housing Activist," in Patel and Thorner, Bombay, pp.179-80.

ON HUNGER: CIVILIZATION

1 McMahon, Paul. *Feeding Frenzy: The New Politics of Food*. London: Profile Books, 2013.

2 Smith, Adam. *Wealth of Nations*, Book IV: On Systems of Political Economy, Chapter V: On Bounties. W. Strahan and T. Cadell, London 1776.

3 Malthus, Thomas. "An Essay on the Principle of Population." Electronic Scholarly Publishing, p. 9.

4 Ibid. p. 5.

5 Ibid. p. 44.

6 Ibid. p. 114.

7   Townsend, Joseph. "A Dissertation on the Poor Laws." London: Printed for C. Dilly, 1786, p. 23.

8   Engels, Friedrich. *The Condition of the Working Class in England*. Germany: Otto Wigand, 1845, p. 102.

9   Stead, William T. "The Maiden Tribute of Modern Babalyon." The Pall Mall Gazette. Lowood Press, 1885.

10   Riis, Jacob. *How the Other Half Lives: Studies Among the Tenements of New York*. New York: Charles Scribner's Sons, 1914.

11   Lenin, V. I. *Imperialism: The Highest Stage of Capitalism*. Sydney: Resistance Books, 1999, p. 84.

12   Davis, Mike. *Late Victorian Holocausts*. London: Verso Books, 2001.

13   McMahon, Paul. *Feeding Frenzy: The New Politics of Food*. London: Profile Books, 2013, p. 18.

14   Sorokin, Pitirim. *Hunger as a Factor in Human Affairs*. Gainesville: University of Florida Presses, 1975.

15   Snyder, Timothy. *Bloodlands: Europe Between Hitler and Stalin*. New York: Basic Books, 2010.

16   Russell, Sharman Apt. *Hunger: An Unnatural History*. New York: Basic Books, 2006.

17   Ibid. pp. 96-97.

18   *Maladie de Famine, Recherches cliniques sur la famine executes dan le ghetto de Varsovie*. Bulmash Family Holocaust Collection. American Joint Distribution Committee, 1946.

19   Roosevelt, Franklin Delano. "State of the Union Address to Congress." Speech. Washington, D.C., January 11, 1944.

20   United Nations. "Universal Declaration of Human Rights." United Nations General Assembly, 1948.

21   Becker, Jasper. *Hungry Ghosts: Mao's Secret Famine*. New York: The Free Press, 1996, p. 138.

22   Ibid. p. 292.

23   Ibid. p. 293.

ON HUNGER: COMPETITION

1   Borges, Jorge Luis. "Tlön, Uqbar, Orbis Tertius." First published in *Sur*, May 1940.

2   Lionaes, Aese. "Nobel Peace Prize 1970 Presentation Speech." Speech. Oslo, Norway, December 10, 1970. Nobelprize.org.

3   Kissinger, Henry. Speech. Rome, Italy, November 5, 1974.

4   Ehrlich, Paul R. *The Population Bomb* (Revised). New York: Ballantine Books, 1971, p. xi.

5   Ibid., p. 130–131.

6   Meadows, Donella H., Dennis L. Meadows, Jørgen Randers, and William W. Behrens III. *The Limits to Growth*. Universe Books, 1974.

7   Sor Juana Inés de la Cruz. "Obras completas de Sor Juana Inés de la Cruz: Lírica personal." Mexico City: Fondo de Cultura Económica, 1951, p. 228.

8   United Nations. The Challenge of Slums: Global Report on Human Settlements 2003. UN Habitat. London: Earthscan Publications, Ltd, 2003, p. 43.

9   Ibid., p. 34.

10   Walton, John K. and David Seddon. *Free Markets and Food Riots: The Politics of Global Adjustment*. Cambridge: Blackwell Publishers, 1994.

THE UNITED STATES: INDUSTRIES OF HUNGER

1   Kaufman, Frederick. "The Food Bubble: How Wall Street starved millions and got way with it." *Harper's* magazine. July 2010.

2   McMahon, Paul. *Feeding Frenzy: The New Politics of Food*. London: Profile Books, 2013. P 67.

3   Starrs, Tom. "Fossil Food: Consuming Our Future." Center For Ecoliteracy. June 29 2009. Web.

4   Ziegler, Jean. "Burning food crops to produce biofuels is a crime against humanity." *The Guardian*. November 16 2013.

5   Lemaître, Frédéric. Demain, la faim! France: Grasset & Fasquelle, 2009.

6   United States. Public Papers of the Presidents of The United States: George W. Bush, Government Printing Office, 2009.

7   Zoellick, Robert. "A Challenge of Economic Statecraft." Speech. Center for Global Development, Washington, DC, April 2 2008. Worldbank.org

8   Faiola, Anthony. "The New Economics of Hunger." *Washington Post*. April 27, 2008.

9   Brown, Lester. "The New Geopolitics of Food." *Foreign Policy*. April 25, 2011.

10   Zurayk, Rami. "Use your loaf: Why Food Prices Were Crucial in the Arab Spring." *The Guardian*. July 16 2011.

11   Cargill Corporate Brochure, 2001.

12   Ziegler, Jean. *Betting on Famine: Why the World Still Goes Hungry.* New York: The New Press, 2013. P. 110.

13   "US Allows Child Slavery Suit Against Nestle, Cargill." Organized Crime and Corruption Reporting Project. 25 October 2018.

14   Kaufman, Frederick. "How Goldman Sachs Created the Food Crisis." *Foreign Policy.* April 27, 2011.

15   *A Place at the Table.* Dir. Kristi Jacobson and Lori Silverbush. Participant Media, 2012.

16   Neel, James V. "Diabetes Mellitus: A 'Thrifty' Genotype Rendered Detrimental by 'Progress'?" *American Journal of Human Genetics.* 1962 Dec; 14(4): 353–362

17   Lustig, Robert H. "The Toxic Truth About Sugar." *Nature* Magazine 482, February 2, 2012. P. 27-29.

18   Schlosser, Eric. *Fast Food Nation: What the All-American Meal is Doing to the World.* New York: Penguin, 2002. Introduction.

19   Patel, Raj. *Stuffed and Starved: The Hidden Battle for the World Food System.* New York: Melville House, 2012. P. 16.

20   Olshansky, Jay, et. al. "A Potential Decline in Life Expectancy in the United States in the 21st Century." The New England Journal of Medicine 352 (March 17, 2005): 1138-1145.

21   Adams, Stephen. "Obesity Killing Three Times as Many as Malnutrition." *The Telegraph.* December 13, 2012.

ON HUNGER: INEQUALITY

1   McMahon, Paul. *Feeding Frenzy: The New Politics of Food.* London: Profile Books, 2013, ch. 2.

2   Statistics drawn from graph in "For Richer, For Poorer." *The Economist.* October 13, 2012.

3   Beddoes, Zanny Minton. "For Richer, For Poorer." *The Economist.* October 1, 2012.

4   Buffet, Warren. Interview with Alison Kosik. CNN Money. September 30, 2011.

5   Diouf, Jacques. "Address by Mr. Jacques Diouf." Speech. Rome, Italy, June 3, 2008, p. 4 in English transcript.

6   Stiglitz, Joseph. "Of the 1%, By the 1%, For the 1%." *Vanity Fair.* May 2011.

7   Congressional Budget Office. "Trends in Family Wealth, 1983–2013." Congress of the United States Congressional Budget Office, p. 1.

8   Oxfam Media Briefing. "The Cost of Inequality: How Wealth and Income Extremes Hurt Us All." Oxfam. January 18, 2013.

9   Manrique, Jorge. "Verses Written on the Death of his Father." Tr. Edie Grossman.

ARGENTINA: THE WASTE OF HUNGER

1   Walsh, Rodolfo. *Operation Massacre.* Tr. Daniella Gitlin. New York: Seven Stories Press, 2013. Prologue.

2   Global Food: Waste Not, Want Not. Institution of Mechanical Engineers. January 2013. p. 2.

3   Ibid. p. 2

4   Ibid. p. 3

5   "Global Food Losses and Food Waste: Extent, Causes, and Prevention." FAO. May 16, 2011. p. 5

6   Gunders, Dana. "Wasted: How America is Losing Up to 40 Percent of Its Food from Farm to Fork to Landfill" National Resource Defense Council. Aug. 2012"

7   "Eco Pulse 2012 Report" The Shelton Group. August 16, 2012.

8   Smithers, Rebecca. "UK households wasting less food, figures show." *The Guardian.* Nov. 15th, 2011

9   Clerc, Denis. Foreword to Francois de Ravignan's La faim, pourquoi? Paris: La Découverte, 2009.

10   Henriques, Gisele and Raj Patel. "Policy Brief No. 7: Agricultural Trade Liberalization and Mexico." Food First (Institute for Food and Development Policy). August 2003. p. 2.

11   Footnoted in: Breman, Jay. *The Labouring Poor In India.* Oxford: Oxford University Press, 2003. p 13

12   Footnoted in: Central Intelligence Agency. The World FactBook. Washington D.C., 2002. p. 80.

13   Davis, Mike. *Planet of Slums.* London: Verso Books, 2006. p. 18.

14   Graeber, David. "On the Phenomenon of Bullshit Jobs: A Work Rant." Strike! Magazine no. 3. August 2013.

ON HUNGER: CHARITY

1   McNamara, Robert S. "Address to the Board of Governors." Speech. World Bank Group, Nairobi, Kenya, September 24, 1973.

2   Eagleton, Terry. *Why Marx Was Right*. New Haven: Yale University Press, 2011, p. 68.

3   "ANTI-HUNGER PROGRAMME: A twin-track approach to hunger reduction: priorities for national and international action." Food and Agriculture Organization of the United Nations, 2003.

4   "OCHA On Message: Humanitarian Principles." United Nations Office for the Coordination of Humanitarian Affairs. April 2010.

5   "The History of U.S. Food Aid." USAID.gov. July 8, 2004.

6   Sen. Hubert H. Humphrey, in naming P. L. 480 the "Food for Peace" program. *Wall Street Journal*, May 7, 1982.

7   Barrett, Christopher B. and Daniel G. Maxwell. *Food Aid After Fifty Years: Recasting Its Role*. New York: Routledge, 2005.

8   Natsios, Andrew S. "Modernizing Food Aid: Improving Effectiveness and Saving Lives." House Committee on Foreign Affairs Hearing on February 14, 2018.

9   Clinton, Bill. Speech. Council on Foreign Relations, Yale Club, New York, NY, June 17, 2002.

10   "ANTI-HUNGER PROGRAMME: A twin-track approach to hunger reduction: priorities for national and international action." Food and Agriculture Organization of the United Nations, 2003.

11   "The Millennium Development Goals Report 2013." The United Nations. 2013, p. 4.

12   "#RecipeForDisaster: Join the Fight Against Food Waste" World Food Programme.

13   "How Solving Hunger Builds a More Secure World." World Food Programme. July 6, 2012.

14   Wilde, Oscar. *The Soul of Man Under Socialism*. A.L. Humphreys, 1912, pp. 3–4.

15   Galaz, Mábel. "CR7 lucha contra el hambre mientras sueña con el Balón de Oro." El País. January 3, 2013.

16   Thurow, Roger and Scott Kilman. *ENOUGH: Why the World's Poorest Starve in an Age of Plenty*. New York: Public Affairs, 2009, p. 229.

17   Ibid. 234.

18   Rocha, Zildo. Helder, O Dom: uma vida que marcou os rumos da Igreja no Brasil (Helder, the Gift: A Life that Marked the Course of the Church in Brazil). Rio de Janeiro: Editora Vozes, 2000, p. 53

19   Zizek, Slavoj. "Fat-free chocolate and absolutely no smoking: why our guilt about consumption is all-consuming." *The Guardian*. May 21, 2014.

20   "Declaration of Nyéléni." La Via Campesina. February 27, 2007.

SOUTH SUDAN: DEVELOPMENTS OF HUNGER

1   Smith, David. "South Sudan president accuses officials of stealing $4bn of public money." *The Guardian*. June 5, 2002.

2   Fleshman, Michael. "Fixing the humanitarian aid system." Africa Renewal Online (Un.org). January 2006.

3   "Paying the Price: How US farm policies hurt West African cotton farmers—and how subsidy reform could help." Oxfam America, 2007, p. 2.

4   Thurow, Roger and Scott Kilman. *Enough: Why the World's Poorest Starve in an Age of Plenty*. New York: Public Affairs, 2009, p. 61.

5   Remarks to the Council on Foreign Relations on December 1, 2005.

6   Cheney, Dick, et. al. "Reliable, Affordable, and Environmentally Sound Energy for America's Future: Report of the National Energy Policy Development Group." National Energy Policy Development Group. May 2001.

7   Moeller, Robert. Presentation at National Defense University, 19 February 2008.

ON HUNGER: METAPHORS

1   Amery, L. S. *The Leo Amery Diaries*. Ed. John Barnes and David Nicholson. London: Hutchinson & Co., 1988, p. 950.

2   Sen, Amartya. *Poverty and Famines: An Essay on Entitlement and Deprivation*. New York: Oxford University Press, 1981, p. 1.

3   Ibid. p. 7.

4   Sen, Amartya. *Development as Freedom*. New York: Knopf, 1999, p. 153

5   Ibid. p. 162.

MADAGASCAR: FORCES OF HUNGER

1   Jung-a, Song, Christian Oliver, and Tom Burgis. "Daewoo to Cultivate Madagascar Land for Free." *Financial Times*, November 19, 2008.

2   De Schutter, Olivier. "Report of the Special Rapporteur on the right to food: Mission to Madagascar." United Nations General Assembly, Human Rights Council. Nineteenth session, Agenda item 3. 26 December 2011, pp 3–4.

3   Odhiambo, Michael Ochieng. "Commercial pressures on land in

Africa: A regional overview of opportunities, challenges and impacts." International Land Coalition, 2011, p. 1

4   Deininger, Klaus and Derek Byerlee. "Rising Global Interest in Farmland: Can It Yield Sustainable and Equitable Benefits?" The World Bank. Washington, D.C., 2011.

5   Pearce, Fred. Interview with Tom Templeton. "Fred Pearce: Land grabbing has more of an impact on the world's poor than climate change." *The Guardian.* May 19, 2012.

6   "Awakening Africa's Sleeping Giant Prospects for Commercial Agriculture in the Guinea Savannah Zone and Beyond." The World Bank, 2009, p 2.

7   Pearce, Fred. *The Land Grabbers: The New Fight Over Who Owns the Earth.* Boston: Beacon Press, 2012, ch. 1.

8   Ibid., ch. 8.

9   "Madagascar, Daewoo e neocolonialismo." Beppe Grillo. November 27, 2008.

10   "Producing More." Monsanto.com

11   McMahon, Paul. *Feeding Frenzy: The New Politics of Food.* London: Profile Books, 2013, ch. 9

12   Martin II, William J., Roger I. Glass, John M. Balbus, and Francis S. Collins. "A Major Environmental Cause of Death." *Science* magazine (334). October 14, 2011.

13   Funk, McKenzie. ""Will Global Warming, Overpopulation, Floods, Droughts and Food Riots Make This Man Rich? Meet the New Capitalists of Chaos." *Rolling Stone* (62). May 27, 2010.

14   Fletcher, Laurence. "Hedge fund couple split businesses after separation." Reuters, October 12, 2011.

15   "Down on the Farm," Oakland Institute. February 14, 2014.

16   Brown, Lester. "The New Geopolitics of Food." *Foreign Policy.* April 25, 2011.

17   Eagleton, Terry. *Why Marx Was Right.* New Haven: Yale University Press, 2011, p. 6.

18   Michel, Serge, Michael Beuret, and Paolo Woods. *China Safari: On the Trail of Beijing's Expansion in Africa* (International Edition). New York: Bold Type Books, 2010.

19   Quoted in "The New Sinosphere: China in Africa." Ed. Leni Wild and David Mepham. Institute for Public Policy Research. 2006.

20   Schneidman, Witney and Joel Wiegert. "Competing in Africa: China, the European Union, and the United States." The Brookings Institute. April 16, 2018.

FINAL THOUGHTS

1   "What Causes Hunger?" The World Food Programme. November 5, 2013.

2   Sandbu, Martin. "The Tobin Tax Explained." *Financial Times.* September 28, 2011.

3   Pearce, Fred. *The Land Grabbers: The New Fight Over Who Owns the Earth.* Boston: Beacon Press, 2012, p. 1.

4   Hessel, Stéphane. Indiginez Vous! Tr. Damion Searls. Reprinted in *The Nation*, March 7–14, 2011, p. 17.